Views of American Economic ⟨⟩ ...n: The Industrial Era

Volume Two
Views of American Economic Growth: The Industrial Era

Edited by

Thomas C. Cochran
*Professor of History
University of Pennsylvania*

Thomas B. Brewer
*Assistant Professor of History
University of Kentucky*

McGraw-Hill Book Company
New York/St. Louis
San Francisco
Toronto
London
Sydney

26205

Preface

■ Economic history as a self-conscious discipline is about a hundred years old. Until World War II its practitioners, although often trained as economists, dealt with records and statistics in much the same way as historians. Since then, however, the pressures of world changes and exciting new theories have generated two important additions to the older methods.

The postwar emphasis on improving the living standards of underdeveloped areas led to fresh analyses of the causes of rapid industrialization, and hence to a combination of economic theory with history called the study of "economic development." In the course of examining exotic non-European cultures, many of the classic economic assumptions were challenged, and the scope of inquiry had to be greatly expanded. As two distinguished economists have observed: "The really fundamental problems of economic growth are noneconomic."[1] This broader cultural involvement is illustrated in this volume by a number of selections dealing with politics, business, and social organization.

The other recent emphasis, often called the "new economic history," has arisen

[1] Norman S. Buchanan and Howard S. Ellis, *Approaches to Economic Development* (New York: Twentieth Century Fund, 1955), p. 405.

because of the interest inspired by John Maynard Keynes, Simon Kuznets, and others in the performance of economics as a whole, an interest in how interrelated factors function in "macroeconomic," or overall, models. When young economists with this interest turned to history as a testing ground for their theoretical assumptions, they soon found that much of the necessary information had either not been preserved or had never been collected. Consequently they place their "primary emphasis on reconstructing measurements which might have existed in the past but are no longer extant, on the recombination of primary data in a manner which enables them to obtain measurements that were never before made, and on finding methods of measuring economic phenomena that cannot be measured directly."[2]

While selections in this book illustrate both of these recent trends, still more are of the older narrative type of economic history. This choice is dictated by the assumption that students should first become generally acquainted with existing facts or data before using them more precisely in theoretical operations. A secondary consideration is that much of the "new economic history" writing necessarily deals with narrowly defined problems and is in mathematical, or econometric, form which requires special training for full

understanding. The editors hope, however, that the spirit of theoretical interest in economic development and the overall functioning of the economy permeates the book in unobtrusive ways, and that economists giving analytical, mathematical lectures may find the narrative history a useful background.

Generally, whole chapters or articles have been reprinted, but in all cases the selections seem long enough to do justice to the thinking of the author and to win a place in the memory of the reader. Besides identifying the author and the importance of the selection, the introductions afford an opportunity for noting generalizations and hypotheses arising from the writings of other scholars excluded because of space limitations or the mathematical complexities involved in the presentation of their work.

As any book of readings has to be highly selective, it is impossible to touch on all the topics that should be included in a comprehensive textbook. Yet, accompanied by lectures that fill in the material omitted in the selections, this and the accompanying volume may serve either as basic or supplemental reading for courses in American economic history, growth, or development. A brief note at the end of the volume lists standard works on American economic history to which the student may turn for additional reading.

Thomas C. Cochran
Thomas B. Brewer

[2] Robert William Fogel, "The Reunification of Economic History with Economic Theory," *The American Economic Review*, LV (May, 1965), p. 92.

Contents

Views of American Economic Growth: The Industrial Era

Chapter One

Political and Social Factors in Industrial Development

■ Strong American faith in the stability of government and the security of property rights—even the Civil War seemed to pose no lasting menace to capitalism as a system, regardless of what its outcome might be—was a major stimulant to long-range investment and hence to economic development. But to say that entrepreneurs were encouraged by faith in ultimate protection by government is not to say that they were always encouraged by what government was doing.

The relations between business and government in nineteenth-century America were complex and changing. In the succession of new communities, territories, and states there was usually an early phase, particularly in the North, when the only men with the specialized knowledge and skill to administer political and legal institutions were likely to be lawyers and a few experienced land operators and traders. The pioneer farmer, in general, lacked the education, time, and interest needed to organize politics. As the community grew, however, the pioneer political administrators became more and more engrossed with their professional and business concerns, and civic responsibilities tended to be delegated to less able men who were willing to devote their time to such affairs; and these local politicians tried to make money from the opportunities offered them, which meant political corruption.

In the older cities much the same process had taken place. Control by leading merchants and lawyers had given way during the early nineteenth century to control by professional politicians, whose chief interest was often in benefiting themselves through promoting the welfare of a particular political party. The corrupt situation that was thus created was aggravated by the influx of large numbers of immigrants from 1845 on, for these newcomers regularly became attached to the party in power locally by favors or small gifts that kept them from desperate want. Quickly they became naturalized voters and began voting for their benefactors, and they were not likely even to know the long-run economic needs of the community.

The result of all this by the 1870s was a deterioration of American political administration which in many instances interfered with economic growth. It did this by making government expensive and unreliable and by discouraging the development of the kind of intelligent economic planning and regulation that government agencies are capable of under better circumstances. On national, state, and local levels timid and venal legislators and administrators were organized and protected by bosses who calculated first what was best for the political machine and only second what was needed by the business community. On the one hand, a legislature tended to be a market in which a business leader could buy a desired law; on the other, it was a highly competitive sellers' market in which he felt he was paying an unfair price.

In the 1870s the professional, religious, and business elite of the big cities were organizing, through clubs and special committees, to bring about greater economy and efficiency in government and either to eliminate bosses or at least to make them more responsive to the interests of the economic leaders. Indeed, a general tide of upper-middle- and upper-class protest against a venal democracy based on the control of immigrant and other lower-class votes was beginning to rise. This protest became conspicuous first in separate municipal, state, and national reform efforts and ultimately in the national Progressive movement, the goal of which was to reform government at all levels. To those who believed that government favorable to business was an essential ingredient in American economic development, the better alignment of politics with the long-run needs of business was becoming of central importance.

Business Wins at Washington

■ The following selection describes the first successes, in the 1880s, of the leaders of national business over the party bosses in Washington. At this stage national businessmen chiefly wanted economy in Federal administration and protection from state interference. Later, mostly after 1900, they would favor some regulation by the Federal government in order to stimulate exports and check cutthroat domestic competition—an improved consular service, the Open Door policy, and effective railroad and food and drug regulation, for example.

Thomas C. Cochran and William Miller
The Business of Politics*

While industrial business was being consolidated into great units and winning for itself unassailable national supremacy, the business of politics, for a decade and a half after the Civil War, levied a heavy toll upon it. The general public, through federal, state, and local taxation, continued, of course, to contribute the largest amounts toward the support of professional politicians. But industrialists and railroad men especially were forced to pay extraordinary sums for political benefits, and frequently were blackmailed by threats of regulation or withdrawal of government aid. Faced with dissolution under the sectional and religious pressures of the fifties, the two-party system had now been firmly reestablished, with the new Republican party almost as strong in the federal government as the Democrats were later to become in the "Solid South." Victory in the war and paternalistic legislation during the conflict had won for the Republicans a staunch nucleus of party regulars, and expanding government functions had given Republican leaders much new patronage to barter for the support of opposition bosses as well as thousands of new officeholders to tax for lavish contributions to party chests. The politicians in power, therefore, could treat businessmen simply as customers, selling political support at the highest price the traffic would bear, depending mainly upon a nation's gratitude and party discipline for the perpetuation of their tenure.

As the relations between government and business became more and more complex, however, and agrarians and

reformers organized protesting blocs within the major parties and radical "third" parties outside them, the older spoilsmen lost their grip. They alienated businessmen by the audacity of their pecuniary demands, the public by their unremitting high taxes, and all respectable elements in society by their unrelieved record of corruption. The depression following the panic of 1873 made political levies continuously more burdensome, so enlarging the ranks of the disaffected that by the 1880's the opponents of the spoilsmen were strong enough to take control into their hands. Symbolizing the change in American politics was civil service legislation in the states and Congress, beginning first on a very small scale to remove government jobs from party control. This relieved government employees from party taxation, forcing politicians thereafter to go to industrialists and railroad men for more and more of their campaign funds. It permitted directors of national corporations, therefore, to exercise more control over the personnel of party tickets, the policies of party platforms, the actions of victorious candidates. Just as they had begun to bring order out of business anarchy, so great industrialists and railroad men began to end political piracy, no longer having to go to the governmental market to bid against one another for favors.

There was no unanimity among industrial businessmen in the 1870's and 1880's in the things they sought from political bargainers or political henchmen. Some wanted cheap money, others dear; some high tariffs, others low; some railroad regulation, others none; some subsidies and lavish grants, others strict economy. But discussion of such problems was now reserved for party councils. Politicians continued to fight bitterly for

* Reprinted with permission of The Macmillan Company from *The Age of Enterprise: A Social History of Industrial America* by Thomas C. Cochran and William Miller. Copyright 1942 by The Macmillan Company, pp. 154–180.

the spoils of office, but only in terms of personalities, conflicts over real issues being settled before they appealed to the voters—and settled almost always in the same way by Republicans and Democrats. Both recognized that industrial businessmen had become the best source of party funds, and both were eager, therefore, to serve them, the Republicans as the "ins" to maintain control of patronage and graft, the Democrats as the "outs" to strengthen their challenge for the spoils.

While in national affairs both parties thus were yielding to businessmen, in the states, especially the commercial farming areas of the Northwest, dissent from the trend of national politics grew constantly more violent. By winning in the national judiciary power similar to that which they exerted in the legislative and executive departments, however, railroad men and great industrialists were able ultimately to ward off agrarian uprisings.

"Nothing Counts except to Win"

The combination of a great war and a rapid expansion of business after 1861 greatly extended the activities of political government and multiplied political office-holders. New excises entailed a host of new tax collectors. High tariffs made the customhouses hum with unwonted activity. Army and navy contracts opened employment to purchasing agents, inspectors, bookkeepers, clerks. Government munition factories gave work to thousands; homesteads and railroad grants occupied surveyors, recorders, clerical assistants; new internal revenue taxes, the growing budget, the expanding population, the constantly increasing immigration once the war was over, created new jobs in the Treasury, the post office, and the ports. The phenomenal growth of American cities with their new requirements in police and fire protection, their construction of sewage and lighting sys-

tems and new public buildings, their paving of streets, their administration of myriad state laws and municipal ordinances added thousands more to public pay rolls. Some of these jobs ended with the war, but most of them continued after 1865; and all were filled on the recommendations of ward or district leaders, city or state bosses, Senators in Washington or the national chairmen of the parties. In the decades after the Civil War politics thus became one of the great businesses of the nation, steadily employing thousands of workers, seeking profits like any other enterprise in a competitive society.

It has become customary to call the Republican party after the Civil War the party of "Big Business," the Democratic the party of reform. At no time, however, did either party have a monopoly of bankers, industrialists, railroad men, or reformers; and until the 1880's both were managed by politicians mainly for the benefit of politicians. Nothing shows this more clearly than the way in which the latter rigged the collection of customs "to annoy, vex and deplete" importers.[1] The excise on whisky, the politicians used not to supply the government with revenue, thus reducing other taxes, but to support their state machines—notably in Illinois, Indiana, Wisconsin, and Missouri.[2] The Democratic Tweed Ring in New York, the Republican Gas Ring in Philadelphia, the bosses of Washington, San Francisco, Cincinnati, and St. Louis, all taxed businessmen severely only to line their own pockets and those of their political

[1] Under the revenue law in force until 1874 whole shipments could be condemned for fraud on the basis of discrepancies that the importer could not prevent. Half of the money received from such condemnation was to be divided between the informant and the customs officials. (Carlos Martyn, *William E. Dodge*, Funk & Wagnalls, 1890, p. 290; Matthew Josephson, *The Politicos, 1865–1896*, Harcourt Brace, 1938, pp. 96, 153–154.)
[2] Allan Nevins, *Hamilton Fish*, Dodd, Mead, 1936, pp. 762–763.

partners. Certainly the Reconstruction governments in the southern states functioned for no business but that of the carpetbaggers, making industrialists and railroad men wary about venturing into the region. "A party," said Secretary Seward, "is in one sense a joint stock company in which those who contribute the most, direct the action and management of the concern."[3] Until the early 1880's contributions to both parties came mainly from officeholders and from candidates who depended upon the parties for support. Until then, therefore, the parties were run for their benefit, as was the government, which could not operate without them. "What are we here for," exclaimed a delegate at the Republican National Convention in 1880, "except the offices?"[4] "The source of power and the cohesive force" in American political parties, said James Bryce, "is the desire for office and for office as a means of gain."[5]

In the age of Johnson and Grant politicians dealt in federal lands, mining and lumber resources, protective tariffs, mail contracts, subsidies, and pensions. They could regulate business, tax it, or protect it from regulation or taxation. Some critics of American politics in this period have complained that in distributing their favors the politicians acted for the benefit of Big Business. But we have seen what it cost Huntington, for instance, to get land grants for the Central and Southern Pacific, what it cost him to avoid paying his government loans. In November, 1877, Huntington wrote to his colleague, Colton:[6]

You have no idea how I am annoyed by this Washington business, and I must and will give it up after this session. If we are not hurt this session it will be because we pay much money to prevent it, and you know how hard it is to get it to pay for such purposes; and I do not see my way clear to get through here and pay the January interest with other bills payable to January 1st, with less than $2,000,000 and probably not for that. . . . I think Congress will try very hard to pass some kind of a bill to make us commence paying on what we owe the government. I am striving very hard to get a bill in such shape that we can accept it, as this Washington business will kill me yet if I have to continue the fight from year to year, and then every year the fight grows more and more expensive; and rather than let it continue as it is from year to year, . . . I would rather they take the road and be done with it.

Jay Cooke of the Northern Pacific, Ames and Durant of the Union Pacific, Tom Scott of the Texas & Pacific, all had similar tribulations. The politicians were eager to do business with Big Business men only because the latter offered the largest fees; in an age of fearful competition, such businessmen vied with one another in bribing legislatures, administrators, judges to gain any advantage over their rivals. Stevenson of Ohio said in 1873:[7]

The House of Representatives was like an auction room where more valuable considerations were disposed of under the speaker's hammer than in any other place on earth.

A party needed only votes to win seats in Congress and in state and local legislatures in order to carry on this business of politics. And as long as a party had its share of the spoils it could control sufficient votes. Not only was every officeholder forced to contribute money to the party chest, but he had constantly to work for the party ticket, to drum up votes at election time, to work for the district between elections. The twenty-

[3] Charles A. Beard, *The Rise of American Civilization*, vol. II, Macmillan, 1928, p. 7.
[4] James Bryce, *The American Commonwealth*, vol. II, Macmillan, 1888, p. 106.
[5] *Ibid.*, p. 102.
[6] Stuart Daggett, *Chapters on the History of the Southern Pacific*, Ronald, 1922, pp. 211–212.
[7] Josephson, *op. cit.*, p. 118.

five hundred customhouse employees in New York City were the backbone of the Conkling organization. The internal revenue collectors operating from St. Louis were the zealous agents of Logan of Illinois and Morton of Indiana. Ben Butler in Massachusetts, Zach Chandler in Michigan, Simon Cameron in Pennsylvania, each had his army of postal clerks and federal marshals trumpeting for the Republican stalwarts in his state. Add to them city and county officials— each not only a voter but a procurer of voters whose job depended upon his proficiency in the ward—and it is not difficult to understand how party loyalty was achieved and party discipline maintained.

Party funds were used to rent offices and halls, to pay clerical help, to print posters and pamphlets, for traveling expenses. Where this combination did not guarantee the necessary votes, they were sought through bribery and fraud. "There are men in New York whom you can buy to make a false oath for a glass of beer," declared Henry Butts, who investigated naturalization frauds during Tweed's regime.[8] Such oaths were required in the manufacture of citizens out of aliens and were made by the thousands when the machine was in danger. Between October 8 and October 23, 1868, for instance, Judge Barnard of the New York State Supreme Court naturalized 10,093 men, said the *Tribune*, "with no more solemnity than, and quite as much celerity as, is displayed in converting swine into pork in a Cincinnati packing house."[9]

From time to time in the 1870's businessmen rebelled against the excesses of bossdom, organizing "liberal" movements in self-defense. In 1871 Democratic lawyers, bankers, and industrialists like Samuel Tilden, August Belmont, and W. F.

Havemeyer formed the New York Citizens' Committee to oust Tweed. In the same year Republicans like A. T. Stewart, William E. Dodge, W. and J. Sloane, and Arnold Constable combined to protest against Conkling and his Republican henchmen in the New York Customhouse. As soon as they achieved their immediate objectives, however, such movements collapsed. Merchants, manufacturers, bankers, and lawyers had other businesses than politics to attend to. Besides, they themselves cut too many corners to tolerate absolutely honest administrators. What they wanted, as Horatio Seymour put it in a letter to Tilden in 1871, was "men in office who will not steal but who will not interfere with those who do."[10] Such men, however, were hard to find, especially among professional politicians.

The End of the Spoilsmen

The Republican party emerged from the war period as the savior of the Union, the emancipator of the Negro, the grantor of homesteads, railroad lands, and high tariffs. It had, therefore, strong emotional and material claims upon the affections of the American people. On the other hand, the Democrats, as the older party, had on their side traditional allegiances, old members and machines. While the loss of the South during radical reconstruction decimated their resources, the Democrats maintained their ranks in the North and controlled many states and municipalities. Between them, therefore, the two parties monopolized political offices and traded them as members of business pools traded market rights and divided profits. In Philadelphia, for instance, in 1881, Republican reformers appealed to the Democrats to support their candidate for Receiver of Taxes

[8] M. R. Werner, *Tammany Hall*, Doubleday, Doran, 1928, p. 135.
[9] *Ibid.*, p. 134.

[10] De Alva S. Alexander, *Political History of the State of New York*, vol. III, Holt, 1906, p. 311.

against the regular Republican ticket put up by the Gas Ring. For a share in the booty of the Ring the Democratic bosses refused. They preferred allowing the Republican organization to win rather than to jeopardize the whole system of political business by supporting an independent reformer.[11]

By the 1880's, however, the conditions that had permitted Republican Stalwarts to entrench themselves in the federal and state governments had run their course. The war was long since over. Reconstruction was complete. Southern Democrats had retrieved their civil and political rights, and federal troops supporting the carpetbag governments had been removed. In addition, the old Stalwarts themselves were dying or retiring from politics. Oliver P. Morton died in 1877, Zach Chandler in 1879, Logan in 1886. Simon Cameron, boss of Pennsylvania, seventy-eight years old in 1877, abdicated in favor of his son. In 1881 Conkling, refused patronage by Garfield, resigned from the Senate. In 1883 Ben Butler bolted from the Republican party to become Democratic Governor of Massachusetts, the next year becoming Greenback candidate for the Presidency.

In national affairs the Democrats had had no opportunities to develop such corruptionists as dominated Republican ranks, but many Democratic state and local machines had been second only to the carpetbag governments in their quest for political booty. As early as 1874, however, in the key state of New York, the "liberal" elements in both parties rewarded Democrat Tilden with the governorship for his prosecution of the Tweed Ring. In 1876 Lucius Robinson, a director of the reformed Erie Railroad, was elected in Tilden's place despite Tammany's opposition, and in 1882 Grover Cleveland became chief executive of the state. By 1884 the nation had

followed the example of New York, sending Cleveland to the White House, the first Democrat to reside there since Buchanan.

Each of these political changes was a measure of the control businessmen were gaining over the major parties. American industry in the late seventies and eighties was employing each year more and more capital and labor, strengthening its pressure groups, clarifying its interests. Spencerian philosophers were spreading broadcast the ideal of progress through business competition, and businessmen were making the claims of the philosophers seem but the clearest common sense. "Life [in America] in the last forty or fifty years," wrote Godkin of the New York *Nation* in 1882, "has grown easier, pleasanter, and more luxurious. Life in the United States to the average man is a sort of paradise."[12] President Harrison in his inaugural address in 1889 spoke of American progress and prosperity as[13]

so magnificent in extent, so pleasant to look upon, so full of generous suggestion to enterprise and labor. God has placed upon our head a diadem and has laid at our feet power and wealth beyond definition and calculation.

The younger political leaders like New York's Tom Platt and Maine's "Czar" Reed had been bred in this atmosphere of expanding business enterprise, while "reconstructed" southerners like Joseph Brown and Henry Grady were spreading its gospel through the South. "A nervous energy permeates all classes of people and all departments of trade and the spirit of enterprise never sleeps," declared a southerner of Atlanta in 1881. "We have challenged your spinners in Massachusetts and your iron makers in Pennsylvania," boasted Grady. "We have sowed towns and cities in the place of theories,

[11] Bryce, *op. cit.*, p. 374.

[12] *The Nation*, vol. XXXV, pp. 348–349.
[13] Josephson, *op. cit.*, p. 441.

and put business in place of politics."
Augusta boasted of being "the Lowell of
the South"; Columbus, "the Pittsburgh of
the South"; Atlanta, "the legitimate offspring of Chicago": "Yes sir-ree, it's a
regular little old metropolis . . . 89,000
people in the last census—and *Progress?*
Gen-tle-men, *Progress? I'll say Progress!*"[14]

Besides "reconstructed" southerners,
northern businessmen like Stanford of
the Central and Southern Pacific and
Depew of the New York Central were
themselves entering Congress in the
1880's. And after the passage of the
Pendleton Civil Service Act in 1883 the
new politicians came increasingly to depend upon such businessmen to finance
machine work. At the same time old
ward heelers were being supplemented
at election time by ambitious clerks and
salesmen. Garfield had complained in
1870 that businessmen "want a representative in Congress that they can own
and carry around in their pantaloons
pocket." By 1880, however, he was asking
and receiving the "assistance in the
canvass of Rockefeller's force of five
hundred oil-selling agents located all
about Indiana."[15] In 1884 the Democrats
also enlisted business aid. " 'What about
this man Cleveland?' wrote James J. Hill,
the western railroad builder, to Tilden.
'He is all right,' replied the corporation
lawyer. Hill thereupon sent Manning
[Cleveland's manager] $10,000—and
telegraphed his associates in the West
'to get busy' for Mr. Cleveland."[16]

The transition from political business to
business politics was not an abrupt one.
It became evident roughly about 1876
with the Tilden-Hayes campaign when the
bosses of each party felt the need to
conciliate the electorate with candidates
who were unassailable as "good machine

men." It was complete by 1888 when
Harrison was teamed with the New York
banker Levi Morton to run against the
New York gold Democrat Cleveland. In
February, 1877, just before Grant left
office, the western capitalist John H. Van
Alen wrote that[17]

no permanent revival of business . . . can be
hoped for until important reforms are effected
and an administration shall be organized on
principles widely different from those which
have governed the present one.

By 1882 those "reforms" had been so
thoroughly "effected" that Henry Demarest Lloyd, after observing that "the
Standard [Oil Company] has done everything with the Pennsylvania legislature
except to refine it," could complain:[18]

Rings and bosses are rising to the top in the
evolution of industry as in that of politics. . . .
A few individuals are becoming rich enough to
control almost all the great markets, including
the legislatures.

And by 1889, according to William Allen
White,[19]

a United States senator . . . represented something more than a state, more even than a
region. He represented principalities and powers
in business. One senator, for instance, represented the Union Pacific Railway System, another the New York Central, still another the
insurance interests of New York and New Jersey. . . . Coal and iron owned a coterie from
the Middle and Eastern seaport states. Cotton
had half a dozen senators. And so it went.

Harrison's cabinet was sometimes
called the "Businessman's Cabinet" because it included the merchant John
Wanamaker and the marble king of
Vermont, Redfield Proctor. But it was in

[14] C. Vann Woodward, *Tom Watson, Agrarian Rebel*, Macmillan, 1938, pp. 86, 115, 123.
[15] Josephson, *op. cit.*, pp. 113, 291.
[16] Joseph G. Pyle, *Life of James J. Hill*, vol. I, Doubleday, Page, 1917, p. 426.

[17] Josephson, *op. cit.*, p. 239.
[18] *Ibid.*, p. 344.
[19] William Allen White, *Masks in a Pageant*, Macmillan, 1928, p. 79.

the Senate that the change in American politics could now be seen most clearly. Among the great businessmen there by 1889 were the lumbermen McMillan and Stockbridge of Michigan and Philetus Sawyer of Wisconsin. From Ohio had come Calvin Brice, director of banks and railroads, and H. B. Payne, father of the Standard Oil magnate; from Nevada, James Fair, the "Bonanza king," and John P. Jones, owner of silver mines. California sent the gold miner and newspaper publisher George Hearst. Together with William B. Allison of Iowa, Donald Cameron of Pennsylvania and Nelson Aldrich of Rhode Island—each a representative of banks, railroads, and other utilities—these men constituted a ruling clique that through the committee system of legislation controlled every bill that tried to run the gantlet of the Senate. And presiding over their activities was Vice President Levi Morton, who ranked with Belmont and Morgan as one of the greatest bankers in the land.

This august body was labeled the "Millionaires' Club" by contemporaries. What its members thought of themselves and their colleagues was felicitously expressed some years later by Senator Hearst:[20]

I do not know much about books; I have not read very much; but I have travelled a good deal and observed men and things and I have made up my mind after all my experiences that the members of the Senate are the survivors of the fittest.

The Defense of National Business

The contradictions in party records might confuse the voting public, and the silence of party platforms on many basic issues might only add to the confusion, but

periodically even the politicians of the ruling business interests had to go to the public for votes. Simply for the right to continue in office, therefore, they had from time to time to make concessions to this public, passing laws which did not directly favor the leading interests. Big Business men were willing to yield such laws to keep their own politicians in power and also to forestall more stringent legislation later. Against the strict enforcement of these laws, however, the leading interests had to protect themselves, and in almost every instance the machinery they created for this purpose proved successful—but not always before business was forced to resort to expensive corruption and to make expensive compromises. To remove the sting from the Granger legislation of the late sixties and early seventies, for instance, agents of the railroads had to bribe the commissioners and legislative committees selected to regulate rates, or railroad politicians had to arrange to get friendly legislators elected or friendly commissioners appointed. In the meantime, the companies were forced to wage costly court trials until ultimate victory was won. Similar expenses were incurred by great national corporations in their efforts to sidetrack or defeat state legislative attacks upon their charters, or state suits alleging that their charters had been circumvented or ignored.

That business politicians were ultimately successful in defeating these early popular attacks upon Big Business corporations was clearly shown by the repeal of the "Granger" laws in Minnesota, Iowa, and Wisconsin within two years after they had been passed. The growing demand throughout the nation for *federal* regulation of railroads and industrial "trusts" also showed the strength of Big Business resistance in the states, while the Supreme Court's decision in the Wabash case in 1886 gave final legal sanction to such resistance, declaring that the states

20 Josephson, op. cit., p. 445.

could not regulate, even within their own borders, any traffic that involved interstate commerce. Since these defeats for the opponents of Big Business only aroused stronger and stronger demands for federal action, however, new concessions had to be made by business politicians. Between 1874 and 1885, more than thirty measures were introduced in the House of Representatives providing for the regulation of interstate railroads; and some of these measures actually were passed, only to die in the Senate. By 1885, however, as memorials and petitions from chambers of commerce and citizens in eastern states were added to the flood of anti-railroad arguments and literature that had been coming from the Middle West for more than a decade, even the Senate had to yield. Its initial response was the appointment of the Cullom Committee to conduct a thorough investigation into all phases of the problem of federal regulation of the railroads. In 1886 this committee made its report, concluding:

It is the deliberate judgment of the Committee that upon no public question are the people so nearly unanimous as upon the proposition that Congress should undertake in some way the regulation of interstate commerce.

This recommendation, combined with the Wabash decision forbidding the states to continue with their regulations, set the stage for the Interstate Commerce Act, signed by President Cleveland on February 4, 1887.

The Interstate Commerce Act was greeted with cheers throughout the farm regions of the West and by small businessmen everywhere. But the cheers were premature. The Act was to be administered by the Interstate Commerce Commission, simply a fact-finding commission with no coercive powers. The Commission could issue "cease and desist" orders to interstate railroads charged by shippers or state commissions with giving discriminatory rates, rebates, or drawbacks to favored corporations, or with levying monopoly rates for short hauls, or with pooling traffic with other companies to keep up rates in competitive territories. But the commission had to appeal to the federal courts to enforce its orders; it could not enforce them itself. Thus the machinery was established for the obstructionism which the railroads soon became adept in employing. The commission's orders would be received, the accused railroad would pretend to comply with them, in the meantime continuing its old practices. The commission would then appeal to the courts for an injunction against the offending railroad, and the railroad would appeal the injunction. The court would hear the appeal and render its decision. Then the loser—either railroad or commission—would appeal to a higher court and finally to the United States Supreme Court, where a final disposition of the case would be made, on the average about four years after the original complaint was instituted. During all that time, the railroads would continue with impunity their old rate schedules, their pools, their systems of rebates and drawbacks, sometimes, indeed, making them even more burdensome upon complaining shippers in retaliation for their accusations. And in the end, the complainants would get no redress whatsoever. Between 1887 and 1905 the Supreme Court heard sixteen cases brought before it under the Interstate Commerce Act. In fifteen it found for the railroads.[21]

The "trust" movement among manufacturing corporations, as we have seen, came later in America than the development of interstate railroad systems, and efforts to regulate the "trusts" were commensurately delayed. By 1887, however,

[21] William Z. Ripley, *Railroads: Rates and Regulation*, vol. I, Longmans, Green, 1912, p. 463.

Louisiana had instituted suit against the Cottonseed Oil Trust and Nebraska against the Whiskey Trust. In 1888 New York attacked the Sugar combine, and in 1890 Ohio sued the giant of them all, the Standard Oil Company. All these actions were "successful," the "trust" being ordered dissolved in each case. In the meantime, in 1888 the House Committee on Manufactures began an extended investigation into various "trusts," and under Populist auspices a great "anti-trust" drive had gotten under way in the West with Kansas in the lead. In 1889 that state passed the first state "anti-trust" act; by 1893 it had been followed by others in fifteen states and territories.

The House investigation succeeded only in postponing congressional action on the "trust problem" and arousing heated discussions of it in many of the new periodicals and journals of the time. It was a problem fraught with complications, most of which the legislators did not understand. It was clear, however, as in the case of the railroads, that the politicians had to take some action. Senator Sherman defined Congress's predicament when he declared in 1890:[22]

They had monopolies and mortmains of old, but never before such giants as in our day. You must heed their appeal [the American people's] or be ready for the socialist, the communist, the nihilist. Society is now disturbed by forces never felt before. Congress alone can deal with the trusts, and if we are unwilling or unable there will soon be a trust for every production and a master to fix the price for every necessity of life.

Congress showed how willing it was to deal with the problem, passing without a murmur of dissent in July, 1890, the Sherman "antitrust" act which declared illegal any combination in restraint of trade or any attempt at monopoly. Sherman had little to do with writing the act that bears his name. It was written mainly by Senators Edmunds and Hoar, the latter remarking of Sherman: "I do not think he ever understood it."[23] Sherman, however, introduced the bill into the Senate and was active in pushing its adoption.

The Interstate Commerce Act was a sop to the malcontents in American political society, the minimum concession by Big Business politicians to a balking electorate. The act was "a delusion and a sham," admitted Senator Aldrich himself, ". . . an empty menace to great interests, made to answer the clamor of the ignorant and the unreasoning."[24] The Sherman Act was a similar device designed to meet a similar situation. Of its passage through the Senate, Republican Senator Orville Platt of Connecticut declared:[25]

The conduct of the Senate . . . has not been in the line of honest preparation of a bill to prohibit and punish trusts. It has been in the line of getting some bill with that title that we might go to the country with. The questions of whether the bill would be operative, of how it would operate, . . . have been whistled down the wind in this Senate as idle talk, and the whole effort has been to get some bill headed: "A Bill to Punish Trusts" with which to go to the country.

If the Sherman Act "were strictly and literally enforced," said Senator Cullom, "the business of the country would come to a standstill."[26] And Mr. Dooley, commenting on the Act, said: "What looks like

[22] Louis M. Hacker and Benjamin B. Kendrick, The United States Since 1865, Crofts, 1939, p. 282.

[23] Josephson, op. cit., p. 459.
[24] Nathaniel W. Stephenson, Nelson W. Aldrich, Scribner's, 1930, p. 68.
[25] Louis A. Coolidge, An Old Fashioned Senator: Orville H. Platt, Putnam's, 1910, p. 444. For a divergent explanation see John D. Clark, The Federal Trust Policy, Johns Hopkins, 1931, pp. 29 ff.
[26] Shelby Cullom, Fifty Years of Public Service, A. C. McClung, 1911, p. 254.

a stone-wall to a layman is a triumphal arch to a corporation lawyer."

While both acts were designed for circumvention, however, and national business interests in fact had no difficulty in getting around them, they proved to be expensive nuisances that Big Business would have much preferred to avoid. Moreover, they were constant reminders that the protective armor of *laissez faire* had been dented at last, no matter how slightly, by the importunities of a harassed public. It was not long, therefore, before a movement was under way for the repeal of both acts. The Sherman Act, however, soon became an effective instrument in fighting labor organizations, and repeal talk was quieted. And by 1892 the better part of political wisdom, as far as the Interstate Commerce Act was concerned, also seemed to be for business to *use* the new government agencies for their own purposes rather than to attempt to crush them. That at least was the opinion of Attorney General Olney, who was so close to railroad men that he had accepted the Attorney Generalship from Cleveland only after getting permission from President Perkins of the Chicago, Burlington & Quincy. In December, 1892, Olney wrote to Perkins:[27]

My impression would be that looking at the matter from a railroad point of view exclusively it [repeal of the Interstate Commerce Act] would not be a wise thing to undertake. . . . The attempt would not be likely to succeed; if it did not succeed, and were made on the ground of the inefficiency and uselessness of the Commission, the result would very probably be giving it the power it now lacks. The Commission, as its functions have now been limited by the courts, is, or can be made, of great use to the railroads. It satisfies the popular clamor for government supervision of the railroads, at the same time that that supervi-

sion is almost entirely nominal. Further, the older such a commission gets to be, the more inclined it will be found to take the business and railroad view of things. It thus becomes a sort of barrier between the railroad corporations and the people and a sort of protection against hasty and crude legislation hostile to railroad interests. . . . The part of wisdom is not to destroy the Commission, but to utilize it.

While national business interests were fighting lesser competitors and their agrarian allies on the battlefield of regulation, the bankers were also forced to energetic defensive measures against legislative meddling with the currency, and the protected manufacturing interests had to fight constantly against downward revision of the tariff. Both of these groups, in the end, proved as successful as the railroads and the "trusts" in maintaining their strong positions in our political set-up. Against the bankers, the representatives of the commercial farmers and the silver miners of the West succeeded in passing various currency and coinage bills in the seventies and eighties. And in 1890, in return for their votes on the McKinley Tariff, the "free silverites" got the Sherman Silver Purchase Act, which greatly enlarged the coinage of silver and the circulation of "silver" legal tender certificates. By 1893, however, under pressure from President Cleveland, who blamed the Silver Purchase Act for the decline of government gold reserves, the Sherman Act was repealed and the country returned to a single gold standard. This was a signal victory for the bankers who had tried so hard to convince the American people that "dear" money was the only "sound" money, that legislative tinkering with exchange was "immoral," that gold alone was the only "true" standard of value. Coming just when the panic of 1893 burst upon the land, this repeal set the stage for the dramatic struggle of 1896, when the bankers and their industrial allies in the East and Middle West ably defended their

[27] Josephson, *op. cit.*, pp. 525, 526. See also I. L. Sharfman, *The Interstate Commerce Commission*, vol. I, Commonwealth Fund, 1931–1937, p. 35.

victory, sending down to a crushing defeat William Jennings Bryan and his free silver, debtor agrarian followers.

In defense of the "gold standard" bankers had to fight only silver miners and debtor farmers. In defense of high tariffs, industrialists had to fight the farmers, practically all the shipowners in the country and their banker allies as well as some manufacturers. The Standard Oil Company, for instance, being a great user of tin cans for kerosene and other products, carried on an unremitting warfare against the tin schedule. Despite the strength of the opposition, however, the high-tariff principle was maintained even more successfully than the "gold standard" right up to 1913, though a few concessions were made to special groups. Before 1890 the demand for a reduced tariff received important Congressional recognition only in the act of 1882 creating a presidential Tariff Commission to investigate the needs of American industry, in the innocuous act of 1883, and in the Mills bill of 1888 which passed the House as a low-tariff measure. Of the Tariff Commission appointed by President Arthur, Senator Aldrich explained that[28]

there was a representative of the wool growers on the commission; there was a representative of the iron interest on the commission; there was a representative of the sugar interest on the commission; and those interests were very carefully looked out for.

If the Tariff Commission was packed from the start with men picked by the protected interests themselves, the Mills bill was made safe in a different way. Introduced into the House as a Democratic measure in response to Cleveland's "tariff issue" message of 1887, this bill was passed by the Democratic majority. In the Senate, however, at the urgent behest of James M. Swank, secretary and leading lobbyist of the Iron and Steel Association, the bill

was amended so drastically that nothing remained but the enacting clause, to which the Senate added what was virtually its own tariff measure. In April, 1888, Swank had written to Senator Morrill:[29]

To amend the Mills Bill in the Senate (in any form) would be a victory for the Democrats, who would make the most of it in the Presidential campaign. No matter how nearly perfect the Senate might make the Mills Bill it would still be the Mills Bill.

So adamant was the Senate, therefore, in insisting upon its version, and so firm was the House in objecting to it that the two-headed bill was allowed to die in the conference of the two houses.

Having resisted the efforts of the Democrats to win popular favor by reducing the tariff, the Republicans in the next election went all out to elect their own President and Congress. Money was spent like water, and illicit voting was rife; and in the end the indefatigable Matt Quay was able to notify Harrison that he had won out. "Providence has given us the victory," exclaimed Harrison when he learned the news. "Think of the man," Quay later expostulated to A. K. McClure. "He ought to know that Providence hadn't a damn thing to do with it." And he added that he supposed Harrison "would never know how close a number of men were compelled to approach the gates of the penitentiary to make him President."[30]

When the Republicans returned to Washington victorious after this hectic campaign, they were faced not only with the tariff question once more but with the huge surplus of idle government funds in the Treasury, piled up during a decade of prosperity from internal revenue, large customs receipts, and the parsimony of the Cleveland regime. To meet both situations the McKinley Tariff was passed.

[28] Stephenson, *op. cit.*, p. 431, note.

[29] Josephson, *op. cit.*, p. 404.
[30] *Ibid.*, p. 433.

Rather than reduce the tariff to an average rate sufficient to meet the financial needs of the government, at the instigation of Senator Randall, Democrat from Pennsylvania, Congress enacted the most prohibitory protective duties in our history on certain schedules, while reducing revenue duties and broadening the free list only for the importation of goods which could not possibly be produced in the United States and could not, therefore, compete with any American products. Western opposition to this measure was angry and articulate, but westerners were bought off with the Sherman Silver Purchase Act.

By 1894, however, depression once again had sapped the confidence of the nation. Agrarians had learned the futility of the Interstate Commerce Act and the Sherman Anti-trust Act, and the Silver Purchase Act had been repealed. Populists had won many seats in Congress, Cleveland was once more in the White House, and the westerners had found in William Jennings Bryan the greatest orator of his day to tell their story to the nation. In such an atmosphere the Wilson Tariff was introduced in the House, moderately reducing rates on most commodities and carrying the hated income-tax provision. After many amendments had been proposed and defeated, the bill came to a vote and was carried only after revealing deep fissures in the ranks of both parties.

Then the interests in the Senate got to work on it. When it finally emerged from "the mysterious recesses of the Democratic steering committee," it had become the Wilson-Gorman Tariff, representing, as Senator Aldrich admitted, "a switch to Protection, incorporating increases from 10 to 300 percent in a long list of items."[31]

Thus the "Millionaires' Club" in the Senate emasculated the last opposition measure of the three decades after the Civil War. But it was left to the Supreme Court in 1895 to administer the *coup de grâce*. The income-tax provision of the Wilson-Gorman Tariff Act had somehow weathered the storm of the Senate's attack; but it was immediately challenged in a suit which promptly came to the Supreme Court. By a five-to-four decision it was declared unconstitutional. This verdict, said Justice Harlan in his dissenting opinion, "did monstrous, wicked injustice to the many for the benefit of the favored few in particular states." The St. Louis *Post-Dispatch* declared:[32]

Today's decision shows that the corporations and plutocrats are as securely intrenched in the Supreme Court as in the lower courts which they take such pains to control.

[31] Josephson, *op. cit.*, p. 545.
[32] Elmer Ellis, "Public Opinion and the Income Tax," *Mississippi Valley Historical Review*, vol. XXVII, p. 240.

The Urban Problem

■ In developing countries, the United States included, construction has always been the largest major category of investment, and in the United States from 1850 to 1900, the essentially municipal items of construction—homes, streets, water supply systems, sewers, offices, and public buildings—cost more than factories and railroads combined.

Since lower railroad rates made it wise to concentrate business operations at junction points, large cities became the chief consumers of all these investments in construction and therefore the most important influence on the allocation of capital in the economy.

As the nineteenth century drew to a close, and particularly after the coming of electric lighting and traction, it became clear to many private taxpayers that the economic affairs of municipal government were too important to be left to a hierarchy of bosses based on the support of the poorest wards.

Edward C. Kirkland, professor emeritus of Bowdoin College, deals primarily with the basic elements of urban growth and the new problems it gave rise to, and only incidentally with some of the efforts at reform.

Edward C. Kirkland
Building American Cities*

Urban Growth and the Welfare of the Economy

To those who believed that the welfare of the American economy depended upon the production of capital goods, the decade of the eighties brought forebodings. The most obvious support for this theory had been the construction of the railroad network. Its constantly extending mileage had given employment and business directly to thousands; it had also stimulated auxiliary activities such as the iron and steel industry and the engineering trades. Now railroad expansion was slowing down. What was to take its place? What power was now to pull the economy forward?

Though the answer was by no means obvious, the new generative factor was the growth of American cities. There had been cities, of course, in the colonial era, and in the first half of the nineteenth century population had gone cityward as well as westward. But after the Civil War the railroads and the industrialization of the economy compelled urbanization at rapid speed. In 1860 the number of places

in the United States with a population of 8,000 or over was 141; in 1900, it was 545. At the same time there was a progressive increase in the absolute totals of urban dwellers. Whereas in 1860 just over 5,000,000 people lived in cities, in 1900 the urban population was just under 25,000,000. The eighties was the decade *par excellence* of urban growth; for those ten years the Federal Census reported "A very large increase in urban population."[1]

The startling accessions of population to cities came from two migrations: one from the country to the city and the other from abroad. On the whole the former, at least in quantitative terms, was probably the more important. Since the country-city migration was merely a population displacement within the national boundaries, it is hard to estimate its net effects. In 1891 the *Commercial and Financial Chronicle*, brooding over the decline of New Hampshire and Massachusetts small towns, expressed distress at this "decay" and "the melancholy story of the farming towns" but added that so long as Massachusetts "as a whole, is showing such vigor, there is no room for lamentations

* From *Industry Comes of Age: Business, Labor and Public Policy, 1860–1897*. Copyright © 1961 by Holt, Rinehart and Winston, Inc. Used by permission of the publishers, pp. 237–261.

[1] *Twelfth Census of the United States. 1900,* I, *Population,* Pt. 1, p. lxxxiii.

over the drift of population away from the barren hillsides."[2] On the other hand, immigrants from abroad represented an addition to the economy. These were producers and consumers the United States had not had before. And they came fast and numerously in the late nineteenth century. In 1882 their number, 788,992, set a record up to that time and one not to be surpassed until 1903.[3]

Though not all immigrants went to cities, and the enlarging population, wherever located, was a stimulus to the economy, there were differences between cities and rural regions which were of profound importance. The compacting and concentration of population stimulated economic activities, for example urban transportation and the provision of electricity from a central station, which a dispersed population in those days could neither have called into being nor supported. Where people were gathered in communities, standards of taste, convenience, and economic necessity compelled other improvements. For instance, officials of Augusta, Maine, complained in 1880: "The method of keeping . . . the main street in condition, is to haul on gravel in the summer and grade up in places where needed. In the fall and spring this makes a road-bed of 6 or 8 inches of mud. . . . Then in the spring our streets are scraped and the gravel that was hauled in is again carted out."[4] This was a road condition to which country dwellers had become, perforce, reconciled. It was humiliating to an aspiring city if "not a single paved street exists."

Furthermore, in the country the building of houses and barns was apt to be assimilated to the partially self-sufficing regime of the farm; in the urban communities it was set apart and organized into commercial construction, the building industry. In 1900, 63 per cent of the establishments in the building trade were located in the country's 209 cities and construction expenditures on farms constituted less than 10 per cent of the nation's total.[5] Finally, in the city considerations of the relation between sanitation and health, to mention no other factors, raised problems that had to be met by community rather than individual or familial action. The provision of pure water and the disposal of waste meant that in the city reliance upon public policy in social and economic matters came earlier and went deeper than elsewhere in the United States.

The problem and challenges inherent in these figures and circumstances induced in some a state of ecstasy. As F. C. Howe of Cleveland was to write: "The possibility of a free, orderly, and beautiful city became to me an absorbing passion. . . . I had an architectonic vision of what a city might be. I saw it as a picture. It was not economy, efficiency, and business methods that interested me so much as a city planned, built, and conducted as a community enterprise. . . . The city was the enthusiasm of my life. And I saw cities as social agencies that would make life easier for people, full of pleasure, beauty, and opportunity."[6] Whatever Howe might dream, the city wore a very material aspect. It had to be built. To some extent the increase in municipal debt mirrored this necessity. Though such debts might occasionally represent operational costs they were primarily capital expenditures. In 1860 net municipal in-

[2] Commercial and Financial Chronicle, LII (February 7, 1891), 221–222.
[3] Bureau of the Census, Handbook of Historical Statistics, 1789–1945, pp. 33–34.
[4] Census Office, Tenth Census of the United States–1880, XVIII, Report on the Social Statistics of Cities, Pt. 1, p. 7.

[5] Twelfth Census of the United States. 1900, VII, Manufactures, Pt. 1, p. cclvi; R. W. Goldsmith, A Study of Saving in the United States (Princeton: Princeton University Press, 1955), I, 619.
[6] F. C. Howe, The Confessions of a Reformer (New York: Charles Scribner's Sons, 1925), pp. 113–114.

debtedness in the country was estimated at $200,000,000; in 1880 it was $725,-000,000, and in 1902 $1,433,000,000.[7] Whereas early in the period these sums were fed into the economy via city subscriptions to railroad securities or other forms of railroad subsidy, the revulsion against the railroad-aid policy in the hard times after 1873 meant that municipal expenditures for other purposes became more important.

Unhappily for purposes of historically measuring and tracing such expenditures, statistical data cannot be pushed very far back into the nineteenth century. But the investment in municipal water works in 1905 was estimated at "considerably more than a billion dollars";[8] in gas works, plants and distributing systems, the sum in 1900 was $567,000,506, about twenty times what it had been in 1860.[9] In 1860 neither central electric power stations nor electric railways existed. In 1902 the issued capitalization and funded debt of electric stations selling power in the commercial market was $627,515,875;[10] At the same date for street railways the capitalization and funded debt was $2,308,-282,099.[11]

The Choice of Public or Private Enterprise

Cities could turn over the provision of municipal services to private enterprise or furnish them at first hand through municipal ownership and operation. Though state legislatures restricted the capacity of cities to go into debt and otherwise limit their functions, cities remained public corporations chartered for public purposes.[12] In favorable circumstances the legal hindrances to activity were not excessive. In 1897 the appellate division of the New York Supreme Court, validating New York City's issue of bonds for the construction and ownership of a subway, asserted that it was a principle of our nation's policy "to foster and protect private enterprise." Nonetheless the municipal ownership of a subway system was neither "socialism nor paternalism." There were other purposes cities could fulfill by their energy and expenditure. It was futile to formulate "a complete definition of 'a city purpose' . . . in view of the fact that reasons may arise which we are unable to foresee or now consider."[13] In the same decade the justices of the Massachusetts Supreme Court unanimously approved a wide area for the municipal provision of public services.[14]

If the city chose to fulfill its functions through the agency of a private corporation, the transfer of responsibility was usually effected by the grant of a franchise, either from the state or city government depending upon the date and jurisdiction. Such contractual documents permitted a private corporation to acquire property through eminent domain and to use the streets to lay pipes, install conduits, put down rails, or string wires. "The political science of the street is of fundamental importance in most municipal problems," commented one expert.[15] Since the streets were generally not wide enough to accommodate competitors, a franchise was usually equivalent to a monopoly

[7] Paul Studensky, *Public Borrowing* (New York: National Municipal League, 1930), p. 13; *Commercial and Financial Chronicle*, XX (May 15, 1875), 463–464.
[8] D. F. Wilcox, *Municipal Franchises* (Rochester, N.Y.: The Gervaise Press, 1910), I, 399.
[9] *Twelfth Census of the United States. 1900*, X, *Manufactures*, Pt. 4, p. 705.
[10] Bureau of the Census, *Special Reports: Central Electric Light and Power Stations, 1902*, p. 16.
[11] Bureau of the Census, *Special Reports: Street and Electric Railways, 1902*, p. 11.

[12] Simon Sterne, "Administration of American Cities," J. J. Lalor, ed., *Cyclopedia of Political Science* (New York: Charles E. Merrill & Co., 1886), I, 460, 463–464.
[13] Sun Printing & Publishing Association *et al.* v. Mayor, etc. of City of New York *et al.*, 152 *New York*, 257; 46 *Northeastern Reporter*, 500.
[14] Opinion of the Justices to the House of Representatives, 150 *Massachusetts*, 592.
[15] D. F. Wilcox, *op. cit.*, II, 806.

grant.[16] The franchise grant might or might not contain time limitations, rate and service regulations, provisions for recapture, or provide for payments by the grantee. In other words, it roughly resembled the earliest railroad charters.

The Improvement of Streets

Even the most confirmed advocate of private enterprise admitted that streets were a legitimate responsibility of government.[17] Expenditures for this purpose were, of course, not large so long as the making of streets did not depart widely from that of country roads. Cities graveled their streets or, as in Philadelphia, used an abundant supply of local materials for cobblestones. Though these methods had the advantage of cheapness, such streets were dirty, rough, noisy, uneven, damaging to traffic and uncomfortable for riders. The rationale for innovation was not long in coming. "Smooth and clean highways are a wise investment from every point of view, and that so long as the work is done in a thorough and scientific manner, the result is worth having, regardless of cost. No city should think itself rich enough to prosper without them, and no city is so poor that it can not afford them if it has any reason whatever for continued existence. Good roadways are cheap at any cost, and bad ones are so disastrously expensive that only a very rich country, like the United States, can afford them."[18]

Apparently about the time of the Civil War, eastern cities became aware of the possibilities and advantages of paving their streets with small granite blocks. Soon

quarries in Massachusetts and Maine, along the coast or accessible to it, became interested in the paving-stone industry. A specialized craft of stone cutters recruited from Yankees and immigrants from the British Isles began hammering out the "New York block" eight to twelve inches long, seven to eight inches deep, and three-and-one-half to four-and-one-half inches wide. Coastal sailing vessels distributed the product to cities up and down the Atlantic and there were even some shipments to the interior.[19] On the whole cities without easy access to quarries relied upon other materials. After the mid-seventies pioneer communities in the Midwest were laying down brick pavements, a material far superior to wooden blocks, which in spite of their tendency to decay and heave, were also a contemporary fashion. Chicago was noted for its "floating pavements" of cedar block, "which are said to rise with the floods of water filling the roadways after heavy rainfalls."[20] Finally, taking a cue from the experiences of Paris and London, American cities about 1870 began the use of asphalt. At first the raw material came from the great Pitch Lake deposit in Trinidad; by the end of the century the refining of American crude oils was producing a domestic supply.[21]

Though cities owned the streets and could improve them through their own officials and employees, the task could also, without a franchise, be turned over

---

[16] E. J. James, The Relation of the Modern Municipality to the Gas Supply (A Paper read before the Philadelphia Social Science Association. February 11th, 1886), p. 8; M. D. Hirsch, William C. Whitney, Modern Warwick (New York: Dodd, Mead & Company, 1948), p. 436.
[17] Charles E. Perkins, Memo, Jan. 26, 1885, Perkins Private Letters and Memos, R. C. Overton.
[18] Dr. Albert Shaw, quoted by N. P. Lewis, "Modern City Roadways," Popular Science Monthly, LVI (March, 1900), 525–526.

[19] Sixth Annual Report of the Bureau of Industrial and Labor Statistics for the State of Maine, 1892, pp. 204–206; Sixteenth Annual Report of the Bureau of Industrial and Labor Statistics for the State of Maine, 1902, p. 47; R. T. Berthoff, British Immigrants in Industrial America (Cambridge: Harvard University Press, 1953), pp. 78–81.
[20] Lewis, loc. cit., p. 530; V. S. Clark, History of Manufactures in the United States, 1860–1893 (New York: McGraw-Hill Company, 1929), p. 494.
[21] Lewis, loc. cit., pp. 534–539; R. W. Hidy and M. E. Hidy, History of Standard Oil Company (New Jersey): Pioneering in Big Business, 1882–1911 (New York: Harper & Brothers, 1955), pp. 445, 773 n. 8.

to private contractors. Like all jobs, these contracts were much sought after and there frequently grew up a political alliance between the city government and favored contractors. The latter provided a labor force, frequently Irish or Italian, and the labor force provided voters at election time.[22]

Water and Sewerage

Cities had also to face the problem of providing abundant supplies of water for their own use, for fire fighting, for industrial purposes, and for their own populations. After research during the closing decades of the nineteenth century had validated the germ theory of disease, the water had to be pure. Building dams and aqueducts, installing pumping apparatus to raise the water to standpipes or high basins, laying out an elaborate distribution system of water mains was an expensive business. Generally speaking, whether the municipality should build and own the works or turn the job over to a private corporation depended upon the empirical consideration of what was the less painful way of raising the money. On the one hand municipal officials and citizens were loath to increase city debt; on the other, private capitalists, though they were sometimes granted subsidies and a monopoly of providing water service, hesitated to invest in enterprises in the determination of whose rates social and sanitary considerations were more important than the law of supply and demand.[23] Though ancient Rome had undertaken the task of water supply and classical precedents meant a great deal to Americans, more influential in the United States was the example of its two leading cities. In Philadelphia the Fairmount works opened in 1799–1801, and in New York, where the original Croton system was opened in 1842, water works were municipal undertakings. Since New York had earlier experimented with private enterprise, its eventual choice of public ownership and operation was all the more influential.[24]

Interlocked with the water problem was the provision of improved sewage facilities. In some instances, as in Chicago and Milwaukee, the sewers emptied into the lakes from which the cities drew their water supplies; everywhere the wider employment of water closets raised problems of disposal. Slowly and quarrelsomely, most municipalities brought themselves to provide facilities through the sale of bonds and the levy of assessments upon abutting property owners. In Chicago the heroic measure of reversing the flow of the Chicago River, into which most waste was dumped, away from Lake Michigan and into the Mississippi was completed in 1871 at the cost of $3,000,000.[25]

Lighting

The provision of modern lighting facilities had, of course, to wait upon the course of invention. In 1816 Baltimore, the first American city to do so, introduced illuminating gas made from coal. In the seventies a dual transformation affected the gas industry. The Standard Oil group became definitely interested in piping and selling natural gas, used primarily for

[22] Hirsch, op. cit., pp. 455–456; R. F. Foerster, *The Italian Emigration of Our Times* (Cambridge: Harvard University Press, 1919), pp. 353–355.
[23] Blake McKelvey, *Rochester, The Flower City, 1855–1890* (Cambridge: Harvard University Press, 1949), pp. 32, 125, 135–136, 263–265; Bayrd Still, *Milwaukee, The History of a City* (Madison: State Historical Society, 1948), pp. 247–248; William D. Miller, *Memphis during the Progressive Era, 1900–1917* (Madison: American History Research Center, 1957), pp. 68–69.

[24] *Tenth Census of the United States. 1880*, VIII, *Report on the Social Statistics of Cities*, Part 1, pp. 565, 812–813; Nelson M. Blake, *Water for the Cities* (Syracuse: Syracuse University Press, 1956), pp. 44–62, 100–171.
[25] Still, op. cit., pp. 241–242, 363–365; Bessie L. Pierce, *A History of Chicago* (New York: Alfred A. Knopf, 1940), II, 330–334.

industrial and heating purposes, and also in the production of gas oil, a derivative from petroleum, which was used to produce water gas, a product with superior illuminating qualities.[26] These changes, of course, soon confronted the competition of electric lighting. Frank Brush's invention of an improved arc light devised a source of illumination peculiarly fitted for the outdoors. The Edison incandescent light early in the eighties was designed for interior use, and it was not until a later date that it competed with the arc light for street illumination. In any case, the advent of electrical lighting slowed the expansion of gas as an illuminant. In many ways the problems connected with lighting were like those of providing water. There was a dual market for the product—a private one, homes and businesses, and a public one, street lighting. Both gas and electricity had to use the streets, the one for mains, the other for wires or conduits.

Urban Transportation

As cities grew in population and enlarged in area, a new problem emerged—urban transportation. Before the Civil War the omnibus and the horse-car furnished public conveyances. Horse-car lines were often adjuncts to speculation in suburban real estate. But these methods were hazardous, uncomfortable, and inefficient. They so heightened street congestion, already intense enough, that a person could proceed on foot more quickly to his destination.[27] More rapid means of locomotion had been introduced into the city incidental to the search by steam railroads for convenient urban terminals. Though railroads secured franchises permitting them to lay rails along the streets, such documents were usually foresighted enough to prohibit locomotives from traveling along city thoroughfares and to insist that there steam should give way to mule or horse-power.[28]

One obvious solution for the dilemma was to construct roadways at different levels and to permit locomotives and cars to travel the elevated one. Still there were real business uncertainties in such undertakings. In view of the proclivity of steam trains to jump the track or to run off bridges, elevated railroads threatened dangers.[29] There was also considerable doubt whether people would take the trouble to walk upstairs for improved transport.[30] Whatever the attitude of passengers, abutting property owners were quickly aware that an iron elevated structure along the street and the frequent passage of noisy trains was likely to diminish rather than enhance the value of their property. Nevertheless the need was so great that a Rapid Transit Commission appointed by the Mayor of New York recommended in the early seventies for two of the north and south avenues in the city an elevated system capable of carrying 15,000 passengers a day.[31] By the next decade elevated roads had demonstrated their success. Eastern cities imitated New York, and in the early nineties Chicago, destined to become the city of "El's," already had its lines.[32]

Eventually the elevateds were electrified. So were the surface lines. Cities, unless

[26] Twelfth Census of the United States. 1900, X, Manufactures, Part 4, pp. 713–714: Hidy and Hidy, op. cit., pp. 171–172, 451, 738 n. 5.
[27] Harry J. Carman, "The Street Surface Railway Franchises of New York City," Studies in History, Economics, and Public Law (New York: Columbia University Press, 1919), pp. 29–30 note; Massachusetts: Twenty-fourth Annual Report of the Board of Railroad Commissioners, 1893, pp. 103–104.

[28] Carman, op. cit., pp. 17–20, 33–35.
[29] "Report on the Meigs Elevated Railroad," Massachusetts: Eighteenth Annual Report of the Board of Railroad Commissioners, 1887, pp. 125–130.
[30] Henry C. Brown, Valentine's Manual of Old New York, 1926 (New York: Valentine's Manual Inc., 1925), p. 21; Commercial and Financial Chronicle, XVIII (April 4, 1874), 339–340.
[31] Brown, op. cit., pp. 19–22; James J. Swank, "Statistics of the Iron and Steel Production of the United States," Tenth Census of the United States, 1880, II, 150.
[32] Pierce, op. cit., III, 218–220.

in special circumstances like San Francisco's, discarded the use of an endless cable beneath the pavement to tow cars and relied, particularly after Sprague's demonstration in Richmond, upon an overhead electric wire or an underground one with which a shoe from the car made contact.[33] By the nineties there "was an active 'boom' in electric railway building" and speculation. "It is stimulated by the apparent cheapness of electricity as compared with horse power, by the expectation of large profits, and in some cases probably by the hope of successful deals in the securities of the company."[34]

Private capitalists solicited and secured the franchises for these networks of urban transportation and operated the completed enterprises. Whereas local capital had once undertaken this task, capitalists without local ties moved into the enterprise.[35] A hope of steady dividends prosaically earned from operations was hardly their aim. Instead they applied to urban transportation the most dubious devices of speculation and personal enrichment developed in the railroad world: the construction company, the lease, consolidation, stock-watering and Wall Street speculation. In some cases those practicing these arts in the new area were railroad men; for instance, in the eighties Jay Gould applied his unquestioned talents to the New York elevated system. He transferred its complicated affairs to the arena of Wall Street, journalistic rumors, and the courts. Eventually the growing returns from the consolidations he put together placed the stock on a dividend basis and made it one of the "blue chips" in the Gould estate.[36]

In street railways a national "syndicate" appeared, originating in Philadelphia. Its leaders, Peter A. B. Widener and William L. Elkins, started their business careers, as had John D. Rockefeller, in the provision trades. Clearly this occupation as a training ground and reservoir of capital possessed a magic of its own. Dabbling in politics, Widener, Elkins, and others had by 1884 gathered within their Philadelphia Traction Company at least half the street car lines of the city. Elkins, who had invested in oil and had sold out to the Standard, once remarked, "Give me the Broadway franchise and the coal-oil trade of Philadelphia and I will retire."[37] Actually this was a rather limited objective. In 1886 the Philadelphia group, with the alliance of broker Charles T. Yerkes, invaded Chicago. In the resulting process of consolidation and leasing, the capitalization of the various enterprises roughly doubled and cable cars superseded the horse-drawn ones.[38]

In New York City William Collins Whitney, a graduate of Yale and a reform anti-Tweed Democrat who had married a Standard Oil fortune, formed an alliance with T. F. Ryan, a Virginia farm boy now a broker. Whitney once remarked of his associate, "If Ryan lives long enough, he'll have all the money in the world."[39] Whitney and Ryan called to their assistance the Philadelphians Widener and Elkins and were also fortunate enough to retain as counsel Elihu Root to plot a path through the intricacies of New York law and politics, though in the latter area Whitney himself was adroit enough. These capitalists went ahead to consolidate all the surface lines of New York City. The first instrument was the Metropolitan Traction Company, a holding company incorporated in New Jersey. Like holding

[33] Hirsch, op. cit., pp. 426–427; Stearns Morse, "Slots in the Streets," New England Quarterly, XXIV (March, 1951), 4–11.
[34] Massachusetts: Twenty-fourth Annual Report of the Board of Railroad Commissioners, 1893, p. 105.
[35] Ibid., p. 106.
[36] Julius Grodinsky, Jay Gould: His Business Career, 1867–1892 (Philadelphia: University of Pennsylvania Press, 1957), pp. 288–314.

[37] B. J. Hendrick, "Great American Fortunes and their Making: Street-Railway Financiers," McClure's Magazine, XXX (November, 1907), 32–37.
[38] Ninth Biennial Report of the Bureau of Labor Statistics of Illinois, 1896, pp. 56–58.
[39] Hirsch, op. cit., p. 466.

companies elsewhere, it exchanged its stock for the concerns it acquired; it also leased enterprises. In 1893 their corporate means of expansion became the Metropolitan Street Railway Company of New York. Whatever the legal form, the battle for consolidation was waged in the city and state governments and with frequent recourse to the courts. A trail of injunctions and receiverships marked this continual litigation. Nor were the vacillations of securities on Wall Street forgotten.[40]

Though Whitney's brother became the urban transportation magnate of Boston through his own efforts, the Widener-Elkins-Whitney-Ryan syndicate at the end of the century were reputed to have built up the street railway systems in New York, Chicago, Philadelphia, and Pittsburgh and in at least one hundred cities and towns from Maine to Pennsylvania. In addition they had become influential in gas and electric-lighting companies as far west as Omaha and as far south as St. Augustine. The united capitalization of their street railways was a billion dollars and of their lighting companies $300,000,000.[41]

The Movement for Municipal Ownership

By the end of the nineteenth century there was a considerable movement for government ownership of certain industries. In its national phase this movement, which sometimes touched the railroads, focussed on the telephone and telegraph. But the objective eliciting the most expenditure of words and effort was the municipal ownership of public utilities. In one sense this is surprising, for earlier circumstances had certainly cast a dark shadow over the wisdom of enlarging both the sphere of municipal activity and the size of municipal debts. The experience of communities

in financing railroad expansion had not turned out well; debt repudiations and scaling wrote an epitaph to the policy. What is more, events in New York City immediately after the Civil War unveiled a most discouraging example of municipal enterprise.

There the municipality had fallen into the merciless hands of a group of unsavory officials, whose leader was William Marcy Tweed, boss of Tammany Hall. With great persistence and courage, reform elements opposed to Tweed in 1871 finally rid the city of his tyranny and documented a noisome record of graft and corruption. The methods of the Tweed Ring in looting the city and enriching itself had diversity and also a certain simple charm. A favorite device was to suggest to contractors who worked for the city that they increase their bills and kick back the surplus to the conspirators. Thus a County Court House which really cost about $3,000,000 was made to stand on the books at $11,-000,000. Toward the end of their rule, Tweed and his associates were taking as their own about 85 per cent of the city's expenditures. "If to the amount stolen outright is added the amount extravagantly and wastefully expended in sinecure offices, the performance of unnecessary work, fraudulent contracts, it is safe . . . to say that one-half the city debt of $130,000,000 represents absolute plunder," concluded Lalor's *Cyclopedia of Political Science*. An investigating committee estimated that if a private corporation had run the city, it could have done so for about one-tenth the stated costs.[42] Incidentally most of Tweed's expenditures were for unquestioned "public" purposes.

The Tweed experience bit deep. Methods of improvement, advocating city home rule

[40] *Ibid.*, pp. 223–224, 226, 421–468; Philip C. Jessup, *Elihu Root* (New York: Dodd, Mead & Company, 1938), I, 146–153, 185–187.
[41] Hendrick, *loc. cit.*, p. 33.

[42] Sterne, *loc. cit.*, pp. 464–465; J. F. Rhodes, *History of the United States from the Compromise of 1850* (New York: Macmillan Company, 1928), VII, 16–25; E. P. Oberholtzer, *A History of the United States since the Civil War* (New York: Macmillan Company, 1922), II, 581–595.

and centralized and responsible city government, seemed inadequate to stem the "evils arising out of our attempts to rule the large populations of our cities, made up of foreign and floating elements, through a government in form republican." The real cure, some felt, was the abandonment of democracy in the city and the restriction of the ballot to those owning property.[43] Americans were not allowed to forget the bearing of this episode upon municipal and state ownership. In 1891 Godkin, editor of the *Nation* and a fanatic for laissez faire, answered the question, What is the State? with an answer complete for New York City, "the little Tammany junta."[44]

If one were likely to forget this equation, events in Philadelphia reminded him of it. Acting on the assumption that gas lighting was a public function and should not be delegated to a private corporation, the city in 1841 took over the gas plant and entrusted its management to twelve trustees appointed by the Councils of the city government. Most paradoxically this arrangement was known as the "gas trust." It became a political machine. It employed 15 per cent more workers than necessary. Since it never established a depreciation fund, the original plant decayed and the mains leaked so badly that it was impossible to maintain pressure. Few extensions of service were made, and the coal used for the gas was purchased at extravagant prices. Finally, in 1880 a committee of investigation concluded: "One could not conceive a large business plant, run upon business principles, in such a condition without reflecting unfavorably upon its owners." After a decade of struggling with direct municipal operation, the Councils leased the city gas

properties in 1897 to the United Gas Improvement Company for $10,000,000. This concern, a trust of quite a different character, owned plants in other cities. For a time the improvements in service and modernization which it introduced gained wide popular approval for it.[45] Be that as it may, the Philadelphia story of public ownership was characterized by one crusader for public ownership as "the most disastrous failure of its kind in the country. It was a huge inescapable argument against the advocates of public ownership. . . ."[46]

Despite such discouragements the advocates of municipal ownership had made considerable headway. The group was composed of college professors, mostly economists, who led a far from routine academic existence: John R. Commons and Richard T. Ely of the University of Wisconsin, E. J. James of the University of Pennsylvania, Edward W. Bemis, from the University of Chicago and eventually a consultant to cities desiring to install municipally owned gas works, and Frank Parsons, a lecturer in the law school of Boston University and a freelance teacher elsewhere.[47] Of the reformers, Parsons was the most important. His *The City for the People*, published in 1899, crammed together in encyclopedic style arguments in

[43] Robert P. Porter, "The Municipal Debt of the United States," *Galaxy*, XXIV (September, 1877), 399, 404; *Commercial and Financial Chronicle*, XXII (May 27, 1876), Investors' Supplement, p. iii; XXIV (February 10, 1877), 123–125.
[44] E. L. Godkin, "The Economic Man," *North American Review*, CLIII (October, 1891), 500.

[45] Leo S. Rowe, "The Relation of Philadelphia to the Gas Supply," *Municipal and Private Operation of Public Utilities. Report to the National Civic Federation* (New York: National Civic Federation, 1907), Pt. II, v. 1, 588–664; Edward W. Bemis, "Municipal Operation *versus* Private Operation of Municipal Monopolies," *Report to the National Civic Federation*, Pt. I, v. 1, 149–155.
[46] John R. Commons, *Myself* (New York: Macmillan Company, 1934), pp. 111–112; Frederic W. Spiers, "The Philadelphia Gas Lease," *Municipal Affairs*, I (December, 1897), 718–729; W. S. Outerbridge, Jr., "History of the Philadelphia Gas Trust," in E. W. Bemis, *Municipal Ownership of Gas in the United States* (Baltimore: American Economic Association, 1891), pp. 155–169.
[47] Commons, *op. cit., passim*; R. T. Ely, *Ground under Our Feet, An Autobiography* (New York: Macmillan Company, 1938), *passim*; Arthur Mann, *Yankee Reformers in the Urban Age* (Cambridge: Harvard University Press, 1934), pp. 126–144.

behalf of municipal ownership. Though its obliviousness to differing contexts or circumstances and its insistent note diminish its persuasiveness, the book reveals one intellectual prop of the group as a whole, reliance upon foreign precedents: Germany's railroads, Berlin's telephone, Glasgow's tramways and gas and electric works. A later volume by Parsons discovered the usefulness of New Zealand precedents.[48] Along with professors, American portraitists of Utopias played their part. In 1888 Edward Bellamy published *Looking Backward, 2000–1887.* An advocate of nationalized industries, Bellamy proposed as one preliminary step the public ownership of local public utilities.[49] Bellamy inspired an organized movement, whose Nationalist clubs and their agitation were one explanation for the passage in Massachusetts in 1891 of a statute permitting cities and towns to own their gas systems.[50]

A contemporary of Bellamy was Henry George. The classic statement of his position, *Progress and Poverty,* appearing in 1879, had focussed upon the evils arising from monopoly in land and proposed to abolish them by a single tax upon its unearned increment. Among the many converted by George's philosophy was Tom L. Johnson, a Cleveland millionaire with a fortune derived from, among other sources, street railways. Johnson saw monopoly in public utilities as one explanation for poverty. As a successful candidate for mayor of Cleveland, he devoted his immense knowledge and convictions to an attack upon urban monopoly or "Privilege." Since Cleveland was forbidden by law to own street railways, Johnson proposed as

a solution the lease of the existing private lines to an operating company of five trustees appointed by the mayor of the city. The lines were to be limited to an agreed return upon their stock, and the rates they charged were placed upon a sliding scale, with a minimum of three cents, depending upon the level of earnings. To bludgeon the old companies into this agreement, Johnson threatened to build competitive lines on parallel streets and charge a three-cent fare.[51] There were mayoralty campaigns elsewhere—Chicago, for instance—which were won on the issue of municipal ownership.

In his ten-years war, Tom Johnson had the support of the Cleveland *Plain Dealer.* This was symptomatic, for the campaign for municipal ownership had considerable journalistic backing. For several years, before he established his Municipal Ownership League and ran for mayor of New York in 1905, William Randolph Hearst had been heating up the issue. In his early career in San Francisco he had been the advocate of municipal ownership of the city's water works; when he invaded New York with the New York *Journal* in the nineties he attacked the Gas Trust and proposed a municipal gas works.[52] Certainly the conjunction of the professional reformers and the notorious editor of sensationalism was puzzling. Still it was not the first time in history that the dragon and St. George were on the same side.

Leaders to be effective had to have followers, and journalists had to have readers who could be persuaded. Generally the crusaders for municipal ownership pictured themselves as relying upon the

[48] Mann, *op. cit.,* pp. 139–141; L. S. Rowe, *Problems of City Government* (New York: D. Appleton and Company, 1908), pp. 330–349.
[49] Sidney Fine, *Laissez Faire and the General-Welfare State. A Study of Conflict in American Thought, 1865–1901* (Ann Arbor: University of Michigan Press, 1956), pp. 296–300.
[50] Bemis, *Municipal Ownership of Gas,* pp. 9–10; *Commercial and Financial Chronicle,* XLVIII (June 1, 1889), 713–714.

[51] F. C. Howe, *op. cit., pp. 85–137;* Tom L. Johnson, *My Story* (New York: B. W. Huebsch, 1915), pp. 107–119, 156–166, 184–294; Herbert Croly, *Marcus Alonzo Hanna, His Life and Work* (New York: Macmillan Company, 1923), pp. 82–83.
[52] John K. Winkler, *William Randolph Hearst, A New Appraisal* (New York: Hastings House, 1955), pp. 136–142; Mrs. Fremont Older, *William Randolph Hearst, American* (New York: D. Appleton-Century Company, 1936), pp. 204–210, 561.

"people" and it would be folly to deny that Hearst's sensational journalism had more positive influence in the crowded sections of New York than in the homes of tycoons.[53] But businessmen also had a stake in efficient municipal services and in low prices for them. They might use water, gas, and electricity in large quantities in business and industrial establishments. Also, since they paid wages, they were interested in lowering the cost of living for wage receivers. If street transportation were not available and cheap, they might have to erect company housing near places of work.[54] So even the apostles of laissez faire were willing to grant to municipalities a range of activities vouchsafed to few other forms of government.

Thus Charles E. Perkins, president of the Burlington Road, thought that "the inhabitants of a small, compact community, like a city, in the exercise of local self-government . . . may wisely and economically combine to procure gas, water, horse-cars, and perhaps other conveniences, granting special privileges in the streets, which are limited in number and extent, and limiting prices in consideration of such privileges. . . ."[55] An executive of the New York Edison Company, concerned as to where to draw the line between the permissible and the forbidden, concluded: "Good roads, it is conceded, must be provided by the commonwealth, as also sewerage; water supply is usually, though not always, considered a municipal function; lighting, communication and transportation are on debatable ground; there are few in this country who approve

public bakeries or store-houses, although bread is a necessity of life. Somewhere within this range is the point where democracy becomes socialism. It is important to limit the function of the municipality at that point, and not be misled by the phrase that 'a city is a business corporation.' . . .The real limits of municipal activity must be found in an alert and wholesome public opinion which will prevent steps that lead by easy reaches into socialistic enterprises, pure and simple."[56]

Vague and fatuous though this distinction was, it had as much touch with reality as the prodigies of reconciling fact and theory undertaken by the advocates of municipal ownership. The strength of their attachment to municipal ownership and of their belief in democratic government confronted them with a dilemma when they looked realistically at the level of politics and political administration in the cities of America. So American advocates of municipal enterprise were compelled to dismiss the Philadelphia gas trust as "that parody on popular government" or elaborate a doctrine of purification in which theory refined fact. Thus it was private enterprise that corrupted city governments, and the responsibility of public enterprise would act as a cleansing agent.[57]

The main thread of their argument was not, however, circular or contradictory. Obviously a franchise was a privilege, a thing of value. Its recipients proceeded to capitalize it. Thus Whitney's consolidation in 1901 of New York street railways issued securities to a par value of $165,000,000; the net value of the physical property was $60,000,000. The differential was the capitalized value of the franchises which Whitney thought, being combined, were worth a good deal more than when they

[53] Abram Hewitt to V. H. Rothschild, October 23, 1871, Allan Nevins, ed., Selected Writings of Abram S. Hewitt (New York: Columbia University Press, 1937), p. 387.
[54] Testimony of William Steinway, Report of the Committee [on Education and Labor] of the Senate . . . 1885, II, 1087.
[55] C. E. Perkins to the Cullom Committee on the Interstate Commerce Act, September 21, 1885, Perkins Papers and Memos, R. C. Overton.

[56] R. K. Bowker, "Public Control, Ownership or Operation of Municipal Franchises? With Special References to Electric Lighting," Municipal Affairs, I (December, 1897), 606.
[57] John R. Commons, "Municipal Electric Light," Municipal Affairs, I (December, 1897), 668–671; Bemis, Municipal Ownership of Gas, p. 17.

were separate.[58] It was performances such as these that gave substance to the frequent charge against the private managers of urban utilities that their stock was heavily watered. Without doubt there were many unfairnesses and short-cuts in this matter of capitalization. Also, as elsewhere in the economy, managers and investors were capitalizing on the basis of estimated earnings rather than actual investment.

Favoritism and extortion were not the whole explanation of this over-capitalization. While certain utilities such as water and gas works had been long enough in existence to be stabilized and the results of their operation anticipated, electricity as light and electricity as power for street railways were new arrivals. Technical advances and manufacturing changes were so rapid that costs, including that for equipment, fell rapidly; experience with these new industries was so lacking that there was a blindness to proper charges for depreciation. As in the case of new industries, there was a spectacular increase in patronage and use. In short, since over-optimism was common, business misjudgments about capitalization and profits understandably resulted.[59] The ideological case for capitalizing prospective earnings was posited, as in manufacturing, upon a certain check by competition. But of course in municipal utilities such competition was unfeasible. So advocates of municipal ownership correctly emphasized the inherent monopoly of public utilities as an explanation of their high and discriminatory charges.

Achievements of Municipal Ownership

In terms of adoption municipal ownership had considerable success. In provision of sewers it was universal; "Copies of sewer

franchises are like rare books, hard to get."[60] In the case of waterworks, of the 3,326 installations in the United States in 1899 only 46.27 per cent were owned and operated by private owners, while 53.73 per cent were owned and operated by the communities in which they were located. At the same date, of the 965 gas works, 1.45 per cent were municipally owned; of the 3,032 electric light plants 15.17 per cent were municipal.[61] In street railways, private enterprise swept the boards. When the National Civic Federation investigated the merits of public and private operation early in the twentieth century, it was compelled to turn to publicly owned tramways in England for a yardstick of performance.[62] As to the reasons for these variations the concentration of municipally owned gas and electric works in the smaller places gives a hint. Individuals as opposite as Tom Johnson and Charles E. Perkins believed the close oversight of operations justified municipal enterprise in such communities.[63] Waterworks which did not require a large labor force were less vulnerable to the spoils system and hence more acceptable to voters. Though private enterprise was historically entrenched in the gas business, electric light and power arrived later, at a time when the municipal ownership movement had acquired momentum.

In terms of comparative economic performance, it is hard to come by a dispassionate appraisal of the merits of public and private municipal enterprise during this period. The contemporary literature abounds with exceptions, assumptions, and short-run judgments. Though much ink had already been spilled on matters

[58] Hirsch, op. cit., pp. 459–460.
[59] E. S. Mason, The Street Railway in Massachusetts: The Rise and Decline of an Industry (Cambridge: Harvard University Press, 1932), pp. 12, 21.

[60] Wilcox, op. cit., I, 451.
[61] Fourteenth Annual Report of the [U. S.] Commissioner of Labor, 1899. Water, Gas, and Electric-Light Plants under Private and Municipal Ownership, p. 13.
[62] Report to the National Civic Federation, Pt. I, v. 1, p. 13n.
[63] Charles E. Perkins to the Cullom Committee, September 21, 1885, Perkins Papers, R. C. Overton; Howe, op. cit., pp. 135–136.

of rates, service and efficiency, the National Civic Federation, when it undertook an investigation in 1907, headed the introduction to its resulting volume with the assertion that until the Federation took up the matter "no definite effort had been made to determine impartially and scientifically the relative merits of private and public ownership and operation of public utilities."[64] However, in 1888 A. T. Hadley, an economist and president of Yale, had dared to appraise contemporary accomplishments. Sensitive to the larger context surrounding the movement for municipal ownership abroad and in America, he concluded: "What the advocates of state ownership really fail to show is the combination of liberal policy and wise administration in the same instance. . . . This is a damaging omission. As far as it exists, it renders the argument for state management of industry totally inconclusive. . . . Successful administration is found, but without the more liberal policy which is the main argument for government activity. Liberal policy is sometimes found, but is almost invariably accompanied by mistakes in administration."[65]

Regulation of Municipal Enterprise

Between private and public ownership lay the compromise of public regulation of private enterprise. As we have seen, state and nation turned to this middle way in the case of railroads, but champions of municipal ownership would have none of it. Tom Johnson, for instance, believed monopoly was more than a match for a prying or regulatory government. It would always win.[66] Moderates were more sympathetic to regulation, for state ownership "may be compared to a man who protects himself against a boy with a snowball by killing the boy. The social industrialism is no more necessary than the homicide is."[67] At different times in different jurisdictions legislation which had once let the government give franchises free or without stipulation, exacted, for this money-making privilege, a flat fee or a percentage of receipts, or stipulated the franchise must be sold at auction to the highest bidder.[68] Franchise grants were limited in duration and the city was authorized to recapture the property after a certain period. Rates and services were also regulated. All this resembled the old effort to regulate railroads through provisions in their charters.

As in the case of railroads, the regulatory movement gravitated into the hands of that new governmental discovery, the commission. In Massachusetts, for instance, street railways were placed under the control of the Massachusetts Railroad Commission when it was established in 1869.[69] Through the decades the degree of regulation over both means of transportation revealed the same evolution: rate-making changed from recommendations to mandates, and the Commission could prescribe measures for public safety and comfort, and finally in the nineties place severe limitations upon the methods of capitalization.[70] In 1885 the Commonwealth established a Board of Gas Commissioners and two years later changed its name to the Board of Gas and Electric Light Commissioners. Explicitly accepting the monopoly character of these new enterprises, the General Court authorized these Boards to investigate rates upon complaint and if they deemed proper, order a reduction in price and, in the case of gas, an improvement in quality.[71] The

---

[64] Report to the National Civic Federation, Pt. I, v. 1, p. 12.
[65] A. T. Hadley, "Some Difficulties of Public Business Management," Political Science Quarterly, III (December, 1888), 581–582.
[66] Howe, op. cit., pp. 132–134.

[67] G. K. Holmes, "State Control of Corporations and Industry in Massachusetts," Political Science Quarterly, V (September, 1890), 436.
[68] Hirsch, op. cit., pp. 442–444, 447–450; Mason, op. cit., pp. 134–137.
[69] Mason, op. cit., p. 134.
[70] Ibid., pp. 138–143.
[71] Acts and Resolves . . . of Massachusetts . . . 1885, pp. 769–772; Acts and Resolves . . . of Massachusetts . . . 1887, pp. 992–993.

anti-stock watering statutes of the Commonwealth also caught within their drag-net the gas and electric utilities.[72]

As in the case of the railroad commission, these regulatory agencies put great emphasis upon reports, publicity, and complaints of wrong from individuals. But a panegyrist of this device confessed it was of limited utility. It would work neither in a "corporation-ridden state" like Pennsylvania, nor "in South Carolina half of whose population ten years of age and over is illiterate." The prerequisites to success were "that a large body of the people of the state shall be intelligent and educated; that they shall be devoted to reading and discussion; that associated efforts shall be habitual and frequent; that population shall be considerably dense; and that resentment against wrong and whatever limits the common welfare shall be quick and energetic."[73] This proviso seemed to require, as in the case of most utopias, the regeneration of mankind or at the very least their elevation to the standard homo sapiens had attained in Massachusetts.

Urban Building

Private expenditures for residential and business purposes were the most important contribution American cities made to the economy.[74] An index of the dollar value of building permits in terms of 1913 dollars reveals how important this stimulus was. The index reached a peak in 1890 which was not approached again until 1925.[75] Such figures, as usual, obliterate distinctions. But so can the impression-

istic, qualitative observations of travelers. In an oft-quoted sentence Lord Bryce, after excepting a few historic American cities, remarked, "American cities differ from one another only herein, that some of them are built more with brick than with wood, and others more with wood than brick."[76] Actually, building followed a straight-line evolution from wood to brick to stone. For stone was the prestige building material, granite enjoying the highest favor. Governmental buildings—customs houses, post-offices, courthouses, and jails—were built of it, as were buildings having a public aspect—banks, hotels, churches, markets, and railroad stations. Since granite was hard to work and therefore expensive, those with lesser means turned to softer stones, and brownstone fitted the prescription perfectly. Since its chief deposits lay along the lower Connecticut River, it could be shipped cheaply by water; the large blocks, straight from the quarry, were easily worked up and fitted near the spot of construction. Brownstone fronts dominated the domestic architecture of Boston's Back Bay and flowed like a chocolate tide along the avenues and cross streets of New York.[77] The birthplace of Theodore Roosevelt had a brownstone front; Commodore Vanderbilt gave the material a certain cachet when he built his palace on Fifth Avenue of it. To the Commodore, granite, like the law, was "too slow," and he wanted the building done before he died.[78] Of the stone buildings in New York, over three-

[76] James Bryce, The American Commonwealth (New York: The Macmillan Company, 1915), II, 880.
[77] "Report on the Building Stones of the United States and Statistics of the Quarry Industry, 1880," Tenth Census of the United States. 1880, X, 127, 282–286, 316–326; Eighty Years of Progress of the United States (New York: L. Stebbins, 1861), II, 355.
[78] Carleton Putnam, Theodore Roosevelt (New York: Charles Scribner's Sons, 1958), I, 20; Wayne Andrews, The Vanderbilt Legend: The Story of the Vanderbilt Family, 1794–1940 (New York: Harcourt, Brace and Company, 1941), p. 220.

[72] C. J. Bullock, "Control of the Capitalization of Public Service Companies in Massachusetts," American Economic Association Quarterly, X (April, 1909), 385–386, 398–404.
[73] Holmes, loc. cit., p. 437.
[74] Goldsmith, loc. cit., p. 619.
[75] John R. Riggleman, "Building Cycles in the United States, 1875 to 1932," Journal of the American Statistical Association, XXVIII (June, 1933), 178.

quarters had brownstone fronts,[79] and its use penetrated even to Chicago.[80] The slate quarries, which furnished fire-proof roofing, and the lime quarries, whose product was processed in kilns to make interior finish plaster, were associated industries. All in all, the number of building stone quarries in the United States increased from 1,444 in 1850 to 5,764 in 1902.[81]

Houses with brownstone fronts usually had side and rear walls of brick. In some communities, for example Philadelphia, brick had been the traditional material for super-structures of the more pretentious early buildings. By century's end, even the slums of Philadelphia were brick single-family houses.[82] Since the costs of transportation increased rapidly with the distance such heavy materials were carried, nearly every city was rimmed with clay pits from which its buildings had been dug. Every state in the Union, except two in the Far West, reported brickyards. Nonetheless there was a tendency for the industry to gravitate to deposits of superior clay and to utilize at these locations brick-making machinery.[83]

In the United States even the interior structure of stone and brick edifices— flooring, beams, roofs—was generally of wood. Furthermore there were factors which made it the preferred material for the whole building. Forests were abundant. Moreover a revolutionary new technique

for building houses and working wood kept prices down. In the 1830's an ingenious migrant from New England to Chicago invented the balloon frame. Previously a frame house had been composed of heavy timbers fitted together; the balloon frame used a multitude of lighter pieces and relied upon the exterior boarding to give the structure rigidity and strength. The house utilized the principle of the box.[84] Later, multiplication and refinement of woodworking machinery released workers from making blinds, sash, doors, and mouldings by hand in a shop during the winter and transferred this task to a shop using machinery all the year round,[85] thus doing the work more cheaply and in some instances performing prodigies hand workers could not attempt.[86]

The census of 1880 observed that, "Having a larger and more rapidly-increasing population than any other country that is noted for its consumption of iron, we are consequently the largest consumers of nails and spikes in the construction of dwellings and public buildings, stores, warehouses, offices and similar structures."[87] So pronounced were the advantages of wooden construction that great American cities clung to it even after the Chicago fire of 1871 demonstrated its danger.[88]

Whatever the building façade, the interior was mechanized. The American stove, "works of real art," "handsome,

[79] "Report on the Building Stones of the United States," loc. cit., p. 314.
[80] Ibid., p. 296; John Drury, Old Chicago Houses (Chicago: University of Chicago Press, 1941), pp. 67, 98.
[81] Twelfth Census of the United States. 1900, Special Reports. Mines and Quarries, 1902, pp. 785–788.
[82] "Report on the Building Stones of the United States," loc. cit., p. 33; James Ford, Slums and Housing, with Special Reference to New York City (Cambridge: Harvard University Press, 1936), I, 267.
[83] V. S. Clark, History of Manufactures in the United States, 1860–1893 (New York: McGraw-Hill Company, 1929), pp. 493–494; Commercial and Financial Chronicle, XXII (May 27, 1876), 508–510.

[84] Siegfried Giedion, Space, Time and Architecture (Cambridge: Harvard University Press, 1941), pp. 269–276.
[85] F. R. Hutton, "Report on Machine Tools and Wood-working Machinery," Tenth Census of the United States. 1880, XXII, 178–290; Testimony of Gabriel Edmonston, Report of the Committee [on Education and Labor] of the Senate . . . 1885, I, 548.
[86] John Maass, The Gingerbread Age: A View of Victorian America (New York: Rinehart, 1957), passim.
[87] Swank, loc. cit., p. 151.
[88] Ford, op. cit., I, 267; Edith Abbott, The Tenements of Chicago, 1908–1935 (Chicago: University of Chicago Press, 1936), p. 10.

bright, cheerful, healthful, and clean,"[89] and one of the early triumphs of American mass production, gave way to an industry of steamfitting and heating apparatus. The same domestic mechanization created the indoor bathroom and toilet, thus benefiting the porcelain industry.

American construction now began to utilize new materials of the industrial age. In New York City Peter Cooper, the ironmaster, decided to support the floors of his Cooper Union on horizontal rolled iron beams. By 1859 his plant was rolling beams 4 feet long and 9 inches deep.[90] Somewhat earlier Harpers rebuilt their burned down publishing plant with one seven stories high, using iron beams supported by iron columns; instead of brick or stone, it had a cast-iron front.[91] By the eighties architects were considering the feasibility of a building whose support was a metal frame or cage and whose walls were simply filler between the beams and columns. In 1885 the plans of a Chicago engineer, W. LeBaron Jenney, materialized in the ten stories of the Home Insurance Company building, the "first skyscraper."[92] Of course steel had now superseded iron. Whereas the census of 1880 had mentioned neither iron nor steel for buildings, the census of 1900 noted the production of 856,983 tons of structural shapes of iron and steel. Unhappily it did not specify what proportion went into buildings.[93]

The construction industry stimulated the economy directly. Materials had to be manufactured and put together or in-stalled. Occupations ranging from sophisticated manufacturing such as wood working to the handicrafts of carpenter, mason, painter, plumber, and plasterer boomed. In 1900, expenditures on construction turned out an annual product valued at $1,946,000,000.[94] In the sixties an American calculator had surmised by extrapolation from data then available that there was "a vast annual demand for 130,000 new houses" and foresaw that the better construction and luxuries of a "modern house" with "modern improvements" constantly increased the expenditure per house. For the decade as a whole he put their total cost at $1,300,000,000. This was quite unlike the course of affairs in the "old and stationary countries of Europe," where "old cities" were already built and there was consequently "no active and continued demand for labor and capital to provide new dwellings to accommodate swelling numbers."[95]

The American ideal of owning one's home was deep-seated. Home ownership conferred prestige, showed others that the owner was getting ahead and reassured him that he was "Americanized."[96] In farming the dream was widely realized; in urban living, much less so. In New York City in 1900, rented homes constituted 87.9 per cent of the total; in Chicago 74.9.[97] Since urban population was notably on the wing, it relied on rented properties. Builders of all sorts relied in large part on borrowed money. The owner did not issue stock, he encumbered the property with a mortgage. Though most figures for construction in the late nineteenth century contain a good deal of surmise, it seems

[89] Swank, loc. cit., p. 150.
[90] Allan Nevins, Abram S. Hewitt with Some Account of Peter Cooper (New York: Harper & Brothers, 1935), pp. 114–119.
[91] Giedion, op. cit., pp. 129–138; Brown, op. cit., pp. 8–9.
[92] Giedion, op. cit., pp. 138–142; Pierce, op. cit., III, 499–500; C. M. Green, American Cities in the Growth of the Nation (London: John De Graff, 1937), pp. 119–120.
[93] Twelfth Census of the United States. 1900, VII, Manufactures, Pt. 1, p. cxlix; X, Manufactures, Pt. 4, p. 61.
[94] Ibid., VII, Manufactures, Pt. 1, p. clxiii; Goldsmith, loc. cit., p. 619.
[95] Eighty Years of Progress of the United States, p. 355.
[96] Abbott, op. cit., p. 363.
[97] G. P. Watkins, "The Growth of Large Fortunes. A Study of Economic Causes Affecting the Acquisition and Distribution of Property," Publications of the American Economic Association, VIII (1907), 75; Abbott, op. cit., p. 366.

reasonably accurate to say that the non-farm mortgage debt rose from $3,811,-000,000 in 1890 to $4,661,000,000 in 1900.[98] While the major share of this mortgage debt was held by individuals, savings banks and insurance companies under legal restrictions were also large holders.[99]

Such arrangements facilitated home ownership without funds; they also aided speculative tenement building. Builders who went into this operation generally bought the land from an owner, borrowing money from him for the purchase; the latter frequently lent a portion of the funds for the purchase of material. When the building was done, the builder tried to sell it as soon as possible to an investor who would put in some money of his own and purchase the mortgages accumulated along the way. Land owner and builder hoped to make their gains by marking up the value of the property in the course of these transactions.[100]

By the mere fact of its existence, the city regulated the kind of edifices it had. Even with minimum planning, the city had to lay out the pattern of the streets. In Philadelphia the rectangular system or gridiron went back to its founder, William Penn. Between 1808 and 1811, three commissioners appointed by the New York state legislature laid out the gridiron plan of north and south avenues and cross streets for New York City and applied it from the old town of crooked streets on lower Manhattan to 155th Street. Chicago also had the gridiron. While this design had the advantage of fixing precise boundaries for property and thus facilitat-

ing its conveyance, it necessarily determined the size of the conventional lot: in New York, 25 feet frontage and 100 feet in depth, and in Chicago "the shoestring lot," also with a 25 foot frontage but often 125 feet deep. Both sizes were ill-adapted for tenement construction, a tenement being a house occupied by three or more families.[101] When multi-family houses were built with higher standards they came to be called apartment houses and furnished abode for the well-to-do and middle classes.[102]

Although tenements appeared in New York as early as the 1830's, it was in the seventies, as congestion deepened, that the typical brick tenement, five or six stories high, appeared, occupying most of the front part of the narrow lot. Since Chicago lots were a little deeper and the city could spread out over the prairie, tenements there became wooden houses two or three stories high. There was one on the front of the lot, one in the rear on an alley, and sometimes one between.[103]

Families were crowded into these dwellings until the density of population per square mile became record-making. In 1893 well over half the population of New York City lived in tenements; in thirty-two acres of the eleventh ward, there were 986.4 persons per acre, a density which only parts of Bombay approached.[104] The crowded urban regions by their filth and lack of ventilation bred more than their share of mortality and illness; to them also were ascribed prostitution, drunkenness, crime, poverty, and the break-down of family life. The more conservative feared they were seed beds of social discontent and revolution.

[98] Leo Grebler, David Blank, Louis Winnick, *Capital Formation in Residential Real Estate* (Princeton: Princeton University Press, 1956), pp. 443–444.

[99] D. M. Fredericksen, "Mortgage Banking in America," *Journal of Political Economy,* II (March, 1894), 208–209.

[100] Robert W. DeForest and Laurence Veiller, editors, *The Tenement House Problem* (New York: Macmillan Company, 1903), I, 357–378; *Eighty Years of Progress of the United States,* p. 357.

[101] Ford, *op. cit.,* I, 83–84, 259–261; Abbott, *op. cit.,* p. 171.

[102] Brown, *op. cit.,* pp. 25–26; Pierce, *op. cit.,* III, 57–58, 500; Homer Hoyt, *One Hundred Years of Land Values in Chicago* (Chicago: University of Chicago Press, 1933), pp. 136–137.

[103] Abbott, *op. cit.,* pp. 190–193.

[104] Ford, *op. cit.,* I, 187.

Charity societies, settlement houses staffed by professors, divines, and social service workers, and individual reformers such as Jacob Riis protested the growth of slums.[105] The particularities of their indictment and proposed remedies would seem to fall within the "public purpose," the responsibility for which in other matters majority opinion had often assigned to city governments. Some European precedents, to which American reformers were usually attuned, pointed in the same direction. But though there were many who asserted that private philanthropy and the self-denial of rich men would remove the slum, rare was the proposal to do so through municipally owned housing.[106] For local authorities to spend public money "competing with private enterprise in housing the masses is bad principle and worse policy." Since housing was not a "natural monopoly,"[107] public housing lacked that justification.

The answer was regulatory legislation. In New York after years of investigation and report, the legislature passed the first tenement house law in 1867. Successive years saw amendments or new acts until the passage of a general tenement house act in 1901, "the most significant regulatory act in America's history of housing." It was widely copied elsewhere. This act "would not have been possible except for the vogue of restrictive legislation that so largely dominated American thought at the opening of the twentieth century."[108] Whereas in 1867 it had been thought sufficient to give each sleeping room ventilation by transom to another room or hall and to prescribe one toilet or privy

for each twenty occupants, by 1901 the law restricted tenement houses to 70 per cent of the lot, required for every room a window opening upon street, yard, or court, compelled the installation of running water and a private toilet in each apartment, and prescribed a certain minimum of cubic feet of space for each occupant. The evolution of these requirements had been accompanied by a tightening of administration through the Board of Health or Building Department and had culminated in a Tenement House Department in 1901.[109] Some provisions of the act were to govern only future construction; others were to compel the alteration of "old-law tenements."

As in other aspects of the economy, the regulatory movement headed into a dilemma. If pushed far enough to accomplish the sanitary and social objectives sought for, it might so increase expenses of construction and hence rents as to defeat its purposes. For a while housing reformers were able to console themselves with the reflection that alterations in "old-law tenements" benefited the landlords by decreasing vacancies and increasing the rents which the occupants ought to be willing to pay.[110] But as congestion continued and new-law tenements were not constructed fast enough, and as apartments in old-law tenements continued in use into the twentieth century, regrets that regulation had not started earlier and chiding landlords for greed hardly seemed an adequate clarification of the situation.[111] What the reformers wanted was expansion under standards which the community could approve. But one employer had noted in the eighties, "Capitalists consider tenement houses a poor investment, paying poor returns."[112]

[105] Ibid., I, 123–124, 172–175, 182, 199.
[106] Ibid., I, 159–162, 175–178, 197–198; E. C. Kirkland, Dream and Thought in the Business Community, 1860–1900 (Ithaca: Cornell University Press, 1956), pp. 44–45.
[107] E. R. L. Gould, "The Only Cure for Slums," Forum, XIX (June, 1895), 498; G. A. Weber, "Improved Tenement Homes for American Cities," Municipal Affairs, I (December, 1897), 752.
[108] Ford, op. cit., I, 154, 205.

[109] Ibid., I, 154–155, 217–223; Weber, loc. cit., pp. 748–749.
[110] DeForest and Veiller, editors, loc. cit., pp. xiv, xvi, xxvi.
[111] Ford, op. cit., I, 202, 204.
[112] Testimony of William Steinway, loc. cit., p. 1087.

Chapter Two

Railroads and Economic Growth

■ Between 1849 and 1854, the greatest American railroad-building boom of all time, in proportion to the length of existing track, gave much of the eastern United States a connected railroad system. A salesman could travel by rail between all the major Northern cities and down the East Coast to Charleston and Savannah or inland to Atlanta and Chattanooga. Orders could be telegraphed to wholesalers or factories and delivered by railroad freight or more rapidly, by a number of railroad express companies.

The expansion of this network, until by the 1890s it reached the limits of the continental United States, and the interweaving of branch lines to service farm areas comprised the great physical achievement of the last half of the nineteenth century. Next to the total of building construction railroad construction consumed the most capital, and it bound the United States together politically and ushered in a more mature phase of industrialism.

As the building process continued,

many railroads came to compete for the same traffic. This led to rate wars and generally low charges between competitive points, for which the roads tried to compensate by high rates between non-competitive stations. In addition, large shippers served by several roads could get rates even lower than those made public by threatening to take their business away from any road that held out for higher rates. Thus by the 1870s the railroad rate structure was extremely irregular, favoring the large shipper over the small and the big city with railroad competition over the small town served by a single road.

Whether the resulting concentration of industry in metropolitan areas and the building up of larger firms stimulated or hindered economic growth is a complex and probably unanswerable question. As suggested in the selection by Professor Fogel in the preceding volume, the necessity of the railroad for economic growth and its contribution to aggregate demand are often exaggerated. It is conceivable that water transportation reinforced by highways and an earlier development of self-propelled highway vehicles might have done the work of the railroad; it is probably sound to regard no invention as indispensable. But the processes would unquestionably have been different and would have produced a differently balanced economic society.

Aside from its profound economic and political effects, the railroad represented an important element in the business organization of an industrial society. It first raised such critical managerial problems of the large corporation as methods of control, delegation of authority, and channels of internal communication. Railroad securities dominated the stock exchanges and led to new procedures for both initial distribution and subsequent selling of stocks and bonds. The basic rhythms of business life were altered in each community reached by the railroads, and men's imaginations were stimulated to new dreams of economic greatness.

The Railroad as an Innovation

■ By merely increasing the volume of migration, the railroad undoubtedly had an innovating effect. The migrant to a new area gets new ideas, sees new ways of doing things, and usually, gives a lift to the initiative and enterprise of the community he enters. Large and continuous migration may well be the most important differential factor between the economic development of the United States and that of Western Europe.

The historian and sociologist, Leland H. Jenks, professor emeritus of Wellesley College, analyzes many other innovating effects of the railroad and appends a theoretical discussion of the nature of entrepreneurship.

Leland H. Jenks
Railroads as an Economic Force in American Development*

I

Any attempt to discuss the way in which railroads have promoted the rise of the American economy must assume some theory of economic evolution. The following analysis is based upon Schumpeter's theory of innovations.[1] Briefly this theory holds that economic evolution in capitalistic society is started by innovation in some production function, that is, by new combinations of the factors in the economic process. These innovations may center in new commodities or new services, new types of machinery, new forms of organization, new firms, new resources, or new areas. As Schumpeter makes clear, this is not a general theory of economic, much less of social, change. Innovation is an internal factor operating within a given economic system while the system is also affected by external factors (many of them sociological) and by growth (which means, substantially, changes in population and in the sum total of savings made by individuals and firms). These sets of factors interact in economic change. "The changes in the economic process brought about by innovation, together with all their effects, and the response to them by the economic sys-

tem" constitute economic evolution for Schumpeter.[2]

Railroad development has had three phases or moments which have involved innovation in distinctive ways. I shall consider (1) the railroads as an idea, (2) the railroad as a construction enterprise, and (3) the railroad as a producer of transportation services.[3]

II

By the railroad as an idea is not meant the original design of steam locomotion on rails. It pertains to the inception in particular areas of particular projects, conceived as likely to be appropriate opportunities for business enterprise. In this sense the idea of any major innovation, such as the railroad, is a potent economic force. For once railway projects have been conceived and plans for their execution elaborated, it becomes easier for other innovating ideas to be entertained.[4] On the one hand, the sociopsychological deterrents against entering upon new ways are lowered. On the other, the characteristics of the prospective future are altered; they assume an aspect more favorable to men and firms with new plans than to men and firms whose posi-

* Reprinted by permission from The Journal of Economic History, IV (March, 1944), pp. 1–20. Note: This article is an elaboration and extension of a paper delivered at the meeting of the Mississippi Valley Historical Association, Washington, D. C., December 28–31, 1938.
[1] Joseph A. Schumpeter, Business Cycles (New York and London: McGraw-Hll Book Company, 1939), Vol. I, esp. chaps. iii and vii, idem, The Theory of Economic Development (Cambridge: Harvard University Press, 1934), chaps. ii and vi; idem, "The Instability of Capitalism," The Economic Journal, XXXVIII (1928), 361–86. Cf. the theory of Allyn A. Young, "Increasing Returns and Economic Progress," ibid., 527–42.

[2] Business Cycles, I, 86.
[3] These distinctions are hinted at but not developed in Business Cycles, I, 130–36. They are not to be construed precisely as stages or periods, although each was relatively more conspicuous in certain decades than in others.
[4] Three types of obstacles to innovation are distinguished in Business Cycles I, 100: hostility to the new idea, absence of facilitating economc functions, and inhibitions against entering upon a relatively incalculable course. Young, in The Economic Journal, XXXVIII (1928), 534, stresses the need to remake human material in terms of new skills and habits and in terms of redistribution of population.

tion is established. Thus early railway projects were attended by a retinue of satellite innovations.

The first railway projects emerged in the United States in the thirties in a situation in which the psychological risks had already been appreciably lowered by the general passion for internal improvements displayed in a plethora of projects for canals, turnpikes, plank roads, bridges, banks, and other enterprises.[5] The earliest railways paralleled, supplemented, or improved transport systems that were already in being.[6] The real railway revolution dates from the forties, prior to the California gold discoveries, in projects to cross the Appalachians, to link the seaboard with the interior, the Ohio Valley with the Great Lakes, and, breaking away from the contours of water transport, to unite distant points by more direct routes.[7] It was the determination to build railroads in advance of traffic that gave the "railroad idea" prolonged force in American economic life. The conviction that the railroad would run anywhere at a

profit put fresh spurs to American ingenuity and opened closed paddocks of potential enterprise.

Innovations are the work of enterprisers. For the railroad as idea, the role of entrepreneurship was pretty much identical with promotion; and the promoter was rarely limited in outlook to the railroad itself. In action, he was omnicompetent and omnipresent. His imagination leaped readily from the concrete problem of securing authority for a right of way to visions of a countryside filled with nodding grain, settlements of industrious families, and other evidences of progress and civilization. Each railway project involved the sanguine judgment of enterprising individuals and groups in particular, local situations that a certain line would be of direct or indirect pecuniary advantage to themselves. It was linked to specific plans for town promotion and real-estate speculation, to combinations for contracting services and supplies or for exploitation of resources, in anticipation of the actual movement of traffic by rail. But as projects multiplied they collectively acquired a symbolic function, dramatizing broader purposes. The railway projector became an exemplification of the power of steam, of the advantages of the corporate form of business organization, of the ability of man to master his environment. The early railway promoter was not only a potential economic agent; he embodied the dream of developing communities, regions, the continent.

Thus, as the barriers to new projects were periodically lowered by the inception of new railway systems, the first moment of the railroad as an economic force was manifested in a wavelike profusion of new enterprises of many sorts. Moreover, its effects in the United States were not exhausted in a decade or so, as they were in England. The railroad idea was periodically renewed for region after region and route after route, as national develop-

[5] Carl Russell Fish, *The Rise of the Common Man* (New York, The Macmillan Company, 1927), chaps. iv and v.
[6] One thinks of the Boston & Lowell, New York & New Haven, Philadelphia & Columbia, Allegheny Portage, the original Baltimore & Ohio, and the lines connecting Albany with Buffalo.
[7] The most dynamic set of American innovations consisted in plans to build railways in anticipation of traffic. Lewis Henry Haney, *A Congressional History of Railways in the United States to 1850* (Madison: University of Wisconsin, 1908), p. 31. Congressional land grants were a factor, as in the case of the Illinois Central, the first large system built through sparsely settled territory. Paul Wallace Gates, *The Illinois Central Railroad and Its Colonization Work* (Cambridge: Harvard University Press, 1934). Canal building had, however, in the old Northwest, anticipated the railroad less successfully in building ahead of population. Frederic L. Paxson, *History of the American Frontier, 1763–1893* (Boston and New York: Houghton Mifflin Company, 1924), chap. xxx. For early systems and projects, cf. Caroline E. MacGill et al., Balthasar Henry Meyer, editor, *History of Transportation in the United States Before 1860* (Washington: Carnegie Institution of Washington, 1917); J. L. Ringwalt, *Development of Transportation Systems in the United States* (Philadelphia: The Author, 1888).

ment, at least facilitated by the earlier railroads, widened the horizons of enterprise.

III

The second moment of the railroad as an economic force came with the actual construction of new lines. The statistics of net mileage added in each year from 1837 to 1937 give a quantitative measure of this contribution of the railroad to development, as appears on the accompanying charts. Two general statements are strikingly supported by these data.[8] In the first place, railway building proceeded in an undulating pattern, paralleling closely the general contours of major business cycles until the First World War. From 1850 to the nineties, omitting the years of the Civil War, the rise and fall in new construction in fact led by a perceptible interval most other indices of

[8] The data for these charts are derived from the United States Treasury Department, Bureau of Statistics, *Statistical Abstract of the United States, 1900* (Washington; United States Government Printing Office, 1901); *ibid., 1914,* p. 637; and *ibid., 1937,* p. 379. Chart II is adapted from Simon S. Kuznets, *Secular Movements in Production and Prices* (Boston and New York: Houghton Mifflin Company, 1930), pp. 191, 526-27.

business conditions.[9] In the second place, there was a long-run trend in new railway construction, which was predominantly upward in absolute figures from the late 1840's to about 1890. The rate of this upward trend tended to slacken with the aggregate movement approximating graphically a logistic curve, but, for the whole period, expansion of railway plant averaged about 10 per cent a year. The trend since 1890 has been irregularly downward, bearing the aspect of a reversed logistic curve. The early persistent succession of fresh waves of railway construction, arising largely in the development of new areas in the American

[9] This correlation was initially based upon inspection of the mileage data in comparison with the chart in Schumpeter, *Business Cycles, II,* 465, and the analyses of business conditions in Willard Long Thorp, *Business Annals* (New York: National Bureau of Economic Research, 1926) and National Bureau of Economic Research, *Recent Economic Changes* (New York: McGraw-Hill Book Company, 1929), II, 892. More decisive support is provided by John E. Partington, *Railroad Purchasing and the Business Cycle* (Washington: The Brookings Institution, 1929). As Partington includes orders for replacements as well as for original basic construction, he finds that orders of railway capital goods led business-cycle changes as late as 1907. Throughout this period, he finds, railway earnings followed, instead of preceded, changes in purchases.

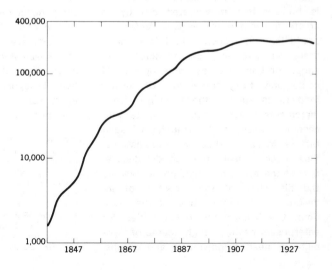

Chart I. Miles of Railroad in Operation, 1837–1937

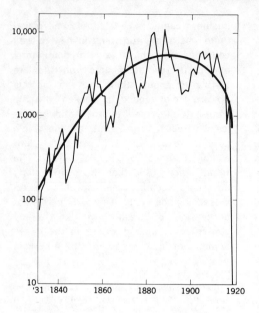

Chart II. Net Annual Change in U.S. Railroad Mileage, 1831–1916

West and South, must be regarded as one of the basic phenomena in the total economic growth of the United States, while the logistic curve of total experience presents in outline a picture of an industry passing from youth through adolescence to maturity.

But how did railway construction as such act as an economic force? How could it be a pace setter? The answer is broadly that it operated directly to create a demand for various factors of production. In response to this demand there were rises in prices or increases in supply or both. Increase of supply could come only from some sort of further innovations, such as the drawing of fresh increments of land, labor, or capital into economic uses or the transfer of such factors to more effective combinations. This process meant the periodic dislocation of the economic structure as well as the disruption of the activities of individuals and communities. At the same time it enhanced the opportunities for enterprisers having a high degree of flexibility, pioneering individuals and groups,

the agents of innumerable innovating firms and procedures.

The land for railroad construction was largely new land, previously not of economic use. It cost virtually nothing to the railway companies, and not very much to anyone else.[10] Socially the land devoted to railroad purposes more than paid for itself by the increment in productivity of adjacent land. This was so obvious to everyone connected with railway building that periodic land booms came to communities even before the rails were laid. The speculative activity thus diffused in anticipation of railroad construction may have brought many creative innovations in its wake. But, by distracting labor and enterprise from productive to parasitic

[10] Frederick A. Cleveland and Fred Wilbur Powell, *Railroad Promotion and Capitalization in the United States* (New York: Longmans, Green and Company, 1909), pp. 199–200. "In the Southern States, and the Mississippi Valley . . . all the real estate required for way, and for depots, stations, etc., are generally gratuity to the roads." *American Railroad Journal*, XXV (January 3, 1852), 13. Cf. James Blaine Hedges, *Henry Villard and the Railways of the Northwest* (New Haven: Yale University Press, 1930), *passim.*

activities, it frequently delayed the realization of the plausible hopes upon which railroad projects were primarily based.

The demand for labor initiated a chapter in the history of immigration and colonization.[11] It also disciplined migratory and local labor power to co-operative industrial effort. But it had wider repercussions. Laborers were paid wages and the wages were spent for goods. They went to market to buy the produce of American farms and mills. Thus the demand for labor stimulated the spread of market economy and the more extensive production of goods and services for distant markets, and thereby contributed to the spread of economic specialization.

The demand for capital functioned in

parallel to the demand for labor. I am speaking of real capital, of goods, of the picks and shovels, sleepers and steel rails, engines and rolling stock and bridgework and culverts and ordinary building material, which make up the physical plant of a railroad. The construction moment of railway history brought an initial demand for these durable goods.[12] Hence there was a chance for the innovator in the lumbering industry, in quarries, in iron mills and carriage works. Indeed these industries were hard put to keep pace with railway construction. Until the later eighties, every boom period found American factories unable to meet the demand for rails, and there were heavy importations from England and Wales. As late as the nineties, over one-fifth of the total output of pig iron in the United States was being rolled into railroad bars.[13]

Much of this demand for durable goods turned eventually into a demand for labor in mine and quarry and mill, into wage payments to labor. And these wages too were spent for consumers' goods and

[11] Gates, *The Illinois Central Railroad*, pp. 89, 94–8. Despite its crucial importance, the subject of labor supply has been too frequently neglected by railway historians. Adequate data for labor employed in new construction are available only for a few large lines such as the Central Pacific, Union Pacific, and the Illinois Central. On each of these, upwards of 10,000 men were employed at the peak of construction. Probably a thousand men were needed for every hundred miles. Assuming that twice as many miles were in progress as were completed in any given year, the figure of 200,000 men is reached as the maximum employed at any one time in the construction of these railways. This figure was not attained until the eighties, by which time the census reported 250,000 officials and employees of railroads, presumably engaged directly or indirectly in transportation service.

[12] Cf. files of railway periodicals for advertisements of manufacturers and dealers in railway materials and supplies. Ringwalt, *Development of Transportation Systems in the U. S.*, pp. 132–36, 210.
[13] For details, cf. *Statistical Abstract of the U. S.*, 1902, p. 380, and corresponding tables in earlier volumes.

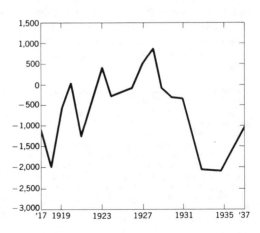

Chart III. Net Annual Change in U.S. Railroad Mileage, 1917–1937

meant widening markets, increased specialization, and, presumably, greater productivity.

Thus the initial impetus of investment in railway construction led in widening arcs to increments of economic activity over the entire American domain, far exceeding in their total volume the original inputs of investment capital. To this feature of modern capitalism, John Maynard Keynes and others have applied the term "multiplier."[14] It is believed that for present-day England the efficiency of the multiplier may suffice to double the impact of a new investment in construction. For nineteenth-century United States, its efficiency seems to have been considerably greater than that.

I have spoken of inputs and investment. In our economy the demand for land and labor and capital has meant another demand, a demand not for an independent factor of production, but for something equally essential, a demand for money capital.[15] In fact, without a supply of money capital there could have been no effective demand for any of the real factors, no railways, and no stimulus from them for economic development. Hence it is convenient to think of the building of railroads as an investment of money capital. To this investment there corresponded in the long run the accumulation of savings. That saving came first and investment in the railroads afterwards is a proposition for which there is little historical evidence, at least in the United States. It is true that the practice of

thrift as an individual and family responsibility was built into our social system by the Puritans. But the savings thus made in the middle of the nineteenth century went largely into land, into improvements on the farm, into the mill, the private business, and, in relatively small amounts, into public securities. Few railroads were originally financed by direct subscription of the shareholders at par in ready cash.[16]

In final analysis, the funds for railway construction came from the extension of credit by American banks and from foreign exchange supplied by European investors. This was accomplished by many devices which called into play the charitable cupidity of contractors and iron manufacturers on both sides of the Atlantic, and the lively anticipations of property owners in the area which the railroad was to develop.[17] Some of the shares were sold at a heavy discount to local residents, but more were given outright for land, for legal and legislative services, for banking accommodation, or as a bonus to promote the sale of bonds. Frequently there was a construction company, analogous to the Crédit Mobilier, which took all the securities in payment for the road and operated it pending the completion of construction. Since the books of these organizations have been conveniently mislaid, it will always be impossible to ascertain what our railroads

[14] John Maynard Keynes, *The General Theory of Employment, Interest and Money* (London, 1936), chap. xi; R. F. Kahn, "The Relation of Home Investment to Unemployment," *The Economic Journal*, XLI (1931), 173–98.

[15] Admittedly "money capital" constitutes merely a vehicle or instrumentality, the means of acquiring command over the several factors of production. More commonly it is spoken of as long-term credit or capital funds. But sometimes an instrument becomes so important that it exerts influences by itself and requires consideration on its separate account.

[16] These were chiefly railroads built in the thirties and forties. Cf. Frank Walker Stevens, *The Beginnings of the New York Central Railroad* (New York and London: G. P. Putnam's Sons, 1926). Even in these cases, as we know from accounts of the crises of 1854 and 1857, the subscribers carried their shares on bank loans. Cf. Schumpeter, *Business Cycles*, I, 325–50.

[17] Cleveland and Powell, *Railroad Promotion and Capitalization*, is still the most adequate account for aspects before 1900. Cf. William Z. Ripley, *Railroads; Finance and Organization* (New York: Longmans, Green and Company, 1915), pp. 10–52; Cleveland and Powell, *Railroad Finance* (New York: D. Appleton and Company, 1912), chaps. ii–iv and the very rich bibliography; Charles F. Adams, Jr., "Railroad Inflation," *North American Review*, XVIII (1869), 138–44.

really cost originally in money capital. The construction companies turned over whole blocks of securities to manufacturers and contractors in payment for goods and services. These enterprises usually seem to have pledged the securities with banks for working capital in the process of supplying the goods. In New York and elsewhere, speculators and specialists in railway finance, operating also on bank loans, facilitated this inflationary process by their dealings in stocks and bonds and daily risked the credit of the railway companies in their furious contests of bulls and bears.

The American banking mechanism did not have to bear this periodic strain alone. Every burst of new railway construction, in the thirties, in the fifties, at the close of the Civil War, through the eighties, and again from 1904 to 1907, meant new investments from abroad by British, Dutch, and German capitalists.[18] Schumpeter states that the boom from 1866 to 1873, which doubled our railway mileage, was entirely financed by an estimated two billion dollars of capital imported during those years.[19] It is incorrect to suppose, as he apparently does, that any such amount of foreign money was at that time invested directly in the railways. British, Dutch, and German investors were then buying nearly half of the Civil War debt, chiefly in 5–20's and 10–40's, to the amount of more than a

billion dollars par. The railroads obtained directly only about half a billion. The purchase of government bonds by foreigners, however, released savings and bank resources for railway, industrial, and commercial promotion in the United States. In no subsequent period was the impact of foreign capital as momentous; but it is easy to exaggerate its importance. Although something like one-fifth of the nominal value of American railroads was foreign-owned in 1873, the whole volume of foreign claims amounted to only 6 or 7 per cent of national wealth.[20] While in the course of subsequent fluctuations foreign ownership of railroad securities may have reached the proportions of one-third in 1890 and nearly as much just before 1914, yet at these later dates it constituted a smaller proportion of the total national wealth than it had in 1873. According to the estimates, foreign investments did not keep pace with the growth of the national wealth.

It would be desirable to measure more precisely the investment of money capital at successive periods. Available figures of railway capitalization are entirely unsatisfactory for historical purposes. Apart from the obscurities of early railroad finance already mentioned, tabulations and estimates do not carefully and regularly include net floating debt or exclude intercorporate securities. The pathology of early stock watering has no necessary connection with the "overcapitalization" from which most railroad systems have suffered in recent years. This overcapitalization is entirely compatible with real historical investment as large as the nominal capitalization. But the available statistics give no adequate clue, before the last few decades, when such amounts actually were invested.

Whatever the source or timing of the

---

[18] This paragraph is based upon original research in London and the United States, made possible by a sabbatical from Wellesley College and a grant from the John Simon Guggenheim Memorial Foundation. An introduction to the subject is available in Cleona Lewis, *America's Stake in International Investments* (Washington: The Brookings Institution, 1938), chap. ii; Ripley, *Railroads; Finance and Organization*, pp. 1–10; and Leland H. Jenks, *The Migration of British Capital to 1875* (New York and London: Alfred A. Knopf, 1927), chap. iii and pp. 169, 255–59 and notes. Before the Civil War the share of foreign investors was smaller than it became later. In only a few cases was it an initiating factor in railroad development.

[19] Schumpeter, *Business Cycles*, I, 335.

[20] Lewis, *America's Stake in International Investments*, p. 560.

application of money capital, the financing of railroad construction encouraged innovations in financial enterprise: the development of stock exchanges and their techniques; the specialization of firms, old and new, in investment banking and in security brokerage; the specialization of banking institutions (especially trust companies) as trustees and registration agents for securities, and as agents for distributing capital and interest payments; the rise of legal firms specializing in corporation law and in adjusting construction activities to the intricacies of the American political system.

New financial techniques and innovations in corporate structure were involved when established railway companies became agents in the flow of capital. By the early fifties the Pennsylvania was using its credit to supply funds for the building of western connections which it only informally controlled.[21] With the establishment of the Pennsylvania Company in 1869, the holding company became a permanent feature of the American scene. In many cases initial construction was of the sketchiest sort and by the seventies it was an established practice, of which foreign security holders bitterly complained, for companies to invest their earnings in necessary improvements and extensions. This financing of corporate growth from within may fairly be claimed to be an American innovation in capitalistic technique, which has only recently been diffused to the British Isles.

With financial innovation came a transformation of the role of the enterpriser in connection with particular railway systems. In the initial moments of construction, the typical enterpriser was still pretty much the omnicompetent pioneer, the individual of imagination, daring, and energy. Like General W. J. Palmer of the Denver and Rio Grande, he considered

himself an agent of civilization, an embodiment of collective purpose.[22] No aspect of the task of railway building was too technical for his consideration and none too petty. In looking for the enterpriser of particular lines, official titles should not deceive. There was usually one man or a small informal group of unspecialized associates who could get things done, who could deal effectively at the same time with laborers, suppliers, politicians, and the local citizenry, and could command the confidence of sources of credit. At the construction moment, administration of a large formal organization was not necessarily involved. The mechanism of subcontracting provided a pattern for the cooperation of innumerable lesser enterprisers of a similar type.

Such enterprisers were rarely able, however, to cope with recurrent financial involvements. The elaboration of the superstructure of railroad securities sooner or later compelled a more formal division of tasks and responsibilities in the continuance of construction. In some cases this involved a shift of the center of decision from the engineer-promoter to financial and legal experts either within or outside the railroad organization.[23] The financier-enterpriser assumed many guises, now entering upon new construction to win stock-exchange battles, now basing a

[21] Pennsylvania Central R. R. Co., *Annual Reports, passim.*

[22] William J. Palmer, *The Westward Current of Population in the United States* (London, 1874), and Glenn Chesney Quiett, *They Built the West* (New York and London: D. Appleton-Century Company, 1934), chaps. ii–vi, throw light upon the career of this neglected enterpriser.

[23] N. S. B. Gras, *Business and Capitalism* (New York: F. S. Crofts and Company, 1939), pp. 246–59, 272–75, indicates the "normal" process by which financial capitalists became involved in industry. He is correct, I believe, in implying that the opportunity and need have not been confined to the late phases of the construction moment. From the standpoint of innovation, the emergence of the financial enterpriser in the railroads is not to be identified with the rise of special departments within the organization. The latter, or their heads, may be simply part of a formally established group functioning as management-enterprise. See section IV below.

program of calculated expansion upon a re-ordering of company accounts, now entering belatedly, as did William Rockefeller in Northwestern, the race for competitive bigness.[24] There was inescapably a narrowing of horizon; the financier-enterpriser could decide freely only problems stated in financial terms, and he focused his attention chiefly on relations with potential intermediaries and rivals for the supply of capital.

Thus the second moment of the railroad as an economic force came with a demand for the factors of production in new construction, accompanied by the rise of new techniques and institutions of finance, by the aggregation of capital in mobile forms, and by the gradual displacement of the omnicompetent type of enterpriser.

IV

The third moment to be surveyed is that of the railroad as a going concern, a complex of tracks and engines and cars and managers and employees engaged in the business of carrying passengers and freight. By rendering this transportation service, the railroad in operation has doubtless added directly to the real income of the United States, and indirectly to economic expansion.[25] There appears to be no satisfactory technique for giving a precise measure to the extent of this

contribution. It seems that the railways carried irregularly increasing ton-miles of freight until 1929, while the aggregate of passenger-miles expanded until 1920. The quanta involved, said to be from 13 billions of freight in 1870 to 450 billions in 1929, are certainly enormous.[26] But the available figures, at least before 1890, are neither accurate nor complete. There have been important changes in the composition of traffic. As Pigou points out, any attempt to measure differences in real income between situations involving substantial variations in the use of productive factors and in the composition of demand is theoretically at least precarious.[27] For contemporary comparison, Holmstrom has worked out a technique by which "virtual costs" (operating and maintenance charges plus interest on replacement cost of ways and works plus depreciation and profits) are equated with "direct benefits" on the one hand and "consumer costs" plus public subsidies on the other.[28] In view of the defective character of the data and the violence

[24] Max Lowenthal, *The Investor Pays* (New York: Alfred A. Knopf, 1933).
[25] Ringwalt, *Development of Transportation Systems in the U. S.*, pp. 382–85, and Henry V. Poor, *Influence of the Railroads of the U. S. in the Creation of its Commerce and Wealth* (New York, 1869) are representative of early discussions. "Our new railroads increase the value of farms and open new markets for their products. They lessen the time and cost of travel. They give a value to commodities otherwise almost worthless. They concentrate population, stimulate production, and raise wages by making labor more efficient. Our existing railroads are computed to create more wealth every year than is absorbed for the construction of new railroads." *Commercial and Financial Chronicle*, XVI (January 11, 1873), 41.

[26] Attempts to use railway data in connection with the study of changes in real income and "productivity" are exemplified by Arthur F. Burns, *Production Trends in the United States since 1870* (New York: National Bureau of Economic Research, 1934), and Spurgeon Bell, *Productivity, Wages, and National Income* (Washington: The Brookings Institution, 1940). A brief factual summary of the role of the railways in the economic system after the First World War is provided by the Bureau of Railway Economics, *The Railways and Economic Progress* (Miscellaneous Series No. 50, Washington, 1929). The theory there suggested that the "economic contribution" of the railways is measured by the volume of their expenditures of all kinds is, however, at variance with the premises of this paper. Incidentally, this is an unusual place to find a theory popularly associated with New Deal economics. On railroad expenditures, cf. Partington, *Railroad Purchasing and the Business Cycle*.
[27] A. C. Pigou, "Comparisons of Real Income," *Economica*, New Series, X (May, 1943), pp. 93–8.
[28] J. Edwin Holmstrom, *Railways and Roads in Pioneer Development Overseas* (London: P. S. King and Son, 1934), chap. i. Cf. E. A. J. Johnson, "New Tools for the Economic Historian," *The Tasks of Economic History*, supplemental issue of *The Journal of Economic History*, December, 1941, pp. 30–8.

of price fluctuations in the United States, there is little hope of applying these means of measurement to the historical problem.

It is commonly assumed that the great contribution of railroad transportation came from the reduction of shipping costs. As compared with pre-motorized forms of highway transportation, the advantage of the railroad has always been obvious. There is no convincing evidence, however, that railways have ever carried freight at lower costs either to shippers or to society than canals or waterways.[29] The advantages that early railways showed over canals, such as speed, flexibility of service, and special adaptability to short hauls, are analogous to those of modern highway transport over the railroad. It was far more important that the railroad brought transportation to areas that without it could have had scarcely any commercial existence at all. At a later epoch, the motor highway provides means to achieve this result, at least in British colonial areas, at lower initial social cost. But historically, the very existence of most American communities and regions, of particular farms and industrial firms and aggregates, was made possible by the railroad.

Holmstrom's study of the cost characteristics of various forms of transportation brings other considerations to the forefront of analysis. He shows that the traffic potential of the railroad per unit of installation is even now far greater than that of any other form of transportation that he considers. For colonial areas in the early 1930's, for example, he computes that human porters could carry a maximum of 1,450 ton-miles of freight per annum; heavy animals, 3,600; "horsed wagons," 118,800; tractor trains, 1,000,-000; and broad-gauge railways, 3,613,-500.[30] Thus an initial and continuing potential contribution of the railroad has come from the volume of traffic it has been able to carry.

The converse of this proposition is the fact that the railroad constitutes a case of increasing return, with special features that give a decisive bent to its impact upon economic structure. Its social costs per unit of traffic decrease rapidly with traffic density.[31] A familiar manifestation of this condition was the well-known shift from passengers and light traffic as principal sources of revenue in the early railroad days to bulk traffic. Any isolated railroad system would tend to expand along those lines. But as new railroads in the United States became linked to previously existing lines, and as the innovation of freight-car interchange was established after the Civil War, a principle of acceleration was manifested enabling newer lines to begin farther along the cost curve. Between 1890 and 1941 the average actual haul of each ton of freight became 50 per cent longer (increasing especially during the First World War and the 1930's); there was an increase of more than 100 per cent during the same period in the distance traveled by the average passenger. These are revealing data about the long-run function of the

[29] General treatments of the economic significance of improved transportation are also found in D. Philip Locklin, Economics of Transportation (Chicago: Business Publications, 1938), chap. i, and Cleveland and Powell, Railroad Finance, chap. i. On comparative costs of service, cf. MacGill, History of Transportation in the U. S. before 1860, pp. 574–82; Haney, Congressional History of Railways in the U. S., chap. iii.; Charles H. Ambler, A History of Transportation in the Ohio Valley (Glendale, California: The Arthur H. Clark Company, 1932), pp. 358 ff.; Harold Kelso, "Waterways versus Railways," The American Economic Review, XXXI (1941), 537–44.

[30] Holmstrom, Railways and Roads in Pioneer Development Overseas, p. 56. Palmer, The Westward Current of Population in the U. S., relates that in 1866 the stage line from the terminus of the Kansas Pacific in Topeka carried six passengers daily to Denver. Two years later, daily trains carried westward one hundred to five hundred passengers daily.
[31] Holmstrom, pp. 104–12.

railroad in the economic system.[32] Such expansion is, however, not a measure of innovation; the recent increase reflects to no small degree adjustments by railroads to other innovations in the economic system. What is significant about the principle of increasing return in the railroad is that it indicates directions in which railway transportation affects the economic structure.

That the railroad tends to attract factors of production to its right of way needs no comment; this perception lay at the heart of the American railroad innovation. As Holmstrom points out, however, this supply of potential traffic does not distribute itself at random. It is polarized first about line terminals, and secondarily about traffic intersections.[33] There is a further tendency. Irrespective of rate differentials, the service of the railroad is of greatest advantage to large shippers requiring a fairly regular flow of traffic.[34] Thus railroad transportation provides a considerable addition to the external economies that firms can realize from large-scale operations. Such phenomena as the ecological structure of wholesale trade, the localization and concentration of primary processing establishments, and the vertical integration of production units in spite of their geographical separation are thus functionally related to railroad transportation service. In more concrete terms, attention may be directed to the initial localization of the textile industry in New England, the development of the factory system in some other industries at points remote from water power and dependent upon rail supply of coal, the establishment of stockyards in Chicago and other terminals, the rise of assembly plants, and generally

the concentration, at terminals convenient to the source of supply, of industries processing and reducing the bulk of raw materials. In all these respects, railway transportation has worked in the same direction as, but in different areas from, water transport. It has functioned differently from the realized and probable tendencies of highway traffic.

The organization of railway enterprise itself early displayed the same tendencies to differentiation that it encouraged in other industries. On the one hand, the railways transferred to other enterprises part of their business. First in individual railway lines, and gradually on a more national scale, came the innovation of express companies, specializing in the rapid transmission of small items of high value. Opportunity arose for Pullman and other specialists in high-cost passenger service. On the other hand, individual railways themselves engaged in other business activities. If their land departments developed in order to implement construction, they proved of more value in augmenting traffic density to remunerative levels. Reading and other companies acquired anthracite fields in the interest of controlling the supply of bulk traffic between terminals. A great deal of change in the internal structure of railway organizations was merely a function of their expansion, involving innovations of a highly derivative and adaptive character; but other changes involved the positive quest of increasing return. The extension of particular systems by purchase, lease, and contract did not invariably contemplate development, but often aimed at controlling for the benefit of original lines the supply of traffic at terminal points. The consolidation movement and much resistance to it on the part of particular companies may be interpreted from this point of view.

It must be clear that to yield real income and participate in expansion are not the same as to be a force for economic

[32] United States Interstate Commerce Commission, *Statistics of Railways in the United States, 1941* (Washington: United States Government Printing Office, 1943), pp. 159–60.

[33] Holmstrom, pp. 265–66, 273.

[34] *Ibid.*, pp. 271–72.

development. On the economic structure, the impact of the railway as a going concern was most decisive in the early years of the expansion of each system and in many respects came from the network as a whole rather than from any particular part. In time many other forces reinforced the polarizing tendency of the railroad. Urban centers tended to generate conditions that made for their own growth into metropolises. The returns to railways from increasing density tended to increase at slackening rates. Change in the railways gradually became more a matter of adjustment to external innovations than a primary source of disturbance to the economic structure.

As early as the eighties, railway systems that had been daring ventures only a decade before found themselves embarking on extensions and improvements, not as acts of innovating faith, but to enable them to handle traffic that had been offered them or to keep somebody else from getting the business.[35] In region after region development initiated by the railroad outran the plans of the projectors. The business of the railroad came increasingly to consist not in starting something but in keeping pace with what others were doing. That the railway would carry freight at known rates and with gradual change in the quality of service came to be part of the normal expectations of every business firm, a stable part of an environment which, of course, might still be disturbed by other innovations.[36] While the real income accruing to society from railway transportation probably continued to grow until 1929, the railroad

functioned decreasingly as a pace setter or as an inciting force in the expansion of which it was a part.

By the time of the financial reorganizations of the nineties, many American railways manifested signs of belonging to an industry that has reached maturity.[37] The signs became more widespread in the first decade of the present century with the completion of the last cluster of new systems. For enterprises in general, Oxenfeldt thinks "newness of economic consequence" can be assumed to have worked itself out within a year of establishment.[38] This seems too short a period for the railroad. Although the bulk of improvement in the early years of American railway systems is properly classed as "construction," the leverage of increasing return in this field involves such extensive relocation of productive forces that opportunity for major business decisions may recur for several years after "completion" of the system.[39]

That some innovations have been made by railroads since 1910 must be conceded. Both technological and organizational changes are involved in the recent rapid increase in ton-miles of freight handled per employee and per unit of capital, in the increased capacity of cars, in speed of train units, in locomotive efficiency, etc. The National Resources Planning Board, however, takes the view that potentialities in this direction are thus far more an idea than an actuality.[40]

Consolidation looms as the source of the most important innovations in the

---

[35] For instance, new financing was sought by the Grand Trunk of Canada in the seventies and the Norfolk & Western in the eighties to make it possible to handle traffic already being offered. It was not always an extension that was involved but more often double-tracks, sidings, rolling stock, and improvements in the right of way.

[36] Schumpeter, Business Cycles, I, chap. ii, presents a representative theoretical analysis of this "equilibrium" position to which railway enterprises have been approximating.

[37] E. G. Campbell, The Reorganization of the American Railroad System, 1893–1900 (New York: Columba University Press, 1938).

[38] Alfred R. Oxenfeldt, New Firms and Free Enterprise (Washington: American Council of Public Affairs, 1943), p. 75.

[39] The degree to which in recent decades public regulation has restricted this opportunity as far as pricing of services is concerned has been the subject of a suggestive inquiry by the National Resources Planning Board. Transportation and National Policy (Washington: United States Government Printing Office, 1942), esp. pp. 87–128.

[40] Ibid., pp. 60–5.

near future. In 1933 only 16 per cent of the time of a typical freight car from shipper to consignee was consumed in hauling; 37 per cent of the time was attributable to railroad terminal movement; and a total of 84 per cent was spent in terminals.[41] Co-operation among carriers could improve this condition, but changes of innovational consequence seem to wait upon government action.

But what has been the role of the entrepreneur in the railroad as a going concern? What is the source of innovation in an enterprise almost wholly concerned with rendering transportation service? The rise of a line organization with few staff features was an early aspect of railway operations, and was well established by the eighties. The Pennsylvania Central seems to have led the way in the practice of promotion from within, a practice that developed rapidly into seniority policies at all levels and the establishment of railroading as a career. For a couple of decades after the Civil War, the training thus afforded made the Pennsylvania an important source from which new companies drew top executives who often developed entrepreneurial talents as individuals. Thomas A. Scott, who rose from the ranks to the presidency of Pennsylvania, was of pioneering quality. As horizons of opportunity narrowed, however, selection from within tended to bring competent administrators of a more routine sort to top executive positions, men who had spent so many years mastering the complexities of detailed management along established lines that they had little interest in changing those procedures. This tendency has been marked in many railroad systems, and is associated with the shift to adaptive change as the principal relation of the railroads to economic expansion in recent years.

Nevertheless, some innovation has taken place, and it can occasionally be traced to pioneering leadership. Large organizations as such, however, apart from their degree of maturity, set up certain hazards to innovation. To continue operations they require the delegation of specialized authority and responsibility to a considerable number of individuals. An innovation disturbs their tasks and their relations with each other quite as much as it does economic relations and activities outside the organization. This disturbance to internal equilibrium is not adjusted through market mechanisms and bargaining transactions. It involves planning activity. Decisive importance can scarcely be allowed to attach to individuals who conceive new ideas, even when this duty is delegated to them as a specific task. The locus of decision tends to spread to a group that includes persons in a position to know and deal with prospective internal disturbances which are only partially of an economic character.[42] It is not clear that this development has explicitly gone far in railroad organization. As an innovation in the role of entrepreneurship itself, it is emergent in some newer large-scale industries. The extent to which the management-enterpriser type, as we may call it, has actually functioned in railroads informally and without explicit recognition deserves inquiry.

V

This general interpretation of the role of the railroad as an economic force suggests what might be undertaken in greater

[41] *Ibid.*, p. 41.

[42] An introduction to the sociological theory of organization can be found in Chester I. Barnard, *The Functions of the Executive* (Cambridge: Harvard University Press, 1938). Cf. T. N. Whitehead, *Leadership in a Free Society* (Cambridge: Harvard University Press, 1936), chaps. vi and viii. The problem at a lower level of enterprise structure is analyzed in F. J. Roethlisberger and William J. Dickson, *Management and the Worker* (Cambridge: Harvard University Press, 1939), chaps. xxiv and xxv.

detail to apply the innovation theory to the history of particular companies and of the railroad system as a whole. What was the impact of the railroad upon technological, locational, structural, and organizational alterations in particular firms, industries, and regions? Parallel inquiries could be made regarding the part played by other major innovations, such as the more recent rise of the electromotive industries. It is not a question of applying the facts of economic history to verify an economic theory. It is a question of using a theory as a tool to coherent understanding of the facts. Economic historians seem increasingly willing to make use of conceptual aids for this purpose. It is one of the most prominent symptoms of what may be a wider tendency to employ analytical procedures in historical studies.

For the study of long-run change, the innovation theory stresses two important aspects of historical process: (1) the distinction between innovating (disturbing, inciting, evolutionary) change and various types of adjustment (including expansion), and (2) the distinctive role of entrepreneurship. The first of these aspects provides the framework for systematic exploration of the relation between changes in several sectors of the economy, in so far as these can be interpreted in economic terms. The breakdown of the railroad innovation into three "moments" is only a convenience that may be peculiar to transportation. In any case, the distinction between innovating and adaptive change is a device that should become more serviceable to the historian as it is sharpened by application to a number of particular situations. It does not necessarily require the economic historian to take into account other than economic events and processes. Indeed, its logical adequacy can only gain from rigorous limitation to the items that are considered to be a part of an economic system.

The emphasis upon entrepreneurship as the crucial factor in capitalistic evolution involves both theorist and historian in considerations that go far beyond the limits of economics. Schumpeter is explicitly aware of this fact, and insists that in his conception the economy is not isolated but functions in a larger universe which requires in the first instance sociological analysis for its interpretation. The theory of innovations is neither a "great man" nor a "better mousetrap" theory of history. The innovator is a person whose traits are in some part a function of his sociocultural environment. His innovation is a new combination of factors and elements already accessible. It relates in every phase to previously developed business and monetary habits, technological skills, and variable tastes, none of which can be regarded as functions of economic activity alone. Thus Schumpeter's theory involves the question of the sociological factors favorable to the emergence of entrepreneurship. In a recent work he has presented a partial analysis of such factors.[43] Further analysis seems to be called for, at least so far as American capitalism is concerned, analysis that will come to closer grips with the special features of American social structure and the various influences which made for a strong entrepreneurial bias in the "social character" of the nineteenth-century American.

Despite his sociological sophistication, however, Schumpeter tends to think of his entrepreneur pretty much as a deviant person—a particular individual or at most a family. This approach tends to make highly problematical the existence of any entrepreneurship in a bureaucratic enterprise such as the railway, whether under private or public ownership. It must be recognized that innovations in a social economy would work themselves out by

[43] Joseph A. Schumpeter, *Capitalism, Socialism, and Democracy* (New York: Harper and Brothers, 1942), chaps. xi–xiv.

mechanisms other than under capitalism. But not all of such differences would be peculiar to socialism. Practically, large-scale organization offers a new type of social resistance to innovation. At the same time, as Schumpeter himself vigorously argues, the large organization offers real support to technological change, at least, by mobilizing resources for its systematic planning.[44]

It is possible that there is a real social lag in conceptions of the entrepreneurial function. The question deserves to be considered whether policy formation by group action is an obstacle to innovation, not inherently, but only because of certain peculiarities in our culture. Is the entrepreneurial role in large organizations increasingly the function of a co-operating group? Is it true that this tendency is not absolutely new but can be discerned in earlier phases of modern industry; that it is less important in entrepreneurial studies to single out the contributions of one individual than to ascertain the personal composition of the group with which he usually interacted and the way in which the members compensated for their respective shortcomings and were adjusted to each other? In so far as there is validity in affirmative answers to these questions, a practical problem of much importance falls upon the large organizations of the present day, that of cultivating social techniques for facilitating innovations. But there would be a broader social problem, that of developing personalities whose practical imagination and responsibility for decision will be stimulated rather than frustrated by membership in policy-determining groups. This would be a task for the family and other educational institutions and for socializing processes in the wider society.

[44] *Ibid.*, pp. 96–8. Schumpeter seems to regard this change as more than adaptational. In so far as it is innovational, however, it functions less to develop capitalist structure than to further its incipient transformation into something else.

Railroads and Local Development

■ The enterprises of a local area are a function of its connections with the outside world. In Shangri-la in the high Himalayas, if it ever existed, the makers of goods must have had few worries about outside competitors. In New York City, by contrast, only those manufacturers who could meet national and world competition could survive. Leonard J. Arrington of Utah State University, the principal Mormon economic historian, shows how the wise Mormon leaders foresaw the disruptive effect of the railroad on their relatively self-sufficient economy and planned in the interests of a balanced society to resist some of the competitive pressures brought by better transportation. The principles illustrated in the Arrington discussion could be applied to any isolated community faced with the coming of the railroad in the nineteenth century. Some enterprises, including farmers in general, would profit greatly, a few types of production would die from the new pressures of outside competition, and everyone would be more involved in a national money economy.

Leonard J. Arrington

The Transcontinental Railroad and Mormon Economic Policy*

An improvement in transportation facilities produces many types of social change. More intricate division of labor, geographic specialization, extension of the market, greater mobility of capital and labor, replacement of local monopoly with regional and national monopoly—these are some of the changes which result from the introduction and use of a major transportation facility. Religious, political, and economic ideologies are transformed, and local customs, beliefs, habits, and other forms of social differentiation are replaced by a new cosmopolitanism in thought and action. As the transcontinental railroad moved west in the 1860's, for example, the self-sufficient family and village economies widened into a national commercial organization. National commerce, in turn, involved regional and local specialization and a high degree of interdependence. Never was an economy of such magnitude knit together so quickly and so securely as the economy of the United States during the first few years after the end of the Civil War.

As with other sections of the country, the territory of Utah was profoundly influenced by the junction of the Pacific railroads at Promontory, near Ogden, on May 10, 1869. That a social revolution did not occur in Utah, that Utah was not immediately absorbed into the national free trade area, and that the economic and social changes in Utah were never as great as those which transformed other western states, can be attributed largely to the action of the leaders of the Mormon church who exercised a dominant influence in the determination of the economic policies of the territory at the

time of the completion of the transcontinental railroad. While their efforts may appear to us to have resembled bare hands pounding against stone walls, and while the advance of eastern competitive capitalism must have descended like an avalanche upon their theocratic "welfare state," Mormon officials attempted to make effective use of the limited weapons at their disposal. Through an agency called the "School of the Prophets," Mormon leaders carried out an economic action program which delayed and mollified the absorption of the unique Mormon commonwealth into the broader social economy of the nation.

The prime objective of Mormon policy was to establish the Kingdom of God on earth. Although most Mormons believed that they were living in the "last dispensation," and some, including leaders, retained carriages in which to drive to Jackson County, Missouri—site of the New Jerusalem in Mormon theology—to prepare for the Second Coming of the Savior, nevertheless, the care with which they planned their society demonstrates that Mormon leaders adopted the long-run point of view.

Latter-day Saints acted as though they were building for eternity and had an eternity in which to build. To Mormon leaders, twenty or thirty years was an insignificant period in the life of a people. They were thinking in terms of results which might take a hundred years to achieve.[1] The "time limit" of Mormon policy seems to have been considerably longer than that which typified nineteenth-century capitalistic America.

The activities of the Mormons during

---

* Reprinted by permission from *The Pacific Historical Review*, XX (May, 1951), pp. 143–157.

[1] Richard T. Ely, "Economic Aspects of Mormonism," *Harper's Monthly Magazine*, CVI (April, 1903), 677.

their first twenty years in the Valley of the Great Salt Lake indicate that they were concerned primarily with building up the resources of the Basin area; of secondary consideration was the immediate maximization of individual incomes. The Mormon people were determined to occupy the Great Basin area, and to develop its resources in such a way as to enable it to support the largest number of adherents. This attitude is exemplified by the early attempts to develop the iron industry, by the efforts to turn alkali soils into sugar beet fields, and by the network of irrigation canals built at a tremendous cost of human labor to carry water to thirsty crops. Brigham Young, leader of the Mormon colony, had launched the group upon a slow, but deliberate, well-planned growth in which the improvement of agricultural production, the stimulation of home industry, and the orderly development of mineral resources for local use were the essential economic ingredients. The development of a highly specialized economy was opposed, partly because it would make the Latter-day Saints economically dependent upon a nation whose citizens had persecuted them in the past and might do so in the future, and partly because a specialized economy exalted trade and exchange, which were regarded by the Mormons, as by Adam Smith, as unproductive. Brigham Young demonstrated, on many occasions, his scorn for the selfish, profit-seeking attitude of merchants, traders, and "speculators" who seemed to him to be more interested in quickly changing capital opportunities than in building a home in the West and developing its abundant resources.

Two basic problems faced Mormon leaders as the Pacific railroad approached the borders of their commonwealth. The first problem, of course, was the manner in which to deal with the flood of cheap imports which was certain to follow in the wake of the railroad. There was great concern among Mormon leaders lest "dumping" from the East destroy "home industry" and put profits into the hands of non-Mormon merchants and traders who might use them against the interests of the Saints. Also, the arrival of cheaper manufactured goods would be certain to disemploy a considerable number of Mormons working in local industries.[2] Capitalist economics has repeatedly shown that such workers, if sufficiently mobile, would find work eventually in other fields or regions. For Mormon leaders, however, the telling point was that it would be difficult for them to find desirable employment in "Zion." There would be little outlet for added employment in an expanded agriculture. Utah's high-cost irrigation agriculture could not compete with the extensive agriculture of the prairies. Indeed, cheap wheat from Kansas and Nebraska might force Utah's agriculture to contract. Moreover, new local manufactures could hardly have been expected to be put on a paying basis unless special measures were adopted to stimulate and protect them. Mormon workers could have found employment in mining, of course, but the life of a western miner was hardly suitable for a Latter-day Saint. While, therefore, the local industries which were in danger of being destroyed would appear to have been uneconomic, and their destruction economically desirable, this may not have been true except in the short run, and the preservation and development by church subsidy of local "infant" industries, from the long-run

[2] A study of the editorials appearing in the church newspaper, The Deseret News, during this period indicates that Mormon leaders were clearly aware of the economic implications involved in the approach and completion of the Pacific railroad. One editorial, for example, introduced the problem as follows: "The railroad is going to make a great change in affairs here, and our people should moderate their expectations and prepare themselves for the alteration which appears inevitable." Deseret News, May 21, 1868.

point of view of Mormon leaders, may have been economically justifiable.

The second basic problem facing Mormon leaders as the Pacific railroad drew ever nearer to Zion was the probability of a tremendous expansion in mining in the Great Basin. The coming of the railroad would make the extensive mineral deposits in the Wasatch Range profitable to work. By concentrating on mining, Utahans could probably pay for imports from the East, Midwest, and the Great Plains. The destruction of local industry and the probable contraction of Utah's agriculture would find ample compensation in the increase in mining. Comparative advantage, for Utah Territory, clearly seemed to lie in the exploitation and exportation of the abundant mineral ores. What was the attitude of church leaders to mining development?

Church policy with respect to mining had been set as early as 1849. The policy was not one of opposition to mining per se, for Brigham Young and other leaders fully realized the importance of iron, coal, and lead in the building of an advanced economy. Nor did the church oppose the mining of precious metals, as such, for a group of "missionaries" had been sent under church leadership to California in 1849 to mine gold for the Saints. Church mining policy was based upon the proposition that the building of the Kingdom required the orderly, balanced development of local resources by a unified people for the support of a permanent society. Mining and the "gold fever" were not allowed to dominate the thoughts and activities of the Latter-day Saints. The disintegrating moral influences and social losses of the "gold fever" were, of course, important considerations. Of equal importance was the fact that a permanent society could not be built upon mining. Mines become exhausted; ghost towns develop; people move away; societies decay. Cultivating land, tending flocks, developing local industries using

local resources—these were the activities which church leaders thought produced stable, happy societies.

An important consideration in the 1868–1872 period was that almost all of the rich deposits in the Great Basin area were owned by non-Mormons. Most of them had been opened up, at considerable government subsidy, in the 1860's by General Patrick O'Connor and his troops of California volunteers. The profit involved in the expansion of mining would go, not to the church, but to the "enemies" of the church. In addition, the commencement of large-scale mining operations in Utah was certain to attract a swarm of non-Mormon miners, workers, and speculators from outside the territory.[3] Mormon leaders were determined that their Promised Valley would not be converted into a rip-roaring mining camp, despite the apparent short-run economic advantages associated with such a conversion.

Church leaders placed repeated emphasis on the fact that Utah mines must be used directly in the building of the Kingdom. This implied exploitation of mines and other resources under church direction, and parallel development of manufacturing so that mineral resources would be processed primarily by local industry. The latter procedure would increase employment and income within the territory, and at the same time guard against early exhaustion of mineral reserves. These seem to have been the

[3] "If Mormons have seemed to oppose the development of mines by Gentiles, it is because they have realized the probability of the influx of a great population, which, through the influence of lying priests and politicians, might seek to re-enact the scenes of Missouri and Kansas. If there were some competent power to make a treaty for the Gentile population, which would be honored, and if it were to be stipulated that the Mormons would receive fair and honest treatment forever at their hands, the latter would not raise a voice in opposition to their coming." Editorial, "The Mormons and Mining," in the Mormon (but not church) Salt Lake Herald, September 18, 1887.

considerations in the minds of Mormon leaders when they voiced apprehension over the development of Utah mines by eastern capitalists.

Utah's economic policy crisis in 1869 was pin-pointed by the Godbeite heresy.[4] Godbe, a prominent Mormon merchant and confidant of Brigham Young, felt that the time was ripe for the absorption of the Mormon "priesthood economy" into the larger capitalistic economy of the nation. Godbe and a group of Mormon intellectual "liberals" began a campaign for coöperation with the Gentiles, elimination of social and economic insularity, and development of mining. The success of the Godbeite movement would have meant triumph for free enterprise, "foreign trade," and competition. It would also have involved the end of the unique Mormon experiment to set up an "economy of faith and plenty."[5] As Werner wrote, "The Godbeite schism was nothing more than the inevitable struggle between Brigham Young's ideas and individualistic big business."[6] Though they undoubtedly had their influence, the Godbeites failed to get Mormon support for their program of appeasement, one-sided adjustment, and assimilation. Mormon economic policy, in 1869 and immediately thereafter, was devoted to the preservation of the theocratic commonwealth which had been carefully nurtured by church leaders with the three-fold aim of unity, welfare, and economic independence.

As the Latter-day Saints faced the problems of 1868–1869, what steps did they take to mitigate the undesirable adjustments which the coming of the railroad entailed? And what agency was competent to translate church policy into an effective economic action program? In large measure, the agency which prevented the complete triumph of the eastern capitalist was the School of the Prophets, which countered an energetic and financially powerful laissez-faire capitalism with a vigorous, well-organized, socially minded, and theocratically directed program of economic action. The School of the Prophets was organized late in 1867 by Brigham Young and was patterned after a similar organization established by Joseph Smith, first Prophet of the Mormons, in Kirtland, Ohio, in 1833. The Salt Lake "School" was composed of over nine hundred leading adults in the Mormon church, and was "parent" to branch "schools" established in many Mormon settlements in the intermountain region. Not a school in the usual sense, the School of the Prophets was a forum or town meeting in which problems of the church and community were discussed and appropriate action taken. The meetings were directed by the First Presidency and other general authorities of the Latter-day Saints church, who frequently used the meetings to impart instructions to line officers of the church. The School of the Prophets resembled in many respects an economic planning conference. In its meetings the economic problems posed by the coming of the railroad were amply discussed and measures were taken to accomplish the desired objectives. It was in the School of the Prophets that the Godbeite heresy was ventilated,[7] and it was the school which voted to disfellowship Godbe and his group of "liberals" from the church.[8]

The existence of this group, its power,

[4] A discussion of Godbeite economic aims by a friendly writer is found in *Tullidge's Quarterly*, I (1880), 14–64.

[5] The phrase is from a chapter heading in Nels Anderson, *Desert Saints: The Mormon Frontier in Utah* (Chicago, 1942).

[6] M. R. Werner, *Brigham Young* (New York, 1925), 432.

[7] *Tullidge's Quarterly*, I, 28. It is not contended that the School of the Prophets devoted its attention exclusively to temporal matters. The school also discussed theology, church government, church history, and other spiritual matters.

[8] On October 26, 1869, William S. Godbe, E. L. T. Harrison, and Eli B. Kelsey were excommunicated by the Church High Council in Salt Lake City for apostasy.

and its manifold activities, cast doubt on the oft-repeated assertion that Brigham Young was a dictator and that every worthy economic endeavor of the Utah Mormons was the product of his fertile brain and restless enterprise.

The School of the Prophets played a major part in the economic policy decisions of 1868–1869 in Utah. Indeed, there are strong grounds for believing that the school may have been instituted, at least in part, expressly for the purpose of meeting the problems created for the Mormons by the approach and completion of the Union Pacific Railroad.[9] The school was disbanded in August, 1872, at which time the economic forces which compelled its attention may be said to have been adjusted, at least to the satisfaction of church leaders.

The economic policies of the School of the Prophets—and the programs initiated by the school for the purpose of bringing those policies into effect—may be summarized as follows:

First, the school attempted to prevent, or minimize, an influx of those who might threaten the morality of the community or destroy its basic structure and function. The first problem in this connection was that created by the construction of the railroad itself. The school thought it important to prevent "the swarms of scalawags that the construction of the railroad would bring. . . ."[10] One member revealed the school's feeling when he wrote to a Mormon missionary in England:

. . . you can form some estimate of what the result would be to our cities and settlements of 5,000 or 6,000 Irish, German, and other laborers crowding through our peaceful vales. It is not the men actually working on the line that I should fear so much, though no doubt they would cause some trouble, and raise a muss occasionally, but it would be the bummers, gamblers, saloon and hurdy-gurdy keepers, border ruffians, and desperadoes generally, who prey upon the laborers, whom I should fear most.[11]

The school's solution to this problem was to sponsor a contract, taken in the name of Brigham Young, to construct the Union Pacific Railroad from the mouth of Echo Canyon to Ogden—a distance of some ninety miles.[12] That contract would, as one member stated, "free" Utah of all the "evidences of civilization" referred to above.[13] It would have been "better," in his opinion, "for the Saints to do the work for nothing, if necessary, than to let outsiders do it, as it would cost us more to preserve our cattle and horses from thieves, and our families from insult, than to roll up our sleeves and go and do the work ourselves."[14]

Another advantage of the railroad contract, from the standpoint of the School of the Prophets, was that it would make certain that the income earned under the contract would inure to the church and its members. "Had the Gentiles had the contract," wrote George Reynolds, "they would have traded with Gentiles, and over-flooded us with traders not of us, who would have crowded into the Territory and made all the money—if any—that is to

---

[9] Shortly after the organization was effected, Brigham Young made the statement that the School of the Prophets was "the place where correction may be given and explanations made upon all matters which pertain to the temporal and spiritual lives of the Saints." Journal of Discourses, XII, 159.

[10] L. D. S. Journal History (hereafter referred to as "JH"), May 22, 28, 29, 1868.

[11] Letter of George Reynolds to George F. Gibbs, dated June 4, 1868, and printed in the Latter-day Saints Millenial Star, XXX, 443.

[12] "Last Friday [May 22, 1868], and also yesterday [May 28, 1868] the first class of the School of the Prophets had under consideration the best measures to adopt to get the work of grading the railroad before the people, and they engaged upon it. The plan of operation, the letting of contracts, and many of the minutiae, were critically discussed. Its advantages to us just now as a people were presented in a very favorable and satisfactory light." Letter of Samuel W. Richards to Franklin D. Richards, Millenial Star, XXX, 410.

[13] Letter of George Reynolds, op. cit.

[14] Ibid.

be made."[15] With the contract in the hands of the School of the Prophets, however, "The *spending* of the means [wages and other income] after it is earned, will be as carefully looked to by our advisers as the *getting* of it."[16]

The School of the Prophets also minimized an influx of undesirable "outsiders" by seeking to deflate the reports on Utah's mineral wealth, thus diminishing the prospect of a "rush" of miners to Utah. Where the expansion in mining provided additional employment, Mormon laborers were urged to do the work rather than make it necessary for the mining industry to import labor from outside the territory.[17]

Second, the school established locally owned "coöperative" enterprises[18] designed to prevent unemployment and make the Mormon community less dependent on imports from the East. George Q. Cannon, Apostle of the Church, articulated the need for the establishment of these enterprises in a series of editorials in the church's *Deseret News.* "The railroad," wrote Cannon, "will not be an unmixed benefit to us unless we prepare for it. It will not put an abundance of money in circulation unless we lay the foundation of branches of business that will bring it to us." When the demand ceases for the labor to construct the railroad, "and we have no products that can be transported at a profit for which money can be had in return, we will be in a worse position than if we had no railroad; for the ease with which the country can then be drained, at speculator's own prices, of breadstuffs and such articles as we now produce will be a detriment to us. . . ."

"We must take the necessary steps to create new industries. . . . Our manufacturers, mechanics and merchants should endeavor to shape their various branches of business so as to be prepared for the coming change. Home manufacture must be extensively and persistently pursued." The railroad, he said, must be used to import raw materials rather than consumers' goods, in order that intraterritorial employment might be maintained. "As for capital to carry out these plans, there is no people better situated than we to obtain it by co-operation—a principle that has been found to work well in carrying on many branches of business."[19]

As the result of the efforts of the School of the Prophets, the following enterprises were established at this time: 1 The Utah Manufacturing Company. This "coöperative" was organized under the sponsorship of the school in 1868 to manufacture wagons, carriages, and agricultural machinery.[20] Approximately fifty tons of timber, iron, steel, paints, trimmings, etc., costing an estimated $50,000, were imported by this firm in the spring of 1869.[21] Many creditable carriages, wagons, and sleighs had been produced by the fall of 1869,[22] and the company engaged in manufacturing operations for at least two years, after which it seems to have been continued under the name of the Deseret Carriage & Wagon Company, which was still manufacturing wagons and carriages in 1881.[23]

2 The Dinwoodey Furniture Company. Parallel to the establishment of the carriage enterprise, the school discussed the

[15] *Ibid.*
[16] Letter of Samuel W. Richards, *op. cit.*
[17] *Deseret News,* October 8, 9, 1870.
[18] Though "coöperative" in spirit, and sometimes in name, the Mormon enterprises of this period were not constructed according to true coöperative principles. See Hamilton Gardner, "Coöperation Among the Mormons," *Quarterly Journal of Economics,* XXXI (May, 1917), 461–499.

[19] "The Railroad—Changes It Will Produce," *Deseret News,* August 10, 1868.
[20] JH, May 28, 29, 1868.
[21] JH, March 13, 1869; *Deseret News,* October 26, 1868.
[22] JH, October 5, 1869, p. 3.
[23] *Deseret News,* November 22, 1881. The transactions of the Utah Manufacturing Company are found in the company's ledger book in the Church Historian's Office, Salt Lake City.

propriety of organizing a companion "coöperative" enterprise to manufacture furniture.[24] Many meetings were held to carry out this purpose, and finally the "coöperative" idea was dropped and its chief backer, Henry Dinwoodey, expanded his "private" furniture-manufacturing enterprise to accomplish the objectives contemplated by the school. The Dinwoodey Furniture Company, still a powerful organization in Utah, was a successful manufacturer of many types of furniture until the relative decline in freight rates after 1907.[25]

3 Silk associations. One of the industries which the school hoped would provide income and employment to the people— especially women and children—was the silk industry. The school devoted a great deal of time to stimulating this industry.[26] George D. Watt was called on a "mission" to organize coöperative silk associations in the wards and settlements throughout the territory.[27] Silk production and silk manufacture were carried out with some success, but the industry never attained the export status for which its advocates hoped.

4 The Provo Manufacturing Company. After preliminary discussion of the possibilities of wool manufacture in Utah,[28] a meeting of the school was held in June, 1869, in Provo, at which the members "resolved to build the large [woolen] factory by coöperation. An organization was effected. . . . After the meeting the ground was laid out and corners set."[29] One hundred thousand dollars worth of machinery for the Provo Woolen Mill was ordered from the East soon afterward,[30] and the company became one of the leading dollar-earning manufacturing enterprises in the territory, exporting as far east as Cincinnati and St. Louis.

5 Several minor manufactures were encouraged; among them, a bucket and pail factory,[31] and ink and match manufacturing.[32]

The school was very critical of Mormon suppliers and buyers who refused to patronize these local enterprises. Consistent trading with competing eastern firms made the culprit *persona non grata* in the organization and endangered his fellowship in the church. Investment in these enterprises, though admittedly risky, was urged strongly on Mormon capitalists, and Brigham Young, as President of the Church, also invested part of the common fund of the community (tithing) in most of them.

Third, as the school discussed the possibilities and prospects of export manufactures, it was agreed that wage reductions were a necessary prerequisite to the placing of local industry on an export basis. Substantial agreement on this matter was reached in 1869 at the time when many of the enterprises referred to above were beginning their operations.[33] At an important meeting of the school in July, 1869, at which the members of the Church First Presidency, several members of the Council of Twelve Apostles, and a full membership of the school were present, a decision was

[24] JH, May 28, 29, 1868.
[25] It is interesting to note that Mr. Dinwoodey was in New York City at the time of the railroad junction in May, 1869. He imported immediately afterward the first commercial supply of manufactured furniture brought to Utah from the East. This furniture was unloaded at Ogden and carried by ox team to Salt Lake City for sale. Mr. Dinwoodey also imported, via the railroad, a planer, a mortising and shaping machine, additional steam engines, and other facilities for manufacturing furniture of native timber. *Deseret News*, June 22, 1869; Salt Lake *Telegram*, December 20, 1923. Inferiority of local materials caused the gradual abandonment of furniture manufacturing in Utah after the above-mentioned decline in freight rates made importation of the finished product feasible.
[26] JH, March 16, March 30, October 31, November 7, December 26, 1868; April 3, 1869.
[27] JH, November 20, 1868, p. 1.
[28] JH, December 15, 1868.

[29] JH, June 1, 1869.
[30] JH, May 27, 1871.
[31] JH, December 19, 1868.
[32] JH, December 26, 1868.
[33] See JH, March 27, June 5, June 12, 1869.

reached to elect a committeeman from each trade. The committeeman was expected to submit to his trade the proposition that wages be reduced "in order that Utah might be able to compete with the manufactures of the States."[34] The reactions of the tradespeople to this proposition are not chronicled, and the extent to which the school was successful in reducing wages is not known. There seems, however, to have been a willingness on the part of many Mormon mechanics and artisans to make sacrifices for the cause of building up Zion. It is interesting to note that wage reduction was the first policy of the church which the Godbeites undertook to criticize in print.[35]

Fourth, another requisite to the success of larger-scale valley industry was the establishment of interior branch railroads. The prime need was the construction of a thirty-seven mile railroad from the Union Pacific terminal at Ogden to Salt Lake City. This road was commenced by the Utah Central Railroad Company—a "church" company—soon after the completion of the Union Pacific Railroad to Promontory. The financing of the Utah Central Railroad was handled largely by members of the School of the Prophets and was discussed several times in meetings of the school.[36] Later Mormon efforts resulted in the construction of the Utah Southern, Utah Southern Extension, Utah Northern, and Utah Eastern railroads.

Fifth, to the extent to which imports were necessary and desirable, the School of the Prophets attempted to canalize them through a church-established wholesale trading concern: Zion's Coöperative Mercantile Institution. This institution, and the "coöperative" movement of which it was a part, has occupied a great deal of space in the historical literature dealing with Mormonism, yet it is not generally realized that Zion's Coöperative Mercantile Institution was a product of the discussions of the School of the Prophets. One of the rules of the school was the following stipulation: "In all matters, their [the members'] dealings should be as much as possible with those in full fellowship in the Church of Jesus Christ of Latter-day Saints, but they must not deal with their enemies. . . ."[37] Before the organization of the School of the Prophets, church leaders had conducted, in 1865–1866, a "boycott" against merchants who were hostile to the interests of the Latter-day Saints.[38] As the Pacific railroad entered Utah Territory, however, a general boycott on Gentile business and trading establishments was inaugurated.[39] This policy of not trading with "outsiders" (i.e., non-Mormons) was discussed in the School of the Prophets before its proclamation to the Church-at-large, and plans for the establishment of a wholesale trading concern were expedited. President Brigham Young told the school that he had "tried to control the merchants, but could not do it . . . they would go to hell, if they did not turn a short corner."[40] The school voted "that those who dealt with outsiders should be cut off from the Church."[41] An examination of the minutes of High Council meetings in Salt Lake City and elsewhere might show the extent to which this was done. A few days later, in October, 1868, the general boycott was presented to the semiannual conference of the church in Salt Lake City. Brigham

---

[34] JH, July 3, 1869.
[35] Tullidge's Quarterly, I, 18.
[36] JH, January 15, July 30, August 6, 1870; May 20, 1871.
[37] JH, September 19, 1868.
[38] B. H. Roberts, A Comprehensive History of The Church of Jesus Christ of Latter-day Saints: Century I (Salt Lake City, The Deseret News Press, 1930), V. 209–211.
[39] Ibid., p. 223. The boycott did not prevent leading Mormons from remaining on friendly terms with a few "Gentiles," such as, for example, F. H. and S. H. Auerbach. This fact somewhat qualifies the absoluteness of the general boycott against "outsiders."
[40] JH, October 3, 1868.
[41] Ibid.

Young vividly stated the new church policy as follows: ". . . we are going to draw the reins so tight as not to let a Latter-day Saint trade with an outsider. . . ."[42] The assembled Saints sustained this protective course. Within two weeks the School of the Prophets had drawn up, discussed, and given final approval to the preamble and constitution of "Zion's Cooperative Institution,"[43] and in November the school approved the by-laws of that institution.[44]

In order to prevent "undesirable" competition among Mormon stores in the Salt Lake area, the school appointed a committee to establish uniform prices for these stores.[45] As outlets for the goods imported by Z.C.M.I., retail coöperative stores were established in each of the one-hundred-odd settlements in Mormondom. These retail coöperatives had a working monopoly on the local market, and all nonlocal goods were to be purchased through Z.C.M.I. Being, in their initial stage, community enterprises, they do not appear to have abused their monopolistic positions. Their establishment and operation were, in many cases, functions of the local branch of the School of the Prophets.

Church officials deemed it essential to the success of the coöperative enterprises that the Mormon people give exclusive patronage to these Mormon firms. Many members, including a brother of Brigham Young, were brought before the school and rebuked for violating the principle of "coöperation," and patronizing non-Mormon establishments.[46] The strength of the social sanctions applied to enforce solidarity and unity in this matter is illustrated by the following excerpt from the minutes of the School of the Prophets: "Bro. ——— was charged with having bought goods from a Jew. He confessed, asked forgive-

ness and promised not to do so any more."[47] The Mormon historian, B. H. Roberts, comments on this policy and its relation to the coming of the railroad as follows:

By a policy of no trade intercourse with non-"Mormons" made effective [as by the School of the Prophets and the other agencies at the command of the Church], the Latter-day Saints could preserve themselves, no matter what the influx of new population might be. . . . It was a time of war—a struggle for community existence, and as a measure of self-preservation until the danger was past, and normal conditions restored, "the no trade intercourse" policy with Gentiles was naturally to be expected.[48]

Sixth, another problem confronting the church when the transcontinental railroad was completed was that of preventing the railroad from acquiring title to land on which the Saints had settled. Until 1869 the Saints had no "legal" property rights in Utah. The railroads were given alternate sections of land along their right of way, except where property rights were already vested in private citizens. As soon as this danger to the vested interests of the Saints appeared (March, 1869), the School of the Prophets appointed a committee to "post" themselves on the land question and "report to the people what steps were necessary to take to preserve their homesteads being claimed by the railroad companies."[49] This committee made periodic reports to the school,[50] and there appears to have been a minimum of injustice done to people of Utah as a result of the efforts of this committee and the School of the Prophets.[51]

[42] Roberts, loc. cit.
[43] JH, October 24, 1868.
[44] JH, November 14, 1868.
[45] JH, December 12, 1868.
[46] E.g., JH, November 28, 1868; May 22, 29, 1869.
[47] JH, November 28, 1868. See also Nels Anderson, Deseret Saints: The Mormon Frontier in Utah (Chicago, 1942), 258.
[48] Roberts, op. cit., p. 228.
[49] JH, March 20, 1869.
[50] JH, March 20, April 24, May 8, 1869; December 9, 1871.
[51] The activities of the local or branch Schools of the Prophets are also of great interest. The Cedar City School of the Prophets, for example, "debated and decided such matters of com-

It had been confidently predicted by leading politicians and preachers that the railroad would mean the end of Mormonism. It was widely believed that Mormon society would succumb, much as other local societies and institutions had succumbed, to the "march of civilization" which followed in the wake of the railroad. Indeed, the strongly supported national antipolygamy legislation which had come to a head in the late 'sixties was momentarily abandoned in the hope that such measures would no longer be necessary when the transcontinental railroad was completed. Brigham Young, however, said that it was a poor religion which couldn't stand a railroad.[52] In full realization of the fact that they were fighting a rear-guard action, Mormon policy makers fought the indicated shift to mining, the seemingly inevitable increase in imports, and the relinquishment of control over business institutions to eastern capitalists. Though these policies undoubtedly were carried out with less success than church leaders desired, they also were unquestionably more effective than non-Mormons—and some Mormons—had anticipated. The Mormon church, itself, did not seem to grow appreciably weaker; and the religion of the Saints was not "mineralized." Their faith did not go down into the mines, there to remain. The Mormons remained a "peculiar people." Utah did not become, at least immediately, an economic province

whose chief function was to supply raw materials to the industrial East. There was a noticeable tendency in that direction to be sure, but Utah managed to avoid, for the next thirty years at least, the "colonial" status which characterized early Montana, Nevada, Colorado, and Wyoming. Utah, whose geography and resources were not greatly different from those of surrounding states, represented, during the succeeding three decades, a quite different type of social economy. There can be little doubt that church policies were influential in accomplishing this result.

The School of the Prophets during its five-year existence served a useful economic purpose by reducing the dislocations and injustices incident upon the economic change brought by the railroad. From the standpoint of the Mormons, the School of the Prophets was a useful economic service agency, for it established protective economic institutions and consolidated the weight of public opinion behind those institutions. It activated local producing and marketing enterprises, and it implemented policies which aimed at preserving the unity, welfare, and economic independence of the Mormon people. While it cannot be said to have been successful in achieving all of its objectives, the school lessened and eased the inevitable adjustments in Utah's economy and prevented other adjustments which were regarded as undesirable. An essential institution in the church's program of economic solidarity, the School of the Prophets managed to prevent, for good or for ill, the immediate and complete assimilation of Mormon institutions, in the years immediately after 1869, by the dominant laissez-faire institutions of nineteenth-century America.

It is doubtful if there is another illustration in recent American history in which a social group of comparable size[53] suc-

munity concern as appointment of water-masters, nomination of school trustees, opening of roads, repair of fences, changing the course of ditches, chastisement of erring members, guarding of stock herds, directorship of the coöperative store, personnel of entrants under the Federal land laws, and other public questions." Wells A. Hutchins, "Mutual Irrigation Companies in Utah," Utah Agricultural Experiment Station *Bulletin* No. 199 (May, 1927), 17–18.
[52] Samuel Bowles, *Our New West* (Hartford, 1869), 260. According to Bowles, Brigham Young's exact words were that Mormonism "must, indeed, be a ———— poor religion, if it cannot stand one railroad." Bowles was quite definite, though certainly wrong, in answering that "they [the Mormons] will find out that it cannot and will not." *Ibid.*

[51] There were approximately 75,000 adherents to the Latter-day Saint faith in Utah Territory in 1869.

cessfully withstood such a social and economic revolution as that which the railroad would have produced in Utah if alert and stubborn church leadership had not adopted the measures referred to above. Other groups (including the Mormons, before this period) had preserved cultural homogeneity and economic self-sufficiency in the face of similar encroachment by moving on to new promised lands and new Utopias. The problems accompanying the junction of the Pacific railroads at Promontory in May, 1869, were met by Mormon leaders with the type of economic action which is usually associated today with what is known as "defensive economic warfare." Whatever the merit of the Mormon solution to the economic policy crisis of 1869, it is clear that the rugged, wasteful, and often short-sighted free-enterprising individualism of eastern capitalism, which had replaced local institutions almost everywhere else in the nation, was not permitted to destroy completely the unique social and economic institutions of Mormondom. Another third of a century was to pass before the Mormon frontier in the intermountain West was to make substantial accommodation to the more powerful institutions characteristic of America at the turn of the century.

Problems of Railroad Competition

■ An industry in which producers have to invest large amounts of capital per worker or per unit of product cannot stand cutthroat competition. This means it cannot afford to have in its midst competitors that are not trying to pay returns on invested capital and therefore can sell for prices much lower than those necessary for a level of returns that will attract new capital for improvement and expansion. In the railroad situation the bankrupt or nearly bankrupt line that was paying nothing to its stockholders or bondholders was the dangerous competitor; such a line could force the potentially profitable companies into ruinous competition. But even prosperous lines could get into money-losing competitive rivalry through their freight agents' bargaining with favored customers.

The railroad companies' solution was to get together, pool the traffic, and then divide it at profitable rates. Each line's share had to be negotiated annually, could not be enforced by law, and hence was always vulnerable to secret violation by an unscrupulous competitor. Albert Fink, discussed in the following selection by David Gilchrist of the Eleutherian Mills Hagley Foundation, was the leading student and advocate of railroad pooling. When it became evident that, under pressure from shippers, the Federal government would pass some type of regulatory act, Fink and other railroad leaders sought to have the act legalize pooling. Unfortunately, the Interstate Commerce Act of 1887 forbade pooling and attempted to maintain uniform rates by an unenforceable legal fiat. The result was more than twenty years of confusing court rulings and inconclusive remedial legislation; ultimately the law gave the Interstate Commerce Commission effective control of rates and recognized the validity of joint rate agreements made by the roads.

David T. Gilchrist
Albert Fink and the Pooling System*

Having cleared its path so far, society went back to its work, and threw itself on that which stood first—its roads. The field was vast; altogether beyond its power to control offhand; and society dropped every thought of dealing with anything more than the single fraction called the railway system. This relatively small part of its task was still so big as to need the energies of a generation, for it required all the new machinery to be erected—capital, banks, mines, furnaces, shops, powerhouses, technical knowledge, mechanical population, together with a steady remodelling of social and political habits, ideas and institutions to fit the new scale and suit the new conditions. The generation between 1865 and 1895 was already mortgaged to the railways, and no one knew it better than the generation itself.[1]

To Henry Adams the railroad was the shaping influence of the post-Civil War era. In 1865 there were 35,085 miles of railroad in operation in the United States.[2] By 1880 the rail system had grown to 93,262 miles, nearly half of which had been built in the decade 1870–1880.[3] Before 1865 the growing western cities of Chicago, Cincinnati, Indianapolis, St. Louis, Detroit, Toledo, Peoria, Columbus, and Cleveland were linked to the eastern seaboard by one or more railroads.[4] After the war, roads were built fanning out from the older population centers into the untapped prairie states. The flood of postwar settlers did not become the subsistence farmers of the old Northwest, at least not for long.

European demand for wheat, corn, and meat products had, even by the middle 1850's, begun to bring about a change in western farming. Large-scale single crop farming became profitable so long as the crops could be brought cheaply to market by rail. Because the transportation charges often determined the marketability of their products, the farmers were peculiarly sensitive to railroad policy. Monopolistic marketing groups allied with the railroads were important causes of the farm protest movement of the Grangers in the late 1860's and early 1870's.[5] The railroads provided an easy target upon which agricultural discontent concentrated, especially in areas served by a single road. The result was a spate of restrictive railroad legislation throughout the so-called Granger states.[6] In the depression following the Panic of 1873, railroad competition was intensified.[7] Rate wars both in the West and among the great trunk lines to the seaboard lowered the rates to a level well below that envisioned by even the most radical of the Grangers.[8] By 1875, Charles Francis Adams, Jr., a leading expert on the railroads and a Massachusetts Railroad Commissioner, wrote of the movement as a "phenomenon of the past."[9] After 1875 the railroads became more of a problem

* Reprinted by permission from Business History Review, XXXIV (Spring, 1960), pp. 24–49.
[1] Henry Adams, The Education of Henry Adams (New York, 1931), p. 240.
[2] U.S. Department of Commerce, Bureau of the Census, Historical Statistics of the United States —1789–1945 (Washington, 1949), p. 200.
[3] Report of the Select Committee on Interstate Commerce, 49th Cong., 1st Sess., Senate Report No. 46, Part I (Jan., 1886), pp. 9, 15.
[4] George Rogers Taylor and Irene D. Neu, The American Railway Network, 1858–1890 (Cambridge, 1956). Maps following the text show the railway network in 1861.

[5] Solon J. Buck, The Granger Movement (Cambridge, 1913), pp. 9–19. Also Henrietta M. Larson, The Wheat Market and the Farmer in Minnesota, 1858–1900 (New York, 1926), pp. 74–93.
[6] Buck, The Granger Movement, p. 7 and map opp. p. 61 show the extent of the movement. Pages 123–237 describe Granger railroad legislation in detail.
[7] William Z. Ripley, Railroads Rates and Regulation (New York, 1912), p. 22.
[8] Larson, The Wheat Market, pp. 122–123. Significant reductions in through rates began first. On the local lines the decline was slower but continuous after 1875.
[9] Charles Francis Adams, Jr., "The Granger Movement" in North American Review, Vol. 120 (April, 1875), p. 395.

to themselves, as far as rates were concerned, than to their customers.

The first really large-scale American capitalists were occupied with uniting segments of the locally built railroads into effective units for long-distance transportation. Originally railroads had simply linked local markets in a well-defined territory.[10] Variety in rail gauges emphasized a spirit of exclusiveness intended by the original builders.[11] In July, 1866, at the insistence of the railroad interests, Congress passed a law authorizing railroad companies chartered by the states to carry passengers across state lines and to connect with railroads of other states.[12] The post-Civil War era was characterized by the consolidation of small local lines into larger complexes, often with surprising and unforeseen consequences.

By 1874, four great trunk lines extended their services between Chicago and the eastern seaboard. Either through direct ownership or alliance with other railroads these trunk lines linked New York, Boston, Philadelphia, and Baltimore with the principal cities along the Great Lakes and the Mississippi and Ohio Rivers. Over 90 per cent of all commerce between the West and the seaboard cities was estimated in 1876 to be by rail.[13] Fierce competition among the trunk lines for this valuable cargo was the inevitable result of the consolidation of the railroad network. Each new link seemed to add another competing, though often devious, route between East and West. Joseph Nimmo, Jr., in his *First Annual Report on the Internal Commerce of the United States* noted that:[14]

The control exercised by the great trunk railroad companies over their competitive traffic is from year to year growing weaker, and the local or non-competitive traffic is continually being invaded by the increasing influence of the various elements of competition. There is a constant demand for the construction of branch roads cutting across existing trunk roads, and forming new competing lines. These branch roads in some cases eventually form parts of great trunk lines between different sections of the country. . . . So long as the lateral lines are confined to local traffic, they usually pursue a policy of neutrality in so far as it may be practicable for them to do so, but in reality every new railroad is a competitor of all other roads through development of new sources of supply to the various markets of the country.

So serious had railroad competition become by the middle 1870's that plans for cooperation and federation were undertaken among the roads to preserve the value of their property. Where competition was keen the shippers frequently forced the rates down to a level that threatened the solvency of the lines. But where there was little or no competition the rates were comparatively high and shippers blamed the railroads for the disadvantage they suffered in competing with their more fortunate brethren.

Railroad cooperation was motivated by a desire to maintain the profitability of the lines. Popular demand for railroad regulation was motivated chiefly by a desire to wipe out arbitrary rate discriminations. Paradoxically the solution to both problems lay in much the same direction. The need for a rational and equitable rate structure was the heart of the railroad problem. Regional associations of railroads and at least temporary pooling of traffic were the means by which this rate structure was devised. A study of the career of Albert Fink, the central figure in railroad pooling, will illustrate the means by which the railroads were eventually enabled to deal witn their customers in a mutually satisfactory manner.

Henry Adams said that with the coming of the railroad "life took on extravagance."

[10] *First Annual Report on the Internal Commerce of the United States,* House Exec. Doc., 44th Cong., 2d Sess., No. 45, Part 2 (June 30, 1877), p. 19.
[11] Taylor and Neu, *Railroad Network,* pp. 19, 30–32, 83.
[12] *First Annual Report Internal Commerce,* p. 175.
[13] *Ibid.,* p. 8.
[14] *Ibid.,* p. 78.

It was a rare individual that did not lose his sense of proportion amidst the "extravagance" of the post-Civil War decades. The economy seemed almost beyond the comprehension and control of the men who managed it. Some men by keeping their attention fixed on the realities of their situation steadily contributed to the solution of major business problems. Albert Fink grew up with American railroading. His career developed logically from the specialized fields of railway building and engineering to operation and management and culminated in the generalized activity of finding broad solutions for railroad problems in railway associations.

Born in Lauterbach, Hessen-Darmstadt, in 1827, Fink was the son of an architect. He received a classical education in secondary school. At the Polytechnic school in Darmstadt, from which he graduated with honors in 1848, he took a course in engineering and architecture. For about a year following graduation Fink worked with a contracting firm near Frankfurt am Main, but he left this work to prepare himself for emigration to America.[15]

Albert Fink's first American job was in the drafting office of the Baltimore & Ohio Railroad under Benjamin H. Latrobe. At the age of twenty-five and only three years after his arrival in America, Fink designed a bridge to cross the Monongahela River at Fairmont, West Virginia, which when completed was the longest iron railroad bridge in the country.[16] Later Fink was placed in charge of construction on the section from Grafton to Moundsville, West Virginia, where he acquired valuable field experience.

Although the Louisville and Nashville Railroad was chartered in 1850, the problem of accumulating enough capital to complete a line between the two cities was not solved until 1857.[17] In that year the L. & N. hired Albert Fink as construction engineer to help build its line through the hilly country between Louisville and Nashville. Not only did Fink devote himself to his specialty of iron bridges, but he designed the main freight and passenger station at Louisville and lent his talents to design and build the Louisville Courthouse as well.[18] In 1859, he was made Chief Engineer and Superintendent of the Road and Machinery Departments.[19] Thus, on the eve of the Civil War, Fink was responsible for the actual operation of the principal rail link between the North and the Cotton Kingdom. When war came the L. & N. sided with the Union and provided a valuable highway of supply into enemy territory. In spite of frequent damage by enemy patrols, Fink kept the road open by means of constantly mobilized repair parties. Throughout the war the L. & N. remained in profitable operation.[20] Instead of the almost total impoverishment suffered by the majority of southern railroads the L. & N., aside from considerable physical damage, was enriched and expanded by the war.[21]

Between 1865 and 1875 the L. & N. expanded its mileage from 286 to 920 miles by building and by consolidation of other roads. "Up to the close of the war our road was operated exclusively as a local one," stated the Annual Report of

[15] Transactions of American Society of Civil Engineers, Vol. XLI (June, 1899), pp. 626–638. Memoir prepared by O. Chanute, Rudolf Fink and H. G. Prout, pp. 626–627. Rudolf Fink, brother of Albert Fink, became president of the Norfolk & Western Railroad. Another brother, Henry, worked for the L. & N.

[16] Ibid., p. 627. Also "American Engineering as Illustrated at the Paris Exhibition—The American Bridge Building" in Railway World, Vol. V (June 7, 1879), p. 533.

[17] Thomas D. Clark, The Beginnings of the L. & N. (Louisville, 1933), p. 47.

[18] Julius H. Parmelee, "Fink, Albert (Oct. 27, 1827–April 3, 1897)," Typewritten manuscript of an article for Dictionary of American Biography in Bureau of Railway Economics Library, Washington, D.C.

[19] A.S.C.E., Transactions, Vol. XLI, p. 629.

[20] Joseph G. Kerr, Historical Development of the Louisville and Nashville Railroad (n.p., 1926), pp. 20–43.

[21] Jean E. Keith, "The Role of the Louisville and Nashville Railroad in the Early Development of Alabama Coal and Iron," Bulletin of the Business Historical Society, Vol. XXVI (Sept., 1952), p. 167.

1868. "We are now competing with the various other transportation companies for the through traffic of the entire South."[22] During this period Fink completed his last major engineering project, a mile-long, 27-span bridge over the Ohio at Louisville.[23] In 1870, he became a vice president of the L. & N. and as chief operating executive began to concentrate on the financial details of railroading.

As an officer of the railroad, Fink developed a technique of cost analysis that was to have an important effect on his subsequent career. Writing of the period just prior to the passage of the Interstate Commerce Act of 1887, William Z. Ripley noted that only a few companies ". . . such as the Pennsylvania, the Union Pacific and the Louisville and Nashville, had indeed attempted to systematize their accounts."[24] The system worked out by Fink attracted nationwide attention with the publication of the L. & N.'s *Annual Report 1873–4*.[25] More than a recital of the facts and figures of L. & N. business for the previous year, this *Report* was actually a lesson in railway economics and a carefully prepared defense of railroad rate-making policies with an eye to the experience of railroads in the Granger states.

To estimate the value and economy of a road, Fink pointed out, the detailed figures covering a period of years for each section of road operated would be necessary. The proportion of net to gross earnings was not a reliable figure. He illustrated his argument with figures for the various branches of the L. & N. where operating costs varied greatly. "The disregard of the facts," he warned, "in esti-

mating the cost and value of railroad transportation with a view to judging the reasonableness of railroad tariffs has led to many erroneous conclusions, which appear now fixed in the public mind."[26] In some states the mistaken notion that there was a uniformity in the cost of transportation had resulted in legislation enforcing uniformity of compensation. Fink pointed out that the proper basis for rail tariffs was the cost of service and from this necessarily followed the "impossibility of enacting general laws establishing tariffs applicable to *more than one road*."[27] Such factors as the volume of business, cost of construction, maintenance, fuel, interest charges etc., all varied considerably even on the various branches of the L. & N. Although the charter of the L. & N. set maximum legal rates from 7 cents to 10.2 cents per ton per mile the actual charge made by the road was an average 2.172 cents.[28] The natural forces of competition prevented a higher charge, a factor over which the railroad's managers had no control:[29]

Different localities are more or less favored in regard to transportation facilities, either by nature or the enterprise of man. It can not be maintained that it is the duty of the common carrier to equalize the existing inequalities at his own expense. All that is required of him is not to create them himself arbitrarily. He must treat all alike that are situated alike. . . . He may be obliged to carry freight at a lower rate to some localities than to others, but this in itself does not constitute an injustice or injury to the shipper in a less favored locality, as long as the charges made are reasonable in themselves and alike to all in the same situation.

Competition among the railroads was the chief source of rate discrimination. Where rail and water routes competed, the

[22] Kerr, *Historical Development of the L. & N.*, p. 63.
[23] Kincaid A. Herr, *The Louisville and Nashville Railroad, 1850–1952* (Louisville, 1943), p. 24.
[24] Ripley, *Railroads Rates and Regulation*, p. 44.
[25] Louisville and Nashville Railroad, *Annual Report, 1873–4* (Louisville, 1875), "Report of the Vice-President and General Superintendent," pp. 21–67, plus tables.

[26] *Ibid.*, p. 39.
[27] *Ibid.*, p. 32.
[28] *Ibid.*, p. 59.
[29] *Ibid.*, p. 57.

community had the benefit of lower rates than its inland competitors. This result of natural factors could not be considered unjust. However, where a large shipper was given advantages not given a smaller shipper, though unit costs of transportation were no different, unjust discrimination resulted. Fink suggested that if the railroad companies could agree among themselves to stop competition to junction points "one of the most fruitful causes of complaint against discrimination in railroad tariffs would at once be remedied; but it would be at the expense of the benefit of competition."[30] This was a suggestion Fink was soon to have the opportunity to test.

The impact of the depression which followed the Panic of 1873 was especially hard in the South. Southern capital resources were limited and railroad building came to an almost complete halt. Traffic along the railroads shrank to a point that endangered the solvency of almost every line.[31] Along with the general business depression came a series of rate wars among the railroads fighting each other for what little business was offered. A cooperative venture was needed to prevent a wave of railroad failures.

In September, 1875, a convention of the Southern Railway and Steamship Association met in Atlanta.[32] The purpose of the meeting was to discover some means of curbing competition, maintaining rates and ending the threat to the financial security of southern railroads. Albert Fink had resigned from the L. & N. in July and was making plans for a vacation trip to Europe.

Although he was unable to attend the convention he wrote a letter to J. E. Brown, the convention president, in which he outlined a plan for cooperative action.[33] On the basis of Fink's suggestions the southern pool was formed; he was elected the first commissioner of the Southern Railway and Steamship Association as well.

Fink's plan was to divide the traffic between junction points among the competing railroads. The portion allotted each road was to be based on previous experience as recorded by the statistical branch of the Association. Rates were to be set by special committees for each junction point on which the roads concerned were to be represented. The portion of pooled traffic allotted each road was to be revised at the end of each year and a new allotment assigned on the basis of business obtained by "fair competition," i.e., by not cutting rates. The first question in the formation of such a pool, Fink noted, was ". . . whether each individual road is willing, in case of conflict, to surrender the necessary authority to that tribunal to decide all questions of difference?"[34]

"There is only one power," he wrote, "that can compel adherence to compacts of this nature—it is that of 'self-interest.' "[35] The success of the scheme depended upon the members' willingness to hold the level of rates steady and not to circumvent the pool by means of secret rebates to shippers. Independent action on the part of a single road could ruin the whole structure.

All decisions on rates and pooling were to be unanimous. But the commissioner was given considerable power in the settlement of disputes. In case of disagreement the commissioner was to settle the matter on its merits. Should the members still not concur in his judgment an outside arbitrator was to be called in and his decision

[30] Ibid., p. 58.
[31] Henry Hudson, "The Southern Railway and Steamship Association," Railway Problems, William Z. Ripley, ed. (Boston, 1907), p. 99.
[32] Proceedings of the Convention of the Southern Railway and Steamship Association held at Atlanta, Georgia, September 16 and 17, 1875 and October 13, 1875 (Atlanta, 1875).
[33] Ibid., pp. 10–16. Fink's letter was dated Sept. 14, 1875.
[34] Ibid., p. 10.
[35] Ibid., p. 14.

was to be final.[36] The main work of the Association was carried out by the statistical department and the various rate committees.

The southern pool seems to have justified the hopes of its originator, Albert Fink. After a difficult beginning, the plan proved successful and remained in existence more or less in its original form until 1887, when the Interstate Commerce Act of that year forbade pooling.[37] It did reduce the number and severity of the rate wars in its territory. There were few complaints of unjust rates or discriminations.[38] The process of joining unconnected lines and thereby creating new routes between competitive junctions continued despite the pooling of traffic.[39] The pool remained as a stabilizing factor, its allotments changed only by proven demand for new routes while the rates were maintained at a profitable level, preventing sudden ruin by quixotic shifts in traffic. So successfully did the scheme harness the revolutionary forces acting upon railroad organization that, according to Joubert, consolidation and combination of railroad companies took place at a slower rate in the South than elsewhere.[40]

The suggestion that competition could result in anything but good was a somewhat novel one for a businessman of the period to make. But the apostasy of Albert Fink went further than this. In a letter to Joseph Nimmo, Jr., author of the *First Annual Report on the Internal Commerce of the United States*, he declared, "Whether this cooperation can be secured by voluntary action of the transportation companies is doubtful. Governmental super-

vision and authority may be required to some extent to accomplish the object in view."[41] From the outset, Fink was aware of the monopolistic, noncompetitive nature of his pooling experiment and believed in the logic and justice of governmental supervision.

It was undeniable that competition had greatly reduced the freight rates. But Fink told Nimmo that the "true and proper plan . . . to cheapen transportation is to concentrate the business of the country upon the fewest number of railroads."[42] Fink wanted a scientific answer as to whether or not the railway network was adequate. From his position in the southern pool the southern network seemed more than adequate.

Growth and change in the internal trade of the United States was taking place at such a rate that venture capital went into railroads in ever-increasing volume long after 1876. Business expectations in the so-called Gilded Age were not based on statistics. The large amounts of capital available for railroad speculation greatly increased the difficulty of rationalizing the rate structure, as Fink was to learn when he came to deal with the territory of the great trunk lines.

———————

Railroad competition was nowhere more intense than between the Midwest and the eastern seaboard. Albert Fink had noted that a change in the freight rate between Chicago and New York altered the rate structure of the Southern Railway and Steamship Association. The rate structure of the whole country, he believed, was based on the rates between these two cities.[43]

In August, 1874, three months before the Baltimore and Ohio Railroad com-

[36] *First Annual Report Internal Commerce* (appendix pages 16–19 describe the agreement and organization), p. 18.
[37] William H. Joubert, *Southern Freight Rates in Transition* (Gainesville, Florida, 1949). Joubert's book contains the most extensive estimate of the pool's accomplishments. See pp. 51–63.
[38] *Ibid.*, p. 62.
[39] *Ibid.*, p. 45.
[40] *Ibid.*, p. 63.

[41] *First Annual Report Internal Commerce* (appendix pages 1–16), p. 12. Letter dated Louisville, May 1, 1876.
[42] *Ibid.*, p. 7.
[43] *Ibid.*, pp. 9–10.

pleted its line into Chicago, the presidents of the four trunk line roads: the New York Central and Hudson River; the New York, Lake Erie and Western; the Pennsylvania; and the Baltimore and Ohio, met at Saratoga, New York, in an effort to make peace and forestall another rate war which a new line into Chicago would inevitably touch off.[44] Although an agreement was reached, conditions were not conducive to peace and it was not observed. A foreign antagonist, the Grand Trunk of Canada, entered the fray in 1875 by means of a service from Chicago via the Michigan Central into Canada and back into the United States to Boston, New York, and the other seaboard cities via the Central Vermont. During 1876 the bitterest of all rate wars up to that time was fought.[45] Enormous losses in revenue were suffered by all the roads involved. Not only the protagonists lost, but the investing public as well. Confidence in American railroad securities was severely shaken.[46]

Much of the warfare was directed toward diverting freight away from New York to Boston, Philadelphia, and Baltimore. Vanderbilt's New York Central fought desperately for its share of the trade. While New York merchants profited by the low rates resulting from such warfare, their advantage was largely at Mr. Vanderbilt's expense. It is not surprising, therefore, that they were upset at the nature of the agreement devised to prevent further losses by the Central. The first part of a general compromise was reached when the four trunk lines signed the Seaboard Differential Agreement on April 5, 1877.[47] Differentials had been tried before, but never had they been placed on such a

fixed basis.[48] Rates on eastbound freight to Philadelphia and Baltimore were to be 2 and 3 cents per 100 pounds lower respectively than New York. Rates to Boston were to be no less than those to New York. On all westbound traffic, differences on third-class and fourth-class freight were to be the same as on eastbound, while first-class and second-class differentials from Philadelphia and Baltimore were set at 6 and 8 cents. Business interests in New York charged that the natural advantages of that great port had been sacrificed in order to purchase railroad peace.

A second agreement, designed to reinforce the first, went into effect in July, 1877. This was the pooling of all westbound freight from New York among the four trunk lines. Under the pooling agreement the New York Central and the Erie received 33 per cent, the Pennsylvania received 25 per cent and the remaining 9 per cent was allotted to the Baltimore and Ohio.[49] To keep statistics on the allotments to the pool and to study detailed rate questions, a permanent organization called the Trunk Line Association was established. In most respects this Association was similar to the Southern Railway and Steamship Association. Similarly, its organizer was Albert Fink.

Fink had reached New York on his way to Europe in time to be called in by the Trunk Lines' representatives to consult with them on their projected plans for settling the rate war. He impressed them so much that he was asked to serve as commissioner of an association organized along the lines he suggested.[50] Maintenance of rates at a profitable level was the main object in view. Pooling and the differentials were simply the means of creating a peaceful atmosphere in which a rational and profitable rate structure could be determined. During the first year, Fink and

[44] Lee Benson, *Merchants, Farmers and Railroads* (Cambridge, 1955), p. 39.
[45] *First Annual Report on Internal Commerce*, p. 62.
[46] Benson, *Merchants, Farmers and Railroads*, pp. 49–50.
[47] John B. Daish, *The Atlantic Port Differentials* (Washington, 1918). Text of the agreement is found on pp. 2–3.

[48] *Ibid.*, pp. xiv-xv.
[49] Benson, *Merchants, Farmers and Railroads*, p. 47.
[50] *Ibid.*, p. 46. A.S.C.E., *Transactions*, p. 634.

the railroad representatives gathered traffic statistics and improved the system of regional rate committees.

The process of making railroad tariffs was not a hurried one. As Ripley has pointed out in his authoritative book on railroad rates, "Tariffs are not made out of hand; they grow."[51] Tariffs are based on experience and to be reasonable and just the experience should be "normal" or peaceful. The rate theory used in the trunk line territory was simple enough, although, in practice, matters to be considered in setting each rate were complex. The rate between Chicago and New York was considered the "base rate." All rates to the seaboard were expressed in percentages of Chicago to New York.[52] Distance determines cost of service to a great extent and the trunk line tariff was a modified distance tariff. A tariff map of the trunk line territory (there is such a map in Ripley's book) looks like a contour map of the United States extending from the eastern seaboard west to the Mississippi and Ohio Rivers.[53] Like great irregular, concentric rings, the contour lines of equal rates circle New York in ever-rising succession as they extend westward. Beyond Chicago these lines represent rates exceeding 100 per cent of Chicago to New York. The north-south irregularities in many cases follow the line of an important north-south railroad with frequent junctures with east-west trunk lines along its route. Ripley is almost poetic in his description of this system:[54]

Since his time [Albert Fink's] by reason of cooperative action for a generation, the confusing maze of railway lines has now [1912] been reduced to a single comprehensive system. Cross-currents of trade hither and thither have been united or articulated in such a way as, speaking in terms of freight charges, to cause the great internal commerce of the country to flow downhill toward the seaboard in an orderly and reasonable way. The inequalities incident to commercial competition have been modified, or, to revert to our original figure, eroded; so that one may literally speak of the products of the country as flowing, like rivers, in more or less natural channels over the railway lines from the great interior basin towards the Atlantic seaboard.

A tariff map of this area, if it had been drawn in 1878, would have shown great sloughs cutting through the contours along the routes of the trunk lines. These would represent the effect of rate warfare. Competition beyond the western termini of the trunk lines resulted in all manner of rate-cutting, the losses from which the western roads expected the trunk lines to share.

At a meeting of railroad executives, representing both the trunk lines and the western roads, held at Saratoga in August, 1878, it was decided to form a Western Executive Committee to pool traffic and establish rates on freight in which they had a mutual interest.[55] In November of the same year, Fink suggested that because the rates from western points were in part dependent upon trunk line rates a joint executive committee be set up with headquarters in New York. Working sub-committees in the various junction cities, composed of representatives of interested member lines, were organized to do the basic work of pooling traffic and determining rates, subject to approval of the Joint Executive Committee.[56] Final arrangements establishing the Joint Executive Committee were made at a convention of eastern and western railroad executives held at

---

[51] Ripley, *Railroads Rates and Regulation*, p. 101.
[52] *Ibid.*, p. 363.
[53] *Ibid.*, opposite p. 364.
[54] *Ibid.*, p. 367.

[55] Joint Executive Committee, *Proceedings of the Railway Convention held at Saratoga, August 20–24, 1878* (New York, 1880). Pamphlet bound with the *Proceedings and Circulars of the Joint Executive Committee, 1878*, p. 77.
[56] Joint Executive Committee, *Proceedings*, Meeting, Nov. 8, 1878, p. 7.

Chicago, December 18 and 19, 1878.[57] Albert Fink was elected chairman, a position he held in addition to that of Trunk Lines' commissioner. A detailed agreement was signed by the member roads. Article 12 of this agreement provided that in case any question brought before the committee did not receive unanimous action it was to be referred to the chairman "who shall decide the case on its merits, and whose decision shall have the same force and effect as the unanimous vote of the Committee."[58] Should any party then remain unreconciled there was provision for arbitration. The chairman of the Joint Executive Committee was thus in a position to wield considerable power over the rate-setting policies for a very large and important area of the country.

In practice the Joint Executive Committee was largely a creature of the Trunk Line Association. Its executive meetings were usually called on the recommendation of the Trunk Line Executive Committee. Thanks to the leadership of Albert Fink the regional subcommittees performed their specialized tasks of rate-making and pooling despite the numerous rate wars and fundamental disagreements among railroad executives higher up. Their work could be truthfully compared to that of a diplomatic corps carefully planning peace, in spite of frequent wars raging about them.

Pooling of eastbound traffic from Chicago, St. Louis, Indianapolis, Peoria, Louisville, and Cincinnati was organized during the first year.[59] The *Proceedings and Circulars* of the Joint Executive Committee were published and open to the public.[60] There was nothing conspiratorial

about pooling. Fink could never understand why it did not appeal to the common sense of *all* railroad executives, men who were in a position to see the high cost of other alternatives. But in railroad finance there were speculators who were not interested in a stable rate system. These men were looking for bonanzas from market fluctuations. Rate wars were a useful means of creating a fluid market and manipulating the value of railroad securities.

In 1879, Albert Fink was called upon to describe and defend the trunk line rate and pooling system before the Hepburn Committee of New York State and the Committee on Commerce of the United States Senate. These were the first of many such appearances he made prior to the passage of the Interstate Commerce Act in 1887.

The Hepburn Investigation first focused attention on pooling and helped arouse both the public and the merchants against it. Farmers, millers, and manufacturers of upstate New York combined with the merchants of New York City to bring about the investigation. The New York merchants believed that their trade was being diverted to other cities by the effect of the differentials, while the upstate people claimed that the railroads charged them arbitrarily high rates at the same time they granted bargain rates to shippers from outside the state.[61] In the course of the investigation many instances of secret and discriminatory rate-making were revealed, but it became obvious that the larger shippers and not the railroads controlled the situation wherever significant competition existed.

Simon Sterne, investigation counsel, questioned Fink before the Hepburn Committee on June 20 and 21, 1879.[62] Much

[57] J.E.C., *Proceedings*, 1878. *Proceedings of a Convention of Officers of Eastern and Western Railroads held at the Grand Pacific Hotel, Chicago, December 18 and 19, 1878* (Chicago, 1878), see especially pp. 5–8.
[58] *Ibid.*, p. 7.
[59] *Report on the Internal Commerce of the United States*, 45th Cong., 3d sess., House Exec. Doc. No. 32, Part 3 (Dec. 1, 1879), p. 168.
[60] *Ibid.*, p. 170.

[61] Benson, *Merchants, Farmers and Railroads* is the best study of the origin of the Hepburn Investigation. See especially Chap. VI.
[62] New York Assembly, *Proceedings of the Special Committee on Railroads* (Albany, 1879), Vol. I, pp. 481–541, 556–636.

of his questioning was on the subject of the peculiar competitive situation of the railroads. Why, he asked, were railroads different from other businesses in regard to competition? Fink replied that they were not different except in competition with each other. Railroad competition with water routes was normal. Sterne was searching for general principles of railroad economics:[63]

Q. Do you think there is a law as to railroads?

A. Yes; there is a law as to railroads, that the public should be served alike by common carriers; if that law is to be carried out, it is necessary that you eliminate the element of competition as between these railroad companies; you cannot have the two at the same time.

Fink was asked to explain the operation of the Trunk Line Association and the Joint Executive Committee. He pointed out that the latter organization was the rate-making power of the trunk lines.[64] His office, he explained, consisted of from 60 to 65 clerks who collected statistical information for use in the pooling allotments and rate-making. The budget for the whole office including his own salary was about $5,000 per month. This amount was shared mostly by the four trunk lines, but a part was paid by the western roads.[65]

The Hepburn Committee was particularly interested in the position of the New York Central. Fink told the committee that the Central would certainly be ruined by all-out competition over any extended period of time, despite its great resources. By driving its competitors to bankruptcy, the Central would not force them out of operation. In receivership, with no interest or dividends to pay, competitors could easily force the Central into the same position.[66] Though the differentials might be

objectionable they were a necessary concomitant to railroad peace.

In New York State the Erie Canal assured low through rates during most of the year by its competition for freight with the railroads. But once rail competition forced the railroad rates below those of the canal, New York would lose all advantage it could legitimately claim over the other seaboard cities. Fink pointed out that both as to distance and actual cost of service Philadelphia and Baltimore possessed far greater advantages than were secured to them by means of the differentials.[67]

Fink's testimony made a deep impression on the Hepburn Committee and upon its counsel, Simon Sterne. Here was a railroad man who talked facts and did not lose his temper trying to justify railroad actions. His arguments made sense and his logic destroyed a great deal of the indictment that the railroads were exercising an irresponsible censorship over the affairs of the business community. There were injustices that could not be denied, mostly on a local level and frequently attributable to the bargaining position of large shippers in places like Buffalo where one road could be played against another. The committee was impressed by the fact that the railroads were subject to competing forces beyond the reach of state government and that pooling seemed to be the only way to control this competition.[68] "The business of transportation," the committee stated in its Report, "requires the greatest freedom of management of any business extant."[69]

National railroad legislation had been under discussion for several years when

[63] Ibid., p. 563.
[64] Ibid., p. 575.
[65] Ibid., pp. 570–571.
[66] Ibid., p. 565.

[67] Ibid., Vol. IV, pp. 106–119, Exhibit No. 1 for June 21, 1879.
[68] Closing argument of Simon Sterne on behalf of the Chamber of Commerce and the Board of Trade and Transportation (New York, 1880), p. 29. Part of Hepburn Comm. Proceedings.
[69] New York Assembly, Report of the Special Committee on Railroads (Albany, 1879), p. 75.

Albert Fink appeared before the Senate Committee on Commerce in 1879.[70] The Reagan Bill had passed the House of Representatives in December, 1878, and thorough investigation was being conducted by the Senate as to the merits of this bill. Fink attacked the Reagan Bill as a kind of Granger law aimed at the symptoms of trouble not the actual causes. It was based, he said, on the assumption that the rate structure was unfair. "No serious difficulty," he told the committee, "is experienced by the competing railroad companies in the country in agreeing upon and establishing tariffs entirely satisfactory to the commercial community and to the people."[71] The problem was to ensure that these tariffs were maintained. No provision of the Reagan Bill ensured this. Briefly he explained the trunk line rate structure and showed that nowhere would the long haul be charged less than the short haul on through traffic.

One provision of the Reagan Bill that Fink welcomed was the requirement that rates be made public.[72] This, he thought, might tend to make rail tariffs more permanent. The bill forbade pooling, but provided no protection against rate warfare to which the roads would inevitably resort to secure the portion of traffic to which they believed themselves entitled.

Fink suggested to the committee what he thought was a proper transportation law. He would have retained the first two sections of the Reagan Bill, which provided that the railroads must offer equal facilities without discrimination and which outlawed rebates and drawbacks.[73] To those sections he wanted to add the following:[74]

Sec. 3.   That all competing railroad companies shall jointly establish a tariff for all competing points.

Sec. 4.   That the tariff so established shall be submitted to a commission of experts appointed by the Federal Government, and if they find that the tariff is just and equitable and based upon correct commercial principles, and not in violation of the common laws governing common carriers, then such tariff shall be approved, and shall become the law of the land, until changed in the same manner by the same authority.

Sec. 5.   In cases where railroad companies cannot agree upon such tariffs, or upon any other questions such as might lead to a war of rates between railroad companies, the questions of disagreement shall be settled by arbitration, the decision of the arbitrator to be enforced in the United States Courts.

This suggestion is surprisingly similar to the actual rate-making and rate-revision process before the Interstate Commerce Commission today. Fink admitted that his amendments to the Reagan Bill were offered on his own responsibility. What the railroad managers and proprietors might think of his suggestions he was "not prepared to say." But as Fink put it, they were just as anxious as the public that the "object of the Reagan Bill be carried out."

The House Committee on Commerce held hearings on the Reagan Bill in January, 1880. On this occasion Fink repeated much of what he had said to the Senate Committee eleven months before.[75] However, he added some remarks in defense of pooling, possibly because he was disturbed by a growing public opposition to pooling as a monopolistic device. "The plan I propose," he said, "prevents that very centralization and absorption of the roads under absolute control of one or few persons. It makes the separate, individual existence of these roads possible, and puts a check upon the consolidation of roads. . . ."[76]

[70] Albert Fink, *Argument Before the Committee on Commerce of the Senate of the United States on the Reagan Bill* (New York, 1879), p. 28.
[71] *Ibid.*, p. 5.
[72] *Ibid.*, p. 7.
[73] *Ibid.*; Reagan Bill is found on pp. 23–28.
[74] *Ibid.*, p. 12.

[75] Albert Fink, *The Railroad Problem and its Solution* (New York, 1880) is a reprint of his testimony.
[76] *Ibid.*, p. 24.

In the year 1880, 115 railroad companies lost their identity in larger combines.[77] Unrestricted competition was one of the principal causes of railroad failures and the usual fate of a bankrupt or weakened road was to be swallowed up by one of its former competitors at a bargain price.[78] While there was wisdom and justice in a great deal of railroad consolidation there were instances of roads being ruined and disappearing in the maze of a speculative empire. The members of a voluntary federation which maintained the rates stood a better chance of surviving to perform the services for which they were built or of being purchased at a fair price.

In May, 1880, after a successful year for the pooling system, Albert Fink notified the Joint Executive Committee that he had fully attained the personal objectives he had in mind when he helped organize the pool. Experience had established the practicability of the pooling method and Fink could not conceive of the possibility of returning to "the former methods and mismanagement of the transportation business."[79] Events proved his optimism somewhat premature.

When testifying before the House Commerce Committee in January, Fink had warned that the new line being built into Chicago by the Grand Trunk of Canada might very well touch off a series of rate wars.[80] The situation was analogous to that of 1874 when the Baltimore & Ohio was building into the same city. In August, Fink announced to the Joint Executive Committee that the Grand Trunk had been invited to become a member of the Trunk Line Association.[81] On this occasion he

reaffirmed his conviction that the surest method of maintaining rates was to be found in the perfection of the pooling system. What had been done so far in regard to eastbound traffic he regarded as "merely a crude beginning." Pooling the traffic of connecting roads was the next step.

At this stage of its development the Trunk Line Association had only one coercive measure at its command. When a line resorted to rate-cutting, the Association could immediately order the rates on competing lines lowered to the new level.[82] This action was usually accompanied by a warning from Commissioner Fink in which he enumerated in detail the revenues that would be lost by the rate cut. Frequently this method brought about a reform. But at times it was difficult to detect rate-cutting or to what extent rates had been lowered. This was due to the various forms of subterfuge developed to hide cut rates.

Rebates were concealed by such tricks as billing freight from a more distant point than actually shipped, methodical underbilling of weight or false classification of cargo. Such methods provided a convenient and hard-to-detect way of affording special consideration to important shippers. To combat these dodges Fink established a system of freight inspection, but he did not expect miracles. His system was not characterized by Prussian efficiency. He was content simply to show the railroads a way to prevent wars. Only time and costly experience, he realized, would convince them.

With the relative success of two years during which there were no major rate wars, Fink recognized that the abolition of rebates and bargain rates might create discontent among the large class of shippers who had grown accustomed to special favors and windfalls. He warned the mem-

[77] Edward G. Campbell, *The Reorganization of the American Railroad System* (New York, 1938), p. 12.
[78] Stuart Daggett, *Railroad Reorganization* (Boston, 1908), pp. 341–342.
[79] J.E.C., *Proceedings*, 1880, p. 117.
[80] Fink, *Railroad Problem*, p. 64.
[81] J.E.C., *Proceedings*, 1880, pp. 151–152.

[82] Trunk Line Association, Freight Department, *Proceedings and Circulars of the . . . Association*, 1880, pp. 47–48.

bers of the Joint Executive Committee at a meeting in April, 1881:[83]

They [the shippers] will appeal through Board of Trade meetings to the prejudices of the people, and complain that the action of the railroad companies in their efforts to establish and maintain a reasonable and properly adjusted tariff throughout the country, is arbitrary and wrong, and should not be permitted.

The apparent lack of flexibility in the rate structure made shippers restive and dissatisfied. As early as February, 1881, Fink looked ahead to a time of trouble. He was sure the rate system was flexible, all too flexible. The rates would not be maintained, he warned the Trunk Line Executives, once the roads entered the season (when the lakes and canals could be used) when their capacities were not fully occupied.[84] By June, as he had predicted, the whole system was demoralized because "the pooling arrangements were incomplete or violated."

To deal with this general rate war a special meeting of the Joint Executive Committee was called for August 10, 1881. At the special August meeting Fink told the Joint Executives that since June 17 eastbound traffic had been carried for less than one half the average cost of transportation.[85] The freight solicitors who were busy securing freight at whatever rate was necessary to get the tonnage were at the heart of the problem. Freight agents allowed the solicitors such liberty because they thought that no better bargain could be made and because they forgot in the heat of competition that only their united efforts could secure a remunerative rate for the business.[86] At the special August meeting the Joint Executive resolved to restore the tariff in effect

June 15, 1881, but this was an unstable and ineffective armistice.[87]

On March 2, 1882, the Joint Executive adopted a set of rules for the conduct of the railroad business.[88] These were largely a reaffirmation of the committee's previous resolutions. However, one important innovation was the appointment of a Joint Agent at all points where traffic was pooled. This agent was to have the power to examine the members' books and bills of lading. All authority to vary rates was withdrawn from the lines and soliciting agents. This power was to be vested in the chairman of the Joint Executive Committee acting with the advice of the committee.

Two weeks after this important meeting, Albert Fink went to Washington to testify before the House Committee on Commerce once more. Pressure for federal legislation had greatly increased since his last appearance. Representative Reagan remarked that there had been "too or three times as many petitions for this legislation as ever came to Congress before."[89] Less credulous about the petitions than Reagan, Representative Washburne remarked that "someone had distributed these petitions broadcast over the country." Although they came from 35 different states the petitions were all identical.[90] Fink observed that it was "fashionable to hold the railroads responsible for everything nowadays." The railroad transportation system, he observed, ". . . has worked a greater revolution in our modern civilization than any other single event recorded in history. It could not be expected that such a revolution could take place without friction."[91]

[83] J.E.C., Proceedings, 1881, p. 29.
[84] T.L.A., Freight Dept., Proceedings, 1881, p. 157.
[85] J.E.C., Proceedings, 188, pp. 76–77.
[86] Ibid., p. 87.

[87] Ibid., p. 96.
[88] Ibid., 1882, pp. 22–24.
[89] Albert Fink, Argument . . . before the Committee on Commerce of the United States House of Representatives, Washington, March 17 and 18, 1882 (Washington, 1882), p. 4.
[90] Benson, Merchants, Farmers & Railroads, p. 226.
[91] Fink, Argument March 17 and 18, 1882, p. 3.

As he had predicted to the Joint Executives, the pressure against pooling from Boards of Trade and merchant groups was much increased. He was closely questioned about railroad earnings during the period of successful pooling in an attempt by the committee to verify the accusations that pooling resulted in inordinate profits. Fink told the committee that during 1880, when pooling was most effective, profits were only about 5 per cent on the capital invested.[92]

While the public was concerned over pooling as a conspiracy to assure the railroads of large profits, Fink was more concerned over the lack of conviction among railroad proprieters that pools would benefit them:[93]

Many railroad managers still cling to the idea that they are autocrats, as far as the control of their property is concerned, and that they can dictate terms and force compliance, although the dearly-purchased experience of many years should have shown them that this is not the fact. . . . They do not recognize that they have not the right to use their own property to injure the property of others, and that by their wrangling among themselves for the carriage of a few tons of freight they offset the public interest by creating all the unjust discriminations that arise from purely selfish acts of disagreement between these private corporations.

In 1881, railroad management was a more serious threat to Fink's rate structure and pooling system than public disapproval. Jay Gould, for example, has been accused of setting off the rate wars of 1881 and 1882 in his efforts to profit by speculations in the securities of the Wabash and the Central of New Jersey.[94] The New York Central was forced to protect itself from Gould, whose hand could be seen in many a project directed against

that road. Gould's influence in the building of the West Shore and in the extensions of the Delaware, Lackawanna and Western are two examples. Almost the only power in the securities market sufficiently strong to cope with Gould was William H. Vanderbilt. Vanderbilt was not a speculator nor was he an empire builder like his father, the Commodore.[95] Basically he was conservative. His stock market moves were made either to preserve the value of his property or to improve it. His support of the Trunk Line Association was probably dictated by the same motives.

The undisciplined jungle of high finance greatly contributed to Albert Fink's problems. In the early 1880's enough speculative capital was available to build the Nickel Plate and the West Shore roads which paralleled Vanderbilt's Lake Shore and the main line of the New York Central. The Delaware, Lackawanna and Western, with Gould's encouragement, began building into Buffalo.[96] This new construction meant fresh competitive forces in the trunk line territory to which the members would have to adjust. To Vanderbilt it meant a direct challenge to his property, a kind of blackmail he was virtually forced to nullify by purchase. In October, 1882, he did buy control of the Nickel Plate, but he left the West Shore to collapse of itself. The conduct of such men as Gould or the so-called "Seney crowd" brought forth the counterforce of investment conservatism characterized by J. Pierpont Morgan. Where Gould was a chaotic influence, Morgan was a conservative, nearly despotic one.

The year 1884 was a crisis year for American railroading. The West Shore was completed and operating, although it showed signs of financial weakness. Vanderbilt was unwisely giving his support to the construction of the South Pennsylvania Railroad, a project backed by

[92] *Ibid.*, p. 7.
[93] *Ibid.*, p. 29.
[94] Julius Grodinsky, *Jay Gould, 1867–1892, His Business Career* (Philadelphia, 1957), pp. 364, 366–368.

[95] *Ibid.*, pp. 209–223, 355–376.
[96] *Ibid.*, p. 221.

Andrew Carnegie and others interested in breaking the Pennsylvania Railroad's monopoly of the steel traffic from Pittsburgh.[97] It was rumored that in retaliation interests allied with the Pennsylvania were quietly buying up the securities of the weakened West Shore.[98] The D. L. & W., abetted by Gould, cut rates on eastbound and westbound traffic.[99] The Trunk Line system was in a shambles as the roads abandoned their agreements in order to participate in a competitive free-for-all.

In January, 1884, Fink, with the approval of the Joint Executive Committee, sent a letter to Samuel Sloan, president of the D. L. & W., warning him that unless his road agreed to join the Trunk Line pool the western connections would not feel obliged to handle D. L. & W. freight.[100] Sloan had been offered a share in the westbound pool based upon traffic his road had obtained during the previous ten months during which he had operated with cut rates.

"Boycotting pure and simple" the New York Evening Post labeled this trunk line threat, and "used in precisely the same spirit with which the trade unions employ it."[101] To the Evening Post Fink replied, "The Lackawanna can adopt and conform to the rules and regulations under which railroad companies exchange business with each other, but, not desiring to do so, it cannot expect to extend its operations and become a forwarder of freight beyond the line of its own road."[102] Boycotting was the strongest measure the Trunk Lines had yet used. It was a sanction that required the cooperation of the connecting lines. It was successful for a short time only.

The West Shore filed bankruptcy proceedings in June, 1884.[103] Vanderbilt was in Europe, out of sorts with the railroad business and in no mood to buy up this competitor. Construction on the South Pennsylvania was proceeding slowly. Speaking of a visit to the office of the Trunk Line Commissioner during this period, Charles Francis Adams, Jr., remarked, "It struck me as a somewhat funereal gathering. Those composing it were manifestly at their wits' ends. . . . Mr. Fink's great and costly organization was all in ruins and no one felt any faith in new experiments. . . . They reminded me of men in a boat in the swift water above the rapids of Niagara."[104] The rate war raged through the summer of 1884 and on into the following year.[105]

Relief came during the summer of 1885. On board his yacht the Corsair, J. Pierpont Morgan conferred with Chauncey Depew, recently elected president of the New York Central, George B. Roberts, president of the Pennsylvania, and Frank Thompson, Robert's chief lieutenant.[106] Morgan volunteered his services, at the risk of his personal fortune as it turned out, to enable the Central to acquire the West Shore and the Pennsylvania to gain control of the South Pennsylvania. The latter part of this plan was never consummated although all work on the South Pennsylvania ceased, which was just as satisfactory to the Pennsylvania. Thus Morgan, the banker and investor, brought about railroad peace by consolidation. It was a kind of railroad "burden of empire" since neither the Central nor the Pennsylvania wanted the roads they acquired. Gould, the villain of the piece, sold out his eastern railroad hold-

[97] George H. Burgess and Miles C. Kennedy, Centennial History of the Pennsylvania Railroad (Philadelphia, 1949), pp. 408–412.
[98] Herbert L. Satterlee, J. Pierpont Morgan (New York, 1940), p. 220.
[99] Grodinsky, Gould, pp. 371–372.
[100] J.E.C., Proceedings, 1884, pp. 8–11.
[101] Evening Post, Jan. 12, 1884. Reprinted in J.E.C., Proceedings, 1884, p. 23.
[102] Ibid., p. 30.

[103] Satterlee, Morgan, pp. 221–222.
[104] Report of the Senate Select Committee on Interstate Commerce, 49th Cong., 1st Sess., Senate Report No. 46, Part 2 (Jan. 18, 1886), pp. 1,207–1,208. (This report is usually called the Cullom Report.) Quoted in Grodinsky, Gould, p. 504.
[105] Cullom Report, Part 2, p. 104.
[106] Satterlee, Morgan, pp. 223–227.

ings during the market rise occasioned by the rumors of peace negotiations.[107]

A new Trunk Line Agreement was signed in November, 1885. It was hoped that its more stringent provisions would strengthen the system and make it permanent.[108] The addition of the signatures of three new member roads indicated, in part, the factors that had made the maintenance of rates so difficult, especially during the years 1884 and 1885. Building and consolidation of railroads was a continuing disruptive element.[109]

On March 17, 1885, the Senate passed a resolution for the appointment of a select committee of five senators "to investigate and report upon the subject of the regulation of transportation by railroad and water routes."[110] A committee was duly appointed, headed by Shelby M. Cullom of Illinois.[111] The five senators traveled from city to city throughout the country hearing testimony on all phases of the transportation problem. Most of the important figures interested in railroad reform appeared before the committee. The report and testimony of the Cullom Committee represent the last careful investigation of the subject prior to the passage of the Interstate Commerce Act.

Railroad pooling was not castigated by the experts. Simon Sterne, who at the time of the Hepburn Investigation had charged that pooling was not only a discriminatory device, but was illegal as well, testified in favor of pooling under government supervision.[112] Arthur Twining Hadley, author of a leading study on railway economics

and later president of Yale, said that legalized pools would greatly increase the chance that they could be used as a power for good.[113] Most contemporary students of the railway problem favored some form of pooling. To forbid pooling, warned Charles Francis Adams, Jr., former Massachusetts Railroad Commissioner, then president of the Union Pacific Railroad, would result in warfare and end by bankrupting most of the railroads in the country.[114]

As a result of his experience with the Hepburn Committee and subsequent events, Albert Fink greatly feared the influence of large shippers against railroad pooling. The testimony of Charles A. Pillsbury before the Cullom Committee illustrates the basis for his fear.[115]

Mr. Pillsbury. As far as our own business is concerned and I think I represent the millers and large shipping interests here [Minneapolis] —we have no complaints to make.

The Chairman. None whatever?

Mr. Pillsbury. None whatever. We think we are getting fully as low freights as the railroads can afford to take the goods for, *if not lower*. [Italics added]

Pillsbury was the spokesman for a virtually monopolistic organization of Minneapolis millers. Between 1875 and 1885 competition had nearly halved the railroad rates in this area.[116] The millers were used to rebates. Through ownership of the grain elevators along the various routes to their mills they controlled the marketing and shipment of grain.[117] In the absence of pooling, Pillsbury and his group had the initiative in setting the rail rates. He told the committee that he felt "an effective pool would hurt the milling interests."

When Albert Fink came to testify before

---

[107] Grodinsky, *Gould*, p. 508.
[108] T.L.A., *Proceedings*, 1885, pp. 70–73. The agreement and a description of the organization in *Cullom Report*, appendix pp. 237–244.
[109] Signers of the new agreement were the Grand Trunk of Canada, New York Central, Delaware, Lackawanna & Western, Erie, Pennsylvania, West Shore and Baltimore & Ohio.
[110] *Cullom Report*, Part 1, p. 1.
[111] Other members were Orville H. Platt, Conn.; Arthur P. Gorman, Md.; W. Miller, N.Y.; and Isham G. Harris, Tenn.
[112] *Cullom Report, Part 2, p. 72.*

[113] *Ibid.*, p. 202.
[114] *Ibid.*, p. 1,204.
[115] *Ibid.*, p. 1,240.
[116] Larson, *The Wheat Market*, p. 122.
[117] *Ibid.*, p. 147.

the Cullom Committee he no longer asked that the government legalize and regulate pooling. He noted that there had come to be a greater tendency to forbid the measures he favored than to aid the railroads in carrying them into effect.[118] Railroad associations, he believed, ". . . were more in accordance with right and justice and with the institutions of the country than the measures which have been adopted in some of the States for the control of the railroads."[119] He tried to dispel the bogey that pooling was for the purpose of bilking the public. "The laws of competition in making tariffs have unrestricted sway, pool or no pool, and are the surest safeguard against extortionate rates." At another point in his testimony he came back to the same theme. "The object of the pooling agreements is to enforce the agreed and published tariffs. They have nothing to do with the making of tariffs."

A major rate war was in progress at the time Fink testified before the Cullom Committee. The conference on board Morgan's *Corsair* had not taken place. The renewed and improved Trunk Line Agreement was a thing of the future. There were no significant glimmerings of peace to brighten the stormy railroad world. But Fink closed his remarks with an expression of faith in the ultimate success of reform through voluntary railroad associations:[120]

It is . . . better to leave these matters in their present shape and let the roads fight it out as best they can for a while longer. It is a very expensive way of learning, but after the lesson is once learned, the institution will, perhaps, be more permanent than if based upon laws which are in advance of the intelligence and understanding of the people and, I may say, of the railroad men themselves.

The Cullom Committee did not "deem it prudent to recommend the prohibition of pooling" in its *Report* to the Senate. And in a spirit that characterized the attitude of the period toward social legislation, the committee did not recommend that pooling be legalized.[121] Albert Fink might have believed that the committee had found his arguments convincing because the results were those he had sought. But in the negotiations between the Senate and House Committees on Commerce over the provisions of an act to regulate interstate commerce, the views of Representative Reagan prevailed and an antipooling clause was inserted.[122] When the Interstate Commerce Act was finally passed in 1887, it brought an end to the pooling system. Twenty years later Senator Cullom remarked on pooling, "Whether it is right or wrong, I do not know even to this day."[123]

Right or wrong, pooling was not a wholly satisfactory means of preventing excessive railroad competition. By outlawing pooling the government did deprive the railroads of a peacemaking device which had, at times, proved effective. But not all of Albert Fink's contributions to the organization of railroad peacemaking disappeared with the pooling system. His ideas and techniques for rate-making continued in the railroad associations and regional rate committees he created. Perhaps his most lasting contribution to railway reform was his systematizing of railroad thought through the use of statistics. Pooling was, after all, simply a device to create the conditions necessary to rationalize the rate system. Railroad tariffs are constructed in much the same manner today, and more in the scientific manner Fink advocated.

[118] *Cullom Report,* Part 2, p. 126.
[119] *Ibid.,* Part 2, p. 114.
[120] *Ibid.,* Part 2, p. 126.

[121] *Cullom Report,* Part 1, p. 201.
[122] Shelby M. Cullom, *Fifty Years of Public Service* (Chicago, 1911), pp. 321–322.
[123] *Ibid.,* p. 322.

Chapter Three

The Business Structure of Industrialism

■ Unquestionably, there is a close relation between the business structure—by which we mean the number and size of firms, their types of management, their relations to each other in the market, and their means of finance—and the overall rate of national economic development. For example, nations that have been slow to industrialize tend to have family-run companies in which managerial jobs are allotted on the basis of kinship, and certain parts of the market tend to be regarded as the preserve of a particular firm. Obviously, enterprises operating under such conditions are likely to be inefficiently operated and are unlikely to compete aggressively for more of the market.

In contrast, United States businessmen have been leaders in developing the professionally managed firm that seeks to dominate the entire national market for its products. As in other nations, small business has been family-run, but with the coming of large banking, public utility, and railroad corporations in the early nineteenth century, the idea of selecting managers of proved ability without regard to family connections began to take hold. By 1900, many large industrial firms were being controlled on the board of directors by the founding family but managed by nonrelatives, by men who might be called professional careerists. And family ownership of large firms was giving way itself to nonfamily corporate ownership. This same transition was also taking place in Western Europe, but the smaller markets of the European nations, their greater regard for family status, and less movement of population all tended to perpetuate family enterprise.

The rise of the big nonfamily company was partly a result of technological change.

As machinery became ever larger and more costly, single families either could not finance an enterprise, a railroad, for example, or did not want to commit so much of their capital to one undertaking. Other forces also made for bigness. Most mechanized processes showed decreasing cost per unit as volume increased. Even if the existing machines were being fully utilized, more machines could reduce unit cost in relation to various types of managerial, marketing, and overhead expense. Bigness also led to a more secure com-

petitive position in the market, and a big company could strive to improve its relative position by marketing and price competition even if the effort led temporarily to losses.

Whether the American path to industrial leadership was the best one available is too complex a question to answer, but the resulting business structure, at least, has come to be admired and to a degree copied in both capitalist and socialist economies.

Changes in Business

■ The new business world produced by the rise of large industrial companies can best be seen as superimposed upon, but not replacing, the old world of small business. Wholesale and retail trade, brokerage, finance and service— the major sectors of business—continued much as they always had, still carried on in 1900 by nearly a million and a half small companies. But the big companies were the exciting new development responsible for great decreases in price and increases in production in industries such as steel, oil, and machinery.

Numerous histories of single companies have been written; Alfred D. Chandler, Jr., of Johns Hopkins University, is one of the few historical scholars who have written on the factors producing structural changes in business as a whole.

Alfred D. Chandler, Jr.
The Beginnings of "Big Business" in American Industry*

Criteria for Selection and Analysis

The historian, by the very nature of his task, must be concerned with change. What made for change? Why did it come

when it did, and in the way it did? These are characteristically historians' questions. For the student of American business history, these basic questions can be put a little more precisely. What in the American past has given businessmen the oppor-

* Reprinted by permission from Business History Review, XXXIII (Spring, 1959), pp. 1–31.
Note: This study was supported by the Sloan Research Fund of The School of Industrial Management and the Center for International Studies, Massachusetts Institute of Technology.

tunity or created the need for them to change what they were doing or the way they were doing it? In other words, what stimulated them to develop new products, new markets, new sources of raw materials, new ways of procuring, processing, or marketing the goods they handled? What encouraged them to find new methods of financing, new ways of managing or organizing their businesses? What turned them to altering their relations with their working force, their customers and competitors, and with the larger American public?

The question of what constitutes the dynamic factors in American business history, dynamic in the sense of stimulating change and innovation, can be more clearly defined if the country's land, natural resources, and cultural patterns are taken as given. Land and resources were the raw materials with which the businessmen had to work, and the cultural attitudes and values helped set the legal and ethical rules of the game they had to play. Within this cultural and geographic environment a number of historical developments appear to have stimulated change. These provide a framework around which historical data can be compiled and analyzed.

The following major dynamic forces are visible in the American business economy since 1815: the western expansion of population; the construction and initial operation of the national railroad network; the development of a national and increasingly urban market; the application of two new sources of power: the internal combustion engine and electricity, to industry and transportation; and the systematic application of the natural and physical sciences, particularly chemistry and physics, to industry through the institutionalizing of research and development activities.

The first, the westward expansion, appears to have provided the primary impetus, except possibly in New England,

to business innovation in the years from 1815 to about 1850; the building of the railroads appears to have been the major factor from the 1850's to the late 1870's; the growth of the national and urban market from the 1880's until a little after 1900; the coming of electricity and the internal combustion engine from the early 1900's to the 1920's; and, finally, the growth of systematic and institutionalized research and development since the 1920's.

These five factors are essentially aspects of fundamental population changes and technological advances. There were, of course, other factors that encouraged business innovation and change. The coming of the new machines and mechanical devices may have been a more important stimulant to innovation in New England than the growth of her markets and sources of supply in the expanding South and West. Wars usually precipitated change. The business cycle, flow of capital, government policy and legislation all played a significant part in business innovation. But such political and financial developments appear to have intensified or delayed the more basic changes encouraged initially by fundamental population shifts and technological achievements.

The purpose of making such a list is, however, not to argue that one development was more dynamic than the other. Nor are these five factors to be considered as "causes" for change; nor are they "theses" to be argued as representing reality, nor "theories" to provide an overall explanation of change or possibly of predicting change. They are, rather, a framework on which historical information can be tied and inter-related. They provide a consistent basis upon which meaningful questions can be asked of the data.

This framework and these questions are, it should be emphasized, concerned only with fundamental changes and innovation in the business economy. They do not deal with the day-to-day activities to which businessmen must devote nearly all of their time. They are not concerned with the continuous adaptation to the constant variations of the market, sources of supply, availability of capital, and technological developments. Nor do they consider why some businesses and businessmen responded quickly and creatively to the basic population and technological changes and others did not. But an understanding of the continuous response and adjustment would seem to require first an awareness of the meaning of the more fundamental or "discontinuous" changes.

Since historical compilation and analysis must be selective, it is impossible to undertake any historical study without some criteria either implicit or explicit for selection. Further study and analysis, by indicating the defects of this approach and framework, will suggest more satisfactory ones. In the process, an analysis and interpretation of change in the American business past should come a little nearer to reality.

The purpose of this article then is, by using the framework of basic, dynamic forces, to look a little more closely at the years that witnessed the beginnings of big business in American industry. What types of changes came during these years in the ways of marketing, purchasing, processing, and in the forms of business organization? Why did these changes come when they did in the way they did? Was the growth of the national market a major prerequisite for such innovation and change? If not, what then was? How did these innovations relate to the growth of the railroad network or the coming of electricity and the internal combustion engine?

In addition to secondary works on this period, the data used in seeking answers to these questions have been annual and other corporation reports, government documents, articles in periodicals, histories, and biographies concerning the 50 largest industrial companies in the country in 1909. Nearly all these companies, listed in Table I (see page 100), had their beginnings in the last years of the nineteenth century.

Major Changes in American Industry at the End of the Nineteenth Century

Between the depression of the 1870's and the beginning of the twentieth century, American industry underwent a significant transformation. In the 1870's, the major industries serviced an agrarian economy. Except for a few companies equipping the rapidly expanding railroad network, the leading industrial firms processed agricultural products and provided farmers with food and clothing. These firms tended to be small, and bought their raw materials and sold their finished goods locally. Where they manufactured for a market more than a few miles away from the factory, they bought and sold through commissioned agents who handled the business of several other similar firms.

By the beginning of the twentieth century, many more companies were making producers' goods, to be used in industry rather than on the farm or by the ultimate consumer. Most of the major industries had become dominated by a few large enterprises. These great industrial corporations no longer purchased and sold through agents, but had their own nationwide buying and marketing organizations. Many, primarily those in the extractive industries, had come to control their own raw materials. In other words, the business economy had become industrial. Major industries were dominated by a few firms that had become great, vertically integrated, centralized enterprises.

In the terms of the economist and sociologist a significant sector of American industry had become bureaucratic, in the sense that business decisions were made within large hierarchical structures.

Externally, oligopoly was prevalent, the decision-makers being as much concerned with the actions of the few other large firms in the industry as with over-all changes in markets, sources of supplies, and technological improvements.

These basic changes came only after the railroads had created a national market. The railroad network, in turn, had grown swiftly primarily because of the near desperate requirements for efficient transportation created by the movement of population westward after 1815.[1] Except for the Atlantic seaboard between Boston and Washington, the construction of the American railroads was stimulated almost wholly by the demand for better transportation to move crops, to bring farmers supplies, and to open up new territories to commercial agriculture.

By greatly expanding the scope of the agrarian economy, the railroads quickened the growth of the older commercial centers, such as New York, Philadelphia, Cincinnati, Cleveland, and St. Louis, and helped create new cities like Chicago, Indianapolis, Atlanta, Kansas City, Dallas, and the Twin Cities. This rapid urban expansion intensified the demand for the products of the older consumer goods industries—particularly those which processed the crops of the farmer and planter into food, stimulants, and clothing.

At the same time, railroad construction developed the first large market in this country for producers' goods. Except for the making of relatively few textile machines, steamboat engines, and ordnance, the iron and nonferrous manufacturers had before 1850 concentrated on providing metals and simple tools for merchants

and farmers. Even textile machinery was usually made by the cloth manufacturers themselves. However, by 1860, only a decade after beginning America's first major railroad construction boom, railroad companies had already replaced the blacksmiths as the primary market for iron products, and had become far and away the most important market for the heavy engineering industries. By then, too, the locomotive was competing with the Connecticut brass industry as a major consumer of copper. More than this, the railroads, with their huge capital outlay, their fixed operating costs, the large size of their labor and management force, and the technical complexity of their operations, pioneered in the new ways of oligopolistic competition and large-scale, professionalized, bureaucratized management.

The new nation-wide market created by the construction of the railroad network became an increasingly urban one. From 1850 on, if not before, urban areas were growing more rapidly than rural ones. In the four decades from 1840 to 1880 the proportion of urban population rose from 11 percent to 28 percent of the total population, or about 4 percent a decade. In the two decades from 1880 to 1900 it grew from 28 percent to 40 percent or an increase of 6 percent a decade. Was this new urban and national market, then, the primary stimulant for business innovation and change, and for the coming of big business to American industry?

Changes in the Consumers' Goods Industries

The industries first to become dominated by great business enterprises were those making consumer goods, the majority of which were processed from products grown on the farm and sold in the urban markets. Consolidation and centralization in the consumers' goods industries were well

[1] The factors stimulating the growth of the American railroad network and the impact of the earlier construction and operation of this network on the American business economy and business institutions are suggested in Chandler, *Henry Varnum Poor—Business Editor, Analyst, and Reformer* (Cambridge, 1956), especially chaps. 4, 6–9.

under way by 1893. The unit that appeared was one which integrated within a single business organization the major economic processes: production or purchasing of raw materials, manufacturing, distribution, and finance.

Such vertically integrated organizations came in two quite different ways. Where the product tended to be somewhat new in kind and especially fitted for the urban market, its makers created their businesses by first building large marketing and then purchasing organizations. This technique appears to have been true of the manufacturers or distributors of fresh meat, cigarettes, high-grade flour, bananas, harvesters, sewing machines, and typewriters. Where the products were established staple items, horizontal combination tended to precede vertical integration. In the sugar, salt, leather, whiskey, glucose, starch, biscuit, kerosene, fertilizer, and rubber industries a large number of small manufacturers first combined into large business units and then created their marketing and buying organizations. For a number of reasons the makers of the newer types of products found the older outlets less satisfactory and felt more of a need for direct marketing than did the manufacturers of the long-established goods.

Integration via the Creation of Marketing Organization/ The story of the changes and the possible reasons behind them can be more clearly understood by examining briefly the experience of a few innovating firms. First, consider the experience of companies that grew large through the creation of a nationwide marketing and distributing organization. Here the story of Gustavus F. Swift and his brother Edwin is a significant one. Gustavus F. Swift, an Easterner, came relatively late to the Chicago meat-packing business. Possibly because he was from Massachusetts, he appreciated the potential market for fresh western meat in the eastern cities.[2] For after the Civil War, Boston, New York, Philadelphia, and other cities were rapidly outrunning their local meat supply. At the same time, great herds of cattle were gathering on the western plains. Swift saw the possibilities of connecting the new market with the new source of supply by the use of the refrigerated railroad car. In 1878, shortly after his first experimental shipment of refrigerated meat, he formed a partnership with his younger brother, Edwin, to market fresh western meat in the eastern cities.

For the next decade, Swift struggled hard to carry out his plans, the essence of which was the creation, during the 1880's, of the nation-wide distributing and marketing organization built around a network of branch houses. Each "house" had its storage plant and its own marketing organization. The latter included outlets in major towns and cities, often managed by Swift's own salaried representatives. In marketing the product, Swift had to break down, through advertising and other means, the prejudices against eating meat killed more than a thousand miles away and many weeks earlier. At the same time he had to combat boycotts of local butchers and the concerted efforts of the National Butchers' Protective Association to prevent the sale of his meat in the urban markets.

To make effective use of the branch house network, the company soon began to market products other than beef. The

[2] Swift's story as outlined in Louis F. Swift in collaboration with Arthur Van Vlissingen, *The Yankee of the Yards—the Biography of Gustavus Franklin Swift* (New York, 1928). The United States Bureau of Corporations, *Report of the Commissioner of Corporations on the Beef Industry, March 3, 1905* (Washington, 1905), is excellent on the internal operations and external activities of the large meat-packing firms. There is additional information in the later three-volume *Report of the Federal Trade Commission on the Meat Packing Industry* (Washington, 1918–1919). R. A. Clemen, *The American Livestock and Meat Industry* (New York, 1923) has some useful background data.

"full line" soon came to include lamb, mutton, pork, and, some time later, poultry, eggs, and dairy products. The growing distributing organization soon demanded an increase in supply. So between 1888 and 1892, the Swifts set up meat-packing establishments in Kansas City, Omaha, and St. Louis, and, after the depression of the 1890's, three more in St. Joseph, St. Paul, and Ft. Worth. At the same time, the company systematized the buying of its cattle and other products at the stockyards. In the 1890's, too, Swift began a concerted effort to make more profitable use of by-products.

Before the end of the 1890's, then, Swift had effectively fashioned a great, vertically integrated organization. The major departments—marketing, processing, purchasing, and accounting—were all tightly controlled from the central office in Chicago. A report of the Commissioner of Corporations published in 1905 makes clear the reason for such control:[3]

Differences in quality of animals and of their products are so great that the closest supervision of the Central Office is necessary to enforce the exercise of skill and sound judgement on the part of the agents who buy the stock, and the agents who sell the meat. With this object, the branches of the Selling and Accounting Department of those packing companies which have charge of the purchasing, killing, and dressing and selling of fresh meat, are organized in the most extensive and thorough manner. The Central Office is in constant telegraphic correspondence with the distributing houses, with a view to adjusting the supply of meat and the price as nearly as possible to the demand.

As this statement suggests, the other meat packers followed Swift's example. To compete effectively, Armour, Morris, Cudahy, and Schwarzschild & Sulzberger had to build up similar integrated organizations. Those that did not follow the Swift model were destined to remain small local companies. Thus by the middle of the 1890's, the meat-packing industry, with the rapid growth of these great vertically integrated firms, had become oligopolistic (the "Big Five" had the major share of the market) and bureaucratic; each of the five had its many departments and several levels of management.

This story has parallels in other industries processing agricultural products. In tobacco, James B. Duke was the first to appreciate the growing market for the cigarette, a new product which was sold almost wholly in the cities.[4] However, after he had applied machinery to the manufacture of cigarettes, production soon outran supply. Duke then concentrated on expanding the market through extensive advertising and the creation of a national and then world-wide selling organization. In 1884, he left Durham, North Carolina, for New York City, where he set up factories, sales, and administrative offices. New York was closer to his major urban markets, and was the more logical place to manage an international advertising campaign than Durham. While he was building his marketing department, Duke was also creating the network of warehouses and buyers in the tobacco-growing areas of the country.

In 1890, he merged his company with five smaller competitors in the cigarette business to form the American Tobacco Company. By 1895 the activities of these firms had been consolidated into the manufacturing, marketing, purchasing, and finance departments of the single operating structure Duke had earlier fashioned. Duke next undertook development of a full line by handling all types of smoking

[3] Report of Commissioner of Corporations on the Beef Industry, p. 21.

[4] Some information on James B. Duke and the American Tobacco Company can be found in John W. Jenkins, James B. Duke, Master Builder (New York, 1927), chaps. 5–7, 10. More useful was the United States Bureau of Corporations, Report of the Commissioner of Corporations on the Tobacco Industry (Washington, 1909).

and chewing tobacco. By the end of the century, his company completely dominated the tobacco business. Only two other firms, R. J. Reynolds & Company and P. Lorillard & Company, had been able to build up comparable vertically integrated organizations. When they merged with American Tobacco they continued to retain their separate operating organizations. When the 1911 antitrust decree split these and other units off from the American company, the tobacco industry had become, like the meat-packing business, oligopolistic, and its dominant firms bureaucratic.

What Duke and Swift did for their industries, James S. Bell of the Washburn-Crosby Company did during these same years in the making and selling of high-grade flour to the urban bakeries and housewives, and Andrew J. Preston achieved in growing, transporting, and selling another new product for the urban market, the banana.[5] Like Swift and Duke, both these men made their major innovations in marketing, and then went on to create large-scale, departmentalized, vertically integrated structures.

The innovators in new consumer durables followed much the same pattern. Both Cyrus McCormick, pioneer harvester manufacturer, and William Clark, the business brains of the Singer Sewing Machine Company, first sold through commissioned agents. Clark soon discovered that salaried men, working out of branch offices, could more effectively and at less cost display, demonstrate, and service sewing machines than could the agents.[6] Just as important, the branch offices were able to provide

the customer with essential credit. McCormick, while retaining the dealer to handle the final sales, came to appreciate the need for a strong selling and distributing organization, with warehouses, servicing facilities, and a large salaried force, to stand behind the dealer.[7] So in the years following the Civil War, both McCormick and Singer Sewing Machine Company concentrated on building up national and then world-wide marketing departments. As they purchased their raw materials from a few industrial companies rather than from a mass of farmers, their purchasing departments were smaller, and required less attention than those in the firms processing farmers' products. But the net result was the creation of a very similar type of organization.

Integration via Horizontal Combination/ In those industries making more standard goods, the creation of marketing organizations usually followed large-scale combinations of a number of small manufacturing firms. For these small firms, the coming of the railroad had in many cases enlarged their markets but simultaneously brought them for the first time into competition with many other companies. Most of these firms appear to have expanded production in order to take advantage of the new markets. As a result, their industries became plagued with overproduction and excess capacity; that is, continued production at full capacity threatened to drop prices below the cost of production. So in the 1880's and early 1890's, many small manufacturers in the leather, sugar, salt, distilling and other corn products, linseed and cotton oil, biscuit, petroleum, fertilizer and rubber boot and glove industries, joined in large horizontal combinations.

In most of these industries, combination was followed by consolidation and

[5] The story of Bell is outlined in James Gray, *Business Without Boundary, the Story of General Mills* (Minneapolis, 1954), and of Preston in Charles M. Wilson, *Empire in Green and Gold* (New York, 1947).
[6] The early Singer Sewing Machine experience is well analyzed in Andrew B. Jack, "The Channels of Distribution for an Innovation: the Sewing Machine Industry in America, 1860–1865," *Explorations in Entrepreneurial History*, Vol. IX (Feb., 1957), pp. 113–141.

[7] William T. Hutchinson, *Cyrus Hall McCormick* (New York, 1935), Vol. II, pp. 704–712.

vertical integration, and the pattern was comparatively consistent. First, the new combinations concentrated their manufacturing activities in locations more advantageously situated to meet the new growing urban demands. Next they systematized and standardized their manufacturing processes. Then, except in the case of sugar and corn products (glucose and starch), the combinations began to build large distributing and smaller purchasing departments. In so doing, many dropped their initial efforts to buy out competitors or to drive them out of business by price-cutting. Instead they concentrated on the creation of a more efficient flow from the producers of their raw materials to the ultimate consumer, and of the development and maintenance of markets through brand names and advertising. Since the large majority of these combinations began as regional groupings, most industries came to have more than one great firm. Only oil, sugar, and corn products remained long dominated by a single company. By World War I, partly because of the dissolutions under the Sherman Act, these industries had also become oligopolistic, and their leading firms vertically integrated.

Specific illustrations help to make these generalizations more precise. The best-known is the story of the oil industry, but equally illustrative is the experience of the leading distilling, baking, and rubber companies.

The first permanent combination in the whiskey industry came in 1887 when a large number of Midwestern distillers, operating more than 80 small plants, formed the Distillers' and Cattle Feeders' Trust.[8] Like other trusts, it adopted the more satisfactory legal form of a holding company shortly after New Jersey in 1889 passed the general incorporation law for holding companies. The major efforts of the Distillers Company were, first, to concentrate production in a relatively few plants. By 1895 only 21 were operating. The managers maintained that the large volume per plant permitted by such concentration would mean lower costs, and also that the location of few plants more advantageously in relation to supply and marketing would still reduce expenses further. However, the company kept the price of whiskey up, and since the cost of setting up a distillery was small, it soon had competition from small local plants. The company's answer was to purchase the new competitors and to cut prices. This strategy proved so expensive that the enterprise was unable to survive the depression of the 1890's.

Shortly before going into receivership in 1896, the Distillers Company had begun to think more about marketing. In 1895, it had planned to spend a million dollars to build up a distributing and selling organization in the urban East—the company's largest market. In 1898, through the purchase of the Standard Distilling & Distributing Company and the Spirits Distributing Company, it did acquire a marketing organization based in New York City. In 1903, the marketing and manufacturing units were combined into a single operating organization under the direction of the Distillers Securities Company. At the same time, the company's president announced plans to concentrate on the development of brand names and specialties, particularly through ad-

---

[8] The major sources of information on combination and consolidation in the distilling industry are Jeremiah W. Jenks, "The Development of the Whiskey Trust," Political Science Quarterly, Vol. IV (June, 1889), pp. 296–319; J. W. Jenks and W. E. Clark, The Trust Problem (rev. ed.; New York, 1917), pp. 141–149. The annual reports of the Distilling and Cattle Feeding Company and its various successors provide some useful additional data, as does the Industrial Commission, Preliminary Report on Trusts and Industrial Combinations (Washington, 1900), Vol. I, pp. 74–89, 167–259, 813–848, and Victor S. Clark, History of Manufactures in the United States (New York, 1929), Vol. II, pp. 505–506. Changes in taxes on liquors also affected the company's policies in the early 1890's.

vertising and packaging.[9] By the early years of the twentieth century, then, the Distillers Company had become a vertically integrated, departmentalized, centralized operating organization, competing in the modern manner, more through advertising and product differentiation than price.

The experience of the biscuit industry is even more explicit. The National Biscuit Company came into being in 1898 as a merger of three regional combinations: the New York Biscuit Company formed in 1890, the American Biscuit and Manufacturing Company, and the United States Biscuit Company founded a little later.[10] Its initial objective was to control price and production, but as in the case of the Distillers Company, this strategy proved too expensive. The Annual Report for 1901 suggests why National Biscuit shifted its basic policies:[11]

This Company is four years old and it may be of interest to shortly review its history. . . . When the Company started, it was an aggregation of plants. It is now an organized business. When we look back over the four years, we find that a radical change has been wrought in our methods of business. In the past, the managers of large merchandising corporations have found it necessary, for success, to control or limit competition. So when this company started, it was thought that we must control competition, and that to do this we must either fight competition or buy it. The first meant a ruinous war of prices, and a great loss of profit;

the second, a constantly increasing capitalization. Experience soon proved to us that, instead of bringing success, either of those courses, if persevered in, must bring disaster. This led us to reflect whether it was necessary to control competition. . . . we soon satisfied ourselves that within the Company itself we must look for success.

We turned our attention and bent our energies to improving the internal management of our business, to getting full benefit from purchasing our raw materials in large quantities, to economizing the expenses of manufacture, to systematizing and rendering more effective our selling department; and above all things and before all things to improve the quality of our goods and the condition in which they should reach the customer.

It became the settled policy of this Company to buy out no competition. . . .

In concentrating on distribution, the company first changed its policy from selling in bulk to wholesalers to marketing small packages to retailers. It developed the various "Uneeda Biscuit" brands, which immediately became popular. "The next point," the same Annual Report continued, "was to reach the customer. Thinking we had something that the customer wanted, we had to advise the customer of its existence. We did this by extensive advertising." This new packaging and advertising not only quickly created a profitable business, but also required the building of a sizable marketing organization. Since flour could be quickly and easily purchased in quantity from large milling firms, the purchasing requirements were less complex, and so the company needed a smaller purchasing organization. On the other hand, it spent much energy after 1901 in improving plant layout and manufacturing processes in order to cut production costs and to improve and standardize quality. Throughout the first decade of its history, National Biscuit continued the policy of "centralizing" manufacturing operations, particularly in its great New York and Chicago plants.

[9] Annual Report of the President of the Distillers Securities Company for 1903.

[10] The information on National Biscuit comes largely from its annual reports.

[11] Annual Report of the National Biscuit Company for the Year Ending December, 1901, January 3, 1902. References to centralizing of manufacturing facilities appear in several early annual reports. As this was written before Theodore Roosevelt had started to make the Sherman Act an effective anti-trust instrument and Ida Tarbell and other journalists had begun to make "muck raking" of big business popular and profitable, the Biscuit Company's shift in policy could hardly have been the result of the pressure of public opinion or the threat of government action.

In the rubber boot, shoe, and glove industries, the story is much the same. Expansion of manufacturing facilities and increasing competition as early as 1874 led to the formation, by several leading firms, of the Associated Rubber Shoe Companies—an organization for setting price and production schedules through its board of directors.[12] This company continued until 1886. Its successor, the Rubber Boot and Shoe Company, which lasted only a year, attempted, besides controlling prices and production, to handle marketing, which had always been done by commissioned agents. After five years of uncontrolled competition, four of the five firms that had organized the selling company again combined, this time with the assistance of a large rubber importer, Charles A. Flint. The resulting United States Rubber Company came, by 1898, to control 75 percent of the nation's rubber boot, shoe, and glove output.

At first the new company remained a decentralized holding company. Each constituent company retained its corporate identity with much freedom of action, including the purchasing of raw materials and the selling of finished products, which was done, as before, through jobbers. The central office's concern was primarily with controlling price and production schedules. Very soon, however, the company began, in the words of the 1896 Annual Report, a policy of "perfecting consolidation of purchasing, selling, and manufacturing."[13] This was to be accomplished in four ways. First, as the 1895 Annual Report had pointed out, the managers agreed "so far as practicable, to consolidate the purchasing of all supplies of raw materials for the various manufactories into one single buying agency, believing that the purchase of large quantities of goods can be made at more advantageous figures than the buying of small isolated lots."[14] The second new "general policy" was "to undertake to reduce the number of brands of goods manufactured, and to consolidate the manufacturing of the remaining brands in those factories which have demonstrated superior facilities for production or advantageous labor conditions. This course was for the purpose of utilizing the most efficient instruments of production and closing those that were inefficient and unprofitable." The third policy was to consolidate sales through the formation of a "Selling Department," which was to handle all goods made by the constituent companies in order to achieve "economy in the distribution expense." Selling was now to be handled by a central office in the New York City headquarters, with branch offices throughout the United States and Europe. Of the three great new departments, actually manufacturing was the slowest to be fully consolidated and centralized. Finally, the treasurer's office at headquarters began to obtain accurate data on profit and loss through the institution of uniform, centralized cost accounting.

Thus United States Rubber, National Biscuit, and the Distillers Securities Company soon came to have organizational structures paralleling those of Swift and American Tobacco. By the first decade of the twentieth century, the leading firms in many consumers' goods industries had become departmentalized and centralized. This was the organizational concomitant to vertical integration. Each major function, manufacturing, sales, purchasing, and finance, became managed by a single and separate department head, usually a vice president, who, assisted by a director

[12] The background for the creation of the United States Rubber Company can be found in Nancy P. Norton, "Industrial Pioneer: the Goodyear Metallic Rubber Shoe Company" (Ph.D. thesis, Radcliffe College, 1950), Constance McL. Green, *History of Naugatuck, Connecticut* (New Haven, 1948), pp. 126–131, 193–194, and Clark, *History of Manufactures,* Vol. II, pp. 479–481, Vol. III, pp. 235–237. The company's annual reports provide most of the information on its activities.

[13] *The Fifth Annual Report of the United States Rubber Company, March 31, 1897,* pp. 6–7.

[14] This and the following quotations are from the *Fourth Annual Report of the United States Rubber Company, May 25, 1896,* pp. 4–5, 7–8.

or a manager, had full authority and responsibility for the activities of his unit. These departmental chiefs, with the president, coordinated and evaluated the work of the different functional units, and made policy for the company as a whole. In coordinating, appraising, and policy-making, the president and the vice presidents in charge of departments came to rely more and more on the accounting and statistical information, usually provided by the finance department, on costs, output, purchases, and sales.

Changes in the Producers' Goods Industries

Bureaucracy and oligopoly came to the producers' goods industries somewhat later than to those making products for the mass market. Until the depression of the 1890's, most of the combinations and consolidations had been in the consumers' goods industries. After that, the major changes came in those industries selling to other businesses and industrialists. The reason for the time difference seems to be that the city took a little longer to become a major market for producers' goods. Throughout the 1880's, railroad construction and operation continued to take the larger share of the output of steel, copper, power machinery, explosives, and other heavy industries. Then in the 1890's, as railroad construction declined the rapidly growing American cities became the primary market. The insatiable demand for urban lighting, communication, heat, power, transportation, water, sewerage, and other services directly and indirectly took ever growing quantities of electric lighting apparatus, telephones, copper wire, newsprint, streetcars, coal, and iron, steel, copper, and lead piping, structures and fixtures; while the constantly expanding urban construction created new calls on the power machinery and explosives as well as the metals industries. Carnegie's decision in 1887 to shift the Homestead Works, the

nation's largest and most modern steel plant, from rails to structures, symbolized the coming change in the market.[15]

Also the new combinations and consolidations in the consumers' goods industries increased the demand for producers' products in the urban areas. Standard Oil, American Tobacco, Swift and other meat packers, McCormick's Harvesting Machinery and other farm implement firms, American Sugar, Singer Sewing Machine, and many other great consumer goods companies concentrated their production in or near major cities, particularly New York and Chicago.

The changes after 1897 differed from the earlier ones not only in types of industries in which they occurred but also in the way they were promoted and financed. Combinations and vertical integration in the consumer goods industries before 1897 had been almost all engineered and financed by the manufacturers themselves, so the stock control remained in the hands of the industrialists. After 1897, however, outside funds and often outside promoters, who were usually Wall Street financiers, played an increasingly significant role in industrial combination and consolidation. The change reflected a new attitude of investor and financier who controlled capital toward the value of industrial securities.[16] Before the depres-

[15] Clark, History of Manufactures, Vol. II, chap. 19.

[16] The story of the shift from rails to industrials as acceptable investments is told in Thomas R. Navin and Marian V. Sears, "The Rise of the Market for Industrial Securities, 1887–1902," Business History Review, Vol. XIX (June, 1955), pp. 105–138. Government securities were, of course, important in the years before 1850 and during and after the Civil War, but in the late 1870's and 1880's as in the 1850's, railroads dominated the American security exchanges. As Navin and Sears point out, some coal and mining firms were traded on the New York Exchange, but the only manufacturing securities, outside of those of the Pullman Company, were some textile stocks traded on the local Boston Exchange. The connections between the railroad expansion and the beginnings of modern Wall Street are described in detail in Chandler, Henry Varnum Poor, chap. 4.

sion of the 1890's investment and speculation had been overwhelmingly in railroad
stocks and bonds. The institutionalizing of
the American security market in Wall
Street had come, in fact, as a response
to the needs for financing the first great
railroad boom in the 1850's.

The railroads, however, had made a
poor showing financially in the middle
years of the 1890's when one-third of the
nation's trackage went through receivership and financial reorganization. The
dividend records of some of the new
large industrial corporations, on the other
hand, proved unexpectedly satisfactory.
Moreover, railroad construction was slowing, and the major financial and administrative reorganizations of the 1890's had
pretty well stabilized the industry. So
there was less demand for investment
bankers and brokers to market new issues
of railroad securities.

Industrials were obviously the coming
field, and by 1898 there was a rush in
Wall Street to get in on this new business.
The sudden availability of funds stimulated, and undoubtedly overstimulated, industrial combination. Many of the mergers
in the years after 1897 came more from
the desire of financiers for promotional
profits, and because combination had become the thing to do, and less from
the special needs and opportunities in the
several industries. Moreover, as the financiers and promoters began to provide
funds for mergers and expansion, they
began to acquire, for the first time, the
same type of control over industrial corporations that they had enjoyed in railroads since the 1850's.

The changes in the producers' goods
industries were essentially like those in
the consumer goods firms before the depression. Only after 1897 the changes
came more rapidly, partly because of Wall
Street pressures; and the differences that
did develop between the two types of industries reflected the basic differences
in the nature of their businesses. Like

the companies making consumer goods,
those manufacturing items for producers
set up nation-wide and often world-wide
marketing and distributing organizations,
consolidated production into a relatively
few large plants and fashioned purchasing
departments. Because they had fewer customers, their sales departments tended
to be smaller than those in firms selling
to the mass market. On the other hand,
they were more concerned with obtaining
control over the sources of their supply
than were most of the consumer goods
companies.

Here a distinction can be made between
the manufacturers who made semi-finished
products from raw materials taken from
the ground, and those who made finished
goods from semi-finished products. The
former, producing a uniform product for
a few large industrial customers, developed only small sales departments and
concentrated on obtaining control of raw
materials, and often of the means of
transporting such materials from mine to
market. The latter, selling a larger variety
of products and ones that often required
servicing and financing, had much larger
marketing and distributing organizations.
These makers of finished goods, except
for a brief period around 1900, rarely attempted to control their raw materials
or their semi-finished steel and other
metal supplies. They did, however, in the
years after 1900, begin to buy or set up
plans making parts and components that
went into the construction of their finished
products.

Except in steel, integration usually followed combination in the producers'
goods industries. And for both makers of
semi-finished and finished goods, integration became more of a defensive strategy
than it was in the consumers' goods industries processing agricultural products.
In the latter the manufacturers had an
assured supply of raw materials from the
output of the nation's millions of farms.
In the former, on the other hand, they had

to consider the threatening possibility of an outsider obtaining complete control of raw materials or supplies.

Integration and Combination in the Extractive Industries/

By the early twentieth century nearly all the companies making semi-finished product goods controlled the mining of their own raw materials. The industries in which they operated can, therefore, be considered as extractive. This was also true of two consumers' goods industries: oil and fertilizer. The experience of these two provides a good introduction to the motives for integration and the role it played in the coming of "big business" in steel, copper, paper, explosives and other businesses producing semi-finished goods.

In both the oil and fertilizer industries, control over raw materials came well after combination and consolidation of groups of small manufacturing firms. The Standard Oil Trust, after its formation in 1882, consolidated its manufacturing activities and then created a domestic marketing organization. Only in the late 1880's, when the new Indiana field began to be developed and the older Pennsylvania ones began to decline, did the Trust consider going into the production of crude oil. Both Allan Nevins in his biography of John D. Rockefeller and the Hidys in their history of Standard Oil agree that the need to be assured of a steady supply of crude oil was the major reason for the move into production.[17] Other reasons, the Hidys indicate, were a fear that the producers might combine and so control supplies, and the desire of the pipeline

subsidiaries to keep their facilities operating at full capacity. Although neither Nevins nor the Hidys suggest that the desire to obtain a more efficient flow of oil from the well to the distributor was a motive for this integration, both describe the committees and staff units that were formed at the central office at 26 Broadway to assure more effective coordination between production, refining, and marketing.

What little evidence there is suggests somewhat the same story in the fertilizer industry. Shortly after its organization in the mid-1890's, the Virginia-Carolina Chemical Company, a merger of many small southern fertilizer firms, began, apparently for the same defensive reasons, to purchase phosphate mines. Quickly its major competitor, the American Agricultural Chemical Company, a similar combination of small northeastern companies formed in 1893, responded by making its own purchases of mines. As the latter company explained in a later annual report: "The growth of the business, as well as the fact that available phosphate properties were being fast taken up, indicated that it was the part of wisdom to make additional provision for the future, and accordingly . . . available phosphate properties were purchased, and the necessary plants were erected and equipped, so the company now has in hand a supply of phosphate rock which will satisfy its growing demand for 60 years and upwards."[18] However, neither of these companies appeared to have set up organizational devices to guide the flow of materials from mine to plant to market; nor did the

[17] Ralph W. Hidy and Muriel E. Hidy, *Pioneering in Big Business, 1882–1911* (New York, 1955), pp. 176–188. Allan Nevins, *Study in Power, John D. Rockefeller, Industrialist and Philanthropist* (New York, 1953), Vol. II, pp. 1–3. Nevins adds that another reason for the move into production was "partly to limit the number of active wells and reduce the overproduction of crude oil," Vol. II, p. 2, but he gives no documentation for this statement.

[18] *Annual Report of the American Agricultural Chemical Company, August 14, 1907*; also the same company's *Annual Report* dated August 25, 1902. In addition to the annual reports of the two companies, Clark, *History of Manufactures*, Vol. III, pp. 289–291, provides information. There is a brief summary of the story of the International Agricultural Corporation in Williams Haynes, *American Chemical Industry—A History* (New York, 1945), Vol. III, p. 173.

managers of a third large integrated fertilizer company, the International Agricultural Corporation, formed in 1909.

Defensive motives were certainly significant in the changes in the steel industry. Here the story can be most briefly described by focusing on the history of the industry's leader, the Carnegie Steel Company.[19] That company's chairman, Henry C. Frick, had in the early 1890's consolidated and rationalized the several Carnegie manufacturing properties in and about Pittsburgh into an integrated whole. At the same time, he systematized and departmentalized its purchasing, engineering, and marketing activities. The fashioning of a sales department became more necessary since the shift from rails to structures had enlarged the number of the company's customers.

Then in 1896 the Carnegie company made a massive purchase of ore lands when it joined with Henry W. Oliver to buy out the Rockefeller holdings in the Mesabi Range. As Allan Nevins points out, the depression of the 1890's had worked a rapid transformation in the recently discovered Mesabi region.[20] By 1896, the ore fields had become dominated by three great interests: the Oliver Mining Company, the Minnesota Mining Company, and Rockefeller's Consolidated Iron Mines. A fourth, James J. Hill's Great Northern Railroad, was just entering the field. Frick's purchases, therefore, gave the Carnegie company an assured supply of cheap ore, as well as providing it with a fleet of ore ships. Next, Frick and Carnegie bought and rebuilt a railroad from Lake Erie to Pittsburgh to carry the new supplies to the mills.

Yet the steel company's managers did little to coordinate systematically the mining, shipping, and manufacturing units

in their industrial empire. These activities did not become departments controlled from one central office but remained completely separate companies under independent managements, whose contact with one another was through negotiated contracts. This was the same sort of relation that existed between the Frick Coke Company and Carnegie Steel from the time Frick had joined Carnegie in 1889. If the Carnegie company's strategy had been to provide a more effective flow of materials as well as to assure itself of not being caught without a supply of ore and the means to transport it, then Frick and Carnegie would have created some sort of central coordinating office.

The steel industry responded quickly to the Carnegie purchases.[21] In 1898, Chicago's Illinois Steel Company, with capital supplied by J. P. Morgan & Company, joined the Lorain Steel Company (with plants on Lake Erie and in Johnstown, Pennsylvania) to purchase the Minnesota Mining Company, a fleet of ore boats, and railroads in the Mesabi and Chicago areas. Again, little attempt was made to coordinate mining and shipping with manufacturing and marketing. In the same year, many iron and steel firms in Ohio and Pennsylvania merged to form the Republic and National Steel Companies. Shortly thereafter, a similar combination

[19] The information on the Carnegie Steel Company is taken from Burton J. Hendrick, The Life of Andrew Carnegie, 2 vols. (New York, 1932), George Harvey, Henry Clay Frick, the Man (New York, 1928), James H. Bridge, The Inside Story of the Carnegie Steel Company (New York, 1903).
[20] Nevins, Rockefeller, Vol. II, p. 252.

[21] The experience of the other steel firms comes primarily from their annual reports and from prospectuses and other reports in the Corporation Records Division of Baker Library. A company publication, J & L—The Growth of an American Business (Pittsburgh, 1953), has some additional information on that company. Also, books listed in footnote 26 on the United States Steel Corporation have something on these companies. Two other steel companies listed in Table I made major changes somewhat before and after the period immediately following 1898. One, the Colorado Fuel & Iron Co., established in 1892, quickly became an integrated steel company in the Colorado area. The Bethlehem Steel Corporation was formed in 1904 when Charles F. Schwab, formerly of the Carnegie company and the United States Steel Corporation, reorganized the finances, corporate structure, and administrative organization of the bankrupt United States Shipbuilding Company.

in the Sault Sainte Marie area became the Consolidated Lake Superior Company. These three new mergers began at once to set up their marketing organizations and to obtain control by lease and purchase of raw materials and transportation facilities. In 1900, several small firms making high-grade steel did much the same thing by the formation of the Crucible Steel Company of America. In these same years, the larger, established steel companies, like Lackawanna, Cambria, and Jones & Laughlin obtained control of more supplies of ore, coke, and limestone and simultaneously reorganized their manufacturing and marketing organizations. Like Carnegie and Federal, they at first made little effort to bring their mining and coke operations under the direct control of the central office.

In copper, defensive motives for integration appear to have been somewhat less significant. In the 1890's, mining, smelting and refining were combined on a large scale. During the 'eighties the railroad had opened up many western mining areas, particularly in Montana and Arizona; a little later the new electrical and telephone businesses greatly increased the demand for copper. Mining firms like Anaconda, Calumet & Hecla, and Phelps Dodge moved into smelting and refining, while the Guggenheims' Philadelphia Smelting & Refining Company began to buy mining properties.[22] In the copper industry, the high cost of ore shipment meant that smelting and—after the introduction of the electrolytic process in the early 1890's—even refining could be done more cheaply close to the mines. Of the large copper firms, only Calumet & Hecla and the Guggenheims set up refineries in the East before 1898, and both made use of direct water transportation.

[22] Information on the mining companies came from their annual reports and from Isaac P. Marcosson's two books, *Magic Metal—the Story of the American Smelting and Refining Company* (New York, 1949), and *Anaconda* (New York, 1957); also Clark, *History of Manufactures,* Vol. II, pp. 368–369.

After 1898, several large mergers occurred in the nonferrous metals industries. Nearly all were initially promoted by eastern financiers. Of these, the most important were Amalgamated Copper, engineered by H. H. Rogers of Standard Oil and Marcus Daly of Anaconda, the American Smelting and Refining Company which the Guggenheims came to control, and United Copper promoted by F. Augustus Heinze. United Copper remained little more than a holding company. Amalgamated set up a subsidiary to operate a large refinery at Perth Amboy and another, the United Metals Selling Company, with headquarters in New York City, to market the products of its mining and processing subsidiaries. The holding company's central offices in New York remained small and apparently did comparatively little to coordinate the activities of its several operating companies. The Guggenheims formed a much tighter organization with direct headquarters control of the company's mining, shipping, smelting and marketing departments. On the whole, there appears to have been somewhat closer coordination between mining and processing in the large copper than in the major steel companies.

Lowering of costs through more effective coordination appears to have been a major motive for consolidation and combination in three other businesses whose raw materials came from the ground: explosives, paper, and coal.[23] The

[23] The story of the leading explosives, paper, salt and coal companies comes from annual reports and also from Charles E. Beachley, *History of the Consolidation Coal Company, 1864–1934* (New York, 1934), George H. Love, *An Exciting Century in Coal* (New York, 1955), the company-written, *The International Paper Company, 1898–1948* (n.p., 1948), William S. Dutton, *DuPont—One Hundred and Forty Years* (New York, 1940), and *U.S. v. E. I. DuPont de Nemours & Company et al. in Circuit Court of the United States for the District of Delaware, #280 in Equity (1909), Defendants' Record Testimony,* Vol. I, and for the paper industry, Clark, *History of Manufactures,* Vol. III, pp. 245–252. The American Writing Paper Company, though less successful, had many parallels to International Paper.

mergers that created the Pittsburgh Coal Company in 1899 and greatly enlarged the Consolidation Coal Company in 1903 were followed by a reorganization and consolidation of mining properties and then by the creation of large marketing departments which operated throughout most of the country. The merger of close to 30 paper companies, forming the International Paper Company in 1899, was followed first by consolidation and reorganization of the manufacturing plants, next by the formation of a national marketing organization with headquarters in New York City, and then by the purchase of large tracts of timber in Maine and Canada. These three activities were departmentalized under vice presidents and controlled from the New York office. In all these cases, the central office was responsible for the flow of materials from mine or forest to the customer or retailer.

The explosive industries underwent a comparable sweeping change in 1902 and 1903. Since the 1870's, price and production schedules had been decided by the industry's Gunpowder Trade Association, and almost from its beginning, that Association had been controlled by one firm, the E. I. DuPont de Nemours & Company. However, the member concerns had retained their own corporate identities and managements. In 1902, the DuPonts bought out a large number of these independent companies through exchanges of stock, and then consolidated them into a single centralized organization. In the process, plants were shut down, others enlarged, and new ones built. A nation-wide selling organization was created, and centralized accounting, purchasing, engineering and traffic departments formed. Once the new organization was completed, then the company's executives obtained control of their raw materials through the purchase of nitrate mines and deposits in Chile.

Except possibly in paper, the control of price and production does not appear to have been a major motive for the initial combinations in the extractive industries making producers' goods. In steel before 1901, and in nonferrous metals and coal, there were several combinations, but none acquired as much as 20 percent of the market. Nor is there any evidence that the creators of the different mergers, while they were forming their organizations, were arranging with one another to set over-all price and production schedules. In explosives, control of competition could not have been a significant reason for the 1902 changes since the DuPont company had enjoyed such control since the 1870's. In coal and explosives, and possibly in copper, the major motive for combination, consolidation, and the integration of supply with the manufacturing and marketing processes seems to have been an expectation of lowered costs through the creation of a national distributing organization, the consolidation of manufacturing activities, and the effective coordination of the different industrial processes by one central office. In steel and possibly copper, the desire for an assured supply of raw materials appears to have been more significant in encouraging combination and integration.

Changes and Integration in the Finished Producers' Goods Industries/ Control of price and production was, on the other hand, much more of an obvious motive for combination and resulting consolidation in the industries manufacturing finished products or machinery from the semi-finished materials produced by the extractive firms. Concern over supply, however, was also a cause for change, for after 1898 the users of steel, copper, coal, and other semi-finished materials felt threatened by the growing number of combinations among their suppliers. In any case, between 1898 and 1900 there was a wave of mergers in these industries, largely Wall Street financed, which led to the formation of American Tin Plate, American Wire & Steel, American Steel Hoop, National

Tube, American Bridge, American Sheet Metal, Shelby Steel Tube, American Can, National Enameling & Stamping Company and a number of other combinations among steel-fabricating firms.[24] At the same time, there were many amalgamations in the power machinery and implement businesses, such as American Car & Foundry, American Locomotive, Allis-Chalmers, International Steam Pump, and International Harvester. The largest combination among the copper users, the American Brass Company, came a little later, in 1903, after the Guggenheims, Rogers, and Heinze had completed the major copper mergers.

Nearly all these combinations quickly consolidated their constituent companies into a single operating organization. Manufacturing facilities were unified and systematized, over-all accounting procedures instituted, and national and often worldwide distributing organizations formed. Many set up central traffic and purchasing departments; some even began to assure themselves control over supply by building up their own rolling mills and blast furnaces. As American Wire & Steel and National Tube began to make their own steel, they cancelled contracts with Carnegie and other semi-finished steel producers. This development, in turn, led Carnegie to develop plans for fabricating his own finished products.[25]

The resulting threat of overcapacity and price-cutting led to the formation of the United States Steel Corporation.[26] This giant merger, which included Carnegie, Federal and National Steel, and the first six of the fabricating companies listed above, continued on as a combination. Although the activities of the various subsidiaries were re-formed and redefined, there was no consolidation. United States Steel remained a holding company only, and the central office at 72 Broadway did comparatively little to coordinate the operations of its many subsidiary companies.

After 1901, the fabricators and the machinery manufacturers made little attempt to produce their own steel or copper. Nor did the makers of semi-finished products try, for some years to come, to do their own fabricating. Possibly the metal users realized that even with the formation of United States Steel they were fairly certain of alternative sources of supply. Also they may have found that once they had combined they had enough bargaining power to assure themselves of a supply of steel and other materials more cheaply than they could make it themselves.

While such firms no longer sought to control their basic materials, many, particularly the machinery makers like General Electric, Westinghouse, American Car & Foundry, International Harvester and, a little later, General Motors, began to purchase or set up subsidiaries or departments to make parts and components.[27] Here again the motive was essentially defensive. Since much of their manufacturing had now become mainly assembling, they wanted to be sure to have a supply of parts available at all times. The lack of a vital part could temporarily shut down a plant. However, they expected to take only a portion of the output; a major share was sold to outsiders. One outstanding exception to this pattern was Henry Ford. He came to control his raw materials as well as his parts and com-

---

[24] The best brief summary of these mergers and the formation of the United States Steel Corporation is in Eliot Jones, *The Trust Problem in the United States* (New York, 1924), pp. 189–200. The companies' annual reports and prospectuses provide additional material.

[25] Hendrick, *Carnegie*, Vol. II, pp. 116–119.

[26] The beginnings and the operation of the United States Steel Corporation are outlined in Abraham Berglund, *The United States Steel Corporation: A Study of Growth and Combination in the Iron and Steel Industry* (New York, 1907), Arundel Cotter, *The Authentic History of the United States Steel Corporation* (New York, 1916), Ida M. Tarbell, *The Life of Elbert H. Gary, the Story of Steel* (New York, 1925).

[27] This generalization is based on the annual reports of the several companies.

ponents, and rarely sold such parts to outside companies. But Ford's insistence on having a completely integrated organization from mine to market, concentrated largely in one huge plant, proved to be one of the most costly mistakes in American business history.

Control of parts and accessory units led to a diversification of the types of products these manufacturing companies made and sold. Such diversification brought, over time, important changes in business organization. Even more significant for stimulating product diversification was the new "full line" strategy adopted by a number of these recently consolidated concerns. Such a policy, initiated largely to help assure the maximum use of the new departments, encouraged technological as well as organizational change.

Pioneers in developing "full lines" in the producers' goods industries were the two great electrical companies: General Electric and Westinghouse. Unlike almost any other of the leading American industrial companies in 1900, these two had begun as research and development rather than manufacturing organizations. Because of their origins, they had the skilled personnel and the necessary equipment to move, in the mid-1890's, from making lighting equipment alone to manufacturing many lines of electric traction and power machinery products.[28] Allis-Chalmers, International Steam Pump, and American Locomotive began, shortly after their formation and subsequent consolidations, to develop new lines using electric and gasoline engines.[29] International

[28] As is well described in Harold C. Passer, The Electrical Manufacturers (Cambridge, 1953).
[29] The development of new lines by Allis-Chalmers, International Steam Pump, and American Locomotive is mentioned in their annual reports in the first decade of the twentieth century. International Harvester's similar "full line" policies are described in Cyrus McCormick, The Century of the Reaper (New York, 1931), chaps. 6–9, and United States Bureau of Corporations, The International Harvester Co., March 3, 1913 (Washington, 1913), especially pp. 156–158.

Harvester, building up a number of farm implement lines, also started to experiment with the use of the gasoline engine for machinery on the farm. In this same first decade of the twentieth century, rubber, explosive, and chemical companies began to turn to industrial chemistry in their search to develop broader lines of products.

Continuing diversification came, however, largely in industries where science, particularly chemistry and physics, could be most easily applied. And it was in these industries, and in those which were directly affected by the coming of two new sources of power, electricity and the internal combustion engine, that the major innovations in American industry came after 1900. The chemical, automotive, power machinery, rubber, and petroleum industries led the way to the development of new processes and products, new ways of internal organization and new techniques of external competition as the new century unfolded. The metals industries and those processing agricultural goods have, on the other hand, changed relatively little since the beginning of the century. In these industries, the same firms make much the same products, use much the same processes, and compete in much the same manner in the 1950's as they did in the 1900's. For them the greatest period of change came in the last decade of the nineteenth century.

Conclusion: The Basic Innovations

The middle of the first decade of the new century might be said to mark the end of an era. By 1903, the great merger movement was almost over, and by then the metals industries and those processing agricultural products had developed patterns of internal organization and external competition which were to remain. In those years, too, leading chemical, electrical, rubber, power machinery and implement companies had initiated their "full line" policy, and had instituted the earliest formal research and development departments created in this country. In this decade also, electricity was becoming for the first time a significant source of industrial power, and the automobile was just beginning to revolutionize American transportation. From 1903 on, the new generators of power and the new technologies appear to have become the dominant stimuli to innovation in American industry, and such innovations were primarily those which created new products and processes. Changes in organizational methods and marketing techniques were largely responses to technological advances.

This seems much less true of the changes during the 20 to 25 years before 1903. In that period, the basic innovations were more in the creation of new forms of organization and new ways of marketing. The great modern corporation, carrying on the major industrial processes, namely, purchasing, and often production of materials and parts, manufacturing, marketing, and finance—all within the same organizational structure—had its beginnings in that period. Such organizations hardly existed, outside of the railroads, before the 1880's. By 1900 they had become the basic business unit in American industry.

Each of these major processes became managed by a corporate department, and all were coordinated and supervised from a central office. Of the departments, marketing was the most significant. The creation of nation-wide distributing and selling organizations was the initial step in the growth of many large consumer goods companies. Mergers in both the consumer and producer goods industries were almost always followed by the formation of a centralized sales department.

The consolidation of plants under a single manufacturing department usually accompanied or followed the formation of a national marketing organization. The creation of such a manufacturing depart-

ment normally meant the concentration of production in fewer and larger plants, and such consolidation probably lowered unit costs and increased output per worker. The creation of such a department in turn led to the setting up of central traffic, purchasing, and often engineering organizations. Large-scale buying, more rational routing of raw materials and finished products, more systematic plant lay-out, and plant location in relation to materials and markets probably lowered costs still further. Certainly the creators of these organizations believed that it did. In the extractive and machinery industries integration went one step further. Here the motives for controlling raw materials or parts and components were defensive as well as designed to cut costs through providing a more efficient flow of materials from mine to market.

These great national industrial organizations required a large market to provide the volume necessary to support the increased overhead costs. Also, to be profitable, they needed careful coordination between the different functional departments. This coordination required a steady flow of accurate data on costs, sales, and on all purchasing, manufacturing, and marketing activities. As a result, the comptroller's office became an increasingly important department. In fact, one of the first moves after a combination by merger or purchase was to institute more effective and detailed accounting procedures. Also, the leading entrepreneurs of the period, men like Rockefeller, Carnegie, Swift, Duke, Preston, Clark, and the DuPonts, had to become, as had the railroad executives of an earlier generation, experts in reading and interpreting business statistics.

Consolidation and departmentalization meant that the leading industrial corporations became operating rather than holding companies, in the sense that the officers and managers of the companies were directly concerned with operating activities. In fact, of the 50 companies with the largest assets in 1909, only United States Steel, Amalgamated Copper, and one or two other copper companies remained purely holding companies. In most others, the central office included the heads of the major functional departments, usually the president, vice presidents, and sometimes a chairman of the board and one or two representatives of financial interests. These men made major policy and administrative decisions and evaluated the performance of the departments and the corporation as a whole. In the extractive industries a few companies, like Standard Oil (N.J.) and some of the metals companies, were partly holding and partly operating companies. At Standard Oil nearly all important decisions were made in the central headquarters, at 26 Broadway, which housed not only the presidents of the subsidiaries but the powerful policy formulating and coordinating committees.[30] But in some of the metals companies, the subsidiaries producing and transporting raw materials retained a large degree of autonomy.

The coming of the large vertically integrated, centralized, functionally departmentalized industrial organization altered the internal and external situations in which and about which business decisions were made. Information about markets, supplies, and operating performance as well as suggestions for action often had to come up through the several levels of the departmental hierarchies, while decisions and suggestions based on this data had to be transmitted down the same ladder for implementation. Executives on each level became increasingly specialists in one function—in sales, production, purchasing, or finance—and most remained in one department and so handled one function only for the major part of their business careers. Only he who climbed to the very top of the departmental ladder

had a chance to see his own company as a single operating unit. Where a company's markets, sources of raw materials, and manufacturing processes remained relatively stable, as was true in the metals industries and in those processing agricultural goods, the nature of the business executive's work became increasingly routine and administrative.

When the internal situation had become bureaucratic, the external one tended to be oligopolistic. Vertical integration by one manufacturer forced others to follow. Thus, in a very short time, many American industries became dominated by a few large firms, with the smaller ones handling local and more specialized aspects of the business. Occasionally industries like oil, tobacco, and sugar came to be controlled by one company, but in most cases legal action by the federal government in the years after 1900 turned monopolistic industries into oligopolistic ones.

Costs, rather than interfirm competition, began to determine prices. With better information on costs, supplies, and market conditions, the companies were able to determine price quite accurately on the basis of the desired return on investment. The managers of the different major companies had little to gain by cutting prices below an acceptable profit margin. On the other hand, if one firm set its prices excessively high, the other firms could increase their share of the market by selling at a lower price and still maintain a profit. They would, however, rarely cut to the point where this margin was eliminated. As a result, after 1900, price leadership, price umbrellas, and other evidences of oligopolistic competition became common in many American industries. To increase their share of the market and to improve their profit position, the large corporations therefore concerned themselves less with price and concentrated more on obtaining new customers by advertising, brand names, and product differentiations; on

---

[30] Hidys, *Pioneering in Big Business*, chap. 3 and pp. 323–388.

cutting costs through further improvement and integration of the manufacturing, marketing, and buying processes; and on developing more diversified lines of products.

The coming of the large vertically integrated corporation changed more than just the practices of American industrialists and their industries. The effect on the merchant, particularly the wholesaler, and on the financier, especially the investment banker, has been suggested here. The relation between the growth of these great industrial units and the rise of labor unions has often been pointed out. Certainly the regulation of the large corporation became one of the major political issues of these years, and the devices created to carry out such a regulation were significant innovations in American constitutional, legal, and political institutions. But an examination of such effects is beyond the scope of this paper.

Reasons for the Basic Innovations/
One question remains to be reviewed. Why did the vertically integrated corporation come when it did, and in the way it did? The creation by nearly all the large firms of nation-wide selling and distributing organizations indicates the importance of the national market. It was necessary that the market be an increasingly urban one. The city took the largest share of the goods manufactured by the processors of agricultural products. The city, too, with its demands for construction materials, lighting, heating and many other facilities, provided the major market for the metals and other producers' goods industries after railroad construction slowed. Without the rapidly growing urban market there would have been little need and little opportunity for the coming of big business in American industry. And such a market could hardly have existed before the completion of a nation-wide railroad network.

What other reasons might there have been for the swift growth of the great industrial corporation? What about foreign markets? In some industries, particularly oil, the overseas trade may have been an important factor. However, in most businesses the domestic customers took the lion's share of the output, and in nearly all of them the move abroad appears to have come after the creation of the large corporation, and after such corporations had fashioned their domestic marketing organization.

What about the investor looking for profitable investments, and the promoter seeking new promotions? Financiers and promoters certainly had an impact on the changes after 1897, but again they seem primarily to have taken advantage of what had already proved successful. The industrialists themselves, rather than the financiers, initiated most of the major changes in business organization. Availability of capital and cooperation with the financier figured much less prominently in these industrial combinations and consolidations than had been the case with the earlier construction of the railroads and with the financing of the Civil War.

What about technological changes? Actually, except for electricity, the major innovations in the metals industries seem to have come before or after the years under study here. Most of the technological improvements in the agricultural processing industries appear to have been made to meet the demands of the new urban market. The great technological innovations that accompanied the development of electricity, the internal combustion engine, and industrial chemistry did have their beginning in these years, and were, indeed, to have a fundamental impact on the American business economy. Yet this impact was not to be really felt until after 1900.

What about entrepreneurial talent? Certainly the best-known entrepreneurs of this period were those who helped to create the large industrial corporation. If, as

Table I/ The Fifty Largest Industrials (Numbers Indicate Relative Size According to 1909 Assets)

CONSUMERS' GOODS COMPANIES

Agricultural Processing	Extractive	Manufacturing
3. Am. Tobacco	2. Standard Oil	4. Int'l. Harvester
8. Armour & Co.	26. Va.-Carolina Chem.	10. U.S. Rubber
9. American Sugar	35. Am. Agri. Chem.	12. Singer Mfg. Co.
13. Swift & Co.		
30. Nat'l. Biscuit		
33. Distillers' Securities		
50. United Fruit		

PRODUCERS' GOODS COMPANIES

Agricultural Processing	Extractive	Manufacturing
6. Central Leather	1. U.S. Steel	7. Pullman
18. Corn Products Co.	5. Amalgamated	15. Gen. Electric
21. Am. Woolens	(Anaconda) Copper	16. Am. Car &
	11. Am. Smelting & Refining	Foundry
	14. Pittsburgh Coal	19. Am. Can
	17. Colo. Fuel & Iron	22. Westinghouse
	20. Lackawanna	24. DuPont
	23. Consolidation Coal	29. Am. Locomotive
	25. Republic Steel	36. Allis-Chalmers
	27. Int'l. Paper	44. Int. Steam Pump
	28. Bethlehem Steel	46. Western Electric
	31. Cambria Steel	
	33. Associated Oil	
	34. Calumet & Hecla	
	37. Crucible Steel	
	38. Lake Superior Corp.	
	39. U.S. Smelting & Ref.	
	40. United Copper	
	41. National Lead	
	42. Phelps Dodge	
	43. Lehigh Coal	
	45. Jones & Laughlin	
	48. Am. Writing Paper	
	49. Copper Range	

Joseph A. Schumpeter suggests, "The defining characteristic [of the entrepreneur and his function] is simply the doing of new things, and doing things that are already done, in a new way (innovation)," Rockefeller, Carnegie, Frick, Swift, Duke, McCormick, the DuPonts, the Guggenheims, Coffin of General Electric, Preston of United Fruit, and Clark of Singer Sewing Machine were all major innovators of their time.[31]

And their innovations were not in technology, but rather in organization and in

[31] Joseph A. Schumpeter, "The Creative Response in Economic History," *Journal of Economic History*, Vol. VII (May, 1947), p. 151, and also his *Theory of Economic Development*, trans. Redvers Opie (Cambridge, 1934), pp. 74–94.

marketing. "Doing a new thing," is, to Schumpeter a "creative response" to a new situation, and the situation to which these innovators responded appears to have been the rise of the national urban market.

There must be an emphasis here on the words "seem" and "appear." The framework used is a preliminary one and the data itself, based on readily available printed material rather than on business records, are hardly as detailed or accurate as could be desired. More data, more precise and explicit questions, and other types and ranges of questions will modify the generalizations suggested here. For the moment, however, I would like to suggest, if only to encourage the raising of questions and the further compilation and analysis of data, that *the* major innovation in the American economy between the 1880's and the turn of the century was the creation of the great corporations in American industry. This innovation, as I have tried to show, was a response to the growth of a national and increasingly urban market that was created by the building of a national railroad network— the dynamic force in the economy in the quarter century before 1880. After 1900 the newly modified methods of interfirm and intrafirm administration remained relatively unchanged (as did the location of major markets and sources of raw materials) except in those industries directly affected by new sources of power and the systematic application of science to industry. In the twentieth century electricity, the internal combustion engine, and systematic, institutionalized research and development took the place of the national urban market as the dynamic factor in the American industrial economy.[32]

[32] This point has only been considered briefly here, but has been developed at some length in my "Development, Diversification and Decentralization," in *Postwar Economic Trends*, ed. R. E. Freeman (New York, 1960).

Monopolistic Competition

■ For many decades students of business and economics assumed that an industry dominated by two or three firms would have very little price and quality competition. Pricing and the introduction of innovation, that is, would be much the same as in the case of a monopoly. Harold Passer, a Harvard-trained industrial economist, shows in the following discussion of the electrical manufacturing industry that rapid technological change, usually present in a young industry, may, in spite of duopoly, produce vigorous competition in both price and quality of the products. Passer's demonstration is modified, however, by his finding that new firms attempting to break into the dominated market generally do the innovating and upset the existing situation. Passer also provides an excellent description of the way in which an entirely new technology—in this case, electricity—finds its way into the commercial market.

As with the history of other general business topics, there has been little writing on that of monopolistic competition. A discussion of the theory in relation to historical evidence can be found, however, on pp. 27–50 of *The Tasks of Economic History*, a supplement to *The Journal of Economic History*, December, 1943.

Harold Passer
The Electrical Manufacturers*

It is now appropriate to summarize this study of the electrical manufacturing industry, stressing the general concepts, tendencies, and trends which run through it all. In addition, a few pages are devoted to suggestions which may be of use in the formulation of the public policies concerning industrial markets. It may seem presumptuous to advance the viewpoint that public policy in 1953 can in any way profit from an analysis of industrial experience in the several decades prior to 1900. Nevertheless, on the assumption that there are repetitive patterns in industrial development and that good public policy must take account of long-run as well as short-run objectives, it is hoped that a study in economic history of this kind will have relevance to modern economic problems.

Competition

Competition in the electrical manufacturing industry during the period 1875–1900 can be summarized by listing in table form the principal factors which determined the nature of that competition. For analytical purposes, the industry can be thought of as composed of two segments: the equipment producers and the lighting-element producers. It has been shown that the competition which existed in arc carbons and incandescent lamps differed appreciably from competition in the heavy-equipment items such as dynamos and motors. Competition in the two markets was interrelated, of course, and the distinction between the two segments of the

* Reprinted by permission of the publishers from Harold Passer, *The Electrical Manufacturers, 1875–1900: A Study in Competition, Entrepreneurship, Technical Change, and Economic Growth.* Cambridge, Mass.: Harvard University Press, Copyright, 1953, by the President and Fellows of Harvard College, pp. 349–365.

industry should not be overemphasized. Some of the firms which produced lighting elements also produced equipment. Another tie between the two markets was provided by the customers, who were present in both markets. Thus on the supply side and on the demand side, the markets were interconnected. Nevertheless, it is convenient to treat the segments of the industry and the corresponding markets separately and then to discuss the consequences of the interrelationships.

Table 1 lists the principal determinants of competition in the electrical manufacturing industry. It will be recalled that the competitive patterns in arc carbons and incandescent lamps were similar. In each case, the product was not durable, and therefore regular purchases by the lighting companies were necessary. The fact that the product was a capital good meant that there was an emphasis on cost. In addition, the product was homogeneous, or nearly so, relatively simple to make, and not subject to rapid technical change. The carbons and lamps could be produced, in the early years at least, without expensive or complicated equipment. The necessary raw materials were readily available. Patents were not significant in either the product or the manufacturing process. In these conditions—a standardized product sold mainly to business firms, relatively free entry, many buyers, and more than fifteen sellers—the market closely approached the economist's concept of pure competition. The competition was almost entirely in prices, and these were driven down to cost by the additional supply from new firms. But these freely competitive conditions did not prevail for long. The years 1888 marked the end of pure competition in arc carbons, and 1896 saw the termination of pure competition in incandescent lamps.

Table 1/ Determinants of Competition in the Electrical Manufacturing Industry

	Heavy Equipment (Generators, Motors, etc.)	Lighting Elements (Carbons, Incandescent Lamps)
Nature of the product	Durable, heterogeneous capital good; complex; many technical changes	Nondurable, nearly homogeneous capital good;[a] simple; few technical changes
Number of producers	Few	Many
Entry of new firms	Difficult	Easy
Patents	Very important in a.c. power and electric railways	Not important in arc carbons; important in incandescent lamps after 1892

This table follows Professor E. S. Mason's classification of the objective elements which help to explain business practices in an industrial market.
[a] Labeling incandescent lamps as a capital good is justified by the fact that prior to 1900 it was standard practice for central stations to furnish the lamps as well as the current and to make one all-inclusive charge for light. The lamps, like the generators, were a capital good used to produce the consumer good, light.

Similar influences were present in both cases. The concentration in production of the equipment which provided the current for lighting elements was one factor. The large electrical manufacturing firms, which produced arc carbons and incandescent lamps as well as equipment, commonly required that the purchasers of their equipment also buy carbons and lamps from them. After most of the equipment was made by a few firms, the independent manufacturers of carbons and lamps had difficulty finding a market. Another influence was the increased mechanization in the production of lighting elements. The machines and processes, which were often patented, required a greater capital investment than the previous production techniques. Patents on arc carbons were never of importance, but in incandescent lamps, patents served as the framework for the price-output stabilization agreement of 1896 and 1897. In both arc carbons and incandescent lamps, the transition from competition to oligopoly was spurred by the experience of the producers under severe price competition. The low prices and chaotic conditions of 1886 and 1887 in arc carbons and of 1894 and 1895 in incandescent lamps

"taught" the firms that some way must be found to stabilize the industry.

It is difficult to say, in retrospect, whether the public interest was better served by competition or stabilized oligopoly. In favor of competition, it may be said that the rapid increase in supply and the lowering of prices stimulated the demand for the lighting elements by reducing the price of electric lighting and encouraging its substitution for other forms of artificial illumination. In favor of the stabilized oligopoly is the fact that the quality of the product was somewhat higher than before. The severe price competition tended to deteriorate the product. In regard to prices, the effect of the stabilization was less than one might expect. Prices were increased moderately at first, but later continued to fall in accordance with the previous long-term trend. Several reasons can be suggested for this price behavior. One is the identity of interest between the equipment manufacturers, who controlled a large proportion of the arc-carbon and incandescent-lamp production, and the lighting companies. The market for equipment depended upon the profitable operation of the central stations. The existing stations would not expand nor would new lighting companies be formed unless profit prospects were good. The equipment makers were therefore quite willing to supply lighting elements at low prices. A second factor was the influence of potential competition. If prices remained low and profit margins small, the production economies of large-scale operations and the use of efficient production processes, which were usually patented, kept new firms out of the industry. If high prices had been set, the entry of new firms would have been encouraged because the use of small-scale, obsolete manufacturing methods would have been profitable.

Competition in electrical equipment was considerably different from competition in the lighting elements. The product was durable, complex, and heterogeneous. As a durable capital good, it was sold to businessmen who were interested in the cost of light production, not the first cost of the equipment. Price was thus relegated to a position of secondary importance. What counted was the quality of the equipment. This included its life, operating costs, maintenance costs, and general reliability. Rapid technical changes improved equipment quality and decreased further the significance of price.

Patents also influenced competitive conditions. They were a prime cause of the numerous consolidations and mergers which finally resulted in only two full-line producers. Furthermore, patents permitted competition to take place on a system basis instead of with reference to single items of equipment. Manufacturers could refuse to allow the use of particular patented apparatus except as a part of a complete lighting or power system. While this kind of competition was intended to take advantage of certain key patents, it should be noted that the economical and reliable operation of a number of interconnected items of equipment was also involved. The seller could contend, with considerable justification, that he was merely protecting the reputation of his products in requiring that only items of his manufacture be combined into one system.

Considerable emphasis has been given in this study to product competition. Three cases—railway motors, induction motors, and polyphase generators—were examined in detail. The product competition was seen to exist even in the presence of duopoly. Moreover, a strenuous price competition was fostered. It is possible that these results also hold in other industries where the product is a durable good which is highly complicated and heterogeneous. Two important qualifications to this conclusion are necessary, however, because of the evidence upon which it is based. The data on competition in all three types of equipment cover the 1893–1896 period, which was one of depressed conditions in the electrical manufacturing industry. Even with a homogeneous product, a strenuous and perhaps cutthroat price competition might have occurred because of the desperate efforts to maintain sales. The second qualification is that the products of the industry were technologically immature. The product competition which took place may have been as vigorous and unrestrained as it was because the art of manufacturing electrical equipment was so young. It is legitimate to ask whether such competition continued after designs had become standardized. If technological change proceeded at a slower pace in later years, the traditional duopoly case, with a fairly homogeneous product and a recognition of mutual dependence, may have resulted. Product competition based on a static technology, in which product choices are made from a perfectly well-known and unchanging set of alternatives, may have an effect on duopolistic behavior different from that based on a rapidly advancing technology.

It is probable that continuous and unpredictable change in the technology of a product and its manufacture introduces the element of uncertainty which accounts for the competitive rather than the monopolistic behavior of the oligopolists. In his treatment of oligopoly with product differentiation, Professor E. H. Chamberlin recognizes that where the product is not homogeneous, additional uncertainty concerning the effects of a rival's actions is introduced because of "a new unknown— the extent of buyers' preferences for his own product over others, expressed by the shape of the demand curves for the individual products."[1]

To this uncertainty which exists where the products are differentiated but fixed may be added the uncertainty due to the fact that one firm does not know which of various possible "products" will be chosen by its rival. If the products are selected from rapidly changing alternatives rather than from a fixed set of well-known ones, still more uncertainty is introduced. And when the product is a durable, highly complex capital good, there are also all the uncertainties relating to the economical and reliable performance of the equipment.

What is the significance of uncertainty for a theory of oligopolistic behavior? The classical theory of oligopoly, which considered only a homogeneous product, could present no definite results because the only uncertainties considered pertained to the expectations of one firm concerning the price and output policy of its rivals. It was certain, not uncertain, that the buyers would choose the product of one firm over another solely on the basis of price. In these conditions, variations in behavior could not be explained by objective elements but only by differences in entrepreneurial psychology. If it can be shown, however, that uncertainties exist because of market or production factors, then oligopolistic behavior patterns become determinate in terms of forces that economists are accustomed to handle.

Professor Chamberlin made the first step in the direction of such a theory of oligopoly when he considered a differentiated product. If to this is added product variation, a rapidly changing technology, and a durable, complex product, then the uncertainty of the effects of the actions of any firm on its rivals may be so great that all indirect effects may be neglected. If this is true, competition can exist in oligopoly and even in duopoly. And no theory of entrepreneurial psychology, blackmail, or warfare is necessary to explain why the relations among a small group of firms are completely competitive.

In his book on the aluminum industry, Professor D. H. Wallace suggested that a distinction should be made between oligopolistic situations on the basis of whether demand is changing slowly and predictably or rapidly and unpredictably. Another factor he considered relevant was the possibility of developing new variations in the basic product. In aluminum this meant finding new alloys and new uses of the ingot metal. Professor Wallace summarized his views as follows: "In a market characterized by great uncertainty surrounding a rapidly moving demand curve, where there is a large field for profitable development of new variations of the basic product, it seems unlikely that oligopolists would follow policies appropriate to more or less permanent division of the market in fixed proportions."[2]

In Professor Wallace's case, the uncertainty results from the moving demand curve and the changing technology of the product. Another economist who has dealt with the effect of uncertainties on oligopolistic behavior is Professor William Fellner. His view is that the quasi-agreements which are typical of oligopoly do not

[1] E. H. Chamberlin, The Theory of Monopolistic Competition (5th ed.; 1946), p. 101.

[2] D. H. Wallace, Market Control in the Aluminum Industry (1937), p. 338.

usually cover technological change, product variation, and advertising. The reason is that

these variables are apt to be more nearly associated with inventiveness than are the variables regulated by quasi-agreement. The lowering of costs of production, product variation, and gains from advertising are more nearly related to inventiveness than pricing. Inventiveness is the faculty of improving the conditions under which one is operating, by adopting methods which are unpredictable. . . . In all these cases, the essence of the matter is that it is impossible to discount the future changes in relative strength which will be brought about by these manifestations of inventiveness. . . . Therefore, in many cases competition remains less restricted, or possibly even unhampered with respect to these variables, especially if the oligopolistic group is not quite small.[3]

Professor Fellner thus imagines agreements which cover price but not product variation, technological change, and advertising. The theory of oligopolistic behavior which has been put forth in this study differs from Professor Fellner's view in two respects. The evidence in the motor competition does not suggest an agreement on price with the other variables handled competitively. As far as can be determined, the vigorous product competition led to equally unrestrained price competition. It is hard to see how it could be otherwise, particularly where the product is a durable producer's good. To agree on price without agreement on all features of the product would surely be unlikely when product changes have measurable results in terms of the production cost. The complex nature of a durable producer's good, the possibilities of improving that good, and genuine disagreement among engineers regarding the features that the good should possess made any product agreement impossible. The result

was a product-price competition with all variables handled competitively. A second modification of the Fellner theory is that the qualifying phrase, "especially if the oligopolistic group is not quite small," may be unnecessary. The electrical manufacturing industry shows that three firms or even two may compete vigorously.

One additional aspect of competition in the electrical industry should be mentioned. It will be recalled that in the Niagara Falls power development, purchases of electrical equipment were nearly equally divided between General Electric and Westinghouse and that it is highly probable that the Niagara Power Company consciously avoided buying from only one manufacturer because of an interest in maintaining alternative sources of supply. This purchasing policy, supposedly designed to maintain competitive conditions in the industry, was also used by other equipment buyers. After the formation of General Electric in 1892, the Westinghouse annual report stated: "It seems to be the views of your principal customers that all users of electric light and power apparatus must soon recognize that an independent concern, like your company, is essential to their prosperity; and that such a concern, conducted on good business principles should be supported, as failure to do so might lead to such a monopoly in the electric light and power business that consumers would be forced to purchase apparatus upon any terms that might be dictated."[4] A few months later, a Westinghouse advertisement called General Electric the "Electric Trust" and concluded with the remark: "We invite the cooperation and support of all users of Electrical Apparatus who desire to have the benefits of competition."[5]

Westinghouse thus tried to secure business not only on the grounds that its

[3] William Fellner, Competition among the Few (1949), pp. 183–185.

[4] Westinghouse Electric and Manufacturing Company, Annual Report (May 18, 1892), p. 6.
[5] EW, III (July 27, 1892), xiii.

products were good and its prices low, but also because it was the only full-line producer other than General Electric. Potential customers were supposed to recognize that if Westinghouse were to go out of business, they would be able to buy electrical equipment from only one company, which would presumably act as a monopolist.

Whether many buyers based their purchase decisions on a principle as general as maintaining competition is not known. The existence of a competitive ideology among these buyers is probable because they were businessmen and aware of the importance of alternative sources of supply. It should also be noted that the contention of Westinghouse that it would provide effective competition for General Electric would be seriously discounted by an economist who applied the usual oligopolistic reasoning. He would doubt that anything but tacit or explicit agreements between the two manufacturers would result. In contrast to this view, the facts prove that Westinghouse did provide an effective competition. If some of the equipment buyers acted on the assumption that duopoly could mean genuine competition, they cannot, with justice, be accused of unrealism.

Entrepreneurship

The entrepreneurial activities in three branches of electrical manufacturing have been examined. These activities seem to fit the following schema. First, the engineer-entrepreneur must visualize a place in the economy that the product he expects to develop—electric-lighting equipment or electric-power equipment—can occupy. With this vision before him, he must decide what technical features the product should have to insure its commercial success. He then must invent a product which possesses these technical features.

The three-stage schema applies most generally to the very beginning of an industry. Once the product is manufactured and sold at a price greater than cost, and if it gives reliable and economical performance, then the task of pioneer innovation is largely completed. The engineer-entrepreneur no longer is the key person in the firm, and as the industry grows and the producers are successful, the important problems shift to the areas of marketing, finance, and business administration.

The pioneer innovation by an engineer-entrepreneur which creates a new industry can be thought of as requiring an extension of entrepreneurship forward to product markets and backward to factor markets.[6] More is involved than the organization of *existing* factors to produce for an *existing* market. On the input side, labor has to be trained, machinery has to be designed, and raw materials have to be located. Brush had to find a new source of carbonaceous material before he was able to make satisfactory arc carbons. Thomson had difficulty in securing copper wire of sufficient purity, and he had to make his own meters for testing because no meters which met his requirements were on the market. Edison sent exploring parties all over the world looking for the bamboo best suited for lamp filaments. The search ended in Japan, which served as Edison's source of filament material for a number of years. All the engineer-entrepreneurs were handicapped by the lack of a labor force which could make, install, and operate electrical equipment. Edison at one time organized a school in New York to train electricians, and Brush traveled hundred of miles to correct troubles in arc-lighting installations because no one else could determine what was wrong.

[6] For a more extended discussion of this phenomenon, see G. J. Stigler, "The Division of Labor Is Limited by the Extent of the Market," *Journal of Political Economy*, LIX (June 1951), 185 ff., especially p. 190.

On the output side, markets for electrical equipment had to be created. The common procedure was to promote lighting firms and to help them get started in business. The manufacturer provided advice and general supervision and took much of the risk by accepting securities in payment for equipment and by giving cost and durability guarantees. When the electrical manufacturing industry was well established, entrepreneurship could shrink back to the confines of a single firm. The factors and supplies were available; the lighting companies were in existence.

It is legitimate to ask, although not in every case possible to answer, how the various engineer-entrepreneurs happened to become interested in electricity and its commercial applications. It will be recalled that Edison and Westinghouse had done inventing and manufacturing in other fields before taking up work in electric lighting and power. Edison was an engineer-entrepreneur on a full-time basis when he turned to the electric light. He made the move consciously and chose electric lighting as the best of a number of alternatives. Westinghouse was also fully occupied in innovational activities and was led from work in railroad switching and signaling devices to electrical manufacturing. Once in the latter field, he saw the commercial possibilities of alternating current. The entrepreneurial activities of both Edison and Westinghouse in the electrical industry should thus be viewed as the result of deliberate choices by experienced engineer-entrepreneurs who were looking for new areas in which to use their talents profitably.

Unlike Edison and Westinghouse, the other important engineer-entrepreneurs—Brush, Thomson, Sprague, and Stanley—confined themselves to the electrical industry, in which they had their first experience in innovational activities. Their decisions to enter the industry grew out of noncommercial backgrounds, and consequently a brief discussion of these backgrounds is necessary to an understanding of their choice of electrical manufacturing as a career.

Brush was interested in scientific literature while still a boy and constructed crude apparatus such as telescopes and microscopes to study natural phenomena. His interests included electricity and especially the arc light. He constructed his first arc light while still in his teens and thereafter set for himself the goal of making the arc light of commercial value.[7]

The story of Thomson is similar to that of Brush. From the age of ten, Thomson was intensely interested in scientific and mechanical subjects. Among other things, he made a camera, a static machine, and a telegraph. He cast type metal, carried on chemical experiments, and read voluminously in scientific books and periodicals. All this activity preceded his graduation from high school. After graduation, he joined the staff of the school and taught chemistry while he carried on electrical experiments. He then lectured at the Franklin Institute and was given the opportunity to test arc-lighting dynamos. This contact with arc lighting combined with what he saw in Paris led him to begin the manufacture of arc-lighting equipment on a commercial basis.

Sprague was introduced to electricity at the Naval Academy and at the 1876 Centennial Exhibition in Philadelphia. During his two years at sea, he found time to invent nearly sixty devices including a telephone, a telegraph, a motor, and a method for transmitting pictures by wire. On returning to the United States, he sought opportunities for electrical work here and abroad and finally resigned from the Navy to enter Edison's employ. His study and experiences led him to believe that the field of the future was electric motive power, and he organized a firm in 1884 to carry out the application of electric power to industry and transport.[8]

[7] Brush, "Some Reminiscences of Early Electric Lighting," pp. 3–5.
[8] Sprague, "Digging in the Mines of the Motors," pp. 695–697.

Unlike Brush, Thomson, and Sprague, Stanley's early life is quite obscure. After a short time at Yale, he left to enter electrical work. Although he was interested in several problems, he thought the crucial need was for a cheaper system of distribution, and he believed that alternating current could meet that need. As early as 1883, he made an entry in a laboratory notebook which showed that he was working on an a.c. distribution system.[9] By the spring of 1885, he was beginning to understand that parallel connection of transformers was the key to an a.c. system which would operate satisfactorily. He described his thought processes during this period in an article he wrote many years later.

I realized that if we could make a transformer that would regulate the energy transformed by slight variations of its induced counter electromotive force in the same manner that a shunt-wound motor regulated for energy transferred by variation of its rotational counter electromotive force, the problem would be beautifully solved. I saw this analogy faintly at first, but soon with strong and clear conviction. I was very much excited by it. It seemed too simple and too easy to be true. I was almost afraid to believe or speak of it, for I had experienced a good many disappointments and was in a nervous and overworked condition; but as my convictions grew and strengthened I gained courage. Then I clearly saw that the solution was found. I told Mrs. Stanley, and, although she did not understand a word about it, she saw it too.[10]

After working for Westinghouse on a.c. problems for about five years, Stanley formed his own company to make a.c. equipment.

It can be seen that Brush, Thomson, Sprague, and Stanley followed similar paths in entering the electrical industry. They had unusual scientific and inventive interests early in life. After literally years

of experimenting with various kinds of electrical apparatus, each engineer-entrepreneur selected one type of electrical equipment which he thought could achieve commercial use. He then carried on development work and organized a firm to make and sell that equipment.

One further aspect of entrepreneurship in the electrical industry should be briefly noted. As a general rule, the radically new developments came not from old, established firms, but from new firms and independent engineer-entrepreneurs. Arc lighting was brought to the commercial stage by Charles Brush. Edison made practical the incandescent light. Westinghouse introduced alternating current for light and power. Sprague pioneered in electric traction, and Stanley in high-voltage alternating current. In some of these cases, existing firms that could have carried out the innovational work were unable to see any commercial value in the innovations. Edison could see no economic worth in alternating current. Edison, Brush, and Westinghouse were not innovators in electric traction. General Electric and Westinghouse were hesitant in pushing toward higher transmission voltages. The idea of abandoning the locomotive principle did not occur to any of the electrical manufacturing firms of 1897.

There were, however, important exceptions to the rule that pioneer innovations require independent engineer-entrepreneurs and new firms. Thomson-Houston innovated in electric traction, although an outsider, Van Depoele, gave considerable assistance. Paine, a member of the General Electric sales force, accomplished a major innovation in the use of a.c. power. And a group of financiers were mainly responsible for the Niagara power development. They envisioned a power project which was far beyond anything then in existence, and they translated that vision into reality by directing and coördinating the activities of engineering experts and manufacturing firms.

In spite of these exceptions, the

[9] Stanley, "Alternating Current Development in America," p. 566.
[10] Ibid., p. 568.

tendency of pioneer innovations to be the work of newcomers to the industry is general enough to receive special attention. Two studies similar to this one reveal the same tendency. In his work on the radio industry, Professor W. R. Maclaurin found that new firms were of critical importance. None of the established companies manufacturing electrical or communications equipment or operating telegraph or telephone systems thought radio was of any commercial value.[11] Similarly, A. A. Bright, Jr., includes material in his book on the electric-lamp industry which indicates that several of the new non-incandescent sources of light were not developed by General Electric or any of the other incandescent-lamp producers. Neon lighting was introduced into the United States by a newly organized subsidiary of a French firm, because General Electric refused to develop neon lighting on the grounds that incandescent lamps were superior.[12] In 1936, a Dutch firm offered General Electric and Westinghouse a license to make and sell a new type of photoflash lamp. Both companies rejected this offer. A small American firm, the Wabash Appliance Corporation, took the opportunity instead and by 1940 was supplying three-fourths of the domestic market in flash bulbs.[13]

It seems reasonable to conclude that for the commercialization of technical advances, society must depend on independent engineer-entrepreneurs and new firms. The reasons for this are several. New technical developments require new understanding. Engineer-entrepreneurs who have spent years in a particular field may find it difficult, if not impossible, to shift to another field. The time which would be needed is one limitation; the fresh point of view required is another. The personal qualities of engineer-entrepreneurs also

are relevant. Such men tend to have faith in their own ideas to the exclusion of all others. This faith is necessary for success, but it precludes success in all but a few lines of endeavor for any one man.

New firms are needed because existing companies, especially if they are successful, tend to become bureaucratic. Mistakes are penalized; initiative is unrewarded. Success in a particular product creates a vested interest in that product, and there is considerable hesitancy about entering new fields. Another factor is the reputation of the company. It fears to try radically new developments when it has a record of excellent product quality at stake. Influenced by all these things, the company management may honestly feel that particular inventions have no chance of commercial success and that any resources devoted to them would be wasted.

Entrepreneurship in a new industry involves decisions which are extremely speculative and require strong faith in the future of the industry. A new firm which is small and unhampered by traditions and records of the past and an engineer-entrepreneur who has devoted himself to making commercial some new product, no matter what resistance he meets, are the functionaries through which scientific advances become of value to society. Many times the proposals of these engineer-entrepreneurs may be completely unsound and of no economic merit. It is not possible to tell beforehand, however, which of the proposals will achieve commercial success and which will not. All should be given an opportunity to appear on the market. The decision on the merits of the proposals then can be made by consumers acting through the market mechanism.

Technical Change

Technical change in the electrical manufacturing industry can be described in terms of several broad trends. One was the increasing complexity of the product.

[11] W. R. Maclaurin, Invention and Innovation in the Radio Industry (1949), pp. 21–29, 243–245.
[12] Bright, The Electric-Lamp Industry, pp. 370–371.
[13] Ibid., pp. 340–341.

The first electric system—arc lighting—was from a technical standpoint quite simple. A series circuit has a minimum of complications. Constant current meant that no fuses were required. Use in street lighting made meters, other accessories, and individual control of the lamps unnecessary. The next electric system—incandescent lighting—was much less simple. The parallel network was very complicated, especially after the three-wire and feeder-main techniques came into use. Fuses were required. In the central stations, ammeters and voltmeters were needed to check operations; in the homes and offices, a meter measured electric energy consumed. Switches, junction boxes, and numerous other devices were part of the system. The third electric system to come into use was alternating current, which was applied to both lighting and power. Complex relations, unknown to d.c. systems, had to be considered. Phase and frequency problems arose. Switching and intersystem connections became a special study. Devices were invented to change alternating to direct current, to convert from one frequency to another, and to alter the number of phases.

The transition from simple to complex systems and equipment can be interpreted as proceeding hand in hand with the training of people to design, manufacture, sell, install, and operate the apparatus. In the beginning, only a simple system could have achieved commercial success. As knowledge of electricity and electrical equipment increased, and as this knowledge became widespread, the more complicated systems could give economical and reliable performance. These more complicated systems fitted electricity into an ever-growing number of uses. The replacement of gas street lighting was relatively simple. Substituting electric lighting for interior gas illumination was less so. Most complicated of all was the general displacement of mechanical methods of power transmission.

Increasing complexity as a facet of technical change can thus be thought of as resulting from the necessity to conform to the degree of electrical knowledge. Other facets of technical change can be viewed as due to market forces. One of these forces was the pressure to reduce cost so that electrical equipment could come into more widespread use. The increase in size of individual items of equipment (generators, motors, transformers), the double-carbon arc lamp, the copper-plated carbons, the high-resistance lamp, the three-wire system, the feeder-main system, the efficient generators, the introduction of alternating current, the use of higher transmission voltages, the turbo-generator units—all these resulted from the efforts to decrease costs. The electrical manufacturers realized that only if costs were lowered could their products triumph over gas, oil, candles, horses, cables, belts, ropes, countershafts, and isolated steam-power plants.

Another market force affecting technical change was the desire to expand the market for electrical apparatus by making it suitable for more uses. Arc lights were reduced in intensity and enclosed to permit use in interior illumination. Incandescent lights were manufactured in large sizes for large-space lighting and in small sizes for surgical instruments and flashlights. The development of alternating current permitted the extension of lighting networks so that incandescent lights could be substituted for oil and candles as well as for gas. In transportation, larger motors and the multiple-unit system of control made electric power more economical than steam in elevated and interurban railways and led to the development of subways. In industry, motors of varied characteristics spurred the application of electric motors to more and more uses.

One further aspect of technical change in electric equipment should be mentioned. Concomitant with the trend toward diversity was a trend toward standardization. Because electrical equipment typically operates as part of a system, certain features of all apparatus on one system must be the same. The apparatus is supplied with energy from a central source and must be constructed with certain characteristics before it can make use of this energy. Arc lamps had to be designed for a certain amount of current, incandescent lamps and d.c. motors for a certain voltage. All the components of an electric-railway system had to be suitable for operation on one voltage. With the advent of alternating current, factors in addition to current and voltage had to be taken into account. The frequency and phase characteristics of the meters, transformers, a.c.-d.c. converters, and so forth, had to match the characteristics of the circuits to which they were connected. In all these system constants—current, voltage, frequency, and phase—the change was from many values to few. Early arc-lighting systems operated on a number of different current values. By 1900, nearly all used 9.6 amperes. The d.c. voltages also differed widely at first. For light and power, 110–220 volts became standard; and in electric-railway systems, 500 volts was nearly universal by 1890. In frequency, 60 cycles for lighting and 25 cycles for power were eventually accepted as standard. In phase, the three-phase system had largely displaced the two-phase and monophase systems by 1900. The fact that the design engineers were willing to treat these system characteristics as constants eventually led to production economies in equipment manufacture and encouraged the expansion of central-station circuits.

Economic Growth

The growth of the electric manufacturing industry was very rapid. Annual sales increased from a negligible amount in 1875 to over $100,000,000 twenty-five years later. The principal reason for this rapid growth was that the products of the industry were readily substitutable for other, less effective ways of doing things. Every new product is a substitute for something, but the substitution will take place much faster if a minimum amount of shift or alteration in the economic structure is necessary. In lighting, artificial illumination supplied from a central source was common in streets and homes. The electric light, arc and incandescent, provided a better light at a cost comparable to gas for these same uses. Street railways were widespread. The electric motor was a better kind of motive power than horses and mules because its cost was lower and it enabled cars to travel faster. Mechanical power was widely used in industry. Electricity was a more economical means of transmitting this power than cables, belts, chains, shafts, and compressed air.

The growth could thus be much faster than if streets and homes had not been lighted from a central source, if public-transportation systems had not been in existence, or if the only power used in industry had been human or animal. The rapid expansion in the use of electricity was possible because of the economic and technical changes that had preceded it and paved the way for it.

This part of the growth of the electrical industry resulted from a substitution of electricity where very little change in economic and technical procedures was required. Later, electricity replaced devices and methods where substantial alterations were required before it could be used. Alternating current permitted the formation of lighting companies and the employment of a system type of illumination where only non-system illuminants, such as kerosene lamps and candles, had previously been economic. Alternating current thus brought about the spread of incandescent lighting to small communities and the outlying areas of large cities which were so thinly settled that gas was not feasible. Similarly, the electric street-car, because of its speed, permitted the.

extension of street railways to areas which could not be served by a public-transportation system when only animal power was available. Here the electric railway was substituted for non-system forms of transportation, such as private vehicles or taxicabs. In elevated railroads, electric power allowed, for the first time, the abandonment of the locomotive principle. The multiple-unit idea, combined with a clean form of power, eventually made possible an entirely new kind of urban transportation, the subway. Other applications of electric power were equally revolutionary. Electricity made mechanical power feasible in the home, a place where the only power had been human. The development of the electric sewing machine, the electric washing machine, and later all the other electric home appliances brought about significant changes in the daily life of the average housewife. Electric power also made available water powers which had been previously inaccessible and completely altered techniques of production. In all these uses, the substitution of electricity for other techniques involved major economic changes. These were the creative effects of the introduction of electricity into the American economy.

Another aspect of economic growth in the electrical industry was the trend within firms to expand from single products or closely related groups of products to the entire line of electrical apparatus. Brush started in arc lighting and spread into incandescent lighting, batteries, electric power, and electric-railway equipment. Thomson-Houston also began in arc lighting and later expanded into d.c. incandescent lighting, d.c. power, electric railways, a.c. incandescent lighting, and a.c. power. Edison was initially only in d.c. incandescent lighting but eventually went into d.c. power apparatus, electric-railway equipment, and arc-lighting systems. Westinghouse first manufactured d.c. incandescent-lighting equipment and then expanded to include a.c. incandescent lighting, d.c. power, electric railways, arc lighting, and a.c. electric power. Thus the economic growth of electrical manufacturing firms has meant not only an increase in sales, assets, employees, physical capacity, and profits, but also in the number of products manufactured. By 1900, there were two full-line producers. These companies manufactured nearly every kind of electrical apparatus other than communications equipment.

The existence of only two full-line producers after more than two decades of growth was largely the result of patents. The mergers and consolidations were prompted by the desire to avoid patent conflicts and the hope of obtaining a strong position in the industry through control of important patents. Patents also made possible the independence of Westinghouse. The 1896 patent agreement between Westinghouse and General Electric strengthened these two firms at the expense of the rest of the industry and hastened the trend toward duopoly.

Suggestions for Public Policy

Two suggestions concerning industrial markets grow out of this study. The first is that free access to resources and free markets should be maintained. Innovations should be allowed to compete for consumer support, and the success of an innovation should be determined in the market place. Individuals who have faith in their ideas and who are willing to spend their time and invest their own and other people's money in developing new products should be allowed to do so, no matter how unsound their ideas may appear to be. The history of the electrical industry proves that many attempts to develop new products will seem preposterous, absurd, and a waste of resources. But the only way to find out whether this is true is to let the development of the new product proceed to the commercial stage and then submit the product to a market test. In the end, it was the consumers who proved Edison right and his critics wrong when he said he could develop a practical incandescent lamp. Similarly, the consumers proved that Westinghouse was right in advocating alternating current and that his critics (who included Edison) were wrong.

The fact that radical innovations usually seem valueless to established companies means that, in most cases, engineer-entrepreneurs have to found new firms to market the new product which they have developed. New firms thus play a critical role in economic progress and should be encouraged. They can present their products to the consumers, who then will judge whether further production is justified.

The second suggestion concerns policy on monopolies. One problem that has puzzled economists is this. If there is a monopoly in a certain industry, would the public interest be served by breaking up this company into two or three firms? Answers based on traditional oligopoly theory are in the negative, because tacit agreements resulting from recognition of mutual dependence lead to a pattern of action very similar to the original monopolist's price and output policies. It is here suggested that forming a small number of firms out of a single firm may result in genuine and effective competition under certain conditions. These conditions relate to the nature of the product and the amount of technical change taking place. If the product is durable, complex, and a capital good, and if technical change in the product and the techniques of making it are reasonably rapid, then the prospect of securing effective competition by establishing only a few firms is good. It would be important that the engineering talent of the original firm be divided about equally among the companies which are created and that each of these organizations be headed by an ambitious and aggressive leader. Free access to basic patents would have to be given to the various firms in order that they could start on an equal footing. On the basis of this study alone, it is not possible to say that any such scheme could succeed or exactly how it should be carried out. But this study does indicate that further analysis of oligopolistic behavior in areas where that behavior has been competitive would be fruitful. If the factors which produce genuine competition under oligopoly could be segregated and identified in a number of industries, general principles could be derived. In particular instances of monopoly, these principles would be of considerable assistance in determining whether competition could be obtained by establishing several firms in place of one.

Financing the Big Company

■ The older, family-owned industrial companies, starting from small beginnings, had usually expanded by reinvestment of earnings. Among private enterprises before 1850 only transportation companies, banks, and urban public utilities had been financed by widespread sale of securities. The national government and state and local governments sold bonds, a business that was greatly stimulated by the Civil War issues.

From the 1870s on, the older types of private security issues became larger and larger, and some big industrial companies also found it possible to sell stocks or bonds to the public. As a result, investment banking, essentially the wholesale marketing of new securities, became more and more important, and access to the services of leading investment firms became necessary for the expansion of many big companies, particularly for raising the tens of millions of dollars often needed by railroads and public utilities.

The ensuing influence wielded by investment bankers over the big-business sectors of the economy led some German and American economic historians to call the stage of economic growth the country was in around 1900 the stage of "finance capitalism." In the following selection George W. Edwards, former professor of economics at the City College of New York, uses the broader term "security capitalism," which may be applied without regard to the power attributed to the bankers. The trend of recent scholarship has been to lessen the importance of the influence of the investment bankers of the time in the overall trends of the economy. It should be remembered that all but a few hundred of the million and a half American firms of 1900 carried on their operations independently of any connection with Wall Street or investment bankers.

George W. Edwards
Development of American Security Capitalism*

The years following the panic of 1873 to the crisis of 1907 marked the developed stage of security capitalism in this country. The period may justly be called the Morgan Era for over these years the House of Morgan came to dominate the financial system. In general, the economic tendencies operating in the previous period continued over these years. American manufacture increased its output, and technical improvements transformed both production and consumption. Free land was still available, and thousands of new acres were brought into cultivation. Foreign trade changed in nature, for, where formerly exports consisted largely of raw materials and foodstuffs, there was now a growing increase in the proportion of manufactured goods. In the railroad field, the great trunk lines were formed.

The struggle for a gold currency continued, and the sound money program supported by Eastern bankers was finally adopted by Congress. In the words of the secretary of the treasury, on the day of the resumption of specie payment "By five o'clock the news was all over the land and the New York bankers were sipping their tea in absolute safety."[1] However, in the ensuing years the supporters of sound money were hard pressed to hold their gains. Uncertainty as to the future of the currency, due to the passage of the Bland-Allison Act in 1878 and the Sherman silver legislation in 1890, continued over this period, and at times checked the flow of capital.

* Reprinted by permission of the publishers from *The Evolution of Finance Capitalism* (New York: Longmans, Green and Company, 1938), Courtesy of David McKay Company, Inc., pp. 161–188.

[1] Beard, Charles A. and Mary R., *The Rise of American Civilization*, New York 1927, Vol. II, p. 331.

At the height of the political campaign of 1896 the *Chronicle* observed that:

There has been no lack of investment funds any more than there has been a lack of capital to engage in reproductive enterprises. The real trouble has been that in view of the pending uncertainty—an uncertainty at once menacing the standard of values and threatening to derange all values—neither the investor nor the capitalist was willing to tie up his money or to let it go far out of his reach.[2]

The Gold Standard Act of 1900 placed the United States on a sound money basis where it remained until March 1933.

In this period the social opposition to security capitalism became intense and the system was attacked in granger acts, and also federal legislation particularly against the trusts. These laws came under the critical review of the Supreme Court, which, by weakening the impact of the Sherman Act, restricting the operations of the Interstate Commerce Commission and the Federal Trade Commission, limiting federal taxation and railroad legislation, became a most important bulwark protecting developed security capitalism from the attacks of its enemies.[3]

Development of Corporate Organization

While the corporation had existed in the period before the Civil War and had developed in the years immediately following, it was however only after the panic of 1873 that this form of business organization came not only to dominate the

economic structure but to be "the master institution of civilized life."[4] Corporate financing was stimulated by the development of bond issues secured by the corporate mortgage. This instrument now included careful provisions for foreclosing on pledged property in case of default and for enabling a company to redeem its bonds prior to maturity through the use of call features, and by the nineties the corporate mortgage reached its modern form.[5]

Another important change in corporate practice was replacing the individual trustee by the corporation, generally a trust company organized specifically for this purpose. The unreliability of an individual as a transfer agent for bonds was demonstrated in the heavy reverses suffered from fraudulent transactions, and the investing public lost confidence in individuals as trustees.[6] There was also a growing practice of issuing collateral trust bonds supported by a block of stocks or bonds which had to be deposited with a trustee acting in behalf of the bondholders.[7] Individual trustees were therefore replaced by corporate trustees.

Another development in corporate organization was the growing use of the holding company. This legal device had already been used in railroad finance as early as 1833, but the first pure holding company in the modern sense of the term was developed between 1868 and 1872 by special acts of the Pennsylvania legislature.[8] These companies were given "full power and authority to hold and own securities of any form, either as collateral or otherwise, and to dispose of the same

[2] *Commercial and Financial Chronicle*, Supplements Vol. 63, October 17, 1896, State and City Supplement—"The Municipal Bond Market," p. 4.
[3] Lerner, Max, "The Supreme Court and American Capitalism" in the *Yale Law Review*, 1933, pp. 668–701; Smith, James Allen, *The Spirit of American Government*, New York 1907, and *The Growth and Decadence of Constitutional Government*, New York 1930. An extreme economic interpretation of the decisions of the Supreme Court is that of Myers, Gustavus, *History of the Supreme Court of the United States*, Chicago 1912.

[4] Veblen, Thorstein, *Absentee Ownership and Business Enterprise*, New York 1923, p. 86.
[5] Stetson, Francis L., and others, *Some Legal Phases of Corporate Financing, Reorganization and Regulation*, New York 1917, p. 13.
[6] Smith, James G., *The Development of Trust Companies in the United States*, New York 1927, pp. 291–295.
[7] Noyes, Alexander D., *Forty Years of American Finance*, New York and London 1909, p. 296.
[8] Bonbright, James C., and Means, Gardiner C., *The Holding Company*, New York 1932, p. 59.

at pleasure."[9] A number of these holding companies played an important part in the railroad and the utility industries. The Pennsylvania Company was formed to aid the financing of the Pennsylvania Railroad system, and the United Gas and Improvement Company developed the first permanent gas and electric system. The State of Massachusetts also granted a special charter for the formation of the American Bell Telephone Company.[10] Holding companies were created by special legislative acts until 1889 when New Jersey amended its general corporation law permitting a corporation to hold the stocks of other companies, and in time other states followed the same practice.[11] The significance of this measure is well stated by Mead:

For momentous consequences, this statute of New Jersey is hardly to be equalled in the annals of legislation . . . the little state of New Jersey, containing 2 percent of the population and 1 and 3/10ths percent of the wealth of the United States, by the simple act of amending its corporation law, nullified the antitrust laws of every State which had passed them.[12]

The growing intricacies of corporate practice developed a class of lawyers who specialized in this field. John B. Dill began his lecture at the Harvard Law School with the statement that "I am the lawyer for a billion dollars of invested capital."[13] William Nelson Cromwell, of Sullivan and Cromwell, in the biography which he prepared for Who's Who stated that he was an "officer or counsel of more than twenty of the largest corporations of the United States and one of the organizers of the United States Steel Corporation" and that he had "reorganized Northern Pacific Railway and many others

and put all on a paying basis."[14] Another important corporation lawyer was Joseph Choate, who performed what was then considered a great service for security capitalism in presenting the arguments in favor of invalidating the income tax.[15]

Internationalization of American Security Capitalism

The United States was evolving from the stage of purely national to that of international capitalism, and in consequence its foreign political relations were becoming more important. It is generally held that the stage of international economy of the United States began during the Great War, but actually it was under way two decades earlier. Even before the turn of the century the United States entered upon a policy of overseas expansion which extended its power to the Caribbean and to the Pacific. American security capitalism, similar to British security capitalism, did not stand to gain from an aggressive foreign policy. In 1896 the United States in supporting the Monroe Doctrine came close to conflict with British internationalism over Venezuela. American banking security capitalism strongly opposed the belligerent stand of its government. Commenting on Cleveland's ultimatum to Great Britain, J. P. Morgan said:

I have labored to build up such relations of confidence between the United States and the money markets of Europe that capital from there could be secured in large sums for our needs, and here is a threatened disaster that will put an end to our borrowing.

Fortunately the clash was averted.[16]

Following the Spanish-American War, the American government took an active part in the financial affairs of Cuba. The

[9] Ibid., p. 59.
[10] Ibid., pp. 61–64.
[11] Ibid., p. 64.
[12] Meade, Edward, Trust Finance, New York 1903, p. 39.
[13] Sullivan, Mark, Our Times, vol. II, New York 1927, p. 318.

[11] Ibid., p. 319.
[15] Pollock vs. Farmers Loan and Trust Co., 157 U. S. 429.
[16] Seitz, Don Carlos, Joseph Pulitzer, New York 1927, p. 201–205. J. P. Morgan was also opposed to the war with Spain. Seldes, George, Iron, Blood and Profits, New York 1934, p. 6.

Platt amendment provided that the Cuban government was not to contract any public debt if its ordinary revenues were inadequate, and also that the United States Government could intervene for the preservation of Cuban independence in the maintenance of a government adequate for the protection of life and property. The amendment gave the United States control over the finances of Cuba, and this power was exercised on several occasions. Likewise the United States Government intervened in Santo Domingo in 1907 when its finances were in a demoralized condition. The United States Government facilitated the flotation of a loan by the National City Bank to the government of Haiti, and also took a hand in the reorganization of the finances of Nicaragua. In almost every case American intervention resulted in a settlement of the financial difficulties of the country and in the improvement of the credit position of the nation. Unlike the policies of the European powers, the protectorates established by the United States over foreign territories were temporary. In the Far East, American banking capitalism came near being seriously involved in an imperialistic venture but fortunately did not carry the policy through. In the period immediately preceding the Great War, the State Department for a time took an active interest in regulating the flow of American capital to China. "That diplomacy," noted one writer, "represents the maximum point to which diplomatic assistance to private investments has been extended by the American Government."[17]

Changing Function of Commercial Banking

The trend of commercial banking in this period may best be traced by studying the changing financial position of the national banks. The national banks at first made extensive use of the privilege of issuing circulating notes permitted under the National Bank Act, and these notes constituted about 20 percent of the total liabilities of the national banks. However, the proportion declined sharply, and by 1910 was only about six percent of the total liabilities. The deposits of these institutions were almost entirely in the form of demand deposits. In 1905 the comptroller of the currency ruled that national banks were not prohibited from operating savings departments, but little advantage was taken of this ruling.[18] The proportion of securities to total earning assets reached a high figure in 1870 due to the large holding of government bonds after the Civil War; the proportion dropped until 1890, and thereafter moved irregularly upward.[19] A growing proportion of the loans of the national banks were based on stocks and bonds as collateral. By 1892 security loans constituted 29.72 percent of total loans, in 1901 they reached a peak of 41.47 percent and then receded but by 1910 still accounted for 37.17 percent.[20] The exact proportion of the security investment assets in the form of direct security holdings and security loans of all the commercial banks of the United States to their total assets in the period before the passage of the Federal Reserve Act has been variously estimated. Dr. Anderson in his study of bank earning assets for 1909 estimated that, exclusive of real estate loans, more than one-half of bank credit was applied to the purchase

[17] Finch, George A., "American Diplomacy and the Financing of China," in the American Journal of International Law, Vol. 16, January 1922, p. 25.

[18] Willis, H. Parker, and Steiner, William H., Federal Reserve Banking Practice, New York 1926 p. 659. State banks, on the other hand, increased the proportion of their time deposits to total deposits from 11 percent in 1896 to 16 percent in 1909. Compiled from Statistics for the United States by A. Piatt Andrews for the National Monetary Commission, Vol. XXI, p. 151.
[19] Dr. Jacob Hollander commented on the increase in the security investments of commercial banks in "The Security Holdings of National Banks" in the American Economic Review, December 1913, p. 793.
[20] Computed from Report of the Comptroller of the Currency, 1920, Vol. II, p. 774.

of bonds or the granting of loans on stocks and bonds.[21] Writing in 1914, C. W. Barron, a financial editor, claimed that two-thirds of the funds extended by commercial banks were used for investment purposes and only one-third for commercial transactions.[22] It is thus clear that even before 1914, as a result of the changing nature of the entire financial system, the so-called commercial bank was broadening its function and was becoming an important institution of developed security capitalism.

American economists and bankers themselves generally accepted the orthodox theory of banking which maintained that commercial banking must be conducted separately from investment operations.[23] However, A. Barton Hepburn, Chairman of the Chase National Bank, as far back as 1893 properly stated that "the purely commercial function as formulated in text books and laid down by the course as the business of the bank, fails fully to describe the banking of today. Banks of discount and deposit have become large owners of securities."[24]

Growth of the Stock Exchange

Over these years the stock exchanges also expanded rapidly. The successful opening of the Atlantic cable in 1866, the adoption of the stock ticker in 1867, and the installation of telephones on the floor of the New York Stock Exchange in 1878 were mechanical improvements which acceler-

ated the growth of security capitalism.[25] The Open Board of Brokers was formed in 1864 as a competitive organization to the New York Stock Exchange, and there was also a Government Bond Department which traded in the securities of the federal government. In 1869 the Exchange, the Open Board and the Government Bond Department, all merged into the New York Exchange. The Exchange now grew in importance, and from 1870 to 1910 the number of stocks listed on the Exchange rose from 143 to 426, while the number of bonds increased from 200 to 1,013.[26] The volume of trading on the Exchange, although small when compared with that of later years, nevertheless, showed a rapid increase. The volume for a single day rose to an early peak of 700,000 shares on November 28, 1879. In December 1886 the million-share mark was attained, and on April 30, 1913 the volume rose to 3,281,226 shares, a record that was to stand until 1916.[27]

In addition to the New York Stock Exchange there were several other security markets in New York City. The New York Mining Stock Exchange traded in mining and other stocks from 1876 to 1883 when it became the New York Mining and National Petroleum Exchange of New York. This financial market later added other securities as those of the railroads, and by the nineties its business was about a third of that of the New York Stock Exchange. The Curb Exchange also expanded its volume of business.[28]

Unlike European financial centers, New York in the period of developed security capitalism did not absorb the interior stock exchanges and these have continued

[21] Anderson, Benjamin, The Value of Money, New York 1936, pp. 510–511.
[22] Barron, C. W., The Federal Reserve Act, Boston 1914, pp. 68–69.
[23] See views of William Scott, E. M. Patterson, and F. A. Cleveland. Cited in Moulton, Harold G., Principles of Money and Banking, Chicago 1916 Part II, pp. 456–460.
[24] Hepburn, A. Barton "State and National Bank Circulation" in the Annals of the American Academy of Political and Social Science, Vol. 3, p. 577.

[25] Meeker, J. Edward, The Work of the Stock Exchange, New York 1930, p. 68.
[26] New York Stock Exchange Bulletin, Vol. 3 February 1932, p. 1.
[27] Chronicle, Vol. 29, supplement, November, 29, 1879, p. III; Ibid. Vol. 43, December 18, 1886, p. 739; Ibid. Vol. 72, April 30, 1901, p. 865.
[28] No definite figures are available for the Curb, as the volume of sales was not reported before 1921.

in importance particularly in Baltimore, Boston, Chicago, Philadelphia and San Francisco.[29]

Rise of Investment Banking

The most important change in financial organization occurred in the field of investment banking. The significant trend of this period was the transfer of the control of American capitalism in many fields from speculative capitalists to banking capitalists. In this respect American differed from British security capitalism, and partook rather of the nature of German security capitalism. To a large extent this difference was due to the relative extent of the supply of capital. In England there was sufficient capital even in the early years to finance the needs of industry, which obtained its funds largely from the resources of individual entrepreneurs. On the other hand, in Central Europe and in the United States, the financial resources of the industrialists were insufficient to meet the needs of the vast enterprises being formed. It was therefore necessary for the investment banker to mobilize not only the funds of the public but also to contribute a proportion of the necessary capital out of his own resources. Under these conditions, it was inevitable that the banker should obtain extensive control over the managerial policies of the enterprises in which he placed his own funds. Thus close relations between industry and investment banking became at first a dominant feature of American security capitalism in the developed stage.

The course of security capitalism in the

years immediately after the Civil War was marked by the private wars of the Fiskes and the Drews which may be likened to the anarchy prevailing under feudalism of the Middle Ages, with the distinction that, whereas under the feudal system the people lost their lives, under security capitalism they lost their money. The investment banker brought a semblance of order out of this chaos, and for a time was able to restrain the ruthless feuds of security capitalism. The transfer of control from the speculative capitalist to the investment banker meant the transition from financial feudalism to financial nationalism. As the growth of nationalism in the fifteenth and sixteenth centuries ended the private wars of the barons, and at least within the confines of the nation brought law and order, so the coming of banking capitalism in the eighties instituted a system of stabilized finance. The captains of industry were no longer sovereigns in their own right but now ruled by the grace of the higher power of the investment banker.

This close relation between industry and finance brought about the combination movement in both fields. The expansion of industry was made possible by the development of intercorporate relations through agreements, pools, interlocking directorates, voting trusts and holding companies. At the same time, to raise the funds for these giant corporations it was necessary to mobilize the financial resources of the nation into concentrated financial combinations. This combination movement was brought about not so much by concentration, that is, the fusion of like units in the form of a number of investment banks, but rather by a policy of integration or the development of a close relation among unlike financial units. Thus the large investment banking houses extended their influence over insurance companies and trust companies in order to obtain dominance over capital resources and over commercial banks to

[29] *Chronicle*, Vol. 46, 1888, p. 304. A study of the amount of the listings of these exchanges made by the *Chronicle* in 1888 showed that the Baltimore exchange on its complete returns had listings of $9,875,000 in bonds and $2,802,000 in stocks. Boston, on incomplete figures, showed $13,141,000 in stocks.

direct their credit resources.[30] By 1912 integration had progressed to the point where 180 individuals representing 18 investment banking houses, commercial banks and trust companies, through holding 341 interlocking directorates controlled 112 corporations with total resources of over $22,000,000,000.[31]

A number of investment banking houses gained in strength over these years. Palgrave, writing in the New York *Forum*, recognized in addition to the Morgan firm the importance of other houses, as Kuhn Loeb, Speyer, J. & W. Seligman and Brown Brothers, in the comment that "there is a considerable moral fibre in the United States, and it would be difficult to find higher examples of business qualities than among its first-rate men."[32]

Rise of the House of Morgan

Until almost the end of the seventies the house of Morgan was conducted as an old-style private banking establishment.[33] Its primary function was to place American securities among foreign investors. At home it participated in the various syndicates which handled United States Government bonds, but in these groups it was still a follower and not yet the leader.

The Morgan firm was unsuccessful against Jay Cooke in bidding for the issue of United States Government bonds in 1871. But in 1873 it broke the Cooke monopoly by forcing the secretary of the treasury to provide for equal participation in the flotation of the loan between the Morgan-Morton syndicate (including Barings) and the Cooke syndicate (including Rothschilds). It was thus a Morgan victory, since the house had asked only for equal participation while Jay Cooke had opposed any division.[34] In 1877 the house of Morgan took part in the refunding of the Government bonds, but the banking group was known as the "Belmont Syndicate."[35] This transaction was, however, important in that Drexel, Morgan took the place of Jay Cooke, and became the American associate of Rothschilds.

The eighties however, marked the early preeminence of the Morgan firm.[36] In addition to its normal banking operations, the firm now initiated policies which were to influence the entire economic system of the United States.

Influence over Supply of Credit and Capital

The broad significance of Morgans in the development of American security capitalism can best be understood by noting the two underlying policies of the house. The first policy advanced its influence over the supply of the credit and the capital resources of the financial system; the second policy extended its influence

---

[30] 62nd Congress, 2nd and 3rd Sessions, Banking and Currency Committee, United States Congress, House of Representatives, "Money Trust Investigation," 1912, pp. 89–90.
[31] United States Banking and Currency Committee (House, 62nd Congress, 2nd and 3rd Sessions), *Investigation of the Financial and Monetary Conditions of the United States, Hearings*, hereafter called *Money Trust Investigation*.
[32] *Forum*, April 1893, p. 198.
[33] Drexel and Company of Philadelphia was really the parent firm, and Drexel, Morgan & Company, the New York firm, was started in 1871. By 1894 the importance of the former firm had declined, and J. P. Morgan the elder then formed the firm of J. P. Morgan and Company of New York. See testimony of J. P. Morgan, the younger, before the Senate Committee on the Munitions Industry, *Hearings* S. Res. 206 Part 25, p. 7479. The outstanding study of the firm is Lewis Corey, *House of Morgan*, New York 1930.

[34] Oberholtzer, E. P., *Jay Cooke*, Vol. II, p. 366.
[35] *Bankers Magazine*, July 1877, p. 172.
[36] Recognition of its growing importance is seen in the cable sent by Cyrus W. Field to Junius Morgan as follows: "Many of our business men seem to have lost their heads. What we want is some cool-headed strong man to lead. If you should form a syndicate in London to buy through Drexel, Morgan & Company good securities in this market I believe you would make a great deal of money and at the same time entirely change the feeling here." Corey, op. cit. p. 132.

over the sources of the demand for capital. While a growing proportion of the capital of the American investing public was placed directly in securities, most of these resources continued to be invested indirectly through investment institutions such as savings banks, commercial banks, trust companies and life insurance companies. For the most part, the Morgan firm made little or no attempt to tap the capital resources of the savings banks and they generally remained independent of investment houses. However, other institutions of indirect investment, as commercial banks, trust companies and life insurance companies, came under the influence of the Morgan firm. This relationship was aided by the fact that the American financial system in practice followed the Continental system of mixed rather than the British system of specialized finance. In the course of time, trust companies extended their activities to include both commercial as well as investment banking operations, and life insurance companies in turn, through buying control of trust companies and of commercial banks, indirectly performed the operations of these institutions. This mixed financial system therefore made possible the extensive integration of the structure which took place in the closing decade of the nineteenth century. Influence over these institutions of indirect investment was needed to give the investment banker the assurance of a market for new issues, and syndicate subscriptions were allotted to these financial institutions.

It was particularly advantageous for investment houses to gain control of commercial banks and trust companies. These institutions were important not only because they possessed capital resources but also credit facilities essential for carrying securities until finally marketed. Influence over the banks was exercised through interlocking directorates. J. P. Morgan became vice-president and director of the National Bank of Commerce, and thereby gained close contact with that institution. This bank in turn was closely interlocked with the First National Bank headed by George F. Baker, an ally of Morgan. The Morgan firm through stock ownership and interlocking directorates also obtained an interest in the Chase, the Liberty, the Hanover and the Astor National Banks, and in addition developed a considerable interest in a number of out-of-town banks.[37] Interest was also extended to a group of important trust companies. J. P. Morgan & Company had representation on the boards of directors of the Union, the Commercial and the Fidelity Trust Companies, and in addition organized the Bankers Trust Company. Through the First National Bank a close relation with the Manhattan Trust Company was maintained.[38] In 1909 the Morgan firm obtained an interest in the Guaranty Trust Company which was then added to the Morgan group.

To meet the government attack on the security operations of the national banks connected with Morgans and other investment banks, separate companies known as affiliates were formed. In 1908 the First National Bank, the keystone of the Morgan system of commercial banks, organized the First Securities Company by declaring a dividend of 100 percent which was issued in the form of stock in the securities company. The two organizations were bound together under an organization agreement between George F. Baker on behalf of the trustees and J. P. Morgan acting for the stockholders. In similar manner in 1911 the National City Bank formed the National City Company by paying a 40 percent dividend to the stockholders, and thus providing $10,-000,000 of stock in the new institution.[39]

[37] *Bankers Magazine*, Vol. 63, September 1, 1900, p. 434.
[38] *Chronicle*, February 17, 1900, p. 306, July 28, 1900, p. 163; *Bankers Magazine*, Vol. 63, November 1901, p. 880.
[39] Money Trust Investigation, Part 20, p. 1423.

The great life insurance companies were veritable reservoirs of financial resources, and the large investment houses made every effort to develop close contacts with these companies. Because of this resultant intimate relationship the insurance companies were described as "the financial annexes to Wall Street interests" in the "Armstrong Report" on insurance companies.[40] The house of Morgan developed connections with the Mutual Life Insurance Company, and acquired an interest in the New York Life Insurance as well as in the Equitable Life Assurance Company.[41] The latter institution had been controlled by Thomas F. Ryan who, in the words of the biographer of Dwight Morrow, "was not considered a man of sufficient calibre to execute so large a responsibility."[42] Morgan, therefore, assisted by George Baker and James Stillman, took over Ryan's interests.[43]

Investment Banking and Federal Government Financing

The investment banker is primarily a middleman, or a merchandiser of securities and thus he desires to obtain as large a supply of securities as he can market. The Morgan firm, therefore, developed relations with three sources of demand, the United States Government, the railroads, and industry. As mentioned before, the firm took an active part in the flotation of the various issues of the federal government after the close of the

Civil War. The influence of the Morgan firm in floating federal government securities became increasingly important with the passing of the years, from its competition against Jay Cooke, its secondary position in the Belmont syndicate to its leadership in the critical federal financing of the nineties.

The relations between the Morgan firm and the federal government in the famous "gold loan of 1895" were the subject of bitter controversy. From the perspective of over forty years it is now possible to view the episode objectively.[44] The panic of 1893 was followed by one of the worst depressions in American history. Unemployment gripped the industrial centers, a large number of the railroads were in receivership and the confused currency legislation of Congress raised serious doubt as to the ability of the United States to maintain the gold standard.

Financial conditions abroad were unsatisfactory as an aftermath of the Baring failure, and Europe was drawing heavily on our supply of gold. Throughout 1894 the gold reserves of the treasury at various times were seriously depleted.[45] In order to replenish the government's gold stock, the treasury throughout 1893 sold several bond issues to the public, but they were not well received.[46] These public issues gave no relief since they did not replenish the government gold fund, and the gold supply fell to the desperately low level of only $42,000,000 in February, 1895. In this crisis President Cleveland and Secretary Carlisle were forced to decide whether to obtain the necessary financial relief through another public loan sold to the investors at large or through a private loan by a banking syn-

[40] See State of New York—Report of the Joint Committee of the Senate and Assembly of the State of New York Appointed to Investigate the Affairs of Life Insurance Companies, 1907.
[41] For an account of the internal controversy over the Equitable Life Assurance Society, see Sullivan, op. cit. Vol. III, pp. 41–44.
[42] Nicholson, Harold George, Dwight Morrow, New York 1935, pp. 152–153.
[43] In 1915 these holdings were turned over to T. Coleman DuPont, and later through the efforts of Dwight Morrow the Equitable was converted from a stock to a mutual company. Ibid. p. 154.

[44] New light is thrown on these negotiations by the careful study of James A. Barnes, John G. Carlisle, Financial Statesman, New York 1931.
[45] McElroy, Robert, Grover Cleveland, the Man and the Statesman, Vol. II, New York 1923, pp. 78–79.
[46] Chronicle, January 20, 1894, pp. 105–106; February 3, 1894, p. 199.

dicate. The latter policy alone would give the assurance of obtaining the necessary gold from abroad. The government in despair turned for help to Morgan who rushed to Washington to confer with Cleveland and Carlisle. As a result of these negotiations Morgan agreed to raise a private loan of $50,000,000 with the understanding that the payment should be made in gold of which half was to be obtained from abroad. Morgan was aided by the Deutsche Bank, by August Belmont and by James Stillman, President of the National City Bank.[47]

When the details of the negotiations were announced, bitter criticism was levied at both Cleveland and Carlisle. In these negotiations one senator saw "the iron band of contraction wielded at the dictation of England," and the *New York World* held that the syndicate was made up of Jews and non-Americans. It was particularly charged that the terms of the loan were exorbitant.[48]

The actual terms of the issue were on a 3.75 percent basis, while the outstanding bonds of the United States Government were selling on a 3 percent basis. The issue however was conditioned by the requirement that one-half of the gold had to be obtained from abroad.[49] The action of the Morgan syndicate enabled the federal government to avoid the step of suspending gold payment and abandoning the gold standard. Cleveland and Carlisle on their part, in seeking to maintain the gold standard, had no alternative but a private loan from the banking syndicate. The fact that the country, at that time, had no central bank, made it necessary to deal with a banking syndicate having sufficient foreign support to import gold.

Rebuilding of Railway Finance

The original reason for Morgan's active participation in railroad finance was primarily due to his realization of the need of protecting the interests of the investors, particularly foreign investors, in American railroad securities. Throughout the seventies losses were heavy, and in 1876 39 percent of all the railroad bonds were in default, while in 1879, 65 roads with capitalization of $234,000,000 were sold under foreclosure.[50] As a result of these conditions, the European market for American railway securities was practically closed, and the free flow of capital from Europe to America was checked. A German banker stated that an American railroad bond could not be sold "even if signed by an angel."[51]

In this emergency the house of Morgan determined to take the leadership in the financial reorganization of the railroads. In the end this policy was to lead the house not only to take merely an external financial interest in the railroads but also to participate actively in the managerial policy of many of the systems. Throughout the sixties the railroads were mainly controlled by the speculative capitalists. The only important invasion of this field by banking interests was the ill-fated venture of Jay Cooke in obtaining control of the Northern Pacific. For years Gould and Fiske not only ruled their own railroad domains absolutely, but even

---

[47] Stillman claimed considerable credit for the success of the negotiations. Burr, Anna R., *Portrait of a Banker—James Stillman 1850–1918,* New York 1927, p. 116.

[48] Even Alexander Dana Noyes, financial editor of the *New York Times,* felt that the bankers had driven a hard bargain. See Noyes, op. cit. pp. 234–235. This opinion of Noyes, a conservative commentator, is frequently quoted in radical literature. See also Nevins, Allan, *Grover Cleveland,* New York 1932, pp. 662–665.

[49] The banking syndicate made its profit mainly from the appreciation of the issue in the open market, since it was purchased at a price of 104 and rose as high as 123. *New York Tribune,* May 11, June 27, September 22, 1895.

[50] *Bankers Magazine,* Vol. 34, February, 1880, p. 654; British *Bankers Magazine,* 1876, Vol. 36, p. 141.

[51] Oberholzer, op. cit., Vol. II, p. 418.

made successful forays into the territories of other powerful railroad barons, including that of Cornelius Vanderbilt, who notwithstanding all his financial strength was forced to give ground. The conservative bankers of the East strongly disapproved of these financial raids, but lacked the courage to check them.[52] Morgan, however, was determined to meet force with force, and with his intervention the Gould-Fiske interests were thoroughly whipped in the battle for control of the Albany and Susquehanna Railroad.[53] The defeat of the Gould-Fiske interests brought relief to harassed security capitalism, and this contest waged not only by litigation but by force of arms made Morgan the acknowledged leader of the new banking capitalism.[54] The victory of the security banker over the speculative security capitalist was decisive, and the latter now disappeared as an important factor in the railroad field.

With his influence over a number of eastern lines now established, Morgan gradually extended his sway over the western roads. Many roads were in a demoralized financial position. To a large extent this condition was due to the economic feudalism which permitted ruthless competition among systems dominated by separate railroad presidents acting as lords over their respective territories. There was urgent need of replacing this chaos with order, and the strong hand of Morgan forced many of the railroad barons to accept his sovereignty. In January 1889 the leading railroad presidents assembled in the Madison Avenue home of Morgan, and at the conclusion of this meeting Morgan made the following significant public announcement:

I am authorized to say, I think, on behalf of the banking houses represented here that if an organization can be formed practically upon the basis submitted by the committee, and with an executive committee able to enforce its provisions, upon which the bankers shall be represented, they are prepared to say that they will not negotiate, and will do everything in their power to prevent the negotiation of, any securities for the construction of parallel lines, or the extension of lines not approved by that executive committee. I wish that distinctly understood.[55]

The financial press of the time referred to this meeting as "the bankers' triumph and the presidents' surrender." This conference signified the transfer of the control of the railroads from the hands of the industrial capitalist to those of the investment banker. Not only were the finances of many of the railroads to be directed by the bankers but also the management of these vast systems passed into their hands.[56]

The New Haven Defeat

The most serious reverse suffered by J. P. Morgan in the field of railway finance came toward the close of his career in the unsatisfactory results of his plan to combine the transportation system of New England. Morgan had been a director of the New York, New Haven and Hartford Railroad for a number of years, and under his guidance the road prospered until the close of the century. Morgan then decided to apply his policy of railroad combination successful in the past in other territories to the entire New England area. To carry out the plan the resources of the New Haven, then in an excellent financial position, were used. All forms of transportation, including railroads, steamship lines and trolley lines were bought up.[57] The most important acquisition was that of the Boston and Maine which was soundly

[52] Corey, op. cit. pp. 111–112.
[53] Ibid. pp. 110–112.
[54] Ibid., p. 112.

[55] Corey, op. cit. p. 170.
[56] Dewing, A. S., "Theory of Railroad Reorganization," American Economic Review, VIII (1918), p. 779.
[57] Brandeis, Louis D., Other People's Money, New York 1914, pp. 179, 193.

capitalized and efficiently managed.[58] On the other hand, worthless property was also purchased. One railroad operating at a loss, was acquired at a cost of $1,-500,000.[59]

The effect of these operations may be seen in Table 1 on page 127 showing the financial position of the New Haven in 1903 and in 1909.

From this table it is seen that in 1903 the financial position of the New Haven was excellent, with the ratio of funded debt to total capitalization at a low of 7.93 percent and with fixed charges fairly well covered at 184.21 percent. By 1909 the funded debt had been increased to $234,900,000, and consequently the ratio of funded debt to total capitalization rose to 52.15 percent while fixed charge coverage fell to 149.08 percent. Dividends on the inflated stock were at first paid from surplus then from short-term borrowings, were later reduced and finally suspended altogether. The press and the Interstate Commerce Commission were bitter in their denunciation of the Morgan policy. The critical but calmer conclusion of Professor W. Z. Ripley on the New Haven episode was as follows:

The New Haven disaster goes far to justify the popular distrust of any undue concentration of power. . . . Once and for all in New England the question seems to be settled that even an honest transportation monopoly is inimical to the best public interest.[60]

Influence over Industry

In addition to the extension of influence over the forces of the demand for capital in the field of national government and of railroad financing, Morgan & Company also extended its power to certain fields of industrial financing, particularly the steel business. In this field Morgan encountered another powerful leader of industrial capitalism in the person of Andrew Carnegie, who was a firm believer in the competitive system, and who entered into bitter competitive fights. In a memorandum to his partners Carnegie wrote:

Put your trust in the policy of attending to your own business in your own way and running your mills full, regardless of prices and very little trust in the efficacy of artificial arrangements with your competitors, which have the serious result of strengthening them if they strengthen you. Such is my advice.[61]

Carnegie threatened Morgan with competition not only in steel but in railroads, for he instituted surveys for his own road from Pittsburgh to the Atlantic seaboard.[62] Morgan then determined to buy out Carnegie. After considerable negotiation, Carnegie agreed to take $447,000,000 for his properties.[63] Thus a leading industrialist capitalist passed from the scene.[64] The Carnegie properties now formed the basis of the billion-dollar United States Steel Corporation, whose board of directors included a large representation of Morgan interests.[65] This deal was another victory for banking capitalism over industrial capitalism, and was so recognized by the press of the day.

Outside of the steel business Morgan & Company in these years made little effort to penetrate the other major fields of industry. The petroleum industry by this time was dominated completely by John

[58] Interstate Commerce Commission Reports, Vol. 31, June–October 1914, p. 47.
[59] New York Times, May 20, 1914, November 10 and 23, 1915.
[60] Ripley, William Z., Railroads, Finance and Organization, New York 1915, p. 473.

[61] Tarbell, Ida M., Life of Elbert H. Gary, New York 1933, p. 114.
[62] Sullivan, op. cit. Vol. II, pp. 347–349.
[63] Tarbell, op. cit. p. 121.
[64] Carnegie in retirement continued to criticize banking security capitalism severely, lashing out against the "Wall Street gamblers." Chronicle, Vol. 48, March 30, 1907, p. 714.
[65] Tarbell, op. cit. p. 118.

Table 1/ Financial Position of the New Haven Railroad (1903 and 1909)

Items	(Million Dollars)	1903	1909
1	Operating revenues	47.3	54.3
2	Total income	10.5	24.3
3	Fixed charges[a]	5.7	16.3
4	Funded debt	14.5	234.9
5	Total capitalization[b]	182.9	450.4

Ratios		(Per Cent)	
A	Total income to fixed charges	184.21	149.08
B	Funded debt to total capitalization	7.93	52.15
C	Total income to total capitalization	5.74	5.39

[a] Includes rents for leases.
[b] Includes capitalization of leased rentals at rate of 6 per cent.
Source: Compiled from Poor's *Manual of Railroads*, 43rd Annual Number, 1910, p. 64.

D. Rockefeller. As an industrial capitalist he differed from Carnegie in that the latter believed in competition while the former aggressively pushed the policy of monopoly. The enormous profits from the petroleum industry furnished sufficient resources to finance the expansion of the Rockefeller interests, and thus they were independent of the bankers. The Rockefeller interests even entered the banking field, and obtained a substantial interest in several financial organizations, particularly the National City Bank.[66]

Henry Clews paid tribute to the financial power of the Standard Oil group in the statement that "This combination controls Wall Street almost absolutely. Many of the strongest financial institutions are at their service in supplying accommodations when needed."[67]

Rockefellers and Morgans, as the respective leaders of industrial and banking capitalism, at times had conflicting interests and came close to open warfare, particularly during the fight over the Northern Pacific, but in every case an open clash was avoided.

In this period Morgan and Company made little effort to finance the new industries which were then coming into existence. For example, in 1908 the Morgan firm was offered the financing of William C. Durant, who was a leader in the new automobile industry. Durant was seeking additional capital and asked Morgan and Company to underwrite $500,000 for which loan he offered stock in his company as collateral.[68] Durant fell into a controversy with E. L. Stetson, counsel for Morgans, and with George W. Perkins, an active partner of the firm. In the conversation Durant stated that the time would come when 500,000 automobiles would be sold annually. Perkins commented: "If he has any sense he'll keep such notions to himself if he ever tries to borrow money." The underwriting was therefore denied. In the course of time the stock which Durant offered as collateral for the loan was to pay $35,000,000 in dividends and was to attain a value of over $200,000,000. Durant in later years founded the General Motors Company and became its President. However, during the difficulties of 1920 control of the company passed from Durant to the DuPont interests.[69] Even in the pre-war period Henry Ford became the leading industrial capitalist in the automobile field. In the postwar period he not only retained his independence of banker control, but even extended his influence over certain major banking institutions. Like Carnegie, Henry Ford was an outspoken critic of banking capitalism.

[66] Money Trust Investigation, Part 22, pp. 1581–1591.
[67] Clews, Henry, *Fifty Years in Wall Street*, New York 1908, p. 702.
[68] McManus, Theodore F., and Beasley, Norman, *Men, Money and Motors*, New York 1924, pp. 103–104.
[69] Nicolson, op. cit. p. 156.

Growing Demand for Capital

The demand for capital came to some extent from the federal, state and municipal governments but largely from the railroad, industrial and utility corporations and from real estate. The trend of the national debt over these years was generally downward. This decline was checked by the financing of the Spanish-American War, the indemnity to Spain and the construction of the Panama Canal. All told, however, the national debt increased but slightly.

The debt structure of the state governments was very sound. The unfunded debt showed no increase and the proportion of the unfunded to gross debt was never high. The net debt generally declined and showed little increase until the turn of the century when it began the rise which continued throughout the war and postwar period. However, population also increased over these years, and as a result the net debt per capita remained at a low figure. The state governments always had a goodly amount of assets which could be deducted from their gross debt, and the proportion of such deductions to the gross debt was always high. The statistics on the amount of the tax base or the assessed valuation of the property on which taxes could be levied are incomplete, but they indicate the rapid increase in assessed valuation of such taxable property. As a result of the more rapid increase in the tax base compared with the increase in the net debt of the states, the tax base covered the net debt at a rising ratio. Thus the various trends in the finances of the state governments were very satisfactory.

Municipal debt rose sharply. In 1870 the total debt was $516,000,000 and by 1880 it had increased by $305,000,000, but over the next decade municipalities adopted a pay-as-you-go policy and debt rose only by $105,000,000. After 1890, however, municipal borrowing rose sharply

and by 1902 the total debt was $1,630,-000,000. The 1912 figures show a municipal debt more than double that of 1902 or $3,476,000,000.[70]

Financial Position of the Railroads

The volume of railroad financing was by far the most important form of corporate investment over these years. The statistics on American railroads before 1890 are incomplete, and owing to differences in the methods of keeping accounts, it is unwise to compare the financial statements before and after this date. The following ratios show the financial position of the railroads from 1880 until 1889.

Table 2/ Railroad Finance, 1880–1889 (Percent)

Years	Total Income to Interest	Funded Debt to Total Capitalization	Property to Funded Debt
	A	B	C
1880	236.58	48.36	194.54
1885	189.46	49.65	186.88
1889	186.73	51.78	178.07

Source: Compiled from Poor's *Manual of Railroads* for these years.

From 1880 to 1890 the financial position of the railroads was not satisfactory, as may be seen by the fact that the total income to interest declined. The proportion of the funded debt to total capitalization increased and the property protection of their funded debt declined.

The trend of railway finance may be studied more accurately after 1890, for after that date the Interstate Commerce Commission presented annual figures for all the Class I railroads. Due to the rapid extensive development of the United

[70] Hillhouse, Albert M., *Municipal Bonds*, New York 1936, pp. 34–35.

States the operating revenues of the railroads from 1890 to 1910 expanded to 261 percent, while operating expenses were at about the same level (263 percent) and so the ratio of operating expenses to operating revenues remained fairly satisfactory at an average of 66.2 percent for the period. Also the ratio of operating income to operating revenues was maintained at the high average of 33.7 percent for the period. This ratio indicated that the roads had the satisfactory sum of 33 cents of operating income left over from the revenues after paying for all operating expenses. Total income rose to 244.9 percent or greater than the upswing in fixed charges which rose to only 159.3 percent. As a result the ratio of the total income to fixed charges rose from 132.6 percent in 1890 to 204 percent in 1910, which was very satisfactory. Also the amount of net income or the balance left over after fixed charges rose more sharply than operating revenues and so the ratio between these two items increased from 9.6 percent in 1890 to 18.8 percent in 1910. This ratio signified that operating revenues could fall 18.8 percent before the coverage of the fixed charges was impaired and indicated a satisfactory margin of safety. While net income, or the balance available for dividends, rose to 511.9 percent, the dividends actually paid by the roads increased to 402.3 percent, and so the ratio of net income to dividends paid rose from 127 percent in 1890 to 147 percent in 1910. This ratio shows that the roads more than earned their dividends over these years.

It was fortunate that the course of earning power was satisfactory, for the trend of railroad capitalization over these years was unsound. From 1890 to 1910 the roads increased their funded debt from $4,462,000,000 to $10,388,000,000, their total debt including capitalized leased rentals from $5,978,000,000 to $12,638,000,000 and their total capitalization from $10,157,000,000 to $20,700,000,000.[71] As a result of the greater increase in the total debt as compared to total capitalization, the ratio between these two items rose from 58.8 percent in 1890 to 61.0 percent in 1910. By 1890 the proportion of debt to total capitalization was already high but increased further in the years which followed. Fortunately the total income increased rapidly and it was possible at the time to carry the heavy debt without serious difficulty.

In part, the increase in total capitalization was due to the need of funds for the construction of additional operating mileage, which rose from 163,597 in 1890 to 240,831 in 1910.[72] The total stated value of railroad property over these years rose from $7,755,000,000 to $14,387,000,000.[73]

Foreign Financing

The trend of the capital movement between the United States and foreign countries began to change in the early eighties. The first important foreign loan was made in 1879 when an issue of $3,000,000 was granted to the Province of Quebec.[74] Between the years 1896 and 1900 $100,000,000 of American capital was exported to Canada.[75] In 1899 Morgan's floated a loan to the Mexican Government and there was also considerable American investment in Mexican railroads.[76] In the early years of the century the New York market granted loans to various continental countries as Germany, Russia and Sweden.[77] The most important single

---

[71] *Statistics of Railroads*, Interstate Commerce Commission, 1890, p. 12; 1910, p. 15.
[72] Ibid.
[73] Ibid.
[74] *Bankers Magazine*, Vol. 33, April 1879, p. 745.
[75] Ibid. *The Economist*, Vol. 59, January 26, 1901, p. 119.
[76] *Chronicle*, April 27, 1901, Vol. 22, p. 60.
[77] *Bankers Magazine*, October 1900, pp. 496, 637.

case of foreign financing in these years was America's extensive participation in the flotation of the British government loans issued to finance the Boer War. During 1900 and 1901 Morgan and Company floated successive loans in large amounts for this purpose.[78] Later England bought back a large part of her securities, and by 1903 the *Chronicle* expressed the opinion that "practically all these securities have gone back to England."[79]

After the beginning of the century the United States took an active though generally unsuccessful part in financing the Far East. Kuhn, Loeb and Company and Edward Harriman participated extensively in financing Japan during its conflict with Russia.[80] Harriman apparently had a grandiose plan of a round-the-world railroad, and for this purpose negotiated with both the Japanese and Russian Governments. In 1905 Morgan and Company took over the Belgian interest in the American China Development Company, but later the entire American participation in the Company was bought out by the Chinese Government.[81] An American banking group headed by Morgan and Company, including Kuhn, Loeb, the National City Bank and Edward Harriman, on the insistence of the state department, and even of President Taft personally, gained its admission into the international banking loan to China in 1911.[82] In 1913 President Wilson withdrew all official support of American banking in its far-eastern finan-

cial operations and thus forced the American group to retire from this field.[83]

Changing Sources of Capital Supply

Throughout this period foreign capital in the United States continued large in amount but of declining importance. While foreign capital had a large and even a majority interest in the leading railroads in the early nineties this participation was sharply reduced by 1905.[84]

In the last quarter of the century the supply of domestic capital increased rapidly, coming both from the profits of the wealthy class and particularly from the growth in the material prosperity of the middle class. As in other countries this group formed the social foundation of developed security capitalism. National wealth rose from $43,600,000,000 in 1880 to $65,000,000,000 in 1890 to $88,-500,000,000 in 1900 and to $186,300,-000,000 in 1910 and likewise national income rose from $7,400,000,000 in 1880 to $31,400,000,000 in 1910. Estimates of the total volume of saving are always difficult but the trend may be seen from the total assets of the financial institutions of the United States from 1873 to 1911. The assets of these institutions including banking institutions as national banks, savings banks, private banks, loan and trust companies and also life insurance companies, rose slowly from a total of $3,091,000,000 in 1873 to only $3,817,-000,000 in 1880. However by 1890 the total rose to $7,096,000,000, by 1900 it was $12,528,000,000 and by 1910 it reached $26,326,000,000.[85] These insti-

---

[78] *Chronicle*, Vol. 71, August 11, 1900, pp. 258, 261; Ibid. Vol. 72, August 27, 1901, p. 796; Ibid. Vol. 74, April 19, 1902, pp. 802–803; See speech of Chancellor of the Exchequer, April 23, 1903; *Economist*, Vol. 61, May 9, 1903, p. 832.
[79] *Chronicle*, Vol. 77, December 5, 1903, p. 2132.
[80] Croly, Herbert David, *Willard Straight*, New York 1924, pp. 239, 297. Willard Straight, consul general at Mukden, later acted for Morgan's in their Far-eastern financial operations.
[81] Ibid. p. 287; Nearing, Scott, and Freeman, Joseph, *Dollar Diplomacy*, New York 1925, p. 37.
[82] MacMurray, John, *Treaties and Agreements with and Concerning China*, Vol. I, New York 1921, p. 800.

[83] The statement of President Wilson is reproduced in the *American Journal of International Law*, Vol. 7, pp. 338–339.
[84] Ripley, op. cit. p. 5.
[85] Some students of the subject believed that the increase in saving funds as indicated in these figures did not represent a growth of the actual saving of the lower classes. It was pointed out that the size of deposits in Con-

tutions of indirect investment over the years transferred a growing proportion of their assets into security investment. The total for all the financial institutions rose from 18 percent in 1890 to 24.7 percent by 1910.

A growing proportion of individual investors turned from indirect to direct investment and from real estate mortgages to securities. Until the end of the nineteenth century only fragmentary figures on the distribution of security holdings are available. In 1880 it was estimated that the public debt was held by 71,587 individuals.[86] The shares of the national banks in 1886 were held by 223,583 persons of whom 117,974 or more than one-half held ten shares or less.[87] In 1897 war loans of $200,000,000 issued by the United States Government were taken up in 320,000 separate allotments.[88] The first extensive figures on security holdings, as compiled in 1899, showed that 54 railroad companies reported 282,160 stockholders and 56 industrial companies showed 338,824 stockholders or a total of 110 corporations with 626,983 stockholders.[89] The number of bookholders of corporate shares in the United States rose from 4,400,000 in 1900 to 7,500,000 in 1913.[90] Over the same period the average number of one hundred dollar par value

shares per stockholder declined from 140 shares to 87 shares.[91] These figures indicate the growth of the popularization of security capitalism in the pre-war period.

There was also a widening of the geographic distribution of security holdings. This distribution of security holdings was no longer confined to the East, but began to spread throughout the West. Frank A. Vanderlip, as vice-president of the National City Bank, stated in 1905 that:

The whole great Mississippi Valley gives promise that at some day distant perhaps it will be another New England for investments. There is a developing bond market there which is of constant astonishment to Eastern dealers.[92]

Public interest in security investment varied with the course of security prices, but since the general trend of security prices over these years was upward, a favorable public attitude towards security capitalism was created.

As a result of the rapid conversion of the assets of the institutions of indirect investment into securities, and the growth of direct investment in securities by individual investors, the proportion of securities to total wealth rose sharply. It was estimated that the outstanding securities amounted to one-third of the total national wealth.[93] This proportion was about equal to that of the leading nations of Europe and thus the United States, by the beginning of the century, had reached about the same maturity in the evolution of security capitalism as these older countries.

Results of Security Capitalism

The developed stage of security capitalism brought with it the usual evils of overcapitalization of assets, deterioration in

---

necticut banks from 1880 to 1910 showed that the total of accounts less than $1,000 decreased from nearly one-half of the total amount of deposits in 1880 to a little over one-third by 1910. This decrease, it is stated, took place notwithstanding the fact that total saving increased almost 400 percent and that the number of depositors increased nearly 200 per cent. Epstein, Abraham, "Darker Phases of American Prosperity" in the New Republic, Vol. 57, February 6, 1929, p. 314.
[86] Adams, Henry C., Public Debts, New York 1887, p. 47.
[87] Chronicle, Vol. 43, December 11, 1886, p. 685.
[88] Annual Report of the Secretary of the Treasury, 1898, p. XXXVIII.
[89] Chronicle, 1909, p. 521.
[90] Estimates of Warshow, H. T., "Distribution of Corporate Ownership in the United States," in the Quarterly Journal of Economics, Vol. 39, November 1924, p. 28.

[91] Ibid. p. 28.
[92] Chronicle, Supplement Vol. 81, Bankers and Trust Section, October 21, 1905, p. 94.
[93] Conant, Charles A., "The World's Wealth in Negotiable Securities," in the Atlantic Monthly, Vol. 101, January 1908, p. 97.

the quality of the securities based on these assets, the issuing of fraudulent statements, consequent security price depreciation, intermittent maladjustment between saving and investment with the resultant sharp security price fluctuations and financial panics.

In the case of certain specific railroads there was serious overcapitalization. Within a seven-year period the bonded debt of the Chicago and Alton was raised from $33,900,000 to $114,000,000.[94] Within a ten-year period the bonds of the Cincinnati, Hamilton and Dayton were increased from $12,000,000 to $48,000,000, while the unfunded debt rose from $200,000 to $10,000,000.[95] In neither case was there any corresponding increase in earnings to justify the higher capitalization. In fact, the underlying assets often depreciated in value and as Sterne declared:

The original bonded indebtedness, representing ties that have rotted, rails that have been sold, cars that have broken up, bridges and engines that have disappeared, remains a charge upon the road in the shape of bonds bearing interest.[96]

Overcapitalization was also a characteristic of much of the industrial financing of the late nineteenth and early twentieth centuries. In the case of the so-called "Sugar Trust," the outstanding bonds of $10,000,000 were based on plans estimated at $7,740,000 and the additional capital stock of $75,000,000 represented no tangible value.[97]

A further illustration was the United States Steel Corporation, which had a total capitalization of $1,403,450,000 consisting of $303,450,000 in bonds, $550,000,000 in preferred stock and $550,000,000 in common stock. The physical valuation of the property, as estimated in the report of the United States commissioner of corporations, was placed at $682,000,000, which did not even cover the bonds and preferred stock.[98] This corporation is a good illustration of the interpretation of overcapitalization as given in the introductory chapter. It was there stated that the test of overcapitalization is whether or not the future earning power of the corporation is adequate to support the volume of securities which have been issued. During the early years the earnings of the United States Steel Corporation were insufficient to justify the heavy capitalization. However, in time the expanding profits of the Corporation were sufficient to place even the common stock on a satisfactory earning basis. Judged therefore by actual earnings the United States Steel Corporation eventually was not overcapitalized. The conservative financial press was strong in its denunciation of overcapitalization, and the *Chronicle* stated that:

the floating of many of these concerns, however, at enormously inflated valuations and the issue of stocks upon such fictitious basis cannot be too strongly condemned—a more forceful objection to these combinations can be found in the extravagant overcapitalization adopted by the promoters. In most of the schemes offered to the public for subscription the bonded debt and preferred stock are fully equal to, and often in excess of, the real value of the property represented, while the common stock is simply a bonus which is divided between the promoters and the original proprietors.[99]

The course of a security boom is generally marked by a deterioration in the quality of new securities and the widespread speculative trend of these years was no

[94] Ripley, op. cit. p. 112.
[95] Ibid. p. 113.
[96] Sterne, Simon, "Recent Railroad Failures and Their Lessons," in the *Forum*, 17, March 1894, p. 27.
[97] Lloyd, Henry Demarest, *Wealth Against Commonwealth*, New York 1894, p. 33.
[98] Cotter, Arundel, *United States Steel*, New York 1921, p. 201.
[99] *Chronicle*, Supp. Vol. 69, July–December, 1899, Bankers and Trust Supplement, p. 25.

exception. Conant writing in 1904 stated that:

In the case of industrial securities issued on the American market, the character of those issued has tended in many cases to become worse as the issues have increased. When this demand for new securities was small, it was necessary that they should be of the highest character to find a market; when the demand became apparently insatiable, it was natural that shrewd and sometimes unscrupulous promoters should set themselves to provide a supply.[100]

Financial statements in this period were unreliable, and the issuing of untrue earning statements was a common practice. When the Atchison, Topeka and Santa Fe went into receivership in 1894, an independent audit revealed that while the statements from 1891 to 1894 showed satisfactory surpluses, actually the books had been falsified to cover an average annual deficit of over $1,250,000 for these years.[101]

As a result of unsound financial practices there were frequently serious losses to the holders of securities.

Losses were especially heavy in oil and in mining stocks. Marvin Scudder, who compiled lists of obsolete and extinct securities, stated in 1904 that "out of something over one million face value of such old mining stocks which have come to hand from estates in the past ten years, I have recovered exactly $12 on one certificate."[102] Real estate bonds also brought heavy losses. One company placed on its bonds in large letters, the words: "United States of America" and in even larger letters the words "savings bonds." The company even employed clergymen to sell its bonds, and when it failed the receiver was not able to find sufficient money in the treasury even to retain an accountant to go over the books.[103]

In the last quarter of the nineteenth century a number of cities overexpanded their debt and in many cases defaults followed. After the panic of 1873 Houston, Pittsburgh, Elizabeth and Rahway defaulted on their obligations. The panic of 1893 again precipitated extensive municipal default but from that year until 1926 the volume of municipal default was relatively small. There was also a marked drop in municipal defaults arising out of acts of invalidity due to technical legal irregularities. In the seventies and even eighties many municipalities took advantage of some small irregularity in the issuing of their bonds subsequently to declare their obligations void. However, these acts in time decreased and by the beginning of the century the practice was negligible. As early as 1885 the American investor began to suffer losses on foreign government bonds and the *Chronicle* for that year bemoaned the fact that: "For the first time a large body of American investors find themselves affected in purse by the action of a foreign government."[104]

Notwithstanding their considerable losses on individual securities, the holders of American issues as a class derived a net gain over these years. The value of common and preferred stocks appreciated markedly over these years. An investment in the stock of the average corporation which had both common and preferred stocks listed on the leading stock exchanges showed a growth in value from 100 in 1886 to 1,102 for common stocks and to 822 for preferred stocks by 1910.[105]

[100] Conant, Charels A., *Wall Street and the Country*, New York 1904, pp. 24–26.
[101] Dewing, op. cit. p. 788.
[102] *Chronicle*, Vol. 78, May 28, 1904, pp. 199.

[103] Atwood, Albert W., "Unsound Real Estate Bonds," *Harper's Weekly*, Vol. 59, August 29, 1914, p. 214.
[104] *Chronicle*, op. cit. Vol. 41, July 18, 1885, p. 62.
[105] Bosland C., *The Common Stock Theory of Investment*, New York 1937, p. 23.

Chapter Four

Agriculture and Labor in an Expanding Economy

■ In the years before World War I, American agriculture presented an increasingly complex pattern. To the old export staples of cotton, corn, cane sugar, tobacco, and wheat were added new regional specialties, such as dates and citrus fruits, and new field crops, such as sorghum and soybeans. Meat animals, which had previously been marketed mainly on the hoof and slaughtered for local consumption, now were shipped alive by rail to central slaughtering and packing plants, and the dressed fresh meat was sent east and to Europe pro-

tected by refrigeration. At the same time, exports of all the staples continued to play an important role in American economic growth. Even in 1914, semifinished and finished manufactures made up less than half of American exports. In partial return for agricultural exports the nation received European manufactured goods and machinery which speeded economic development.

The westward movement of farmers to new land continued throughout the nineteenth century and into the early twentieth, but with changing destinations. Up to the middle eighties, Kansas, Nebraska, Minnesota, and the Dakotas were the principal new farming areas; from 1850 on, the Pacific Coast also attracted farmers; and in the early twentieth century, Oklahoma and west Texas had waves of pioneer farm settlers.

In all the new farming areas, available land at an attractive price was inevitably the reason for settlement, but the process of settlement has been overidealized as one of poor men with little capital becoming farm landowners or at least farm tenants with the expectation of easy progression to ownership. Recent study of the details of settlement has cast doubt on whether landowners or even tenants were a majority of the adult-male population in new agricultural areas. It would appear that the small initial population of a new agricultural area was likely to be made up largely of men interested in land speculation or exploitation of natural resources and that in the first large wave of settlers more than half the people either could not afford to set up as farmers or had other interests—in mining, manufacturing, trade, or services. For example, in the Black River Census District of Trempealeau County, Wisconsin, in 1850, when settlement had just begun, there were only 63 farm owners or managers out of 235 people gainfully employed.[1] In short, recent scholarship reveals the history of the westward movement as a story of business and labor as well as a tale of the spread of independent farming.

[1] Merle E. Curti and Associates, *The Making of an American Community* (Palo Alto, Calif.: Stanford University Press, 1959), p. 63.

The Prairie West

■ Establishing a farm on the Western plains, anywhere from Illinois to Colorado, was an arduous and costly process. The sod was so resistant to initial plowing that extra teams of horses, mules, or oxen had to be hired; timber for building had to be bought and transported long distances; and as one went west, crop yields became more and more uncertain. In an important article published in 1935, Paul W. Gates, of Cornell University, attacked the ideas that free land could mean free farming settlement and that a turn to farming out west could be an escape from economic woe for unemployed Eastern workers.[2] The article coincided with a general revision of ideas about the economic meaning of the frontier. In the following selection, Professor Gates points out that $500 would be a minimum cost of settlement, and two or three times this sum might be average. By the time they reached their destination, westward migrants generally lacked such capital. As a result they were forced either to rent from an established landlord or to serve as laborers. Because of the high costs of settlement, free land never had much meaning for the would-be farmer without capital.

[2] "The Homestead Act in an Incongruous Land System," *American Historical Review*, vol. 41, pp. 652–681.

Paul W. Gates
Frontier Estate Builders and Farm Laborers*

To the simple democratic society of the American frontier consisting mostly of small farmers, as Frederick Jackson Turner described it, should be added two types, the one common, the other small in numbers but profoundly important in shaping land-ownership patterns, political action, and the beginnings of a cultured society. The first of these types includes the farm laborers, some of whom became farm tenants. The other type is the capitalist estate builder who took with him a "seemingly endless appetite for power and for land," as Arthur Moore put it.[1] It was these capitalist estate builders, whether cattle barons, land speculators turned developers, or men who went west with the set purpose of creating great plantations operated by tenants or hired hands, who made possible the employment of thousands of laborers.

The capitalist developer, big and little, was first revealed indirectly in 1860 when the Bureau of the Census presented statistics showing the number of farm laborers—statistics as noteworthy in their way as those showing the extent of farm tenancy in 1880 or the statement of the superintendent of the census in 1890 that the frontier was gone. Notwithstanding America's much-boasted opportunities, its seemingly limitless supply of public lands, its ever-expanding and newly opening frontier, the farm laborer, ordinarily a landless person whose economic status was less secure than that of the European peasant, was shown to exist in large num-

bers, not only in the older and well-developed communities, but in the new states and middle border territories.

Consider for a moment Iowa, only fourteen years a state, still but lightly touched by settlement, not able to boast two people to the square mile, with less than a third of its land in farms but the bulk of its public lands already in private ownership. Despite the slight development of this state, largely concentrated in the eastern counties, its obvious frontier status, its abundance of raw unimproved prairie, Iowa in 1860 reported 40,827 farm laborers—6 per cent of its population. More to the point, out of every hundred persons engaged in agriculture, twenty-three were farm laborers. Or look at Kansas, which had neither attained the dignity of statehood nor acquired anything but a thin veneer of settlement along its eastern border in the six years since it had become a territory. Census enumerators found here 10,400 farms and, surprisingly, 3,660 farm laborers. Nineteen out of every hundred persons engaged in agriculture were farm laborers. For the states of the Old Northwest the percentage of farm laborers among the total number of people engaged in agriculture ranged from 20 to 28.

Throughout the rest of the century, the number of farm laborers grew rapidly in the newer states of the Upper Mississippi Valley, while in the older states it fluctuated up and down and took a violent upward turn in the last decade. In proportion to the total number of persons engaged in agriculture, the number of farm laborers reached a high point in 1870. The census for that year shows that the percentage of farm laborers in the total number of persons engaged in agriculture was 30 in Minnesota, 32 in Nebraska, 33

* Reprinted by permission of the copyright owners, the Regents of the University of Wisconsin, from Walker D. Wyman and Clifton B. Kroeber, The Frontier in Perspective, 1957, the University of Wisconsin Press, pp. 144–163.
[1] Arthur Moore, The Farmer and Rest of Us (Boston, 1945), 131.

in Wisconsin, 34 in Kansas, and 37 in Iowa. All these states had fairly stable and well-developed areas by 1870; but all except Iowa also had portions not yet out of the frontier stage. With so many farm laborers in new as well as old communities, no picture of the West can be considered complete without attention to their social and economic background, the reasons why they existed in such numbers. But Western historians have not been concerned about them. The stereotype of the mortgaged farmer is familiar to all students of Western lore, but the farm laborer has not been the subject of rowdy ballads, he does not appear in the fiction of the frontier, nor is he to be found in the works of Turner, Paxson, Riegel, or Billington.

Statistics of farm labor for these years in new states and territories are so startling that it seems desirable to look into their compilation to determine just who in the opinion of the census enumerators fitted into this category. Analysis of the original census schedules shows that older boys of farm families who were over fifteen years of age and were living at home were not infrequently listed as farm laborers. Undoubtedly they performed heavy routine work on the farm, but I have not thought of them as laborers, since they rarely drew wages and since they could expect to inherit a share of the farm some time in the future. Offsetting this factor was the exclusion of migratory workers who were employed for the harvest season but were not at the time of enumeration living with the farmers who had previously engaged them or were thereafter to do so. Clearly, the timing of the census was important in the matter of enumerating farm laborers. The first of June, the date for which information was collected, was not the busiest time for farmers in the Corn Belt, because crops were already in, haying had not begun, and wheat was not yet ready for harvest. A month or six weeks later,

enumerators would have found greater numbers of hired hands to list.[2]

By 1870 the census takers were collecting information respecting the value of compensation, including board paid hired hands the previous year. True, this information was not processed and published, but a sample study of Poweshiek County in central Iowa shows that of 1,634 farmers owning land, 932 paid out for labor the previous year sums ranging from $5 to $2,000, the average being over $150. In nine townships in this county, payments to farm laborers, including the value of their board, amounted to $234,000.[3]

The census schedules also furnish information on the emergence of farm tenancy, a midway step from laborer to farm owner, which is particularly valuable since we have no specific data on tenancy as such until 1880. Some years ago in a colloquy on land speculation at a meeting of the American Historical Association, this writer ventured to suggest to Dr. Joseph Schafer, superintendent of the State Historical Society of Wisconsin, that in his examination of the profits and losses in speculation, he may have underestimated the rents speculators collected; this suggestion was scoffed at for intimating that tenancy existed on the fron-

[2] Information on the use of migratory laborers is meager, but the *Davenport Gazette* (Iowa), published in an important river port, is helpful in its issues of July 13 to 18, 1868. Daily mention is made of the demand for farm hands, for which as much as $3 and $4 per day was being paid. A stampede of city workers was reported which so depleted the community that construction projects could not be carried on. On the 18th, the steamer Dubuque was reported as bringing in 75 field hands, who within thirty minutes after arrival were engaged at $3.50 to $3.75 a day. Later reports of the movement north of wheat harvesters indicate that migratory labor was a major feature of agriculture in Illinois, Iowa, Wisconsin, and Minnesota.

[3] The original census schedules of Iowa and Wisconsin are in the Iowa Historical and Art Department, Des Moines, and the State Historical Society of Wisconsin, Madison, where they were used for this paper.

tier or that rents could have been collected for land use.[4] Dr. Schafer was a tartar in argument, but the fact remains that tenancy did exist on the frontier, it was not uncommon in Wisconsin in the fifties, and it does have to be taken into account in any consideration of the frontier process. In the absence of detailed census compilations, we can learn much about tenancy from earlier census schedules, the county deed records, local newspaper advertisements, and correspondence of land dealers and landlords.[5]

The censuses of 1850, 1860, and 1870 show a sharp increase in the number of farms in excess of five hundred acres, the expanding volume of hired hands previously alluded to, and numerous "farmers" and farm laborers who owned no real or landed property but did have personal property such as horses, mules, oxen, milch or beef cattle, and hogs. Some of these "farmers" and farm laborers may have been attempting to buy farms they were operating, but whether they were or not, they were at the time tenants. Analysis of the 1870 census listings of farmers and farm laborers in two lightly developed western Iowa townships and one well-settled central Iowa township shows that of 184 persons (excluding children) listed as engaged in agriculture, ninety-six owned land and eighty-eight owned no real property, but fifty-seven of these latter owned personal property and were presumably tenants. Thirty-one "farmers" and farm laborers listed no property of any kind. Of the agricultural population of these three townships (Belvedere, Ashton, and Shiloh), 53 per cent owned farms and 47 per cent owned no land.

Farm land was being rented to tenants in Ohio, Indiana, and Illinois as early as the 1820's, but the practice did not become common for nearly a generation.[6] After the frenzy of land speculation in the thirties, many investors, caught with heavy obligations in a falling market, with interest and tax costs growing, offered to rent their land to squatters or newly arriving immigrants too poor to buy, partly to protect their property but also to get at least the taxes out of them.[7] As early as 1842, Solon Robinson, the well-known agricultural writer, in describing the attractions of the flat lands of northwestern Indiana to immigrants, said: "No matter if you have no money, you can rent land very low, and will soon be in a condition to let land instead of hiring it."[8] By the middle of the century, tenancy was emerging everywhere in the prairies of Indiana, Illinois, and eastern Iowa and a little more slowly in Wisconsin. From northern and eastern Indiana, the Military Tract and the central prairie counties of

[4] For his study of the land speculation of Charles Augustus Murray, who bought 20,000 acres in Grant and LaFayette Counties, Wisconsin, in 1836, Dr. Schafer used the conveyance records at the county seats to determine when the various parcels of land were sold and at what prices. He concluded that Murray had not done as well as if the money had been invested in gilt-edge securities. Since leases ordinarily were not recorded, he had no way of knowing whether any of the land had been rented or what income might have come from rents. In regard to farm tenancy in 1880, these two counties ranked close to the top among Wisconsin counties. The state figure for 1880 is 9 per cent; figures for Grant and LaFayette are 14 and 18 per cent. For Schafer's treatment see his The Wisconsin Lead Region (Madison, 1932), 148–154.

[5] Notices of Wisconsin farms for rent in the fifties were found in the Janesville Gazette, the Janesville Democratic Standard, the Baraboo Sauk County Standard, and the Eau Claire Free Press. The papers of Catlin and Williamson, Cyrus Woodman, and J. Richardson & Co. in the Wisconsin State Historical Society and of Allen Hamilton and George W. Ewing in the Indiana State Library are useful.

[6] Solon J. Buck, Pioneer Letters of Gershom Flagg (Springfield, Illinois, 1912), 22–46; Indiana Oracle and Dearborn Gazette (Lawrence, Indiana), Oct. 4, 1823. Nicholas Longworth had 27 tenants on his farms near Cincinnati in 1850. Ophia D. Smith, The Life and Times of Giles Richards, 1820–1860 ("Ohio Historical Collections," Vol. VI [Columbus, 1936]), 45.

[7] Paul W. Gates, Frontier Landlords and Pioneer Tenants (Ithaca, 1945), 3.

[8] Herbert A. Kellar (ed.), Solon Robinson, Pioneer and Agriculturist ("Indiana Historical Collections," Vol. XXI [Indianapolis, 1936]), I, 351.

Illinois, and the eastern counties of Iowa came many reports of persons renting land who lacked the means to buy. Renting was so common in La Salle County, Illinois, that the local newspaper in its price current listed farms as renting from $1.25 to $1.50 an acre. In eastern Iowa, where improved land also was renting at the same prices, a dealer in 1852 advertised thirteen farms for sale or rent. Elsewhere newspapers discussed the growing practice of share renting.[9]

In mid-century Indiana, a move to define the rights of landlords and tenants developed into a major political battle. Bills to give landlords a lien on crops raised by their tenants had the support of legislators from the prairie counties, where landlordism flourished, but were opposed by the Democratic representatives from the small-farm counties of southern Indiana. Opponents, perhaps not aware of how far landlordism had already developed in the richer counties of the north, said that any such measure would stimulate landlords to enlarge their domain, "increase their subordinate tenancies," and strike at "our true policy to encourage every man to become a land owner." It was legislation "in favor of capital, the rich, and against labor, the poor." Another Hoosier opponent of the measure proposed an amendment to give landlords liens on the furniture, the wife, and the children of the tenant! Session after session of the legislature gave consideration to the question from 1857 to 1881, but not until the latter year was action completed.[10]

The growth of tenancy was stimulated by the granting of lands to railroads to aid in their construction. Two early beneficiary railroads—the Illinois Central and the Burlington and Missouri—after making their selections of land, found squatters on them who could not easily be dispossessed without creating ill feeling, but who were not in a position to pay the price asked for their claims. The Burlington officials found that the easiest policy to follow in such cases was to rent the land to the squatters for one to three years at a nominal price of twenty cents an acre with the hope that such improvements as the squatters made would enable the land to bring a good price when the lease expired and legal action might be taken to evict, if necessary. In 1878, the Burlington was renting Nebraska land which had been farmed during the past year for $1 an acre and idle lands for fifty cents an acre; its land in Iowa was then being rented for as much as $1.25 to $2 an acre. Railroad land-grant policy, like the government policy of permitting—and, indeed, encouraging—extensive speculation in Western lands, hastened the coming of tenancy to the West.[11]

The rapid alienation of public land and swiftly rising land values helped to accelerate the renting of land in the sixties

[9] Letter of J. W. Schreyer, June 22, 1846, in Indiana Magazine of History, XL (Sept., 1944), 294; Anon., A True Picture of Emigration: Of Fourteen Years in the Interior of North America (London, 1838), 60; Florence E. Janson, The Background of Swedish Immigration, 1840–1930 (Chicago, 1931), 141–142; Harvey L. Carter, "Rural Indiana in Transition, 1850–1860," Agricultural History, XX (April, 1946), 114; La Salle, Illinois, Independent, March 4, 1854; G. C. Beman, Groton, Lee Co., Iowa, Jan. 12, 1853, to D. Kilbourne (Kilbourne MSS. in the Iowa Historical and Art Department); Davenport Gazette (Iowa), Jan. 29, Nov. 25, 1852; Oct. 6, 1853; March 26, May 5, 1858; Sioux City Register (Iowa), March 17, 1860, and March 15, 1862.

[10] Brevier Legislative Reports, 1852, 1857, 1859, 1861, 1865, 1881; Laws of Indiana General Assembly, 1881, p. 565; Indianapolis State Sentinel, Jan. 14 and 23, 1857; Monticello Herald, April 1, 1875.

[11] Peter Daggy, Land Department, Illinois Central Railroad, Nov. 30, 1865, to C. E. Perkins; J. M. King, Clarinda, Iowa, June 21, 1865, to Perkins; J. D. McFarland, Lincoln, Nebraska, Nov. 25, 1868, to A. E. Touzalin; W. W. Baldwin, Land Commissioner, Burlington and Missouri, Aug. 23, 1879, to R. A. Crippen, Burlington Archives, Newberry Library. The correspondence of Edward Hayes of Oak, T. S. Goddard of Hastings, R. A. Crippen of Corning, Iowa, land agents of the B & M, contains allusions to numerous instances of the railroad's leasing to tenants on a cash or share-rent basis.

and seventies. In 1880, when statistics of tenancy were compiled, the figures for the public-land states, particularly those which still contained land available for homestead, alarmed land reformers. In Illinois 31 per cent and in Iowa 23 per cent of all the farms were tenant operated. The counties of greater land values and higher productivity had tenancy rates ranging into the high 30's and 40's. More surprising was the swift emergence of tenancy in the border counties of Kansas and Nebraska, where the land had been in private ownership no more than twenty-three years, much of it less than fourteen years. Here the tenancy figures ranged from 25 to 40 per cent. In the states of the Upper Mississippi Valley, the percentage of people engaged in agriculture who were either tenants or farm laborers ranged from 32 in Minnesota to 53 in Illinois.[12]

The early appearance of tenancy and agricultural labor in the amount that has been shown in or close to frontier areas, together with their rapid increase, provides convincing evidence that government land policy was not producing the results its defenders claimed. In view of the oft-repeated objective of American land policy—to assure a nation of free-holders—how is it possible to account for the early appearance of farm laborers and tenants in frontier communities?

Paradoxically, the fact that cheap, and finally free, land was to be had in the American West has a direct bearing on the appearance of farm laborers and tenants in that section. Government land prices were progressively reduced from $2 an acre in 1800 ($1.64 for cash) to $1.25 in 1820, to 60¢ to $1 by the use of military bounty land warrants of 1847–55, to as little as 12.5¢ in 1854, until finally,

in 1862, free land could be obtained. European peasants and debt-ridden farmers in older sections of America were lured west by the vision of cheap or free farms that they confused with cheap or free raw land.

Nor was it sufficiently noted that the cost of farm making was increasing as settlers moved into the tough-sodded, poorly drained, and timberless prairies, where in competition with construction and railroad building they either had to pay high wages for custom work such as breaking, harvesting, and threshing or buy expensive labor-saving equipment. Custom plowmen, using the heavy breaking plow pulled by a number of yoke of oxen, charged $2 and $3 an acre for breaking prairie. Lumber for the house, fencing, and perhaps a barn could no longer be "hooked" from neighboring government- or absentee-owned tracts and had to be brought in at heavy expense from the Mississippi River mill towns or Chicago. A yoke of oxen, wagon, plow, stove, chains, ax, shovel, grindstone, scythe or cradle, together with seed, funds to maintain the family until the first crop came in, fees for filing land-office papers, or money to make the down payment on a railroad tract, brought the amount needed to start farming to $500 at the minimum; safer estimates were two or three times that much. Land agents and representatives of the land-grant railroads warned prospective emigrants in the East and in Europe that they should bring some capital with them to the West.[13]

Notwithstanding these well-meant warnings, immigrants continued to reach the

---

[12] To arrive at these percentages I added the number of tenant farms (presumably farmed each by one tenant) to the number of farm laborers and computed what percentage that total was of the number of people engaged in agriculture. The figures are from the Tenth Census, Agriculture (Washington, 1883), passim.

[13] Guide to the Lands of the Northern Pacific Railroad in Minnesota (New York, 1872), 22; Arthur F. Bentley, The Condition of the Western Farmer as illustrated by the Economic History of a Nebraska Township ("Johns Hopkins University Studies in Historical and Political Science," Eleventh Series, No. 7 [July, 1893]), 28; Clarence H. Danhof, "Farm Making Costs and the 'Safety Valve': 1850–1860," Journal of Political Economy, XLVI (June, 1941), 317ff.; Paul W. Gates, Fifty Million Acres: Conflicts Over Kansas Land Policy, 1854–1890 (Ithaca, 1954), 223.

outer edge of settlement destitute, unable to start farm making. We need not probe their disillusionment when their scant resources proved insufficient to enable them to take advantage of the government's free homestead policy. They could still cherish the dream of owning a farm while they worked for others.

Immigrants newly arriving in the West soon learned that unless they quickly established a claim to land, their chances of making good selections would be minimized, perhaps lost to other more foresighted settlers or to speculators. The settler and the speculator were catching up with the surveyor, especially in Iowa, Kansas, and Nebraska, and land when offered or opened to entry was quickly snatched up. Consequently, a first step toward farm ownership was to select a tract, establish a claim upon it, and hope that it could be held for two or three years without cost even though the claimant was not actually living upon it or abiding by the provision of the pre-emption or homestead acts. Frontiersmen moving early into newly opened communities found they could sell their claims with but slight improvements for $50 to $100 to later comers and then go a little farther west and make another selection. Claim making, a species of land specula-tion, was indulged in by many who gradually acquired a little livestock and equipment through sales of claims or through outside earnings and were ready in a few years for more permanent farm making. A combination of claim specula-tion and temporary work on railroad con-struction jobs or building projects in grow-ing urban centers was common. That many immigrants also took agricultural jobs as hired hands in areas close to, if not right in, the frontier is not as well known.

Some students and readers of fiction relating to Western pioneer life have enter-tained the notion that Western farmers never really prospered but were in a more or less chronic state of depression that was aggravated by periods of unusually low prices and near crop failures with resulting acute distress. Perhaps more attention has been directed to the agrarian reaction to such distress and the causes thereof than to periods of favorable prices and bountiful crops that brought early prosperity to many. Certain it is that in no comparable period did such large num-bers of immigrants to a new region gain ownership of the farms they were im-proving and live well upon those farms as in the fifty-year period from 1850 to 1900 in the Mississippi Valley. Boomer literature of the time tells of numerous cases of individuals in Illinois, Kansas, or Nebraska who made enough on one good crop to pay for their land and equipment. That there were such cases cannot be denied, but whether they were typical it is impossible to say. We do know that industrious, skillful farmers blessed by good fortune did succeed not only in subduing the usual 80- to 160-acre tract of wild land to grain production and live-stock use, but in many instances in developing even larger farms. This was accomplished not alone by the head of the family and his children, but with the aid of hired men.

The census schedules of 1870 reveal thousands of instances of farmers with no more than 160 acres employing one or two laborers.[14] These farmers did not attract the attention of journalists or travelers of the time, and, consequently, it is more difficult to reconstruct their opera-tions than those of the larger capitalist farmers, whose operations were on a much bigger scale and who individually employed numerous farm hands.

The American West proved attractive not only to poor immigrants but also to men of means interested in developing not

[14] Paul S. Taylor, "The American Hired Man: His Rise and Decline," Land Policy Review, VI (Spring, 1943), 3–17; LaWanda F. Cox, "The American Agricultural Wage Earner, 1865–1900: The Emergence of a Modern Labor Problem," Agricultural History, XXII (April, 1949), 94–114.

single family farms but estates of thousands of acres worked by laborers and tenants. Large capitalistic enterprises in the pioneer West are not unknown to historians, but most attention has been centered on the bonanza wheat farms of the Red River Valley of Minnesota and Dakota and on cattle ranching in the Great Plains. Carried out on a grand scale and with a dramatic flourish, they drew the attention of journalists and other commentators of the time and consequently found their way into most histories of the West.[15] Their day was short, their long-range influence not great, and they deserve a mere footnote in history compared with the quieter, more pervasive, and longer-lasting investments by masterful and aggressive capitalists in the Corn Belt, who came not merely to speculate nor to develop a bonanza farm but to create rent-producing estates composed of numerous farms operated either by hired hands or by tenants.

These estate builders were to be found in practically every portion, one can almost say in every county, of the Corn Belt. Their homes, in highly stereotyped and stilted engravings, the number of acres they owned, and the moral qualities of the owners all are presented in the numerous county atlases and biographical volumes that were the rage in the Gilded Age. Their investments ranged from a few thousand to hundreds of thousands of dollars and, for a score or more, to one or two millions.[16] That is not to say that they brought capital in this amount with them when they first ventured into the West. Much of their capital was made in the West.

The cattle ranchers and drovers who flourished in Indiana and Illinois in the forties, fifties, and sixties and in Iowa and Missouri a little later dominated great areas of the prairies for a time. They built upon their first investments by shrewdly buying the surplus stock of neighbors, fattening them on the prairie bluestem with the addition of a little grain, and then driving them to Chicago, Indianapolis, or the East, wherever they could get favorable prices. Later they brought in cattle from Missouri and Texas. Their profits were invested in land when it could be bought "dirt-cheap" to assure an abundance of grass and grain for their operations. Slowly, they turned to grain feeding and grain production and improved livestock, using meantime an increasing number of hands. By mid-century the operations of the successful cattle kings were being conducted on a huge scale, with herds of cattle numbering in the thousands, fields of corn covering thousands of acres, and scores of hands to carry on the business. Their holdings in land increased to 5,000, 10,000, 20,000, even 40,000 acres.[17] For every giant farm of this size there were a score or more of smaller operators with holdings

[15] Harold E. Briggs, *Frontiers of the Northwest* (New York, 1940), 509–522; and Fred A. Shannon, *The Farmer's Last Frontier, Agriculture, 1860–1897* (*The Economic History of the United States*, David, Faulkner, Hacker, et al. [eds.], Vol. V [New York, 1945]), 154–161.

[16] In Illinois alone a compiler found in 1892 the following "millionaires" whose wealth was largely made in farm lands: Matthew T. Scott, Orlando Powers, L. B. Casner, Estate of John Shaw Hayward, John C. Proctor, George Pasfield, Horatio M. Vandeveer, William H. Ennis, W. H. Bradley. In Missouri the outstanding millionaire landowners were David Rankin and five heirs of Milton Tootle; in Nebraska, Stephen Miles; in Minne-

sota, J. A. Willard and A. H. Wilder; in Indiana, William H. English and the Estate of Moses Fowler. Other identifiable millionaires in these states added materially to their wealth through farming operations and land improvement. *American Millionaires: The Tribune's List of Persons Reputed to be Worth a Million or More* (June, 1892), reprinted in Sidney Ratner, *New Light on the History of Great American Fortunes. American Millionaires of 1892 and 1902* (New York, 1953).

[17] Gates, *Frontier Landlords and Pioneer Tenants, passim.*; "Hoosier Cattle Kings in the Prairies," *Indiana Magazine of History*, XLIV (March, 1948), 1–24; "Cattle Kings in the Prairies," *Mississippi Valley Historical Review*, XXXV (Dec., 1948), 379–412.

ranging from one to four thousand acres.[18]

These bonanza farms, located as they were in Corn Belt counties with high land values, soon became as outmoded as the sickle and cradle. Farm workers proved irresponsible when hired at low wages. They were careless with tools, they slighted their tasks, overworked or abused the draft animals, drank heavily, and often engaged in fisticuffs. On slight provocation they quit their jobs, knowing that equally good opportunities were available elsewhere, and they demanded high wages when the peak of employment was reached in the harvest season. Old Isaac Funk, who accumulated a fortune of two million dollars in his land and cattle business in McLean County, Illinois, said in 1861 that no one could afford to hire men to grow and market grain at prices then prevailing. Their wages were too high and they worked too little, thought Funk. Another Illinois landlord, in deploring the wage of two dollars a day being paid to harvest hands in 1862, held that "cheap farm laborers" were essential for the winning of the Civil War.[19] The best agricultural laborers wanted to become tenants or owners and would remain in employment only as long as was necessary for them to accumulate the resources for starting on their own.

Continuing immigration into the prairies with its resulting pressure upon the supply of land, skyrocketing values, taxes and assessments forced more intensive land use. Ranches with grain as a side issue could no longer be economically justified, and for a time the bonanza farms became grain farms with cattle as a side issue. Before long, central administration of the

land was abandoned. The big farms were divided into small holdings and assigned to tenants. Though the workers might prove poor farm hands, it was seen that, given a share in the returns of farming, they were more responsible, more willing to exert themselves, more careful with their tools, horses, and oxen, and with their housing accommodations. In the transition to full tenancy the landlord might provide everything but maintenance for the operator and pay him eight or ten cents a bushel for the corn he produced. In 1870, a tenant who furnished his own team was paid fifteen cents for each bushel of corn, fifty cents for each bushel of wheat, and twenty-five cents for each bushel of oats he produced. A more common practice was for the tenant to pay the landlord one third to one half of the crops or a cash rent for each acre of cultivable land.[20]

The day of the Corn Belt cattle kings was short, as was their career as bonanza farmers. As entrepreneurs developing their estates they made jobs available for many workers who later were permitted, if not encouraged, to become tenants. In the tenant stage of land development some of the landlords continued to expend their surplus from rents in additional improvements, so that their constructive period lasted throughout the first generation and, indeed, well into the second. In the process of change, some land was sold; more, through inheritance diffusion, passed to a larger number of landlords. Analysis of the assessment records or the current

[18] The Census of 1880 shows 2,916 farms in excess of a thousand acres in the ten states of the Upper Mississippi Valley.
[19] New York Tribune, July 30, 1861 and Aug. 11, 1861; C. H. Moore to Dr. John Warner, July 21, 1862, Moore-Warner MSS., Clinton, Illinois; Country Gentleman, March 10 and May 5, 1864; July, 1865.

[20] Columbus State Journal (Ohio) in Davenport Gazette (Iowa), Aug. 12, 1855; 1 Miscellaneous Record, 434, Logan County Recorder's Office, Lincoln, Illinois; James MacDonald, Food from the Far West (London, 1878), 142–148; Appendix, "Agricultural Interests Commission, Reports of the Assistant Commissioner" (London, 1880), Parliamentary Papers, 1880, XVIII, 18, 38–39; Bloomington Bulletin (Illinois), March 4, 1887. On the Fowler lands in Indiana, in return for breaking land and putting it in corn, tenants were paid 25¢ a bushel for the corn they raised in the first five crop years. Benton Review, June 11, 1885.

platbooks of Corn Belt counties reveals a century later how tenaciously third- and fourth-generation descendants of the old cattle kings have clung to their possessions.

Side by side with these modern holdings are other equally large estates which sprang from another type of investment on the frontier, that of the capitalists who came west to create permanent estates like that of the Wadsworth family in the Genesee country of New York by buying and developing extensive areas. Some of these capitalists concentrated their attention entirely upon farm making, while others bought and sold real estate, acted as agents for eastern capitalists wishing to invest in the growing West, or perhaps ran a bank and made loans to squatters. Profits and fees they invested in land improvements. A number took construction contracts on railroads, receiving land instead of cash in payment. They were careful to keep their titles clear, to pay the taxes before liens were issued, and to protect their timber against the prevalent custom of "hooking." With all these side issues, they kept before them the goal of land development.

Extensive improvement of their holdings required these estate builders to seek out workers to break the prairie, fence, erect tenant houses for the families of workers and barracklike constructions for single men, to seed, cultivate, harvest, shuck, thrash, and haul the grain to market. To assure themselves an adequate labor supply, and subsequently to attract tenants, these entrepreneurs had at times to advertise, distribute handbills in eastern communities, and in a number of instances publish pamphlets describing the opportunities their lands provided to immigrants.[21] Workers could not save much from the low wages paid them, but

many pioneers did make their start by accumulating small funds from such earnings and investing them, perhaps while still holding the farm job, in near-by land on which they might at the same time make some improvements.

For the Western immigrant who was anxious to have a farm of his own but who lacked the means to acquire it, it was distinctly better to be a tenant than a farm laborer. He could, when he attained this status, feel he was moving toward his goal. Now he shared with the capitalist proprietor the profits from farming, but he also shared the losses. Furthermore, he was usually required by his lease to make capital improvements upon the rented land, and the cost would be deducted from the rent. Every improvement he made raised the value of the land and pushed farther away the possibility of his buying it. If he paid cash rent, continued improvement of the land was certain to be followed by a higher rent charge; if he paid share rent, the landlord might—and in the eighties did—exact a larger portion of the grain. Tenancy was no happy choice to the immigrant looking for the free or cheap land about which he had heard so much, but unless he was willing to go far beyond the railroad into areas lacking social facilities and market opportunities, there was no other alternative.

Some landlords were willing to pay for much of the cost of breaking and fencing, to provide machines and even credit to carry their tenants through harvest. Others insisted on the tenants' making all the improvements, which they then might own or at least have the right to sell to other tenants, subject to the approval of the landlord. Advertisements for tenants were increasingly common in the prairie newspapers, but more ominous from the point of view of the tenant were advertisements of renters looking for land.[22] Eviction for

[21] Sioux City Register, Jan. 12, 1861; Margaret Ruth Beattie, "Matthew Scott, Pioneer Landlord-Gentleman Farmer, 1855–1891" (Thesis, Cornell University Library, 1947), 58ff.; Jacob Van Der Zee, The British in Iowa (Iowa City, 1922), 57ff.

[22] The Champaign Gazette (Illinois), clipped in the Bloomington Pantagraph (Illinois), Jan. 23,

sloth, failure to make required improvements, poor farming, and cheating the landlord increased as hordes of new immigrants looking for land to rent came in from central Europe. The pressure for places to rent made it possible for the landlord to exact more and to allow the tenant less. Farmers of older American stock found the role of tenant increasingly unbearable. Disillusioned by their meager returns and unwilling to compete with the new wave of European immigrants, they abandoned their rented places in Illinois and Iowa by the thousands in the seventies and eighties for a new try at ownership in western Kansas or Nebraska, or perchance in the Dakota country. It was this emigration of older American tenants from the Corn Belt that was responsible for the increasingly conservative character of agrarian politics in Illinois and Iowa. These disillusioned and frequently angry tenants who emigrated farther west carried their resentment with them and made the area in which they settled fertile ground for the Populist agitator.[23]

Meantime, the capitalist estate builders, having divided their holdings into small tenant farms, were emerging as farm managers. Where they had erected tenant homes, set out fences, and established orchards they needed to protect their investment by making certain that proper care and maintenance were provided. They naturally wanted for their tenancies good farmers who would keep the weeds down, get their crops in and harvested at the right time, protect the timber if any, and pay their cash rent promptly or turn

in a fair landlord's share of the grain. Good tenants assured better yields and hence more share rent. Both landlords and tenants were driven to exploit the land by their need for high returns to meet costs of farm improvements, new implements, and perhaps livestock. Rotation, the use of alfalfa or clover, prevention of erosion were all subordinated to the production of grain, with declining fertility the natural—though not immediately apparent—result. Much the same thing can be said of farm owners who were struggling to raise funds out of their crops to purchase new equipment, to fence additional land, to drain the low places, or to enlarge their original two- or three-room houses to accommodate growing families. Economic circumstances were largely responsible for a pattern of land use that disregarded the lessons of the past in older states, was exploitative and destructive of values. In defense of the capitalist estate builders, it should be added that some of them early showed concern for proper land management by insisting upon rotation of crops; the use of alfalfa, clover, and lime; the elimination of weeds; and careful use of pastures.

Elsewhere the operations of capitalist estate builders, whose individual and family holdings ran as high as 60,000 acres and in one case to 200,000 acres, have been described. Few of these "feudal lords," as George Ade called them, would sell unless faced with disaster.[24] They instilled in their children a deep respect for the land they had improved and sought by every possible legal device to restrict the right of alienation. Because of their great success in retaining ownership of their many farms, the names of Scully, Moore, Davis, Vandeveer, Ennis, Funk, Fowler, Wearin, Rankin, and Lawrence-Lowrie are as familiar today to the residents of the prairie states as were the names of the great planters of South

1879, reported "The demand for farms to rent far exceeds the supply, and men are compelled to seek other localities to get places." Monticello, Indiana, *Prairie Chieftain*, Nov. 4, 1852; *Bloomington Pantagraph*, Feb. 8, 1854 and Nov. 5, 1856; Watseka, Illinois, *Iroquois County Times*, Oct. 21, 1875; *Malvern Leader* (Iowa), Feb. 8, 1883; Feb. 26 and March 5, 1885.

[23] Chester McArthur Destler, "Agricultural Readjustment and Agrarian Unrest in Illinois, 1880–1893," *Agricultural History*, XXI (April, 1947), 104–116; Gates, *Fifty Million Acres*, 244ff.

[24] George Ade, "Prairie Kings of Yesterday," *Saturday Evening Post*, July 4, 1931, p. 14.

Carolina and Georgia to the ante-bellum residents of those states.

With all the plethora of information the Bureau of the Census had gathered, the problem of multiple ownership of tenant farms received no attention until 1900. Something of the concentration of ownership of tenant farms, the heritage of the capitalist estate builder in the nineteenth century, may be seen in the census data of that year. The figures are not complete and are made less useful by the fact that they are compiled on the basis of residence of owner; but in the absence of anything better we must use them. For the states of the Upper Mississippi Valley, 3,800 landlords appear as owning 32,646 farms. Five hundred and fifty-one of these landlords had an average of 12.8 farms each, and 122 owners had an average of 35.5 farms each. In Illinois 34 landlords are shown owning 1,115 farms, or an average of 32 each.[25]

Ownership of Tenant Farms by Owners Living in Upper Mississippi Valley, 1900

	Number of Owners	Number of Farms Owned
Owned one farm	419,900	419,900
Owned two farms	39,124	78,248
Owned three to five farms	12,070	39,831
Owned five to ten farms	3,127	21,263
Owned ten to twenty farms	551	7,052
Owned twenty or more farms	122	4,331
Total (plural ownership)	54,994	150,725

Since one landlord owned 322 farms in Illinois and an additional 845 farms in Missouri, Kansas, and Nebraska but had his residence in the District of Columbia, it is easy to see how deceptive, how inadequate, the census data is.

The estate builder brought much-

[25] Census of 1900, Agriculture, Part I, lxxxviii; Howard A. Turner, The Ownership of Tenant Farms in the North Central States (United States Department of Agriculture Bulletin, No. 1433 [Sept., 1926]), 10.

needed funds to the West, developed substantial areas, and provided early employment and housing facilities for many newly arrived immigrants who lacked means to begin on their own. He aided others in getting started by lending them funds to commence farming as a tenant or owner; by furnishing them the necessary farming implements, seed, and food until harvest; and by providing livestock on a partnership basis. Much of the risk in these operations was his. Frequently, he undertook such investments with borrowed capital on which he paid 10 to 15 per cent interest. Taxes bore heavily on him, as the residents of his community seeking better schools and roads raised his assessments on tangibles that could not be hidden. Poor crops or low prices or, worse still, a combination of both might so reduce his income as to make it impossible for him to meet his obligations. One bad year he could take, perhaps two, but a larger combination of bad years was disastrous. The late seventies marked the final defeat of a number of large farm operators, and this was the result of poor prices, unfavorable weather, high interest rates, and perhaps poor management.

This paper may have indicated that society on the frontier and in areas a generation beyond the frontier stage was more complex, had a wider range of economic well-being, than Frederick Jackson Turner thought. The early appearance of farm laborers and tenants, many of whom were never to rise to farm-ownership status, and of great landed estates, whose owners brought wealth with them and added much to it, did not make for a "fundamental unity in its [frontier's] social structure and its democratic ideals. . . ." Concepts of the homogeneity of frontier society, similarity of frontier outlook, common addiction to democratic principles, may well be questioned.

Ante-bellum Democratic senators of the Upper Mississippi Valley appeared to be more concerned with their own land speculation schemes or the welfare of fur, lumber, mining, and railroad companies than with the fortunes of their farmer constituents; and they did little to loosen the reactionary control southern slave owners had over their party. The land-owning aristocracy early moved into politics via the Whig and Republican parties and fought as vigorously for privilege as did eastern conservatives. It was a combination of prairie landlords—Isaac Funk, Jesse Fell, Asahel Gridley, and David Davis—who had an important share in bringing the Republican nomination to Lincoln in 1860. Their activities contributed to fasten protection, the gold standard, land subsidies to railroads, and an incongruous land system upon the country. When the Democratic party in the Middle West recovered from its debacle, it was in the hands of Bourbons no more liberal in their outlook than the Republican officeholders they sought to displace.

The appearance of the Greenback and Populist parties seemed for a time to offer promise of effective agrarian leadership, but a combination of upper-class landowning families that directed the Greenback and Granger parties and a will-of-the-wisp search for a magic commodity price formula by the Populist party offered no aid to the farm laborer searching for a route to ownership or to tenants struggling to retain their step on the ownership ladder. While Western newspapers were bewailing the fate of Irish tenants, they gave no heed to the emergence of the tenant class at home whose rights were less secure, whose plight as serious. The landlords and successful farmers were in the saddle politically, and though they might erupt in condemnation of financial lords of the East, railroad magnates, or tariff-minded manufacturers, they did nothing to assure fixity of tenure, fair rent and compensation for improvements to tenants; in Illinois they joined together to beat down levels of wages paid to farm workers.[26]

At the close of the nineteenth century the agricultural laborers and tenants outnumbered full owner-operators of farms in five of the states we have studied, and in all the Upper Mississippi Valley the numbers of farm laborers and tenants were fast growing. Agrarian reform movements offered nothing to improve their lot. It was not until the twentieth century that the status of the tenant was substantially bettered with his gradual accumulation of livestock, equipment, and investment in improvements, which has made him a substantial farmer with an equity worth thousands of dollars.

[26] A Farmers Union meeting in Mason County, Illinois, in 1885 resolved "not to exceed fifteen dollars per month, by the year, for the best farm labor, . . . that for the limit of six months, the limit of wages be eighteen dollars per month . . . that we pay no more than $1.50 per day for driving header wagon in harvest; $1.50 per day for labor in haying, and from 50¢ to $1.00 for common labor, to be regulated by time and circumstances." *Mason County Democrat*, Jan. 16 and Feb. 6 and 20, 1885.

Origins of the AFL

■ In spite of their large numbers—even in 1900 there were still about as many laborers on farms as in industry—farm workers took little or no part in efforts at organization. The labor movement was an urban affair, and was largely confined, before the 1930s, to skilled workers outside of factories.

The American Federation of Labor, the first enduring national labor organization, was a product of conflict that rose within the labor movement between 1878 and 1886, a period of prosperity interrupted only briefly by minor depression from mid-1883 to mid-1885. Shortage of skilled labor in this great industrial upswing, particularly from 1879 to 1883, gave skilled workers increased bargaining power and encouraged organization. In efforts to recruit and organize an increasingly varied group of workers, a struggle developed between leaders who wanted to use organization for idealistic purposes, such as cooperative production, the end of the wage system, or fighting the evils of drink, and those who wanted to use their strength purely and simply to gain higher wages and shorter hours. The struggle gradually hardened into a fight between the old reformist Knights of Labor and the trade unions.

In carrying the story of this struggle to the final break between the two factions and the founding of the AFL by the trade unions in 1886, Gerald N. Grob, of Clark University, contributes to an understanding of the mechanics of the early labor movement. From 1887 on, the American Federation of Labor gradually gained strength by attracting the skilled craftsmen to its businesslike program, whereas the more idealistic Knights of Labor declined precipitously from a high of 700,000 members and then, in the Depression of the 1890s, disappeared as an effective organization.

Gerald N. Grob
The Knights of Labor and the Trade Unions, 1878–1886*

The year 1886 was destined to be a crucial one in the history of the American labor movement. The eight-hour crusade, the numerous strikes, the Haymarket bomb, the entrance of workingmen into the political arena at the state and national levels, and the mushroom growth of labor organizations all contributed to the agitation and excitement of the year. Yet the importance of these events was overshadowed by a development that was to have such far-reaching implications that it would determine the future of the labor movement for the succeeding half century. That development was the declaration of war by the trade unions

against the reform unionism of the Knights of Labor.

The struggle between the Knights and the other unions represented a clash of two fundamentally opposing ideologies. The Knights of Labor, on the one hand, grew out of the reform and humanitarian movements of ante-bellum America, and was the direct descendant, through the National Labor Union, of the labor reform tradition of the Jacksonian era. Banking on the leveling influence of technological change, its leaders sought to organize the entire producing class into a single irresistible coalition that would work toward the abolition of the wage system and the establishment of a new society. "We do not believe," a high official of the Knights remarked, "that the emancipation of labor will come with increased wages

* Reprinted by permission from The Journal of Economic History, XVIII (June, 1958), pp. 176–192.

and a reduction in the hours of labor; we must go deeper than that, and this matter will not be settled until the wage system is abolished.''[1] The leaders of the Knights therefore emphasized education and co-operation, and they bitterly opposed their constituents' participation in such affairs as the Southwest and stockyards strikes of 1886, as well as the very popular eight-hour movement of that same year.

The reform ideology of the Knights, in turn, had an important impact upon the development of its structure, which followed a heterogeneous rather than a homogeneous pattern. Minimizing the utility of organization along trade lines, the Order emphasized instead the grouping of all workers, regardless of craft, into a single body.[2] Highest priority therefore was given to the mixed local assembly, which included all workers irrespective of their trade or degree of skill. Neither a trade, plant, nor industrial union, the mixed assembly could never be more than a study or debating group. Including many diverse elements (even employers), it could not adapt itself to meet the problems of a specific industry or trade. The mixed assembly might agitate for reform or participate in politics, but it could never become the collective bargaining representative of its members.

Given the predominance of the mixed over the trade local, the structure of the Knights inevitably developed along geographical rather than jurisdictional lines, and the district assembly, which included

mixed as well as trade locals, became the most characteristic form of organization. The highest governmental body of the Knights—the General Assembly—was not intended as a medium for collective bargaining. Indeed, its very inclusiveness precluded such a possibility.

The trade unions, on the other hand, rejected the broad reform goals of the Knights, emphasizing instead higher wages, shorter hours, and job control. Such objectives were clearly incompatible with an organizational structure such as that developed by the Knights. Eschewing the multitrade local that had been so prevalent during the 1860's and was being perpetuated by the Order, the trade unions began to stress the craft-industrial form of organization both at the local and national levels. A relative scarcity of labor, together with a rapidly expanding economy, had created a favorable environment for the trade unions. Gambling on the hope that the rise of a national market made organization along trade rather than geographical lines more effective, union leaders chose to concentrate upon the task of organizing the workers along trade lines into unions designed for collective bargaining rather than social reform.[3]

Therefore, given the inherent differences in ideology and structure, the conflict between the Knights and the trade unions was, if not inevitable, certainly not an unexpected or surprising development.[4] Undoubtedly the antagonistic personalities of partisans on both sides hastened an open rift.[5] Yet the hostilities between the

[1] The Laster, IV (Nov. 15, 1891), 3.
[2] For the antitrade unionism of the national leadership of the Knights see the Journal of United Labor, I (June 15, 1880), 21 (hereinafter cited as JUL); Knights of Labor, Proceedings of the General Assembly, 1880, p. 169; 1884, pp. 716–17; 1897, p. 37 (hereinafter cited as K. of L., GA Proc.); Terence V. Powderly, Thirty Years of Labor: 1859 to 1889 (Columbus: Excelsior Publishing House, 1889), pp. 155–56; Powderly Letter Books, Catholic University of America, Washington, D.C.; Powderly to James Rogers, Dec. 19, 1892; Gerald N. Grob, "Terence V. Powderly and the Knights of Labor," Mid-America, XXXIX (January 1957), 41–42.

[3] See Lloyd Ulman, The Rise of the National Trade Union (Cambridge: Harvard University Press, 1955), pp. 348–77.
[4] See Carrol D. Wright, "An Historical Sketch of the Knights of Labor," Quarterly Journal of Economics, I (Jan. 1887), 155; Cigar Makers' Official Journal, XI (June 1886), 6; The Carpenter, VI (Feb. 1886), 4, (Apr. 1886), 4.
[5] Norman J. Ware emphasized the importance of conflicting personalities. Ware, The Labor Movement in the United States, 1860–1895 (New York: D. Appleton and Company, 1929), pp. 162–63, et passim.

Knights and the trade unions cannot be explained solely in terms of personalities, for the conflict was not simply a struggle for power between two rivals. It was a clash between two fundamentally different ideologies—with the future of the labor movement at stake.

I

The contest between trade unionists and reformers for control of the labor movement developed on two planes. Commencing first as an internal struggle within the Knights, it eventually expanded and soon involved the national unions. Within the Knights the struggle revolved around the unresolved question as to which form of organization best met working-class necessities. On the surface the issue of mixed versus trade locals was simply a structural problem. In reality, however, the differences between the two forms indicated the existence of a fundamental cleavage in ultimate objectives, for the mixed assembly could be utilized only for reform or political purposes, while the trade assembly was generally a collective bargaining organization.

Although the national leadership of the Knights regarded the mixed assembly as the ideal type of unit, a large proportion of its local assemblies were trade rather than mixed. The first local, composed of garment cutters, was strictly craft, and remained so to the end. Most of the other locals that followed were also trade assemblies.[6] On January 1, 1882, according to the *Journal of United Labor*, there were 27 working districts and over 400 local assemblies. Of the latter, 318 were trade and only 116 were mixed. Thirteen additional districts, not functioning, had 53 trade and 87 mixed locals, attesting to the relative instability of the mixed

form of organization. Of the 135 locals attached directly to the General Assembly, 67 were trade and 68 were mixed.[7]

Despite the wide latitude given them to organize trade local assemblies, the trade element within the Knights nevertheless found it difficult to function efficiently. Local trade assemblies, no matter how inclusive in their particular area, were often ineffective when operating in a market that was regional or national rather than local in character. So long as employers could find a ready supply of nonunion labor elsewhere, efforts at collective bargaining by locals would be ineffective. The only solution lay in national organization, and the trade exponents within the Knights pressed for national and regional trade districts that would transcend the limited geographical area normally encompassed by the local or district assembly.

The General Assembly, therefore, meeting in January 1879, authorized the establishment of autonomous national trade districts within the framework of the Knights. But only nine months later the Assembly completely reversed itself by declaring that trade locals were "contrary to the spirit and genius of the Order," and it returned exclusive jurisdiction over all locals to the district assembly of their area.[8]

In December 1881, however, the Federation of Organized Trades and Labor Unions, predecessor of the American Federation of Labor (A.F. of L.), held its first convention. Of the 107 delegates present, no less than 50 came from the Knights.[9]

The following September the General Assembly heard the secretary of the

[6] See Wright, "An Historical Sketch, Knights of Labor," p. 146.

[7] Ware, *Labor Movement*, p. 158. The statistics on trade locals in the Knights are unsatisfactory and misleading, since many of them admitted workers belonging to different trades.
[8] K. of L., GA Proc., Jan. 1879, pp. 69–70, 72; Sept. 1879, pp. 98, 129.
[9] Federation of Organized Trades, *Proceedings*, 1881, pp. 7–9 (1905 reprinting).

Knights warn that trade sentiment was growing rapidly. "Many Trades Unions have also written me," he remarked, "stating that they were seriously meditating the propriety of coming over to us in a body, freely expressing the opinion that their proper place was in our Order."[10] To prevent any mass exodus from the Order to the rival Federation, and also to recruit members from the trade unions, the General Assembly enacted legislation authorizing and encouraging the formation of national and regional trade districts. This move was reaffirmed and even extended at the meetings of the General Assembly in 1884 and 1886.[11]

While permissible, at least in theory, the establishment of trade districts was not a simple matter. The basic philosophy of the Knights militated against organization along craft lines, and the establishment of autonomous trade units within the framework of the Order aroused strong opposition. "I do not favor the establishment of any more National Trade Districts," Terence V. Powderly, head of the Knights from 1879 to 1893, told the General Assembly in 1885, "they are a step backward."[12] Other reform unionists, echoing Powderly's sentiments, charged that trade districts violated the fundamental principles of the Knights.[13] Holding tenaciously to their reform concepts, the leaders of the Knights were insistent in their demands that organization should not proceed along trade lines.

Applicants for trade districts therefore could not always be certain that charters would be granted them, even though they had met all the formal requirements. In some cases charters were granted without any questions. Window Glass Workers' Local Assembly (L.A.) 300 was chartered as a national trade district at a time when such districts were contrary to the laws of the Knights, and the telegraphers were organized nationally in 1882 as District Assembly (D.A.) 45. For a while these two were the only national districts, although before 1886 there were two district assemblies composed of miners, five of shoemakers, three of railroad employees, and one each of printers, plumbers, leather workers, government employees, and streetcar employees. Between 1883 and 1885 the General Assembly went on record as favoring the establishment of trade districts of shoemakers, plate-glass workers, and plumbers.[14] On the other hand, after sanctioning the formation of builders' districts in 1882, it refused the following year to permit these districts to be represented on the General Executive Board.[15] Even while passing legislation authorizing trade districts, the General Assembly refused to allow woodworkers, cigarmakers, and carpenters to organize trade districts. Furthermore, it passed a resolution stating that no charter for a trade district would be granted unless the applicants could demonstrate to the satisfaction of the General Executive Board that the craft could not be effectively organized under the system of mixed or territorial districts.[16] The attitude of the board, however, was often conditioned by the antitrade unionism of its officers. In 1886, for example, it refused to sanction the request of five building trade locals that they be permitted to withdraw from D.A. 66 and organize their own district. At the same time it em-

[10] K. of L., GA Proc., 1882, pp. 296–98. See also the statement of the General Executive Board in ibid., p. 334.

[11] Ibid., pp. 364, 368; 1884, pp. 705–7, 776; 1886, pp. 265–66.

[12] Ibid., 1885, p. 25.

[13] See the JUL, VII (June 25, 1886), 2100; John Swinton's Paper, Sept. 6, 1885; K. of L., GA Proc., 1884, pp. 716–17.

[14] K. of L., GA Proc., 1883, pp. 438, 443, 502; 1884, p. 787; 1885, pp. 127, 133; JUL, V (Dec. 10, 1884), 856.

[15] K. of L., GA Proc., 1882, pp. 325, 347; 1883, pp. 445, 498.

[16] Ibid., 1882, pp. 311, 351; 1883, pp. 439–40, 498, 502.

powered a New Hampshire local to change from a trade to a mixed assembly.[17]

Trade units, generally speaking, were authorized usually in efforts to attract workers to join the Knights. Thus the International Trunkmakers Union came into the Order as a trade district.[18] Once inside, however, workers found it considerably more difficult to secure trade charters. After affiliating in 1882, to cite one case, the plumbers later left the Knights when they encountered difficulty in obtaining a charter for a national trade district, and they established the International Association of Journeymen Plumbers, Steam Fitters, and Gas Fitters.[19]

The hostility of the national leadership of the Knights was not the sole obstacle to the formation of trade units. Mixed and territorial districts, which were first in the field and were already established as functioning organizations, were also antagonistic toward trade districts. If the latter were formed, not only would a mixed district suffer a loss of membership to a trade district, but it would also surrender its absolute jurisdiction over a given territorial area, since the autonomous trade district would exercise control over the entire craft in that area.

The General Assembly and the General Executive Board often supported the mixed and territorial districts in disputes with trade districts. Frequently the district's consent was a prerequisite to secession and the establishment of a trade district. This consent was not easily obtained. In 1886 D.A. 30 of Massachusetts turned down an application by four of its locals for permission to withdraw and form a national trade assembly of rubber workers.[20] While the General Assembly supported a district court decision that members of trade locals could not be compelled to join mixed locals, the General Executive Board refused to force trade members of mixed locals to transfer to trade assemblies.[21]

Even after obtaining a charter, trade districts encountered difficulties with the mixed district in their areas. Dual jurisdiction often led to friction, though in theory the system of mixed and trade districts appeared perfectly harmonious and compatible. For example, D.A. 64 of New York City, composed of workers in the printing and publishing business, became embroiled in a rivalry with D.A. 49 (mixed). In 1883 D.A. 64 failed to get exclusive jurisdiction over all workers in the trade. Soon afterward D.A. 49 charged that the printers were accepting locals not of their trade, and that these locals had also withdrawn from D.A. 49 without permission. An investigation by the secretary of the General Executive Board disclosed that D.A. 64 had been initiating lithographers, typefounders, pressmen, and feeders in order to strengthen itself as a bargaining unit, and that it had not engaged in raiding forays against D.A. 49. Although the Board upheld D.A. 64, the decision did not resolve the rivalry, and the two districts continued their feud.[22]

With the single exception of L.A. 300, trade districts did not enjoy any appreciable measure of success between 1878 and 1885.[23] The far-reaching reform goals

[17] Ibid., 1886, pp. 126–27.
[18] Ibid., 1883, p. 506; 1884, p. 619. This was also the case in the affiliation of the harness workers. JUL, IV (June 1883), 511; (July 1883), 520–21. The Knights also aided the barbers, horse railway men, miners, railway men, and ax makers in attempts to get them to join.
[19] New York Bureau of Labor Statistics, Annual Report, V (1887), 202–3.

[20] Quarterly Report of District Assembly No. 30 . . . July . . . 1886 (Boston, 1886), p. 69. For a somewhat similar case see New York Bureau of Labor Statistics, Annual Report, V (1887), 202–4.
[21] K. of L., GA Proc, 1885, pp. 102–3, 140; 1886, p. 130.
[22] Ibid., 1883, pp. 467, 508; 1884, p. 617; 1885, pp. 125, 135; 1887, pp. 1714, 1757.
[23] Even the successful career of L.A. 300 cannot be attributed to the Knights. It was due primarily to the skilled nature of the trade which permitted the window glass workers to organize thoroughly, restrict output, and regulate apprenticeship requirements. See Pearce Davis,

of the Knights and its structural inclusiveness left the advocates of trade organization in the position of a perpetual minority. The expansion of the Knights into the more sparsely populated regions of the South and West, moreover, further diminished trade influence, since the mixed assembly was dominant in rural areas. Lacking a majority, the trade members were unable to establish a central strike fund or concentrate on collective bargaining, and they found that their immediate goals were being subordinated to and sacrificed for more utopian objectives.

II

The struggle between trade unionists and reformers within the Knights, however, was completely overshadowed by the rupture of relations in 1886 between the Knights and the national unions. The latter, stronger and more cohesive than the trade districts of the Order, were better able to take the lead in the conflict between reform and trade unionism. Disillusioned with labor reformism, the trade unions acted upon the premise that the traditional programs of the past were no longer suitable to the changing environment, and they led the assault against the Knights of Labor in 1886.

During the early 1880's, however, it was by no means evident that the Knights and the national unions were predestined to clash. The Federation of Organized Trades and Labor Unions permitted district assemblies of the Knights to be represented at its annual conventions,[24] and many trade union leaders also belonged to the Order.[25] Local unions and

assemblies often co-operated in joint boycotts, and expressions of friendliness by the national unions toward Powderly and other officials of the Knights were not uncommon.[26] The International Typographical Union expressed appreciation in 1882 for the aid given it by the Knights in a number of cities, and then went on to adopt resolutions recommending co-operation with other labor organizations and permitting its members to join any body that would further the interests of the craft in their particular locality.[27] In other words, the national unions regarded the Knights as a valuable economic ally.

In turn, the Knights vehemently denied having any hostile designs upon the trade unions, and in a number of prominent cases before 1885 it acted accordingly.[28] Nevertheless, with its structural inclusiveness and reform ideology, it was perhaps inevitable that the Order, in its efforts to bring all workingmen into a single organization, would undercut trade union organizational efforts. Thus the General Assembly authorized a committee in 1883 to confer with union representatives in the hope of incorporating all the trade unions within the Knights.[29]

In the absence of any national or international union, the absorption of local unions by the Knights in the form of trade assemblies created no friction. Indeed, isolated local unions were eager to affiliate with such a powerful national organization.[30] By 1886, therefore, the

The Development of the American Glass Industry (Cambridge: Harvard University Press, 1949), pp. 126–30.
[24] Federation of Organized Trades, Proceedings, 1882, pp. 5, 16, 20, 23.
[25] For a partial list of trade union leaders belonging to the Knights see The Painter, II (Feb. 1888), 3.

[26] See Iron Molders' Journal, XIX (June 30, 1883), 9; XX (June 30, 1884), 10; XXI (Nov. 30, 1885), 14; Amalgamated Association of Iron and Steel Workers, Proceedings, 1882, p. 955; The Craftsman, II (Jan. 17, 1885), 2, (Aug. 15, 1885), 2.
[27] International Typographical Union, Proceedings, 1882, pp. 43, 58, 62, 78, 83, 87.
[28] See K. of L., GA Proc., 1882, p. 270; 1884, pp. 707, 787; 1885, pp. 73, 138.
[29] Ibid., 1883, pp. 460, 467, 505–6. See also Powderly Letter Books, Powderly to J. P. McDonnell, Sept. 24, 1882.
[30] Ohio Bureau of Labor Statistics, Annual Report, IX (1885), 28; Grace H. Stimson, Rise of the Labor Movement in Los Angeles (Berkeley: University of California Press, 1955), p. 45.

Knights claimed nearly eleven hundred local assemblies, many of which undoubtedly represented local trade unions having no parent national union.

When, however, the Knights began to organize workingmen in trades already having national organizations, friction was quick to arise. The trouble that followed the Order's expansion into the realm of the trade unions was not simply a jurisdictional rivalry between similar organizations. As discussed above, the Order and the national unions had opposing conceptions of the legitimate functions of the labor movement, which in turn had led to different structural forms. The expansion of the Order's mixed units thus served to undermine the economic functions of the trade unions, since the heterogeneous character of the former prevented them from exercising any appreciable degree of economic power. Furthermore, the structural diversity of the Knights caused trouble when its trade assemblies sought to perform tasks that logically fell within the purview of the trade unions.[31] The national unions, moreover, took the position that geographical trade assemblies were inadequate to meet the challenge of a nationalized economy, and in fact were little better than mixed district assemblies. In defense, union officials generally refused to consent to a mutual recognition of working cards,[32] and they demanded that the Knights cease interfering in trade affairs.[33]

The Knights, however, did not heed the warnings of the national unions, and its organizers continued their sporadic work in trades having national unions. "Every week," John Swinton reported in 1885, "Trade Unions are turned into Local Assemblies, or Assemblies are organized out of Trade Unions."[34] As early as 1881 a district leader attempted to capture a typographical union local, and by 1884 there were over forty local assemblies of printers in the Knights.[35] The over-zealous activities of the Order's organizers also led to trouble with the Bricklayers and Masons International Union.[36]

The trade unions continuously charged that the Order had accepted scabs and unfair workers.[37] It is probable that the unions greatly exaggerated this grievance, but there is little doubt that the existence of two labor organizations, each purporting to accomplish different ends, created a disciplinary problem. Intraunion disagreements frequently concluded with one party seceding and joining the Order as a local assembly. Thus the trade unions found that the Knights were attracting dissidents who normally might have remained in the union.[38]

Despite the proselytizing activities of the Knights, there was no general conflict with the other unions before July 1885.

---

[31] Differences over wages, hours, and working conditions frequently ensued between trade assemblies and local and national unions, especially since no formal co-ordinating bodies existed. For an example of such a disagreement see K. of L., GA Proc., 1884, pp. 703, 764, 768.
[32] Iron Molders International Union, Proceedings, 1882, pp. 15, 54–55.
[33] See the National Labor Tribune, July 7, 1883, cited in John R. Commons, ed., History of Labour in the United States (4 vols: New York: Macmillan Company, 1918–1935), II, 353. "With other trade unionists," Gompers recalled, "I joined the Knights of Labor for the purpose of confining that organization to theoretical educational work and to see that the Trade Unions

were protected from being undermined or disrupted." Gompers Letter Books, A.F. of L.—C.I.O. Building, Washington, D.C., Gompers to N. E. Mathewson, Oct. 10, 1890.
[34] John Swinton's Paper, Apr. 12, 1885.
[35] JUL, II (Sept.–Oct. 1881), 158; John Swinton's Paper, Mar. 2, 1884.
[36] Bricklayers and Masons International Union, Proceedings, 1884, p. 9; Powderly Papers, Henry O. Cole to Powderly, Mar. 9, Apr. 28, 1883.
[37] The Carpenter, III (Feb. 1883), 3; International Typographical Union, Proceedings, 1884, p. 12.
[38] For typical examples see The Carpenter, III (Oct. 1883), 2; VI (Mar. 1836), 4; VIII (Feb. 15, 1888), I; Robert A. Christie, Empire in Wood: A History of the Carpenters' Union (Ithaca: Cornell University Press, 1956), pp. 50–51; John Swinton's Paper, Feb. 1, 8, 1885; K. of L., GA Proc., 1885, pp. 106, 109, 140.

At this time the membership of the Order was slightly over 100,000, and examples of clashes with the trade unions were generally the exception rather than the rule. When differences did arise, the trade unions often made conciliatory efforts at peaceful adjustment. Thus the convention of the International Typographical Union agreed in 1884 to its president's suggestion that he confer with Powderly in order to iron out existing grievances, although it refused to sanction a proposed amalgamation with the Order.[39]

In only one major case—that involving the Cigar Makers International Union—did the differences between a national union and the Knights erupt in open hostilities before 1886. Historians, placing much emphasis upon this particular conflict, have credited Adolph Strasser and Samuel Gompers, the leaders of the Cigar Makers, with the dual responsibility of helping to precipitate the internecine war between the national unions and the Knights, and then founding the A.F. of L. as a rival national federation.[40]

While the national unions generally supported the Cigar Makers in its struggle with the Knights,[41] it is improbable that sympathy for the Cigar Makers would have led to a fight with the Order. Undoubtedly Strasser and Gompers exerted great efforts to induce the unions to lend them support. The fact is also incontrovertible that both were determined, forceful, and sometimes ruthless men. Nevertheless, their efforts would have been useless unless a solid basis of discontent had already existed. In other words, for the unions to break with the Knights, there must have been more compelling reasons than simply the activities of two individuals.

III

To understand the conflict that split the labor movement, the rapid growth of the Knights after 1885 must be examined. In the twelve months between July 1885 and June 1886 the Order's membership increased from 100,000 to over 700,000. This growth, at least in part, came about at the expense of the other unions. In many cases workers abandoned their trade unions to join the Knights. The Journeymen Tailors National Union found that many of its locals had transferred to the Knights, resulting in a considerable loss of membership. A vice-president of the Amalgamated Association of Iron and Steel Workers complained in 1886 that some sublodges in his area had been disbanded because of inroads by the Order.[42] Further difficulty was caused by overzealous organizers who made determined efforts to transform trade unions into local assemblies. In February 1886 the secretary of the Journeymen Bakers National Union protested against such activities. "We never knew," responded the secretary-treasurer of the Knights, "that the K. of L. was proscribed from bringing into its fold all branches of honorable toil."[43]

The Knights, in other words, had adopted an organizational policy diametrically different from that of the trade unions. The traditional concept of organization held by the A.F. of L. (the representative of the trade unions) required that federal labor unions (local units including workers of all trades having no separate unions of their own) be

[39] International Typographical Union, *Proceedings*, 1884, pp. 12, 65–66, 70, 72, 102.

[40] See especially Ware, *Labor Movement*, pp. 258–79, 285, *et passim*, and Commons, *History of Labour*, II, 401–2.

[41] *Iron Molders' Journal*, XXII (Mar. 31, 1886), 14; *The Craftsman*, III (Aug. 7, 1886), 2.

[42] John B. Lennon, "Journeymen Tailors," *American Federationist*, IX (Sept. 1902), 599; Amalgamated Association of Iron and Steel Workers, *Proceedings*, 1886, p. 1793.

[43] New Haven *Workmen's Advocate*, Dec. 10, 1887.

splintered into separate homogeneous craft units as soon as there were enough workers in that locality to form such bodies. The aim of such a policy was to develop the collective bargaining potentialities of the various trades. The Knights, on the other hand, sought to reverse this strategy and proceed in the opposite direction, and it encouraged the combining of trade units into mixed assemblies, which at most were reform or political units. Beneath the structural and organizational differences of the two groups, therefore, lay opposing goals.

To what extent did the Knights encroach upon the domain of the trade unions? Peter J. McGuire of the Carpenters claimed that between 150 and 160 trade unions, including the Molders, Boiler-Makers, Bakers, Miners, Typographical, and Granite Cutters, had grievances against the Order.[44] Only in the case of the Bricklayers and Masons International Union, however, is the evidence fairly complete. In response to a survey conducted in the summer of 1886, the union's secretary received eighty-seven replies. Eight locals reported the existence of bricklayers and masons assemblies within their jurisdiction, four claimed the Knights were working for subunion wages, and three asserted the Knights were working longer hours. "But there are a large number of such men scattered throughout the country who belong to mixed assemblies," the secretary reported—and herein lay the union's major grievance.[45] The complaints of the Bricklayers and Masons were echoed by most of the other major national unions.[46]

In general, the national unions were fearful of the Knights for two closely related reasons. The mixed assembly, in the first place, was incompatible with trade union goals. In theory both structural forms could exist side by side, each pursuing its own ends. Thus the mixed assembly could concentrate on reform and politics, while the trade unions could develop their collective bargaining functions. This *modus vivendi*, however, presupposed that workers could belong simultaneously to both trade unions and mixed assemblies. At a time when the labor movement's primary problem was to organize and stay organized, such an assumption was unwarranted, and trade union leaders recognized the mutual hostility of the mixed assembly and trade union.

In the second place, trade union officials opposed the chartering of trade assemblies within the Knights for the reason that these units had proved incapable of developing collective bargaining and other union institutions. Furthermore, the geographical and regional organization of the Knights meant that there was little hope for the mature evolution of the national trade assembly. Since local trade assemblies were often ineffective when operating in an environment marked by a nationalized economy and the geographical mobility of labor, trade union leaders argued that these units were attempting to perform functions that logically belonged to the national unions, and in the long run tended to undermine the standards of membership and employment that the unions had struggled so fiercely to establish.[47]

By the spring of 1886 relations between the trade unions and the Knights had so

---

[44] K. of L., GA Proc., 1886 special session, pp. 50–51.
[45] Bricklayers and Masons International Union, Proceedings, 1887, pp. 70–75.
[46] Iron Molders' Journal, XXII (Feb. 28, 1886), 10, 14 (Apr. 30, 1886), 8 (Aug. 31, 1886), 6; XXIII (Dec. 31, 1886), 7; The Craftsman, III (May 15, 1886), 3; Granite Cutters' Journal, X (Apr. 1886), 3; The Carpenter, VI (May 1886), 2; Cigar Makers' Official Journal, XI (Apr. 1886), 6; Printers' Circular, XXI (June 1886), 66; International Typographical Union, Proceedings, 1886, pp. 90, 93–94; Iron Molders International Union, Proceedings, 1886, pp. 16, 25, 31.
[47] See The Craftsman, III (Feb. 6, 1886), 2 (Mar. 20, 1886), 1; The Carpenter, XXIV (Dec. 1904), 5.

deteriorated that a collision appeared imminent.[48] Five prominent unionists therefore called for a meeting of union leaders to arrange a settlement of differences, while at the same time Powderly summoned the General Assembly in a special session to consider, among other things, the troubles with the trade unions. The conference of trade union officials then appointed a committee of five to draw up a plan of settlement. Under the moderating influence of McGuire, who played the leading role, the committee drew up a "treaty," which it submitted to the General Executive Board of the Knights on May 25, 1886.[49]

By the terms of this treaty the Knights would refrain from organizing any trade having a national organization, and also would revoke the charter of any existing trade assembly having a parent union. In the second place, any workers guilty of ignoring trade union wage scales, scabbing, or any other offense against a union, would be ineligible for membership in the Order. Third, any organizer who tampered with or interfered in the internal affairs of trade unions would have his commission revoked. Finally, local and district assemblies were not to interfere while trade unions engaged in strikes or lockouts, and the Knights would not be permitted to issue any label or trade-mark where a national union had already done so.[50]

On the surface it appears surprising that the trade unions, which claimed to represent about 350,000 workers (although their actual membership was about 160,000), would present such a document to an organization having 700,000 members. Yet the treaty was neither a bargaining offer nor a declaration of war.[51] It was rather the logical outcome of the duality that had pervaded the labor movement since the Civil War. Under its terms the labor movement would be divided into two separate and distinct compartments. The Knights of Labor, on the one hand, would continue its efforts to abolish the wage system, reform society, and educate the working class. The national unions, on the other hand, would be left paramount in the economic field, and the Order would no longer be permitted to exercise any control over wages, hours, working conditions, or the process of collective bargaining. In other words, trade unionism and reform unionism had come to a parting of the ways.

In one sense the treaty was an expression of the fear of the skilled workers that they were being subordinated to the interests of the unskilled.[52] Yet the polarization implied in such an interpretation should not be exaggerated, for it cannot be said that the Knights themselves represented the unskilled workers. The Order was not an industrial union, nor did it emphasize collective bargaining. It was rather a heterogeneous mass that subordinated the economic functions of labor organizations to its primary goal of reforming society. The mixed assembly, while including workers of all trades and callings, was in no sense an industrial

[48] *John Swinton's Paper*, Mar. 21, 1886; Illinois Bureau of Labor Statistics, *Biennial Report*, IV (1886), 160–61.
[49] Bricklayers and Masons International Union, *Proceedings*, 1887. pp. 63–66; *The Carpenter*, VI (May 1886), 2 (June 1886), 3; *Cigar Makers' Official Journal*, XI (June 1886), 7; K. of L., GA Proc., 1886 special session, pp. 1–2; Powderly Letter Books, Powderly to P. J. McGuire and Adolph Strasser, May 11, 1886.
[50] A.F. of L., *Proceedings*, 1886, p. 16 (1905–06 reprinting).

[51] Cf. Ware, *Labor Movement*, p. 284.
[52] Perlman has interpreted the conflict between the Knights and unions largely as one between skilled and unskilled workers. Commons, *History of Labour*, II, 396–97. Undoubtedly the skilled workers feared the Knights. The Knights, however, was not necessarily an organization of unskilled workers, as the large number of trade assemblies would indicate. While the unions jealously guarded their autonomy and independence, the conflict that developed in 1886 was more than simply a struggle between the skilled and unskilled, although this aspect was an important element.

union, since it was not organized either by industry or factory. Moreover, the trade unions had never excluded the unskilled from the labor movement; they simply maintained that organization along craft lines was historically correct. "In truth," remarked Gompers, "the trade union is nothing more or less than the organization of wage earners engaged in a given employment, whether skilled or unskilled, for the purpose of attaining the best possible reward, [and] the best attainable conditions for the workers in that trade or calling."[53]

The General Assembly of the Knights, in turn, submitted its own proposals to the union committee. Its terms included protection against unfair workers, a mutual exchange of working cards, and the holding of a joint conference before either organization presented wages and hours demands to employers.[54] Clearly the Assembly's position was in fundamental disagreement with that of the trade unions. The latter had demanded unitary control over the economic field, while the Knights had demanded equal jurisdiction over membership and working standards. Thus neither side evinced willingness to compromise over basic issues.

Although failing to conclude a settlement with the trade unions, the special session of the General Assembly did not close the door to further negotiations. For the time being, therefore, the conflict remained in abeyance. While matters were pending, however, the Knights made a determined effort to end friction by intensifying its campaign to bring the national unions under its control. The national unions, however, recognized that the structure of the Knights was incom-

patible with trade union objectives, and the policy of the Order was only partially successful. Some of the smaller unions, including the Seamen's Benevolent Union, the Eastern Glass Bottle Blowers' League, and the Western Green Bottle Blowers' Association, joined the Knights.[55] The American Flint Glass Workers Union, on the other hand, refused to go along with the other glassworkers because of an earlier dispute with the Order.[56] In New York City the Knights made a determined but unsuccessful attempt to capture the German shoemakers and the Associated Jewelers.[57] Most of the larger and more important unions emphatically rejected the Order's overtures. The members of the Amalgamated Association of Iron and Steel Workers overwhelmingly defeated a referendum on the subject, while a similar poll conducted by the secretary of the Bricklayers and Masons resulted in the same conclusion. The Iron Molders' convention turned down the merger proposal by a vote of 114 to 27.[58] Furthermore, the Typographical Union, the Carpenters, the Plumbers and Gas Fitters, the coal miners, and the Stationary Engineers all rejected the invitation to join the Knights.[59]

At the regular meeting of the General Assembly in October 1886 further negotia-

[53] Gompers Letter Books, Gompers to George H. Daggett, Jan. 4, 1896. See also Gompers to Albert C. Stevens, Nov. 1, 1889; Gompers to Frank D. Hamlin, May 6, 1890; Gompers to Charles W. Nelson, Apr. 29, 1892.

[54] K. of L., GA Proc., 1886 special session, pp. 53, 55, 67.

[55] JUL, VIII (Aug. 20, 1887), 2476; K. of L., GA Proc., 1887, p. 1334; John Swinton's Paper, July 25, 1886; David A. McCabe, The Standard Rate in American Trade Unions (Baltimore: The Johns Hopkins Press, 1912), pp. 155–56. The glassworkers probably joined the Order in the hope of emulating the success of L.A. 300.

[56] Iron Molders' Journal, XXII (Feb. 28, 1886), 10; Cigar Makers' Official Journal, XI (Aug. 1886), 6; Secretary of Internal Affairs of the Commonwealth of Pennsylvania, Annual Report, XVI (1888), Pt. III, Section F, pp. 18–19.

[57] The Carpenter, VI (Oct. 1886), 1.

[58] Amalgamated Association of Iron and Steel Workers, Proceedings, 1886, pp. 1807–08, 1818–19, 1846; 1887, pp. 1959–62; Bricklayers and Masons International Union, Proceedings, 1887, pp. 71, 76; Iron Molders International Union, Proceedings, 1886, pp. 17–20.

[59] John Swinton's Paper, June 20, 1886; The Carpenter, VI (Oct. 1886), 1. See also Locomotive Firemen's Magazine, X (Mar. 1886), 141.

tions between the trade unions and the Knights again ended in failure. The action by the Assembly in ordering all workers holding cards in both the Knights and the Cigar Makers International Union to leave the latter under pain of expulsion[60] was interpreted by both sides as constituting a final break and an open declaration of war.[61] The trade union committee therefore issued a call on November 10, 1886, for all unions to send representatives to a convention in Columbus, Ohio, on December 8, to form an "American Federation or Alliance of all National and International Trade Unions." Out of this meeting came the A.F. of L. Completely dominated by the national unions, the December convention excluded assemblies of the Knights from membership, and then proceeded to establish the new organization on a firm foundation.[62]

Thus by the end of 1886 the die had been cast, and the Knights and national unions prepared for war. Why had all negotiations failed? Undoubtedly the intractability of leaders on both sides contributed to the difficulties, but there were also those who had made sincere efforts to head off the impending conflict. The trade unions, furthermore, had encountered jurisdictional rivalries with the Knights, but this has been an endemic problem of the labor movement, and one which has not always had an unhappy ending.

The conflict between the Knights and the trade unions, then, had a much broader significance than the negotiations between them indicated, and represented the culmination of decades of historical development. The Knights, growing out of the humanitarian and reform crusades of ante-bellum America, emphasized the abolition of the wage system and the reorganization of society. To achieve this purpose it insisted on the prime importance of the mixed assembly, which would serve as the nucleus of an organization dedicated to reform. The trade unions, on the other hand, accepted their environment, and sought to take advantage of the relative scarcity of labor and the rising scale of production. Hence they emphasized the collective bargaining functions of labor organizations, thus tacitly accepting the workers' wage status.

Perhaps grounds for compromise did exist, but neither side was prone to make any concessions. The national unions, by insisting upon strict trade autonomy as a *sine qua non* of settlement, were in effect demanding that the Knights should virtually abandon any pretense at being a bona fide labor organization. It is true that the unions could have organized as national autonomous trade districts if the Knights had been ready to grant permission. The leaders of the Knights, however, were unwilling to permit their organization to be transformed into what the A.F. of L. ultimately became. Indeed, after 1886 many national trade districts left the Order because of their inability to function within the framework of that body.[63]

[60] K. of L., GA Proc., 1886, pp. 200, 282.
[61] See Joseph R. Buchanan, The Story of a Labor Agitator (New York: The Outlook Company, 1903), p. 314.
[62] Bricklayers and Masons International Union, Proceedings, 1887, pp. 79–80; A.F. of L., Proceedings, 1886, pp. 13–15. A committee from the Knights was also present at the trade union convention in December 1886 but no agreement was reached. See A.F. of L., Proceedings, 1886, pp. 17–18; K. of L., GA Proc., 1887, pp. 1445–47.

[63] The shoemakers, miners, machinists, garmentworkers, carriage and wagonworkers, and potters all seceded from the Knights after 1886 because of their inability to function efficiently within the existing framework of the Order. For evidence on this point see the following: The Laster, I (Mar. 15, 1889), 1; Shoe Workers' Journal, XI (July 1910), II; United Mine Workers of America, Proceedings, 1911, I, 581; JUL, VIII (May 19, 1888), 1; Journal of the International Association of Machinists, VII (July 1895), 238; Garment Workers, III (Sept. 1896), 4; Carriage and Wagon Workers Journal, II (Jan. 1, 1901), 113; United States Industrial Commission, Report of the Industrial Commission (19 vols: Washington, D.C., 1900–02), XVII, 59, 209; Theodore W. Glocker, The Government of American Trade Unions (Baltimore: The Johns Hopkins Press, 1913), p. 54.

The national unions, moreover, were not encouraged by the experiences of trade districts within the Knights before 1886. Finally, there was the simple element of power, and both the trade unions and the Knights, as established organizations, were adamant in their refusal to surrender any part of it.

Between reform and trade unionism, therefore, existed a gulf that the leaders of the 1880's were unable to bridge. By 1886 this chasm had widened to such a degree that co-operation between the two seemed virtually impossible and war seemed to be the only solution. Reform and trade unionism had at last come to a parting of the ways, and upon the outcome of the ensuing struggle hinged the destiny of the American labor movement.

Chapter Five

Changing Foreign Economic Relations

■ From the late 1820s through the rest of the nineteenth century a fairly steady stream of foreign investment flowed to the United States, most of it English. In the early part of this period state bonds for public works were the favorites, then railroad securities, and then, in the late 1870s and the 1880s, investments in Western cattle ranches. These agricultural investments and some other investments, in American public utilities and breweries, for instance, continued into the 1890s, the decade which brought to a close the period of important foreign investment in

the United States. The reasons for a decline in the westward flow of capital become clear from a look at interest rates in the United States money market. In 1870 good railroad bonds were yielding nearly 8 per cent interest; by 1890 the same type of bonds yielded only about 4.5 per cent, and by 1900 less than 4 per cent. The American rates were no longer attractive to the foreigners or, for that matter, to all domestic investors.

The same trends toward easier money and lower interest rates were also present in Europe. To capitalists in all the leading industrial nations, which now included the United States, the securities of still under-developed areas on which interest rates were high, even if payment was somewhat uncertain, became increasingly attractive. As always, investments in new areas were looked upon as useful in opening up markets for the export of manufactured goods. The financiers of the European nations increased their investments in Asia, Africa, and mainland South America; United States capitalists turned initially to the nations bordering the Caribbean Sea and to Canada. As the rate of real capital formation in relation to national income slowly declined in the United States, Americans became larger and larger suppliers of capital for external investment, until after 1914 they supplanted the British as the great source of international funds.

A broad view of American economic development shows that the United States benefited from being an attractive area for foreign investment during its period of rather acute capital scarcity, and that as domestic saving became adequate in relation to the opportunities offered for investment, the inflow of foreign capital diminished. Such a sweeping general truth should not, however, obscure the fact that capital interchanges in bank deposits and security sales are always taking place between the leading nations, and may or may not generate considerable net flow of funds in a given year.

The Passing of the Old Order

■ While the largest part of foreign investment in the United States had been in railroads and government securities, British investors had always had an interest in Western land; and in the late 1870s a boom in Western cattle raising, brought about by improved transportation facilities and increasing rainfall, led to extensive British, as well as eastern American, investment in ranches. It is ironic that these risky ventures, which were generally unprofitable after 1886 because of diminished rainfall, involved some of the most prestigious and conservative capitalists of both England and the United States.

For the British, these investments differed in one important respect from most of the earlier types. Buying the bonds of American governments or railroads, for example, had never involved any direct British controls over management; many of the ranches, however, were British-owned and -run. This had important effects. The English and Scotch managers aroused the kind of local resentment against foreign capitalists that is often observed in under-developed areas. Foreign ownership increasingly seemed to the hardworking western farmer to threaten his hold on his own land or to kill his hope of moving to better land some day. As a result, legislation restricting foreign ownership began to be passed after 1887.

In discussing this course of events, Roger V. Clements, of the Manchester (England) Joint Research Council, focuses on what is, to be sure, a series of minor incidents in American economic history; yet the new growth of the restrictive attitude in the United States was symbolic of the changing stage of American development.

Roger V. Clements
British Investment and American Legislative Restrictions in the Trans-Mississippi West, 1880–1900*

British investments in the West during the latter part of the nineteenth century brought charges of exploitation and fostered western resentment against alien control. The Plains farmers, a class particularly aggrieved by the extension of alien ownership, were already suffering from a variety of afflictions, most of them of domestic origin. The rapidity of settlement between the Missouri and the Rockies had distorted the accustomed framework of economic life. Railroads were sometimes too few, sometimes too many. Marketing facilities were often monopolistically controlled. Many troubles, too, could be traced to the environment, for the Plains farmer lived in a harsh and unlovely setting in which he faced shortages of timber and water. These and other evils added resentment and fear to western life and sharpened the hunt for devils.

When alien ownership was complained of, it was alien ownership of land which created the greatest jealousy and resentment. Of chief concern was the fact that supplies of land were giving out; indeed, for practical purposes they were exhausted by about 1890. The dream of Utopia was vanishing. The farmer who had endured with grasshoppers for company and a sod hut for home was especially sensitive to whatever threatened his hold on the land he had or appeared to cripple hope of some day acquiring better land. Whether he was prosperous or poor, his homestead represented life itself. In mortgaging it he mortgaged his future more fundamentally than the industrial entrepreneur who employed borrowed

capital. The disposition of the land, his own and the public domain, became a vital problem to the western farmer in the 1880's and 1890's.

In fastening upon the land British investment antagonized the homesteader, the democrat, and the American. It was worse than the bitterly resented eastern control, for it was alien and its absentee features more prominent. Moreover, though in the aggregate British investment and invasion of traditional values were less than those which had an eastern origin, individual cases were often on a grander scale and more prominently publicized. The farmers' attitude toward the operations of outside capital—especially British capital—grew more critical, although isolated instances may be given to the contrary: when, for example, a lecturer confessed the dependence of the farmer upon capital;[1] or when western men initiated a British lending business in Texas;[2] or when a normally hostile newspaper acknowledged the useful achievements of British capital in the West.[3]

British estates in America were owned both by individuals and by companies. Although men like Lord Dunraven and William Scully each controlled several thousand acres, individuals were often

* Reprinted by permission from The Mississippi Valley Historical Review, XLII (September, 1955), pp. 207–228.

[1] In discussing the high hopes of the immigrants it was confessed that "capital only can accomplish these fine things." Colorado State Grange, Annual Report (1890), 45.
[2] The Texas Land and Mortgage Company. J. Evetts Haley, Charles Goodnight, Cowman and Plainsman (Norman, 1949), 344–45.
[3] "English capital has done much toward developing the Western country, and there is much to commend in the enterprise which brings millions of dollars to put into the land, ditches and cattle along the foothills." Laramie Weekly Sentinel, June 9, 1883, quoted in Notes of Herbert O. Brayer (Colorado State Archives, Denver).

credited with the ownership of great tracts which actually belonged to corporations of which they were merely directors. Such erroneous beliefs created an impression that British-held land was in the possession of individual aristocrats, whereas most of it was in reality owned by corporations.[4] The extent of this corporate activity was indicated by the incorporation in Britain of twenty-one major western cattle companies by the end of 1883.[5] Among them were the famous Matador and Prairie companies. The latter in its heyday ranged 100,000 cattle over at least 1,000,000 acres of land, and its capitalization was put at $2,500,000. In the spring of 1884 the brokerage firm of Tait and Denman estimated the Scottish investment in cattle at $25,000,000.[6] The area within which British companies operated stretched from Texas to the northern plains of Montana. There was no leasing system and in its absence Americans and British evolved essentially the same methods of acquisition and control. Landholdings were enlarged by having workhands file claims on water holes and courses and then transfer their rights to the employer.[7] The railroad lands which were bought or leased included in effect the intermingled sections of public land. Local communities

became alarmed at the scale of these alien acquisitions, and their growing opposition, together with increasing settlement, led the cattle companies to take the defensive by building wire fences about their domains.

The eagerness with which newspapers gave prominence to rumored transactions involving millions of acres and millions of dollars led to an agitation of the public mind not altogether warranted by the facts of the case.[8] Official investigations and lists of alien landholdings published as congressional reports apparently confirmed perfervid imaginings. The subsequent admission of one of the chief anti-alien spokesmen that considerable error attended his computations was less avidly seized upon.[9] Even so, these investigations revealed the British control of at least 20,000,000 acres in large lots, chiefly in the West, and newspapers made additions to the lists.[10] In 1884 the St. Paul *Pioneer Press* estimated that Englishmen owned nearly 500,000 acres in Iowa and Minnesota.[11] The Girard *Herald* of Kansas, publishing its own version of the official lists, bitterly contrasted the vast holdings of the "land gods," largely noblemen, with the landless condition of American "sovereigns."[12] In 1892 it was pointed out by a Colorado paper that English holdings in America were larger

---

[4] Lists included Sir Edward Reid, the Marquis of Tweeddale, the Duke of Sutherland, Lord Dunmore, Lord Houghton, Lord Dunraven, and Sir John Kay. "Ownership of Real Estate in the Territories," *House Reports*, No. 3455, 49 Cong., 1 Sess., 2. This kind of person, however, was mainly concerned with American lands as a member of the board of a company, like the Marquis of Tweeddale as chairman of the Capitol Freehold Land and Investment Company. Lewis Nordyke, *Cattle Empire: The Fabulous Story of the 3,000,000 Acre XIT* (New York, 1949), 74.

[5] Herbert O. Brayer, "When Dukes Went West," *Westerners Brand Book* (Denver Posse), No. 4 (Denver, 1948), 66–67.

[6] *Cong. Record*, 48 Cong., 1 Sess., 4773 (June 3, 1884).

[7] The activities of the Scottish Prairie Cattle Company in this regard are described in John Clay, *My Life on the Range* (Chicago, 1924), 128–29.

[8] British cattle companies were accused of keeping Oklahoma closed to settlement. See the picture of a rather ordinary looking log hut captioned "English Ranch in Oklahoma," in A. P. Jackson and E. C. Cole, *Oklahoma! Politically and Topographically Described: History and Guide to the Indian Territory* (Kansas City, 1885), 60–61.

[9] Senator Preston B. Plumb of Kansas. *Cong. Record*, 49 Cong., 1 Sess., 7955 (August 4, 1886).

[10] See *House Reports*, No. 3455, 49 Cong., 1 Sess. A slightly different version appears in *Cong. Record*, 48 Cong., 1 Sess., 2359 (March 27, 1884).

[11] Jacob Van der Zee, *The British in Iowa* (Iowa City, 1922), 116.

[12] Girard (Kansas) *Herald*, March 16, 1889. This list included the Earl of Beaconsfield, who had been dead some years.

than the area of Ireland.[13] The farmers' *Alliance Handbook*, by throwing in the land grants of railroads in which aliens were interested and making a generous estimate of alien-held mortgages, credited foreigners with control over 150,000,000 acres.[14] The famed bimetallist, William H. Harvey, assisted in reviving discussion in the 1890's with his *Coin's Financial School up to Date* and its map—a wonderful exaggeration—purporting to show their estates in the West.[15]

The menace of land monopoly and of land speculation was an ancient one, yet it had been only in the 1870's that even those most clearly affected, the pioneering farmers, began to perceive its full gravity. Complaint rose in volume, stimulated by the agricultural depression and the shortage of good land. Much of the complaint, though with small success, was directed against the railroad grants. Alien offenders were singled out for castigation even in the beginning, for they were among the few in the Far West who then could afford to invest in large undertakings. From 1874 for over a decade indignation was expressed in Colorado over Lord Dunraven's possession of several thousand acres in Estes Park. The Land Office revealed that his lordship's agent had intimidated American settlers in order to silence their testimony about the fraudulence of the nobleman's claims.[16] Similar reports were made concerning a Scottish company's methods of

acquiring immensely valuable timber land in California.[17]

It was, however, the movement of settlers into western Nebraska, Kansas, and Texas and into eastern Colorado which first made general this hostility to British enterprise. A tempest developed between 1883 and 1887 as settlers came up against the fences of the cattle companies. The large size of British outfits drew upon alien heads most of the wrath. The Prairie Cattle Company and the Arkansas Valley Land and Cattle Company were each said to have fenced a million acres in Colorado, and long reaches of the Arkansas River were denied to smaller cattlemen.[18] Though the Americans involved far outnumbered the aliens, the large part that British companies played in these conflicts was assiduously publicized. In official documents the lists of alleged fraudulent fencing claims always carefully distinguished the British cases; in Congress the foreign character of some of the actors in the drama was indefatigably stressed.[19] Newspapers also played up popular anti-alien sentiment along these lines. Comment was unsympathetic in Colorado and Wyoming when it was learned that the people in Britain were worried: "Our English and Scotch cousins are deeply interested in

[13] *Field and Farm* (Denver), October 22, 1892.
[14] *Handbook of Facts and Alliance Information* (Washington, 1890), 64.
[15] William H. Harvey, *Coin's Financial School up to Date* (Chicago, 1895), 110, 112. The pictures were those of Lords Houghton and Dunraven, the Duke of Marlborough, Lady Churchill, and Baroness Burdett-Coutts. The map showed practically the whole of South Dakota, Nebraska, and New Mexico as owned by these people. Reproductions appear in the Boston *Herald*, January 27, 1895.
[16] Greeley *Tribune*, May 26, 1874; Denver *Tribune*, May 26, 1874. "Report from Commissioner of the General Land Office concerning Entries of Public Lands by the Estes Park Company and Other Foreign Corporations," *Senate Exec. Docs.*,

No. 181, 48 Cong., 1 Sess., 2; Secretary of the Interior, *Annual Report*, 1886 (Washington, 1886), 72.
[17] Secretary of the Interior, *Annual Report*, 1887 (Washington, 1887), 162–64; California State Board of Forestry, *Biennial Report*, 1888–1889 (Sacramento, 1890), 146; San Francisco *Evening Bulletin*, March 31, 1888.
[18] "Letter of the Commissioner of the General Land Office on the Subject of Unauthorized Fencing of Public Lands," *Senate Exec. Docs.*, No. 127, 48 Cong., 1 Sess., 18, 31, 33–34, 38. See also "Unlawful Occupancy of the Public Lands," *House Reports*, No. 1325, 48 Cong., 1 Sess., 2.
[19] Representative Lewis E. Payson of Illinois asserted in the House that American citizens were excluded from the public lands "for the reason that they are fenced in by foreigners, Americans having no interest in the fencing whatever." *Cong. Record*, 48 Cong., 1 Sess., 4769 (June 3, 1884).

these fences, for it was their money which built them, and it is only natural that they should complain about the interference of 'those blawsted Hamericans, you know.' " Instead of trying to allay these apprehensions, some newspapers threatened that old vigilante methods might be used to avenge the deaths of wire cutters.[20] Editors and readers did not tire of the subject, for a year later re'erence was still made to the continued oppression of settlers by the fences of alien corporations.

In Texas, relations between cattle companies and nesters had deteriorated so far that the demoralized condition of the state in 1887 was ascribed to this conflict, and analogies were drawn with "Bleeding Kansas."[21] A special session of the Texas legislature in January, 1884, attempted to define the rights of enclosure and to set adequate penalties for fence cutting.[22] In earlier years Congress had taken cognizance of the fencing problem and had carried out investigations, but not till after the Democratic victory of 1884 was a bill passed making such fences illegal and authorizing the Executive to remove obstructions from the public domain by military force. In August, 1885, President Cleveland, acting under the provisions of this bill, ordered the removal of fences on public land.[23] The rejoicing which greeted this order was somewhat premature,[24] but the issue did become less important. Furthermore, Bri-

tish cattle companies in particular suffered from the slump in cattle prices and from the hard winters of 1885–1886 and 1886–1887. Of the nine chief companies, with a paid-up capital of $18,000,000, only one issued a dividend in 1886 and none at all in 1887.[25] The fortunes of the few that struggled on to liquidation continued to be so erratic that in 1904 they were termed a "sporting investment."[26] Everywhere they gave way to the encroachments of the settlers; only in Texas was their resistance sufficiently stout to keep antagonism alive.

The debate on the disposition of the western domain had meanwhile passed to a more important phase: the right of aliens, particularly absentees, to own land. The campaign against British land investments was conducted at all levels—in the press, in Congress, in state legislatures, and by labor and agrarian organizations. A basic assumption was that the homestead laws expressed the wisdom of the founding fathers and were the prime condition of the continued success of the Republic. Traditional doctrine asserted that a prosperous landowning yeomanry was the backbone of the country in war; more modern doctrine taught that a healthy and extensive agrarian economy was the foundation of peacetime national progress. The approaching exhaustion of the public lands together with a swarming population suggested that the homestead tradition must soon be at an end. In any case the aim of the homestead laws had been perverted by lax administration and prodigal grants to railroads. Greater vigilance was needed, therefore, against alien landholders. Revolution itself was

---

[20] Laramie *Daily Boomerang*, September 12, 1884, quoting Denver *Tribune Republican*.
[21] Clara Barton to President Grover Cleveland, February 19, 1887, Papers of Grover Cleveland (Division of Manuscripts, Library of Congress).
[22] Texas Legislature, *House Journal* (1884), 3–5, 17, 182.
[23] *Statutes at Large of the United States*, XXIII (1884), 321–22; XXIV (1885), 1024–25.
[24] For example, in 1889 the decision in a case concerning an English company sanctioned fences built upon its land, despite their enclosure of intermingled government sections. United States v. Douglas-Willan Sartoris Co., 3 Wyo. 287–310 (1889), 22 Pacific 92.

[25] *Economist* (London), XLVI (March 17, 1888), 388.
[26] *Ibid.*, LXII (March 5, 1904), 404. The change in emphasis of these companies from cattle to the disposal of the land did nothing to endear them to the advancing settler, especially in Texas. The Prairie, Hansford, Matador, Swan, Texas, and Western ranches still remained in 1904.

conceivable if the land monopoly was not attacked, for the best "safeguard against public disorder, tumults, and riots," said to be "a generally distributed ownership of lands and homes," was not being secured.[27]

Such fears lodged in the minds of western farmers in the late 1880's and 1890's as they observed the engrossment of large estates by alien absentees. Apprehensions were heightened by the special terrors which the British name conjured up. "British" stood for the subjection of other peoples, for financial power, and for aristocratic institutions. It was believed dangerous for American soil to pass into the hands of foreigners "whose birth and education create and foster sentiments inimical to the country from which they are attempting to derive wealth."[28] In Colorado in 1887 it was asserted that British ownership of large bodies of land was "contrary to the spirit of independence."[29] A reported transfer of ownership of a large tract of land, including irrigation canals, to an English syndicate in 1892 was regarded in Kansas as an exemplification of the oft-repeated comment that "England by stratagem and purchase [is] getting back what she lost in war."[30]

Many Alliance men showed greatest concern over the two baneful systems which they believed the Britons sought to establish on American soil: an economic system of landlordism and a social system of aristocracy. Tenancy had been rare enough in earlier years for the tradition to become firmly held that the American farmer, by definition, owned his farm. Yet the problem was soon the concern of the secretary of the interior, and in 1885 official currency was given to the report

that the United States, with 570,000, led the world in number of tenant farmers.[31] Tenancy of this sort was labeled "un-American," and the hunt for scapegoats soon discovered them in the British owners of American land.

The lists of alien landowners published by Congress showed a preponderance of titled Englishmen. English workers, it was said in the Senate, believed that the English upper classes were building a more monstrous aristocracy in the United States than that which was in retreat in Britain.[32] British lack of sympathy for American democratic institutions and British designs upon them and the people were presumed if not proved, and harsh treatment of subject races did not go unremarked. In particular Hibernian sufferings provided awful warnings of the fate that awaited America. States passed resolutions of sympathy for Michael Davitt and Ireland, and of encouragement for Gladstone.[33] The redoubtable Mrs. Mary E. Lease lashed British tyranny and spoke in commemoration of Robert Emmett. Not without reason all of Ireland's ills were blamed upon the system of absentee aristocratic landlordism. Westerners entertained an apocalyptic vision of a future in which all the violent evils of Ireland —the midnight eviction, the firebrand, and gunfire at night—would occur in

[31] Secretary of the Interior, Annual Report, 1883 (Washington, 1883), xxxii–xxxiii. For a symposium on the subject in 1886, including statements by a member of Parliament and Henry George, see North American Review (New York), CXLII (January, February, March, April, 1886), 52–67, 153–58, 246–53, 387–401.

[32] Cong. Record, 48 Cong., 1 Sess., 4774 (June 3, 1884). The commissioner of the General Land Office reported that this "un-American system" established "conditions of feudalism in baronial possessions and comparative serfdom of employees." Secretary of the Interior, Annual Report, 1886, p. 70. The Iowa Alliance was apprehensive of "the vicious European landlord system." Farmers' Alliance (Independence, Iowa), December 17, 1891.

[33] See for example Colorado Legislature, House Journal (1881), 661–62; ibid. (1883), 773–74; ibid. (1887), 2235.

[27] These were the arguments of Representative Lewis E. Payson. House Reports, No. 3455, 49 Cong., 1 Sess., 1–4.

[28] Ibid., 4.

[29] Denver Republican, February 21, 1887.

[30] Girard Western Herald, March 26, 1892.

America, if upon her soil aristocratic English landlordism were tolerated.

Examples nearer home were used in support of the claim that English land-lordism was more extortionate and cruel than any other. William Scully, an Anglo-Irishman with extensive holdings, was said to be drawing $200,000 annually by 1885 from tenant farmers in Illinois, Kansas, and Nebraska. He appears to have been a bad landlord, refusing to make improvements himself in order to evade taxation; giving no compensation to tenants for their improvements; and encouraging a low type of occupant. The wide area of his operations was poorly maintained and underdeveloped.[34] He was the "Lord Saunders" of Sarah M. Brigham's cautionary story entitled "Waverland: A Tale of Our Coming Land-lords," published in serial form in 1890 in the Western Herald of Kansas. In his London club and in his country house, the English landlord of the story squandered the rents drawn from a country whose institutions and ideals he contemned. And at the nadir of human hopes was the Irishman who, evicted from his native cot, found himself the tenant of the very same landlord in democratic America.[35]

Tenancy itself was a subject of wide-spread concern. The increase in farm-renting was expected to lead to the formation of a degraded tenant class, but an even worse threat to American hopes and traditions lay in the substitution of foreigners for natives on these rented farms. Scully did this, but the impression was fostered that it had occurred on a much larger scale and would be even greater in the future. Governor James S. Hogg of Texas anticipated that vast British estates in Texas would be subdivided among inferior foreign tenants who would surrender American politics into the hands of aristocratic landlords by being compelled to vote in their interests.[36] A speaker in Congress pictured honest, patriotic American citizens dispossessed by servile, alien minions.[37] The National Economist, organ of the Alliance, emphasized the radical nature of the change that would darken American society should this development be unchecked.[38] Whether native or foreign, so depressed a tenantry, subservient to the monopolistic, aristocratic landlords, cut right through the cherished ideals of opportunity, progress, and freedom.

Wrought-up public sentiment against alien interests was responsible in December, 1883, for the introduction in the House of Representatives of a bill to prohibit the acquisition of territorial land by absentee aliens or by companies in

[34] Paul W. Gates, "Land Policy and Tenancy in the Prairie States," Journal of Economic History (New York), I (May, 1941), 81. Scully's system was referred to as a matter of course as "the English system." Report of select committee to inquire into the amount of land owned by aliens in Kansas. Kansas Legislature, House Journal (1889), 383.
[35] Girard Western Herald, November 1, 1890. The same idea was suggested by Terence V. Powderly, Thirty Years of Labor (Columbus, 1889), 340–41. Scully was exceptional, and the land brokerage and mortgage business of the Close Brothers, for example, in Iowa and Kansas, bigger than that of Scully, apparently brought no opprobrium, although they made a good profit out of their tenants. It was pointed out, too, that American law sanctioned Scully's behavior; and it was even suggested that as their last step toward irresponsible domination the foreign landlords had dictated the eviction laws of some of the states, with the result that "it is easier to evict a family today in Kansas than it is in Ireland." Quoted in Girard Western Herald, December 5, 1891.

[36] Robert C. Cotner (ed.), Addresses and State Papers of James Stephen Hogg (Austin, 1951), 98, 179–80.
[37] A one-armed veteran was imagined as seeking a home and being "confronted there by the minions of some lisping lord or the satraps of some capering count, and is kept from that land which his valor and blood have secured to us." Cong. Record, 48 Cong., 1 Sess., 4782 (June 3, 1884).
[38] "The hold of this deadly monster [English landlordism] is at last being loosened on the green sod [Ireland], but it has seized upon the fresh energy of America, and is steadily fixing its fangs into our social life, until even now thousands of so-called free Americans are as much the vassals of English masters as the most oppressed of Ireland." National Economist (Washington), I (June 29, 1889), 229.

which more than 20 per cent of the stock was held by aliens. The chief backers of the measure were Senator Preston B. Plumb of Kansas and Representative Lewis E. Payson of Illinois. In the debate most of the customary arguments about aliens and alien ownership were in evidence: Irish sentiment, chauvinism, dislike of aristocracy, suspicion of British ambitions, as well as concern for the thwarted aspirations of the small farmer. A noted Irish supporter, Representative William McAdoo of New Jersey, introduced a related bill, and Representative William E. Robinson of New York called for an inquiry into the purchase of land by "foreign noblemen, so called."[39]

By 1884 hostile opinion had forced anti-alien planks into both Democratic and Republican platforms, and in January, 1885, an extended debate followed the report of the House committee on public lands. In this debate arguments were heard about the danger of alien institutions, of the importation of foreigners to inhabit these estates, of the possibility that through foreclosure on the railroads the ownership of a hundred million more acres would pass out of American hands. The animus of the report was against alien ownership and control, not against the investment of alien money. The notion that the contemplated legislation would drive out capital was scouted.[40] A bill was finally agreed upon by the two houses of Congress and signed by President Cleveland in March, 1887. It forbade any absentee alien, or resident alien who had not declared the intention of becoming a citizen, to gain possession in the future

of real property in the territories, except property acquired by inheritance or through the collection of debts previously contracted. Likewise, at least four fifths of the stock of any corporation thereafter acquiring real estate in the territories had to be held by citizens. Nor could any company, native or foreign, own more than five thousand acres of land, except those building transport and communication services.[41]

This legislation won the approval of most opinion, particularly in the East. Several territories on becoming states enacted similar legislation of local application. Mining territories and states, however, objected to the application of the law to mining property and carried on a continuous campaign for its amendment. But when amendment came, a decade later, it did not alleviate an anti-alien grievance of the farmers. Foreign money-lenders had been a special target for farmers' abuse in the early 1880's.[42] It was contended that alien mortgages aimed not so much at the repayment of the money-debt as at the ultimate possession of the land. Yet, since the West needed capital, the act was amended in 1897 to reassert the right of alien mortgagees to enforce contracts by taking possession of the real property for a maximum period of ten years.[43] But the amendment was not in line with the wishes of western agrarians who believed that the original act itself was inadequate. Many of them thought it should have included the states as well as the territories, and they gave strong support to Representatives William C. Oates of Alabama and William P. Hepburn of Iowa, who persistently advocated in Congress a federal restriction on alien ownership

[39] At the same time Robinson asked for a variety of measures: a pension for "the sole surviving grandchild of the author of the Declaration of Independence"; an investigation of the bombardment of Alexandria; and an examination into reports of the presence of a British spy in the United States Post Office Department. *Cong. Record*, 48 Cong., 1 Sess., 97 (December 11, 1883).
[40] "Land Titles to Aliens in the United States," *House Reports*, No. 2308, 48 Cong., 2 Sess., 1–4.

[41] *Statutes at Large of the United States*, XXIV (1887), 476–77.
[42] See, for example, Des Moines *Iowa Weekly People*, February 6, 1879, for the attitude of the Iowa State Grange.
[43] *Statutes at Large of the United States*, XXIX (1897), 618–19.

of real property in both the states and the territories.[44]

Reinforced by poor seasons and a swelling sense of wrong, farmer organizations waxed after 1887. For several years agitation about the ownership of large estates by absentee aliens was an important part of their activities. The Greenbackers of Iowa were already condemning land monopoly in 1879, and with the adoption of the National Greenback Labor platform at Indianapolis in May, 1884, the party specifically demanded the prohibition of alien landownership, individual or corporate. The Granges made a similar transition; but it was slower because of the philosophy and character of the organization. The Colorado State Grange, for example, lashed the monopoly of land by the wealthy in the 1870's, but as late as 1885 it had not reached the point of specifying aliens. The Wisconsin Grange, however, petitioned Congress in 1887 for restrictions on foreigners, and three years later the Michigan Grange argued elaborately the danger of alien investment in real property.[45] In its national conferences the Grange was alert to the threat by the end of 1886. At the 1889 session it passed a resolution deploring the wide extent of alien landownership and the possibility of a repetition of Ireland's ills in America.[46]

The issue was most adequately brought into public discussion by the entry of the farmer into an independent role in politics. To the Alliance man and the Populist, the anti-alien planks of Democrats and Republicans in 1884, the act of 1887, and even the state legislation, were all

inadequate. The complete prohibition of landownership to the alien became an article of agrarian faith. The platform of the National party of Iowa, a forerunner of the People's party, assaulted "English cunning" and foreign landownership.[47] Another transitional body, the Union Labor party, took a similar stand. Under the editorship of C. W. Macune, the *National Economist* built up a campaign during 1889 in issue after issue, reaching a climax in August. Then it revealed on its front page the "modern plan of conquest" which British investors were pursuing in America.[48] By the time the National Farmers Alliance and Industrial Union and the Knights of Labor met in St. Louis in December, 1889, the prohibition of absentee alien landownership was solidly embedded in radical agrarian doctrine. Henceforth the demand for national measures appeared regularly in platforms of the emergent Populist party at its annual conventions, and it was one of those provisions which could always rally support, South or West, when agreement faltered on other objectives.[49]

By the end of 1889, not Alliance men alone, but even Granges were demanding that these aims be achieved by state legislation.[50] In response to this feeling many trans-Mississippi states enacted anti-alien laws which involved sometimes a complete reversal of older policy, for several states had had positive guarantees

---

[44] Missouri, for example, backed Oates, and Iowa suggested a constitutional amendment to forbid real property to aliens. *Cong. Record*, 50 Cong., 1 Sess., 2894 (April 12, 1888); *ibid.*, 51 Cong., 2 Sess., 1756 (January 22, 1891).

[45] *Cong. Record*, 49 Cong., 2 Sess., 386 (January 6, 1887); *ibid.*, 51 Cong., 1 Sess., 1135 (February 7, 1890).

[46] *Journal of Proceedings of the Twentieth Session of the National Grange of the Patrons of Husbandry* (Philadelphia, 1889), 106–107.

[47] Independence (Iowa) *National Advocate*, January 27, 1887.

[48] *National Economist*, I (August 17, 1889), 337–38. The Texas State Alliance had already taken a similar stand in August, 1886. Solon J. Buck, *The Agrarian Crusade* (New Haven, 1920), 114.

[49] John D. Hicks, *The Populist Revolt* (Minneapolis, 1931), 428, 431, 433, 438, 443. It appeared again in 1896. William J. Bryan, *The First Battle* (Chicago, 1896), 275. One of General James B. Weaver's claims to leadership, according to an admirer, was that he had opposed the sale of millions of acres to Britons.

[50] *Journal of Proceedings of the Twenty-third Session of the National Grange of the Patrons of Husbandry* (Philadelphia, 1889), 147.

of alien property rights.[51] The general features of these new laws were similar. Usually non-resident aliens were singled out. Corporations wholly or partly controlled by alien capital were generally understood to be included in the restrictions but frequently they were explicitly mentioned. In such cases a certain percentage of the stock was fixed which, if held by aliens, was to give the corporation an alien character. Kansas, Minnesota, and Missouri set this figure as low as 20 per cent, following the federal law, while Iowa and Washington more liberally designated 50 per cent.[52] In every instance the operations of mortgage companies—their right to enforce contracts by foreclosure sales and their right of ownership of real estate, usually for a short term of years—were safeguarded, though sometimes a lack of precision necessitated the passage of more definitely worded guarantees later. Here again is evidence that despite the bitter attacks made upon the alien moneylender and his motives, the Westerner had to recognize his services. The value of foreign capital in urban and industrial development was frequently acknowledged by excepting urban lots either in the original laws, as in Colorado and Iowa, or by later amendments, as in Minnesota and Nebraska.[53]

Most anxious to keep open supplies of alien capital were the mining interests.

It was pointed out with reference to Montana and Idaho in 1889 and to Utah in 1895 that an advantage of statehood would be the gaining of exemption from the federal prohibition on alien capital.[54] Territories which became states in these years, escaping the operation of the federal law of March, 1887, as often as not passed anti-alien laws; but like Colorado in 1887, Idaho in 1891, and Arizona in 1912, they exempted mineral lands from the prohibitions of these acts.[55] In Washington, where an English firm, the Moss Bay Iron and Steel Company of America, was attempting to utilize the mineral resources of the state, the constitution of 1889, while imposing the usual restrictions on alien property rights, excepted "lands containing valuable deposits of minerals, metals, iron, coal or fire clay, and the necessary land for mills and machinery to be used in the development thereof and the manufacture of the products therefrom."[56] Even the strongly agrarian state of Kansas allowed foreigners to possess coal-, zinc-, and lead-bearing

[51] Kansas, in 1888, and California, in 1893, had to amend their constitutions in order to restrict alien property rights. Iowa had legislative guarantees of alien property rights from 1873.
[52] See Kansas Legislature, Session Laws of 1891 (Topeka, 1891), 7–10; General Laws of the State of Minnesota (Minneapolis, 1887), 323–24; Laws of Missouri (Jefferson City, 1895), 207–208; Iowa Legislature, Acts and Resolutions (Des Moines, 1888), 125–26; Session Laws of the State of Washington (Olympia, 1890), 288–91.
[53] Colorado Legislature, Laws Passed at the Sixth Session (Denver, 1887), 24–25; General Laws of the State of Minnesota (Minneapolis, 1889), 220; General Laws of the State of Minnesota (Delano, 1897), 197–98; Nebraska Legislature, Laws, Joint Resolutions, and Memorials (Omaha, 1889), 483–86.

[54] Mining needs were so paramount that the delegate in Congress from Montana rejected a suggestion that aliens be given full freedom to make any investment only so long as they were resident. Mining needed capital, absentee or not. Proceedings and Debates of the [Montana] Constitutional Convention (Helena, 1889), 268. See also "Address to the People of Utah," Francis N. Thorpe (ed.), Federal and State Constitutions, Colonial Charters, and Other Organic Laws (7 vols., Washington, 1909), VI, 3701; and Governor George L. Shoup's proclamation calling Idaho's convention, Proceedings and Debates of the Idaho Constitutional Convention (2 vols., Caldwell, 1912), I, x.
[55] General Laws of the State of Idaho (Boise City, 1891), 108–109, 118–19; Arizona Legislature, Acts, Resolutions, and Memorials (Phoenix, 1912), 350–51.
[56] Thorpe (ed.), Federal and State Constitutions, VII, 3979. For the iron company, see Joseph Daniels, "History of Pig Iron Manufacture of the Pacific Coast," Washington Historical Quarterly (Seattle), XVII (July, 1926), 184–85. For the hopes roused in Washington by this English activity, see Samuel R. Mohler, "Boom Days in Ellensburg, 1888–1891," Pacific Northwest Quarterly (Seattle), XXXVI (October, 1945), 293–95.

land when it passed its anti-alien law of 1891.

The geographical distribution of this state legislation emphasizes the largely agrarian character of the agitation against British land investments. On the whole the Rocky Mountain states were less strenuous in their campaign. Montana, Utah, Nevada, and New Mexico failed to make an enactment; Idaho passed a comparatively liberal measure; Colorado first amended its anti-alien law and then within four years of its original formulation repealed it. The agrarian states of Nebraska, Missouri, Oklahoma, Texas, Kansas, Iowa, and Washington, on the other hand, had the most stringent provisions. The disinterest of North and South Dakota may be ascribed to the few instances of British activity there, and that of Wyoming to the predominance of cattle interests and to the comparatively happy relations between English and American cattle barons.

The agrarian character of the driving force behind the campaign against the absentee alien owner of real property was evident in the several states. In Texas a bill was considered as early as January, 1884, but despite an eloquent appeal in its behalf it was defeated on the ground that the issue was not among the purposes of the special session in which it had been introduced.[57] But a resolution calling for an investigation into the extent of alien ownership was adopted, and in a few years the upswing of the settlers' discontent overcame the big British interests and their sympathizers. Feeling against the British companies was intensely bitter and in 1889 the Texas Alliance repeated the demand for their ejection from Texas soil.[58] Although not

an Alliance man, Governor James S. Hogg was firmly against monopolies, friendly to the farmers, and hostile to alien landholding. When running for governor in 1890 he attacked the British cattle companies whose broad acres, he foresaw, would soon be in demand by settlers. After election he renewed his appeal for legislation and several bills materialized, one of which, severely restricting alien property rights, was passed and approved in 1891.[59] When the courts subsequently set it aside because of a fault in drafting, correction of the act was made one of the purposes of the special session of the following year. In this session Hogg succeeded in getting little else of his program enacted. But on the alien measure he was apparently least assailable, though his opponents argued that he was driving capital away from the state.[60] Despite their entrenched position in the Panhandle, the British companies could not withstand the overwhelming hostility of the settled eastern parts of the state.

Several trans-Missouri commonwealths took action in 1887 during the time of ferment in which railroad laws, antitrust laws, usury laws, and the like were being promoted and sometimes enacted. Nebraska was most speedy in passing antialien legislation despite a close vote in the senate. Two years later, however, conservatives managed to safeguard alien interests in manufacturing, railroads, and moneylending.[61] In Kansas, newspapers

[57] Texas Legislature, House Journal (1884), 12, 54, 56.

[58] Buck, Agrarian Crusade, 114; National Economist, I (September 7, 1889), 386. British companies dominated the Texas Panhandle and relations were poor there. "A whole half dozen—or

there-abouts—of blarsted Britishers landed on our shores last Saturday night and have for three or four days this week been looking over the Panhandle with a view to purchasing the rest of it." Tascosa (Texas) Pioneer, May 12, 1888. I am indebted to Professor Raymond E. Lindgren of Occidental College for this reference.

[59] Cotner (ed.), Addresses and State Papers of James S. Hogg, 98, 117–18; Texas Legislature, House Journal (1891), 52, 80, 602, 880, 897.

[60] Revised Civil Statutes of the State of Texas (Austin, 1912), 6–7; Texas Legislature, House Journal (1892), 2; Cotner (ed.), Addresses and State Papers of James S. Hogg, 20–21, 179–80.

[61] Nebraska Legislature, Senate Journal (1887),

discussing British guilt in connection with the currency "crime" did not forget the more evident control over the lives of American farmers implicit in British ownership of American land. Kansas farmers strongly supported the Populist policy of federal legislation against alien landownership, a stand affirmed by resolutions and by petitions to Congress from local Alliances.[62] As in the implementation of the rest of the farmers' program, state machinery was used, but efforts to pass an anti-alien law in 1887 were stalled in committee by constitutional difficulties.

The difficulties were removed in November, 1888, when a resounding popular vote in Kansas approved an amendment to the state constitution to permit regulation of alien property rights. A plethora of bills followed the governor's appeal for appropriate action at the next meeting of the legislature.[63] A committee of the house made a scathing attack upon alien landowning in Kansas. Their favorite target of abuse was William Scully, who figured prominently, though involuntarily, in this campaign. From the counties in which his lands lay came the strongest support for the legislation. A senate bill, modeled on the federal law and demanding American incorporation of any company doing business within the state, made most progress but final agreement could not be reached.[64] In 1891 harmony prevailed and a bill was enacted; but by that time the agricultural depression had reached new depths and support outside the legislature was less positive. Kansas then desperately needed capital, and even

land monopoly was attractive when land values were crashing.[65] It was not until 1901, however, after several years of prosperity had been enjoyed, that the state law was repealed.[66]

Colorado, like Nebraska, was successful in early passage of an act to prevent nonresident aliens from gaining title to real estate, though all but agricultural land was carefully exempted from its provisions. In Colorado there was not merely an appreciation of the private and public advantages which British capital wrought but also a concentration of British interests. Furthermore, the conviction grew that the state legislation of 1887 had been instrumental in diverting masses of capital to other states, to Colorado's loss.[67] The next session saw the adoption of a liberalizing amendment, and in 1891 the entire act was repealed, amidst the plaudits of the Republican press and the silence of even the chief Democratic paper.[68]

In the Minnesota legislature, Ignatius Donnelly organized his caucus of farmers at the beginning of the 1887 session to deal with corruption, monopoly, and interest rates. A fruit of this agitation was the introduction in the senate of a bill to restrict alien property rights. Although it was unusual for opposition to be expressed in 1887, the Republican St. Paul *Daily Globe* promptly dubbed the measure "A Foolish Bill."[69] It was passed, but by 1900 it had been considerably modified.

After the turn of the century, the hostility to alien landownership persisted primarily in those areas where frontier conditions continued to exist. When Okla-

32, 293, 1399. Perhaps it was not coincidental that three of the seven house opponents of the bill were British-born. Nebraska Legislature, *House Journal* (1887), 182, 385, 637, 795, 1748.
[62] *Girard Herald*, February 22, 1890; *Cong. Record*, 51 Cong., 1 Sess., 1045 (February 3, 1890), 1791 (February 27, 1890).
[63] Kansas Legislature, *House Journal* (1889), 61, 383.
[64] *Ibid.*, 382–83, 411, 1093, 1167; *Girard Herald*, March 28, 1891.

[65] Kansas City *Times*, July 23, 1891. Of course farmers hoped that the legislation would put cheap land on the market.
[66] Kansas Legislature, *Session Laws of 1901* (Topeka, 1901), 1.
[67] *Field and Farm* (Denver), July 27, 1889; Denver *Republican*, February 7, 11, 14, 1891.
[68] Colorado Legislature, *House Journal* (1889), 461, 2292, 2437; *ibid.* (1891), 317, 1139, 1447.
[69] St. Paul *Pioneer Press*, January 4, 1887; St. Paul *Daily Globe*, January 28 and 29, 1887.

homa became a state in 1907, for example, its constitution, framed under the influence of the farmers' leader, William H. Murray, included limitations on the rights of aliens to own land, and these provisions were amplified by legislation in 1908.[70]

The efficacy of all this legislation, state and federal, is difficult to assess. The federal act of 1887 created a bewildering situation for many investors who had not expected the legislation and also for those unable to determine the extent of its application. Business transactions were delayed. The Rio Arriba Land and Cattle Company, for example, which had recently been formed in London and had agreed to purchase land in New Mexico, refused to fulfill the terms of the contract until after it was decided judicially that the act could not prejudice an agreement made prior to its passage.[71] President Cleveland's private secretary was beset with urgent appeals from a New York attorney for information as to the exact hour of the President's approval of the bill, in order that he might clarify certain transactions involving aliens and the transfer of real estate.[72] The State Department was at once besieged with inquiries about the true significance of the act. In court cases the legislation was invoked to throw a shadow on the validity of transfers of

property by aliens, while state laws were also utilized for the same purpose.[73] These uncertain conditions for investment stimulated the British representatives in America to collate the various laws governing alien property rights. The *Economist*, a British publication, attempted a summary of the effects of applicable laws, and the British Foreign Office also found it necessary to keep track of the new legislation enacted by the states.[74]

While the effects of the anti-alien legislation may have been exaggerated in some quarters, the laws quite clearly required study by promoters and capitalists; and the managers of English properties in the United States carefully reported them to the home offices.[75] New ventures in absentee ownership were now more difficult, and though the laws had no retroactive force the limitations on the future operations of existing businesses were handicaps. Consequently these laws sometimes accomplished their object indirectly by persuading Englishmen to assume American citizenship.[76] The change in allegiance subjected these people more completely to American control, assuring the attainment of a chief aim of the agrarian agitation.

More striking success was achieved by the extent to which the legislation checked

[70] *Proceedings of the Constitutional Convention of Oklahoma* (Muskogee, n.d.), 17–18, 160, 289. In his address as president-elect of the convention William H. Murray said: "In my native state there is a tract of five million acres of land owned by one British subject. Let us write it into the Constitution that no alien shall own land in the State of Oklahoma." See also Thorpe (ed.), *Federal and State Constitutions*, VII, 4330, and Oklahoma Legislature, *Session Laws* (Guthrie, 1908), 481–83. For a similar measure adopted by the first legislature of the new state of Arizona in 1912, see Arizona Legislature, *Acts, Resolutions, and Memorials* (Phoenix, 1912), 350–51.

[71] *Prospectus of the Rio Arriba Land and Cattle Company, Ltd.* (London, 1888).

[72] Simon Sterne to Daniel S. Lamont, March 5, 1887 (letter and telegram), and March 10, 1887, Papers of Grover Cleveland.

[73] See, for example, Gorman Mining Co. v. Alexander, 2 S. D. 561–62 (1892), 51 Northwestern 346; Oregon Mortgage Co., Ltd. v. Carstens, 16 Wash. 165–71 (1896), 47 Pacific 421; and Omnium Investment Co., Ltd. v. North American Trust Co., 65 Kan. 50–52 (1902), 68 Pacific 1089.

[74] *Economist*, XLV (November 5, 1887), 1402–1403; XLVI (April 28, 1888), 532–33; XLVI (December 15, 1888), 1573; LI (April 15, 1893), 446.

[75] Estelle D. Tinkler, "History of the Rocking Chair Ranch," *Panhandle-Plains Historical Review* (Canyon, Texas), XV (1942), 27.

[76] The most prominent case was that of William Scully. Homer E. Socolofsky, "The Scully Land System in Marion County," *Kansas Historical Quarterly* (Topeka), XVIII (November, 1950), 338. A small ranchman in New Mexico whose business required at times the purchase of new land also took this step. William French, *Some Recollections of a Western Ranchman* (New York, 1928), 240–41.

some British enterprises. General William J. Palmer, of the Rio Grande Western Railway Company, was hampered in his business dealings with British investors by the Colorado statute, which he described as "conclusive and prohibitory," and he looked forward to the repeal of "the absurd demagogical law."[77] On the passage of the federal law of 1887 the mining territories protested that it would do them great harm by stopping the flow of capital to them, and within a short time the governors of Wyoming, Idaho, Montana, Dakota, and Utah asserted that this gloomy prophecy had been fulfilled.[78] It was said that mining and other deals on the point of consummation in Europe had been canceled.[79] The report of a special commission appointed by Congress to look into the extent of alien mining interests in the territories a year after the passage of the act confirmed the belief that large projected purchases within the territories had fallen through and that capital had been withdrawn in order to comply with the limit set on alien-held corporation stock.[80]

All agreed that the prosperity of the territories had suffered severely from the stoppage of foreign investment which was supposed to have been caused by the federal anti-alien law. Consequently, the argument for statehood in Montana, Idaho, and Utah, for example, was stoutly buttressed by the claim that as states they would be released from the restrictions on alien capital which the federal

law imposed upon them as territories. Many of the new states admitted after 1887, however, provided for control of foreign investments, but as some of these were found to be too effective the most rigorous were gradually tempered. The opinion became so widely held in Colorado that the local law had deprived the state of any part of the dazzling influx of British capital into the United States that the law was repealed in 1891.[81] In Kansas, the experience of her neighbors was drawn upon to cast doubt upon the wisdom of enacting an alien law in the year that the Colorado law was repealed.[82]

Yet the restrictive effects of these laws can be overemphasized and complaints that they virtually shut off British investments cannot always be accepted at face value. To a radical like "Coin" Harvey the extent of British investment in 1899 still seemed threateningly great, and indeed it grew rather than diminished in the decade before 1914.[83] The laments of the territories were sometimes inspired by local patriotism rather than by reliable information. It was disingenuous, for example, to blame the federal law for the refusal of Britons in 1887 to invest in the Harney Peak (Dakota) Tin Company, Ltd., for at that time their unwillingness was due instead to their suspicions of the promoters.[84] Companies could be incorporated in the state in which they did business and still retain their British character. It was at once suggested that the 20 per cent maximum limit put upon alien-held stock in a territorial company would be but laxly applied, and companies with a far higher proportion of British

---

[77] William J. Palmer to Dr. William Bell (a British friend of Palmer and a large investor in the Southwest), February 19, 1891, Papers of Dr. William Bell (Colorado State Archives, Denver).
[78] Secretary of the Interior, Annual Report, 1887, pp. 850, 869, 925.
[79] The flotation of mining companies was abruptly checked in London. Philadelphia Weekly Press, April 23, 1887. According to the New York Herald, quoted in Girard Herald, April 28, 1887, Stephen W. Dorsey's attempts to sell lands in London were nullified.
[80] "Report of Committee on Mines and Mining [1889]," Senate Reports, No. 2690, 50 Cong., 2 Sess., 2–4, 9–14, 19.

[81] For an example of a complete reversal of attitude, compare the editorials in Denver Republican, February 21, 1887, and February 7, 1891. See also Field and Farm (Denver), July 27, 1889.
[82] Kansas City Times, July 23, 1891; Field and Farm (Denver), March 7, 1891.
[83] Herbert Feis, Europe the World's Banker (New Haven, 1930), 13, 21–22, 25.
[84] Senate Reports, No. 2690, 50 Cong., 2 Sess., 12. See also Statist (London), XX (November 12, 1887), 538.

participation continued to function in the territories.[85] After 1890 most of these territories had become states, and their own legislation, if they had any, was usually more liberal than the federal statute, itself modified in 1897. Even in the states where strict legislation was in force, means of evasion were not unknown. The states seldom prosecuted foreign companies for infringement of the anti-alien acts, and unless the state took action there was no case against an alien property holder. As for the territories which remained under Washington's tutelage, the experience of Dr. Nathan E. Boyd in raising money for the Rio Grande Dam and Irrigation Company in New Mexico in 1896 demonstrated that methods could be evolved for insuring both British investment and a measure of control in enterprises in the territories.[86]

The numerous exceptions made in the laws indicate that powerful interests were not wholly in sympathy with a complete embargo on alien capital. Even the farmers realized the need for capital, whatever its source. Governor Hogg, ten years after his victory in passing the Texas anti-alien law, visited England to secure money with which to develop his oil wells.[87] So long as British investors were prepared to take into account the laws regulating the area in which they wished to locate, they were not seriously handicapped in running their enterprises. Moreover, the era of large land companies, which had excited the storm, had passed, and public opinion supported alien investments in mining, the other chief western industry. So far as there was a dwindling

of British interest in cattle, land, and mines, it should be ascribed mainly to climatic vagaries and to economic stagnation in England after the Baring crisis at the end of 1890 and in America after 1893.

As with so much else of the Populist program, while complete success eluded the grasp of the farmers, the changes they wished regarding alien real property holding came about to a large degree. Much had been accomplished in the fields of legislation and public opinion by the late 1880's even before Populism became a powerful force. By the end of the century most states had restricted alien rights. More important, economic patterns were already changing in the 1890's, and British investments in western real estate were both less extensive and less blatant than a decade before. Eastern capital, too, had become more available.[88]

Some credit for the greater timidity or reticence of British capital must be ascribed not only to concrete legislation and to the hostility of farmers to specific businesses but also to the doubtful conditions for investment in America created by agrarian discontent, starting as far back as 1883 with the fencing imbroglio.[89] To the bitter attacks launched upon aristocratic land monopolists were added assaults upon Lombard Street financiers and upon the gold standard, which became more important as currency questions became the dominant theme. One of the principal attractions to Britons in conducting enterprises in the trans-Mississippi West had been the stability

[85] Denver Republican, April 4, 1887. The Old Guard Mining Company of Arizona Territory announced its formation in May, 1887. Statist, XIX (May 14, 1887), 518. Despite reports that investments had been given up, shares do not appear to have been forced on the market.
[86] "History of the Rio Grande Dam and Irrigation Company," Senate Docs., No. 104, 56 Cong., 2 Sess., 3–5.
[87] Cotner (ed.), Addresses and State Papers of James S. Hogg, 26, 500–503.

[88] In 1901, Governor Miguel A. Otero of New Mexico turned from a long preoccupation on behalf of a particular British enterprise in his territory to address an eloquent appeal to the East for investments. Secretary of the Interior, Annual Report, 1901 (Washington, 1901), Part III, 407–408.
[89] R. H. Inglis Palgrave, "An English View of Investment in the United States," Forum (New York), XV (April, 1893), 192–93. Scottish land and cattle brokers were agitated in 1884. Cong. Record, 48 Cong., 1 Sess., 4773 (June 3, 1884).

and respect for property rights characteristic of American society in the past. But the Bryan program seemed to represent repudiation and despoliation, while the agrarian measures and propaganda raised grave doubts in Britain as to the continuance of the earlier favorable conditions and helped to make the West a less desirable field for investment. Colonies, besides presenting new opportunities for exploitation, could be expected to show that proper respect for British rights which Americans were apparently beginning to forget. As had happened when state debts were repudiated following the Panic of 1837 and after the Civil War, British capitalists were more cautious in investing money in America after 1890, and by 1900 the question of alien investments in the trans-Mississippi West had ceased to be a serious issue.

The Coming of the New Order

■ Late in 1893 Americans faced two new realities: the United States had recently become the largest industrial producer in the world, and the country was in a deepening depression. The first reality obviously suggested the cure for the second: use the great economic power of the United States to open overseas markets and spread American trade. By 1895, as the depression lingered, journalists, intellectuals, politicians, and business leaders were talking of the dependence of a now mature domestic economy, one that was assumed no longer to have the stimulation of the expanding frontier, on developing export sales. American access to the markets of underdeveloped nations, formalized as the Open Door policy, has remained a guiding principle of American foreign relations.

William Appleman Williams, of the University of Wisconsin, is one of a number of writers, who in recent years have emphasized the importance of these economic factors in American foreign policy, an importance that scholars writing before 1950 had tended to minimize.

William Appleman Williams
Imperial Anticolonialism*

A continuance of the present anarchy of our commerce will be a continuance of the unfavorable balance on it, which by draining us of our metals . . . [will bring our ruin]. In fact most of our political evils may be traced up to our commercial ones, and most of our moral to our political.

James Madison to Thomas Jefferson, 1786

[Our recent policies] have hastened the day when an equilibrium between the occupations of agriculture, manufactures, and commerce,

* From The Tragedy of American Diplomacy by William Appleman Williams. Copyright © 1959 by William Appleman Williams. Published by arrangement with the World Publishing Company, Cleveland and New York, pp. 23–44.

shall simplify our foreign concerns to the exchange only of that surplus which we cannot consume for those articles of reasonable comfort or convenience which we cannot produce.
Thomas Jefferson, 1809

American factories are making more than the American people can use; American soil is producing more than they can consume. Fate has written our policy for us; the trade of the world must and shall be ours.
Albert J. Beveridge, April, 1897

Even protectionist organs are for free trade in China, where freedom is for the benefit of American manufacturers. Even anti-Imperialists welcome an Imperial policy which contemplates no conquests but those of commerce.
London *Times*, 1900

America's traditional view of itself and the world is composed of three basic ideas, or images. One maintains that the United States was isolationist until world power was "thrust upon it," first to help Cuba, then twice to save the world for democracy, and finally to prevent the Soviet Union from overwhelming the world. Another holds that, except for a brief and rapidly dispelled aberration at the turn of the century, America has been anti-imperialist throughout its history. A third asserts that a unique combination of economic power, intellectual and practical genius, and moral rigor enables America to check the enemies of peace and progress—and build a better world—without erecting an empire in the process.

Not even Joseph Stalin maintained that America's record in world affairs was exactly the reverse of this common view, and for Americans to do so would be to mistake a candid and searching re-examination of their own mythology for a tirade of useless self-damnation. The classical ideas about American foreign policy are not all wrong: the United States did come to full, active involvement in international affairs by degrees; it has been anti-imperialist in some respects at certain times; and periodically it has con-

sciously acknowledged various limitations on its power. But the need for critical self-appraisal seems apparent upon considering the implications of the accepted interpretation. For if America were in fact all and nothing more than the traditional ideas declare it to be, then it would experience but minor difficulties and suffer no crises. Such a combination of power, morality, and technique would have established the millennium long before the Bolshevik Revolution.

In beginning such a re-evaluation of twentieth-century American diplomacy it is illuminating to recall that Americans thought of themselves as an empire at the very outset of their national existence —as part of the assertive self-consciousness which culminated in the American Revolution. Though at first it may seem surprising, when contrasted with the image of isolationism which has been accepted so long, in reality that early predominance of a pattern of empire thought is neither very strange nor very difficult to explain. Having matured in an age of empires as part of an empire, the colonists naturally saw themselves in the same light once they joined issue with the mother country.

However natural, attractive, and exhilarating, such a commitment to empire nevertheless posed a serious dilemma for the founding fathers. Political theory of that age asserted the impossibility of reconciling democratic republicanism with a large state. Up to the time of the American Revolution at any rate, the British could remain ignorant of—or evade—that issue. Self-governing Englishmen never had to cope with the problem of integrating their conquests into their domestic social and political economy. Americans were not so fortunate, for any expansion they undertook immediately enlarged the mother country. Led by James Madison, they sought to resolve the contradiction between their drive for empire and their politics by developing a theory of their own which asserted that democratic republicanism could be improved and sustained by just such an imperial foreign policy.

Probably taking his cue from David Hume, an Englishman who attacked Montesquieu's argument that democracy was a system that could work only in small states, Madison asserted that expansion was the key to preventing factions—themselves primarily the result of economic conflicts—from disrupting the fabric of society. Institutional checks and balances could help, and were therefore necessary, but they were not enough in and of themselves. Expansion was essential to mitigate economic clashes by providing an empire for exploitation and development and to interpose long distances (and thus difficulties and delays in sustaining initial antagonisms) between one faction and the rest of the nation and the government itself.

Madison thus proposed, *as a guide to policy and action in his own time*, the same kind of an argument that the historian Frederick Jackson Turner formulated a century later when he advanced his frontier thesis which explained America's democracy and prosperity as the result of such expansion. Madison's theory was shared (or borrowed) by many other American leaders of his time. Thomas Jefferson's thesis that democracy and prosperity depended upon a society of landholding and exporting freemen was a drastically simplified version of the same idea. Perhaps Edward Everett of Massachusetts most nearly captured the essence of the interpretation and argument in his judgment that expansion was the "*principle* of our institutions." In 1828–1829, Madison himself prophesied a major crisis would occur in about a century, when the continent had filled up and an industrial system had deprived most people of any truly productive property. His fears proved true sooner than he anticipated. For in the Crisis of the 1890's, when Americans *thought* that the frontier was gone, they advanced and accepted the argument that new expansion was the best, if not the only, way to sustain their freedom and prosperity.

The Crisis of the 1890's was a major turning point in American history. It marked the close of the age of Jacksonian laissez faire and provided the setting for the death scene of the individual entrepreneur as the dynamic figure in American economic life. At the same time, it was the cultural coming-out party of a new corporate system based upon the corporation and similar large and highly organized groups throughout American society.

Since it affected all Americans in one way or another, most of them either offered or accepted some kind of an explanation of the crisis. A great many, perhaps the majority, took the somewhat fatalistic view that the American system was so successful that it produced more than it could use, causing it to slow down every so often until the slack was taken up. Another large group argued that the system was somehow out of kilter, but disagreed over what could and should be done to improve it. Most of the critics thought a few modifications and reforms would take care of the trouble. A much smaller number, composed of socialists and other radicals, asserted that the existing system ought to be scrapped for a new one. Though the radicals never mustered enough strength to act on their proposal, they did provide some helpful ideas for the reformers.

It is often argued, therefore, that the history of the Crisis of the 1890's (and subsequent American development) revolves around a struggle between those who stressed the need to reform the system and others who argued that conditions would improve faster if it was left alone. Carried over into the realm of foreign affairs, that interpretation points to the conclusion that Americans were not very concerned with questions of foreign policy. The difficulty with that part of the analysis is that it does not correspond with the facts. Americans were very agitated about foreign policy in the 1890's and sustained their interest after the depression ended. While it is apparent that much of American history in the twentieth century concerns purely domestic issues, it also is true that foreign affairs are a significant part of the story.

Perhaps the most important aspect of the relationship between domestic and foreign affairs is the fact that both the reformers and the conservatives agreed that foreign policy could and should play an important—if not crucial—part in recovering from the depression and in preventing future crises. This broad consensus was based upon two ideas. The first, held by manufacturers, bankers, farmers, and most other specific groups in the economy, explained the depression and social unrest as the result of not having enough markets for their specific product—be it steel, capital, or wheat. Hence each group looked at foreign policy as a means of getting markets for their merchandise or services. The second idea was much broader and took account of the particular outlook of all special interests. It explained America's democracy and prosperity in the past as the result of expansion across the continent and, to a lesser degree, overseas into the markets of the world. Either implicitly or explicitly, depending on the form in which it was presented, the idea pointed to the practical conclusion that expansion was the way to stifle unrest, preserve democracy, and restore prosperity.

The generalization about the relationship between expansion, democracy, and prosperity became most well-known as the frontier thesis advanced by Frederick Jackson Turner in 1893. But the most fascinating aspect of the idea was that it was put forth, in slightly different versions, by other intellectuals at just about the same moment that Turner published his essay. One of them was Brooks Adams, brother of the famous Henry Adams and close friend of such political leaders as Theodore Roosevelt, Henry Cabot Lodge, and John Hay. Another was William Graham Sumner, an economist and sociologist who believed almost frantically in the virtue and viability of the old order of laissez-faire individualism.

In response to the Crisis of the 1890's, therefore, Americans developed a broad consensus in favor of an expansionist foreign policy as a solution to their existing troubles and as a way to prevent future difficulties. Special interests pushed expansion from their particular point of view, while the intellectuals unified such separate analyses in one general interpretation. The idea of expansion became even more pervasive because Turner, Adams, and Sumner evoked responses from different ideological and political groups in the country. Turner's statement of the frontier thesis, for example, appealed to the wing of the reform movement which favored using antitrust laws and political reforms to preserve democracy and prosperity. Adams, on the other hand, had his largest following among other reformers who accepted the large corporation and the giant banks but wanted the national government to regulate and control them in behalf of the general welfare.

Sumner's role is more difficult to judge. For one thing, his influence was connected with that of Herbert Spencer, the British philosopher of laissez faire. For another, and unlike Turner and Adams, Sumner did not himself advocate an expansionist foreign policy. But one of his central ideas asserted that it was "the opening of the new continents and the great discoveries and inventions which have made this modern age. . . . The chief source of new power, however, has been the simplest of all, that is, an extension of population over new land." This explanation implied further expansion, just as his defense of laissez faire sanctioned such action as a natural right. In any event, Sumner's influence—whatever it amounted to—affected the more conservative section of American society which insisted that the principles and practices of laissez faire offered the best answers to all economic and social problems.

Those specific pressures and general ideas in favor of expansion rapidly gained strength after 1890. By 1895, many individuals and groups were stressing the importance of expansion as a way to solve domestic economic problems. The editors of *Harper's* magazine outlined the approach rather bluntly as early as 1893. "The United States will hold the key," it explained, "unlocking the gates to the commerce of the world, and closing them to war. If we have fighting to do, it will be fighting to keep the peace." Others saw expansion as a way to avoid labor unrest—or even revolution. "We are on the eve of a very dark night," warned businessman F. L. Stetson in 1894, "unless a return of commercial prosperity relieves popular discontent." A bit later, Senator William Frye was even more specific. "We must have the market [of China] or we shall have revolution."

By the winter of 1897–1898, the expansionist outlook dominated American thinking on foreign affairs. Western farmers who wanted markets for their unsold produce and commodities joined forces with silver miners and railroad magnates. Jerry Simpson, a sometime radical politician from Kansas, expressed such concern in one anguished cry: "We are driven from the markets of the world!" Along with many other Populists, Simpson also supported the campaign for a big Navy. Midwestern flour millers and Southern cotton growers agitated for the same kind of diplomacy favored by giant oil corporations, steel barons, and textile manufacturers. James J. Hill sought to provide regular freight shipments (and hence revenues) for his railway system by lining up such interests in a general campaign for expansion across the Pacific.

Even the traditional policy of tariff protection was questioned and modified by Americans who saw reciprocity treaties as a way of getting into foreign markets. When it was organized in 1895, for example, the National Association of Manufacturers devoted over half its original program to the problems of expanding foreign markets. One of its specific proposals favored reciprocity treaties as a "practical method of extending our international commerce." And within a year the organization had established special commissions to push business expansion in Latin America and Asia. Its leaders also emphasized the role of such expansion in preventing labor unrest and in making it possible to obey the laws on child labor and yet earn a profit.

While he was president of the N.A.M. in 1897, Theodore C. Search summarized the general feeling within the business community. "Many of our manufacturers have outgrown or are outgrowing their home markets," he explained, "and the expansion of our foreign trade is their only promise of relief." Similar organizations, such as the Pan American Society and the American Asiatic Association, concentrated on promoting an expansionist foreign policy in one particular area. As the *Journal of Commerce* observed in 1897, more and more American economic leaders were fixing their eyes on "the industrial supremacy of the world." A growing number of bankers also began to consider overseas economic expansion as a way of putting their idle capital to work. Some favored direct loans to foreigners while others preferred to finance the operations of American firms. That difference of opinion led to conflict between some bankers and the industrialists over the question of what kind of expansion to undertake, but both groups did agree on the need for overseas activity.

Such general and active support for economic expansion is often neglected when considering the coming of the Spanish-American War. It is customary to explain the war as a crusade to save the Cubans, or to interpret it in psychological terms as a release for national frustrations arising from the depression. But while it may be granted that economic leaders preferred not to go to war as long as they could attain their objectives without it, and although it may be useful to talk about Americans developing a national compulsion to punish Spain for mistreating Cuba, it is equally apparent that such interpretations do not take account of several key aspects of the coming of the war. For one thing, it is clear that various groups saw war with Spain over Cuba as a means to solve other problems. Many agrarians viewed it as a way to monetize silver at home and thus pave the way for a general expansion of their exports to the sterling areas of the world. Some labor groups thought it would ease or resolve immediate economic difficulties. And many important businessmen, as contrasted with the editors of some business publications, came to support war for specific commercial purposes as well as for general economic reasons.

Although there were other reasons for the businessmen's attitude, four factors appear to have played the most important part in the developing outlook within the business community. First, the businessmen were convinced by the late summer of 1897 that recovery was being generated by overseas economic expansion. The jump in agricultural and manufactured exports (which actually began in October, 1896) and the turn of the international gold balance in favor of the United States during 1897 provided the basis for that interpretation. Hence they became even more convinced of the need for an active foreign policy. Second, changes in the Cuban situation affected some of them directly. Not only had the rebels come to appear less reliable to deal with in connection with American interests, but the Cuban conservatives (some of whom were

Spaniards) began to change their anti-American position. Crystallized (and symbolized) by Senator Redfield Proctor's trip to Cuba which ended with a dramatic interventionist speech to the Congress, these two considerations prompted many American businessmen to replace their earlier indifference about saving the Cubans with vigorous support for action to protect American enterprise in the island. The irony was that many influential Americans now came to favor intervention as a counterrevolutionary move designed to prevent radicals from controlling Cuba.

Third, and perhaps most important of all, the large group of American leaders who saw economic expansion as the solution to social and economic problems were deeply agitated by indications that the European powers and Japan were going to divide China among themselves. Most Americans looked to Asia, and to China in particular, as the great market which would absorb their surpluses. It is beside the point that this did not happen; at issue is the nature of American thought and action at that time. As a result, a growing number of Americans began to think about a war with Spain more in terms of the Philippines than Cuba itself. To some extent, moreover, other businessmen who concentrated their activity in Latin America saw a more vigorous European diplomacy as a threat to their interests in that region, and so became more interested in taking Cuba as a move to forestall that possibility. Finally, those who viewed the situation in any of these ways were eased in their fears of a major war by the indications that the European powers did not agree among themselves.

These considerations help explain why, by November, 1897, many economic and political leaders were agitating for "improved trade conditions in Cuba" and for action to prevent the partitioning of China —and also dropping their objections to war as the court of last resort. As early as April, 1897, Albert Beveridge asserted that "the trade of the world must and shall be ours." The next month August Belmont (who was financing rebel bonds) and other key businessmen began to carry their campaign for intervention directly to President McKinley.

Though such businessmen acquiesced in McKinley's request to phrase their public agitation in terms of humanitarian purposes, that does not alter the fact that they were concerned with economic matters. And by March 15, 1898, a special agent sent to New York to sound out the business community found it "feeling militant." He reported that there was "nothing but war talk." Among those so engaged were John Jacob Astor, Thomas Ryan, William Rockefeller, Stuyvesant Fish, and spokesmen for the House of Morgan. It seems clear, therefore, that the specific and general consensus in favor of economic expansion played a significant role in the coming of the war with Spain. President McKinley did not go to war simply because the businessmen ordered him to do so; but neither did he lead the nation into battle against their economic wishes—as often is asserted.

Perhaps even more important to an understanding of twentieth-century American diplomacy is the manner in which the underlying bipartisan agreement on overseas economic expansion resolved the debate over whether or not America should embark upon a program of colonialism. Beginning with Admiral George Dewey's victory at Manila Bay and ending shortly after the election of 1900 (if not sooner), the argument is usually interpreted as a battle between the imperialists led by Theodore Roosevelt and the anti-imperialists led by William Jennings Bryan. It is more illuminating, however, to view it as a three-cornered discussion won by businessmen and intellectuals who opposed traditional colonialism and advocated instead the policy of an open door for America's overseas economic expansion. Discounted in recent years as a futile

and naive gesture in a world of harsh reality, the Open Door Policy was in fact a brilliant strategic stroke which led to the gradual extension of American economic and political power throughout the world. If it ultimately failed, it was not because it was foolish or weak, but because it was so successful. The empire that was built according to the strategy and tactics of the Open Door Notes engendered the antagonisms created by all empires, and it is that opposition which has posed so many difficulties for American diplomacy in the middle of the twentieth century.

At the outset, it is true, the debate between imperialists and anti-imperialists revolved around an actual issue—colonialism. Touched off by the specific question of what to do with Cuba and the Philippines, the battle raged over whether they should be kept as traditional colonies or established as quasi-independent nations under the benevolent supervision of the United States. Though the differences were significant at the beginning of the argument, it is nevertheless clear that they were never absolute. The Open Door Notes took the fury out of the fight. And within five years the issue was almost nonexistent. The anti-imperialists who missed that changing nature of the discussion were ultimately shocked and disillusioned when Bryan became Secretary of State and began to practice what they thought he condemned.

Such critics were mistaken in attacking Bryan as a backslider or a hypocrite. Bryan's foreign policy was not classical colonialism, but neither was it anti-imperial. He had never shirked his share of the white man's burden, though perhaps he did shoulder a bit more of the ideological baggage than the economic luggage. He was as eager for overseas markets as any but the most extreme agrarian and industrial expansionists. As with most other farmers, labor leaders, and businessmen, economic logic accounts for much of Bryan's anticolonialism. Looking anxiously for markets abroad as a way of improving conditions at home, all such men feared and opposed the competition of native labor. It was that consideration, as much as racism and Christian fundamentalism, that prompted Bryan to assert that "the Filipinos cannot be citizens without endangering our civilization."

Bryan's program for the Philippines symbolizes the kind of imperial anticolonialism that he advocated. Once the Philippine insurrection was crushed, he proposed that the United States should establish "a stable form of government" in the islands and then "protect the Philippines from outside interference while they work out their destiny, just as we have protected the republics of Central and South America, and are, by the Monroe Doctrine, pledged to protect Cuba." Opposition spokesmen gleefully pointed out that this was the substance of their own program.

Bryan also supported the kind of expansion favored by such Democrats as ex-President Grover Cleveland and ex-Secretary of State Richard Olney. "The best thing of the kind I have ever heard," remarked Cleveland of Olney's famous assertion that the United States "is practically sovereign on this continent, and its fiat is law upon the subjects to which it confines its interposition." As for Hawaii, Cleveland (and Bryan) wanted to control "the ports of a country so near to Japan and China" without the bother and responsibilities of formal annexation. Informal empire is perhaps the most accurate description of such a program. Both Cleveland and Bryan favored the overseas expansion of the American economic system and the extension of American authority throughout the world.

So, too, did such men as Roosevelt, Hay, and Lodge. At first, however, they stressed the acquisition of colonies, if not in the traditional sense of colonialism, at least in the pattern of administrative colonialism developed by Great Britain

after the Indian Mutiny of 1857. Thus the early arguments between Roosevelt and Bryan were to some point. But the Roosevelt imperialists rather quickly modified their position in line with the argument advanced by such men as Brooks Adams. None of these leaders were motivated by a personal economic motive, but by concentrating on the economic issue, other more important considerations were overlooked. The Roosevelt group defined their economic interest in terms of preventing the stagnation of the American economic system, and their program to accomplish that objective was vigorous overseas economic expansion.

Following the thesis developed by Adams, they argued that the American system had to expand or stagnate. Businessmen agreed, interpreting that general economic analysis in terms of their specific and immediate economic motive for more markets. Imperialism or no imperialism, the nation agreed, our trade must be protected. But defined in that fashion, trade was no longer the exchange of commodities and services between independent producers meeting in the market place; it became instead a euphemism for the control of foreign markets for America's industrial and agricultural surpluses.

Secretary of State John Hay's Open Door Notes of 1899 and 1900 distilled this collection of motivations, pressures, and theories into a classic program of imperial expansion. Based on the assumption of what Brooks Adams called "America's economic supremacy," and formulated in the context of vigorous pressure from domestic economic interests and the threatening maneuvers of other nations, the policy of the open door was designed to establish the conditions under which America's preponderant economic power would extend the American system throughout the world without the embarrassment and inefficiency of traditional colonialism. Hay's first note of 1899 asserted the right of access for

American economic power into China in particular, but the principle was rapidly generalized to the rest of the world. His second note of 1900 was designed to prevent other nations from extending the formal colonial system to China, and in later years that also was applied to other areas.

The Open Door Notes ended the debate between imperialists and anti-imperialists. The argument trailed on with the inertia characteristic of all such disagreements, but the nation recognized and accepted Hay's policy as a resolution of the original issue. In a similar fashion, it took some years (and further discussion) to liquidate the colonial status of the territory seized during the Spanish-American War. It also required time to work out and institutionalize a division of authority and labor between economic and political leaders so that the strategy could be put into operation on a routine basis. And it ultimately became necessary to open the door into existing colonial empires as well as unclaimed territories. But Secretary of State Hay's policy of the open door synthesized and formalized the frontier thesis, the specific demands of businessmen, workers, and farmers, and the theory which asserted that the American economic system would stagnate if it did not expand overseas.

America and the world shared this interpretation of the Open Door Policy at the time it was enunciated. Brooks Adams eulogized Secretary Hay as the realist who industrialized the Monroe Doctrine. The Philadelphia *Press* agreed: "This new doctrine established for China is destined to be as important as the Monroe Doctrine has been for the Americas in the past century. It protects the present, it safeguards the future." Quite aware of the grand design, the Boston *Transcript* spelled it out in blunt accents. "We have an infinitely wider scope in the Chinese markets than we should have had with a 'sphere of influence' in competition with

half a dozen other spheres." Many European commentators acknowledged that the strategy "hits us in our weak spot." Agreeing with the Boston analysis, a Berlin paper summed it up in one sentence: "The Americans regard, in a certain sense, all China as their sphere of interest."

Ex-Secretary of State Olney made it bipartisan. Prepared for the presidential election campaign of 1900, in which he supported Bryan, Olney's statement of the new imperial consensus was at the same time an excellent review of America's new foreign policy. "The 'home market' fallacy disappears," he explained, "with the proved inadequacy of the home market. Nothing will satisfy us in the future but free access to foreign markets— especially to those markets in the East." As one convinced at an early date by Brooks Adams that noncolonial economic expansion was the best strategy, Olney regretted the acquisition of the Philippines. It would have been wiser to have followed Washington's advice of 1796 and the principles of the Monroe Doctrine. "The true, the ideal position for us," Olney explained, "would be complete freedom of action, perfect liberty to pick allies from time to time as special occasions might warrant and an enlightened view of our own interests might dictate." But he was confident that the policy of the open door provided the very best approximation to that ideal.

Americans of that era and their European competitors were basically correct in their estimate of the Open Door Policy. It was neither an alien idea foisted off on America by the British nor a political gesture to the domestic crowd. Latter-day experts who dismissed the policy as irrelevant, misguided, or unsuccessful erred in two respects. They missed its deep roots in the American past and its importance at the time, and they failed to realize that the policy expressed the basic strategy and tactics of America's secular and imperial expansion in the twentieth century.

When combined with the ideology of an industrial Manifest Destiny, the history of the Open Door Notes became the history of American foreign relations from 1900 to 1958.

The most dramatic confluence of these currents of ideological and economic expansion did not occur until the eve of American entry into World War I. For this reason, among others, it is often asserted that the United States did not take advantage of the Open Door Policy until after 1917, and some observers argue that the policy never led to the rise of an American empire. In evaluating the extent to which Americans carried through on the strategy of the Open Door Notes, there are two broad questions at issue with regard to statistics of overseas economic expansion, and they cannot be mixed up without confusing the analysis and the interpretation. One concerns the over-all importance of such expansion to the national economy. The answer to that depends less upon gross percentages than upon the role in the American economy of the industries which do depend in significant ways (including raw materials as well as markets) on foreign operations. Measured against total national product, for example, the export of American cars and trucks seems a minor matter. But it is not possible at one and the same time to call the automobile business the key industry in the economy and then dismiss the fact that approximately 15 per cent of its total sales in the 1920's were made in foreign markets.

The other major point concerns the role of such foreign enterprises and markets in the making of American foreign policy. This effect can be direct in terms of domestic political pressure, or indirect through the results of the American overseas economic activity on the foreign policy of other nations. In the broadest sense of gross statistics, moreover, the overseas economic expansion of the United States from 1897 to 1915 is more

impressive than many people realize. Loans totaled over a billion dollars. Direct investments amounted to $2,652,300,000. While it is true that the nation also owed money abroad during the same period, that point is not too important to an understanding of American foreign policy. For the loans and the investments had a bearing on American foreign policy even though balance of payment computations reduce the net figure. Businessmen with interests in Mexico or Manchuria, for example, did not stop trying to influence American policy (or cease having an effect on Mexican or Asian attitudes) just because their investments or loans or sales were arithmetically canceled out by the debt incurred by other Americans in France.

Another misleading approach emphasizes the point that America's overseas economic expansion amounted to no more than 10 or 12 per cent of its national product during those years. But 10 per cent of any economic operation is a significant proportion; without it the enterprise may slide into bankruptcy. In that connection, the most recent studies by economists reveal that exports did indeed spark recovery from the depression of the 1890's. In any event, the businessmen and other economic groups *thought* the 10 per cent made a crucial difference, and many of them concluded that they could not get it in any way but through overseas expansion.

Other considerations aside, the conviction of these groups would make the figure important if it were only 1 per cent. Or, to make the point even clearer (and historically accurate), it would still be significant if all an entrepreneur did was to pressure the government to support an effort that failed. In that case the economic indicators would be negative, but the relevance to foreign policy might be very high. Such was precisely the case, for example, with the America-China Development Company. It ultimately disappeared from the scene, but before it died it exerted an extensive influence on American policy in Asia during the first decade of the twentieth century.

In another way, overseas economic operations which seem small on paper may mean the difference between survival and failure to a given firm. Faced by the near monopoly control over key raw materials exercised by the United States Steel Corporation after 1903, Charles Schwab had to go to Chile to get the ore supplies that were necessary to sustain the Bethlehem Steel Company. Schwab's investment was only 35 million dollars, but it played a vital role in his own affairs and exercised a significant influence on Chilean-American relations. Or, to reverse the example, economic activity which seems incidental judged by American standards is often fundamental to a weaker economy. This aspect of the problem can be illustrated by the situation in Manchuria between 1897 and 1904, where approximately one-tenth of 1 per cent of America's national product gave the Americans who were involved a major role in the affairs of that region, and provoked them to agitate vigorously for official American support. Their efforts were successful and led to crucial developments in American foreign policy.

It is impossible, in short, to judge the bearing of overseas economic expansion upon American diplomacy—and thus to judge the importance and efficacy of the Open Door Policy—in terms of gross statistics. The important factors are the relative significance of the activity and the way it is interpreted and acted upon by people and groups who at best are only vaguely symbolized by abstract aggregate statistics. And by these criteria there is no question about the great relevance for diplomacy of America's proposed and actual overseas economic expansion between 1893 and 1915—and throughout the rest of the twentieth century.

Still another interpretation which discounts the significance of the Open Door Policy in the early part of the century is based upon America's failure to control Japanese activity in Asia. Though perhaps the strongest argument of its type, it nevertheless fails to establish its basic thesis. Three weaknesses undermine its conclusions: (1) the Open Door Policy was designed to secure and preserve access to China for American economic power, not to deny access to other nations; (2) America's difficulties with Japan between 1899 and 1918 stemmed from a failure of judgment concerning the execution of the policy, not from a flaw in the policy itself; and (3) the United States acted with considerable effectiveness between 1915 and 1918 to prevent Japan from exploiting America's earlier error.

To grasp the full significance of these points it is vital to realize that the Open Door Policy was derived from the proposition that America's overwhelming economic power would cast the economy and the politics of the weaker, underdeveloped countries in a pro-American mold. American leaders assumed the opposition of one or many industrialized powers. Over a period of two generations the policy failed because some industrialized nations, among them Japan, chose to resort to force when they concluded that the Open Door Policy was working only too well; and because various groups inside weaker countries such as China decided that America's extensive influence was harmful to their specific and general welfare.

While that result may be judged a long-term failure, such a verdict should not be confused with an unfavorable conclusion about the policy in Asia between 1900 and 1918. Once it is understood that the Open Door Policy was neither a military strategy nor a traditional balance-of-power policy, then it becomes clear that the troubles in Asia stemmed from President Theodore Roosevelt's confusion on that very point. For in first taking sides with Japan against

Russia in 1904 in an attempt to exhaust both nations and thereby open the way for American supremacy, and then fumbling in an effort to correct his error by controlling the peace settlement, Roosevelt gave the Japanese the initiative and on top of that antagonized them.

Roosevelt's mistake stemmed in large measure from his aristocrat's *noblesse oblige* and his reaction to the theories of Brooks Adams. From a very early date Roosevelt viewed himself as something akin to the country squire of the twentieth century. Adams convinced him of the importance of economic expansion, and reinforced his existing view that the businessmen needed to be controlled. But Roosevelt interpreted such advice in the context of his admiration for the squire in the role of knight of the Round Table, the aristocrat's basic contempt and antagonism toward the peasant who aspires to higher things, and his racist nationalism. Useful insights into the ideology of those prejudices (along with others which matured in connection with the Bolshevik Revolution of November, 1917), and into the way they affected Roosevelt's successors, can be gained by considering them as part of the benevolent American desire to reform the world in its own image.

Chapter Six

Government and the Economy

■ In the early nineteenth century, as seen in Volume I, Chapter 3, government, particularly state government, had been used for planning and constructing many of the public works necessary for internal transportation, and in some areas state banks had supplied needed capital and credit. As private enterprisers became stronger financially, they wanted to take over the state activities that were profitable, and to a large degree they did so. And in the late nineteenth century, they developed strong arguments for complete reliance on private enterprise for economic purposes except in a few areas, governmental aid for the domestic economy by protective tariffs, for example. In this the leaders of business were fortified, in the English-speaking world at least, by classical laissez-faire economic theory and Herbert Spencer's insistence on the necessity of competitive struggle for evolution upward.

In opposition to this philosophy of a divorce between business and the state stood doctrines brought back by American economists who had studied in Germany. These economists argued for a practical view of the use of state power; if the end was desirable and the state could act most efficiently, it should do so. Their ideas produced a school of thought known as institutional economics.

Government participation in economic activity did increase from 1885 on, and the institutionalists provided much of the initial academic justification for this. But apart from theory, the changes brought about by economic development worked in favor of the policies advocated by the institutionalists. Increasing urbanism, which is inevitably accompanied by decreasing self-sufficiency for the individual, and technological change both required added public facilities and so forced a continual expansion of government activity. "Forced" is the proper word, because in many instances American governments resisted expansion of their activities and expenditures as long as possible. The states did not begin to deal adequately with highways and schooling until the 1920s, the Federal government resisted social security and agricultural relief until the 1930s, and adequate national highway planning had to wait until the 1950s.

Meanwhile, a new justification for government participation in economic affairs, particularly Federal government participation, had been provided by the theories of the English economist John Maynard Keynes, later Lord Keynes. Even a brief summary of Keynes's rather complex theorizing is impossible here, but in relation to government activity he argued that investment, essential to economic growth, would follow increased demand and that government could increase demand both by redistributing income downward, through helping labor to secure higher wages and making relief payments, and by spending more money.

The latter proposition marked a basic change in attitudes. In 1932 presidential candidates Herbert Hoover and Franklin D. Roosevelt both preached that depression would be alleviated by a balanced budget and curtailed expenditures; Keynes held that the cure for depression was increased government expenditures and an unbalanced budget. Keynes probably never convinced Roosevelt or many wealthy and conservative men of the complete truth of this doctrine, but politicians in general learned by experience that it worked. After World War II both major parties, in practice if not in principle, used increased spending as a cure for recession. This policy was powerfully aided by a generally increasing level of military expenditure from 1949 on, a level so high that it strongly affected the volume of business. For military purposes government financed most of the new applied research and fostered important technological changes which stimulated civilian consumption.

The Economist's View

■ If certain government expenditures, such as those for education or better health, are looked upon as aids to economic development rather than as burdens on the taxpayer, one can say that as the twentieth century wore on, more Americans learned how to use government constructively. In part the twentieth-century trend of government activity reflected a return to early-nineteenth-century attitudes, a turning away from the distrust of government that developed during the last half of the nineteenth century, when it was corrupt and inefficient. Solomon Fabricant of New York University, for many years director of research of the National Bureau of Economic Research, gives an overall statistical picture of the trend in government expenditure. It is interesting to compare the figures in this selection with those in Professor Broude's article in the preceding volume (Chapter 3, page 122), for the period a century earlier.

Solomon Fabricant
Factors Affecting the Trend of Government Activity*

The causes of the trend of government activity since 1900 must be sought in the tendencies present in the economy of 1900, modified or strengthened by the forces that entered the scene in later years. To get at these, let us take brief stock of the situation in which the twentieth century opened and note the changes after 1900 that seem most significant. We can then ask some pertinent questions. Are the causes suggested by our review themselves reflections of a more basic cause underlying them all? What is needed to confirm the significance of the factors thrown up by analysis of the American experience of a half-century? And what does the future appear to hold in store in the light of this analysis?

Tendencies in 1900

Government's role was a modest one when the twentieth century opened. Yet modest as it was by present standards, government seems to have been more important in 1900 than it had been in earlier decades. In our detailed discussion we could touch only briefly on changes before 1900. The figures on the labor force, it will be recalled, show a rise between 1870 and 1900 in government employment relative to total employment, though perhaps not as rapid as after 1900; and the figures on tax-exempt property trace a rising trend between 1880 and 1900 in the proportion of the nation's capital assets held by government. Information on the ratio of government expenditures (including interest, transfers, etc.) to national income is con-

* Reprinted by permission from The Trend of Government Activity in the United States since 1900 (New York: National Bureau of Economic Research, 1952), pp. 140–152.

flicting but seems also to indicate an increase, though rather slight, between 1890 and 1903. These suggestions are consistent with the general evidence on government activity before 1900, and with details on activities added by Detroit and California in the nineteenth century.

There already existed, then, a record of expansion in government activity.

The forces that had brought that expansion were still alive as the century opened. And other forces were already in motion and soon to add their impetus to the trend of government activity. Many of these were already apparent in 1900. Recall, for example, that the Industrial Commission was uncovering problems and offering solutions to them; that experience was revealing what was needed to amend the monopoly and railroad acts; that the United States had recently entered the international arena; and that Secretary Gage was not yet satisfied with our banking system. Groups were already in the habit of addressing appeals or demands to government for aid and protection.

Tendencies toward further increase in government activity, it therefore seems fair to say, were already present at the turn of the century. But we need not consider the situation of 1900 in detail. The underlying forces are sufficiently well illustrated in our review of changes after 1900, on which we concentrate. For many of the same factors were at work.

Changes after 1900

Population change, always a striking aspect of our national growth, comes first to our attention.

On the one hand, the doubled density of population tended to diminish the relative importance of government activity, with resulting economies in the use of government facilities, such as we have found in our analysis of interstate differences in 1942. And decline in rate of population increase (from 2 percent per annum at the opening of the century to $1\frac{1}{4}$ percent in the 1940's) also may have operated in this direction by tending to cut per capita government outlays on many items of construction and equipment, just as it tends to reduce per capita outlays on residential construction, except for replacement needs.

On the other hand, however, accompanying changes in population composition worked to step up the relative importance of government activity. Decline in number of children per family meant a higher value placed on each child, and a larger amount of money available for each child. Parents wanted longer schooling for their children, and more and better health, sanitation, hospital, and recreational services. Thus the number of school teachers rose more rapidly than the population, despite the decline in the percentage of children in the population. And increase in the percentage of older people in the population, together with urbanization, made the problem of the older worker more serious. Old age and survivors insurance is a recent step by government to meet the problem.

The increase in population and the ceaseless movement westward accompanying it brought also the end of the frontier in 1890.[1] This caught the attention of Frederick Jackson Turner in 1893 and provided a clue to the meaning of American history that fired the imagination of the next generation of historians. Whatever the merits of Turner's theory, the safety valve theory that was its corollary—or even more, the wider spread and less sophisticated reasoning from the simple fact of the frontier's disappearance

—influenced opinions and provided ammunition for proponents of a "positive program" by government. Later, along with decline in the rate of population growth, the end of the frontier came to be a major factor in policies based on the theory of economic maturity and stagnation. But the impression that opportunity had diminished with the end of the frontier did its work long before the 1930's.

More directly, the end of the frontier led to a reassessment of the value of conserving and developing the nation's natural resources. The nineteenth century's "slaughter" of the great eastern forest and its "mining" of the soil seemed to create no problems as long as virgin land lay farther west. The twentieth century came to think otherwise. Federal control, regulation, and development of natural resources, reflected in extensive and increasing expenditures on reclamation and river development, for example, appeared early. Timber reservations and national parks expanded to cover substantial areas. More recently, soil conservation took hold and the Tennessee Valley Authority began its activities. The development was cumulative. "By 1947 Stimson was prepared to admit—perhaps even to claim—what he had denied in 1935, that the principle of TVA, as an adventure in the effective use of national resources, was a direct outgrowth of the position he and other conservationists had taken back in 1912."[2] The three volume report of the President's Water Resources Policy Commission, published in 1950, is the latest in the series of discussions of conservation held in the last half-century. And the work of the Departments of the Interior and Agriculture has grown in correlated ways; for example, the former has studied shale and coal as possible sources of oil supply.

---

[1] Customarily, and rather crudely, defined as the band of land with a population of 2 to 6 persons per square mile.

[2] Henry L. Stimson and McGeorge Bundy, *On Active Service in Peace and War* (Harper, 1948), pp. 43–4.

Ever advancing science and technology also had their impact on government activity. The automobile, for example, stimulated road building and betterment, a task of government already taking on a new lease on life in the early years of the century, even before the auto had become important. (More and better roads, in turn, helped swell the number of automobiles, and thus the need for still more and still better roads.) The automobile created a demand for state and national parks and state police. It led to a reorganization and expansion of rural and suburban schools. Advance in economic science and statistics improved our knowledge of interstate and intrastate differences in needs and capacities and may have helped stimulate the system of state and federal grants-in-aid. It strengthened belief in the possibilities of dealing with social problems by collective action. It made for increase in the statistical and other fact-finding activities of government. Advance in chemical and biological science made possible and stimulated the growth of government work on sanitation, garbage disposal, health, and the control of pests, and plant and animal disease: witness, for example, the growth of state and municipal laboratories for testing water, food, and blood.

Indirectly, the advance and diffusion of science and technology had even more important effects. The main channel was through industrial change, in which increased population density, rise of national income, and other factors already mentioned or to which we refer below, also played a role. Two major developments may be selected for emphasis: changes in agriculture and in size of business operations.

Decline in agriculture relative to other industries, already on the way well before 1900, turned into an absolute decline, in terms of employment, about 1910. Commercialization of agriculture was a parallel process of lessening self-sufficiency and increasing specialization. These trends, stimulated by important changes in technology in and out of farming, illustrate a major theme and contribute to a minor theme of our history.

The major theme is growing economic interdependence. No farm is truly self-sufficient; it is dependent in some degree on supplies from the nonagricultural sphere. Yet the impact of change in the prices of farm products and farm supplies, if not also in tax and interest rates, is small when the farmer produces little for the market and much for himself. Independence diminishes as farms become commercialized. Correspondingly, interdependence increases as urban industries grow in relative importance and as limits on specialization widen with expanded markets. Not only are people more dependent on one another, they come to feel so. Thus was altered the climate of opinion in and out of farming on the need for positive government programs to deal with problems as diverse as public welfare, health, conservation, resource development, and business regulation.

The minor theme is increase in the share of government activity devoted to agriculture. Many industries have risen and declined in our history. Declining industries are as characteristic of an expanding economy as are rapidly growing industries, as Arthur F. Burns has demonstrated.[3] But none has ever had the political influence of agriculture. It is a very large industry; furthermore, in this country it directly controls a disproportionately large number of legislative votes. It benefits also from the fact that so many people's grandfathers were or are farmers. Viewed as the "seed bed" of population, the chief refuge of the independent spirit, and a major segment of the "sound middle class" sustaining democracy, it enjoys a unique position.

[3] *Production Trends in the United States since 1870* (National Bureau of Economic Research, 1934), Ch. 3–4.

Many of the increases we have noted in government activity thus were, in one way or another, to aid the farmer far beyond the degree prevailing in 1900: by mortgage and other credit (recall the provisions of the Federal Reserve Act favoring agricultural credit, the revival of the War Finance Corporation in 1921 to assist in financing and rehabilitating agriculture, the Agricultural Credits Act of 1923, and so on), the wheat and cotton purchase programs of 1929, and the stream of measures instituted in the 1930's.

Increase in the size of business establishment and enterprise, another trend apparent before 1900, gave rise to the Interstate Commerce Commission Act in 1887 and the Sherman Act in 1890. These led the way for a host of other government measures to prevent, combat, or regulate industrial monopolies and public utilities. The Elkins and Hepburn Acts which strengthened the ICC, the antitrust prosecutions, the life insurance investigations, the Federal Trade Commission and Clayton Acts came before World War I. The Cellar Anti-merger Act marks the latest episode. Increasing size of enterprise was important also in supporting the case for government encouragement of trade unions and "small business," for example through provisions of the Clayton Act and antichain store and resale price maintenance legislation.

The drift of people to the cities, so closely associated with the decline in agriculture and its other side, industrialization, deserves a separate word. Indirectly, of course, this truly secular trend influenced government activity in many ways; the insecurity of old age has been mentioned. Here we emphasize its direct influence: the need to provide services which rural life finds unnecessary or takes care of among family chores. Included are many of the great host of expanding municipal services: sanitation, waste removal, water supply, recreation and parks, local transportation.

While these services are mainly to final consumers, they are in fact largely costs to be charged against the attraction of urban incomes. For urbanization, and the industrialization accompanying it, meant higher real income per capita. This trend toward higher income also affected government activity, both by raising demand for government services and by making it possible to meet the costs of providing more such services.

Higher incomes influenced all levels of government. It would be impossible to explain much of the rise in educational expenditures in this country without referring to increased demand for more and better educational services per capita. The percentage of population enrolled in schools, mostly public, rose between 1900 and 1940 from 80 to about 95 for the 10–14 age group, and from 42 to over 75 for the 15–17 group.[4] And the kind of changes in the quality of educational service is obvious to anyone who compares the facilities and equipment of the modern school building and the training of the modern teacher with those of 1900, of which exhibits are still available. Municipal services also grew in quantity, quality, and variety. One simple illustration will suffice: inspection of restaurants and other eating and drinking places rose in relative importance along with higher incomes. State and federal activities also responded to higher incomes. Increase in state hospitals, for example, and in federal social security have been justified in terms both of long-term investment in productive human resources and of decent standards of responsibility for the immediate well-being of those who cannot help themselves. Both ability to invest and standards of responsibility rose with higher income levels.

The recurrence of business depression played its part. We are too close to the

---

[4] Such factors as compulsory school-attendance laws are largely results rather than causes of high enrollments. The more basic factor is undoubtedly income together with urbanization.

great depression of the 1930's, and to its influence on social security, labor, banking, agricultural, and other legislation, to need to emphasize its role. But we need to recall that the government developments associated with the New Deal constituted only the latest, if also greatest, of a series of step-wise movements along an upward trend. In some degree the Populist movement of the 1890's bore its fruit after 1900. The panic of 1907 underscored Secretary Gage's complaint of 1900 and led to the formation of a National Monetary Commission and eventually to the Federal Reserve System. The collapse of 1920–21 started a number of schemes in later years: agricultural legislation has already been mentioned. And the depression of the 1930's made its mark even before 1933: recall the Reconstruction Finance Corporation. Not only depression but also prosperity contributed: by stimulating labor and other movements agitating for the expansion of government activity, and by expanding local government outlays and commitments whose effects persist, in terms of government employment, purchases, and services rendered, even after the boom has passed.[5]

Developments in other parts of the world also contributed to the expansion of government activity in the United States. A number of innovations in social legislation and standards in their application came from Europe. The opening and development of new farming areas abroad played a part in the decline of American farming, and thus in its influence on the rise of government.

Also important, of course, was change in the international situation which brought war and the increased possibility of war. Even before World War II—and certainly for the entire period under review —the trend in the number directly engaged in national defense, including civilians in the nation's military establish-

[5] D. W. Gilbert, "Cycles in Municipal Finance", *Review of Economic Statistics* (November 1940).

ment as well as uniformed men, was steeper than the trend of population. By 1925, at the middle of the period under review, persons engaged in national defense had more than doubled since 1900; before Korea they numbered seven times the 1925 figure. Expenditures (apart from payrolls) grew even more rapidly, as equipment, vehicles, and ships used by the forces became more elaborate and "mechanization" proceeded. To this must be added expansion in the State Department and, in recent years, membership in international organizations and international relief, rehabilitation, and development. The residues of war and of preparation for or against war also must be counted: Veterans Administration activities, a subsidized Merchant Marine, higher tariffs to protect war-born infant industries, a heritage of war plants (Muscle Shoals, which culminated, after some hesitation, in the Tennessee Valley Authority; and the Atomic Energy Commission), the Canal Zone, and expansion of the statistical activities of government. In the conditions and policies determining the magnitude of the peacetime defense effort—that is, the changing international scene and our reactions to it—we have, then, another factor contributing substantially to the growth in government activity.

The century opened with the people largely though not wholly against government "interference" and "paternalism." But then came stimulated growth of the elements in the climate of opinion that look to government to deal with social and economic problems, and lowered resistance to such a program. Socialist ideology gained ground—although more in Europe than here; and in opposition to it there emerged a "positive program for democracy" to ward off radicalism by training the strong forces of government on the great problems of the day. And the problems themselves multiplied.

In addition, confidence swelled in the ability of government to do a job, partly because of changes in the organization and efficiency of government itself. The corruption so much raked over around 1900 lessened with the spread of the merit system and the formation of a professional attitude and skill among government workers. The state government executive was strengthened and its responsibility established. New methods of control and audit were devised, and a budgetary system introduced and expanded. Finally, the waging of a great war persuaded many people that government can do a big job well, and some jobs even better than private enterprise.

With this shift of attitude the ground was paved for the other factors we have noted to work their effects. The change in attitude helped to push farther the role of government in economic life by establishing a condition essential for that advance.

Government's Expansion as a Concomitant of Economic Growth

The various factors in our list have had pervasive influence on government activity. There is hardly any function or activity of government untouched by most of them. In this obvious sense, they are inter-related, operating as joint causes. But they are inter-related in other ways that deserve emphasis.

The factors have operated not only on government activity but also on one another, and through one another on government activity. We have noted some of these connections; only lack of space prevents illustrations in every section and paragraph.

Most important, the various factors we have paraded—with the important exception of the international situation—may be viewed as largely different aspects of one central cause or group of causes. That is the cause or causes of the economic growth—in population, per capita income, and aggregate income— that has characterized the United States

during the last half-century. Change in population composition of the kind we have experienced, the end of the frontier, advance and diffusion of science and technology, industrialization, urbanization, increase in size of enterprise and business cycles were concomitants of that growth and suggest themselves as distinctive characteristics of a growing economy. If this view is sound, the rising trend of government activity also is a concomitant of economic growth.

The developments underlying our economic growth disturbed the security of individuals and groups—the farmer, the older wage-earner, the smaller shopkeeper are examples—and posed serious social and economic problems of adjustment and protection. Economic development multiplied problems of monopoly and industrial relations and finance; created new, and enlarged old costs—of transport, communication, sanitation—involved in the operation of urbanized society; unearthed some resources but depleted others; spurred demand for the services—educational, recreational, health—that expand with increasing income. At the same time, it raised the nation's standards of responsibility for the economic welfare of the groups composing it, thus stimulating government production in general as a channel for the distribution of income as well as government production of the services meeting the particular needs of the groups requiring assistance. Economic development, further, swelled the number of activities in which the private return, but not the social return, compares unfavorably with its cost—examples are conservation and protection. Economic development may have improved government's efficiency in production relative to the efficiency of the private sector in certain areas—or led people to think this true. Finally, economic development may also have created, in Professor Schumpeter's phrase,[6] "growing hostility" to the

[6] Joseph Schumpeter, Capitalism, Socialism, and Democracy (Harper, 1942), Ch. 13.

system of private enterprise and a predisposition towards "interventionism" involving increased government regulation, protection, subsidy, and participation in the production process.

This explanation of the trend of government activity in the United States since 1900 forms a persuasive hypothesis. Like all hypotheses, however, it raises questions that need to be explored before we may accept it confidently.

If increasing government activity was the result of our economic development and a concomitant of economic growth since 1900, there should have been increasing government activity before 1900, when economic growth was rapid. And the evidence does suggest that immediately before the turn of the century government activity was rising in relative importance. However, we do not know how far back the trend goes; nor is it clear whether the trend before 1900 was as steep as it was afterward. It is not unlikely, of course, that developments associated with the very rapid economic growth after the Civil War led to an increase in government activity but with a long lag, that is, not until after 1900; and we have noted this possibility in our discussion: that is one reason why we started with the situation in 1900 and spoke of its "tendencies." But how long the lag may have been we do not know. Nor can we do more than mention the possibility that the lag itself may have been shortened in this century, in part because of the very development and elaboration of the scope, organization, and apparatus of government and the accompanying changes in the habits and attitudes of people.[7]

Again, if increasing government activity in the United States was the result of its economic development, did not other countries, which also grew economically, expand the activities of their governments? Population, income per capita, and aggregate income rose also in most other nations in the western world. And their history, too, shows changed population composition, increased density, technological advance, industrialization, urbanization, increase in the size of enterprise, and the cycle of prosperity and depression. We know that government activity did grow in many other countries. Some of the social legislation we established came from them. And the recent movement toward socialization in England has attracted considerable attention.[8] In 1938 expenditures by government (not including public service enterprises) on goods and services, as a percentage of gross national product, were about 15 percent in the United Kingdom, Sweden, and Canada, as well as in the United States. But no systematic survey has

---

[7] Relaxation of government's grip on economic life has been pointed to as a cause of the Industrial Revolution. If true, economic growth at that time was accompanied by decline in the relative importance of government regulation and supervision in economic life. However, there are a number of reasons why this explanation of what happened then is not necessarily inconsistent with the hypothesis discussed above. Other causes than government action or lack of action may have been important in the eighteenth century. Also, government activity and government regulation are not identical, nor are all types of government regulation similar in their effects. And lags are involved: decline in government regulation can be a cause of economic growth; in turn, the changes associated with economic growth can—later—cause a return to government regulation and increase in government activity generally. (Eventually, to proceed another step, increased government activity may affect the rate of economic growth: some of these activities are designed to do so, as has been mentioned earlier; others may have unintended "side" effects on growth. The net outcome would depend on the kinds of government activity and their relative weights.)

[8] The percentage of workers on government payrolls in Britain has been estimated to be 6 in 1911, 9 in 1921, 10 in 1930, and 25 in 1950 (A. L. Bowley, London and Cambridge Economic Service, Special Memo. 17A, Dec. 1926; D. Dewey, Journal of Political Economy, June 1950; and T. M. Ridley, Journal of the Royal Statistical Society, Series A [General], Part II, 1951).

been made of the course of events that established these levels. The inductions of Adolph Wagner and Henry C. Adams, which led them to formulate their "laws" of "increasing State activities among progressive peoples" and of "public expenditures for progressive peoples" may be said to find support in the history of the United States during the twentieth century; but these "laws" were based on very fragmentary nineteenth century data on government expenditures and taxes in a few countries without the advantage of adequate information on national income, not on the kind of information we have been able to collect for the United States since 1900.[9] The impressions one obtains of vast changes in the role of government abroad need to be systematically checked. What are the similarities and differences between the current level in other countries and ours? What are the similarities and differences between their trends and ours? Have the factors that seem to underlie trends here played a similar role abroad, and how important have they been? With such a comparative study completed, we can be

surer of the causes of developments in this country.[10]

Not all the factors affecting the trend of government activity can be said to be aspects of economic development. We noted the important exception of the international situation, which contributed so much to expansion in our government activity. Some would argue, of course, that international rivalry, and the war, preparations for war, and problems of postwar adjustment created by it, are consequences of economic growth. But important noneconomic factors are involved also. Given international rivalry as an independent factor, however, economic growth and the developments associated with it may have contributed to swelling its effect. Here we can only ask what are the relative weights of these economic and noneconomic factors and how have they influenced one another and worked their effects on the trend of government activity?

Chance, too, has a part, large or small, in all events; and the trend of government activity must therefore in some degree be interpreted as a series of historical accidents. But chance denotes only causes lying outside the system of variables constructed for an analysis. Their importance can be determined, if at all, only by the comparative historical and international analyses suggested above.

[9] Adolph Wagner, Grundlegung der Politischen Oekonomie (Leipzig, 1893), Erster Theil, Zweiter Halbband, p. 894; Henry C. Adams, The Science of Finance: An Investigation of Public Expenditures and Public Revenues (Henry Holt, 1898), Part I, Book I. Adams did not go beyond stating that total public expenditures would tend to increase with economic progress; Wagner explicitly stated his belief that economic progress brings a relative increase in the importance of government activities.

[10] A study of government activity in Western Europe was recently started at the National Bureau of Economic Research by Moses Abramovitz.

More Government in Banking

■ In 1914, for the first time, the United States established a central banking system. While the First and Second Banks of the United States had had some characteristics of central banks, they never developed the needed authority or responsibility.

In spite of very thorough advance study of central banking by special commissions, the system set up by political and business compromises in 1913 and 1914 was deficient in several respects. Whereas the buying and selling of government bonds, called "open-market operations," were a major reliance of the Bank of England, the Federal Reserve Board was not given adequate power over the way this stabilizing device was used by the regional reserve banks. In general, the Board lacked power to control the policy of these banks, as well as authority over the size of stock-market margins. These weaknesses were corrected in the Banking Act of 1935.

The following selection is a chapter from a book written by a father and son who both established reputations as students of money and banking. The late Edwin D. Kemmerer ended his career as a professor at Princeton; his son, Donald L. Kemmerer, is a professor at the University of Illinois. In describing the inability of the Federal Reserve Board to curb the stock-market inflation of 1929, the Kemmerers pose a dilemma that has never been solved: how to check a dangerous rise in stock prices without initiating a downswing in a normal business activity.

Edwin D. Kemmerer and Donald L. Kemmerer

Federal Reserve Bank Open-Market Operations in the 1920's*

World War I was the first major crisis that the Federal Reserve System was called upon to meet. The threat to the nation's financial well-being was clear, and the Federal Reserve Banks responded satisfactorily. Likewise, there can be little doubt that they dealt with the 1920 panic better than the old regime had handled the 1907 panic. During the rest of the 1920's, until 1929, there were several lesser crises to be met and minor problems to be solved, but no major emergency was apparent. The Great Depression of the 1930's was, of course, in the making. On the whole, the Federal Reserve System handled these minor crises and problems well. This it did largely with a new financial tool called open-market operations, which was used with such seeming success that some experts believed that the Federal Reserve System could probably eliminate the more serious aspects of the business cycle and stabilize the price level.[1]

This illusion made the Federal Reserve authorities largely unaware of the underlying financial weaknesses which would manifest themselves after 1929. Thus they used their open-market and rediscount powers sparingly and sometimes belatedly. Perhaps, of course, they could have done little even if they had realized these weaknesses more fully. The country enjoyed the boom of 1927–1929 while it lasted and was in no mood to listen to "prophets of doom." People did not know what the years ahead held for them: that is something which the amateur historian must never let himself forget.

To understand what took place in the 1920's, it is necessary to have a clear grasp of open-market operations. These

* Reprinted by permission of the publishers from *The ABC of the Federal Reserve System*, pp. 91–109, Copyright 1950 by Harper & Brothers.

[1] Board of Governors, *Federal Reserve Policy* (Post-war Studies, No. 8), p. 8.

affect the supply of credit available in the nation's money markets. But first, what are money markets?

The Money Markets

Large corporations and banks in New York and in the interior of the country often have liquid surplus funds on which they would like to earn a return. The banks generally feel that it would be unwise to lower their local rates to attract new borrowers. That raises all kinds of complications. Putting the funds to work elsewhere avoids the difficulties. This is all the more desirable if the funds may be committed for only a short period of time. Where is there such a place? There are money markets in several of the larger cities, but the New York money market is the national market for liquid surplus funds. It is also the largest such market in the world. Who is able to borrow in this market? In general, banks, big merchants and manufacturers, brokers with good collateral, and the government. These all want large amounts of capital at lower-than-ordinary rates or on special terms. Because the lenders are anxious to lend their surpluses, and because the borrowers enjoy excellent credit or have good collateral, the funds are loaned at rates that are normally lower than those offered at the commercial banks. Where in New York is this market?

The New York money market is not one institution where buyers and sellers of funds congregate and bid and offer. It is four specialized markets. These four are the banker's acceptance or bill market, the commercial paper market, the government securities market, and the call money market. There is a fairly definite relationship among the interest rates prevailing in these markets. Funds are easily moved from one market to another. In general, then, the money market is where the "marginal" demand for funds and the "marginal" supply of them meet, to use the economist's terms. It is a highly sensitive market, and changes in it may eventually affect interest and discount rates for all kinds of loans.

It is not necessary for us to know the detailed operations of these four markets. We need only summarize the basic functions of each.

Let us look first at the bill market. The bill, or banker's acceptance, was a European device that became popular after the establishment of the Federal Reserve System. As the name implies, it is a seller's bill to a buyer. It takes the form of a draft on the buyer's bank. The bank "accepts" it, that is, guarantees payment on it, so that the seller may sell it to someone else and get his money immediately. The seller, of course, must take a trifle less than if he waited. How much less? That is the interest rate, known in this connection as the bill rate. Who buys such bills? Anyone may: the market is open. But usually "dealers" buy them and then sell them to banks, savings banks, insurance companies, and business concerns. The largest dealer is the Discount Corporation of New York. The Federal Reserve Banks themselves bought large amounts of bills in the 1920's. As a result, the open-market rate and the Federal Reserve Bank buying rate for bills were about the same.

The commercial paper market is like the bill market except that dealings are in terms of trade acceptances or drafts drawn on a buyer instead of on his bank. The buyer is a well-known merchant or manufacturer like Sears Roebuck or General Electric. He "accepts" the bill, i.e., confirms future payment of it, and then the owner sells it to a commercial paper house. This house, in turn, sells such drafts to its customers. The commercial paper house sells the drafts, it does not endorse them.[2] Except for Federal Reserve

---

[2] Buying bills should not be confused with discounting them or rediscounting them. When

Banks,[3] the same general type of customers buy commercial paper in the open market as buy bankers' bills. Commercial paper generally pays a little higher interest.

Likewise akin to bankers' bills and commercial paper in this period were short-term government securities like Treasury certificates of indebtedness and Treasury notes. Since the government's credit was excellent and maturity was near, the rates on these bills were low. The short-term government issues of the 1920's differed slightly from those of today: there were no Treasury "bills" then. The certificates of indebtedness ran for three months or more, whereas the Treasury notes ran from three to five years. All these securities were sold in the first instance through the Federal Reserve Banks to a wide variety of institutions, companies, and individuals. Subsequent sales took place on the stock exchanges or through such houses as C. J. Devine and Company. These, together with the Federal Reserve Banks, were the government security market.

The call money market is different from the three markets just described. No discounting is done there. It is the market where stockbrokers get funds to finance the margin purchases of customers. A speculator buying securities "on margin" in the 1920's would probably pay for them with funds that were 15 percent his own and 85 percent borrowed "on call." His broker would arrange to leave the

---

banks discount bills, they assume liability for them, but when banks or dealers sell bills, they assume no such liability. More bills were rediscounted than sold in this period because the names on most bills were not well enough known to warrant sale.
[3] The term "commercial paper" is often used loosely, which is confusing. Sometimes it excludes bankers' bills and sometimes it includes them. For example, commercial paper houses do not normally handle bankers' bills. On the other hand, the only kind of "commercial paper" that Federal Reserve Banks may buy in the open market is bankers' bills.

securities as collateral for the money borrowed. The speculator expected the securities to rise in price so that he could sell them and thus make over six times the profit he would have made if he had limited himself to what he could buy with his own funds. The call money loan desks are located in the stock exchange buildings, and rates are set the morning of every business day for new loans and for renewals. Brokers, banks, corporations, and others with money to lend made contact through these desks with those who wanted to borrow funds. Call loans may be terminated on twenty-four hours' notice, and so they are liquid in addition to being well secured. But because they cannot be rediscounted, the rates are sometimes fairly high for a money market loan. Of the four money markets the call money market is the most volatile.

The following table shows the money rates prevailing in these four markets in November, 1926. The average rate for loans to bank customers was 4.70, which is slightly higher than the highest of the money market rates. The rediscount rate for eligible paper of the New York Federal Reserve Bank was 4.0. This rate customarily stood between the bill rate and the commercial paper rate.

The New York money market was a sensitive and important institution. Any action noticeably affecting the demand and supply conditions in this market would usually be felt in changes in interest rates in other financial markets throughout the country. The New York money market was the strategic point at which to effect either stability or changes in interest rates. And the Federal Reserve Banks were in the best position to do this, for they could buy or sell heavily and at will in the money market. Indeed, they were the flexible factor to the money market that the money market was to the banks of the nation. By a change in their policy, therefore, they could sometimes influence the credit situation for the

Table 1/ Money Market Rates, 1926

Treasury certificates, 3–6 months	3.35	percent
Prime bankers' acceptances, 90 days	3.75 to 3.875	"
Prime commercial paper, 4–6 months	4.50	"
Call loans, renewal rate	4.56	"

Source: *Federal Reserve Bulletin*, 1926, p. 829.

entire nation. At different periods in the 1920's the Federal Reserve authorities used this power to achieve certain ends. The occasions will be discussed shortly. The methods they used to influence money rates were not always the same, but they came to prefer open-market operations.

Open-market Operations

Before World War I and immediately afterwards changes in rediscount rates by central banks° constituted the principal method of controlling the money market. In the London money market, in particular, attention had been focused for many years upon the use of the rediscount rate to maintain stability. It was natural, therefore, that during the early years of the Federal Reserve System the rediscount rate was in the foreground in all discussions of the policies of the Federal Reserve Banks. At the time of the abrupt deflation in 1920–1921, the rediscount rate was the principal factor in Federal Reserve control of the market. Yet it was this depression that led to the discovery of open-market operations.

The depression reduced the earnings of several interior Federal Reserve Banks. To avoid a loss, these Banks bought securities with idle funds. That had to be done in New York. Some of the sellers of the securities deposited their receipts in member banks there. With additional deposits, the member banks were able to get out of debt to the New York Federal Reserve Bank, which reduced that Bank's earnings. In other words, several of the Federal Reserve Banks were increasing

their earnings by transactions which then decreased the earnings of the New York Federal Reserve Bank. Such competition between Federal Reserve Banks was undesirable. In addition, all this affected the stability of government securities. But, most important, it was noticed that these operations had a stimulating effect on the supply of credit. At the instance of the Treasury, a policy of coöperation among Federal Reserve Banks was inaugurated.[4] Without going into the evolution of the administrative details, the result was the Open-market Investment Committee of the 1920's.

The Committee was subject to the Federal Reserve Board and consisted of five governors of Federal Reserve Banks, with Governor Benjamin Strong of the New York Federal Reserve Bank as chairman. It was instructed that "the time, character, and volume of all purchases and sales of paper . . . eligible for open market operations shall be governed with a view of their bearing upon the general credit situation of the country."[5] An account was set up in the New York Federal Reserve Bank, and the other Federal Reserve Banks generally participated in all purchases and sales on a pro rata basis.

After 1922 the Federal Reserve authorities relied chiefly on open-market operations when dealing with the money markets. Why did they prefer these to changes in their rediscount rate? Any changes in the rediscount rate or bill-buying rate were only an announcement

[4] R. Westerfield, *Money, Credit and Banking* (New York, 1938), pp. 692–693.
[5] Section 12A, paragraph 3, Amended Federal Reserve Act.

of a change in the credit situation as seen by the Federal Reserve authorities. These changes might or might not have much influence on the attitude of businessmen, depending on the atmosphere of business confidence. And it took time for the announcement's effects to be felt in a country with thousands of individually owned banks. In short, the initiative often remained with member banks.[6] On the other hand, the Federal Reserve Banks found that through open-market opera-

tions in Treasury certificates and notes they could play a more effective part in the disposition of credit. True, they could operate through only two of the four markets, and only one of those usually was significant. That was the government securities market. But funds were transferred readily from one market to another, and so interest rates adjusted themselves fairly quickly.

When the Open-market Investment Committee ordered the sale of government securities, the result was to contract credit in general. This was because the purchasers paid with checks on their own banks, and in the clearing process these checks were deducted from member banks' reserves. Then the member banks had to replenish those reserves. They might do so by pulling their surplus funds out of the money markets, or they might even have to borrow from their Federal Reserve Bank. Interest rates rose in the money market, and perhaps the banks raised their interest rates too. In any

[6] Another reason sometimes advanced in favor of open-market purchases and sales of United States government securities by the Federal Reserve Banks, over changes in the rediscount rates, as a means of controlling the money market, was that the use of the rediscount rate sometimes resulted in sharp and often undesirable psychological reactions. Just as, in taxation, indirect taxes produce revenues less painfully than do direct taxes, so, in the control of the money market, purchases and sales of United States government securities by the Federal Reserve Banks accomplished their purposes more effectively than changes in the rediscount rate and usually with less public irritation and criticism.

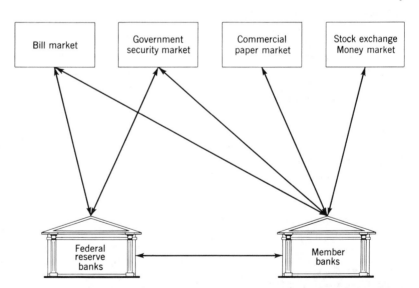

Chart I. The Bill Market and the Government Security Market Have Direct Access to the Federal Reserve Banks, but the Commercial Paper Market and the Call Money Market Have Access Only through Member Banks. (From R. Burgess, *The Reserve Banks and the Money Market*, rev. ed., New York, Harper, 1946, p. 152. Courtesy of the author and the publisher.)

event, the banks had less funds to lend. In this way open-market selling operations curtailed credit.

On the other hand, when the Committee ordered the purchase of government securities, the result was to expand credit. The persons or institutions who had sold the securities received checks drawn on the Federal Reserve Banks. When they deposited these checks in their own banks, their banks' reserves with the Federal Reserve Banks were increased. Their banks could now lend more freely. They might send surplus funds to the money market, where rates would fall, or they might even lower their own local rates to encourage borrowing. Thus open-market buying operations tended to expand credit.

Open-market operations could be used and were used, as we shall see, to moderate or to accentuate the effects of gold imports or of gold exports. The Federal Reserve authorities were now less at the mercy of the vagaries of the international gold standard than before, when changes in rediscount rates were their only defense. The discovery of open-market operations resulted in more planning by the central financial authority. Thus it marks a decline in the automatic gold standard. Virtually no one, however, thought that the new device seriously jeopardized the gold standard. Its prestige was high in the 1920's. Nor do we mean to imply that using open-market operations was a mistake. Their use simply represented an unconscious but significant step from an economy based on the theory of automatic price adjustments to a more planned economy.

Federal Reserve Policy and Business Activity

About 1922 there began to emerge something like a definite policy on the part of the Federal Reserve authorities. As may be seen from Charts II and III, there appears from that time a more or less consistent relationship between the various components of Federal Reserve credit and business activity, as measured by the index of industrial production. While the interests of foreign countries at times played an important part in determining Federal Reserve action, the policies of the Federal Reserve authorities were dominated by domestic considerations. In Chart II the index of industrial production is shown. In Chart III are shown the principal items of Federal Reserve credit outstanding. These are: (1) bills rediscounted, which includes the member banks' collateral loans; (2) bills bought, which means essentially the Federal Reserve open-market purchases of bankers' acceptances; and (3) United States government securities bought, which means the portfolio of open-market purchases of United States government securities held by Federal Reserve Banks.

From the beginning of 1922 through the year 1931, the money market was controlled mainly through the open-market operations of the Federal Reserve Banks, and particularly through purchases and sales by them of government securities. The Federal Reserve rediscount rates rose and fell in accordance with open-market operations. With the exception of the autumns of 1924, 1928, and 1931, Federal Reserve Bank policy was not reflected to any substantial extent in open-market purchases of acceptances. Such purchases were dictated rather by the exigencies of the acceptance market and the desire of the Federal Reserve authorities to develop this market. A discussion of the relationship of the broken line on Chart III, representing the portfolio of United States government securities held in the Federal Reserve Banks, and industrial production (Chart II) will help to explain Federal Reserve policy during the period 1922–1931.

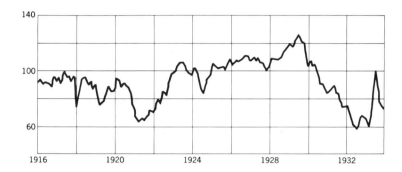

Chart II. Index of Industrial Production, 1916–1934 (1923–1925 = 100). (The index for 1916–1919 is from *Standard Statistics—Basic Statistics*, April 29, 1938, p. 67; that for 1919–1934 is from Board of Governors, *Annual Report*, 1936, pp. 184–189, and *Federal Reserve Bulletin*, June, 1938, p. 526.)

Relationship between Member Bank Borrowing and Federal Reserve Bank Security Purchases/ At the beginning of 1922, much of the world, including England, Sweden, Netherlands, Japan, Italy, Austria, Canada, and Argentina, was in a state of business depression. The United States was emerging from depression; France, Belgium, and one or two other countries were relatively prosperous. Easy credit conditions gave promise of bringing the world out of the depression, and this was particularly true of the United States. An easy credit policy was, therefore, followed by the Federal Reserve authorities, through the increase of Federal Reserve Bank holdings of United States government securities, as shown in Chart III. This policy, along with the gold flowing in during the year, enabled member banks to pay off their indebtedness at the Federal Reserve Banks and, in addition, to increase their reserve balances with Federal Reserve Banks. By the middle of 1922, however, the continued inflow of gold seemed to have been a sufficient stimulus to member bank credit expansion. In fact, the rapid rise about that time in the index of industrial production

seemed to presage another boom. The Federal Reserve easy credit policy was therefore reversed to a relatively firm credit policy, and United States government securities were heavily sold by the Federal Reserve Banks. As the securities were sold, member bank balances were depleted by an equal amount, and this forced the member banks to rediscount with the Federal Reserve Banks, that is, to borrow from them (see in Chart III the rise in bills discounted with the decline in United States government security holdings of the Federal Reserve Banks). Industrial production reached its peak late in the spring of 1923, followed by the downward movement culminating in the "minor depression of 1924" (see Chart II).

By 1924, all of the more important countries, with the exception of Japan, had emerged from the depression of 1921, and the world was in a relatively prosperous condition—a minor depression taking place in the United States. Even though much of the world was prosperous, it appeared to the Federal Reserve authorities safe to follow an easy credit policy, in view of the minor depression in this country, and for the purpose of

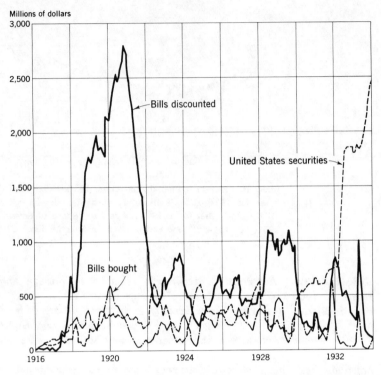

Millions of dollars

Chart III. Principal Items of Federal Reserve Credit Outstanding. (The data were obtained from Federal Reserve Board, *Annual Reports* and *Federal Reserve Bulletin, passim.*)

helping England to return to the gold standard.[7] The Federal Reserve policy, therefore, was to purchase government securities at a fairly rapid rate throughout most of the year 1924.[8] This enabled

[7] Low interest rates here would not be likely to attract surplus funds from England. High interest rates might have done so, thereby threatening England's gold redemption funds just as she was trying to return to the gold standard.
[8] Following is the comment of the Federal Reserve Board concerning its policy during 1924: "At the time when the open-market purchases were made, there was a recession in industrial activity, the attitude of the business community was hesitant, and there was no evidence of the growth of speculation. Open-market purchases during this period served to build up a portfolio of securities and to increase the proportion of outstanding reserve bank credit under the direct control of the federal reserve banks. By these purchases the reserve banks placed themselves in a position, through the subsequent sale of

member banks again to pay off much of their indebtedness to Federal Reserve Banks and to expand credit on a cheaper credit base.

Somewhat alarmed by the spurt in business activity which followed and also by the large amount of speculation in stocks and bonds, the Federal Reserve authorities early in 1925 sold government securities rather heavily and thereby made credit conditions firmer. This, together with an outflow of gold in the spring of 1925, forced member banks once more

securities in case it should become desirable, to cause member banks to discount and to bring a larger part of the outstanding reserve bank credit under the influence of the discount rate." Federal Reserve Board, *Annual Report*, 1924, p. 12.

to rediscount with their Federal Reserve Banks. From the course of the index of industrial production, this tightening of the money market seemed to have the desired effect of leveling off the boom and, in fact, causing a slight recession. Conditions seemed to be fairly well stabilized at a high level of prosperity during 1926 and the first part of 1927.[9] During the summer and fall of 1927, some recession appeared in the index of industrial production for the United States. However, many of the important countries of the world were riding on the crest of boom times, including Australia, England, Germany, and Poland. Only Italy, Japan, and Norway were depressed.

Federal Reserve Credit and Security Speculation/ A striking characteristic of the year 1927, from the point of view of the United States, was the flotation of foreign and domestic securities, which assumed record-breaking volume,[10] and the growing activity in the stock market. (See Table 2.) Still, it did not seem to the Federal Reserve authorities that speculative activity was assuming dangerous proportions. Because of the slight business recession in this country in 1927, the Federal Reserve System eased credit conditions by the purchase of government securities, beginning in the forepart of 1927. This policy was also owing to a desire to help the world maintain the gold standard. We particularly wanted to help England reduce the

amount of deflation necessary to enable her to clinch her recently reëstablished gold standard.[11] At any rate, this easy credit policy was continued by the Federal Reserve Banks throughout the remainder of the year 1927. Instead of member banks using this credit, however, as they had on similar occasions, to reduce their indebtedness to the Federal Reserve Banks, they used it as a basis for the expansion of security loans.[12]

Inflation in the securities market, thus stimulated, was an object of great concern of Federal Reserve authorities, and early in 1928 Federal Reserve policy was again reversed: the Federal Reserve Banks began to sell rapidly their holdings of United States government securities. This was accompanied by an outflow of gold and had the effect of tightening the money market and forcing member banks to rediscount with their Federal Reserve Banks. The boom seemed to have been leveled off by the late spring and early summer of 1928, as the index of industrial production shows. There also had been a significant pause in stock market speculation, in the rise of security prices, and in loans on securities.

In the late summer and fall of 1928, Federal Reserve policy changed once again. A halt was called in the sale of United States government securities; and not only that, but unusually large purchases of bank acceptances were made— more than enough to take care of the seasonal requirements. This so eased the

[9] *Ibid.,* 1926, pp. 1–3, and 1927, pp. 1–3.
[10] Federal Reserve Board, *Annual Report,* 1927, pp. 5–8, and 1928, pp. 1–3.

[11] *Ibid.,* 1927, p. 10.
[12] *Ibid.,* pp. 5–6 and 10–11.

Table 2/ Stock Market Statistics

Item	1922	1925	1927
General Motors stock (high)	15	150	282
September stock averages (1935 –1939 =100)	77	98	135
Brokers' loans, Sept. (in billions)	$1.8	$2.9	$3.9
Annual volume (in millions of shares)	261	460	582

credit situation that member banks were able to reduce their indebtedness at Federal Reserve Banks.[13] There followed a resumption of the stock market boom and of the business boom, as indicated by the extraordinary rise in the index of industrial production (Chart II).

Experiment with "Moral Suasion"/

About the beginning of 1929, the Federal Reserve authorities resumed their tight-money policy by a much larger reduction in holdings of acceptances than the normal seasonal reduction, and also by some sales of government securities. In addition, the Federal Reserve Board attempted to exercise "direct pressure" or "moral suasion" upon the member banks to restrict the wild expansion of speculative credit. Accordingly, the Board addressed two letters to the Federal Reserve Banks, under dates of February 2 and 7, 1929, calling attention to the fact that security speculation was assuming proportions, which made it "incumbent upon the federal reserve banks to give constant and close attention to the situation in order that no influence adverse to the trade and industry of the country shall be exercised by the trend of money conditions, beyond what may develop as inevitable.

"The extraordinary absorption of funds in speculative security loans which has characterized the credit movement during the past year or more, in the judgment of the Federal Reserve Board, deserves particular attention lest it become a decisive factor working toward a still further firming of money rates to the prejudice of the country's commercial interests.

". . . A member bank is not within its reasonable claims for rediscount facilities at its federal reserve bank when it borrows either for the purpose of making speculative loans or for the purpose of maintaining speculative loans.

"The Board has no disposition to assume authority to interfere with the loan practices of member banks so long as they do not involve the federal reserve banks. It has, however, a grave responsibility whenever there is evidence that member banks are maintaining speculative security loans with the aid of federal reserve credit. . . ."[14]

Unfortunately, the country was by this time thoroughly enjoying the speculative spree. It would have taken strong measures by men of great courage and insight to stop it, and it is doubtful if such paragons would ever have been thanked for their efforts. Whether the Board was doing all that might have been expected of it may be debated. In any event, the Board did not have as full control of the situation as might be imagined. Three episodes in 1929 will illustrate this: one shows the independence of individuals, one of member banks, and one even of Federal Reserve Banks.

The bulk of the speculation was being financed by brokers' loans, which were obtained on the call money market. As has been mentioned, in normal times such funds came from New York banks and their correspondents. But in 1927–1929 "others" began putting their funds into this market. These "others" were corporations with surplus funds, investment trusts, wealthy individuals, and even some middle-class persons like college professors. The high interest rate, the liquidity, and the collateral provided made call loans highly attractive. Table 3 shows how brokers' loans increased during this period.[15] Notice the column "Loans for Others" during 1929: it made up more than half the total at times.

Since these loans were not derived from banks, they were largely beyond the con-

[13] *Ibid.*, 1928, pp. 6–7.

[14] *Ibid.*, 1929, pp. 2–3.
[15] The publication of statistics on brokers' loans from February, 1926, on was intended to have a dampening effect on speculation. It did not. Board of Governors, *Federal Reserve Policy*, p. 67.

Table 3/ Composition of Brokers' Loans (in Millions)

Date	Funds of N.Y. Banks	For Out-of-Town Banks	"Loans for Others"	Total
Feb. 3, 1926	$1,222	$1,280	$ 590	$3,092
Jan. 4, 1928	1,511	1,371	928	3,810
Nov. 28, 1928	1,235	1,768	2,287	5,290
Apr. 3, 1929	1,021	1,652	2,889	5,507
July 31, 1929	1,205	1,696	3,058	5,960
Oct. 2, 1929	1,071	1,826	3,907	6,804
Oct. 1, 1930	1,834	602	627	3,063

Source: L. Haney, L. Logan, and H. Gavens, *Brokers' Loans* (New York, 1932), pp. 220–221.

trol of the Federal Reserve authorities. For example, Federal Reserve rediscount and open-market policies caused New York banks to decrease their loans on the call market in the late summer of 1929, but high interest rates only led the "others" to pour more funds into the call money market.[16] No method had been devised to control these funds.

The perverse action of a big bank might neutralize Federal Reserve policies too. When the Board put its tight-money policy into effect early in 1929, call money rates advanced to 9, 12, 15, 17, and finally 20 percent. Some banks timidly withdrew funds from the call money market. Stock prices fell sharply. Presumably this halting of the speculative upsurge was just what the Board was seeking. Yet at this point President Charles Mitchell of the National City Bank of New York, the country's second-largest bank, placed $25 million in the call money market at rates of 16 to 20 per cent. He later told a Congressional investigation committee, "We stepped in there to allay what was becoming a money panic, an inability of the legitimate borrower to borrow for his day's contracts the money that was essential if they

should be maintained."[17] The market recovered in the next few days, and brokers' loans advanced again.

We must remember that banks were within their legal rights in making loans to speculators provided the loans were well secured. Such loans were merely not eligible for rediscount. Some banks borrowed on eligible paper but used the funds to make loans to speculators. That was what the Board was inveighing against in February. Mitchell's excuse for his action in March was that his bank was not in debt to the Federal Reserve Bank at all. The fundamental difficulty lay in the fact that the Federal Reserve System was founded on the theory that bank credit should grow out of self-liquidating paper. But that was never written into the law for member banks, only for the Federal Reserve Banks. As a result, the Federal Reserve authorities were limited in what they could do about speculative loans.

If the Board had really wanted to stop the boom, they could, of course, have raised rediscount rates higher and engaged in open-market selling operations again. At least, so it might be argued. But

[16] The "others" also contributed to the country's distress when the panic began in October, 1929, by withdrawing over $2 billion in one week. Fortunately, the Federal Reserve System and the New York member banks were able to make up part of this. Without them the money panic would have been appalling.

[17] *Hearings before a Subcommittee of the Committee on Banking and Currency*, U. S. Senate, 72nd Congress, 2nd session, on Senate Resolutions 84 and 239, part 6, p. 1816. Mitchell was an A director of the New York Federal Reserve Bank in 1929. Senator Glass demanded his resignation from the position on the ground that he had acted in contempt of the Federal Reserve Board. New York *Times*, March 29, 1929, p. 1.

that presumes agreement in the Federal Reserve councils, where apparently harmony and discipline did not prevail either. It was the general custom at this time that the Federal Reserve Banks, particularly the New York Federal Reserve Bank, should initiate proposals of change in credit policy. The Board would then approve or disapprove of them. The governor of the New York Federal Reserve Bank during most of the 1920's was Benjamin Strong, a man with a persuasive personality and a shrewd grasp of economic conditions. He had more influence than the chairman of the Federal Reserve Board.[18] No proposals were made all during the later part of 1928 while the "bull market" boom was gaining momentum.[19] Perhaps the undue optimism of the period explains this failure of the Federal Reserve Banks; perhaps the illness of Governor Strong after February, 1928, and his death in October explain it.[20] Under the circumstances the action of the Board in February, 1929, was necessary but belated. It was also drastic and rather unprecedented. This does not clear the Board of blame for not acting sooner, but it does clarify the situation somewhat.

By the time the Board took action, they felt that mere raising of rediscount rates would be inadequate. Instead, they favored

"moral suasion" and "direct pressure." By direct pressure they meant denying Federal Reserve credit to banks that were known to be speculating or helping speculators. The New York Federal Reserve Bank, however, was unsympathetic to the policy instituted by the Board early in 1929 and belatedly urged that the rediscount rates be raised instead. The Board objected to that, and a heated controversy over the two methods of dealing with the situation ensued. Meanwhile, the New York Federal Reserve Bank continued to rediscount for member banks even when it knew that those banks had large call loans outstanding. The rediscount rate was 5 percent; call loans were generally 8 percent or more. Such independent action by the New York Federal Reserve Bank, by far the largest of the twelve Federal Reserve Banks, made the Board's policy of direct pressure virtually impossible. The Board relaxed it that summer and let the New York Federal Reserve Bank raise its rediscount rate.[21]

Conclusions

Open-market operations were a new device in the 1920's, and central bank control of the nation's credit was only a few years older. It would be an historical phenomenon if we could point to this as a case where men in a new position of great authority had exercised a new implement of control with courage and wisdom. The Federal Reserve authorities used open-market operations well in handling minor boomlets and recessions, in solving foreign currency stabilization problems, and in sparing the money markets from the severe stringencies they had experienced in most former panics. But they could not avert the major disaster of 1929. Indeed, by their policies of "too little and too late" credit restric-

[18] R. Westerfield, *Money, Credit and Banking* (1938), p. 395.

[19] A. C. Miller, "The Federal Reserve Policies, 1927–29," *American Economic Review*, September, 1935, pp. 452–453. Miller was a member of the Federal Reserve Board.

[20] Carl Snyder, statistician for the New York Federal Reserve Bank, states that it was Strong's plan to raise the rediscount rate steadily and head off the boom that was gathering. "If Governor Strong's plan of restricting credit had been followed, from early in 1928, the later phase of wild speculation could easily have been avoided." *Capitalism the Creator* (1940), p. 228. The New York bank raised its rate from 3.5 to 4 percent on February 8, 1928, to 4.5 percent on May 18, to 5 percent on July 13, and finally to 6 percent over a year later, on August 9, 1929. Most of the other banks followed the lead of the New York bank except for the last increase mentioned.

[21] *Ibid.*, pp. 454–456.

tion,[22] some critics believe they made the panic worse.

Yet perhaps the Federal Reserve authorities have been unjustly blamed for not stopping the 1929 panic. Let us suppose they had been permitted to see, in the late 1920's, what the economic future would bring, and to devise policies to curb stock market speculation. Would they not have encountered strong opposition from the country and then been severely blamed when a depression followed the execution of their policy? They might have softened the depression somewhat, but they would hardly have prevented it. The depression was certainly the product of more than a serious stock market crash. Yet blame for the depression would then have attached largely to the Federal Re-

serve authorities. Criticism of them might have been so severe that their powers would have been greatly curtailed as a result. We shall never know. Once the Board chose its route at the crossroads, it could never know what dangers lay the other way. But it is sometimes healthy to conjecture.

The experience of 1929 did show, however, that the Board needed to have some more specific controls at its command. Since there was not enough self-liquidating paper in the 1920's, banks made speculative and long-term loans.[23] To handle the speculative situation, the Board needed more power over the stock market. They needed more discipline among the Federal Reserve Banks in carrying out open-market operations. And they needed some additional credit curbs, for open-market operations were not the patent cure-all that they had originally been supposed.

[22] The Board could have done more if they had dared to act boldly. From 1918 to 1932 member bank reserve balances never exceeded $2.5 billion, and excess reserves were rarely over a few tens of millions. Between 1927 and 1929 Federal Reserve Banks held a total of $1.5 to $1.8 billion of bills and government securities which could have been offered on the open market.

[23] To some extent the increase in long-term assets held by banks was offset by an increase in their time deposits. *Federal Reserve Bulletin,* 1940, p. 286.

More Government in Industry

■ Presidential administrations have wavered between two contrasting economic policies: maintaining reasonable prices for the consumer by Federal regulation, and attempting to accomplish the same end by ensuring competition between suppliers. The first policy, championed by Theodore Roosevelt, who called it the New Nationalism, has been carried out, for example, by the Interstate Commerce Commission and the Federal Power Commission. The second, championed by Woodrow Wilson as the New Freedom, has been implemented by antitrust laws and their enforcement. Whereas Wilson started with the second policy and, under pressure of wartime demands, swung over to the first, Franklin D. Roosevelt tried regulated cooperation in 1933 but had switched to antitrust by 1939. Arthur M. Schlesinger, Jr., Harvard professor who became a special adviser to Presidents Kennedy and Johnson, shows in the following selection, a chapter from his multivolume history *The Age of Roosevelt,* how the exigencies of depression led in 1933 to the National Industrial　●

Recovery Act, the most extreme attempt at planned and regulated business in the United States. The act initially had broad bipartisan support, including that of the United States Chamber of Commerce and other powerful business organizations, but many groups on both sides of the political fence, including small businessmen and organized labor, turned against its operation.

Arthur M. Schlesinger, Jr.
The Birth of NRA*

The fight to save the banking system opened the Hundred Days; the fight to save the farmers opened the New Deal proper. But throughout the sleepless days and nights of March 1933 a major gap in the recovery program became increasingly vivid and disconcerting. For the heart of the American economy was neither finance nor agriculture but industry; and that heart was only beating faintly. By the Federal Reserve Board index, manufacturing production declined from 110 in 1929 to 57 in 1932—almost 50 per cent. The total value of all finished commodities at current prices had fallen even more— from $38 billion to $17.5 billion. Private construction had crashed from $7.5 billion to a dismal $1.5 billion. As General Hugh Johnson contended to Raymond Moley on the New York train five days after the inauguration, a rise in farm prices without a corresponding stimulation of industrial activity would be fatal to recovery.

But how to go about stimulating industry? Johnson and Moley agreed on one thing: that the industrial program would have to be carried out in a framework of business-government partnership. The General, who had helped mobilize industry for war fifteen years earlier, now advocated a comparable national effort to mobilize

industry for recovery. He had always believed that the War Industries Board contained lessons for peace. "If cooperation can do so much," he had reflected after the war, "maybe there is something wrong with the old competitive system." In a report of December 1918 he wrote that although detailed central controls might not be necessary, the peacetime economy could attain full efficiency only by permitting planning through trade associations in areas where joint action was forbidden under the antitrust laws. In 1919 he tried with Peek to establish what he called "self-government in industry under government supervision" through the short-lived Industrial Board. Business experience in the twenties only confirmed his dislike of unrestrained competition. Depression perfected the indictment. The antitrust acts, Johnson declared, had failed the nation in every crisis. They had to be suspended during the war to enable the country to defend itself. When they were restored in 1919, they set the stage for 1929. They fed the inflation, and they fostered the crash. Unchecked competition had no place in a mechanized and integrated society. "The very heart of the New Deal," he asserted, "is the principle of concerted action in industry and agriculture under government supervision looking to a balanced economy as opposed to the murderous doctrine of savage and wolfish individualism, looking to dog-eat-dog and devil take the hindmost."

Johnson's personal patron and old War Industries Board chief lent the force of his own presumably supernatural economic wisdom to this general view. Bernard Baruch too had favored coordination through trade associations under public supervision in 1919. As early as the spring of 1930, he called for suspension of the antitrust laws to permit collaborative business action against depression. On May 20, 1933, he denounced the Sherman Act, invoked the WIB example, and renewed his call for industrial planning.[1]

II

In the meantime, business itself had gone far to provide "self-government" an organizational basis. The key instrumentality, as Johnson and Baruch had argued in 1919, was the trade association; this was, said Raymond Moley, "the natural means which economic life has sought to find a way out of chaos." (In 1922 Franklin D. Roosevelt himself had become president of one such association, the American Construction Council.) Throughout the twenties, the Federal Trade Commission not only stimulated the spread of these associations but encouraged them to promulgate "codes of fair competition" for their industries. About 150 such codes were adopted between 1926 and 1933. And by 1931 business leaders—especially Henry I. Harriman of the Chamber of Commerce and Gerard Swope of General Electric (another War Industries Board veteran)—were calling for national economic planning through the trade associations.

Beyond the general proposals of Harri-

man and Swope for all industry, the cry for planning arose with special urgency in industries confronting particularly chaotic internal conditions. Oil, for example, was greatly overdeveloped in terms of existing demand as a result of the tapping of new pools between 1926 and 1931. When depression came, the industry itself tried to allocate production, first through voluntary agreements and then through state legislation. As these controls broke down, industry leaders by early 1933, seeing anarchy ahead, began to plead for a federal oil dictator.

In other unstable industries, like coal and the needle trades, the demand for planning came from organized labor. Here the trade association was bypassed in favor of direct resort to government. In the case of coal, which had been a sick industry through the twenties, the United Mine Workers early developed a plan to stabilize the industry through federal licensing, control of production, suspension of antitrust laws, a thirty-hour week and the guarantee of collective bargaining. After the onset of depression, it became apparent to John L. Lewis, the Mine Workers' president, that coal could not be stabilized apart from the rest of the economy. Accordingly he began to urge the extension of these principles to the economy as a whole. (Some coal operators had more drastic views, urging a federal coal dictator and even telling the Secretary of Labor that they would "sell the mines to the government at any price fixed by the government. Anything so we can get out of it.")

The garment industry, with a long history of destructive competition, had similarly produced labor leadership interested in stabilizing production and employment. Like Lewis, Sidney Hillman of the Amalgamated Clothing Workers believed that the disease had spread beyond his own industry and that the time had come, as he said in 1933, for the establishment of "an instrumentality to coordi-

[1] Historical Statistics, Ser. H3, J30, J49; Senate Finance Committee, Investigation of the National Recovery Administration: Hearings, 74 Cong., 1 Sess. (1935), 2409–11; Raymond Moley, After Seven Years, 185; H. S. Johnson, The Blue Eagle (New York, 1935), 93, 101, 114, 153–55, 169, 172, 187–88; C. F. Roos, NRA Economic Planning (Bloomington, Ind., 1937), Ch. 1; A. M. Schlesinger, Jr., The Crisis of the Old Order (Boston, 1957), 181.

nate the industries of this country and with power to put its planning at once into effect."[2]

III

There were, in addition, special labor interests at stake, which made even a conservative American Federation of Labor leader like Matthew Woll call for "national planning which will conceive of the economic activity of the nation as a whole rather than individual parts." In an unplanned system, labor seemed the first casualty of economic crisis. The obvious way to preserve profits was to cut costs; the firm which worked its labor longest and paid it least gained the greatest competitive advantages. "Cutthroat competition," as Hillman observed, "makes the unscrupulous employer the leader in each industry and the rest willingly or otherwise follow." (Businessmen who cut wages had the further satisfaction of knowing they were following the injunction of orthodox economics that the effort to maintain wage rates increased unemployment.)

With the worker—and the responsible businessman—thus at the mercy of the greedy, desperate or doctrinaire competitor, standards of wages and hours, attained after so many years of battle and negotiations, began to crumble away. No state laws existed to provide effective protection for wages; and, where laws regulated working hours, no state had a weekly limit as low as 44 hours even for women. Sweatshops were springing up on every side. Child labor was coming back. The

Pennsylvania Department of Labor and Industry reported that half the women in the textile and clothing industries were earning less than $6.58 a week, and 20 per cent less than $5. In Fall River, Massachusetts, more than half the employees in a garment factory were getting fifteen cents an hour or less. At the same time, the work week in some states was lengthening to sixty, sixty-five, even seventy hours. There stretched ahead only the prospect of longer, grimmer work days and thinner pay envelopes.

In many cases, trade associations hoped through industry agreement to resist the attack on labor standards. But, when the Cotton Textile Institute resolved not to work women at night, 15 per cent of the manufacturers refused to comply, and the agreement broke down. How to protect the responsible employer in his effort to resist the pressure against wages and hours? In New York, laundrymen sought out the National Consumers' League and offered it $10,000 a year if it would inspect and "white-list" laundries maintaining fair wages and hours. But others simply gave up the voluntary effort. George W. Alger, impartial chairman of the cloak-and-suit industry, declared, "I am convinced today that decent industry needs help from law, which it never required before." As the executive secretary of the chemical industry trade association put it, the individual selfishness of employers left legislation as the only method by which unfair practices could be eliminated.

Even before his inauguration, Molly Dewson, once of the Consumers' League, more recently of the Women's Division of the Democratic party, urged on Roosevelt the importance of wages and hours legislation to arrest the downward spiral. When New York passed a minimum-wage law in April 1933, Roosevelt called on governors of a dozen other states to take similar action. But would state action solve a nationwide problem? Hillman had already recommended that the federal government

[2] Moley, "Changing the NRA," Today, June 2, 1934; G. B. Galloway et al., Industrial Planning under Codes (New York, 1935), 21–23; J. T. Flynn, "Whose Child Is the NRA?" Harper's, Sept. 1934; Schlesinger, Crisis, 182–83; Harold L. Ickes, First Thousand Days, 24; Frances Perkins, The Roosevelt I Knew (New York, 1946), 230; House Labor Committee, Thirty-Hour-Week Bill: Hearings, 73 Cong., 1 Sess. (1933), 198–99 (Harriman); Sen. Finance Com., Investigation of Economic Problems: Hearings, 72 Cong., 2 Sess. (1933), 299–301 (Lewis), 875–76 (Hillman).

set up labor boards to control wages and hours in all industries where self-government had broken down. And the American Federation of Labor, unwilling to go quite that far, now threw its support to a measure introduced into the Senate by Hugo Black of Alabama—a bill prohibiting interstate shipment of goods produced by men working more than thirty hours a week.

The case for a limitation on working hours had received its most effective statement in *Jobs, Machines and Capitalism*, a book by Arthur Dahlberg published in 1932. It had won some support in business circles; thus Ralph Flanders of the Jones and Lamson machine tool company wrote that it was "difficult to disagree with Dahlberg's arguments" (though by 1933 both Dahlberg and Flanders concluded that the depression had become too severe to respond to the thirty-hour remedy). From Dahlberg, Black took the theory that technological progress would create a permanent labor surplus unless work was in some manner spread among the entire labor force. And, in addition, Black argued that the thirty-hour week was essential in the present emergency; it would halt the attack on labor standards and, by forcing employers to hire more workers, would reduce unemployment and increase mass purchasing power. Black put no minimum-wage provisions in the bill, apparently in the belief that the Supreme Court had outlawed federal regulations of wage rates; also perhaps because of the American Federation of Labor's continued opposition to minimum-wage legislation. He was confident that as the shorter week tended to create a labor shortage the increase in labor's bargaining power would push wages up. His bill, he predicted, would put six million men back to work, give new strength to organized labor, and provide a permanent means of absorbing the consequences of technological progress.

Organized labor agreed. If Congress did not enact the bill, William Green, the AF of L president, told a Senate committee, labor would exercise its "economic force"; he spoke ominously of a general strike. "Which would be class war, practically?" said Black. "That is the only language that a lot of employers ever understand," said Green; "—the language of force."[3]

IV

The movement for industrial coordination had still another source: the proponents of concentration and control who traced their inspiration back to the New Nationalism of Theodore Roosevelt. Thus a veteran of the Bull Moose crusade like Donald Richberg had never abandoned the dream of what he had termed in 1917 the "democratization of industry." "There might grow, out of our present spreading commercial empires," he wrote in 1929, "a group of industrial republics within our national boundaries"; this, he said, would give democratic government "a new birth in state and nation." The grand objective, as he saw it, was "self-government in industry."

Depression made Richberg call with new vehemence on government to take the lead in bringing about industrial reorganization. "While not advocating the perma-

[3] Matthew Woll and W. E. Walling, *Our Next Step—A National Economic Policy* (New York, 1934), 80; Sen. Finance Com., *Investigation of Economic Problems*, 875 (Hillman); Mary W. Dewson to F.D.R. [Feb. 1933], in Mary W. Dewson, "An Aid to the End," I, 104–5, Dewson Papers; Josephine Goldmark, "The New Menace in Industry," *Scribner's*, March 1933; Senate Judiciary Committee, *Thirty-Hour Work Week: Hearings*, 72 Cong., 2 Sess. (1933), especially 2–11, 21–22, 285; House Labor Committee, *Six-Hour Day—Five-Day Week: Hearings*, 72 Cong., 2 Sess. (1933), especially 14, 17; Ralph E. Flanders, "Limitations and Possibilities of Economic Planning," *Annals*, July 1932; John Chamberlain, "Panaceas for the Depression: Solving It with a Thirty-Hour Week," *New Republic*, March 29, 1933; J. P. Frank, *Mr. Justice Black* (New York, 1949), 89; Charlotte Williams, *Hugo Black* (Baltimore, 1950), 47–49.

nent socialization of business or property," he told a Senate committee, "we believe that an emergency governmental control is now as essential to the national welfare as it would be in a time of war. . . . No man with sufficient intelligence to be worthy of any attention can deny that a planned control of the great essential industries is absolutely essential." When someone asked how far he would extend that control, Richberg answered quickly, "Practically as far as necessary to put the employees back to work by whatever means were necessary. . . . A nationally planned economy is the only salvation of our present situation and the only hope for the future." He proposed a national planning council on top of a pyramid of industrial councils. He differed from Harriman and Swope in resting industrial self-government not on trade associations but on councils made up of managers, investors, and workers and in visualizing a larger measure of federal intervention.

Richberg advanced these ideas in a mood of extreme radicalism. The planning solution, he said bitterly, would probably be intolerable to the masters of industry because of their "insensate greed." "Although the conspicuous money-makers who presume to advise you have proved their ability to make themselves wealthy," he told the senators, "it is far more important for this committee to realize that they have also proved their ability to make millions of people very poor." His only concern, Richberg added, was whether an effective program could be put into effect "before too large a percentage of the people have been starved into either hopeless resignation or desperate revolt."

Within Roosevelt's own circle, Moley favored what he called "a policy of cooperative business-government planning" to combat economic instability and social insecurity. Tugwell had a particularly comprehensive conception of government-business planning. "Self-government in industry" by itself, Tugwell thought, would

only benefit the individual industry. What was necessary was rather "a forced balance among all industries." In *The Industrial Discipline* in 1933 he advanced the idea of coordination through an Industrial Integration Board. Each trade association would have its own planning apparatus; and the Board would reconcile the plans of the affiliated industries with the basic plan laid down by government. Only in this way, Tugwell felt, could the private collectivism created by the new technology be reliably harnessed to the public interest. Nor would he recoil from the War Industries Board model; after all he once favorably described the War Industries Board as "America's War-Time Socialism."

Jerome Frank, Tugwell's ally in the Department of Agriculture, had similar views. He felt that the key mass-production industries should be treated frankly as monopolies and made to adopt intelligent policies; and he contended that the solution of the problems of a profit economy lay in *"an intensification of coordination between all parts of the economy."* "Just as America took an important step forward when it rejected political anarchy and integrated this continent into one nation," wrote Frank, "so it needs now to press forward to a deliberate economic integration." Like Tugwell, Frank would strive for this integration through a new central agency.

The planning philosophy had support in the Senate, notably from Robert F. Wagner of New York and Robert M. La Follette, Jr., of Wisconsin. No member of the Senate had been so consistently alert to the problems of industrial society as Wagner. Even before the depression, he had argued that government had the responsibility and could have the power to maintain employment and stability. In 1931 he called for a public works program, a federal employment stabilization board, and a federal system of unemployment insurance. La Follette at the same time had contended for large public works and relief programs as well as for a national economic council. With the new administration, both Wagner and La Follette were determined to press for new initiative in the industrial field.[1]

V

And so, from diverse sources—from recollections of the war mobilization of fifteen years before, from business hopes for protection of prices and profits, from trade union hopes for protection of labor standards, from liberal hopes for creative national planning, from a collective revulsion against a competitive system which competed at the expense of human decency—opinion was converging on a broad approach to the problem of industrial recovery. With past policies of exhortation and drift discredited, with state socialism undesired and politically excluded, there remained the prospect of a mighty attempt, organized by government, to halt the decline through a massive experiment in national cooperation. Even a writer like John T. Flynn, so soon to be an impassioned critic of the result (and to blame it all on the United States Chamber of Commerce), called in March 1933 for the establishment "without delay" of an Economic Council to "take measures for balanced production through the organization of trades under government supervision."

The nation was more than ready. Many people had an anguished sense of crisis.

[1] Donald Richberg, "Trying to Bury the Big Stick," *Survey Graphic*, Sept. 1929; Richberg, *Tents of the Mighty* (New York, 1930), 196–203; Senate Committee on Manufacturers, *Unemployment Relief: Hearings*, 72 Cong., 1 Sess. (1932), 340; Sen. Com. on Man., *Federal Aid for Unemployment Relief: Hearings*, 72 Cong., 2 Sess. (1933), 453–55; Sen. Finance Com., *Investigation of Economic Problems*, 643–48; Moley, *After Seven Years*, 184; R. G. Tugwell, *The Industrial Discipline* (New York, 1933), 212–16; Tugwell, "New Deal Memoir," Ch. 2; Tugwell, "America's War-Time Socialism," *Nation*, April 6, 1927; Jerome Frank, *Save America First* (New York, 1938), 341–43; Schlesinger, *Crisis*, Ch. 2, pp. 224–26.

For some, society itself seemed confronted by the specter of dissolution. "It is no wonder," said Bernard Baruch, "that the whole of industry seems to have risen en masse to find some way to check it as a matter of stark self-preservation." Alexander Sachs of the Lehman Corporation, a close friend of Hugh Johnson's, summed up the feeling when he said that the entire Western economic order was threatened "not by the destructive impact of external or natural forces, but by a spontaneous disintegration from within." This was not, Sachs said, normal economic depression; it was "economic nihilism, which, from a national point of view, cannot be permitted to go on." The crisis did appear, in a phrase of the day, worse than war. For a moment, all bets were off, all antagonisms adjourned; Americans, it seemed, had to work together or else they would founder together.

The President, preoccupied with banking, agriculture, and relief, did little in his first month to face up to the industrial problem. Then the unexpected passage by the Senate of the Black thirty-hour-week bill on April 6, 1933, ended administration lethargy. "It's the first constructive measure yet passed dealing with unemployment," said William Green with satisfaction. But Frances Perkins, upon whom the burden of policing the measure would fall, was a good deal less satisfied. And the President was particularly repelled by the bill's rigidity; "there have to be hours adapted to the rhythm of the cow," he remarked, thinking of its irrelevance to the dairy industry. In addition, he considered the bill unconstitutional. Yet he sympathized with its objectives; and he did not want to embarrass the Democrats who had voted for it. Above all, he must have sensed the rising demand in the nation for action on the industrial front. "It was," Ernest K. Lindley wrote of the Black bill, "revolution boiling up from the bottom."

In the meantime, a separate clamor had arisen in the Senate for a federal public works program. This was led by Wagner, La Follette, and Costigan and backed by many in the administration (including Miss Perkins, Ickes, Dern, Tugwell, and Richberg, but definitely excluding Douglas, who was strongly opposed). The convergence of the Black bill and the public works drive meant that the administration could no longer put off thinking about a comprehensive plan for industry to parallel its program for agriculture. For some time, plans for industrial recovery had been indiscriminately dumped in the busy office of Raymond Moley at the State Department. Roosevelt now told Moley to get in touch with the people working on business-government cooperation plans around town and come up with some recommendations.[5]

VI

By this time several groups were working independently on the general problem. Because they had shifting and over-lapping membership and engaged in a continual process of cross-consultation, it is difficult to reconstruct the sequence of developments; and the recollections of participants in this respect have proved as confusing as the events themselves doubtless were. It seems evident that two groups were especially important. One centered in Senator Wagner's office on Capitol Hill, the other in the office of John Dickinson, the Undersecretary of Commerce.

Wagner, of course, had been concerned

with employment planning ever since arriving in the Senate. In his group, David Podell, a trade association lawyer, proposed modifying the Antitrust Act through codes of fair competition in the interests of business self-government; Gilbert H. Montague was an expert on the law of business association; Robert M. La Follette, Jr., emphasized public works and national planning; W. Jett Lauck of the United Mine Workers spoke both for the interests of labor and for the UMW approach to economic planning; and Harold Moulton of the Brookings Institution brought an economist's judgment to the reconciliation of the various suggestions. The Dickinson group drew primarily on the ideas and resources of the Executive Branch; along with Dickinson himself, Tugwell, Jerome Frank, and Frances Perkins were its active members. From the start, the two groups were in contact. Thus young Leon Keyserling, a Harvard Law School graduate whom Tugwell brought to Washington in March, came into the discussion as a lawyer on Frank's staff. His contribution at an early meeting impressed Wagner, who then invited Keyserling to come to the Hill as his legislative assistant. After a time, the Wagner and Dickinson groups in effect joined forces and went to work on a common draft.

Moley, who was flooded with other responsibilities, was finding industrial expansion one project too many. At just this point, Baruch and Hugh Johnson, fresh from a hunting trip in South Carolina, showed up in Washington. Moley, running into Johnson in the lobby of the Carlton late in April, begged him to get into the picture: "Nobody can do it better than you. You're familiar with the only comparable thing that's ever been done—the work of the War Industries Board." Johnson needed no urging. He went over to Moley's office that afternoon, took off his coat and tie, unbuttoned his collar, and went to work with furious energy. A year

[5] J. T. Flynn, "The New Capitalism," *Collier's*, March 18, 1933; Johnson, *Blue Eagle*, 153; Alexander Sachs, "National Recovery Administration Policies," in Clair Wilcox et al., eds., *America's Recovery Program* (New York, 1934), 117; Perkins, *Roosevelt I Knew*, Chs. 16, 22; Perkins, letter in *Washington Post*, April 20, 1933; *Time*, April 17, 1933; House Labor Com., *Thirty-Hour-Week Bill*, especially 3–7; Frances Perkins, "Eight Years as Madame Secretary," *Fortune*, Sept. 1941; Ickes, *First Thousand Days*, 21; Tugwell, Diary, March 31, April 2, 3, 1933; Moley, *After Seven Years*, 184–90.

of discussion with Alexander Sachs on the agenda of industrial revival, on top of his own varied business experience, convinced him that he knew exactly what should be done. On only one point did he feel weak—the problem of labor. Then someone spoke of Donald Richberg. Johnson called him in, and they appeared to hit it off from the start.

By early May, there were two main drafts—a Johnson draft, written originally on a couple of sheets of legal-size foolscap, based on a tough government licensing system; it bore the endorsement of Moley, Douglas, and Richberg; and a Dickinson draft, more legalistic, complex, and cautious, looking to industrial self-government through trade associations, and bearing the endorsement of Frank and of the Wagner group. Tugwell liked much in the Dickinson-Wagner draft; but he was also attracted by the fact that Johnson had more power in his bill, with clearer compulsions. Henry I. Harriman, who was in and out of the discussions, preferred the Dickinson-Wagner draft because it made greater use of trade associations; but he also felt, like Tugwell, that the sanctions of the Johnson draft ought to be included. Frances Perkins regarded the public works provisions of both drafts as inadequate.

The President awaited the results of the interminable meetings with impatience. As early as April 12 he had hinted to his press conference about the possibility of a plan designed to secure "the regulation of production or, to put it better, the prevention of foolish over-production." When the United States Chamber of Commerce met in Washington in early May, he called on business to work with government "to prevent over-production, to prevent unfair wages, to eliminate improper working conditions." (The convening businessmen could hardly have been more enthusiastic about the prospect. Of the forty-nine speakers, twenty-seven came out for more government direction of industry. "If we are to save our traditional freedom for the future," said Paul W. Litchfield of Goodyear Tire and Rubber, ". . . we must make substantial concessions to what we have in the past classified as the more radical school of thought.") And in his second fireside chat, on May 7, Roosevelt talked about "a partnership in planning" between government and business, with government having the "right" to "prevent, with the assistance of the overwhelming majority of that industry, unfair practices and to enforce this agreement by the authority of Government." (While they were working on this speech, Moley said, "You realize, then, that you're taking an enormous step away from the philosophy of equalitarianism and laissez-faire?" Roosevelt, silent a moment, replied with great earnestness, "If that philosophy hadn't proved to be bankrupt, Herbert Hoover would be sitting here right now. I never felt surer of anything in my life than I do of the soundness of this passage.")

Three days later, with Johnson and Dickinson still unable to reach agreement, a meeting was called at the White House. Here Roosevelt, after listening to the competing arguments, issued his familiar order that the group lock itself in a room until it could come out with a single proposal. Then Dickinson, Johnson, Wagner, Tugwell, Richberg, Frances Perkins, and Douglas moved over to Douglas's office for the final agony of drafting. There were unpleasant moments: Douglas made a last effort to knock out public works; Dickinson became biting and arrogant toward Johnson; but Tugwell, siding with Johnson in his demand for sanctions, helped resolve the dispute. By May 15, the long struggle was over, and a bill was ready for Congress.[6]

[6] Moley, *After Seven Years*, 184–90; Johnson, *Blue Eagle*, 193–204; J. P. Warburg, "Reminiscences" (Oral History Research Office, 1952), 213, 216, 248, 369–70, 378–80, 493; Tugwell, Diary, April 21, May 30, 1933, and "New Deal

VII

The bill was divided into two main parts. Title I, "Industrial Recovery," proclaimed the intent of the Congress "to promote the organization of industry for the purpose of cooperative action among trade groups." Sections providing for codes of fair competition and for exemption from the antitrust laws embodied the trade association program; a provision for the federal licensing of business showed the influence of the national planners; and Section 7a, pledging collective bargaining, maximum hours, and minimum wages, fulfilled the hopes of labor and the promise of the Black bill. Title II, "Public Works and Construction Projects," calling for the establishment of a Public Works Administration with an appropriation of $3,300,000,000, satisfied the public works advocates. The Act was to be in effect for two years.

The House passed the bill with few changes in just over a week. Most important was a determined attempt, pressed by William Green, to strengthen Section 7a. This section had already had a precarious passage through the drafting process. The trade association group, evidently feeling that organization was a privilege to be accorded only to employers, accepted the idea of 7a with reluctance; even the more liberal among them, like Harriman and Swope, had made no provision for organized labor in their own

Memoir," Ch. 2; Press Conference #11, April 12, 1933, #18, May 5, 1933; H. I. Harriman to F.D.R., May 11, 1933, Roosevelt Papers; F.D.R., *Public Papers* (1933), 157, 164–65; Donald Richberg, *The Rainbow* (New York, 1936), 106–10; "The Birth of the NRA," unsigned memorandum, NRA Papers; Perkins, *Roosevelt I Knew*, Chs. 17, 22; Donald Richberg, *My Hero* (New York, 1954), 163–65; Flynn, "Whose Child is the NRA?"; H. S. Johnson, "Background of NRA," *Saturday Evening Post*, June 30, 1934; Roos, *NRA Economic Planning*, 36–40; E. K. Lindley, *The Roosevelt Revolution* (New York, 1933), 151–61; *New York Times*, May 4, 1933; *Time*, May 15, 1933; Leon Keyserling to author, April 9, 1958.

plans. As a result, 7a was constantly on the verge of being defined out of existence. Only the vigilance of Jerome Frank, Leon Keyserling, and Senator Wagner and the fear of provoking labor opposition kept it in. Now Green took advantage of the House hearings to persuade the Ways and Means Committee to plug possible holes. Language taken over bodily from the Norris-La Guardia Act made explicit the protection of workers from coercion by anti-union employers; and other changes in phraseology specifically exempted workers from having to join company unions as a condition of employment.

In the Senate, however, the bill in general and 7a in particular had a stormier time. The National Association of Manufacturers and the Chamber of Commerce both assailed the labor provisions; and Senator Bennett C. Clark of Missouri came up with an amendment stating that "nothing in this title shall be construed to compel a change in existing satisfactory relationships between the employees and employers of any particular plant, firm, or corporation." The Senate liberals, led by George Norris, were quick to denounce this as an attempt to favor company unions, if not to legalize yellow dog contracts. Clark then astonished the opposition by explaining that Donald Richberg, who had been present during discussions of the amendment, had said he thought it very beneficial. But the liberals, unmoved at this revelation, said that Richberg could not have understood what he was endorsing and voted down Clark's proposal.

The more important part of the Senate discussion, however, turned on another question—the significance of the suspension of the antitrust laws. William E. Borah of Idaho led the attack on the bill from the viewpoint of an old-fashioned antitruster, with cogent support from Burton K. Wheeler and Hugo Black; and Wagner, courteous, wearily patient, ever resourceful, defended the measure. The debate, conducted on an uncommonly high level, opened up basic issues. Borah contended that the suspension of the antitrust acts would infallibly promote the concentration of wealth and power. Wagner replied that the urgent need was to outlaw sweatshops, long hours, and low wages, and that this could only be done by allowing business cooperation. The issue quickly reduced to the question: Could industry be trusted to combine for fair standards for wages, hours, and working conditions without at the same time combining for pools and price-fixing?[7]

VIII

The question of price-fixing rapidly assumed critical importance. It was already clear that many businessmen—including, for example, the Chamber of Commerce group—believed that the bill conferred on industry the power to fix prices and restrict production. Businessmen wired Borah that if the bill did not do this it would be just a labor measure, and they wanted no part of it. Richberg, testifying before the House Committee, said that price-fixing would be permitted. But Wagner, who saw clearly the implications of uncontrolled price-fixing, stated vigorously in the Senate debate, "It is not contemplated that prices shall be fixed, because the fixation of prices is not in conformity with the preservation of fair competition." The bill was not designed, he said, to end competition but to lift its standards—"to make sure the best judgment and the highest ideals of the industry govern its competitive activities, replacing the now low standard of sweatshop, cutthroat competition. . . . The bill does not abolish competition; it purifies and strengthens it."

[7] House Ways and Means Committee, *National Industrial Recovery: Hearings,* 73 Cong., 1 Sess. (1933), 72, 95–96, 117–22; *Congressional Record,* 73 Cong., 1 Sess., 5279–80 (June 7, 1933).

Yet even Wagner made exceptions: sales below cost should be forbidden in the interests of preserving small enterprises against their chain competitors; moreover, cooperation might be necessary to prevent harmful price fluctuations. For these reasons Wagner opposed a Borah amendment flatly prohibiting price-fixing. The real danger, said Wagner, was "monopolistic price fixing"; and this was forbidden in the bill. "What the Senator fears," Wagner said, "can result only from a faithless and disloyal administration of the act." To this Borah, Wheeler, and Black responded in effect that suspension of the Sherman Act made a faithless and disloyal administration inevitable. "Do you mean to tell me," said Black, ". . . that they would meet and agree on minimum wages and maximum hours and never discuss, to any extent whatever, the questions of the price at which they were to sell their goods?" The big interests, added Borah, would always dominate code-making, whatever the language of the bill. But how else, except through the codes, Wagner responded, to outlaw sweatshops and to store up the crumbling position of labor? "I do not think we will ever have industry in order," he said, "until we have nationally planned economy, and this is the first step toward it."

It was a close argument. Given the presumption that a direct federal attack on wages and hours was unconstitutional, the only way that competition could be stopped from grinding labor standards down to ever more squalid levels was through covenants enforceable throughout the industry. Yet, if agreement were permitted on wages and hours for the benefit of labor, how to prevent agreement on prices and production for the benefit of monopoly? Opinion in the Senate swayed back and forth as the debate progressed. Thus Black voted against Title I, for the bill, and finally against the conference report; La Follette, Norris, Wheeler, Costigan, Cutting, and other progressives voted for Title I and the bill, and then against the conference report; Huey Long, after denouncing the bill in unmeasured terms ("The Democratic Party dies tonight, Mr. President. We will bury it"), voted for it and then against the conference report. But the Senate finally adopted the conference report on June 13 by 46 to 39, and the bill was rushed to the President.

The purpose of the bill, the President said on June 16, was to put people back to work. It was to raise the purchasing power of labor by limiting hours and increasing wages. It was to elevate labor standards by making sure that no employer would suffer competitive disadvantages as a result of paying decent wages or establishing decent working conditions. Above all, it represented an historic experiment in government partnership with business. "It is a challenge to industry," Roosevelt emphasized, "which has long insisted that, given the right to act in unison, it could do much for the general good which has hitherto been unlawful. From today it has that right."

"History probably will record the National Industrial Recovery Act," Roosevelt added, "as the most important and far-reaching legislation ever enacted by the American Congress."[8]

[8] *Congressional Record,* 73 Cong., 1 Sess., 5153, 5244, 5245, 5307 (June 7, 1933), 5835, 5838, 5839, 5840, 5845, 5861 (June 13, 1933); F.D.R., *Public Papers* (1933), 246, 252, 256.

The Recognition of Keynesian Economics

■ In the Employment Act of 1946 Congress wrote into law the principles of Federal responsibility for the nation's economic welfare which had often in fact guided policy since 1932. But the basic contradiction that had partially paralyzed Hoover and Roosevelt also entered the wording of the law: the economy was to be *controlled* in the interest of *free* enterprise. Faced in 1945 with a bill that would have provided for Federal planning of capital investment through the Office of the President, the conservatives in Congress had recoiled, and ultimately agreed only to a law so general in its wording and so lacking in new power for the administration that the menace of a planned economy was averted. Yet the act, by providing a three-member Council of Economic Advisers whose duties were to study trends in the economy and advise the President and by compelling the latter to issue an annual economic report to Congress, ensured periodic attention to economic developments which was previously lacking or unformulated.

In the resounding but unimplemented language of the act, the President, as advised by the Council, had the momentous responsibility of acting "to promote free competitive enterprise and the general welfare . . . and . . . maximum employment, production and purchasing power." In the following selection economist E. Cary Brown analyzes the recommendations made by the President and how far they resulted in policies that modified the business cycle or stabilized income in the years following the passage of the law.

As important as better understanding of tools for maintaining prosperity has been the implicit acceptance by both political parties of government responsibility. Arthur F. Burns, President Eisenhower's Chairman of the Council, stated in 1954 that "it is no longer a matter of serious controversy whether the Government should play a positive role in helping to maintain a high level of economic activity. What we debate nowadays is not the need for controlling business cycles, but rather the nature of governmental action, its timing and its extent."[1]

E. Cary Brown
*Federal Fiscal Policy in the Postwar Period**

In the period following the Second World War, stabilization policy has had to cope with both inflations and recessions. A review of this period can throw some light on its success or failure. Was the need for action seen promptly or was there a substantial lag? Was the prescription proper in terms of the seen need? How fast was policy adjusted to the new situation? What mixture of automatic and discretionary policy was used? Was the Administration hampered by the legislature, or was it the reverse? There are so many aspects of policy into which one can probe that some considerable narrowing down of the subject is necessary.

The first limitation is imposed by the title. This essay will deal only with fiscal policy and not with other aspects of stabilization policy, such as money and cost-price relationships. This leaves us with government spending, taxing, and borrowing problems. But, because debt problems are so intertwined with monetary management, and because monetary policy is being discussed in another chapter, this essay will be restricted to taxing and spending policies.

Even this narrowed conception of fiscal policy requires further restriction. In what follows we judge fiscal policy solely by reference to its consequences for economic stability, and not with reference to its effects on resource allocation, income distribution, or growth. Such a judgment cannot, therefore, be final. It would have to await an appraisal of all the results of the fiscal action.

Even so circumscribed, a number of problems remain. We must, for example, agree on what constitutes a fiscal action. The most helpful rule, it seems to me, is that fiscal inaction results from the maintenance at a constant level of real government purchases of goods and services and tax and transfer rates. Thus, if tax yields rise under an unchanged tax structure as income rises, no action is considered to have been taken. Such an interpretation creates some awkward problems. One cannot draw a sharp line between automatic and discretionary policy and expect it to hold up in all situations.[†] What happens to tax yields will inevitably

[1] *The New York Times*, Oct. 19, 1954.
* From *Postwar Economic Trends in the United States*, edited by Ralph E. Freeman. Copyright © 1960, Massachusetts Institute of Technology. Reprinted by permission of Harper & Row, Publishers, pp. 141–188.

[†] Samuelson early pointed out the arbitrary nature of the distinction between automatic and discretionary policy. See Paul A. Samuelson, "Principles and Rules in Modern Fiscal Policy: A Neo-Classical Reformulation," *Money, Trade, and Economic Growth: In Honor of John Henry Williams* (New York: The Macmillan Company, 1951).

Table I / Government Budget Activity in 1947 Prices, Quarterly Totals, Seasonally Adjusted, at Annual Rates*

Year and Quarter	G_T	G_F	$G_{S\ and\ L}$	T	$G_T - T$	$G_T - 0.8T$	T_{Gross}	$T_{Personal}$	$T_{Corporate}$	$T_{Ind.\ Bus.}$	T_{SS}	Transfers	Net Interest Paid	Subsidies less Current Surplus	P_{G_T}	P_{G_F}	$P_{G_{S\ and\ L}}$
(1)	(2)	(3)	(4)	(5)	(6)	(7)	(8)	(9)	(10)	(11)	(12)	(13)	(14)	(15)	(16)	(17)	(18)
1945-1	129.9	120.4	9.6	59.9	70.0	82.0	69.0	26.7	16.2	18.8	7.3	4.3	4.1	0.7	75.9	75.4	81.0
45-2	127.5	118.1	9.6	59.2	68.3	80.1	69.1	26.4	16.2	19.0	7.6	5.2	4.5	0.2	76.4	75.8	81.5
45-3	104.1	94.4	9.9	51.8	52.3	62.7	63.7	25.5	11.2	19.2	7.7	6.1	4.7	1.0	77.0	76.4	82.0
45-4	70.2	59.9	10.3	43.1	27.1	35.7	62.1	25.0	9.6	19.8	7.7	12.2	5.0	1.8	78.6	78.1	82.7
1946-1	43.3	31.3	10.7	34.7	8.6	15.5	56.9	21.8	7.3	20.2	7.5	14.7	5.4	2.1	82.0	84.4	83.8
46-2	34.4	23.0	11.1	38.7	-4.3	3.4	59.8	22.4	9.4	20.6	7.3	13.4	5.4	2.3	87.0	88.6	85.7
46-3	29.9	19.0	11.3	42.6	-12.7	-4.2	59.1	21.2	11.6	19.7	6.5	11.7	5.0	-0.2	96.0	96.8	91.2
46.4	29.9	18.7	11.7	43.7	-13.8	-5.1	58.5	20.6	12.8	18.9	6.1	10.2	4.6	-0.1	99.0	99.0	94.5
1947-1	28.2	16.2	12.2	44.1	-15.9	-7.1	59.0	21.9	12.3	18.6	6.3	10.4	4.5	0.0	99.4	99.5	97.3
47-2	27.8	15.3	12.6	42.3	-14.5	-6.0	57.1	21.6	10.8	18.5	6.2	10.1	4.5	0.3	99.6	99.8	99.3
47-3	28.6	15.7	12.9	38.8	-10.2	-2.4	56.2	21.5	10.8	18.6	5.3	13.6	4.4	-0.6	100.3	100.2	100.8
47-4	29.7	16.0	13.5	42.6	-12.9	-4.4	56.6	21.3	11.2	19.0	5.1	10.3	4.2	-0.6	100.9	100.6	102.6
1948-1	30.5	16.8	13.5	43.0	-12.5	-3.9	57.3	22.0	11.7	18.6	4.9	10.4	4.1	-0.6	102.4	100.6	106.2
48-2	34.3	20.4	13.7	40.6	-6.3	1.8	54.8	19.4	11.7	18.9	4.8	10.1	4.1	0.0	103.9	100.7	110.4
48-3	36.9	23.0	14.2	40.8	-3.9	4.3	54.2	18.5	12.0	18.9	4.8	9.5	4.0	-0.2	106.1	100.8	112.8
48-4	37.5	23.1	14.8	40.8	-3.3	4.9	54.1	18.8	11.1	19.3	4.9	9.1	4.1	0.0	107.2	101.1	113.8
1949-1	40.0	25.1	15.4	38.2	1.8	9.4	53.0	17.4	10.6	19.5	5.4	10.4	4.3	0.0	107.8	102.1	113.8
49-2	41.1	25.6	15.6	37.0	4.1	11.5	52.2	17.5	9.3	20.1	5.3	10.9	4.3	0.0	108.0	103.8	113.7
49-3	40.2	23.8	16.2	38.2	2.0	9.6	53.3	17.4	9.8	20.7	5.3	11.1	4.3	-0.4	108.2	105.6	113.5
49-4	40.0	22.9	16.6	37.7	2.3	9.8	52.8	17.5	9.3	20.7	5.3	11.1	4.3	-0.3	108.4	106.9	113.6
1950-1	38.0	20.4	17.0	33.9	4.1	10.9	58.0	18.4	12.3	21.1	6.2	19.5	4.4	0.2	108.6	107.4	114.0
50-2	36.5	19.2	16.9	43.2	-6.7	1.9	61.6	18.8	14.6	21.9	6.3	13.3	4.4	0.6	109.7	107.7	114.6
50-3	36.3	19.2	17.3	53.5	-17.2	-6.5	67.8	19.0	19.3	23.2	6.3	10.2	4.3	-0.2	112.0	107.9	115.4
50-4	40.0	23.0	17.7	54.5	-14.5	-3.6	69.2	21.2	19.6	21.8	6.6	10.2	4.3	0.2	114.9	109.0	117.2

	(2)	(3)	(4)	(5)	(6)	(7)	(8)	(9)	(10)	(11)	(12)	(13)	(14)	(15)	(16)	(17)	(18)
1951–1	44.0	26.8	18.0	62.7	−18.7	−6.2	77.0	24.7	22.8	22.5	7.0	9.8	4.2	0.3	118.5	114.1	119.8
51–2	49.8	32.0	17.8	58.1	−8.3	3.3	72.7	24.9	19.3	21.5	7.0	10.0	4.1	0.5	121.4	121.2	122.7
51–3	54.6	36.9	17.1	56.7	−2.1	9.2	70.8	25.0	17.0	21.8	6.9	10.0	4.1	−0.1	122.5	122.6	126.5
51–4	58.2	40.6	17.3	59.3	−1.1	10.8	73.2	25.9	18.1	22.2	7.0	9.9	4.0	−0.1	123.0	121.7	128.2
1952–1	58.7	41.0	17.5	62.4	−3.7	8.8	76.3	28.7	17.5	22.8	7.3	9.9	4.1	0.0	123.0	120.7	129.7
52–2	63.0	45.3	17.7	60.9	2.1	14.3	75.1	28.7	15.6	23.6	7.2	9.8	4.1	0.2	122.8	119.9	130.3
52–3	65.4	47.8	17.7	61.2	4.2	16.4	75.3	28.8	15.8	23.5	7.2	10.2	4.1	−0.2	122.0	118.7	130.8
52–4	66.3	48.3	18.2	64.1	2.2	15.0	78.3	29.2	17.4	24.3	7.3	10.4	4.1	−0.3	121.4	117.0	131.6
1953–1	69.1	50.5	18.5	65.7	3.4	16.5	80.3	29.7	18.2	25.0	7.4	10.6	4.1	−0.2	121.0	116.7	132.9
53–2	70.9	52.7	18.1	66.4	4.5	17.8	81.0	30.0	18.4	25.2	7.4	10.6	4.2	−0.2	120.6	116.0	134.4
53–3	69.1	50.9	18.3	65.4	3.7	16.8	79.9	29.8	17.6	25.2	7.2	10.6	4.1	−0.3	121.2	116.0	135.2
53–4	69.3	50.2	19.0	60.6	8.7	20.8	75.3	29.6	13.5	25.2	7.1	11.1	4.2	−0.6	122.0	116.7	135.9
1954–1	65.5	45.9	19.5	58.2	7.3	18.9	73.8	27.1	13.9	24.8	7.9	11.7	4.3	−0.4	123.0	117.5	136.2
54–2	60.8	40.7	19.9	57.7	3.1	14.6	74.5	27.2	14.4	24.9	8.0	12.3	4.3	0.2	124.4	118.5	136.9
54–3	60.2	39.8	20.5	57.3	2.9	14.4	74.1	27.2	14.1	24.7	8.0	12.6	4.3	−0.2	126.1	119.8	137.7
54–4	58.4	37.8	20.7	59.5	−1.1	10.8	76.7	27.7	15.4	25.4	8.2	13.2	4.3	−0.3	127.3	121.0	138.4
1955–1	59.6	38.3	21.2	63.2	−3.6	9.0	80.7	28.9	16.7	26.2	8.8	13.1	4.3	0.1	128.3	122.3	139.0
55–2	59.4	37.7	21.5	64.8	−5.4	7.6	83.1	29.6	17.2	27.3	9.0	13.4	4.2	0.6	129.0	123.2	139.8
55–3	59.4	37.7	21.7	67.7	−8.3	5.2	85.4	30.1	18.3	27.6	9.4	13.4	4.3	0.0	130.0	123.9	140.8
55–4	59.5	37.7	22.0	69.5	−10.0	3.9	87.4	30.3	19.4	28.2	9.4	13.4	4.4	0.1	131.5	125.0	141.6
1956–1	58.8	36.4	22.4	70.0	−11.2	2.8	89.0	32.3	18.4	28.3	10.0	13.8	4.6	0.7	133.0	126.8	143.0
56–2	58.6	36.0	22.6	69.4	−10.8	3.1	89.0	32.6	17.8	28.6	10.0	14.1	4.7	1.0	135.4	129.0	145.6
56–3	58.5	36.1	22.5	68.3	−9.8	3.9	88.1	32.4	16.9	28.6	10.2	14.2	4.7	1.0	137.7	131.0	148.0
56–4	59.4	36.9	22.6	70.7	−11.3	2.8	91.1	32.7	18.8	29.2	10.3	14.3	4.8	1.3	139.4	132.7	150.0

Columns (2)–(4) are from U.S. Department of Commerce, National Income, 1954 Edition, Tables 45, 46 and 49, deflated by the appropriate price index for government goods and services in Table I—Column (16) for all government, Column (17) for the federal government, and Column (18) for state and local government. These indices have been developed by freehand quarterly interpolation of the Commerce Department's annual implicit deflators of government purchases, National Income, 1954 Edition, Table 41, Lines 13–15. This interpolation was based on the quarterly movement of the consumer price index.

Column (5) is from USDC, ibid., Table 45, deflated by the consumer price index.

Column (6) is column (2) minus Column (5).

Column (7) is Column (2) minus 80 per cent of Column (5).

Columns (8)–(15) are from USDC, ibid., Tables 46 and 49, divided by the consumer price index.

* G_T = Total government purchases; G_F = federal government purchases; G_S and $_L$ = state and local government purchases; G_S = state and local government purchases; T_T = total taxes less transfers; T_{Gross} = total taxes; $T_{Personal}$ = personal taxes; $T_{Corporate}$ = corporate income taxes; $T_{Ind. Bus.}$ = indirect business taxes; T_{SS} = social security taxes; P_{G_T} = price index of total government purchases; P_{G_F} = price index of federal government purchases; $P_{G_S \text{ and } L}$ = price index of state and local government purchases.

affect decisions regarding changes in the tax structure. It is, perhaps, best to think of all actions as discretionary, but in one case heavier reliance is placed on automatic yield changes, whereas in others more emphasis is given to revision of tax yields by structural changes.

Our rough measurement of budget changes will rely on the national-income concepts of the Department of Commerce. "Government expenditures" represent their series on purchases of goods and services. Both annual and quarterly data (seasonally adjusted) in 1947 prices* are shown in Table I.

The tax yields and transfer expenditures are also based on national-income concepts. This means that tax yields generally refer to collections, except in the case of the corporate tax, which is based on the accrued liability. Both quarterly and annual data are shown in 1947 prices (Table I),† with a breakdown between federal, state, and local shown in Table II.

The difference between government purchases and taxes less transfers is the national-income concept of the budget surplus or deficit. This figure is charted for each of the subperiods discussed as a rough approximation to the impact of fiscal policy on demand. But it is unsatisfactory for this purpose in two important respects.

First, expenditures are not a wholly satisfactory measure of the effect of govern-

ment activity on demand. Quite aside from many subtle effects government spending may have on economic activity, expenditure may inadequately measure gross effects.[1] The actual impact of government activity may be more closely related, in some instances, to contract awards, for example, instead of expenditures, especially when they are changing rapidly. Even directly induced expenditures may not be counted, as, for example, when post offices are built privately and leased to the government. Expenditure then embraces only the annual lease payment.

Second, this view ignores the fact that the direct effects on total demand of government purchases are probably larger than the direct effects of taxes and transfers, since the latter must work through private disposable incomes before affecting private purchases. A somewhat better idea of the demand effects can be secured, then, if government purchases are compared with, say, 80 per cent of taxes and transfers.[2] In some instances this concept will be followed.

With this advice as our guide to indicate crudely the impact of government fiscal action, we proceed to a chronological review of postwar fiscal action. We then attempt to judge whether the action was reasonable, judged solely from the point of view of its effects on stability. The focus is primarily on the executive branch of the government, the action it recommends, and the action taken. We take at face value recommendations for tax changes, regardless of their motivation. Obviously, in the political process recom-

* At the time this paper was prepared, only annual data in constant prices were available from the Department of Commerce. Now, they have taken an important step forward and developed a quarterly series. Our quarterly series represents the deflation of their quarterly series in current prices by a price index. Our price index represents a rough quarterly interpolation of the annual Commerce price index in the government sector, the interpolation based on the movement of the consumer-price index.

There are some differences between our results and the new Commerce series, but they are not serious. It did not seem feasible at this late stage to incorporate the new data.

† The consumer price index was used to deflate the tax-transfer series.

[1] For a recent discussion of these issues, see Murray L. Weidenbaum, "The Federal Government Spending Process," in *Federal Expenditure Policy for Economic Growth and Stability*, Joint Economic Committee, papers submitted by panelists appearing before the Senate Subcommittee on Fiscal Policy, 1957.

[2] This percentage seems not unreasonable in the light of recent studies of private spending decisions. For further discussion see my paper, "Fiscal Policy in the Thirties: A Reconsideration," *American Economic Review*, Vol. XLVI, Dec. 1956.

Table II / Net Taxes in 1947 Prices

FEDERAL

Period	Personal Tax and Nontax Receipts	Corporate Tax Accruals	Indirect Business Taxes	Contributions for Social Insurance	Transfer Payments	Grants-in-aid	Net Interest Paid	Subsidies less Current Surplus of Gov't. Enterprises	Net Taxes
1945	24,084.2	12,718.8	8,858.6	7,151.0	5,356.4	1,081.2	4,143.4	1,884.0	40,347.6
1946	19,683.0	9,919.5	9,055.9	6,299.9	10,567.5	1,270.7	4,775.6	1,856.8	26,487.7
1947	19,650.0	10,679.0	7,874.0	5,008.0	8,887.0	1,738.0	4,117.0	571.0	27,898.0
1948	17,629.2	10,987.5	7,507.5	4,186.2	7,101.0	1,843.0	3,878.1	598.5	26,889.8
1949	15,181.8	9,193.1	7,648.1	4,628.4	8,206.8	2,088.7	4,056.5	692.8	21,606.6
1950	16,866.4	15,827.3	8,379.8	5,480.0	10,098.1	2,170.1	4,111.0	1,072.5	29,101.8
1951	22,580.6	18,559.1	8,189.1	6,088.1	7,444.1	2,129.3	3,916.6	1,099.9	40,827.0
1952	26,191.0	15,939.8	8,845.2	6,200.4	7,484.0	2,214.4	3,856.5	849.6	42,771.9
1953	26,977.6	16,257.1	9,332.4	6,143.5	8,061.0	2,343.5	3,901.7	701.9	43,702.5
1954	24,221.9	13,844.4	8,353.6	6,739.4	9,543.0	2,394.3	3,982.0	968.7	36,171.3
1955	26,256.9	17,128.0	9,196.3	7,784.3	10,423.3	2,540.6	3,948.4	1,518.5	41,934.7
1956	28,818.2	17,233.5	9,481.0	8,647.1	11,073.4	2,689.7	4,266.5	1,968.2	44,182.0

STATE AND LOCAL

Period	Personal Tax and Nontax Receipts	Corporate Profit Tax Accruals	Indirect Business Taxes	Contributions for Social Insurance	Transfer Payments	Current Surplus of Gov't. Enterprises	Net Interest Paid	Net Taxes
1945	1,849.2	565.4	10,432.0	477.2	1,644.2	939.5	433.7	12,185.4
1946	1,887.7	529.8	10,841.6	559.6	1,880.9	899.1	336.0	12,500.9
1947	1,856.0	604.0	10,784.0	575.0	2,226.0	798.0	253.0	12,138.0
1948	1,990.5	621.7	11,414.4	657.9	2,681.9	757.2	244.0	12,515.8
1949	2,312.8	567.1	12,643.1	750.0	2,688.7	862.5	253.1	14,193.7
1950	2,543.0	714.4	13,647.0	893.4	3,173.0	883.2	264.4	15,243.6
1951	2,571.8	754.4	13,840.7	932.3	2,515.1	939.2	226.8	16,296.5
1952	2,719.5	689.9	14,775.0	1,038.7	2,634.6	965.6	241.1	17,313.0
1953	2,844.5	670.2	15,864.4	1,132.9	2,682.8	1,054.6	270.9	18,612.9
1954	3,156.2	635.5	16,680.8	1,315.1	2,786.5	1,161.4	333.1	19,829.4
1955	3,525.2	798.0	18,177.7	1,389.4	2,947.1	1,324.4	390.6	21,877.0
1956	3,753.5	790.4	19,246.9	1,491.3	3,003.3	1,432.0	444.0	23,266.8

Source: USDC, Tables VIII and IX, divided by consumer price index.

mendations are made that are not wanted for their own sake but because they will make a tidy political record, embarrass the opposition, or lead through political compromise to the desired end result. The fascinating game of fiscal politics is, however, not our subject matter here. Nor are we particularly interested in the quarrels between the executive and legislative branches, although they will appear from time to time. Nevertheless, certain broad judgments must be made of the character of congressional response to administrative recommendations, and they come out in this review.

Appraisal of political action, no matter how academic, cannot help being controversial. Many of the conclusions reached are inevitably matters of judgment. On such matters one cannot expect unanimity. Indeed, our institutional arrangements can be improved and strengthened only through discussion, analysis, and debate.

Immediate Postwar Inflation: 1945 (4)—1948 (2)

The first of the three postwar inflationary periods followed immediately after demobilization. It was characterized by very little unemployment and by excess demand. But what fiscal steps were actually taken?

Expenditure Policy/ Governmental expenditure policy was that of reducing, sharply and rapidly, war outlays to peacetime proportions. These purchases fell by more than half in two quarters, measured in 1947 prices—from a rate of $104 billion in 1945 (3) to $43 billion in 1946 (1)—and remained around $30 billion for the bulk of the period, although they rose somewhat at the end (Chart I). All of the decrease and more was in federal government purchases—from $94 billion to $31 billion in the same period, to a low of $15 billion in 1947 (2). State and local government purchases were beginning their

steady expansion of an average of somewhat more than $1 billion per year (in 1947 prices) throughout the postwar period.

The general policy of the Administration at this time was to minimize purchases of goods and services in order to reduce inflationary pressures. Expanded programs, such as those that had to be undertaken in the first part of 1948 for Marshall Plan aid and defense, were recognized as expansionary, and led to the decision to retain existing taxes.

Taxation and Transfer Policy/ Federal government tax and transfer policy involved several specific legislative decisions in this period. First were the reconversion problems covered in the Revenue Act of 1945 and the GI Bill of Rights of 1945. Second, those connected with the expansive subsequent period in which were enacted two attempted tax reduction measures of 1947; finally, the Revenue Act of 1948 with which this period closes.

1 Reconversion

The Revenue Act of 1945 was the major reconversion tax bill.* Action was initiated on October 1, 1945, following V-J Day, and it was sped to enactment on November 8, 1945. It provided major tax reduction beginning in 1946 at an estimated rate of $6 million per year at prices and incomes ruling at about that time, in the following areas:

a) Corporation taxation—repeal of the excess-profits tax, but continuation of the carry-back of unused excess-profit credit for one year; and reduction of the corporate income-tax rate from 40 to 38 per cent.

b) Personal taxation—reduction by 3

---

* The Tax Adjustment Act of 1945, enacted earlier in the year, was a measure designed primarily to ease the financial position of business firms. It provided for the speeding of tax refunds already due business firms under existing law.

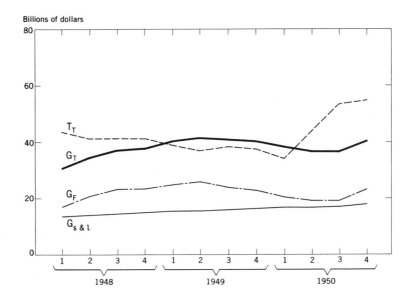

Chart I. Government Expenditures and Taxes, 1945–1948: Seasonally Adjusted Annual Rates in 1947 Prices (Billions)

percentage points in each bracket of personal income tax rates, with a further reduction of 5 per cent of the total tax, and the elimination of the vestige of the so-called victory tax by applying surtax exemptions to the normal tax.

c) Excise taxation—continuation of wartime rates.

d) Social security—postponement to January 1, 1946, of scheduled increase in tax rates from 1 to 2.5 per cent.

Looking back from our present vantage point, we can conclude that they were improper adjustments to the inflationary situation actually faced in 1946 and 1947. The policy error can be attributed primarily to an incorrect forecast of the kind of action needed, not an incorrect reaction to the situation actually expected. Both Congress and the Administration were

under heavy pressure for substantial tax reduction in the face of an expected large increase in unemployment in 1946 and later years. To some extent the Administration resisted these pressures, but they unquestionably helped to shape the program formulated. Had the inflation been clearly foreseen, the administration would surely have taken the line that it later took, namely, that tax reduction in the face of inflationary pressures was unwise.*

* Roy Blough, the chief tax adviser in the Treasury at this time, put a high gloss on the Treasury position. He argued that the Treasury position was not designed to increase effective demand in the face of an expected recession, but rather ". . . to remove from the tax laws three special wartime provisions that Congress had indicated it wished to remove as soon as possible after the close of the war. The Treasury proposed (1) to repeal the excess profits tax . . . ;

Perhaps the thorniest question that arose in discussion of the bill was repeal of the excess-profits tax. Its repeal was a close thing politically, with the weight of the Administration probably decisive. The consequences on inflationary pressures of its repeal are difficult to appraise. On the one hand, various direct controls rested on an uneasy compromise between many groups in the economy—business, labor, farmers, consumers—which was shattered by removal of the excess-profits tax. On the other, a high rate tax, especially with lower rates in prospect, reduced supply incentives, which increased inflationary pressures, subject to the qualification that private incomes after tax would be lowered by the taxes collected.

On balance, short-run direct effects of the tax were probably unimportant. The stimulus to wasteful spending does not seem to have been quantitatively significant.[†] The demand-reducing effects of the tax collections would also have been slight in the short run, given the substantial

---

(2) to reduce the income tax by the 3 percentage points that had been added to each bracket when the 'victory tax' was transformed into the normal tax; and (3) to reduce the excise taxes to their 1942 levels. . . ."—*The Federal Taxing Process* (New York: Prentice-Hall, Inc., 1952), pp. 249–250.

To argue that this was the purpose of the Treasury program is not to excuse it for its consequent inflationary effects on total demand. Secretary of the Treasury Vinson in testimony before the Ways and Means Committee placed major emphasis on reconversion problems, but at the same time indicated the desirability of the legislation as a defense against deflation. See the summary in Randolph E. Paul, *Taxation in the United States* (Boston: Little, Brown & Co., 1954), p. 410.

† The same incentives were present in 1945 and in 1946: in 1945 because the excess-profits tax was repealed as of the end of the year; in 1946 for firms falling below their exemption because the carry-back of unused exemptions was continued in that year. Yet investigation of this period leads to no clear-cut picture of excessive costs being incurred for tax reasons. See the present author and Richard Eckaus, "Operation of the Carrybacks of World War II during the Reconversion Period," *National Tax Journal*, V (September 1952).

liquidity of the reconversion period. The indirect effects in stimulating higher wage demands and the abandonment of various price and wage controls, then, may have been decisive. The early destruction of wartime controls may well have been the most fateful consequence of reconversion fiscal policy.

2 Expansion

In any event, the fiscal stimulation to total demand was sharply reduced through 1945. The over-all government budget deficit shrank from $70 billion at the beginning of 1945 to a surplus of $4 billion in 1946 (2). Throughout the rest of the period until the tax reduction in 1948, the budget surplus was in excess of $10 billion, peaking at $16 billion in 1947 (1). While government budgets might not have been as contractionary as they should have been, their direct impact on demand was still aimed in the proper direction even after allowing for the fact that perhaps 20 per cent of taxes come out of savings.[*]

The federal government's contribution toward stability was even larger than all other governments combined. As already noted, state and local expenditures expanded regularly from 1945 onward, while their tax yields expanded at a slower rate. Thus the federal government had to maintain large budgetary surpluses, larger than we had ever had in our previous history— a truly remarkable achievement. The achievement consisted primarily of holding up the existing tax structure, which in turn no more than held up real tax yields, although some gains were made by the elimination of certain wartime subsidies and the reduction of GI transfer payments.

It is perhaps worthwhile to emphasize the behavior of tax yields over this period. They rose over one-third in current prices —from $46 billion in 1946 (1) to $60

---

* On the assumption that a tax dollar reduces demand by only 80 cents, the government budget would still have been contractive from 1946 (3) through 1948 (1).

billion in 1948 (1). Yet in 1947 prices they remained almost constant—$57 billion in 1946 (1) and again in 1948 (1) just before the cut in personal taxes of 1948. It is commonly believed that progressive personal income-tax yields will automatically rise in real terms as prices rise. Yet such was not the case in this inflationary period. For the nine quarters ending with 1948 (1), the seasonally adjusted annual rate of personal tax yields (federal, state, and local) varied between $20.6 and $22.4 billion in 1947 prices. Federal personal tax collections alone were $19.7 in both 1946 and 1947 on an annual basis. In this period, therefore, these progressive taxes were essentially neutral as price stabilizers.

The story regarding corporate income taxes seems essentially the same, although they dipped more in the reconversion period. Indirect business taxes, as one would expect, fell off slightly both at the federal level and in total. Social security contributions dropped most sharply in real terms, partly from a reduction in the number of covered employees, but primarily from nearly constant money collections. Transfer and net interest payments also fell. One is driven to the conclusion from this brief survey that tax yields did not act as automatic fiscal stabilizers of the price level, effective as they may have been as stabilizers of income. In this period, then, expenditure cuts provided the initial budget surplus, while the *status quo* in the tax structure maintained this position.

For maintaining a deflationary policy, President Truman's administration can take a full measure of credit. Congress did not make the task easy. The first Republican Congress in over two decades was pressing to make good its campaign promise of tax reduction, and the large budget surpluses were an open invitation for such a policy. To achieve a deflationary policy required the indefinite continuance of excise taxes at their wartime rates under the Excise Tax Act of 1947 rather than their automatic reduction as provided by the wartime legislation.* It also required opposition to tax reduction for individuals as provided by Republican-sponsored tax-reduction bills.

The President hewed a consistent line. In his 1947 *Budget Message* he stated:

As long as business, employment, and national income continue high, we should maintain tax revenues at levels that will not only meet current expenditures but also leave a surplus for retirement of the public debt. There is no justification now for tax reduction.[3]

Again in his first *Economic Report* in 1947:

In the present economic situation, it is clear that it would be unsound fiscal policy to reduce taxes.[4]

In his *Economic Report* in July of that year:

Under current economic conditions, the accumulation of a Federal surplus counteracts remaining inflationary influence, reduces the national debt, and leaves us in a better position to deal with changing developments, whether domestic or international.[5]

Despite this counsel Congress passed tax-reduction bills in 1947 and 1948 that provided $4 billion cuts in personal income taxes. The 1947 bills were undertaken, it was said, in order to meet a possible deficiency of demand when Congress was not in session or because of the lag

* In 1945 the Administration recommended reduction of excise taxes to their 1942 rates (Paul, *op. cit.*, p. 410). But by 1947 the President in urging retention of the wartime rates stated: "When the time comes for excise tax revision, the Congress should review the entire group of excise taxes rather than concentrate attention on those that were imposed or increased during the war."—*Budget Message of the President for Fiscal Year 1948*, p. M11.
[3] *Ibid.*, p. M5.
[4] *Economic Report of the President*, January 1947, p. 22.
[5] *Midyear Economic Report of the President*, July 1947, p. 27.

in effective tax reduction after its need was recognized.[6] Both bills, however, encountered Presidential vetoes.

In late 1947 the Administration continued to view its major domestic economic problem as that of countering inflation. Indeed, President Truman called Congress into special session in late 1947 and suggested methods of dealing with it in the special message of November 17. Nevertheless, no legislation resulted.

Again, in his *Economic Report* of January 1948, he advised:

Taxes at present are providing revenues substantially larger than expenditures. It is important to maintain this favorable balance as long as the inflationary trend continues.[7]

But the growing pressure for tax reduction throughout the country was forcing some modification in his original position, and he continued:

However, certain adjustments need to be made immediately in order to protect those in the lower income groups hit hardest by inflation. . . .[8] Certain tax changes now will help those millions of families whose disposable incomes have lagged more and more behind the increased cost of living during the past year and a half.

I therefore propose that the Congress enact legislation extending a cost-of-living tax credit of $40 for each taxpayer and each dependent. To offset this decrease in government revenues [of over $4 billion per year], corporate taxes should be increased sufficiently to yield an equivalent amount.[9]

This surely was a controversial program for dealing with inflation. At best it looked as if demand for output would remain unchanged; and, if corporate taxes were

not as effective in cutting back demand as personal tax reduction was in expanding it, inflationary pressures would be higher. Since the Administration took the view that higher corporate taxes would not reduce investment spending, one can legitimately charge it with proposing an expansionary program, although it would have denied this. In any event, stated in the cloudy way that it was, the President's tax program must surely have weakened the Administration's policy position. Yet pressures were so powerful for tax reduction by then that nothing might have saved it. The Revenue Act of 1948, under which personal income and estate taxes were cut by $5 billion on a full-year basis, became law over the Presidential veto.

Economic activity showed some signs of slackening in the first quarter of 1948—the first such on a seasonally adjusted basis since 1945. Yet there was no clear evidence that the postwar boom was over at the time of the passage of the 1948 legislation. Indeed, the reports of the congressional committees accompanying the bill advocated tax reduction in order to combat inflation! It was argued in these reports that supply would increase through the greater incentives provided by lower taxes and that this would close the inflationary gap.* While one may cavil at the faulty argument,† Congress had come to the position that fiscal action, desirable as

* "By lowering tax rates in both the lower and upper income brackets, your committee's bill will increase the incentives of labor and management to produce, and will increase investors' willingness to assume business risks. For these reasons H.R. 4790 will increase production. This in turn will decrease inflationary pressures."— U.S. House, Committee on Ways and Means, *Report to Accompany the Revenue Act of 1948*, Report No. 1274, January 27, 1948.
† It is, of course, technically possible for tax reduction to be deflationary provided that supply expands enough to more than offset the additional spending resulting from the tax reduction and from the additional income generated by the added output. This is, however, a fairly large order and requires quite extraordinarily elastic supply schedules or extraordinarily low marginal spending-income ratios.

[6] See *Individual Income Tax Reduction Act of 1947*, U.S. House of Representatives, Committee on Ways and Means, Report No. 180, March 24, 1947; and *Individual Income Tax Reduction Act of 1947*, U.S. Senate, Committee on Finance, Report No. 173, May 14, 1947.
[7] *Economic Report of the President*, January 1948, p. 6.
[8] *Loc. cit.*
[9] *Ibid.*, p. 48.

it might be on other grounds, should also be justified by reference to the effects on stabilization. Warped though their analysis was, it was, perhaps, an improvement over completely ignoring the issue.

Withholding rates were changed by the legislation on May 1, 1948, less than a month after the act's passage on April 2, 1948, and disposable income rose sharply in the third quarter of 1948. While consumption also rose somewhat, most of the change in disposable income was reflected in saving. If the consumption effect had been more marked, this tax reduction could be given some blame for reactivating the price rises of the third quarter of 1948. But it appears more reasonable to suppose that the tax reduction did little short-run damage and helped to shore up demand in the subsequent recession.

Thus we come to the end of a curious period. It started with incorrect action taken for the correct reasons: tax reduction to fill up a nonexistent deficiency in demand. Economic intelligence was poor, not the reaction to it. The period ended with correct action taken for incorrect reasons: tax reduction to cure an inflation. Since the inflation had almost ceased to exist, this action turned out relatively satisfactorily.

The Recession of 1949: 1948 (3)—1950 (2)

The signs of the 1948–1949 recession were hard to read. But, after making allowances for this obscurity, one can criticize the Administration for the extraordinarily long time it took to recognize them.

Both the *Midyear Economic Report* and a Presidential message to Congress on July 27, 1948, requested re-establishment of the excess-profits tax ". . . in order to provide a Treasury surplus and a brake on inflation."[10] This fiscal program was

actually a repetition of the ones proposed by the Administration in late 1947 and early 1948, whereby tax burdens would have been rearranged. But, because the personal income tax had been reduced by the Revenue Act of 1948, that portion of the program was dropped and the increase in corporate taxes retained. Later still, in August, Chairman Keyserling of the Council of Economic Advisers testified to the Banking and Currency Committee that inflation was still the major danger.

Even on into 1949 the Administration's legislative program as outlined in the State of the Union Message and supported in the *Economic Report* of January was directed against inflation. The President stated under a heading of "Policies to Combat Inflation": "It is essential to sound fiscal policy to have a budget surplus now. . . ."[11] He then went on to propose an increase of $4 billion per year in added revenues principally from additional corporate taxation but also from estates and gifts, upper and middle brackets of the personal income tax, and perhaps added excises. In addition, he proposed an increase in social security contributions and careful limitation on federal expenditures. This program would, of course, have had a clear-cut deflationary impact. Yet, with almost every index sagging, it was defended vigorously in February 1949 by Chairman Keyserling before the Joint Committee on the Economic Report.

But by the time of the *Midyear Economic Report* of 1949 the weakening of demand had become clear to the Administration. For example, in this report the President noted the absence of inflationary strains. He therefore spoke out against reductions in his expenditure program at that time, but, curiously, he believed that

Under present conditions, immediate tax increases should be limited to raising estate and

---

[10] *Midyear Economic Report of the President,* July 1948, p. 7.

[11] *Economic Report of the President,* January 1949, p. 10.

gift tax rates and closing the loopholes in their administration. . . . At the same time, the tax on transportation of goods . . . should be eliminated. Furthermore, the loss carry-over provisions in the corporate income tax laws should be liberalized. . . . The net effect of these three changes in our tax structure, taken together, will be favorable to the expansion of business activity, without causing a significant net loss in total receipts. No changes in the tax laws which would result in a larger net loss in revenues would be justified at this time.[12]

By the beginning of 1950 the President in his *Economic Report* stated his belief that the economy had passed from inflation to stability and that the process would be completed by the rearrangement of taxes previously recommended. At the same time he decried the current budget deficit, ". . . principally because of the drop in incomes and employment in 1949, the untimely tax reductions in 1949, and the continuing heavy demands of national security programs."[13]

Despite this clumsy activity on the part of the Administration, the actual fiscal behavior of governments taken as a unit and of the federal government alone contributed to stability. Government purchases of goods and services in 1947 prices surged upward by $7 billion from 1948 (2) to their peak of $41 billion in 1949 (2) (Chart II). They continued at nearly this high rate through 1949, only falling back somewhat in the first half of 1950—a rather providential piece of timing. Although most of this change was carried out by the federal government, little credit can be given to its discretionary stabilization policies. The expansion by the federal government was due almost entirely to expenditures dictated by international tensions—an involuntary expansion from the stability viewpoint—and somewhat from increased purchases

[12] *Midyear Economic Report of the President,* July 1949, p. 8.
[13] *Economic Report of the President,* January 1950, p. 11.

of approximately $2 billion per year of agricultural products, an automatic spending response to changes in agricultural prices. State and local governments had a steady and continuous rise in expenditures throughout the period under review— about $3 billion for the whole period.

Net taxes and transfer payments declined sharply, a factor also contributing to stabilization. From 1948 (1) to the trough in 1949 (3), taxes less transfers in 1947 prices fell by $5 billion. This decrease can be attributed to the algebraic result of four major factors:

1 The personal tax reductions provided by the Revenue Act of 1948 took effect for years beginning in 1949, with withholding changes effective on May 1, 1948. The change in annual rate of tax collection amounted to $4 billion.
2 Social security contributions increased over $1 billion.
3 Indirect business taxes increased $2 billion, primarily the result of state and local tax activities.
4 Total yields automatically decreased with changes in national income in 1949, particularly personal and corporate income taxes, but these did little more than offset increases at state and local levels. In total they were of the order of $4 billion.

How much credit can discretionary fiscal policy take for the observed reduction of net taxes, a not inconsiderable factor in cushioning the decline? Almost none, it would appear from the list. The 1948 tax reduction was taken, it was said, to remove inflation, not recession, and probably was undertaken for its own sake. The *increases* in social security contributions and in state and local indirect taxation were surely not designed as anti-recession devices. But the automatic decrease in tax yields was surely an important cushion in 1949, although by 1950 it was little more than offsetting state and local tax increases.

It is an understatement to say that

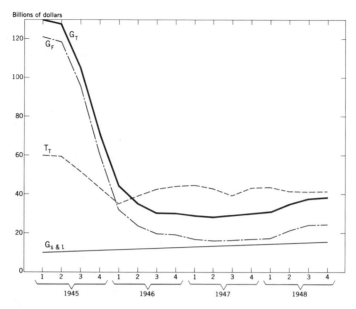

Chart II. Government Expenditures and Taxes, 1948–1950: Seasonally Adjusted Annual Rates in 1947 Prices (Billions)

little credit can be given the Administration for the reasonably stabilizing fiscal behavior observed in the recession. Its policy position was a difficult one to understand. Consider the program it proposed in July 1949 and again in January 1950, and contrast it with the one recommended in January 1948 and January 1949. In January 1948 President Truman asked for a program in which personal tax credits of $40 per capita would be offset by corporate tax increases amounting to about $4 billion in the face of a situation generally regarded as inflationary. To his credit, President Truman firmly opposed over-all tax reduction at this time. But no one would characterize his 1948 program as sharply deflationary. Indeed, the increase in consumption spending from the proposed tax credit would probably have more than offset the decrease in corporate spending from higher corporate taxes. By January 1949 inflationary pressures had slackened. Yet the fiscal program President Truman urged was one of

considerably greater inflationary impact than that proposed in the preceding year. He had dropped personal tax reduction but retained the corporate tax increases. Not until July 1949 and January 1950, when no one had any doubts that the economy was undergoing a recession, did the Presidential fiscal recommendations come back approximately to their position during the inflation—namely, to holding taxes constant. It is difficult to reconcile these two positions of the Administration, or to agree with Caplan that the reaction of the Administration was satisfactory once the economic situation was fully sized up, although such recognition was slow in coming.* The Administration grudgingly accepted a budget deficit. For-

* "Unlike its poor record in diagnosing the turning point in the economy, the record of the government was very good during this phase of the recession."—Benjamin Caplan, "A Case Study: the 1948–1949 Recession," in Policies to Combat Recession, Universities—National Bureau Committee for Economic Research (Princeton, N.J.: Princeton University Press, 1956), p. 50.

tunately, the recession proved to be primarily an inventory turn-around, and little more had to be done to pull the economy out of its slump. Fortunately, also, the Administration's fiscal requests in this period were largely ignored by Congress.

Yet these fiscal recommendations did set in motion a new tax bill in 1950. While recovery seemed under way, there was a sharp rise in unemployment in February, and this hastened action. The tax message of January 23, 1950, contained a detailed program for tax rearrangement that would have resulted in additional revenues of about $1 billion per year. Excise taxes, especially on freight transportation, were to be cut to the extent that tax loopholes were plugged. In addition, $1 billion were to be secured from revised estate and gift taxes and a rise in the corporate income tax from 38 to 42 per cent on large corporations. Surely one would not argue that this program was an expansionary one.

In the House, where the bill was debated for nearly half a year—in and out of committee—it finally emerged as essentially a tax-rearrangement measure, additional revenues coming entirely from the speeding up of corporate tax collections. Excise taxes were cut $1 billion on a broad front, and the balance was sought by raising the corporate tax to 41 per cent and by comprehensive loophole-closing provisions. But the bill also provided for reductions in the holding period (from six months to three months) for long-term capital gains, and expanded, rather than contracted, the percentage-depletion provisions. Its passage came on June 29, shortly after the Korean invasion, which was to force complete reconsideration of fiscal policy.

The Korean War: 1950 (3)—1953 (2)

Hearings were begun in the Senate on July 5 on the House bill with the understanding that, should there be serious war developments, action on the bill would be suspended. Less than a week later Secretary Snyder recommended such suspension; and on July 19 President Truman reported to Congress on the economic problems of the Korean War. He recommended more taxation, an amount that would come as close as possible to matching additional expenditures. His detailed stopgap tax recommendations were contained in a letter of July 29 to the chairman of the Senate Finance Committee. They consisted of the conversion of the House bill to one sharply increasing revenue by $5 billion per year through (1) eliminating the excise-tax reductions and other revenue-losing provisions of the bill, but retaining its loophole-closing features; (2) raising corporate income-tax rates on 1950 incomes to 45 per cent; and (3) increasing individual income-tax rates through removal of the percentage reductions in rates provided under the revenue acts of 1945 and 1948, effective October 1, 1950.*

The House bill was thus revivified. The Senate Finance Committee promptly began work on it and reported out nearly a month later a bill raising $4.5 billion essentially along the lines recommended by the President. Although some important amendments were made to the bill on the Senate floor, notably the amendment instructing the tax committees to prepare a retroactive excess-profits tax as soon as practicable, it became the Revenue Act of 1950. The new law became effective October 1—a remarkably rapid reversal of legislative policy. This speed was possible because a tax bill was already under way, and thus only half of the standard legislative journey had to be traversed. Even then, however, it was nearly three full months before the enactment of the new

* Withholding-rate changes were also made effective as of that date, and only one-fourth of the elimination of percentage reductions in tax rates applied to 1950 incomes.

legislation despite the urgency of the occasion.*

As a consequence, government fiscal action shifted from a budget surplus in 1950 (2) of $7 billion to a surplus of $17 billion in 1950 (3), and of $19 billion in 1951 (1) (Chart III). The surplus continued through 1952 but at a lower rate. Adjusting taxes for the approximate fraction coming out of savings, the direct effects of government fiscal action on demand seem to have been impressively contractive through 1951 (1). This remarkable performance accompanied an expansion of government purchases from a low in 1950 (3) of $36 billion to $50 billion by midyear 1951.

This prompt fiscal action was undoubtedly an important factor in explaining the puzzling price stability of 1951.† After the

---

* Professor Walter W. Heller points to this episode as one justifying, by its prompt response, greater reliance on discretionary policy. Certainly it can be considered as one of the better fiscal performances. But he reports the action as taken in a matter of weeks. Actually, a surprisingly long time was taken despite the prompt recognition of need and the rather noncontroversial nature of the action. See his article, "CED's Stabilizing Budget Policy after Ten Years," *American Economic Review,* Vol. XLVII (Sept. 1957), pp. 634–651.

† Bert G. Hickman in his monograph *The Korean War and United States Economic Activity, 1950–1952,* Occasional Paper 49, (New York: National Bureau of Economic Research, Inc., 1955), attributes the relative stability of the economy after its initial price rise to the inventory decumulation (both consumer and business) that could be undertaken in 1951 after the accumulations of the earlier period. He writes: "The outbreak of the Korean War in June 1950 was followed by eight months of strong inflationary pressure, due largely to abnormally heavy buying by consumers in anticipation of possible future shortages. However, the anticipated shortages did not develop, and early in 1951 consumer demand fell off. . . . In the period (1950–1952) . . . the key to an understanding of trends in economic activity is to be found in the behavior of consumers—that is, in the private, rather than the public, sector of the economy. The wide fluctuations in consumer spending that occurred during 1950–1951 were largely independent of variations in income and were strongly influenced by changing short-term expectations." (p. 203.)

It is our belief that fiscal policy in this period

sharp rise of nearly 20 per cent in wholesale prices from the middle of 1950 to the beginning of 1951, their general course was downward throughout the war period. With some lag, they fed into the consumer-price index. It, in turn, rose about 10 per cent and then remained essentially stable at the higher level throughout the war period, with transportation and rents showing the largest increases.

Two other pieces of fiscal legislation made their contribution to price stability in this period. First, the excess-profits tax called for in the Revenue Act of 1950 was provided in the Excess Profits Tax Act of 1951. Work was begun on it November 15, 1950, following receipt of the President's letter asking for a retroactive tax to July 1, 1950—the beginning of defense mobilization—that would raise $4 billion. Despite the fact that an excess-profits tax is a desperately complicated business, and the tax this time was considerably more complex than that of the Second World War on which it was modeled, it took less than two months to enact—on January 3, 1951. Here again is an impressive legislative achievement, considering the bitter opposition it faced from those who wanted no more taxes, or a higher corporate income tax instead of an excess-profits tax, or a tightening of re-negotiation of war contracts.* The ultimate law was estimated to yield $3.3

---

is deserving of a larger accolade than that given by Hickman, although relative balance is difficult to establish. The data for this period are consistent with the view that there was a gradual restoration of a more normal consumption-income relationship following the heavy consumer purchases in the immediate postwar period. While in any single quarter consumer spending did not relate closely to income, it did over annual periods in a way indicating the importance of fiscal policy in containing the rise in disposable income.

* The procedure for renegotiation of war contracts was amended by the National Military Establishment Appropriation Act of 1950 and the Renegotiation Act of 1951, passed on March 23, 1951.

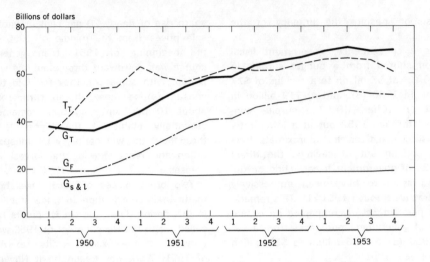

Billions of dollars

Chart III. Government Expenditures and Taxes, 1950–1953: Seasonally Adjusted Annual Rates in 1947 Prices (Billions)

billion by raising the corporate income-tax rate to 47 per cent and providing an excess-profits tax. In computing this tax, taxpayers were permitted a credit based on average earnings in the period 1946–1949 or specified percentages of invested capital, with a minimum of $25,000. A tax of 30 per cent was imposed on taxable excess profits (in addition to the income tax), with a 62 per cent over-all limit on income and excess-profits taxes.

Later in the year the other major piece of fiscal legislation—the Revenue Act of 1951—was enacted. It was started on its way at a time when large deficits faced federal budget makers. Defense expenditures were just beginning to mount toward peak levels. From the low of $19 billion in 1950 (3) federal expenditures in 1947 prices were to rise to $40 billion by 1951 (4) and reach a peak of $53 billion in 1953 (2). In his messages to Congress and the *Economic Report* filed at the beginning of 1951, President Truman asked for substantially additional taxes to keep pace with rising expenditures. His tax recommendations were for immediate enactment of an additional

$10 billion of revenue and for consideration later in the year of further taxes after determination of receipts and expenditures had become clearer. The $10 billion was to be fairly evenly split between the personal income tax ($4 billion), the corporate income tax ($3 billion), and excises, primarily of the demand-shifting variety ($3 billion). In addition, the standard recommendation was made for the closing of loopholes.

Secretary Snyder initiated legislative activity by his appearance before the Ways and Means Committee on February 5 to spell out in detail the administration program. The subsequent history of the legislation was long and stormy, passing the House on June 22 as a $7.2 billion measure, the Senate on September 28 as a $5.5 billion bill, and finally enacted on October 22 to yield $5.7 billion. Approximately $2.3 billion were from the personal income tax, primarily through rate increases that averaged 11 per cent to 12 per cent. Withholding changes became effective on November 1, and one-sixth of the added rates were to apply to 1951 incomes. Corporate income taxes were expected to yield $2.2 billion through an additional 5 percentage points on the income tax that raised it to 52 per cent on income over $25,000. Three-fourths of this rate were to apply to 1951 corporate income. The additional excise-tax yield of $1.2 billion was mainly to come from the old stand-bys—liquor and tobacco—although other commodities shared some of the increases, such as cars, trucks, and sporting goods, and the 3.33 per cent tax on electrical energy was repealed, also effective November 1. In signing the bill the President indicated his dissatisfaction and stated that he would shortly request additional revenues in order to maintain a pay-as-you-go fiscal system.*

The retroactive character of this legislation resulted in a sharp rise in tax revenues in 1951 (4) and 1952 (1), as individuals and corporations adjusted their tax payments and accruals to the higher tax provisions. But from then on the government was making heavy expenditure drains on the economy that were by no means offset by tax yields. The gap between the two was to rise to a peak of nearly $9 billion in 1953 (4) for all governments. For the federal government alone, a deficit of approximately $2 billion was recorded in calendar years 1952 and 1953. President Truman reiterated his request for more revenues in the early part of 1952. In his *Economic Report* he pointed out his initial request in 1951 for $10 billion in revenue, only half of which was met by the Revenue Act of 1951. He therefore requested ". . . at least enough additional revenues to reach the revenue goal proposed last year, by eliminating loopholes and special privileges, and by tax rate increases."[14] But by

* Secretary Snyder had informed the Ways and Means Committee in his appearance on April 2 that the second part of the President's program could be postponed until January 1952, in view of the budgetary developments then expected.
[14] *Economic Report of the President*, January 1952, p. 25.

now Congress evinced no interest in further tax legislation, and, indeed, the degree of stability in the economy was high. Consumer prices were essentially stable, wholesale prices were falling, and unemployment was less than 3 per cent of the labor force. And so it continued through the rest of the year.

On the whole the fiscal performance during the Korean War deserves high marks. Action came promptly after the need for it was correctly ascertained. While more revenue was requested in the later stages of the war than turned out to be necessary, the pressure in this direction was a salutary one. Thus prompt action meant that direct controls could be weak, since their role was merely that of buttressing fiscal and monetary policy, not the other way round as in the Second World War.

Post-Korea and Recession of 1954: 1953 (3)—1954 (4)

After assuming office at the beginning of 1953, the Eisenhower administration embarked on a program designed to end the Korean hostilities, slash spending and taxes, halt price inflation, and eliminate wartime economic controls. This latter action was first taken in February. There was a fear that it would result in an initial sharp upsurge of demand for goods and services, and a tighter money policy was followed. But the upsurge did not take place. Hence it seems doubtful whether these controls had been playing much of an active role in keeping down effective demand. Prices had been relatively stable right along. The wholesale price index had reached a peak in early 1951 and had fallen fairly steadily since that time. Consumer prices had grown very slowly. Yet monetary tightness continued through May of 1953.

Along with these actions went strenuous efforts to cut budget expenditures in order to bring the budget into balance. Yet actual expenditures on goods and services declined very slowly through 1953. In the tax field, the excess-profits tax was scheduled for automatic repeal on June 30, 1953. Chairman Reed of the Ways and Means Committee seized this opportunity to update by six months the automatic reductions in the personal income tax that would have reduced rates to their levels under the Revenue Act of 1950, and considerable political pressure was gathering behind his proposal.* To blunt this pressure, the President sent a message to Congress on May 20, 1953, decrying the budgetary situation and making commitments for tax reduction. Official and semiofficial commentaries have largely ignored his significant statement. It is with a sense almost of rediscovery that it is reproduced in some of its detail here:[15]

Tax receipts will apparently fall considerably short of our necessary expenditures during the next fiscal year. In view of this fact I have come to the conclusion that no reduction in tax rates should become effective during this calendar year. . . . Under present conditions of high business activity, coupled with a budget deficit, a tax reduction would not be consistent with attaining the vital financial objective of a sound dollar.

He went on to recommend:

1. The excess profits tax should be extended as now drawn for 6 months beyond its present expiration date of June 30.

2. The reduction in the regular corporate tax rate from 52 per cent to 47 per cent, now scheduled to go into effect on April 1, 1954, should be rescinded.

3. The increase in the old-age insurance tax from 1½ to 2 per cent on both employees and

employers, now scheduled to go into effect next January 1, should be postponed until January 1, 1955.

4. The reductions in excise taxes, which would take place next April 1 under present law, should be rescinded pending the development of a better system of excise taxation.

5. I believe that a reduction in personal income taxes can and should be made effective next January 1. This reduction will amount to about 10 per cent on the lower and middle incomes, graduating down to between 1 and 2 per cent on the highest brackets. While this reduction is in accordance with existing law, it would have been impossible to accomplish on the basis of the previous administration's budget without additional deficit financing with its resultant inflationary pressures. A reduction will be justified next January only because of reductions in proposed expenditures which the present administration has already been able to make and because of additional economies we expect to achieve in the future.

6. As you know, the Ways and Means Committee of the House of Representatives is currently engaged in a comprehensive reexamination of the existing tax structure. To help achieve this objective, I have asked the Secretary of the Treasury to present by the end of the year recommendations to remove existing inequities of our tax structure, simplify the needless complications which have developed over the years in tax laws, and generally secure a better balance of tax revenues.

Note the heavy emphasis given to pure budgetary considerations rather than to the economic situation as it then appeared or would appear: no tax reduction in 1953 because there would be a budget deficit; tax cuts in 1954 only because of the reduction in expenditures that had been or would be made. There is some oblique reference to "high business activity" and "inflationary pressures," but the latter seem to be equated with the budget deficit. Surely the interpretation given in a subsequent *Economic Report* that ". . . it seemed reasonable to expect that in another six or twelve months the boom might recede and that at such a time some reduction in taxes would become appropriate . . ."[16] seems to be a rationalization after the fact.

The diagnosis, then, was that the situation seemed inflationary. The fiscal program was conformed to this diagnosis and aimed in a deflationary direction for the moment. It was surely a gamble to recommend tax reduction for 1954 at this time, since the future course of the economy was by no means clear. Yet firm action was needed, or premature tax reduction would have been forced on the Administration. At the same time it was made clear by the Administration that it was not holding up taxes permanently. Both Secretary Humphrey and Undersecretary Folsom of the Treasury strongly emphasized the need for ultimate repeal of the excess-profits tax after its temporary six-months' extension, the former before the Ways and Means Committee on June 1, and the latter before the Small Business Committee on May 21. There was no question about the Administration's commitment at this time.

Shortly after these deflationary steps were taken, the economy began to hesitate. GNP slackened off in the third quarter and hit bottom in the fourth at a rate $10 billion lower than 1953 (2). Not until 1954 (4) was it to rebound from this trough to the earlier peak rate of 1953 (2).

The initial drop of $10 billion in GNP was, through 1953, essentially a switch of $8 billion (annual rate) from inventory accumulation to decumulation. This change is attributed primarily to the sharp cutbacks in federal government orders that changed the rate of spending by $13 billion, in 1947 prices, between 1953 (2) and 1954 (4) (Chart IV).* There were

minor changes in other components. Consumer expenditure fell slightly despite the fact that personal and disposable income remained unchanged at seasonally adjusted annual rates. (Government transfer payments rose slightly and undistributed corporate profits absorbed the balance of the change in GNP.) Nonresidential construction remained virtually the same, but the other components of domestic investment fell off slightly. Foreign investment went up by $1.3 billion, and government purchases fell by about the same amount.

Following the deflationary fiscal action of sharp expenditure reduction and postponement of excess-profits tax repeal, expansionary federal action came through automatic changes in the budget—in price supports, transfers, and automatic tax reduction as income fell. These fiscal adjustments were powerful indeed. The developing recession was followed closely by the Administration,[17] but the large tax reductions—excess-profits tax repeal and personal income-tax reduction—previously agreed to in May were undertaken on January 1. Their timing was indeed fortunate. This luck is reminiscent of the 1948 tax reduction that bolstered the 1949 recession. The estimated full-year revenue reduction was $7.4 billion, but the lowered level of economic activity at this time would place it at a slightly lower level. In any event, these reductions were well short of the deflationary impact resulting from the $15 billion cut in expenditures.

Another version of this period is contained in the various economic reports of

---

[16] *Economic Report of the President*, January 1954, p. 52.

* Bert G. Hickman, "The Contraction of 1953–4," *Review of Economics and Statistics*, Vol. 40 (February 1958), attributes the inventory disinvestment to reduced defense expenditures and also to reduced consumer outlays. This latter view seems harder to sustain. The change in

consumer spending was only $1 billion on a seasonally adjusted basis, and clearly should be treated with care. Even if there were in fact such a change, one would not expect inventory decumulation to be timed so closely with it. The linkage of stock of inventories to seasonally adjusted purchases requires considerably more examination.

[17] Robert J. Donovan, *Eisenhower: The Inside Story* (New York: Harper & Brothers, 1956), gives a vivid picture in Chapter 15 of the Cabinet concern and discussion.

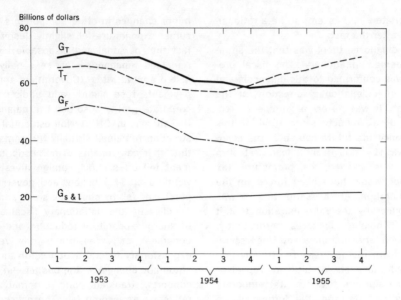

Chart IV. Government Expenditures and Taxes, 1953–1955: Seasonally Adjusted Annual Rates in 1947 Prices (Billions)

the President and the statements of Chairman Burns of the Council of Economic Advisors. In January 1954 the President wrote:

As the year wore on, tax policy was continually reviewed by the Treasury, not only from the viewpoint of moving toward a budgetary balance, but also in the light of the economic situation at large and the part that fiscal policy could play in contributing to economic growth and stability. By late September it was clear that the existing danger of inflation had passed, and that the prospective reduction of Federal expenditure would justify some tax reduction. The Secretary of the Treasury therefore announced in the plainest possible language that the Administration, besides relinquishing the excess-profits tax, would not seek to postpone the reduction of the personal income tax, averaging approximately 10 per cent, scheduled for January 1, 1954.[18]

This "announcement" was apparently made in a speech to the American Bankers Association on September 22.[19] A reading of it does not indicate anything other than a repetition of the Administration's position established by the President's earlier statement as well as the testimony of the Secretary of the Treasury himself.

In January 1955 the *Economic Report* gave a still different version. Special credit is claimed for ". . . the announcement of sizeable tax reductions before it was generally known that an economic decline was actually under way. . . ."[20] The reference seems to be to the Secretary's speech, not the President's statement, since the latter gave no hint that a decline might be under way.* Another curious

[19] Donovan, *op. cit.*, p. 210.
[20] *Economic Report of the President*, January 1955, p. 20.
* Chairman Burns gave the same version of the policy steps in his important talk to the Economic Club of Detroit, October 18, 1954. He stated: "Late in September, 1953, when it seemed plain that an economic decline had already begun but when unemployment figures still continued to move downward for seasonal reasons,

[18] *Economic Report of the President*, January 1954, p. 54.

aspect of this view of the steps taken in policy formulation is that Secretary Humphrey's speech was delivered on September 22, yet the first serious mention of recession in Cabinet meetings is reported to have been on September 25.[21]

At any rate, the commitment entered into earlier regarding tax reduction was timed fortuitously to offset the deflationary effects of the Administration's policy of expenditure reduction. There were other steps, however, which further decreased taxes and others which offset this action of which brief mention should be made.

1 The President pocket vetoed, August 6, 1953, a bill repealing the 20 per cent tax on movie admissions on grounds of revenue loss and unfair discrimination. Its full-year effect would have been about $150 million.

2 The President and Congress failed to implement the freezing of social security taxes called for in the May presidential message. On January 1, 1954, the tax rate rose from 1.5 to 2 per cent, and the yield increased on an annual basis by $1.3 billion.

3 The Administration opposed the Excise Tax Reduction Act of 1954. In his January 1954 budget message the President spoke against lowering total excise-tax yields. Secretary Humphrey made a statement in opposition to the cut before the Ways and Means Committee on March 2, 1954.[22] Nevertheless, this bill became law on March 31, 1954. It reduced revenues by $1 billion through cuts in excise taxes (other than gasoline, liquor, and tobacco) to rates of 10 per cent, with the rate on household appliances reduced to 5 per cent.

4 The Administration opposed further tax cuts in connection with deliberation on the Internal Revenue Code of 1954.[*] Because of widespread unemployment at this time, considerable agitation, largely from the Democratic side, arose for further tax cuts to stimulate the economy.

On the expansionary side was the Internal Revenue Code of 1954, the cornerstone of the Administration's fiscal program, designed to reduce revenues at least $1.4 billion in the first fiscal year of its operation. While it was reasonably well timed as a tax-reduction measure, its major purpose was certainly not to expand purchasing power but to achieve structural tax reform. Secretary Humphrey assured both congressional tax committees that it would have been introduced when it was regardless of the position of the economy, whether receding or inflating. After an acrimonious journey through Congress, this bill became law on April 16, 1954. It made a host of detailed changes, but the largest and most discussed provided a dividend credit equal to 4 per cent of dividends received (after excluding $50 per dividend recipient),[†] permitted more rapid methods of depreciation to be used, increased deductible medical expenses to the excess over 3 per cent of gross income (rather than 5 per cent as previously), and granted limited deductions for child care and for retirement income.

By 1954 (4) GNP had recovered $10 billion to its pre-recession rate of 1953

the Government announced that it would make sizeable tax cuts for individuals and corporations effective in January, 1954, so that people would have more money to spend or invest."—(U.S. News & World Report, October 29, 1954, p. 44.) Burns's later discussion of this period, even when he was no longer a spokesman for the Administration, continues to ignore the role of the President and the commitments the Administration had made. His description differs little from the preceding. See Arthur F. Burns, Prosperity without Inflation (New York: Fordham University Press, 1957), pp. 30–31.
[21] Donovan, op. cit., p. 165.
[22] Annual Report of the Secretary of the Treasury, 1954, p. 242.

[*] President Eisenhower in a speech to the nation on March 15, 1954, Annual Report of the Secretary of the Treasury, 1954, p. 221. Secretary Humphrey stated that "We cannot stand any further loss of revenue" to the Senate Finance Committee on April 7, 1954.—Ibid., pp. 228–229.
[†] The Administration originally asked for a dividend credit which ultimately would have amounted to 15 per cent of dividends received after an exclusion of $100 per recipient.

(2). There was expansion from the low point in consumption and investment, but sharp contraction in the government sector. Consumption spending had risen $11 billion from 1953 (2), almost entirely the result of increases in purchases of non-durable goods and services by an amount exceeding the $7 billion rise in disposable income. Domestic investment was up over $7 billion—residential construction was up substantially, inventory accumulation had recovered most of its recession losses, nonresidential construction remained about constant, but plant and equipment continued to fall. Foreign investment added $2 billion to demand for goods and services.

How much credit can fiscal policy take for the mildness of this recession? Examination of changes in the government's budget position shows it to have expanded in 1953 (4) and 1954 (1) and then contracted. The following seems to have happened. In 1953 (4) automatic tax reduction took place before the expenditure cuts could become effective. By 1954 (1) expenditure reduction began to take hold, but the scheduled tax cuts also went into operation in this quarter and they were substantially offsetting. Thus the combination of automatic and discretionary fiscal changes shored up demand initially, while monetary policy had a chance to stimulate residential construction. As recovery set in, fiscal policy acted increasingly as a drag. Had attention been focused on the shifting budget position of the government at full employment, its discretionary action would have been increasingly deflationary. Indeed, by 1955 the budget surplus was averaging $7 billion in 1947 prices—a sharp change from the $9 billion deficit of 1953 (4). More recovery credit, therefore, must be given to automatic fiscal action than to discretionary policy, with an important assist from foreign investment.*

* I would agree with A. E. Holman's careful appraisal of fiscal policy in this period as ". . . re-

Inflation Once More: 1955 (1)—1957 (3)

After the recovery had gathered force in 1955, wholesale prices began creeping upward, primarily because the fall in farm prices had been brought to a halt. By the middle of 1957 wholesale prices were 7 per cent above their 1955 level. In mid-1956 consumer prices began reflecting these increases, so that by mid-1957 they were 6 per cent above the 1954–1955 level. The pressure on prices seems to have been fed by every sector. GNP rose $67 billion in current prices between 1954 (4) and 1957 (2). Consumer money expenditures expanded $38 billion, but by less than disposable income, which in turn rose less than personal income, thanks to automatic stabilizers. Only 10 per cent of the expansion of consumption was in durable goods. The government sector and domestic investment rose equally in money terms—about $13 billion. While residential construction was actually down, business purchases of durable goods were going ahead briskly. State and local expenditure rose somewhat more than federal, but both components had risen by considerable amounts. Foreign investment, primarily because of the Suez oil shortage, had pushed up $3 billion. A picture of general expansion on all fronts is evident.

The budgetary position of all governments combined had shifted markedly. By 1956 budget surpluses averaged nearly $11 billion per year in 1947 prices. Government purchases had fallen off slightly in real terms—from $60 billion in 1955 (1) to $59 billion in 1956 (4). Hence the direct effect of government fiscal action on demand was deflationary as compared with the preceding recession.

The primary stabilizing effect exerted

markably similar in 1949–50 and 1953–5 . . . ," provided we take account only of the tax side. Inclusion of the expenditure side shows a marked difference. See "The Eisenhower Administration and the Recession, 1953–5," *Oxford Economic Papers*, Vol. 10 (Feb. 1958), p. 53.

by the federal government was through reduction in purchases and in the large automatic increase in personal and corporate taxes yielded by the existing structure. No new enactments of any magnitude were made or recommended,* although the scheduled reductions in excise and corporate taxes (as of April) were postponed in each year, 1955–1957. Indeed, almost every budget message in this period contained hopes for tax reduction, with emphasis on the budget position rather than on the economy. In January 1954 the President stated:

I am anxious to have taxes reduced as fast as that can be done without building up inflationary deficits. It is the determined purpose of this administration to make further reductions in taxes as rapidly as justified by prospective revenues and reductions in expenditures.[23]

In 1955 he held:

Our economy is strong and prosperous, but we should not dissipate our economic strength through inflationary deficits. I have, therefore, recommended to Congress extension for one year of present excise and corporate income tax rates which are scheduled for reduction on April 1, 1955, under present law. . . . Any other course of action would result in either (1) inadequate expenditures for national security, or (2) inflationary borrowing.[24]

And in the *Budget Message* in 1956 the President mused:

So, in the present state of our financial affairs, I earnestly believe that a tax cut can be deemed justifiable only when it will not unbalance the budget, a budget which means pro-

vision for some reduction, even though modest, in our national debt.[25]

The fiscal program of the Administration for dealing with these slowly increasing prices was passive—a holding onto existing spending and taxing structures. Hope was placed on monetary policy and appeals to labor and management to follow non-inflationary price-wage policies.

While this period was a relatively quiet one on the fiscal front, the effects on excess demand and inflation of two major fiscal policies are worth further discussion. The first is the accelerated-depreciation provision of the Internal Revenue Code of 1954. The other is the major highway program initiated in 1956.

Some economists credit the inflationary pressures of 1956–1957 to the boom in purchases of producers' durable goods and credit or blame the accelerated-depreciation provisions enacted in 1954 for this result. That there was such a boom is clear. In real terms producers' durables rose nearly 16 per cent from 1954 to 1956.[26] Moreover, they rose as a percentage of the expanded GNP. Nevertheless, this shift is not entirely out of line with past recoveries. The 1938–1939 recovery resulted in an expansion of over 10 per cent in producers' durables. In 1950 it was considerably more—but this recovery is clouded by the Korean War. From 1949 to 1950 (2) the increase in real terms was slightly over 11 per cent. Whether we can attribute the 1956 bulge to the 1954 depreciation provisions is another question. The determinants of investment are a notably weak spot in economic analysis. Yet some provisional appraisal of this view must be made despite its necessarily tentative nature.

In sum, the data are not inconsistent with this interpretation, although any kind of conclusive testing would require more

* Each year did see the unsuccessful recommendation that postal rates should be raised to eliminate the postal deficit. Not much credit can be given on stabilization grounds, however, since this recommendation was made every year, in prosperity or recession.
[23] *Budget Message of the President for Fiscal Year 1955*, p. M12.
[24] *Budget Message of the President for Fiscal Year 1956*, p. M5.

[25] *Budget Message of the President for Fiscal Year 1957*, p. M17.
[26] *Survey of Current Business*, July 1957, U.S. Department of Commerce, Table 40, p. 25.

formal specification of the investment function. Consider first the timing of producers' durable goods. The pickup in demand for business durable goods came in about the second half of 1955. Since the depreciation provisions were enacted in April 1954, it would seem reasonable for business firms to begin to take advantage of them on a large scale only after study, debate, formulation, and placement of orders, a process that might well take six months to a year or more. But unfortunately this timing is also consistent with the view that the short-term movement of producers' durable goods lags behind the movement in GNP by about this length of time, and that we observe a reasonably normal reaction of these purchases to the 1955 recovery in other sectors of the economy. Note that the trough in producers' durables was not reached until 1955 (1), whereas the GNP trough came in 1953–1954. In 1949 the trough for producers' durables came in 1950 (1), compared with essentially the same quarterly GNP rates from 1949 (1) to 1949 (3).

A second kind of question we can ask is whether the expansion in producers' durables is found in industries that would use and benefit from accelerated depreciation. The regulated industries, rails and utilities, for example, viewed these provisions with many doubts. Here we find that, of the increase in annual rate of purchases from 1954 to 1956 of over $8 billion, half was in manufacturing, over $2 billion in utilities and rails, and nearly $2 billion in trade, service, and the like. This test is also, unfortunately, inconclusive. While these purchases by manufacturing firms represented a 36 per cent increase in 1956 over 1954, the purchases by rails represented 33 per cent, by the communications industry nearly 60 per cent, by trade over 30 per cent, with considerably lower figures (less than 20 per cent) for some of the other major groups. We can only conclude that the data are not inconsistent with this hypothesis, though they certainly do not confirm it.

The other major fiscal issue revolved around the federal highway program. Reference to it was first found in the President's 1955 Budget Message and Economic Report. At this time he requested that the federal government, at a cost of $27 billion, bear nearly all the costs of modernizing interstate highways over a ten-year period. He then intended that the program be financed by an independent authority from the excess of federal revenue from gasoline and lubricating oils over the then current amount of federal grants-in-aid for roads.[27] Over a thirty-year period these revenues would have equaled ten years' expenditure. This proposal was the one developed by the President's Advisory Committee on a National Highway Program headed by General Clay. It was severely criticized in Congress. While termed self-liquidating, it provided for added expenditures of nearly $3 billion per year without any added revenues—only an allocation of existing revenues was called for. The borrowing by the highway authority was to be exempt from the debt limit against which the Treasury was continually bumping. As a government corporation, however, it would have borrowed at higher interest rates than the Treasury. There were other more technical objections raised.[28]

The program as initially formulated was a transparent device, through which Congress quickly saw, for avoiding the debt limit. The Administration seemed to take the old position that borrowing by the Treasury was inflationary whereas borrowing by a government corporation was not.

[27] Economic Report of the President, January 1955, pp. 61–62. The amount of grants-in-aid at that time was $875 million per year.
[28] For detailed discussions see Hearings on National Highway Program, U.S. House of Representatives, Committee on Public Works, (1955); and Hearings on National Highway Program, U.S. Senate, Subcommittee of Committee on Public Works (1955).

It appeared to be wholly unaware that it would have increased inflationary pressures at a time when they could be ill afforded. Attention was focused on the effect on the executive budget. The enormous potential of the program as a counter-cyclical measure was barely discussed.*

Indeed, so much criticism was aroused by this inept financial proposal that Congress developed what was essentially its own program.† While a separate authority was created for managing the highway program, new taxes were voted which would partially, although not wholly, offset the expansionary effects of the additional highway expenditures. The final program provided for average expenditure of slightly more than $2 billion per year, primarily from stretching out the construction period from ten to thirteen years. The added tax revenues were from higher taxes on gasoline and other motor fuels, on tires, and on trucks.‡ It was estimated that they would cover less than half of the federal costs,§ so that over the long run the program would be expansionary. However, since the new taxes were collected faster than the added expenditures could be undertaken, this legislation initially exerted some deflationary pressure.

On the whole, this period was not a particularly attractive one for a fiscal policy.

* A side glance was given it. "Although a steady pace of construction, financed through the sale of bonds to the public, would normally be the best procedure, expenditure and financing plans could be adjusted in the interests of general economic stability."—*Economic Report of the President*, January 1955, p. 62.
† The Administration backed off sharply from its initial proposals. See the testimony of the Secretary of the Treasury before the House and Senate Committees referred to in footnote 28. See also *Economic Report of the President*, January 1956, p. 84.
‡ They added 1 cent per gallon on motor fuels, 3 cents per pound on tires and camelback, 2 per cent of the manufacturer's value of trucks, buses, etc., and $1.50 per 1,000 pounds on trucks and buses weighing over 13 tons.
§ The revenue estimate was $14.8 billion over a sixteen year period.

While the expenditure-tax line was largely held, there was little constructive fiscal action to cope with inflation; and the road program as initially formulated was obviously the reverse.

The Recession of 1957 (4)—1958 (2)

Both the Administration and Republican and Democratic congressional members were driving for tax reduction in 1957 and again in 1958. There was obvious controversy in the Administration at the time of the preparation of the budget for the fiscal year 1958. Upon its release the usual press conference was dominated by Secretary Humphrey rather than the director of the Budget Bureau. Secretary Humphrey openly invited Congress to squeeze more water out of the budget or face ". . . a depression that will curl your hair."[29] Congress took up the challenge and cut down expenditures wherever it could. The Administration was criticized for giving ineffective and vacillating support to its own budget program and for failing to formulate a stronger program to halt the continuing rise of prices. The President did recommend, in the fiscal field:

Government can strengthen the enterprise system at this time by preserving a balanced budget. Accordingly, the Congress should continue tax rates at their present levels, and Federal expenditures should be strictly limited.[30]

Secretary of Defense Wilson had imposed a $38 billion defense-spending ceiling. Since spending in the first half of 1957 was running ahead of that rate, there were sharp cutbacks on order placements in the middle of the year. Moreover, the debt was pressed against the legal ceiling, following a decision not to ask

[29] *Congressional Quarterly Almanac*, Vol. XIII (1956), p. 691.
[30] *Economic Report of the President*, January 1957, p. vi.

for a raise in it. There were slow-ups in expenditure that forced severe financial hardship on many firms. These cutbacks were an important factor contributing to the 1957 recession, but at that moment there was little concern over the consequent slow growth of unemployment from April 1957 onward.

The successful orbiting of the Russian Sputnik in early October was the first major shock requiring fiscal action. The initial reaction of the Administration was to belittle the Russian effort and talk up our own. But talk soon turned to expanding certain aspects of the defense effort. The Republican party had essentially abandoned its position in favor of tax reduction by November. The Democrats, with whom rested control of the Ways and Means Committee, had, however, scheduled tax hearings for January 7, 1958, presumably to discuss methods of reducing taxes. But their position, too, changed as they called for sharp step-ups in the defense program to match the Soviet effort.[31]

The mid-November position of the Administration regarding the forthcoming budget was stated by the President to be that of cutting back sharply many categories of nondefense spending to keep total expenditures in fiscal 1959 at the 1958 level. He also indicated, however, that he would not let budget-balancing considerations limit the defense program.

By the turn of the year the signs of gathering recession became clear. The Administration took an optimistic view of it, nevertheless. The budget it submitted in January was based on income forecasts that were immediately attacked as unrealistically high and were shortly to be proved so. A deficit of $400 million was expected by the Administration for the current fiscal year, and a small surplus of $500 million for fiscal 1959. Because of the Administration's belief that confidence

was the major ingredient for an economic recovery, a recommendation for expansionary fiscal action was missing in the *Budget Message* and the *Economic Report*. The President did propose tax reduction to small business to the tune of approximately $140 million per year, a renewal of a recommendation he had made on July 15, 1957.[*] In addition, government workers were to be given higher pay that would amount to $1.1 billion, and payments to states from the highway trust fund were expected to rise $0.6 billion. But the President also recommended an increase in postal rates of $0.7 billion and the further postponement of the scheduled July 1 decrease in tobacco, liquor, and auto excises, and the corporate income tax. Indeed, both the administrative budget and the cash-consolidated budget were expected to show a small deflationary shift between 1958 and 1959.

A vigorous policy discussion gathered force, picking up speed after the sharp increase in unemployment between December and January.[†] Shortly before the congressional Easter recess, April 4–14, it reached a peak. Pressure for tax reduction seemed irresistible. But apparently congressional soundings at home showed that the public was less concerned about the recession than Congress had thought. A noticeable slackening of pressure for expansionary fiscal policy followed on its return.

The debate covered most of the policy facets. In one group were those favoring tax reduction for its own sake. Some urged various types of income-tax reduc-

---

[31] *Wall Street Journal* (New York), December 3, 1957, p. 3.

[*] It consisted of accelerated depreciation on $50,000 of used property acquired in any year; a partnership option for stockholders of closely held corporations; an option to pay the estate tax over a ten-year period; and ordinary loss treatment, with some maximum, on losses from investment in stock of small corporations. It was, essentially, enacted as Title II of the Technical Amendments Act of 1958.
[†] It rose from 5.0 to 6.7 per cent of the labor force, a seasonably adjusted increase of from 5.0 per cent to 5.8 per cent.

tion from increases in personal exemptions, of primary benefit to low-income groups, to devices aimed at stimulating effort, thrift, and investment by the wealthier. Others favored excise-tax reduction in order to revive demand for specific consumer durable goods, an area of demand notably weak, or to aid the railroad and transportation industry by repealing the tax on freight and passenger transportation. Still others advocated business-tax reduction by way of accelerated depreciation or rate cuts.

A time dimension was also added to the tax-reduction controversy. Since prices had moved slowly upward throughout the recession, there were fears that a recovery would add fuel to these fires. Therefore, some schemes for tax reduction carried terminal dates; for example, a tax-with-holding holiday of a few weeks or months, with appropriate change in tax liabilities in the following April.

Other advocates of expansionary fiscal policy wished to see larger government programs in areas they thought were seriously lagging. Although most favored expansion of the military program, other programs, such as research, education, highways, foreign aid, rivers and harbors, and other public works, did not lack for support.

Throughout the recession, however, the Administration essentially stood pat, relying on automatic fiscal responses and monetary policy to achieve stability. A strategy meeting of the Republican congressional and Cabinet officers early in the year was reported to have reached the decision that both a tax cut and increased public works spending should be considered by summer if there were no midyear economic upturn. But it was expected by this group that business activity would turn upward without such aid. As the recession developed, the Administration seemed to favor a speed-up of existing public works and procurement programs and then, if that failed, a tax

cut.[32] Nevertheless, the Democrats characterized the policies as inactive and inadequate. Stung by their criticism, the President released an *Economic Statement* and a *Fact Paper* on February 12 outlining the steps he had taken to counter the recession. In the fiscal area, primary emphasis was placed on the $.6 billion rise in the highway program, the placing of a higher rate of defense contracts in 1958 than in 1957, the civil public works expansion of $.3 billion, and the announcement of a $2 billion post-office modernization program.[33] This was not, however, a particularly reassuring picture. The expansion in highway spending had been provided in the initial legislation in 1956. The added defense-contract awards represented merely a restoration of the cutbacks of the preceding year, with little or no expansion in defense output.[*] The post-office modernization program of $2 billion was a five-year program, with at most $175 million to be spent in 1958 and that contingent on the passage of the higher postal rates on out-of-town first-class mail that would have collected at least as much in added revenue.[†]

Congressional pressures for more activity mounted in March as action began on bills that would cut taxes, expand highways, housing, and other public works.

[32] For example, in the President's press conference of February 26, 1958, *Wall Street Journal*, February 27, 1958, p. 12.

[33] *Ibid.*, February 13, 1958, pp. 1, 54.

[*] "What is more, high Administration officials are now willing to concede that they overrated somewhat the stimulative effect of the planned 50 per cent increase in defense orders in the current half year over the last half of 1957. They concede that this will mostly just make up for orders not placed last year." *New York Times*, March 9, 1958, p. 54.

"The sharp step-up, disclosed earlier by President Eisenhower as part of his anti-recession program, doesn't represent much additional buying. Instead, it reflects the efforts of the armed services to catch up with their original contract-letting schedules after a delay last summer and fall." *Wall Street Journal*, March 14, 1958, p. 4.

[†] The Administration was not entirely clear at first on this contingency. *Wall Street Journal*, February 12, 1958, p. 3.

The President on March 8 sent the minority leaders of the House and Senate a letter outlining steps that had been taken to cope with the recession, especially those since his February 12 statement. The major items involved a federal extension of exhausted state unemployment benefits through loans to states, acceleration of procurement programs, added capacity for lending under the housing program, and suspension of certain spending limitations under the National Highway Act‡. The extension of state unemployment benefits, estimated to cost $600 to $800 million, while obviously a helpful step in expanding demand, was subjected to criticism. First, it was held that it discouraged states from strengthening their unemployment-compensation programs.* Second, an extension of unemployment benefits was, technically speaking, a measure to soften recessions and not a device to raise full-employment demand and thus stimulate recovery. The highway program, it was estimated, would make possible $600 million in new contracts, but only in the last half of 1958.[34]

The whole program was yet something less than Congress thought desirable. By the middle of March expectations were high that a tax-reduction program would soon be announced. There was much jockeying between the Congress and the Administration to reap the political benefits from priority and a fear on both sides that such competition would produce a premature cut. An agreement between Speaker Rayburn and Secretary Anderson, neither of whom was a strong advocate of tax reduction, to inform each other in advance of any proposals, calmed the atmosphere,[35] as did unofficial estimates

of budget deficits of $1 billion in 1958 and of $5 billion in 1959 without any tax reduction.[36] In addition, several steps were taken or proposed by the Administration to accelerate existing programs. Congress was also busy with further highway bills which involved a speed-up as well as additions to the highway program, a rivers and harbors bill, and a loan program for state and local public works.†

But following the congressional recess in the first half of April a stiffening attitude was plainly evident. The President vetoed the rivers and harbors bill on April 15, belittling its contribution to economic recovery.[37] No attempt was made to pass it over his veto.‡ The farm price-support freeze had been successfully vetoed at the end of March. The highway bill, however, was approved on April 16.[38] By mid-April a deficit of $3 billion in 1958 and $8 to $10 billion in 1959 was in prospect.[39] The crucial action that indicated the shift in congressional sentiment came on the measure to extend certain excise taxes for another year beyond July 1, 1958. It was reliably reported that the House leadership and the Treasury were attempting to develop a legislative procedure ". . . aimed at burying all broad tax cuts for the year."[40] It was successful. The inevitable tax-cutting amendments to this extension act were beaten back in the House. On the Senate floor amendments repealing the excise tax of 3 per cent on freight transportation and of 10

---

‡ The so-called "Byrd Amendment" limited spending to the amount of money in the highway trust fund.
* A statement by 19 academic labor economists takes this view. *New York Times*, March 23, 1958, p. 42.
[34] *New York Times*, March 9, 1958, pp. 1, 54.
[35] *Wall Street Journal*, March 14, 1958, p. 2.

[36] *Ibid.*, p. 1.
† A careful appraisal of these programs is made by Edwin L. Dale, Jr., *New York Times*, April 6, 1958, IV:7. He speaks of one estimate within the government that the added spending for all these programs would equal $1 billion in annual rate by the end of 1958.
[37] *Wall Street Journal*, April 16, 1958, p. 3.
‡ A modified version meeting his objections went to him for signature on June 25. *Congressional Quarterly, Weekly Report*, No. 26, June 27, 1958.
[38] With misgivings, however. *Wall Street Journal*, April 17, 1958, p. 2.
[39] *Wall Street Journal*, April 23, 1958, p. 3.
[40] *Wall Street Journal*, May 12, 1958, p. 8.

per cent on passenger transportation were successful. However, only the freight amendment survived in conference and the President signed the bill. Better news on the economic front sharply reduced interest in expansionary fiscal action.

Present signs give a clear picture that the bottom of the recession was reached by the middle of the year. Little assistance was given by the federal government. Perhaps the reported vigorous differences of opinion within the Administration stalemated any prompt and decisive action.[41] Perhaps the absence of Arthur Burns to carry weight in Cabinet meetings and counter some of the arguments used to support inaction was felt. The carrying out of this passive policy by the Administration resulted in much beclouding of the actual position of the economy through carelessness about seasonal adjustments, unjustified reliance on the "prediction" that things would soon be better, and gross overstatement of the efficacy of the Administration's reaction to the recession. Certainly the policy of holding the fiscal line until the situation clarified was a defensible one and did not need such shabby support. The major criticism to be made is not of the policy itself but of the reasons given in support of it and the ways in which it was implemented. There was complete failure to make a clear-cut presentation of the issues to the public for decision and advice.

Secretary Anderson took his post at the beginning of the recession. He apparently played a key role in the Administration's policy formulation. Yet his economic views were sometimes obscure and not always consistent. On April 24, for example, at approximately the depth of the recession, he published an article on the virtue of increased consumer saving as a device for strengthening the nation.[42] Congres-

sional leaders were also somewhat reluctant to move. Speaker Rayburn obviously had doubts about the efficacy of tax reduction as a recovery device, and Majority Leader Johnson was putting no pressure on him.

Nevertheless, the debate over policy developed interesting objections to fiscal activity. By the time the recession was deep enough for fairly strenuous action to be called for, it had become widely accepted that new public-works programs would be ineffective recovery devices. However, this was partly a question of semantics, since the acceleration of *existing* public-expenditure programs was given first priority. Opposition to tax reduction also took many forms. Some held it to be ineffective in inducing added consumer expenditure, especially if of a temporary character. Others argued that a permanent tax reduction would amount to so little per week as to have no effect in inducing purchases of durable goods. In some cases these arguments were coupled with the view that, since added budget deficits would be inflationary, although no added spending would result, the consequence would be inflation without recovery. And, finally, some thought that tax relief to the employed would not feed the unemployed.

That there is little proved theory regarding the speed of response of consumer spending to changes in disposable income is an unfortunate fact. But what we do know regarding consumer response to income changes would lead to the expectation of some significant additional spending. The argument that it is too small to do any good is an argument for more, not less, tax reduction.* To argue that it would be inflationary without having any effect on spending is to become ensnared in the mythology that deficits per se are

---

41 *Wall Street Journal*, April 25, 1958, p. 8.
42 *Christian Science Monitor* (Boston), April 24, 1958, p. 14. At the same time the President was urging the public to save less and buy anything.

* The significant speech of April 10, 1958, by Howard C. Petersen, president of the Fidelity-Philadelphia Trust Company, and chairman of CED's fiscal subcommittee, gives emphasis to this view. *CED Release*, April 11, 1958, p. 5.

inflationary. Unfortunately, this latter view has cropped up often in public statements over this period both in Congress and the Administration, from the President on down. This view should not, of course, be confused with the quite reasonable one that the added consumer spending from tax reduction may feed in slowly and cause *later* inflationary pressure when other demand recovers. But if this is the fear, there is surely no practical reason why such pressures could not be dealt with later when and if they arose. And, finally, the belief that tax reduction for the employed does not help the unemployed is primarily an argument about the distribution of income. Even on these grounds, however, the distributional difference is not as large as it might seem. Income-tax reduction, provided it induced added consumer spending, would result in the employment of those now out of work. They in turn would receive tax reduction on the wages that they would earn upon re-employment.

But perhaps the most powerful argument as the recession grew was the budget deficit itself. The forecast 1959 budget deficit automatically swelled from near balance to around $10 billion in a very few months in early 1958. The news was received with alarm by many. They took the position that further tax reduction could not be afforded. Others thought that fiscal policy was a failure, since recovery was not promoted by such a large deficit. Here again we see a failure to distinguish between deficits that arise passively from existing programs and those that arise from new legislation or from administrative action which increases government spending or decreases tax rates and yields at existing levels of income. One cushions; the other expands.

Although the economy had turned the corner, the recovery was weak. While there was some indication of need for further expansive fiscal action, none was discussed. On the contrary, following the 1958 elections, the Administration bent every effort to cut expenditures further.

Concluding Observations

What can we conclude from this excursion through approximately a decade of attempted economic stability? What lessons can be learned regarding the use of fiscal policy?

1 Economic intelligence has improved over this period. The slowness with which the 1949 recession was sensed contrasts sharply with the speed with which both the 1953 and 1957 recessions were detected. But with the improvement in knowledge has come increasing ability to distort. Public officials have not yet firmly accepted the view that political decision making will be improved by making available to the public as accurate a description of the existing state of affairs as it is possible to give. Instead, current statistics may be released incompletely; seasonal adjustments may or may not be made, depending on which result is most congenial to current policy positions; and meaningless or misleading comparisons may be emphasized. Oftentimes these data may be given especial emphasis by release through the White House or in press conferences.

This attitude on the part of public officials leads also to the official rewriting of economic history. The economic reports of the President, for example, are, unfortunately, quite worthless as descriptions of the course of fiscal policy. Instead of accepting the backing and hauling, inconsistencies, false starts, action on inadequate information, that characterize actual policy formation, they are written with omniscience and self-justification.

There seems little that can be done to suggest remedies for this situation. Obviously it is desirable to have public servants who assist rather than mislead public discussion. Perhaps an independent statistical body could release these data along with their interpretation of them, so that interested users would have some place to turn.

This administrative attitude toward knowledge has even extended to the creation of the data themselves. The most obvious and recent example is the budget estimate of January 1958. It was administration policy not to recognize a decline in incomes below the preceding year since such a decline would imply inadequacy of policy. As a result, the budget was obsolete by the time of its preparation.

It might lead to greater clarity in fiscal policy if the budget estimating procedure urged by the CED and other groups were adopted. Under such a procedure the "full employment" amounts of revenues and expenditures would be forecast. Such a budget could be supplemented in considerably less detail by one or two alternative budgets that indicated alternative forecasts of economic activity. In this way the politics of budget making could be further channeled toward giving the public more information on which to act.

The importance of such a procedure is heightened by the common failure to distinguish between movements along the aggregate demand schedule (automatic responses) from shifts in the schedule (autonomous changes). In a rapidly changing economic environment it becomes difficult for legislators and the public to know whether changes in the budget position result from modifications in the tax structure or spending rates, or from automatic budget reactions to variations in output.

2 Understanding of economic analysis has advanced considerably over the decade. As long as output was slumping in the last recession, public discussion of fiscal policy was concerned primarily with questions of timing and choice of fiscal instruments. This is as it should be. Some clouding of this impression is found toward the end of the recession, when the size of the budget deficit which was primarily a pas-

sive reaction to the recession frightened some, and when public statements were made that incorrectly equated budget deficits with inflation. But the business community has clearly advanced a great deal from its attitudes in the thirties.

3 Discretionary fiscal policies cannot claim much credit for stabilization operations over this period. The 1945 tax remissions were premature; the 1948 tax cuts were carried out for precisely the wrong reasons; nothing much was undertaken in the 1949 recession except to carry out policies undertaken for other reasons; policy in the early portion of the Korean War was correct and effective; net deflationary fiscal policies were followed in the recession of 1953–1954; little or nothing was undertaken fiscally to reduce the inflation of 1955–1957; and in the 1957–1958 recession fiscal action was relatively slim.

Yet this is too harsh a judgment. There was less moving in the wrong direction as more understanding was acquired. Expenditures, the major shifts in which are marked primarily by changes in defense policy, have tended to be stabilizing factors in recessions and inflations. State and local governments have steadily increased expenditures and taxation throughout the postwar period, but the changes here have been predictable, helping in recessions, hindering in booms. Indeed, the degree of stability, both of price and employment, in the postwar period was extraordinarily high for this country.

4 Automatic fiscal stabilizers have played an enormous role in postwar recessions. They have sharply reduced the secondary repercussions on income from shifts in inventory accumulation or decumulation, thus aiding materially in stabilizing consumer expenditure, and, in turn, business investment in plant and equipment. Taxes and transfer expenditures show great sensitivity in real terms to changes in output. They do not show this same sensitivity to price changes, notably in the 1946–

1948 period. This means that the economy is much less protected automatically against price change than it is against changes in output. Put in another way, automatic fiscal stabilizers are much stronger in reducing output fluctuations than price fluctuations. Their efficacy depends primarily on tax rates.* As between the 1946 tax structure and that at the end of the period, there may have been some slight improvement, mainly from broadening social security coverage. As compared with the thirties and twenties, vast progress has been made. But as compared with, say, the middle of the postwar period, automatic fiscal stabilizers have been reduced.

5 One sees in this period a repetition of the following policy pattern. First, there is a growing awareness of a recession or inflation, but more information must be gathered to be sure of the pattern. By the time of reasonable certainty, the economy is well into the inflation or deflation. In the case of recessions, where the problem arises most vividly, many fiscal instruments are then rejected as being too dangerous in their timing. New public works, for example, have often been placed in this category. Permanent tax reductions have also been viewed with alarm. And temporary reductions carrying a restoration date were rejected in 1958 because, it was argued, the additional purchasing power would be saved rather than spent because of their temporary character. Thus most fiscal instruments are discarded except the speed-up or slowdown of existing expenditure programs, and this procedure may offer inadequate flexibility. Thus discretionary fiscal policy is enormously weakened.

It points up a number of problems. Is there a factual basis for these arguments?

Have we extended our knowledge of the timing of public-works outlays beyond the thirties? What kinds of expenditure patterns can arise under public-works programs? Have adequate plans been formulated? How much do we know about the speed with which permanent or temporary tax reductions feed into disposable incomes and consumer spending? Are there genuine differences between income and excise-tax reductions? Would tax credits for business investment work promptly? Are there other, more flexible, fiscal devices? In a word, much more research on the timing of fiscal policies must be undertaken before we can resolve some of these questions.

Unfortunately, the chance to try a promising fiscal device was rejected in the last recession. The interesting proposal of temporary tax reductions, including withholding tax forgiveness, appears to be the most flexible fiscal change yet proposed. While not new,* it has never received as much support as it did in the 1958 recession. In essence, it permits a sharp, temporary change in the rate of disposable income without a commitment to a permanent change. Any amount of withholding forgiveness can be achieved when coupled with appropriate adjustment of final liabilities in the subsequent April. For example, if the starting income-tax rate were 20 per cent, three months' withholding forgiveness (and one declaration) would result in a computation of final liabilities for the whole year at three-fourths of this rate, or 15 per cent. Half a year's forgiveness would result in the use of 10 per cent as the starting rate. In neither event would the permanent starting rate change.

In principle, it would permit a prompt flexible adjustment to the developing eco-

---

* Much too much credit in this area is given to trivial modifications in the tax structure that improve the timing of tax collections, such as extension of the loss carry-back from one year to two years.

* Albert G. Hart has had this idea for a long time. He spelled it out in a book written jointly with the present writer, *Financing Defense* (New York: Twentieth Century Fund, 1951), pp. 139–141.

nomic situation. It could be carried out on any scale believed desirable—one month or more up to twelve. And it should have powerful leverage, provided consumers will spend the proceeds. On this, further study is needed.

6. The inflexibility of government expenditure is impressive. Major policy changes—Marshall Plan, Korean War, post-Korean War, and post-Sputnik—took a long time appearing as changes in government expenditures. This behavior raises the question whether or not expenditures are a satisfactory measure of the impact of the government on economic activity or whether better series could be developed, such as appropriations, orders, output, or some combination of them.

7 It seems somewhat startling, but, with two exceptions, broad tax reductions or additions were undertaken only when there were (roughly) corresponding expenditure changes. In other words, discretionary tax changes have not been made for stability purposes. The tax reduction of 1948 was undertaken alone, but not to shore up a recession. On the contrary, it represented the giving away of a large budget surplus in an inflationary period. The other possible exception, on a small scale to be sure, was the 1954 excise-tax reduction of $1 billion over administration protests. But since expenditures were being cut by $15 billion at this time, even this reduction is not a genuine exception.

The generalization that all of us have made from time to time—that expansionary fiscal action will be taken promptly in a recession—and that, therefore, there is an inflationary bias in fiscal action is simply not borne out by the facts. Fiscal bias there may be. But the bias toward larger budget deficits in the time of recessions has not been present in the postwar period. In this country, therefore, we cannot take it as obviously true that a properly stabilizing fiscal policy will be undertaken.

Chapter Seven

A New Type of Capitalism?

■ By the early 1950s many Americans, including such well-informed observers as the editors of *Fortune*, thought that the United States had entered a new phase or stage of capitalism. The editors cited such factors as higher wages, fairer labor relations, greater personal security, and more social responsibility by corporate executives.[1] Unquestionably, the need for high-level consumption in an advanced industrial capitalism was more clearly recognized than in earlier decades. This appeared to make management, particularly in industries dominated by large corporations able to control prices, less resistant than formerly to wage and salary increases. Pension funds, social security, and unemployment insurance helped to stabilize the economy in recessions by maintaining certain minimums of investment and consumption. Government-guaranteed mortgages permitted workers to own their homes.

[1] See *U.S.A.: The Permanent Revolution* (Englewood Cliffs, N.J.: Prentice-Hall, Inc., 1951).

Physically, the automobile and to a lesser degree the airplane were relocating population and economic activity. All types of employees could live in the suburbs or even beyond and commute by automobile. Plants, offices, laboratories, and shopping centers were moving to the urban fringes of metropolitan areas and drawing their workers from both the central city and the nearby countryside. Big companies could have many medium-sized plants within easy reach of executives by company airplane, rather than a few gigantic factories.

In some industries government demand for military purposes was more important than that of civilian consumers, and in these industries the government supported a high level of developmental research. Also, many big companies had come to regard research as a necessary aid in the unending race with competitors. As a result, research in general, in the universities as well as in industry itself, proceeded at levels never approached before World War II.

In the mid-1960s it was too early to tell whether these elements added up to a new major stage of capitalism in the United States and in parts of Europe, where they were also present. From 1950 on, growth rates, employment, and stability in business activity had been more satisfactory in the Western capitalist world than they were from 1920 to 1939. In all the leading nations living standards, as measured by the consumption of refrigerators, radios, television, automobiles, and other semidurable goods, were higher than ever before. On the other hand, there were potentially unstable elements in the situation. A trend toward inflation of prices was present in all the economies, and there were continuing difficulties over international payments. Capital formation was proceeding rapidly in some European nations, but showed a tendency to lag in the United States. In the United States the economy was geared to a very high level of military spending, nearly 10 per cent of gross national product. Was the system capable of resisting the forces that had led to financial panics and ensuing periods of stagnation in the past?

The Modern Corporation

■ By the middle of the twentieth century manufacturing, finance, transportation, and public utilities were each dominated by the practices of large corporations. The census still showed that independent retailers were the most numerous businessmen, but big-company executives were the progressive spokesmen and recognized leaders of business. These men lived in a different world from that of the owner-manager or small proprietor. Just how different it was is suggested by the fact that in the following selection Oswald Knauth, a big-company executive himself, as well as a professional economist and a director of the National Bureau of Economic Research, calls the new business system "managerial" as distinct from the old "free" enterprise. The manager who fully recognized the change business had undergone adopted principles and goals quite different from those of the entrepreneur operating in an uncontrolled free market, and the new situation affected the whole range of managerial relations, from those with stockholders to those with labor.

Oswald Knauth
The Transition from Free Enterprise*

Ordinarily managerial enterprise has developed from free enterprise. By 1900, large companies, family-owned and family-operated in most instances, had accumulated such an investment that stability of the economy and a continuity of operation were essential to the maintenance of its value. Many individual companies in the steel, agricultural implement, oil, milling, textile, and shoe industries had attained an importance that made them factors in stabilizing the market. As their owners managed them in their personal interests, they had some of the characteristics of free enterprise, coupled with the power acquired through growth. They were on the border line between free and managerial enterprise.

Take the case of J. Ogden Armour. Ray Stannard Baker in *American Chronicle* suggests that Mr. Armour was lacking in sincerity when he proclaimed the gospel of free enterprise. He none the less acted according to the needs of the meat-packing system which he was creating at the turn of the century.[1]

I recall thinking how curious Mr. Armour's position was. On the one hand he commended competition as the only fair regulator of industry, asserting that the law of supply and demand was the only law that could operate successfully in controlling the cattle, beef and fruit business. On the other hand, he was himself, so far as I could learn, secretly doing his best to prevent competition and build up monopoly in every business with which he was concerned. In other words, he wanted free competition for the people who dealt with him,

and he wanted unrestricted power to do away with competition when he dealt with them.

Well, I liked Mr. Armour, but it seemed clear to me that his likableness had little to do with the hard problems of social injustice we were studying. One of his strange defenses of his situation, in which there seemed an implied admission of the evils of the system under which he was thriving, was that even if he should step aside the man who took his place would be forced to play the game just as he did. He would still have to meet the competitive practices of other packers.

Pressure of events was compelling every man in Mr. Armour's position to do precisely what he had done. Management had to think in the terms of the morrow rather than of the day. The fixity of capital investment, the pressure of stocks flowing from mass production, the multiplicity of skills that go into making the finished product, the need for continuous distribution, all these demanded an integrated organization. When capital equipment became so large, specialized, and unwieldy that it could not be moved easily, its value could be extracted only over a period—in most instances several years. To maintain continuity in the flow of raw materials to the manufacturer and of finished products to the consumers, internal and external conditions had to be shaped.

This decline of the self-regulating, impersonal market was not confined to the United States, but was world-wide. The monetary orderliness imposed by the gold standard was crumbling as managed currencies aimed at local stability were instituted in many countries. International balances no longer adjusted themselves automatically. The accompanying political changes were the collapse in many instances of liberal states and shifts in the balance of power. The institutional frame

* Reprinted from *Managerial Enterprise* by Oswald Knauth. By permission of W. W. Norton & Company, Inc. Copyright 1948 by W. W. Norton & Company, Inc., pp. 25–57.
[1] Baker, Ray Stannard, *American Chronicle* (Scribner, 1945), p. 209.

within which the individual entrepreneur had been accustomed to work out his own destiny was losing its strength as a protective shield. Business had to shore up its own bulwarks. It had to safeguard its markets, its sources of materials and labor, and its relations to foreign as well as to domestic competitors.

These new demands could not be met by individual entrepreneurs, each acting on his own. They required a system in which were coordinated all the steps from the extraction and purchase of raw materials to the distribution of the finished product to the ultimate consumer. Long-range planning took the place of the astute judgments with which the entrepreneur met the problems of the passing hour. Success depended more upon carefully considered policies, designed to fit present realities and to allow for future potentialities, than upon the seizure of momentary advantages. Immediate profit was no longer the sole objective. In its place an established trade position became paramount. Management found that stressing immediate profits led to future losses. Over-shrewdness in driving a bargain with a regular customer aroused antagonism, which might be repaid with interest when the tables were turned. No great managerial enterprise has ever been erected by skillful trading alone. In the long run, value must have been delivered.

The life blood of managerial enterprise is a steady demand. This is sometimes general, but is often localized in a community, class, or group, or in another industry. Chewing gum, soft drinks, prepared goods are consumed by the general public, harvesting machines only by farmers, and locomotives by railroads alone. For each product, however, there is a broad base of demand. In seeking to assure continuity of operation businessmen have found that they had to build up a reputation that would attract and hold customers, have a convenient location, contracts that would ensure sources of

material, trade connections, a complete series of services, research departments, patents, and secret processes. Any trade advantage that might be of use was eagerly followed up and cultivated. The goal was to gain over the market as great a control as possible. The number and importance of the trade advantages determined the degree of this control and some degree was ordinarily achieved. This type of control was reflected in the steadiness of demand and volume rather than in the price.

The coverage of this type of demand is constantly spread by advertising in magazines with nation-wide circulations and over the radio. Thereby manufacturers acquaint the entire country with the virtues of their products. Rapid distribution by post, rail, truck, air, and automobile, together with the ability to supply identical products over a wide area, unify the patterns of demand of urban and rural dwellers in East and West, North and South. The big mail-order houses, chain stores, and some department stores have a national demand for their products that can be forecast. They can place orders many months ahead, and on these manufacturers can count as a backlog for an efficient and economical schedule of production.

Many manufacturers, exasperated by their failure to anticipate the unpredictable orders of wholesalers, assure themselves of a constant market by setting up their own distribution systems. The Coca-Cola Company, oil producers, tire, and radio manufacturers can estimate to a nicety the consumption of each locality. Automobile companies organize intricate systems of distribution that are marvels of efficiency. Standardized services are widely available for the repair of standardized articles. When sales fall below the projected quota, new pressure devices are immediately applied to restore them. Advertising in newspapers and on the radio is intensified. Special inducements are offered. Surveys are made to discover customers' preferences, and then no effort is spared to satisfy expressed desires.

But local and group prejudices run deep and are as difficult to overcome as they are to explain. Regions and groups are partial to certain brands. Utica sheets are popular in one city, Pepperell sheets in another. Pepsi-Cola outsells Coca-Cola in certain localities. It is an expensive and risky process to attempt to break into a market already pre-empted by another dealer. Stocks must be carried and services installed to be ready to meet the demand it is hoped will eventuate. Until that hope is realized, turnover may be so low that products will lose their freshness. Then overhead expense and wages become disproportionately heavy. Thus before consumer acceptance is won, if it is, many months may have elapsed, and the cost may have been ruinous.

On the other hand, if a product cannot be bought for some time, consumers may switch permanently to another. The habits and preferences of consumers are strong, but they are fickle. Perhaps the most serious effect the war had on some companies was to remove their products from the market. Fear that their products would be forgotten explains their feverish exertions to keep their names before the public.

The circumstances giving rise to managerial enterprise in the United States were also at work in other parts of the world to a greater or lesser extent, especially in industrial countries. But governmental policies have differed. In widespread instances, particularly in England, France, and Germany, government invested in industry on a large scale, contributing a substantial portion, often the bulk of the capital, but usually appointed only a minority of the directors. These "mixed" corporations were common in railroads, shipping, public utilities, and munition plants. They are unknown in the United States, where the policy of the antitrust acts is to compel competition, especially in prices. The Department of Justice has attacked even railroads on their adoption of the conference method of fixing rates. Although no railroad is permitted to set its own rates, rates between the same two stations on competing lines must be identical, and all rates must be approved by the Interstate Commerce Commission. Relations between management and government have been at arm's length, if not actually hostile.

With the depression of the thirties, some governmental agencies became more friendly. This tendency grew more pronounced during World War II. Through the Maritime Commission appropriations, the aviation services of the War and Navy Departments, the mail subsidies of the Post Office, the loans of the Reconstruction Finance Corporation, government has lent a helping hand to industry. None the less, managerial enterprises have, in general, remained independent entities.

Everyone who has taken part in the management of an old going concern is impressed with the sheer momentum it has acquired. Orders come in and production goes on as a matter of routine. Driven by constant pressure, the busy executive is occupied with the tasks that flow to him. Each day, each hour brings to him reports, letters, visitors, and meetings. These are problems that require attention and must be settled. Occasionally, he must rise above this mass of detail to examine the operations, tendencies, and policies as a whole.

It is around articles that can be readily produced in any quantity desired and have a widespread demand, that managerial enterprise grows. These may be termed articles of commerce—automobiles, cigarettes, and thousands of others. With these the difficult problem is not production. The vital task of management is that of distribution, and this involves inciting rather than filling the demand. Once a producing unit has been organized, its forces can be guided in one direction as well as in another. Facilities can be expanded, provided the demand is sufficiently strong and permanent. When the increase in output can be made at an equivalent or smaller cost, the basis for this economy of plenty has been laid.

One of the fundamental differences between free and managerial enterprise lies in the relation between demand and supply. The free enterprise economy presupposes a scarcity of goods. An increase in demand leads to the utilization of marginal resources and less efficient methods. This tends to raise costs. Prices respond to the rise of costs until they reach a point where the demand tends to decrease. Then a new equilibrium at a higher price is found.

Managerial enterprise, on the contrary, possesses for all practical purposes an unlimited ability to produce the best sellers among commercial articles. When demand seems to be rising, ingenuity is directed toward meeting it. Productive capacity is stepped up, labor-saving machinery installed, mass methods and economies are introduced. This tends to lower costs and prices. Prices are set at lower levels to induce demand and to bring products within the purchasing range of a fresh set of consumers. Renewed efforts are made to find and invent other uses for articles. From luxuries, they become necessities.

The process spirals. Increased use of articles calls for an increase of co-related facilities and services. New industries are born. As they achieve quantity production, they too have lower costs and can reduce prices. The demand for raw materials encourages a search for new and cheaper sources of supply. The quantities bought are so tremendous that transport can be regularized. New skills are developed, employment rises, and output per worker

multiplies. This culminates in higher wages, higher returns to capital, and lower prices. The economy of plenty is ushered in. The struggle for existence becomes a struggle for advantage. A desire for betterment replaces need as the motive power of individual action. The gloom of the classical economist gives way to the hope for an age freed from poverty. And the potentialities seem only to have been tapped.

Despite the shadowy contours of managerial enterprise, which in many instances is but partially matured, it is quite possible to set up a table of contrasts with free enterprise.

Free Enterprise	Managerial Enterprise
Fluid capital	Sunken capital
Flexibility and mobility	Standardization and a relative rigidity
Concern for the moment	Concern for the future
The identity of ownership	The separation of ownership and management
Unimportance of the individual entrepreneur	Each unit affects the market
Action is adjusted to impersonal market conditions	Market conditions are shaped by policies
Increased demand has its main impact upon price	Increased demand has its main impact upon production
Costs are estimated accurately	Costs are based upon actuarial assumptions
The goal is immediate profits	The goal is a stable and adjustable system, the functioning of which creates profits

Free enterprise operated under the mythical belief that the acts of individuals were consonant with the welfare of the community. This mutuality of benefit was supposed to be achieved through competition on the free and impersonal market. No such preordained harmony can be claimed for managerial enterprise. At times it seems to pursue policies beneficial to itself but harmful to the community. Indeed, Keynes has argued that economic equilibrium may be achieved at a level lower than the highest of which the economy is technically capable. He points out that the balance of productive forces which management attempts to maintain on an even keel does not necessarily bring about full employment of the working population nor the maximum of output. By this he means that the interest of the individual enterprise does not coincide with the national interest, and indeed may be antagonistic to it. Whether such a criticism can be substantiated can be answered only after examining the structure and processes of managerial enterprise internally and externally. And this is our next task.

The Change of the Corporate Pattern

The corporation originated with a group of owners, the participation of each being reflected in the number of his shares. These shareholders selected from their own number a board of directors. These directors comprised the largest and most capable owners, who in turn, again from their own number, selected the active managers. Thus, management and ownership were intimately bound together. This close relation persists in many private corporations whose stock is not ordinarily sold on the market. Indeed, in some of these corporations, an owner cannot dispose freely of his shares. To a lesser degree, it persists in corporations where the managers themselves own or represent large holdings.

In the amalgamations during the first decades of this century, this close owner-management relationship continued to exist. Many of the family industries that entered into these mergers dominated the amalgamations through their large holdings, thereby extending their power. However, with the passage of time, ownership and management began to drift apart. The owner-managers were gradually replaced by men selected for their executive ability, regardless of whether they were stockholders. Stock was sometimes divided among children and grandchildren, or sold to the public. When it was held in trust the owner-management concept was again stretched, the trustee becoming a director primarily to watch over the interests which he held for the benefit of others. Later, the bankers who floated issues to the public often became directors in order to maintain contact with the conduct of the affairs of the company. The personal touch between owner and employee that had characterized small concerns was lost. Employees were counted in the thousands, and were scattered in different localities. The new immigrants who furnished most of the unskilled labor came to be looked upon as a race apart.

Stockholder

This widespread dissemination of corporate ownership has converted the modern stockholder into an absentee owner. Corporations now speak proudly of their large families. The American Telephone and Telegraph Company boasts of having over 600,000 stockholders, no one of whom owns more than one per cent of the total stock. Many corporations have stockholders running into tens and hundreds of thousands. Even their long lists of stockholders understate the breadth of distribution, for many shares are held by dummy corporations, on whose books the holdings are credited to the individual owners. This anonymity cuts the true owner off completely from management. Not being recorded on the books of the company, he receives his reports only indirectly, if at all, and he has no communication or personal relation with management.

Though he may be interested in the enterprise, he cannot find out what is going on. When he anxiously inquires for information beyond that provided in the reports, management is polite, but firm. He is told that his suggestions will be given due consideration, but that he is entitled only to such facts as are made public. The excuse is that the granting of further information would be favoritism and provide one stockholder with inside knowledge unavailable to others. Even for insiders, a correct understanding of all phases of any large enterprise is extraordinarily difficult. Properties may be scattered, and policies intricate, contracts carefully guarded and good will not easy to evaluate. Capital value may appreciate or depreciate substantially before the evidence appears in the balance sheet.

There is a strong tendency to support management blindly. The exception is provided by the case of a few professional obstructionists or reformers. Occasionally an individual will take advantage of his legal right to voice his protest against some policy. But objection is usually futile, and soon forgotten. Many stockholders have such a feeling of frustration that they do not bother even to sign and return proxies. To "get out the vote" for a quorum at the annual meetings of stockholders is difficult. The stockholder usually expresses his lack of confidence in a corporation by selling his shares. He

seldom succeeds in having a new management hired. John D. Rockefeller, Jr., is among the few to have made an effective protest and even he, despite his large minority stock ownership in the Standard Oil Company of Indiana and his great influence, barely succeeded in his campaign to change its management in 1933.

The diversification of investments, though sound from the standpoint of the individual, reduces his need to be actively interested in wise and proper management. Absentee ownership is extended by other circumstances. Investment trusts trade in shares solely for the benefit of their own stockholders. These might be called "hot" shares, for they are always for sale at a price. While an investment trust must publish quarterly a list of the securities it holds, the average stockholder does not compare lists and note the changes. Moreover, in recent years a new profession, the investment counsellor, has arisen, eager to assume responsibility for diverting clients' holdings to the most profitable channels. He is in duty bound to advise the sale of holdings if he deems other investments safer or more promising. Though the evaluation of the business is thus put into trained hands, the concept of ownership as a stake in it is further diluted. From investors who were part owners with active interest in the progress of a corporation, stockholders have thus been transformed into speculators who are claimants on such portions of income as the directors declare in the form of dividends.

Director

The role of directors of corporations has evolved along several lines. Originally the directors were the working mouthpiece of the stockholders. Their duties and responsibilities were not specifically defined simply because there was no pressing need for sharp delineation. By right of ownership and ability, they were the policy-making management. Such assistance as they needed in management at the lower levels was purchased, just as labor was hired and capital borrowed.

As time passed, in the course of averting bankruptcy, negotiating mergers, or financing expansions, a new type of director was introduced. The financiers who made the arrangements had themselves put on the board of directors. The purpose at first was to establish a contact through which they could keep themselves currently informed about the undertaking. But once the barrier of ownership had been let down, directorships too frequently became the means of obtaining advance information. Favors and back-scratching deals were enormously profitable. It was not extraordinary for a man to be a director in thirty or more corporations.

Many of the reasons for infusing new blood into the board of directors were entirely proper. Lawyers, real-estate experts, officials of other corporations with which the concern had intimate relations might become valuable assets. Certain of the more capable managers who had grown up in the business, even though they owned little or no stock, asserted themselves and became directors. However, with the dilution of ownership and management, private deals detrimental to the interests of the stockholders became more feasible.

Abuses, real and alleged, led to prying the lid off corporate affairs in litigation and Congressional investigations. Finally there was set up the Securities and Exchange Commission. Directors found themselves subject to suit by disgruntled stockholders for the company's losses. The business community was startled when the General Motors Corporation and certain of its directors were sued on the ground that bonuses paid officers had been illegal. At first, the case was not taken seriously, for the procedure followed seemed to meet all the requirements. Although the principle of bonuses had

been approved by the stockholders and had the blessing of counsel, the court held that bonuses must bear some relation to the value of the services rendered and that otherwise, they constituted gifts. Witness the following judicial utterance in *Winkelman* vs. *General Motors Corporation:*[1]

If it is shown that there were breaches of duty and the compensation voted in such breaches bore no relation to the services rendered, the directors responsible for voting the compensation may be held personally liable.

The request of the defendants that the case be dismissed was granted only in respect of the bonuses paid in 1931, 1933, 1934, and 1938. In these years they were held not excessive. It was disallowed for 1930, 1935, 1936, and 1937. No bonus had been paid in 1932. Subsequent review resulted in an order by the lower court that the sum of $4,500,000 be returned by the recipients to the Corporation. Even when directors consider some course of action above reproach, they do not venture upon it if their legal advisers believe it may bring them afoul of the law.

Whether directors should direct or whether they should confine themselves to the selection of management and then its critical appraisal is a moot question. As a board of directors is constituted today, it is in no position to manage. The members include large stockholders, representatives of institution-held blocks of stocks, financiers inheriting ancient connections with the corporation, experts of various sorts, and active managers. The last-mentioned group, which is usually about half the total board, are the only members equipped to direct the daily affairs of the enterprise. Indeed, they are the more capable in inaugurating policies as well as carrying them out. But since they make up a large section of the

[1] 39 Fed. Supp., 826 ff.; also 44 Fed. Supp. 960, and 48 Fed. Supp. 485, 490, 500, 504.

board, it is difficult for the board as a whole to act as an impartial tribunal when their ability is called in question. The other members either lack the time or inclination, or are not sufficiently in touch with the company's affairs to direct actively. However, they are men of wide acquaintance, much experience, and with an intense personal interest, both financial and moral, in the success of the enterprise. Hence they are eminently qualified to appraise, with a sure touch, programs and results. Again, their varied contacts give them a wide range of choice if it becomes necessary to select a new management. None the less, recent developments have tended to push each group into the field occupied by the other. Directors are viewed as responsible for the acts of management, yet managers select directors, thereby perpetuating themselves.

At one extreme are the boards of directors chosen entirely from within the organization. The Standard Oil Company of New Jersey has eleven directors, each of whom has worked his way up from within and was chosen for his proficiency in some branch of operation. To be a managing director of this company is a full-time job. Such directors are not permitted to have any other business interests. They select, counsel with, and supervise the executives of the subsidiary companies, decide whether to purchase or sell properties and whether to expand or contract operations. The Dennison Manufacturing Company has gone even further in this direction. It has removed the voting power from the shares owned by the public and concentrated it in a small percentage of shares owned entirely by the two hundred top-flight employees. These employees elect the board of directors from their own number, thereby completely divorcing ownership and management. They are required to surrender their voting shares when they leave the company. Both companies are successful. In each case, these employees have had

to broaden their vision to encompass the affairs of the entire company, and not devote themselves exclusively to furthering their own interests.

At the other extreme is the board of the American Telephone and Telegraph Company, composed of nineteen members, only two of whom are in the active management. The rest are leaders in industry, finance, and public affairs, selected for their prestige as well as their integrity and ability. They represent diverse interests and viewpoints, rather than unanimity. Between these extremes is every conceivable combination.

A recent innovation is the paid director. Men are picked for their wisdom and experience to study the company's affairs and offer their considered opinions. They may be directors in half a dozen companies, receiving a stipend from each, and engaging in no other activity. The idea has merit. There is a place in industry for the broad point of view which the busy executive, immersed in his own technical problems, is unable to supply.

Management

As we have seen, with the passing of the founder-owner-manager there came the separation of ownership and management. The first generation manager had created his own niche. His name was frequently over the front door. The manager of the next generation owed his position to others. He was selected by the directors for his skill, resourcefulness, and reputation and regardless of whether he owned stock in the company. Frequently, the terms of his employment were set forth in an arm's-length contract. Therein his duties, salary, and other provisions contingent upon his success were outlined. At times, the illusion of ownership, as well as the opportunity for extra benefits, was furnished by an option to purchase stock at a fixed price. Again pension rights might be offered in lieu of a higher salary. The contract was for a year but life tenure was implied and expected.

The appointed manager took over a going concern, with traditional ways of doing things. It was up to him to continue its success and to adapt its policies to technological improvements and to changes in public demand and in social outlook. Unlike his predecessor, the owner-manager, his was not the voice of ownership. His loyalty came to embrace the organization as a whole. He had to decide nice questions about sources of supply, the rights and duties of directors, officers, employees, and customers, as well as of stockholders. Relations with the public and government came within his purview.

Alfred McIntyre, President of Little, Brown and Company, wrote on the 110th Anniversary of the company:[2]

In 1937, when Little, Brown and Company celebrated its centenary, I had been with the company for not quite thirty years, and I felt then—at least it seems to me now—that I knew most of the answers to our problems— that generally speaking a decision that seemed sound as of yesterday would seem wise as of tomorrow.

I am proud today as I was then of the company's history, and my associates and I are still influenced in our daily actions by tradition, but a decade of world crisis has taught us that, as Benjamin Franklin once wrote, "In this world nothing is certain but death and taxes." Of course we all have beliefs and prejudices; and as Little, Brown and Company is about to begin its 111th year of book publishing I am convinced of this at least—that to increase the retail prices of books percentage-wise to match increased costs of manufacture is to drive the consumer away from the book stores.

The qualities that lead a person to found a business and bring it to maturity and those that make a good manager are quite different—the former calls for innovation, the latter for statesmanship.

[2] *Publishers' Weekly*, May 19, 1947, p. 2483.

Such terms as "rugged individualist" and "economic royalist" describe the owners of the preceding century better than they do the managers of the present. Managerial enterprise is entwined with the national economy. Its acts are important, not only to itself but also to others and often to the community. It has to succeed or it disintegrates, yet its success cannot be at the expense of the community. No codes of behavior or ethics to cover these, at times conflicting, responsibilities have yet been formulated. Political discernment as well as business sagacity is required.

The degree of success that management must produce to remain in office is surprisingly small. Indeed management must fail obviously and even ignominiously before the dispersed forces of criticism become mobilized for action. Directors are slow to act. This is entirely proper for they cannot upset the entire organization for every blunder. Their hope is that things will somehow right themselves. Besides, it is difficult to determine whether a bad situation is due to causes beyond the control of management or to lack of foresight. The balance sheet may yield no immediate evidence whether affairs are improving or deteriorating. Miscalculations may be temporary. Ideas may be premature. The first Chrysler streamlined model in 1934 found no favor with the public. Later it inaugurated a vogue that eventually transformed the pattern of automobile bodies.

This relative immunity to criticism and accountability gave to managers a position they could—and frequently did—abuse. Having become in their own view the paid employees of the stockholders they failed to assume the responsibilities of their position which was that of a trustee. Indeed, so independent did management frequently become that in many cases it felt justified in withholding vital information from stockholders, though they were the legal owners. There was real ground for this attitude, for the divulging of certain information might be dangerous competitively.

Stimulated partly by the Securities and Exchange Commission and the New York Stock Exchange, and partly spurred from within, managements have drastically altered their policies with respect to secrecy in recent years. For their own protection, they have sought the sympathetic understanding of their stockholders and the public at large. Publicity campaigns have been carried on and annual reports have become veritable fountains of information. The example set by the pioneers in this movement has been followed by many companies which at times seem to vie with one another to see which can tell the most.

This evolution has an unfortunate effect. It puts a damper on imagination and initiative, and makes for an atmosphere not conducive to the taking of risks. Any decision may turn out to have been wrong, and honest mistakes may be twisted into dishonesty by the unscrupulous in litigation. The temptation to yield to timidity is strong. This is the more so because managers know that they are dragging their directors into the shadowy area of interpretation of intent. Management is curiously lonely in its equivocal surroundings. Its relations with stockholders are as unclear as with directors and employees. Directors are its advisers only within limits. At annual meetings they become its critics. Management is estranged from stockholders by the devices of ownership, such as the dummy company. On the surface antagonism rather than mutuality of interest with employees is emphasized by the growth of trade unions, the closed shop, and collective bargaining.

Employee

Some employer-employee relations under free enterprise in the nineteenth century were very good. Others were very bad. The friendliness of the brothers Cheeryble, whose paternal care of employees Dickens recounts in *Nicholas Nickleby*, and the ugliness of the sweatshop were products of the same economy. Under free enterprise, employers paid wages literally out of their own pockets, personally supervised the work, and had a good eye for quality. When the value of the labor that went into a product could be measured a standard for wage rates was set. The employer either paid this rate or ran the risk of losing his employee to a competitor. This standard could be applied to jobs whose labor output was less easily computed, but required a similar grade of intelligence.

As business grew more complex in the transition stage between free and managerial enterprise, these measurements of individual output became less possible. When employers held the whip hand, they could regulate conditions of work and wages to a considerable extent according to their own ability and inclination. Since the individual employee was less necessary to his employer than his job was to him, the employer had the advantage. The temptation was strong to keep wages at a minimum. Also, so far as employers could move their plant and machinery from one locality to another, they could, when pressed, seek a more favorable labor market. Personal relations, however, mitigated some of the harshness of this impersonal market. Goodhearted employers were not uncommon. As long as it was their own money they were dealing out, they could allow themselves the luxury of helping faithful employees in need, looking after them when they were sick, and giving Christmas bonuses after a good year.

As managerial replaced free enterprise, there was less opportunity for personal contact. Employees, especially in the heavy industries, were helpless in their efforts to get better conditions. They did not have the bargaining power necessary to protect their positions. During the last decades of the nineteenth century immigrants were pouring into the United States. To survive, they had to accept work upon such terms and conditions as were offered. Here and there trade unions were formed to give employees some modicum of bargaining power. But they were few and far between and for the most part ineffective. Economic theories, the law, and court decisions stood in their way. Out of this situation grew the claim, fiercely propagated by labor leaders and liberals, that labor was not a commodity to be bought and sold on a purely commercial basis. This claim made headway, for conditions were too distressing to be tolerated in a country with expanding production. It is today declared and accepted statutory policy.

While family concerns were being amalgamated into great systems from 1890 to 1910, the free enterprise attitude toward labor continued, giving the employer an even greater bargaining leverage. The first generation of managers, regarding themselves as representatives of their stockholders, thought of wages as coming out of dividends. Generally their concentration on the mechanics of production and the brilliant results which they achieved made them oblivious to their responsibility to the employees. They had little fellow-feeling for the stream of foreigners who arrived yearly and who could be hired upon any terms they chose to dictate. Even those who were kindly disposed believed they had no right to waste their stockholders' money on wages that were higher than they had to pay. Competition among employers for labor, though stimulated by the westward movement of the population, was insufficient to offset their dominant position. "Business was business." Management justified its low wages by pointing to the impersonality of competition. Occasional strikes were effectively quashed. These and other factors dissipated employee loyalty, a natural concomitant of connection with any institution.

The second generation of managers long clung to the notion that they were primarily responsible to the stockholders. Brought up under free enterprise, they could not immediately modify their viewpoint with the changing conditions of industry. They could hide behind the legal concept of the fictional corporate person and thus rationalize acts for which as individuals they would not have accepted responsibility. Though they were shaping market conditions to a considerable degree, they still thought in terms of free enterprise, under which the entrepreneur had to adjust himself to market conditions. They exaggerated the indefinable risks of competition, and were unwilling to admit that they had moral and social responsibilities to their employees as well as business obligations. The relations between management and employees were at a low ebb during this transition period.

As the position of the individual employee became more and more helpless, the movement toward trade unionism accelerated. Both leaders mobilized the forces of labor in order to match the strong bargaining position of management with an equally effective position of their own. Such stratagems as the strike and the picket line, resulting in a collective bargain, were a necessary part of large scale industry under a free enterprise philosophy.

National unions covering an industry began to be organized at this time. Some states passed laws establishing minimum working conditions and minimum wages and hours, especially for women and children, which in retrospect, seem incredibly low. Occasional investigations by social workers and legislatures revealed the poor living conditions of employees. The conscience of the community was so touched that it approved the promulgation of doctrines that gave to the workers some kind of a chance. Despite bitter opposition by management, the right to organize and to strike, the picket line, and collective bargaining, all gained ground. The present-day effects of these practices are infinitely more widespread than they were in those earlier days.

With a few notable exceptions, employees came to look to their labor leaders rather than to management for the amelioration of conditions. Meanwhile, the growth of production opened up opportunities for a higher living standard. Labor unions capitalized on the liberty afforded by free enterprise. The American Federation of Labor guided by Samuel Gompers accepted the philosophy of free enterprise and concentrated upon getting a larger share of the product for workers. But its power was limited in scope. It achieved a modicum of success, but its field was confined to some of the more highly skilled occupations.

With World War I, a new era began. The urgency of increased production brought to light the weaknesses which past labor policies had fostered. Obviously some kind of a change was called for. Management grudgingly acknowledged this need and sought to meet it by resuscitating personal contacts. Labor leaders were given high positions and great responsibility in government. The National War Labor Board, created in 1918 under the joint chairmanship of ex-President William Howard Taft and Frank P. Walsh, consisted of five representatives of employers and five representatives of labor. The objective was to stipulate fair standards rather than leave matters to the impersonal workings of the market. With the consent of the parties disputes were settled and wage rates were set by order of the Board. Again by mutual consent the right to strike was temporarily suspended. Labor relations counsellors, employed by management to correct injustices, obtained a precarious toe hold. Here and there welfare measures were introduced and working conditions were improved. During this period, wages were raised by competition for workers.

Heavy labor was at a premium. Health hazards received attention. Employers gave dances and picnics for their employees.

But it was too little and too late. The lines had been formed. Loyalty to unions had paid as loyalty to management had not. At the end of the war, emergency regulations and controls were discarded, and unions made the most of the newly found strength of labor solidarity. They asserted their rights with increased confidence. The belief spread that the constant prodding of union leaders had compelled management to grant higher wages and better working conditions than it would have offered without this pressure. During the 1920's the number of union members fell off from the level attained during the war, but remained well above the prewar levels. Managements, fearful of a resumption of growth of unionism, were granting wage increases in line with increasing production, so that, toward the last years of the decade, wages and conditions of employment were probably at the highest level ever known. With the depression, came decreases in wage rates, rising unemployment and a further considerable drop in union membership. But after 1933, the position of the unions had a sharp upturn. Section 7(a) of the National Recovery Act of 1933 assured to employees the right to organize and bargain collectively without interference from employers, and restricted the right of employers to control union activities. This increased the stature which labor had already achieved in 1932 through the anti-injunction provisions of the Norris-LaGuardia Act.

The speed with which the unions gained members and power brought about a novel situation. Not only did union membership within old industries rise more rapidly than at any preceding time, but new industries began to be organized. The Committee on Industrial Organizations was formed in 1935. Government actively promoted unionization and collective bargaining as an end in itself. The privileges accorded to unions by the former Section 7(a) were expanded and codified in the National Labor Relations Act, passed in 1935. As the closed shop and check off were included in an increasing number of labor agreements, the unions attained a higher degree of power and of permanence. In this fashion all employees in a given industry could be compelled to join the union and the income of the union was stabilized. Collective bargaining, which had been inaugurated under free enterprise to give employees some degree of equality, now placed them in many respects in a superior trading position in relation to management. As in a conflict neither management nor unions had any choice except to come to some compromise, the word "bargaining" in the phrase "collective bargaining" lost something of its meaning. The process was accentuated by the formation of the War Labor Board under the chairmanship of William H. Davis. The question of union status was disposed of by maintenance of membership, and the Board devoted itself to settling disputes about wages, hours, and conditions. The most recent striking of balances between these opposed forces in our economy has come with the passage of the Taft-Hartley Act. Here the consequences are daily news and their evolution must await the passage of time.

In effect, the union leader became the employment manager for the industry. Frequently, he passed on terms and tenure of employment, on personnel, on disputed interpretations of rules, on promotions. Though clothed with these vital powers, he stood apart from management and did not share its responsibilities. Yet good wages and working conditions were dependent upon successful and continuous operation. No more could be distributed than was produced. The ability of business to adjust itself to the falling trends of the depression years was limited. The gains labor could win by further fighting were approaching the point of diminishing returns. Improvement once more became linked to increased production as well as to bargaining power.

Under the Congress of Industrial Organizations, entire industries were unionized. Whereas a generation ago strikes had been local and had had small effect, now they frequently closed entire industries and had profound repercussions throughout the national economy. When the coal mines were shut down, transportation and many manufacturing industries were demoralized. A strike did not even have to be in a key industry. Stoppages in subsidiary industries disorganized the major industries they supplied. The carefully built interrelations could be shattered at many points. The same reasoning that justified the right to strike in free enterprise loses its validity when applied to managerial enterprise. The right to strike is denied to government employees on much the same grounds. As long as unions were a minority power within the industry, warfare might achieve constructive results. But when the minority power had grown to be the major power, the battle had been won. Continued warfare ceased to make sense. A fundamental change in relationship had taken place.

Under a free-enterprise economy, the right to strike was the chief weapon in achieving higher wages and better conditions of work. But under managerial enterprise it may be turned into a fearfully destructive instrument in bargaining technique. Free enterprise is based on competition; managerial enterprise on co-operation. Schooled as labor leaders and managers are in the philosophy of bargaining under free enterprise, both find the shift to co-responsibility hard to comprehend and each is loath to admit its inevitability. So rapid have these changes been that the new relationships have scarcely had time to take shape. Only recently has managerial enterprise begun to recognize the employee as an essential part of the production mechanism. The obligation of industry to furnish steady jobs has been conceded by many groups in management and stressed by the Committee for Economic Development.

Several trends are in process of formation:

1 *To pay all workers of the same grade and seniority in an industry at the same rate.* Uniformity of wages and conditions expresses an historic union attitude. It disassociates employment from the state of business and tends to work a hardship on the company unable to meet the standard set. Obviously, such a mechanical rule in part disregards the qualities that make an employee extra valuable.

2 *To give employees a share in profits.* This doctrine is in direct contrast to equal pay for equal work. Here the assumption is that a company should pay wages in accordance with its ability. Consequently, more successful companies should pay higher rates of wages than less successful. As wages are dependent on a company's ability to survive, it must be permitted to make profits. The employee becomes a participant in earnings and has a stake in the business. The application of this philosophy is of necessity vague, though attempts have been made to formulate in advance the proper division of earnings above a stipulated minimum. This emphasis on partnership between employer and employee has been particularly strong in the clothing trades. Under the leadership of Sidney Hillman the Amalgamated Clothing Workers Union has, on occasion, made loans to employers to tide them over a business slump and to maintain employment.

3 *To give steady employment at a guaranteed annual wage.* As John Maurice Clark has brilliantly argued, in *Economics of Overhead Costs*, wages are as regular an expense as any other expense. Similarly grocery bills and rent must be paid by workers in bad times as well as good, in slack and busy seasons. The theory is that after a certain time, the job comes to constitute a vested interest which should be recognized by assuring continuous employment. The Proctor and Gamble Company has demonstrated the practicability of the annual wage for certain types of industry. It must be remembered, however, that demand for soap is more constant than that for many other products. The regular force, defined as employees who have worked for the company two years, are guaranteed forty-eight weeks of work and about 80 per cent of the employees of the company are included under this arrangement. The custom of giving separation pay similarly rests on the theory of an acquired vested interest in the job. In case of dismissal, the loss of this vested interest must be compensated for.

4 *To have a welfare fund administered by the union in the interest of the employees.* Many companies have already instituted a welfare fund. Some manage it themselves while others put it in the hands of a selected group of employees. The amount is usually determined by the management and is dependent upon the profits of the preceding year. The unions hold such a scheme to be inadequate. They demand that a fixed royalty or percentage of payroll be set aside and administered by them. This demand has received a setback in the Taft-Hartley Act,[3] which provides that welfare funds be administered as a trust fund for specified objects jointly by an equal number of representatives of employers and employees, together with neutral representatives as are agreed upon or appointed by a designated court.

5 *To recognize labor's right to participate in management, either on the board of directors or in the management group.* This controversial demand is resisted by certain groups among both employees and management. Labor fears the appointees will lose their identity as representatives

[3] Labor Management Relations Act, 1947; 80th Cong., 1st Sess., HR 3020, Sec. 302, C-5-B.

of labor and will inevitably be drawn into the complex problems connected with the survival and success of the business. Management fears that the presence of a representative of labor would lead to internal conflicts that would endanger the business as a whole. They agree that the divided loyalties of a labor leader on the board of directors would have unpredictable potentialities. To make his voice count, he would have to cease to be an advocate for the particularized interest, and to visualize it as a thread in the entire fabric of the economy.

None of these tendencies has progressed beyond the experimental stage. New relationships are being forged in many industries. Yet all have one thing in common. They are based on the recognition that employees are an integral part of the business. Employees are no longer considered mere hired hands, as they were under free enterprise. Taken together with the evolution of management toward becoming the arbiters of the whole business in contrast to their former role as the representative of the stockholders, these tendencies are crystallizing into a new concept of the position, rights, and responsibilities of employees.

The Impact of Technological and Procedural Change

■ Alfred D. Chandler, Jr., stated in Chapter 3 that the coming of electricity and the internal-combustion engine and the rise of institutionally directed research have been the major dynamic forces in the American business economy in the twentieth century. The next selection is chiefly concerned with the business and economic effects of these basic influences.

Within a few years after the selection was written, the airplane had overtaken the railroad in annual passenger-miles of travel, and by 1961 the airplane total was more than 50 per cent greater. It is worth noting also that by this time all overland carriers except for a few electric lines were using internal-combustion engines.

Thomas C. Cochran

A New Business Environment*

Along with mid-twentieth-century changes in the character of the business cycle and in such basic trends as investment and

* Reprinted by permission of the publishers from Thomas C. Cochran, *The American Business System: A Historical Perspective, 1900–1955*. Cambridge, Mass.: Harvard University Press, Copyright, 1957, by the President and Fellows of Harvard College, pp. 123–139.

consumption came marked alterations in the physical environment of business. Means of business transportation, location of plants and offices, and ways of securing supplies of raw material were all changed as a result of technological progress and total war. Each of these changes presented new problems and opportunities to management.

In spite of dramatic governmental changes involved in the New Deal and World War II, the social and economic importance of the maturity of the giant corporation and its managerial system, or the potential cultural effects of the rise of radio and television, later historians may characterize the period from 1925 to 1950 as that of "the motorization of the United States." The Rooseveltian concept of the welfare state would no doubt be of major importance in times of business recession, and the changes in management and electronic communication would, in time, profoundly and subtly alter human relations, but the automobile was immediate. Like the steam railroad from 1840 to 1880, it changed the face of the nation.

Because of automobiles people not only traveled and sent goods differently, they lived and thought differently. Aside from war the motor industry became the greatest direct stimulant to American capital investment. Directly it drew private capital into rubber, glass, electrical equipment, steel, and other metals; indirectly it was responsible for millions of new suburban homes, stores, offices, and factories, and for massive government expenditures on highways, bridges, and tunnels. During the twenties government construction of roads for automobiles was, except for buildings, the largest type of investment. By 1940 the network of paved highways represented a capital outlay as big as that in railroads, and larger than that in public utilities. Following World War II building construction again became the greatest consumer of capital, but much of the new investment was in locations made accessible only by automobiles and trucks.

Business in the Fields

More and more Americans thought of travel whether for work or play in terms of the automobile. By the forties industrial plants, except those in the biggest cities, provided parking facilities and with some use of other people's cars practically everyone who wanted to could ride to work "privately." And prestige was attached to driving rather than to going by bus. After World War II some transportation companies found waiting buses, ready to start at the end of the shift and go to within a short walk of workers' homes, virtually unoccupied. Consequently, a suburban or even a country location seemed more attractive to labor than one in the central city where parking was difficult. Meanwhile the truck, freeing many companies from the need of rail connections, made it possible to use cheap land.

Office work not directly connected with seeing clients responded to the same influence. Increasingly record-filing, calculating, planning and drafting, and laboratory work accompanied manufacturing in its move to the country. While central cities remained the chief meeting place for financiers, brokers, jobbers, planners, and wholesalers, the retailers and service supplies followed their customers to the country. In order to survive, many big-city department stores found it necessary to open rural or small city branches, and moving-picture displayers built country "drive-ins."

The term "country" perhaps exaggerates the usual shift, which was from a central metropolitan city to its more thinly populated suburban fringe. There was still an advantage in being near the large quantities of labor, the big banks, the suppliers, and the distributors of the metropolis. Distant sites near country towns were likely to be occupied by plants that needed only a moderate amount of labor, run by concerns that could supply managerial and skilled employees from other offices. The head office would ordinarily remain in its original city, from which by telephone, teletype, and airplane it could manage branches in areas of cheap land and unskilled, nonunion labor.

New developments, such as the general

spread of electric lines to country districts, reliable electric pumps, quick-heating electric stoves, radio and television, higher real wages, and federal mortgage credit for homes, aided the automobile in dispersing population. Workers and managers were not only willing but anxious to leave city apartments to become suburban or country home owners. This movement made the building construction business one of the most important in the nation. Without any important new machinery beyond improved bulldozers and gasoline shovels, builders managed to effect some economies by building many houses at once and thereby getting continuous productive work from each of the numerous types of specialized labor. Some progress was also made in factory prefabrication of house panels and units of equipment. As a net result, mass builders like the Levitt brothers could produce houses in large developments near New York and Philadelphia for about two-thirds the cost of individual construction.

But such economies would not have put new houses within the reach of average families whose income was under $4,000 a year in 1950 and whose cash savings were insignificant, had it not been for government-guaranteed mortgages. By a series of acts from 1934 on, the federal government guaranteed mortgages issued by qualified banks for the purchase of small homes. The exact provisions were changed from time to time, but usually the government would guarantee over four-fifths of the price of a small home for nonveterans and, under the Act of 1950, practically the whole cost for veterans. Furthermore, mortgages could run up to twenty-five years with payments of interest and principal arranged so that a uniform amount was paid each month. For the first time in American history the working man with a job but no savings could buy where he chose on reasonable terms. Thus the government partially underwrote the housing boom and the re-

location of business that followed World War II. By 1954, twenty million government-guaranteed loans had been made, covered by thirty billion dollars' worth of mortgage insurance.[1] Federal policies also had an important effect on private lending institutions, which dropped the idea of first and second mortgages repayable only in large amounts and adopted the "packaged" mortgage, with a uniform monthly payment even when no government guarantee was involved.

From the standpoint of the businessman, the automobile and truck had joined with electricity in offering economies from relocation. The nineteenth- and early twentieth-century pattern of plant location had been dictated by rail transportation for materials, products, and workers. Factories had been built at trunk-line junction points, both to gain the lower competitive rates, and to be assured of an adequate supply of labor. Within a metropolitan area the tendency had been to locate at central points where railroad lines converged. Here goods could easily be shipped or received from the various roads, and workers from all parts of the area could reach the plant by train and trolley. But these advantages had to be paid for in high land prices and taxes.

By 1950 trailer trucks with oil-burning Diesel engines could compete effectively even with long-distance rail service. Although it cost more per ton mile to haul the load on a concrete highway, the savings in time, loading, terminal charges, and overhead costs might make the total expense less than by rail. Furthermore, to gain the essential economy of even carload shipments to particular markets was difficult for some medium-sized manufacturers. Trucks gave them a means for shipping small quantities at any time.

In all the major industrial sections, and in many rural areas, electric power could be purchased at reasonable rates.

[1] *Time*, March 15, 1954, p. 100.

The efficiency of small-scale use of electric power, and the cheapness of small shipments by truck enabled little enterprises to live in competition with larger ones. Furthermore, as the economies of mass production led the biggest companies to concentrate on a few standardized models or qualities, there were greater opportunities for the small specialty shop that would make just what the customer wanted at a price only slightly higher than the standard product.

In spite of the fact that all of these factors were operating as early as 1930, the shift to the country was not rapid in the period before World War II. In addition to depression, difficulty in disposing of existing plants or offices except at a large loss in terms of their cost of replacement, and fear of a poorer labor supply in the suburban or country areas were among the factors retarding movement from the older central cities. When it came to moving to or establishing a branch plant in another section of the country, the problem of administrative labor was often a serious deterrent. Unskilled labor might be available in an agricultural region, but the important nucleus of highly skilled or managerial labor would be lacking. If the plant needed a lot of such labor, a move from an older industrial area presented difficulties, and subsequent skilled-labor turnover would be a menace to production.

World War II, however, spread industry into the South and the West. The government offered quick amortization of the cost of new plants as a deduction from taxes or else built the plants and leased them to the operators. Most of the states west of the Mississippi River gained industry at an increasing rate because of the war and kept many of the plants in operation afterward. But the movement away from the older sections is easy to exaggerate. While the value added by manufacture increased almost fourfold in California and Texas between 1939 and 1947, the same figure rose threefold in

Ohio and Illinois, and nearly that much in New York and Pennsylvania.

Of the ten major metropolitan manufacturing areas, ranked by value added by manufacture, Boston, Pittsburgh, and Buffalo each dropped one place between 1939 and 1947, and Los Angeles, Cleveland, and San Francisco–Oakland advanced one place. But the position of the big four, New York, Chicago, Detroit, and Philadelphia, remained unchanged.

Business in Family Machines

Families of the nineteenth century had prized big homes, fine furniture, and good horses, none of which were made by big business. Before the middle of the twentieth century the most valued possessions, for both convenience of living and social prestige, had become electrical household equipment, television, and automobiles, all products of giant companies. These new durable consumer goods had much in common with each other and nearly the whole range of products might be made by one big company. The automobile, by far the most important single product, may exemplify the general character of the entire business.

The great depression demonstrated the maturity and stability of the automobile business. It ceased to be among the most rapidly growing, but it continued to sell cars to people who lacked money for what an earlier generation would have regarded as necessities of food and housing. Instead of falling to near zero, as bankers had feared they might, automobile sales about followed the average for all business.

After brief returns to prosperity in 1937 and 1940 and 1941, the automobile companies between 1942 and 1945 converted their factories to war uses by government order. Consequently, at the end of the war it was difficult to reëstablish full-scale mass production of passenger cars. The 1937 level of passenger-car production was not achieved until late in 1948. Trucks and buses presented a different pattern since they had been turned out continuously for military purposes. From 1946 on, each year set new records in the production of heavy motor equipment.

Gradually catching up with the unusual demand created during the war years and the new prosperity, the industry by the fifties had returned, from the standpoint of production, to what might be called a normal relation to its market. Except for the recession year of 1954, production ran from about seven to over eight million vehicles a year, with passenger-car production 50 per cent above 1929, and truck and bus output up 75 per cent. Although the car and truck had proved to be essentials rather than luxuries during the thirties, their long life made for instability in demand. Even the mere threat of bad times could lead people to decide to keep their old car another year, and if half of the customers of any of the years from 1950 to 1955 should have made such a decision, consumer purchasing would have dropped more than seven billion dollars. The same considerations applied to the other consumer durables. Yet there was little beyond a desire for new things and social prestige behind at least half of the demand.

The automobile emphasized particularly the aspects of mass production associated with direct public consumption. By the middle thirties the industry comprised some thousand factories owned by over 800 companies, as well as thousands of smaller subcontractors and distributors. The producing end of the business used about half the nation's malleable iron, a fifth of the steel output, and around three quarters of all glass and rubber. Large-scale operations and large capital investment characterized the final manufacturing stages of this and other mass-production businesses. The main manufacturing plants of even the smaller companies were very large, normally employing upwards of 5,000 workers, and representing investments of over fifty million dollars each. The industry continued to be dominated by General Motors, Chrysler, and Ford, who produced 80 to 95 per cent of the total, and General Motors came to be the nation's most highly capitalized industrial company. Even the specialized manufacturers of parts usually operated very large plants. While technological improvement continually increased efficiency there was, presumably, no place in the whole productive operation where added size would lead to any considerable saving in direct manufacturing cost.

As a result of many years of engineering effort, the final products and most parts were highly standardized. This, however, presented one of the dilemmas of mass production for the consumer market. To keep down costs it was desirable to make very few changes in design. By never changing a simple model Henry Ford had sold cars in the twenties at incredibly low costs, for less than $600 retail in terms of the 1955 value of money, whereas no new car in the latter year, even after taxes were deducted, could sell for under $1,000. But ultimately even Ford was speared on the other horn of the dilemma, failure to appeal to a changing public taste.

The problem for the manufacturers was to make each year's products different enough so that those who could raise the money would be coaxed to buy, without incurring large costs at the factory for retooling the assembly lines. Although the same situation existed in principle for other high-priced, mass-produced durables, it proved undesirable for several reasons to pay for as rapid a stylistic obsolescence as occurred in the case of passenger automobiles. The other durables might be concealed within the owner's home, but he appeared in public in his automobile, and newness and cost, therefore, became matters of obvious social prestige.

These considerations put a premium on automobile advertising and selling. Since the number of producers was small, and a rapid approach to monopoly by any one firm would have undoubtedly been met by antitrust prosecution, price competition at the factory was minimized. Wholesale prices were administered, as in a monopoly, to seek the level that in the long run would show the largest product from units sold times profit per unit. All producers either reached about the same conclusions or followed the lead of the big three as to price. On the retail front the situation was different. Here, in automobiles and other consumer durable goods, thousands of dealers competed strongly with each other. By 1954 the wise buyer demanded and received large discounts. The entire single-price structure of American merchandising, built by the big retailers of the late nineteenth century, was crumbling. In 1955, it was still too early to see the ultimate trends of this new stage of retail price warfare.

Because of their high cost and long life, consumer durables in general and automobiles in particular spread the practice of installment selling. By the late forties installment sales had put durable-goods purchases largely on a "pay as you go" basis. Late in 1954 a newspaper cartoon showed a banker admonishing a teller arrested for embezzlement, "If you wanted nice things why didn't you get them on installments like the rest of us!"

Having large fixed capital to shelter against the winds of technological change, and earnings available for expansion, automobile companies began to produce airplane parts and electrical equipment such as refrigerators and washing machines. Tire companies went into clothing and numerous specialties, including moving pictures. Large companies in other fields, such as chemicals, also took over the ownership of many kinds of plants, including automobile companies. Thus the big companies diversified their risks, and the American business pattern became a more closely knit fabric of associated interests. Expansion into new fields posed managerial and organizational problems, and made companies like General Motors under Alfred P. Sloan pioneers in new devices for stimulation and control of activity in the giant enterprise.

Rivals in Transportation

Making automobiles, trucks, airplanes, or railroad cars was a different business from operating them. Even aside from private passenger cars it is impossible to assess the size of the business of automotive transport. Common-carrier trucks crossing state lines were regulated and had to report to the Interstate Commerce Commission. In 1949 the ten leading interstate lines had revenues of from eleven to nearly twenty-nine million dollars a year. Single lines operated routes extending from the Mississippi Valley to the West Coast and made deliveries considerably faster than did railroads. Most trucks, however, were not common carriers across state lines, and no reports were made of their use by private concerns. The fragmentary figures that exist indicate that by 1950 trucks and buses ranging from local delivery vans to transcontinental Diesels provided the main form of commercial transportation.

The growth of truck and bus companies was greatly aided by post-World War II highway development. Excellent concrete highways from coast to coast, turnpikes, and four-lane expressways enabled trucks to travel faster than freight trains. And while railroad tracks had to be maintained by the company exclusively for its own use, highways were also used and supported by the public. Essentially the highway was gaining because it was a more flexible transportation device than the railroad track.

As more transport planes became available for civilian use from 1943 on, airlines also gained rapidly on railroads as passenger carriers. World War II with its millions of plane-miles of routine flying largely eliminated the old fear of accidents. Figures demonstrated that a passenger was much safer in an airliner than in a private automobile; the problem for the airlines now became one of providing attractive service. By 1950 plane fares were less than railroad plus Pullman fares, although still higher than coach. Though the lack of adequate transportation to and from airports, usually located on the outskirts of major cities, prevented the growth of much local traffic, long-haul passenger miles equalled a quarter of the figure for Class I railroads. Planes were important carriers of emergency parts, flowers, and luxury foods, but the volume of express or freight business compared to trucks or railroad was negligible.

In all this upsurge, the railroad company was adjusting to a new place in the economy. Benefiting greatly from the prosperity and inflation of the forties and early fifties, the companies reduced their debt to eight and a half billion, compared to nearly twelve billion in 1930; in real or constant value dollars the debt had been cut to less than half. This change in the burden of overhead would allow the railroads to specialize profitably in types of traffic which they could carry with the greatest efficiency and to give up other types to their new competitors. The shift from steam to Diesel engines, more than two-thirds complete by the early fifties, cut fuel bills and schedule time. The railroads also bought into the truck and bus lines and by 1950 came to control about a third of this type of common-carrier business. But there were many phases of the complex competition that had not been resolved. Antiquated union regulations, such as manning requirements for trains; railroad administrative traditions, such as the belief that passenger traffic

must lose money; and government regulations against mergers and combinations with competitive carriers were some of the elements inhibiting the rapid adjustment that would spell self-preservation.

Dynamics of World War II

The United States' contribution in goods to World War I had been largely in raw materials and semifinished products. Relatively little finished war material emerged from American factories before the armistice. As early as 1916 the demands of England and France had brought the United States economy to the normal level of full employment. Additional workers had to be found among those not ordinarily counted as employed. As a result, during 1917 and 1918 it was possible to add only about three million workers, or about 10 per cent, to total employment, including military, and nothing to the 1916 level of national product.

The disappointing immediate results of the effort to increase production were caused by bad harvests, but shifting workers to new tasks or attracting women or retired workers to jobs was a wasteful process. American business leaders realized fully for the first time the rigidities of mass-production processes. As Grosvenor B. Clarkson, one of the Directors of the Council of National Defense explained: "A group of French workmen who had been making automobiles could almost on a day's notice begin making airplanes, and might have one done within a few days. The process of making standardized parts for final assembly into a whole is incomparably different."[2]

A change-over from automobile to airplane motors, for example, meant months of work on blueprints and specifications, then the manufacture of new machine tools for new purposes, and finally elimi-

[2] Grosvenor B. Clarkson, *Industrial America in the World War* (Boston: Houghton Mifflin, 1923), p. 233.

nation of unforeseen, but almost in-evitable, miscalculations in the actual production operation. Furthermore, during 1916 "the condition had become inextri-cably snarled. There was not only that general congestion of the northeastern section, but there were innumerable local entanglements . . . orders were many times placed where they never could be filled."[3] As a result of such delays neither the German enemy nor the Italian or Japanese ally sensed the vast potential war productivity of the United States.

The situation at the beginning of World War II was strikingly different. In 1940 when the United States started to arm, the unemployed were conservatively esti-mated at almost seven million out of a total "normal labor force" of fifty-three million.[4] By 1944 these seven million had been put to work and the total employed workers had increased from forty-seven to over sixty-three million. This 35 per cent increase in the number of employed workers almost exactly coincided with the percentage increase in real national pro-duct or income for the same period. In contrast to the time covered by the United States' participation in World War I, the period from 1940 to 1945 was long enough to yield the fruits of mass produc-tion.

In World War I production of civilian goods had continued; in the second world war plants needed for war material were entirely converted. The conversion to war was far more complete than in any earlier conflict. By 1945 the war effort was consuming 57 per cent of the national income, a situation unprecedented in American history. Civil War costs had barely risen above 25 per cent of national income in the North, and World War I had only approached this amount in 1918. The figures for 1945 give concrete mean-

ing to the twentieth-century phrase, total war.

During the approach and start of World War II government and business mobiliza-tion repeated most of the mistakes of earlier periods, in spite of impressive ulti-mate achievements. "My experience in two world wars . . . ," said Bernard Baruch, business advisor to both Wilson and Franklin Roosevelt, "makes me marvel at the regularity with which errors are repeated. One of the errors that most fre-quently recurs is failure to study and understand the records of past experi-ence."[5] The obstacles to rapid action were much the same in both world wars. American businessmen were not anxious to submit to dictatorial government ad-ministrators, even temporarily, and the President was not willing to delegate ade-quate power to any one man or board until forced to do so by necessity. Further-more, as the conflict in Europe developed, some members of the administration, such as Secretary of Commerce Jesse Jones, were initially opposed to entry into the war or to large-scale advance prepara-tion.[6]

Late in 1940 a relatively powerless Na-tional Defense Advisory Commission was superseded by the more potent Office of Production Management (OPM), headed by William S. Knudsen of General Motors and Sidney Hillman of the Amalgamated Clothing Workers. By the spring of 1941 the pressure of war orders and the rapidly mounting consumer demand of workers with plenty of money were pinching the civilian economy, and an Office of Price Administration and Civilian Supply was created. This agency, headed by economist Leon Henderson, saw normal production of passenger cars, which promised to exceed that of any year save 1929, as the greatest creator of shortages in ma-

[3] Ibid., p. 235.
[4] Historical Statistics of the U.S., 1789–1945, p. 65.
[5] Quoted in Eliot Janeway, The Struggle for Sur-vival (New Haven: Yale University Press, 1950), p. 72.
[6] Ibid., p. 83.

terials for war.[7] Under his urging OPM cut automobile production after August 1, 1941, by 20 per cent.

Within a little more than a month after Pearl Harbor a supreme War Production Board (WPB) was created to direct the existing boards and offices, and Donald M. Nelson, formerly of Sears, Roebuck, was placed at its head with the same type of comprehensive power that Wilson had conferred on Bernard Baruch in March 1918. This centralization of authority did not solve all the problems, but production for war was administered with reasonable efficiency from then on.

While steel and some other industries were loath to expand beyond estimated future peacetime needs, the struggle between business as usual and a government consciously heading for all-out war continued to center on the role of the automobile industry. The motor companies were willing to fill contracts by building new plants with quick write-offs of the expense, or by using surplus facilities, but they were not willing in time of peace to convert the main assembly lines. The industry contended that only automobiles could be efficiently manufactured in their plants, and OPM accepted the situation.

"The period between Pearl Harbor Day and the beginning of WPB on January 15th, 1942," wrote Donald Nelson, "was one of great writhing and thrashing around on the part of the automobile magnates and the functionaries of government who were trying to prepare the nation for war. The industry, without opposing conversion, had wanted to use up certain raw materials and parts for a final splurge in passenger car production —and the truth of the matter is they made out a very good case."[8] But on January 20, 1942, Nelson's WPB stopped further production of passenger cars and light trucks, and the vast power of the

automobile industry was concentrated on war supply. "Historians who wade deeply enough into the facts and figures, the cold engineering statistics of World War II," Nelson wrote, "may some day come to the conclusion that our automotive industry could, alone, have produced almost enough to lick the Axis."[9]

While in both World War I and World War II the greatest business achievement may have been the running of the emergency boards and bureaus, a more obvious one was the organization of shipbuilding. From 1936 on, the United States Maritime Commission had been subsidizing the construction and operation of vessels for approved foreign trades. This had provided a small number of up-to-date ships, but in general the merchant marine capable of navigating rough water was composed of leftovers from World War I or an earlier period. Between 1939 and 1945 American shipbuilders, using many new processes, such as subassembly of large sections at secondary plants, electric welding, and a high degree of standardization, turned out over fifty-six million deadweight tons, an amount about equal to the prewar steam tonnage of the British Empire.[10] In the course of this achievement Henry J. Kaiser's shipyards reduced the time of building a Liberty ship, the standard slow freighter of World War II, from over 300 days to fourteen.

The war accelerated certain business developments already in progress. The need for efficient use of all transportation and labor led to new branch plants in undeveloped areas. On the economic side, the new factories brought lasting industrialization to parts of the South and West. On the business side, new centers presented problems in executive coördination, in managing a team whose players were separated by thousands of miles. Such problems plus close contacts with govern-

[7] Norman Beasley, *Knudsen: A Biography* (New York: Whittlesey House, 1947), p. 322.
[8] Donald M. Nelson, *Arsenal of Democracy* (New York: Harcourt, Brace, 1946), p. 224.

[9] *Ibid.*, p. 212.
[10] Frederic C. Lane, *Ships for Victory* (Baltimore: Johns Hopkins University Press, 1951), p. 5.

ment administrative committees led business to make greater use of committees for control of large sprawling corporations. Standard Oil of New Jersey, for example, reconsidered its entire administrative structure from 1941 on. The result was almost complete adoption of the principle of policy formation by committees. As Frank Abrams, its later chairman, explained, "It stands to reason that if you get five men together and one man is wrong, the mistake is going to be picked up. Or if one man has a good idea, the others will contribute to it and develop it."[11]

Relatively high taxes in the thirties had caused management to consider how the company might be benefited by using money for untaxed items of expense rather than allowing it to accumulate as taxable profit. Excess-profits taxes, up to over ninety cents on the last dollars earned, put a premium on finding ways to spend for the long-run welfare of the company. More public-relations work of all kinds, more research, and more liberal use of executive expense accounts were the usual ways of getting the most out of untaxed dollars. They all had enduring effects on business practice, and on the relations of business to the rest of society.

Though the war, by taking some men away from their normal research, probably retarded the progress of basic science, applied science of certain types was greatly stimulated. An Office of Scientific Research and Development, headed by Dr. Vannevar Bush, put scores of able research men to work on military problems. Ideas with practical utility were passed on to the contractors making the relevant equipment. While the most spectacular and potentially important development was atomic energy, many other advances in motors, chemicals, and elec-

[11] Courtney R. Hall, *History of American Industrial Science* (New York: Science Library Publishers, 1954), p. 414.

tronics had permanent peacetime value, and promoted additional expenditures for company research. Since there is no quantitative measure of either technological or scientific progress, it is impossible to balance these gains against a short-run loss in basic science.

The war undoubtedly hastened the use of atomic fission by several years and resulted in leadership in this area that would probably not have come had America remained at peace. Before 1955 the atom produced no direct business effects beyond a speculative boom in uranium properties, but development of commercial atomic power was imminent. From 1950 on the Atomic Energy Commission encouraged selected teams of industrial scientists to study commercial uses of fissionable materials and reactors, and in May 1952, set up an office to administer industrial participation. As a result certain public-utility companies undertook the construction of plants to be finished in the late fifties.

Shortage of labor and a government friendly to collective bargaining produced a sharp wartime rise in real wages that led to both higher consumption and higher production in the postwar years. Since in the postwar inflation that followed the early abandonment of price controls and rationing, wage rates outran price increases, and the value of inherited wealth and the incomes of people on relatively fixed salaries lagged, it can probably be said that the war brought an advance in economic democracy.

Portents and Promises

The postwar American economy of higher production and higher consumption continued the rapid exhaustion of known resources of many high-grade raw materials. While the age of cheapness and plenty which had made American managers careless about conserving materials had ended for metals like copper, zinc, and tin in the 1920's, the demands initiated by World War II threatened the very basis of the early industrial strength of the nation, high-grade iron ore. The management of firms using these disappearing materials had now to plan on a long-range, world-wide basis for future supplies.

One type of planning was directed toward substitutions. But possibilities were limited and required much development. The northern European nations made gasoline and rubber from coal, and alcohol, food, and clothing from wood, but in the United States synthetic rubber was the only one of these substitutes that was currently economic. Plastics might ultimately replace some sheet steel, but the immediate recourse of the business planners was to new sources of iron ore in Canada and Latin America. The shift toward ore delivered by ocean steamers, in turn, revived the old heavy industry areas of the East Coast, like Baltimore and Philadelphia. Offshore prospecting for oil and sulphur was another example of the business quest for future supplies.

An added generation of experience with the unpredictable character of shifts in industrial demands for raw materials made businessmen at mid-century more philosophical about exhaustion of particular resources than were their predecessors of the twenties. Furthermore, the resources of Canada were in an early stage of exploitation. The writings and speeches of executives of the fifties indicated close attention to the problem of exhaustion of supplies, but relatively little fear that research, exploration, and new technology would fail to find solutions.

The changes stimulated by the war had in common a new emphasis on the place of the big company in relation to external factors. Relations with government, in many cases both at home and abroad, relations with various publics, and provision for continuing supplies of materials all called for long-range planning. None of these considerations were newborn in the war; some companies like Standard Oil had faced all of them since the nineteenth century. But now all large companies were affected, and the questions were posed with a force and insistence usually lacking in earlier years.

Built-in Innovation

■ Innovations requiring new capital investment in themselves and producing widespread effects on investment in the rest of the economy have been an important force, if not the chief force, in stimulating economic development. Until the twentieth century such changes came by chance from the experimentation of individual men in their own homes or laboratories or while they were performing duties in factories or shops. Since the early part of the century the education required for innovation in many fields and the high cost of experimentation have required organized sponsorship of research if a high rate of innovation was to be maintained. From about 1920 on, institutional research and development has been an important factor in business and economic change.

Kendall Birr, of the State University of New York, Albany, supplies a brief historical background of the rise of organized research in the Western world, a movement in which the United States lagged until World War I and did not consistently assume leadership until after World War II. As Professor Birr indicates, research has a tendency to snowball. Companies in industries where technology is rapidly changing necessarily spend the most money on research, and this in turn produces still more rapid change and a still higher rate of investment in research in order to keep up with competitors. In the broad picture, competitive rivalry with the Soviet Union has produced the largest United States expenditures for research. Of the $14 billion spent in research in the United States in fiscal 1960, the government supplied $9 billion.

Kendall Birr
The Roots of Industrial Research*

Scientific research is big business today. According to one estimate, the United States spent about $8 billion in 1956 for scientific research and development. This is not surprising since American research laboratories perform virtually every imaginable scientific and technological operation. They are supported by the federal government, universities, foundations and industrial concerns both large and small. And they play an important role in the economic life not only of the United States but also of other countries throughout the world.

A large part of this research is carried on in industrial research laboratories— 4,834 of them according to a recent survey by the National Research Council. Books and articles on the subject of industrial research flow in endless streams from technical publishers. Several leading educational institutions hold regular conferences on the administration of industrial research and offer courses in the subject.

What is industrial research, this phenomenon of such importance in our present-day society? The term has suffered from a good deal of semantic confusion, and defining it has become a favorite pastime of the more thoughtful practitioners of scientific research. The "industrial" part of the term seems clear enough, but the word "research" has a variety of meanings. "Getting new knowledge, that is just what research is," one veteran of industrial research put it.[1] An academician defined it in a somewhat more sophisticated way; "research may be defined as the application of human intelligence in a systematic manner to a problem whose solution is not immediately available."[2]

There can be little disagreement with such general definitions, but difficulties mount when one tries to distinguish various kinds of research. One common distinction between "fundamental" and "applied" research must be mentioned. The distinction lies not so much in "what" the researcher is doing as in "why" he does it. Fundamental research seeks to extend scientific knowledge, while applied research attempts to explore technology with scientific methods and principles. The former is motivated largely by curi-

* Reprinted by permission of the publishers from *Pioneering Industrial Research* (Washington, D.C.: Public Affairs Press, 1957), pp. 1–27.

[1] T. A. Boyd in a lecture at the University of Wisconsin, Oct. 6, 1950.
[2] David Bendel Hertz, *The Theory and Practice of Industrial Research* (New York, McGraw-Hill, 1950), p. 2.

osity, although the scientist may work in faith that his discoveries will at some time in the future have utilitarian value; the latter is more clearly motivated by considerations of usefulness. Fundamental research adds to understanding about the nature of the physical world; applied research uses this understanding to manipulate and control man's natural environment. Both varieties of research call for a high order of scientific competence, but the results are different. Industrial research laboratories have engaged in both kinds of investigations, but they are quite naturally concerned primarily with applied research.

The difficulties and follies of attempting to develop narrower definitions and make finer distinctions are soon apparent when one examines the kinds of activities research laboratories customarily engage in. So-called "research" laboratories have sponsored fundamental research, applied scientific principles to discover radically new processes or products, developed these processes and products to the point of commercial practicability, seen them through the pilot-plant stage, acted as troubleshooters for market or production difficulties, been responsible for quality control, and even, in a few cases, engaged in routine testing and production control. Obviously, the term "research" covers a wide spectrum of scientific activities. But equally obviously any attempt to distinguish fine gradations in a research hierarchy has little basis in reality since there is little or no agreement on the boundaries between the various types of research.

In the final analysis, industrial research as it developed in the late nineteenth and twentieth centuries involves at least four elements. First, it is nearly always organized research; the term generally does not include the individual inventor or the lone experimenter. Second, industrial research uses scientific methods and scientifically trained personnel. Third, in-

dustrial research is concerned with the natural sciences and technology and excludes such things as the social sciences or market research. Last, the investigations carried on in industrial research laboratories, whether they be fundamental or applied research, are connected in one way or another with industry and are directed primarily toward improving technology and maximizing economic satisfactions. Industrial research in the long run is utilitarian.

The Rise of Industrial Research

In the age of the automobile, plastic chemistry, atomic energy, and modern medicine, it is difficult for the layman to realize that industrial research is a relatively recent development. Yet such is the case. This is not to say that human beings have only recently begun to apply intelligence to the solution of technical problems; technology in the sense of a systematic knowledge of the industrial arts is exceedingly old. However, the application of science to the solution of technical problems is something relatively new.

Historically, science and technology have occupied two separate and largely independent spheres of activity. Science devoted itself to the development of a fuller and more satisfactory philosophical understanding of the world of natural phenomena. Its cultivation was confined largely to members of the educated upper classes who pursued it out of curiosity. It is probably symbolic of its character that science was known as "natural philosophy" and "natural history" until the nineteenth century. By contrast, technology was concerned with the manipulation of things and the production of economic goods. It was essentially a traditional knowledge, handed down from one generation to the next, among eminently practical craftsmen. Innovation was the result of crude empiricism of the cut-and-try variety. Between the two branches of knowledge there was negligible interplay, in part because of the differing social statuses of the scientist and the craftsmen, but largely because science had little or nothing to offer technology.

It would, of course, be an overstatement to say that there was no contact between the scientific and technological traditions in western civilization. There were a number of notable exceptions. Archimedes, for example, mixed the two as he formulated the law of floating bodies and devised new and improved instruments of war. The medieval alchemists combined theorizing about the nature of materials with experimentation out of which grew primitive industrial chemistry. Medicine at various times in history combined the construction of elaborate theories of the nature and operation of the human body with practical information about its actual operation and techniques for combating at least a few of humanity's ailments.

The seventeenth and eighteenth centuries in particular brought some interesting contacts between science and technology. Huygens and Hooke utilized the scientific theories of mechanics in work on clocks and watches; astronomical discoveries had practical implications for navigation; and James Watt found that the theoretical work being done in the field of heat helped him to improve the steam engine. Yet it is fair to say that even in the seventeenth and eighteenth centuries, science was relatively helpless in the face of technological problems.

Despite these practical limitations on the actual contact between science and technology, the belief developed in the seventeenth and eighteenth centuries that science possessed great utilitarian possibilities. This belief found an outstanding exponent in the person of Francis Bacon, whose most recent biographer has dubbed

him the "Philosopher of Industrial Science." Bacon not only argued for a greater amount of empirical research in science but also urged that science could be of practical importance and in his famous description of "Solomon's House" foresaw the cooperative approach which has been such a striking feature of modern scientific research. Robert Boyle, another prominent seventeenth century scientific figure, similarly claimed that practical inventions might well rise out of science. This view of the utilitarian possibilities of science was taken up and widely disseminated in the eighteenth century by the scientific societies which sprang up in western Europe and began the popularization of scientific knowledge.

But before the marriage of science and technology could be consummated, three conditions had to be met. First, science had to develop to a point where there was no question about its usefulness to technology. Second, businessmen and those other people who made the basic decisions in economic life had to realize the importance of science to their economic welfare. Finally, some institutional arrangements had to be made for the conduct of industrial research. These conditions were finally met in the nineteenth century.

The development of science to a point where its principles had application in economic activity occurred at various times, depending on the science and the type of economic activity involved. The importance of science in agriculture was revealed relatively early in the nineteenth century. The work of the German chemist Justus von Liebig in the 1830's was the crucial development in this field, and eventually led to the modern agricultural revolution based on systematic scientific research in agriculture and vigorous efforts to disseminate new and better ideas among the practicing agriculturists. In the broad field of engineering, the convergence of science and technology came in the middle of the nineteenth century when it became apparent that close attention to scientific principles could work significant savings in the cost of construction.

More spectacular was evidence of the utility of science provided by individual industries. The synthetic dye industry is a good example. Although English chemist William Henry Perkin synthesized the first dye in 1856, German chemists soon seized the leadership of the industry, and by World War I they had completely ruined the formerly flourishing business of producing indigo. The scientific feats performed by the German dye-manufacturers and the profits they reaped as a result of their scientific prowess were often cited by the promoters of industrial research as evidence of the profitability of applying science to industry. Carl Zeiss' success in improving optical instruments through the use of scientific talent was another outstanding example of the way in which science could aid industry. The electrical industry was perhaps the prime example of the way in which the discovery of new scientific principles could create a whole new technology independent of any preexisting traditional craft techniques. By the end of the century, the petroleum industry, destined to become a leader in industrial research, had begun to realize that scientifically trained geologists could be of immense help in locating the eagerly sought pools of oil beneath the earth's surface.

Uneven progress in the various sciences meant, of course, that not all industries profited equally from the application of science. The nineteenth century steel industry, for example, made little use of developments in physical metallurgy, in part at least because they seemed to offer little of practical importance, and C. E. Kenneth Mees, one of the most experienced industrial research directors in America and long-time head of research for Eastman Kodak has declared that "to

this day the making of photographic materials is in advance of the understanding of the basic science of the subject."[3] Such industries as textiles would provide further evidence for the generalization that in many industries traditional craft knowledge remained more important than systematic scientific knowledge until relatively recent times. This is not to say that these industries neglected research; it merely means that the research they did was based more on cut-and-try methods than on scientific principles.

The growing realization of the importance of science for industry can be seen in the increasing use of scientifically trained persons in nineteenth century industry. Use of such men was sporadic and scattered, but from the little we know about the subject, it is clear that a growing number of industrialists called on the services of scientifically trained individuals. The French revolutionary government, for example, mobilized French scientists in the 1790's in the defense of the fatherland. The scientists proved of considerable assistance developing new shells, a semaphore telegraphy system, captive observation balloons, and improved methods of producing gunpowder. A half century later, the noted German chemist, Robert Bunsen, was invited to use his knowledge in the study of blast-furnace operation. From 1858 to 1866, Sir William Thomson (later Lord Kelvin), one of England's outstanding physicists, devoted his talents to making a technical success out of the Atlantic cable.

In the United States the influx of scientifically trained men, especially chemists, into industry was steady and striking. In the first half of the nineteenth century Joseph Cloud became assay master at the Philadelphia Mint, while Samuel Luther Dana in a career lasting from 1834 to 1868 with the Merrimack Manufacturing

[3] "The Growth of Industrial Research," *American Ceramic Society Bulletin*, 29:449 (Dec., 1950).

Company of Lowell, Massachusetts, introduced numerous innovations into the textile industry. Shortly before the Civil War, pioneer oil men called on the noted American chemist, Benjamin Silliman, Jr., to analyze their oil samples. The use of scientifically trained men grew more rapidly after the Civil War as chemists moved into the iron and steel industry. By the end of the century, chemists were entering such industries as meat-packing, copper, paper, and others. Still, the prejudice against trained men remained strong, and many scientists reported resistance to their efforts to change traditional methods in the light of theoretical discoveries.

Of even greater importance than the individual scientist who entered industry to utilize his talents were the scientists who personally founded new industries as a result of outstanding inventions or discoveries. Many of the most important inventors of the nineteenth century—Eli Whitney, Oliver Evans, Robert Fulton, Samuel F. B. Morse, Alexander Graham Bell, and Charles Goodyear, to cite only some prominent American examples—were men of little scientific training, basically inventors whose ideas grew out of their knowledge of industrial arts rather than from science. But as the century advanced it became increasingly clear that inventions were flowing from the minds of scientifically trained men who proceeded to exploit their own ideas in business. In Europe, Perkin, the first scientist to synthesize a dye, went into the synthetic dye business himself, and gave practical training to other chemists who often left to found new firms. In the United States, John Wesley Hyatt with the aid of Frank Vanderpoel, a trained chemist, developed celluloid in the 1870's. Chemist Charles M. Hall, experimenting at Oberlin, discovered a practicable method of producing aluminum in the 1880's and spent the rest of his life directing development work on the process. Leo H. Baekeland, a professor at a Belgian school, in the 1890's embarked on a career of independent inventing and promoting which produced a new type of photographic paper and one of the first important plastics, Bakelite. Such inventor-entrepreneurs, who combined technical training with a firm grasp of commercial necessities and possibilities, did much to convince industry of the usefulness of science and, as we shall see, were especially important in the electrical industry.

The final contribution of the nineteenth century to the growth of industrial research was the concept and practice of cooperative organized research. The historically-minded scientist could find bases for such practice in the distant past in the researches pursued at the famous Museum in Hellenistic Alexandria, and the theorist could turn to the preachments of Francis Bacon for encouragement. But in the final analysis it was the developing practice of cooperative research that shaped the modern industrial research laboratory.

In part, cooperative research grew out of the techniques of graduate instruction in science in the nineteenth century universities, particularly in Germany. The essential element in the Ph.D. degree was a piece of original research carried out by the candidate under the supervision of his instructor. The topics of research were generally dictated by the interests and knowledge of the instructor so that in effect, a kind of cooperative research system grew up with instructors acting as heads of research units and utilizing less-experienced students to assist in expanding the frontiers of science. Under the *Privatdocent* system, new Ph.D.'s were often attached to the university in an unsalaried position where they were permitted to gain further teaching and research experience while eking out a living from student fees. The result was the development, particularly in Germany, of specialized research institutes which did a great deal of a kind of cooperative research. This variety of cooperative research received a further stimulus in the latter part of the nineteenth century with the formation of government-supported national laboratories designed to maintain physical standards and do additional research. The first was the German Physikalische Technische Reichsanstalt formed in 1870; the American counterpart, the Bureau of Standards, was organized in 1901.

Perhaps even more important than the example of the universities was the slow but steady establishment of organized laboratories within individual corporations or specific industries. In the United States trained chemists set themselves up in consulting practice or organized laboratories which catered to the varied needs of different clients. Charles T. Jackson, the erratic discoverer of the anesthetic properties of ether, opened a laboratory in Boston in 1836 where he conducted experiments on sorghum, cotton-seed, and other products. His contemporary, James C. Booth, studied in Europe with Wöhler and Magnus and then returned to Philadelphia in 1836 to open a laboratory which became not only a center of industrial investigations but also a leading training school for American chemists. C. M. Wetherill and Frederick A. Genth were other Philadelphians who operated analytical and consulting laboratories before the Civil War. Later in the century Peter T. Austen, Henry C. Bolton, Thomas B. Stillman and Henry Wurtz operated such laboratories in New York while James F. Babcock and Francis H. Storer were active in Boston.

Individual American corporations gradually set up separate laboratories during the nineteenth century, although much of their activity could hardly be considered research in any modern sense of the word. The Pennsylvania Railroad, for example, hired Charles B. Dudley in 1875

to set up testing and specification systems for the railroad; when he left, the Pennsylvania possessed a laboratory with 34 trained chemists. The iron and steel industry early founded laboratories of a kind. R. W. Hunt, a chemist trained in Booth's laboratory, in 1860 established an analytical laboratory at the Johnstown plant of the Cambria Iron Company, and one of the first successful Bessemer steel plants included a chemical laboratory when it was built at Wyandotte, Michigan, in 1863. But the transition from individual to organized scientific research in industry was perhaps best exemplified by Thomas A. Edison's laboratory. By 1876, Edison had already been so successful with his inventions that he was able to leave manufacturing and devote full time to inventing and experimenting. To assist him in his work he established a well-equipped and permanently staffed laboratory in Menlo Park, New Jersey. In 1878 when he began concentrated work on the electric lamp he had a nucleus of about 20 men. Although Edison himself was more an inventor than a scientist and actually had few scientifically-trained men in his laboratory, the fact that he had an *organized* laboratory probably enabled him to gain priority over his competitors in the invention of the incandescent electric lamp. He certainly demonstrated the profitability of organized research and development.

Industrial research burgeoned forth in its modern form in the late nineteenth and early twentieth centuries, primarily in Germany and the United States. In Germany the electrical, chemical and optical industries made systematic use of scientific personnel and set up large-scale laboratories before World War I, while German industry as a whole supported the establishment in 1911 of the Kaiser Wilhelm Gesellschaft, a series of scientific institutes conducting both fundamental and applied research. In the United States, industrial research began to attract an increasing amount of attention in the technical press in the decade preceding World War I, and these years saw the organization of some of the most important industrial research laboratories, notably at General Electric, DuPont, Bell Telephone, Westinghouse, Eastman Kodak and Standard Oil (Indiana). Rapid technical advancement in chemicals and electricity made the need for systematic research apparent, while the growth of large corporations provided economic organizations with sufficient capital to support research and to exploit its results.

But it was World War I which really convinced Western Europe and the United States of the necessity for systematic industrial research. Both England and the United States found themselves cut off from German dyes, chemicals, medicines, and glass. The result was a vigorous effort to bring science to the aid of industry. In the United States existing industrial research laboratories turned toward the war effort, while the government set up the National Research Council to coordinate the activities of American scientists. The results were astounding. Applied reseach during the war gave a tremendous boost to the American chemical industry besides solving innumerable special wartime problems. It was a convincing display of the benefits of industrial research. In the United Kingdom the problems were similar, but the solution was different. There the government formed the Department of Scientific and Industrial Research (D.S.I.R.), an agency which has since played a leading role in encouraging cooperative British industrial research.

Patterns of European Development

Since World War I, research has been an established part of the industrial scene. But its exact character has depended so much on time and place that it is impossible to generalize with any degree of

accuracy. The rate of expansion and the patterns of organization of industrial research have shown significant national variations. Similarly research activity has depended on technological and economic conditions which have varied widely from industry to industry. With such important national and industry differences existing it will be necessary to undertake a brief country-by-country survey. (No attempt is made here to discuss industrial research in the Soviet Union where administrative patterns have diverged sharply from Western practice.)

From about 1900 to 1930, Germany was quite clearly the leading industrial research country in the world. There were a number of reasons for this. German industry was relatively late developing, but when it did begin to flourish in the latter part of the nineteenth century, the application of science was unhindered by obsolescent methods or ideas. In addition, German universities of the nineteenth century were leaders in scientific work; Heidelberg, Berlin, Göttingen, Leipzig and Giessen provided Germany with the best trained scientists of nineteenth century Europe. Furthermore, industrial research in Germany did not suffer from the social stigma that was attached to it by the upper classes in England; instead it offered an outlet to talent in a country where it was increasingly difficult to acquire positions in the state, the university, or the clergy. Government offered its aid also by supporting the Physikalische Technische Reichsanstalt and contributing to the Kaiser Wilhelm Gesellschaft. Finally, Germany had special stimuli for increased research in the 1920's. Industry turned to science for solutions to all kinds of economic problems in an attempt to recoup the losses of World War I.

The golden age of German industrial research in the 1920's gradually gave way to slow decline under the Nazis. While the Nazis made few structural changes in the conduct of German research, they did put ever increasing emphasis on immediate results and permitted long-range fundamental research to languish. Furthermore, the advent of politics into science helped disrupt many a research project while anti-Semitism hampered the flow of talent into the scientific field. The final blows came with the physical destruction of World War II, the invasion of Germany itself, and occupation by conquerors who all too soon fell to quarreling among themselves and thereby split Germany. Nonetheless, industrial research in West Germany has shown amazing recuperative powers. In the decade since the end of the war it has once again become an efficient auxiliary to reviving German industry.

Throughout the turbulent decades of its history German research has shown very persistent patterns of organization. A sizeable part of industrial research has been concentrated in laboratories of the larger corporations. As early as 1900, the four leading German chemical manufacturers were employing over 500 chemists, while one particular company, the Badische Anilin und Soda Fabrik, supported Adolf Baeyer and a group of chemists for 15 years at a cost of $5 million while they developed a practicable synthesis of indigo from benzene via anilin. Chemical firms such as I. G. Farbenindustrie maintained this research lead in later years. Prominent electrical firms, such as Siemens and A.E.G., and leading steel companies, such as Vereinigte Stahlwerke and Krupp, had well-equipped laboratories and competent staffs. A good many of these managed to survive World War II in one way or another. Some were relatively undamaged. Others had a more difficult time. The Zeiss optical works, for example, had the misfortune to be located in the Russian zone, but 84 of Zeiss' ranking managers and scientists were able to escape west and begin anew.

Perhaps Germany's most significant contribution to the organization of industrial research was in the field of coopera-tive research. The most notable example of this was the Kaiser Wilhelm Gesellschaft. Founded in 1911, it drew support from both government and industry but remained independent of both as it set up a series of scientific institutes which conducted both fundamental and applied research. Germany also developed a good many cooperative research associations, especially in industries where plants were small or where cartels, trade associations or special societies existed. Textiles, automobiles, and railway cars provided pre-World War II examples of such cooperative research. In addition, German industry often sponsored work in the universities. While the specific organizations were often disrupted in the holocaust of 1944–45, recent developments in Germany show a continued interest in the cooperative approach. The Kaiser Wilhelm Gesellschaft has been replaced by the Max Planck Society, and a whole new array of cooperative organizations has developed, most of them heavily supported by the government.

Germany's major European rival in the application of science to industry was Britain. While British industrial research has grown steadily since World War I, it has tended to lag behind Germany and the United States, at least until the temporary elimination of one of its rivals in 1945. Several factors have contributed to this situation. British industry, having gained a head start in the Industrial Revolution, has seemed reluctant to change with the times. Much of British industry has been dominated by small firms incapable of supporting very much scientific research. Moreover, British industry has too often been controlled by people with little scientific background or interest. Even the chemical and electrical industries, the chief backers of British industrial research, have had few men of scientific background or interest on their boards of directors. Some people have argued that the British educated classes have been prejudiced against industrial research, favoring instead the more rarefied atmosphere of "pure" research in the university laboratory; but how important this has actually been is impossible to say.

The precise size of the British industrial research effort past or present is difficult to determine; most estimates have been little more than informed guesses. One observer in 1938 set research expenditures of British industry, apart from government assistance, at only about £2 million per year. A survey made in 1945–46 found the situation somewhat improved. By that time British industry was employing about 10,000 scientific graduates and spending perhaps £30 million annually on research and development within its own establishments. The most recent figures reported by the D.S.I.R. reveal total British research expenditures of about £325 million with research being performed by 133,000 persons, 32,000 of whom were qualified in science or engineering. These figures for 1955 are substantial. Yet they are small when compared with American research and development outlay and are clearly inadequate for British needs.

A substantial proportion of British industrial research has been carried out in the laboratories of individual corporations. In 1955 over half of British research was carried out in privately-owned industry, although the British government foots the bill for over 60% of British research. Estimates of the number and quality of these private laboratories have not been very accurate, but there were perhaps 500 of them doing some kind of research and development in 1950. Most of the important work has been concentrated in a relatively few laboratories of the most research-conscious corporations. Aircraft, chemicals, electrical manufacturing, and engineering and shipbuilding have been the British research leaders in recent years. Imperial Chemical Industries, for example, was one of the pioneers in British industrial research, and in recent

years has possessed a highly-developed system of laboratories working on every imaginable type of chemical problem. Within the electrical industry British Thomson Houston, the General Electric Company, Metropolitan-Vickers, and Philips Lamps all have had good-sized laboratories and spent substantial sums in industrial research.

One of Britain's more interesting contributions to the organization of industrial research has been the research association jointly sponsored by the government and a specific industry. Impressed by the virtues of industrial research during World War I, the government set up the Department of Scientific and Industrial Research (D.S.I.R.) with a fund of a million pounds to be spent over a period of years to encourage industrial research. The general plan was to set up cooperative research associations supported jointly by government and industry funds with the idea that the associations would eventually become self-supporting. Initial results were disappointing. Capital was at first inadequate, industry proved reluctant to provide money, and good scientists were dubious about joining an organization with such an uncertain future. Nonetheless the government persisted and managed to organize over 20 associations in the 1920's. While the depression of the 1930's inhibited expansion of the system, only one association failed, two more were added, and income grew slowly but steadily. There was a vast expansion during World War II, and by 1950 the number of associations had reached 42 and total income had risen sevenfold over 1939 to about £3.4 million.

Research associations have been formed to investigate everything from scientific instruments and refractories to laundry techniques and coil springs. Materials research and equipment design and development have been especially important fields of investigation. Much of the research has been fundamental, but there has also been some development work, a good deal of routine technical advice, and even some technical training. The scope of the operation varies widely; staff size may be under 20 or over 500, depending on the association. On the whole these cooperative research associations have proved to be workable and useful in stimulating industrial research, especially in those industries composed of firms too small to support extensive research in their own laboratories.

The government, in addition to its subsidies to the research associations, encourages research in other ways. The D.S.I.R. has operated the National Physical Laboratory since 1918 and the Geological Survey since 1919. It has set up research centers in several specific areas, notably fuels, food preservation, building, forest products, radio, high pressure and high temperature chemistry, water pollution, and road construction. Other government agencies conduct important work in telecommunications, agriculture, medicine, armaments and atomic energy. In addition, the government pays for a substantial amount of research done in industrial laboratories, particularly in aircraft and armaments. To help exploit discoveries made in government laboratories, the Board of Trade established after World War II a National Research Development Corporation, provided with £5 million to develop to the marketable stage inventions resulting from government or government-sponsored research.

Other agencies have also participated in British industrial research. The universities have done their share. The D.S.I.R. administers a system of university science scholarships and research grants while private industry, notably Imperial Chemical Industries, has granted fellowships for university research in particular fields of interest. Some of the research sponsored by the D.S.I.R. research associations has actually been performed in university laboratories. Since World War II a new element has entered the industrial research scene. Two private research institutes, apparently modeled on American counterparts like the Mellon and Battelle institutes, have been founded. Such institutes may find a useful place in performing confidential research which the research associations have been reluctant to handle.

Any discussion of industrial research in France must inevitably revolve around the question of why there has been so little. In the early nineteenth century France was the acknowledged scientific leader of Europe. Yet as the century advanced, France lost ground relative to Germany and England, and following World War I an absolute decline set in. There are a number of reasons for this. For one thing, a large segment of French society has always remained anti-scientific in temper. Furthermore, science has depended heavily on the state for support, and the state has at times been niggardly with its funds. The pitifully inadequate laboratories of great nineteenth century French scientists such as Claude Bernard, Louis Pasteur, and the Curies bear eloquent witness to this. Furthermore, science has generally been considered primarily a part of man's cultural heritage rather than a tool of practical value. This tendency to shun practical applications of scientific knowledge, accentuated by the conservatism, passiveness and secretiveness of French business, has severely limited French contributions to industrial research.

The structure of French scientific research in the twentieth century has clearly been dominated by the state. Government laboratories and the laboratories of nationalized industries have been of great importance. Furthermore, French educational institutions, another important source of scientific research, have been closely under the control of the government. The state in addition in 1939 set up an elaborate organization, the National Center of Scientific Research, supported by state funds but controlled by leading scientists, which has since World War II supported a large staff of scientists, coordinated French scientific research, trained advanced investigators, and encouraged cooperative industrial research. While private industry has tended to lag behind the state, a good many of the more progressive firms have set up their own laboratories. If France has fallen far behind Germany, the United Kingdom and the United States in the twentieth century, some observers have been able to discern signs of a post-World War II scientific renaissance which may slowly bridge the gap.

Italian industrial research has followed a different pattern. Applied science has been steadily emphasized, in part because of the long years of Fascist rule with its emphasis on national self-sufficiency. Mussolini's twenty-three year regime also made the state a prominent element in the scientific scene, and even since World War II, government laboratories and the government-sponsored National Research Council have played an important role in industrial research. The state-supported universities, too, not only have done basic research but also have cooperated closely with industry. Most industrial firms have little time or money for research. True, Montecatini (chemicals), Fiat (mechanical engineering), Pirelli (rubber), and a few others support laboratories that are quite respectable by American standards, but these are exceptions. Small industry has been particularly neglected, for cooperative research has made less headway in Italy than in other parts of Europe.

While other European countries have not developed research organizations of a scope comparable with the four major powers already discussed, some excellent industrial research work is performed in the smaller countries. In many cases applied research is limited and specialized to meet the particular needs of the individual country. Sweden and Norway, for example, have done a good deal of research dealing with their particular raw material and power resources, while

Denmark has concentrated on dairying and other aspects of agriculture. In most of the smaller countries cooperative research has played a very prominent role. Sweden, Norway, the Netherlands, and Belgium all have systems of cooperative research, the Belgian system having been inspired by the British D.S.I.R. The individualistic Swiss provide an exception. In most of these countries the state has contributed substantial support. Norwegian applied research is financed almost exclusively by the government; the Danish government supports agricultural research; Sweden aids research projects through a system of grants made by research councils; the Belgian government supports cooperative research in the same fashion as the British; while the Dutch government makes substantial grants through a national research organization. Again the Swiss form a notable exception. In virtually all of the countries there are close relations between the universities and technical institutes and industry.

If most of the smaller countries have turned increasingly to state aid and various kinds of cooperative research, this has not prevented the establishment of some excellent private laboratories. In the Netherlands, for example, the Philips firm has performed outstanding research in the electrical field since the turn of the century, and Royal Dutch Shell has supported a sizable laboratory. In Switzerland the prominent pharmaceutical firm CIBA spends close to $3 million per year on research. Nor are these merely exceptions. Many other Swiss firms support research, while a recent survey revealed over 50 good-sized industrial laboratories in Sweden.

Industrial research, like the Industrial Revolution, has tended to expand from the major centers of industry to the more peripheral areas. Most of the smaller countries of Western Europe tended to develop industrial research organizations at a later date than did countries like Germany and the United Kingdom. Thus

Austria and Ireland are only now beginning to encourage systematic industrial research. With the expansion of industrialism to other parts of the world has gone the idea of industrial research. Australia, for example, has since World War II copied the British system of governmental encouraged industrial research, while Canada has slowly broken away from its dependence on the United States and the United Kingdom and begun its own programs. More important, research has been seen by the so-called underdeveloped countries as a prime weapon in their struggle to industrialize and compete with the western world in the economic realm. Japan, the earliest of the non-European powers to industrialize, developed an elaborate system of industrial research in the 1930's largely dominated by the government, but drawing partly on German, partly on American practice. Much of the work that was produced was of dubious value, but Japanese technology was making important strides before it was disrupted by World War II. Since the war, there has been a revival of scientific activity, largely sponsored by the government. India has similarly turned to research to assist its program of economic expansion. Inspired by the British C.S.I.R., the Indians have established a series of national laboratories and research institutes as well as co-operative research associations which have begun to attack the multitudinous scientific and technical problems of India's economic development. Even Burma has turned to research. Under a 1953 Point Four grant, American scientists from the Armour Research Institute have been assisting the Burmese to establish a technical institute which would do research in ceramics, metallurgy, and several other fields.

Thus, beginning in the late nineteenth century, scientific methods have been applied to industry and technology in Western Europe and its cultural appendages. The institutions for the promotion of industrial research and the vigor with which research has been prosecuted have varied from country to country. Clearly internal conditions—the state of scientific knowledge, the conditions of industry, political and social factors such as war and the drive for self-sufficiency—have modified and conditioned industrial research. But by mid-century industrial research has become a clearly recognized aspect of science and an activity essential to economic and industrial advancement. Individual countries have had a wide area of choice in how they might utilize and administer industrial research; none could escape the consequences of neglecting it.

The Growth of American Industrial Research

Nowhere has industrial research been more assiduously cultivated than in the United States, and there is available a mass of statistical and descriptive material which presents a clear and reasonably precise picture of its growth and characteristics since World War I. The statistical material is of two types. First, the National Research Council since 1920 has periodically published directories of American industrial research laboratories and has estimated the number of personnel employed in them. Second, periodic attempts have been made to estimate American research expenditures. These figures are less satisfactory than the first, largely because of varying definitions of research, different accounting systems, a reluctance to publicize financial figures, and changes in the price level and the cost of research through the years. Nonetheless, the estimates that have been made are valuable in suggesting the general level and distribution of research efforts.

The picture that emerges from these statistics is one of steady growth during the 1920's, relative stagnation during the depression of the 1930's, and a new and rapid increase in research during World

War II and the subsequent Cold War. Indications are that the 1920's were the seedtime of most American industrial laboratories. Some of the more important ones had been founded before World War I, but interest in research was more widespread and active after that conflict than before. The first fairly comprehensive survey of the National Research Council in 1927 showed nearly a thousand laboratories; by 1931 the number had increased to over 1600. Total personnel had risen from 19,000 to 32,000 in the same interval. The best estimates available indicate that about $166 million were being spent annually for scientific research in 1930, 70% of this by industry, and indications are that most companies engaged in research had increased their expenditures steadily during the 1920's.

The advent of the depression brought a minor setback to industrial research, although not as serious as one might have expected. Between 1931 and 1933 the number of laboratory workers declined by more than 5000, in part because 110 firms discontinued organized research. The smaller firms were apparently the hardest hit. Nonetheless the setback was minor and temporary. By 1938 personnel employed in industrial research laboratories had risen above the 1931 level to total over 44,000, while industry research expenditures climbed over $200 million by 1940, encouraged by the profitability of research and by New Deal tax policies.

World War II brought important changes. There was a sharp increase in the total amount of research. The war effort mobilized scientists of every hue and description, and experience showed that scientists who had previously pursued scientific truth within the cloistered environs of the college campus could be of immense help in solving pressing technical problems. The war, too, emphasized the importance of the cooperative approach to research and brought new experience in the techniques of organized scientific endeavor. Above all, the success of Allied arms and the awesome results of the atomic research brought new prestige to science and a renewed confidence in its utilitarian potentialities.

The net result has been a marked increase in applied research in the United States since the war. The number of persons engaged in research is more than double the pre-war level, and a shortage of trained personnel has become the limiting factor in research efforts and a matter of serious concern. Total research expenditures have risen even faster than the size of the research staff, in part because of the postwar inflation, and in part because of the growing cost and complexity of research. Indications are that we are spending as much or more relative to our gross national product as European nations. Above all, the war and the succeeding years have tremendously increased the role of the Federal government in applied research. With the accent on atomic energy, aircraft, and missile development, the government has increasingly provided funds and shaped the character of research and development. The 1953 survey of science and engineering in American industry sponsored by the National Science Foundation revealed that the Federal government paid for 37% of the research and development carried on in American industry besides spending substantial sums in its own scientific establishment.

Generalizations of this kind, however, cover a great many variations. Statistics on "research" encompass numerous activities. How much is basic research, how much advanced types of applied research, and how much simple production control or trouble-shooting is difficult to say. What is clear is that the amount of basic research is relatively small. A 1952 study of 191 leading American corporations which account for perhaps a third of U.S. industrial research expenditures concluded that 50% of the research and development expenditures in these com-

296/ VOLUME TWO: VIEWS OF AMERICAN ECONOMIC GROWTH

panies went for product improvement, 42% for new product development, and only 8% for basic research. The 1953 survey by the National Science Foundation found only 4% of total industry research and development expenditures going for basic research. Even allowing for a wide margin of error it is clear that it is unusual to find much fundamental research in an industrial laboratory.

General statistics of the numbers of people engaged in research also hide the precise character of the workers. The 1953 National Science Foundation survey showed, for example, that in corporations with more than 1000 employees, there were 180 supporting personnel—technicians, craftsmen, clerical help, and administrators—for every 100 scientists or engineers. Among the technically trained personnel, chemists have traditionally been the most numerous, although in recent years they have been overtaken and passed by engineers, a reflection of the growing importance of aircraft and armaments in the research picture. Physicists, metallurgists, mathematicians, and biological and earth scientists are also hired by industry, but in numbers they lag far behind chemists and engineers.

Industry is not the only agency competing for the services of scientifically trained men. Government and the universities require a share of the available manpower. As of 1954 the United States had around 850,000 persons with professional scientific or engineering training including about 650,000 engineers. Perhaps 192,000 scientists and engineers were engaged in research and development in 1953. Recent estimates indicate that colleges and universities hold around 42,000, some of them engaged full-time in research work. The Federal government employed around 80,000 people in scientific positions in 1951 according to the last available figures. Whether or not this is a proper distribution of available scientists is hard to say. There may be too few in colleges and universities considering that these institutions educate future scientists and carry on a large proportion of America's fundamental research.

Within industry, research workers are by no means evenly distributed. Geographically, research has been concentrated in the northeast and in the large urban centers. In 1950 62% of the personnel employed in industrial research laboratories were located in New York, New Jersey, Pennsylvania, Ohio, Illinois, and Michigan, although the figure had been 73% in 1938 and the intervening twelve years had seen a marked expansion of research in states like California and Texas. The South, despite vigorous and highly-publicized efforts to improve its economy through research, still accounted for only about 4% of U.S. industrial research in 1952.

More important, industrial research has tended to be dominated by big business and large laboratories. From the beginning, established industrial research laboratories tended to grow larger; 244 laboratories which reported in each of the National Research Council surveys from 1921 to 1938 showed a growth in the average number of employees from 32 to 70. This concentration of research in large laboratories is even more marked when one considers that in 1938 the 45 largest employers of research personnel employed half of the U.S. total with individual staffs ranging from 170 to 4000; these same corporations employed a third of the total in 1950, still a substantial percentage. The larger laboratories have been owned by the larger corporations. The afore-mentioned 45 companies included 36 owned or controlled by companies which were among the 200 leading nonfinancial corporations in the United States in the 1930's. The trend has not changed significantly since the war. A 1952 survey revealed that two out of three researchers were employed by companies with more than 5000 employees. This is not to say that small business has found research unprofitable and has not engaged in it; it merely points out that in the total picture, American big business has been the major backer of industrial research.

The most startling variations in the pattern of industrial research appear when one examines the amount of research performed in specific industries. The differences from industry to industry have been and are enormous. Industrial research made its earliest start in the electrical and chemical industries and expanded into petroleum, rubber and other fields. On the other hand, certain industries—textiles, primary metals, furniture, construction, and printing, for example—have never undertaken very much research. The validity of these generalizations has been upheld in virtually every study of American industrial research. In 1938, for example, the chemical petroleum, rubber and electrical industries employed about 57% of the researchers in American industry. By contrast, motor vehicles and agricultural machinery accounted for only $8\frac{1}{2}\%$ and the metals industries for only a bit over 6%. Textiles employed less than 1% of the researchers at work in American industry in 1938. When industries were ranked on the basis of the ratio between research workers and wage earners in 1938, chemicals, petroleum, rubber, and electrical manufacturing again ranked at the top. Nor has World War II changed the situation significantly. A survey of 4800 companies in 1951 showed that a relatively large percentage of the companies in such fields as chemicals, scientific instruments, and electrical equipment maintained research organizations, while relatively few metal fabricators, wood product companies, or printers and publishers engaged in organized research. Of the industrial chemical firms responding to the survey, 68.4% maintained research organizations; only 7.8% of the firms dealing with lumber and wood products had laboratories.

Such generalizations as these can be further substantiated by examining briefly the history of research in specific industries. As we shall see shortly, the electrical industry depending as it did on new scientific ideas for its founding and advancement, early engaged in organized technological improvement. Bell, Westinghouse, General Electric and R.C.A. have become major research leaders. The chemical industry, like the electrical, was an almost wholly new industry based on the discoveries of nineteenth century science rather than on the expansion of time-honored handicraft, cut-and-try techniques. The result has been that the chemical industry in Germany, the United Kingdom, and the United States has been one of the most important backers of research in each of these countries.

The leader of the American chemical industry, DuPont, used research as a method of expanding company interests. In the nineteenth century, DuPont was primarily an explosives manufacturer, but when it embarked on organized research shortly after the turn of the twentieth century it moved into dyes and general organic chemicals. By 1927 it was engaging in some fundamental research as well as a wide variety of more immediately profitable projects. By 1950 the company was carrying on about 1000 different research projects ranging from one-man laboratory work to pilot plant operations spread through 13 different departments and nearly 40 research laboratories manned by close to 2000 scientists and technicians. The research budget in 1950 was running around $35 million per year. In large part this was a reflection of the fact that research at DuPont had paid off spectacularly well; from the laboratories of the company had come dyes, synthetic rubbers, nitro-cellulose lacquers, and most important, nylon and a wide range of other synthetic fibers. If DuPont has been the research giant of the chemical industry, other firms have followed closely. Union Carbide, American Cyanamid, Dow Chemical, Allied Chemical and Dye, and others have all developed substantial research programs.

Other industries closely related to basic chemicals have also engaged in extensive research. Eastman Kodak, for example, was a company founded on the inventions of George Eastman in the field of photographic film, and the company used professionally trained chemists almost from the beginning. The laboratory, established in 1912 as an independent unit, developed into one of the largest and best in the industry. Laboratory discoveries helped the firm branch out from photography into other fields of chemistry. The head of the laboratory, Dr. C. E. K. Mees, has become one of the most noted and articulate of American directors of industrial research.

Pharmaceutical firms also engaged in research at a relatively early date. Some firms employed trained chemists in the nineteenth century, and nearly all found it desirable to enlarge their scientific staffs with the passage of the federal Pure Food and Drugs Act in 1906. By mid-twentieth century such staffs had grown to very large size, and observers have estimated that the pharmaceutical industry spends more for research in relation to its sales than any other American industry. The reason is obvious. A 1947 survey indicated that 54% of the drugs then in use had been unknown ten years before, and in the case of one leading firm, Abbott Laboratories, only 25% of its sales volume in 1951 was made up of items known a decade earlier.

The rubber industry was also an early and vigorous proponent of research. B. F. Goodrich entered the field as early as 1895 and U. S. Rubber began in 1913. While concentrating largely on tires and other rubber products, these companies have shown signs in recent years of branching out into new fields. This process of expansion of interests has characterized the growth of research in the petroleum industry as well. Research was slow to get started; as late as 1923 writers were pointing out the need for it in industry. It was the development of the cracking process in 1913 by Dr. William M. Burton of Standard Oil (Indiana) that really gave an impetus to research. Other companies were reluctant to depend on licenses from Standard and turned to research in an effort to get around the original patents. Some companies became interested in scientific investigation through their search for oil. Gulf Research and Development Corporation, for example, grew out of an interest in geophysical techniques in the discovery of petroleum. Research in turn has led to new fields, such as petrochemicals, as petroleum has become a source for a vast array of products in addition to the fuels and lubricants usually associated with the oil industry. As a result virtually all of the major oil companies have established sizable research laboratories. The Standard Oil Development Company was by far the largest in 1950 with 2600 technical and non-technical employees, but Shell, Standard of Indiana, Gulf and Texaco followed close behind with about 1700, while Socony-Vacuum, Standard of California, Phillips, Humble, Sinclair, Atlantic, and Sun each had more than 300.

The rapidity of the development of research as an organized activity in other fields has varied considerably. The American glass and optical industry, while lagging behind its German counterpart, had well established laboratories in such firms as Corning Glass and Bausch and Lomb before World War I. Producers of non-ferrous metals similarly began research work at a relatively early date; New Jersey Zinc and American Brass both were engaged in research activities before World War I. On the other hand, the iron and steel industry was relatively slow. The major companies such as U. S. Steel, Jones and Laughlin, and Bethlehem, did not begin research in earnest until the 1920's, and then a large proportion of their effort was directed toward empirical improvement rather than the expansion of fundamental theory. The amount and character of research in the machinery field has varied a great deal. While such an industry as automobile manufacturing has always depended on engineering advancement and has had the benefit of research activities among its suppliers in, for example, the rubber and steel industries, it has never been a real leader in fundamental research in the same way as the electrical or chemical industries. The aircraft industry has, of course, always depended heavily on research. It has been somewhat unique, however, in that most of the fundamental research has been performed for it by the government. While most industrial research has been concentrated in manufacturing, food processing firms, most notably meat packers, the large corporations such as General Mills, and important suppliers such as the Continental Can Company have also strongly supported industrial research.

Why have the variations in the amount of research performed in different industries been so great? There seem to be several reasons. In the first place some industries have been pretty clearly "technologically based"; that is, from the beginning their prosperity has depended on a rapidly changing technology founded on scientific principles. The electrical and chemical industries have been such examples. By contrast, such a field as metallurgy has had to depend pretty largely on empirical research untied to any well-developed conceptual framework. While this situation has begun to change in the last two decades, it is probably fair to say that scientific knowledge has not been of central importance to practical metallurgy until quite recently. Scientific research is not particularly attractive when technological change is slow or when science seems to offer little hope of important technical improvements. In the second place, a good many industries have been so organized as to be unable to afford a substantial amount of scientific research. In industries dominated by small firms, effective research has been difficult to conduct. This has been a limiting factor in such fields as textiles and clothing, or in some branches of specialized manufacturing.

A small firm structure is certainly a handicap to research when carried on by individual firms, and research carried on in the laboratories of individual companies has clearly been the dominant form of industrial research in the United States. In the petroleum industry, for example, it has been estimated that 90% of the research is carried on in research laboratories of competitive companies. Estimates of this kind were confirmed by the 1953 National Science Foundation survey which found that only 4.5% of total industrial spending for research and development went for work performed by organizations other than the companies supplying the funds.

Yet the plight of the small businessman is not impossible. Cooperative research can do much to meet the scientific needs of small firms or to supplement the research activities of large companies. One of the most common forms of cooperative research is that carried on by trade associations. In 1953 some 543 cooperative organizations, most of them trade associations, spent over $20 million for research and development. Sixty-six of the organizations operated their own laboratories employing 696 scientists and engineers and spending just under $10 million. The earliest and largest of the separate laboratories was the Underwriters Laboratories (1894); by way of contrast the laboratory of the Association of American Railroads was organized only in 1940. Organizations which have not desired to support their own laboratories have turned to government laboratories, agricultural experiment stations, university research facilities, and research institutes. Association research has included investigations into canning, paper, tanning, meat, baking, fisheries, coffee, laundering, and petroleum. On the whole it is fair to say that cooperative research has been a useful supplement to individual corporation laboratories, but that it has not become a decisive influence on American research nor has it reached the dimensions of some of the European efforts.

Perhaps the United States' unique contribution to the organization of industrial research has been the semi-private non-profit research institute. The earliest and one of the most successful of these was the Mellon Institute. The Mellon Institute grew out of the conception of Robert Kennedy Duncan, an American chemist, and the fortune of the Mellons. The scheme as it was developed shortly before World War I was to establish a well-equipped laboratory with a nucleus of trained personnel. Individual firms would then establish a fellowship for work on some specific problem. The laboratory administration would select the fellow and direct the research; the donor paid the salary of the fellow, the operating charges of the laboratory, and the cost of special equipment and at the same time received title to any results of the investigation. The Mellon Institute has been highly successful. Fellows have investigated everything from phenolic resins to sausage casings. In some cases fellowships have led to the organization of corporation research laboratories; in other cases the fellowships have become virtually permanent fixtures at Mellon.

In recent years the number of non-profit research institutes has increased to twelve. The largest, Battelle Memorial Institute, was founded in 1929 and has since expanded its operations as far as Europe. At Battelle the research project is carried out by the Institute as a whole rather than by a specially established fellowship. The twelve non-profit institutes employed about 6400 persons and reported total research and development expenditures of just over $53 million in 1953.

Closely related to the non-profit research institutes are the independent commercial laboratories. There are several hundred such laboratories, most of them very small, but they did around $33 million worth of business in 1953 and employed over 9300 people. Some of these grew out of the 19th century firms of consulting chemists. Arthur D. Little, Inc., the outstanding example of this genre, did just that. A large proportion of the commercial laboratories have been established since World War II, in many cases to take advantage of government research contracts. Most such laboratories concern themselves with relatively specific and limited projects for which they have special skills, although a few like Arthur D. Little, Inc., are able to handle a surprising variety of problems.

Research organizations such as the non-profit research institute and the commercial laboratory have performed an important function. They have served businesses unable to afford their own laboratories while at the same time they have provided large corporations with special facilities and talents which it would be uneconomical for the large company to provide itself. An increasingly large proportion of their research is paid for by the government—well over half in 1953. The largest industrial patronage comes from medium and larger-sized firms who have more research funds to spend and who seem to be able to do a better job of formulating research problems and utilizing research results than very small firms. Very little of the research is basic; most of the institutes and commercial laboratories sell the kind of applied research services industry and the government seem to want. It is a small but important service.

To some degree the universities have become centers for industrial research. The original impetus came from industry which initiated a policy of contributing research fellowships to the universities, either for general research in a broad area or occasionally for the solution of fairly specific or well-defined problems. Some universities before World War II turned more and more to a campaign to attract industrial research problems, often carried out in semi-independent research institutes. This trend was accentuated by heavy government research contracts during and after World War II. Such extensive use of university facilities for applied research, however, has raised problems which suggest that this may not be a wholly desirable development. In part the problems are administrative; salary differentials easily develop between professors concerned largely with contract research and those carrying the normal program of the university, and this can harm university morale. More important, an excessive interest in applied research can easily divert the university from its major objectives of training scientists and carrying on fundamental research of a kind which is too seldom seen in industrial research laboratories.

While the prime responsibility for American industrial research has remained in the hands of private agencies, the Federal government has expanded its role until at mid-twentieth century it is probably the single most important force shaping the direction and character of research. The Federal government has become involved in research for several reasons. It became a major supporter of agricultural research largely because American farming has been so organized as to be incapable of supporting research through private agencies. The government similarly seemed to be the only organization capable of operating large-scale geological surveys or organizing a nation-wide meteorological service. Most important, the government has become involved in research through national defense. World War II, the subsequent Cold War, and the development of atomic energy all contributed to the growing importance of the government in the research picture. Some of the research has been and is done in federal facilities, most notably in such establishments as the Bureau of Stand-

ards, the Department of Agriculture, or the Atomic Energy Commission. But a very large proportion—over half in 1955 —has been done in industrial or other private laboratories under contract.

From this brief survey of the historical background of industrial research several generalizations emerge. In the first place, industrial research has had a substantial history. It has been the offspring of the marriage of science and industry in the nineteenth century. In the second place, industrial research has not been an isolated phenomenon. Nearly all of the industrially and scientifically advanced countries of the western world have participated, and it is becoming apparent that the so-called "backward" countries of the world are becoming increasingly interested. In the third place, modern industrial research has been organized research. The increasing cost and complexity of research along with the growth of large-scale industrial organization made necessary and desirable an organized, cooperative approach. The lone investigator still plays an important role on the far frontiers of scientific knowledge, but applied research has generally been organized. In the fourth place, it must be noted that the characteristic forms of organization have varied considerably. Universities, private industry, the government, various kinds of cooperative agencies, private research laboratories, and consultants have all had their hands in research. Yet the particular pattern of research has varied from time to time and from place to place in accord with particular historical circumstances. Finally, it is clear that there have been immense variations in the amount of research performed in different industries. In part this has depended on the level of technical advancement in the industry, in part on the organization of the industry and its ability to support large-scale research. But whatever its character, it is clear that industrial research has come to play a major role in twentieth century society.

Chapter Eight

The Big Change in Agriculture

■ Twentieth-century American agriculture falls into three sharply contrasting periods. From 1900 to 1920 farmers enjoyed prosperity from good markets and rising prices. The years 1910 to 1914 were those chosen by the New Deal economists as representing "parity," the relationship between agricultural and industrial prices most satisfactory to the farmers.

Yet evident to anyone who would look deeply was the fact that stimulated by wartime demand, farmers had invested too much capital in raising wheat and other staples and not enough in diversifying to produce the meat, fruits, vegetables, and dairy products demanded by Americans with an increasing standard of living. As both the domestic and foreign markets for American wheat slumped in the twenties, the Western grain farmers were hard hit. With the coming of the Great Depression,

the producers of all the agricultural staples faced ruin.

The New Deal measures restored a degree of stability to agriculture, but a true revolution started with World War II. During the preceding twenty years there had accumulated an unprecedented amount of knowledge regarding higher-yielding and hardier varieties of grain, breeding animals for desired qualities, altering soil biology and chemistry, and proper fertilization. Improved tractors and a great number of specialized machines were available that would produce substantial economies if used in large enough operations. But the unprofitability of most farming and the uneconomically small size of the average farm had discouraged investment of money, brains, or additional labor in agriculture. By suddenly creating an abnormally large demand for food, World War II broke the dam and released this vast store of knowledge and technology. In the twenty-five years from 1940 to 1965 farming in the United States became a scientifically oriented, mechanized industry carried on by a small fraction of the total national labor force.

But a farm problem still remained. Of about 2,000,000 "commercial" farms in 1960, that is, farms with over $2,500-a-year cash income, about 750,000, those with over $10,000-a-year income, could have produced all the needed products. The rest were too small to be efficient under modern conditions. Yet the owners and tenants of these 1,250,000 small farms were kept on the land by their ability to be nearly self-sufficient and by Federal subsidies. Furthermore, they and other farmers, including over a million part-time cultivators, were strong enough politically, through farm organizations and the overrepresentation of rural areas on legislative bodies, to protect their favored position. The shift from regarding agriculture as a way of life that should be preserved to regarding it as a rather capital-intensive industry in which only efficient business units should be encouraged was far from complete.

The Crisis in Agriculture

■ By 1932 the staple-crop farmer appeared to have reached the end of the line. Total farm income, which had run between $10 billion and $11 billion a year from 1924 to 1929, sank to under $5 billion in 1932. Many farmers found it better to use corn for fuel than cart it to market. Only relief payments, a moratorium on mortgage debts, and some plan for the future could keep millions of farmers on their farms. It was in this atmosphere that George Peek, Henry Wallace, and other agricultural experts joined the Roosevelt administration in an effort to rescue the farmer. Gilbert Fite, of the University of Oklahoma, supplies a realistic account of the conflicts of ideas and politics that tend to enter into the formation of any new government economic policy. In theoretical language, these personal attitudes are some of the intervening variables that come between economic problems and the human response to the economic situation.

Gilbert C. Fite
Seven Months in the A.A.A.*

It was understandable for George Peek to feel that he should have a major part in

* From George N. Peak and the Fight for Farm Parity, by Gilbert C. Fite. Copyright 1954 by the University of Oklahoma Press, pp. 243–266.

developing any New Deal for American farmers. No one in the United States had given so much time and money in trying to work out a national agricultural policy. "I had bought it and paid for it and wanted to have something to say about the kind of legislation we were to have," he told Henry Wallace.

Regardless of what one may think of Peek's ideas, his part in publicizing and dramatizing the farm issue had been of inestimable value. And many loyal friends and supporters believed his ideas were sound. They expected Peek to furnish the same kind of aggressive leadership which he had demonstrated so well between 1924 and 1928. He would not disappoint them.

By early December, 1932, George and Georgia, his wife, were back in Washington. They took an apartment at the Carlton Hotel and settled down to help finish the farm fight. Agricultural leaders were then considering emergency legislation along the lines of the allotment plan. It called for benefit payments to growers of basic crops on that portion of their production used in the United States, providing farmers agreed to reduce their output as recommended by the secretary of agriculture. The payment was to be sufficient to bring the average commodity price up to a fair exchange value, or parity. Wheat, cotton, hogs, and tobacco were considered basic, and money to finance the plan was to come from processing taxes. The major farm organizations, meeting in Washington, December 12 and 13, had approved these principles which were incorporated in the Jones bill.

The winter of 1932–33 was a tense and hectic one for Peek. Day after day, throughout December, January, and February, he worked and conferred on the principles of farm legislation. The Peek apartment was always a beehive of activity. Friends and acquaintances came at all hours of the day and night. It was not uncommon for visitors to show up early enough for breakfast or to be there until midnight, or past. The telephone was always ringing, so it seemed. Georgia Peek, who, like her husband, lived and breathed farm relief, not only served as wife and hostess, but as adviser, part-time secretary, and errand boy. If George was too busy to write a particular letter, she would do it, or if papers and plans had to be rushed to a senator or congressman, Georgia hailed a cab and went to Capitol Hill. Working together, the Peeks would sometimes become so engrossed in their task of preparing statements and data that everything else, including meals, was forgotten. "We worked so long over 'Comments' on the Agricultural Bill that we forgot to have any dinner and late at night we ordered up some oyster stew," Georgia Peek wrote in her diary. In some ways the feverish activity was reminiscent of the most exciting McNary-Haugen days. But now the atmosphere was more charged with excitement, and the pressure to do something—just anything—was greater.

Peek had not been in Washington long before it became apparent that he was in sharp disagreement with many of his old friends. The emphasis of Henry Wallace, who was to become secretary of agriculture, of Wilson, Ezekiel, and others on production control caused him deep dismay. After one conference, he declared that "farm leaders were being led off by economists." The winter had been one long, "unpleasant experience," he wrote in March, 1933.

Peek felt that he must fight the acreage-restriction and production-control group with all his might. Never accustomed to fencing, he struck with sledge-hammer blows. His first big punch against the trend of events was delivered on February 14, when he appeared before the Senate Finance Committee. He had been asked to discuss the relation between agriculture and the causes of the depression, a subject of paramount importance to Peek. Backed by pages of facts and figures, he told the senators that a major cause of the depression could be traced directly to low farm purchasing power since 1921. The disparity between agriculture and industry must be corrected, he said, by raising farm prices.

Then he took up the subject of production control. Peek maintained the widely held view that there was really no such thing as overproduction. If people both at home and abroad had sufficient food and clothing, he believed there would be no price-depressing surpluses. Therefore, the objective of any government program should be to maintain parity prices for that amount consumed at home, and somehow find markets for the surplus. Thus Peek took the position that the problem was essentially one of handling the supply after it had been produced, not controlling production.

A homely illustration of the underconsumption theory had been presented to Secretary Hyde in 1931 by a Texas cotton farmer. He urged that the government convert some nine million bales of cotton into blankets and overalls and distribute them to the needy through the Red Cross. The Secretary sat down and did some figuring. He replied that, if nine million bales of cotton were so converted, they would make 1,125,000,000 two-pound blankets, and 2,250,000,000 pairs of overalls weighing one pound each. Roughly, he said, this would be 9 blankets and 18 pairs of overalls for every man, woman and child in the United States. "A family of five," he concluded, "would get forty-five blankets and ninety pairs of overalls!"[1] Hyde was not impressed with this solution.

Peek and all of those who opposed production control undoubtedly represented a majority of American thinking. The idea of forced scarcity was repulsive to most citizens. The files of the Secretary of Agriculture for that period bulge with complaints against policies of restriction. A railroad worker wrote to Henry Wallace

on June 14, 1933: "Perhaps the railroad officials are getting enough to buy sail cloth for their yachts but we shopmen are not able to buy clothes, we are wearing rags and using flour and feed bags for towels and pillow slips. . . . We go to market once in a while to look at the nice vegetables then go home and eat macaroni and oatmeal. Is this the new deal? Give us decent wages and there won't be any surplus of either cotton or vegetables."[2]

Opponents of production control not only criticized the principle, but argued that practically it was impossible. For example, Peek presented figures to show that about 75 per cent of the variation in wheat output was due to factors other than acreage. On this point William Allen White wrote satirically: "What is to be done with the young sow of subnormal intelligence and bad home environment— or the headstrong individualist who would set her own impulses above somber judgment of the Party and insist on having eight or ten little piggies instead of the allotted six?"[3]

Thus, in his testimony, the "Man from Moline" harshly criticized the general policy of production control. Speaking of wheat, he said:

For many years I have protested against the expressed view of those who advocate the restriction of agricultural production to the demands of the domestic market, and I have pointed out the unfavorable effect such a policy would have, not only upon the farmer, but upon our whole economic structure—commerce, transportation and finance. The social effects, too, would be far reaching and destructive. I have pointed out also that the vacuum created in the world's agricultural market by our withdrawal would be—in fact is being— filled by other exporting countries. . . . Such withdrawal would dry up our own resources to the direct advantage of foreign nations.

A little later, he added: "Any plans for the

---

[1] Arthur Hyde to a Texas cotton farmer, August 20, 1931. Files of the Secretary of Agriculture.

[2] Railroad worker to Wallace, June 14, 1933. *Ibid.*
[3] Copy of White's statement in *ibid.*

restriction of agricultural production to the demands of the domestic market involving substantial curtailment of acreage, except occasionally in case of great emergency, as in the case of cotton at present . . . should not be adopted as a permanent national policy." He argued that the government should adopt a program which would remove the price disparity for agriculture and restore foreign markets rather than cut production. These two policies were inseparably linked in his mind.

Having outlined his own views, he then scored the Jones bill. First, he said that, in the form it passed the House, too many basic commodities were included—wheat, cotton, hogs, rice, tobacco, peanuts, and butterfat. Peek believed that only wheat, cotton, hogs, and tobacco should be considered basic, meaning products on which benefit payments would be made. He declared that prices for these exportable crops were disproportionately low, and that "the prices of these commodities are believed to be a controlling factor in establishing prices for other agricultural commodities."

Secondly, he declared that marketing agreements should be added to the bill. This is signally important in light of his later insistence on attacking the surplus problem from this angle. "The purpose of such marketing agreements," he said, "is to put the agencies of government behind private enterprise (corporate and co-operative) in disposing of surpluses and to aid in maintaining for producers the fair exchange value for their commodity." Peek believed that price-raising agreements between processors and other agencies handling farm products and the government could be successful. He said that "if the results secured from these marketing agreements are such as to raise prices of agricultural commodities to the fair exchange value, there may be no occasion for the issuance of adjustment certificates and the collection of taxes from the processor." If under such agreements, however, prices did not rise to parity, then the difference between the fair price and "the prevailing market price should be paid to the farmer by the Government, and the Treasury should be reimbursed by means of an adequate tax on the processor," he declared.[4]

Furthermore, Peek argued that if in a great emergency the government did have to reduce the amount going to market, it should "arrest the harvesting of a part of any commodity by paying to the farmer the local market price, less the cost of completing production." If supply must be reduced occasionally, he said, it should be done in those states and areas producing the surplus. He also thought any restrictive provision should be administered on the state level and not from Washington.

Of course, Peek demanded at all times that farmers should have parity prices on that part of their production used in domestic consumption. In the first domestic-allotment bills, the idea had been to make the tariff effective. But the concept of equality or parity for which Peek had been fighting for ten years was incorporated in the Hope-Norbeck and Jones bills. The tariff idea had been superseded by the ratio-price or parity plan, because, even if the full amount of the tariff could have been added to the price of basic commodities, it would not have been enough in the crisis.

The Peek farm relief principles could be summarized as follows: marketing agreements, plus benefit payments sufficient to bring farm prices to parity; an aggressive program to find export markets; and restriction of production only as a last resort.

During the rest of February, Peek worked on amendments to the Jones bill, but the Senate took no action. It did not

[4] *Investigation of Economic Problems*, Hearings before the Senate Committee on Finance, 72 Cong., 2 sess., February 14, 1933, pp. 108–45.

matter, since Hoover would probably have vetoed any legislation like that passed by the House. Action on agricultural relief had to await the new administration. Most Americans, and none more than Peek, waited impatiently and watched the Hoover regime pass unmourned.

On March 4, while Franklin D. Roosevelt was raising the hopes of millions by his stirring inaugural address, Peek was back in Moline. There, for the first time, he began to get rumors of why he had not been offered the job of secretary of agriculture. Paul Preston, one of his friends who had recently talked with Wallace, explained that Peek would have been asked to serve except for his friendship with Baruch. Secretary Wallace had remarked that President Roosevelt did not completely trust Baruch and his "New York connections." The new Secretary had also expressed the fear, according to Preston, that Peek would resent his appointment and refuse to co-operate. "I explained," Peek said, "that his fears were groundless and I would help in any way I could without stultifying myself."[5] Besides, Peek would rather have had Baruch's friendship and confidence than any public office.

There is no doubt, however, but that later differences between Peek and Wallace stemmed, to some extent, from Peek's resentment against the Wallace appointment. Perhaps Peek would have liked to be secretary of agriculture more than he cared to admit. In any event, he wanted a man in the post who was imbued with Peekian principles. Wallace was looked upon as kind of an outsider, an interloper, by the leaders of McNary-Haugenism. He had not been on the firing lines during the discouraging days when Calvin Coolidge ruled the White House. Peek's friends sensed this feeling, and he revealed it in his book *Why Quit Our Own.* He referred to Wallace as "a dreamy,

honest-minded and rather likable sort of fellow," but one who had "never been an active member of our farm group and had not gone through the days of battle." However, there was no sign of this feeling in the critical spring of 1933. The main thing was to get some farm legislation—at once.

On March 9, at Wallace's request, Peek left for Washington to help frame the new agricultural program. Two days before he had written to "Dear Henry" that he did not care about the details of legislation, but "I want to see the principle of fair exchange value become the law of the land so that never again may agriculture be subjected to another experience of the same kind we have passed through for the last twelve years."[6] On Sunday, March 12, Wallace met with Peek and a large group of farm leaders in his office. After the discussion, the Secretary turned to Peek and asked him if he would administer the new law when it passed. "I said 'no,' " Peek wrote in his diary, "but would be glad to help him in whatever way I could by advice and etc."[7] But he soon changed his mind.

Worry over administration, however, was slightly premature. First the principles of legislation had to be agreed upon, and then Congress must act. On March 16, the administration presented a bill which had been prepared in the Department of Agriculture. Peek appeared before the Senate Agriculture Committee on March 24, and repeated much of what he had told the Senate finance group a month earlier. He emphasized that broad administrative powers must be given to the secretary of agriculture "to deal with the various ramifications in this very complex industry." He thought the legislation must be flexible. No single prescription, he said, would fit every crop.

Peek made it clear again that he con-

[5] Peek Diary, entry for March 4, 1933.

[6] Peek to Wallace, March 7, 1933. Peek Papers.
[7] Peek Diary, entry for March 12, 1933.

sidered marketing agreements, not production control, the most important part of any new legislation. But the hearing revealed that some of the Senators thought otherwise.

Senator Smith: Every element of this bill is to restrict our production to domestic consumption, . . . and we therefore, under these artificial methods can raise the price perhaps to a profitable level for that portion that is sold domestically. That is the logic of it.

Mr. Peek: Senator, your understanding of it is just exactly the opposite of mine. My understanding of it is that we are going to put the power of Government behind the farmers and the processors of farm products, to the end that we may raise prices to a fair level within the United States and meet world competition without having the price break down within the United States.

While Peek belittled the possibility of successful planned production in agriculture, he agreed that some provision for control should be in the bill.

Mr. Peek: It might be well occasionally to go in the particular areas in a particular season, after the prospect of the crop was well in sight, and remove a proportion of the maturing crop and destroy it rather than have that proportion destroy the whole industry. That is what happens with unregulated, uncontrolled supply. . . .

The Chairman: . . . you don't mean to advocate, in order to maintain prices, the destruction of crops that are already produced, do you?

Mr. Peek: I would destroy them before I would let the slight surplus destroy our whole national economy; yes, sir.

The next day Wallace outlined his views on the new farm bill. Unlike Peek, he considered acreage control and regulation of production the cornerstone of the measure. He told the committee:

Production must be balanced with consumption if the price levels are to be maintained at any level that is fair to the farmer. This is particularly true when we face the burdensome carry-overs of cotton and wheat. . . . It is necessary that the administration have not only the authority to control acreage planted, but also to control production marketed, in order to meet the varied circumstances.

However, Wallace did not completely discount the validity of marketing agreements. He said that the bill should provide for them and agreed with Peek that they "may in many instances assure producers a fair return without the necessity for the processing tax and rental or benefit payments." "The marketing agreements," he said, "also afford a means of providing relief for many minor commodities with respect to which acreage or production control and rental or benefit payments are not contemplated."

Despite Wallace's emphasis on production control, he did not favor a permanent policy of reducing output only to domestic demands. "I do not contemplate such reduction of acreage as meaning that we permanently forsake our foreign markets," he declared, "but only that we should face the fact of the existing carry-overs and control the acreage planted with a view of keeping the new production in accord with our potential domestic and foreign markets." But the question of developing additional foreign markets, he said, was "still at the mercy of an undetermined national policy."[8] From this testimony, it is clear that Wallace and Peek agreed in general on what ought to go in the farm bill, but they differed greatly on emphasis and on the possibility of increasing exports.

The Agricultural Adjustment Act, which was signed by the President on May 12, was broad enough to win the hearty support of those whose primary interest was

[8] *Agricultural Emergency Act to Increase Farm Purchasing Power*, Hearings before the Senate Agriculture Committee, 73 Cong., 1 sess., March, 1933. See the Peek testimony, pp. 73–104; and Wallace, pp. 128–49.

acreage control and also that of those who advocated marketing agreements. The law sought to achieve agricultural equality by working toward the restoration of parity prices. The purchasing power of farm commodities was to be raised to the 1909–14 period, with the exception of tobacco, in which case 1919–29 was designated. This was to be done by limiting production and eliminating surpluses, by making direct payments to farmers who participated in the production control programs, and by working out voluntary agreements with processors and distributors of farm commodities in order to get higher prices and eliminate marketing abuses. The program was to be financed by processing taxes. The basic commodities on which benefit payments could be made in return for agreements to curtail acreage or production were wheat, cotton, corn, hogs, tobacco, rice, milk, and milk products.

The law did not lay down any rigid formula for solving farm problems or raising agricultural prices. The secretary of agriculture was given wide powers to meet the various problems as they might arise. Furthermore, the law was flexible in that prices were not set at any arbitrary figure, but were to be maintained at a level fixed in relation to other commodities. The principle for which Peek had fought, equality for agriculture or parity, had been at last written into the law of the land.

Besides including the concept of parity and a provision for marketing agreements, the new law included another Peek-sponsored section. This was part of section 12b which permitted the use of processing taxes to pay losses on exports. Was McNary-Haugenism dead after all? Indeed not, if Peek could implement this part of the act.

It was generally known that Peek would get the number one administrative spot, even before the A.A.A. was approved by Congress. He took over as administrator

on May 15. Peek was a natural choice for the job. Since the act was, in some respects, a sharp departure from previous farm legislation, its success might depend on effective and sympathetic administration. Certainly Peek's ability and experience in both industry and government, plus his devotion to the farm cause, qualified him for the post. And since he had such a large farm following, it was politically desirable to make him a member of the administration team. Besides, Wallace admired and liked his aggressive, hard-fighting friend from Moline, and appreciated what he had done for American agriculture. "I have known few men so determined and so little deterred by setbacks as George Peek in his long battle for the farmer," Wallace wrote in 1934.[9]

An additional reason why Peek was chosen to administer the A.A.A. has generally been overlooked. Many senators and congressmen accepted the idea of acreage restriction only reluctantly. Some of them considered parts of the law positively dangerous. The general knowledge that Peek would head the agency went a long way to allay the doubts, fears, and opposition of men like Senators Pat Harrison and Hubert D. Stephens of Mississippi.[10] Moreover, processors and distributors violently opposed the act, especially the licensing provisions. If they thought the program was going to be administered by a conservative businessman, their opposition might be lessened. Peek recorded in his diary a revealing conversation with an individual who had recently talked to representatives of the packers and other handlers of food products. "I asked him point blank," Peek wrote, "if they would object to the bill if they felt they would receive sympathetic and business-like administration of it. He said 'no,'

[9] Henry A. Wallace, New Frontiers (New York, 1934), 146.
[10] See Peek's account of his talks with Stephens and Harrison in his diary for March 22, 1933.

but that they shuddered at the thought of Tugwell or Ezekiel."[11]

Generally popular, Peek's appointment was hailed as a victory for the conservatives and practical men of affairs in the Roosevelt administration. Here was a man, people said, who would help counteract the influence of theoretical college professors. "How should I address you, Mr. Peek? Doctor or Professor?" asked a publicity man in the Department. In reply, Peek could only snort, "Hell no!"

William Hirth said that Peek's selection was a "happy development" because Wallace's staff was "utterly unfitted" to administer the law, and because "it gives assurance to the farmers of the country that the question of higher farm prices has been placed in the hands of a strong and practical man."[12]

The old farm crowd, sometimes called "Henry's Father's gang" by the young liberals in the department, believed that the Department of Agriculture was too heavily loaded with idealists and social reformers. Had not the Secretary himself said that the new farm bill was "a major social experiment"? And then there was Tugwell, who became under-secretary. Many farmers and their spokesmen considered him radical, if not outright red, and wished that he was back at Columbia University.

But the more conservative farm leaders could relax now that George Peek was running the A.A.A. He was not interested in social experiments. If asked what he planned to do, he was apt to blurt out, "I'm going to try like hell to raise farm prices." In fact, two days after his appointment, he bluntly declared in his first press release, "The sole aim and object of this act is to raise farm prices." To be exact, he repeated it *three* times. That, and that alone, was Peek's idea of the law's purpose, and of his job as administrator. In discussing the profit system and

the government's taking over more business, he characteristically remarked, "Unless it hustles, the Government has more hay down now than it will get up before it rains."

With the clear and undivided objective of lifting agricultural prices, Peek surrounded himself with old friends and other men in whom he had confidence. Charles J. Brand, author of the first McNary-Haugen bill, was brought in as co-administrator. The main administrative divisions under Peek's control were Information and Publicity, Production, Processing and Marketing, and Finance. These were headed by Alfred D. Stedman, Chester C. Davis, W. I. Westervelt, and Oscar Johnston, respectively. These men were not dreamy idealists. Peek also announced that he was going to depend heavily upon men such as Baruch and Lowden for advice.

In the late spring and early summer of 1933 haste was imperative. The growing season was well advanced by the time Congress acted. In many cases crops had been planted and the prospect of further staggering surpluses was frightening. "Wherever we turn to deal with an agricultural commodity, we have in prospect a race with the sun," Peek declared grimly.

Despite the confusion and lack of guideposts, Peek and his associates got the new farm program underway with amazing swiftness. Programs of production control were quickly inaugurated for cotton and wheat, and, a little later, for corn and hogs. Cotton was plowed under, the drouth cut wheat output, and young pigs and bred sows were slaughtered for food and fertilizer. And government checks began flowing into thousands of farm homes. On Thursday, September 15, 22,122 checks were produced, but the number fell off the next day when a broken generator "stalled the machine for five hours!"[13] Looking at the spectacle of hundreds of

---

[11] *Ibid.*

[12] *Missouri Farmer*, Vol. XXV (June 1, 1933), 8.

[13] H. P. Seidemann, memorandum for Mr. Peek, September 18, 1933. Files of the Secretary of Agriculture.

employees busily producing and mailing out checks, a Russian visitor remarked: "Good Lord! This is a Revolution!"[14]

No, there was nothing like it in all of American history. Millions of individualistic farmers were welded into a great co-operative effort through the vehicle of government benefit payments. In explaining that more than 500,000 cotton growers had signed contracts to take over 9,000,000 acres out of current production, Peek told a nationwide radio audience on July 14, "What has transpired . . . marks an epoch in American agriculture." Then he added, "I say history has been made during these days." And so it had been. This early success of the A.A.A. was a tribute to the work and resourcefulness of Peek and those who were working with him.

Peek had a good bit of adaptability in his make-up, and was not the inflexible administrator sometimes pictured. He had enough of a sense of humor and consideration for the opinions of others to get along well unless a matter of major policy was involved. For instance, when former Senator Brookhart was forced on his agency by the President, Peek accepted it despite his belief that Brookhart was not a good selection. Some of the A.A.A. officials watched Peek squirm. When the question of office space came up, someone asked, "Where are you going to put him, George?" With a doleful smile that was a combination of humor, satire, protest, and resignation, Peek instantly replied, "Oh, a way off somewhere in an attic room with a lot of God damn cobwebs in it."

Peek had a half-serious and half-humorous way of conveying his wish that the A.A.A. should take his conservative direction. He did this without asking men outright to change the color of their thinking. Alfred Stedman, his director of publicity, recalls that Peek was sometimes disturbed by his sympathy with the liberal views. One day Peek, noticing that Sted-

man was wearing a reddish necktie, said with a direct look but with a smile to take away the edge, "Your necktie is too red. I will send you one of a better color." A few days later Stedman received in the mail a handsome *blue* necktie, a gift from Peek.

In spite of the progress made in fighting the farm depression, these were extremely unhappy days for George Peek. Fundamental differences between himself and Secretary Wallace, and between their respective followers in the Department of Agriculture, created a tense and disagreeable situation. From the beginning the A.A.A. was torn by internal dissension. Everyone was pulling hard, but in different directions. It is surprising that so much was accomplished.

As mentioned earlier, Secretary Wallace believed that production control was the heart of the law and that this phase should be stressed; Peek placed confidence in marketing agreements and the revival of foreign trade, while an aggressive legal staff of young urban liberals, headed by Chief Counsel Jerome N. Frank, wanted to use the A.A.A. as an instrument of long-range social and economic reform. Under these circumstances, it was natural for conflicts to develop.

Peek later declared that he had been completely surprised at Wallace's emphasis upon production control. But in trying to justify and defend his own position, he must have had a convenient lapse of memory. Before Peek took the post of administrator, both Wallace and Roosevelt had made their views abundantly clear. On April 7, Peek, Lowden, and Baruch were at the White House to confer on the pending farm bill. Referring to the President, Peek wrote, "He and I disagreed on the question of restricted production as a national policy." And Wallace explained to Peek on the day the A.A.A. became law, "it seems to me entirely clear that we ought to undertake acreage reduction in both cotton and corn but the extent to which this ought to go should again depend upon the outcome of our various conferences."[15] The fact that Peek insisted upon "direct access to the President" before he became administrator indicates that he believed he would have fundamental differences with the Secretary. Undoubtedly, Peek expected that, in a showdown on policy, he could win the President's support. And sometimes he did.

Regardless of the conflict of opinion, Peek set out to administer the law along the lines which he favored. He supported the acreage-reduction programs for cotton and wheat more out of duty than conviction. And on the corn-hog program he said, "there seemed nothing to do but go along with it in view of the existing emergency."[16] However, he shuddered at signing death warrants for juvenile hogs. Peek therefore concentrated on finding export markets and negotiating marketing agreements in order to get better prices and to dispose of surpluses. He had his assistants busy drawing up marketing agreements for fluid milk, fruit, tobacco, and other products. The thing to do, he argued, was to get processors and distributors to enter into voluntary agreements to pay parity prices for farm commodities. The first marketing agreement covered the handling of milk in the Chicago area and went into effect on August 1. It determined prices to be paid producers, consumer prices, and fair trade practices. This was typical of the agreements, and others soon followed.[17]

Peek was vitally concerned about increasing the percentage of the consumer's dollar received by farmers. By March, 1933, farmers were only getting 30 per cent of the consumer's dollars spent on farm products while they had received 50 per cent in 1929. It made Peek's blood

boil to see the food industries in 1932 earn more than half their 1929 profits while farmers suffered ruin and foreclosure. Yet when it came to implementing his program, Peek was surprisingly charitable with the processors and handlers of food products. In his first press release on May 15, he declared that as far as the food and textile industries were concerned, he wanted "as little interference with established institutions and methods as is consistent with the fixed purpose of the law."

To supplement marketing agreements, Peek strongly advocated diverting surpluses not marketable at parity prices into special domestic or export channels. He would not admit that foreign markets were permanently lost. Through an aggressive export policy supported by the government, he thought that markets could be found. Peek still believed in the basic features of the McNary-Haugen plan and wanted to implement the two-price system. "It had been our original intention . . . ," he later declared, "to provide in the AAA the needed machinery to run the two-price system—an American price for American consumption and competitive foreign prices for exports." On September 20, he wrote Secretary Hull that "a strong, persistent, and well-planned policy looking toward the revival of international trade" should be undertaken at once. Since he based his policies partly on the assumption that foreign markets could be opened for surplus farm commodities, Peek brought himself into further conflict with Secretary Wallace, who held no such views.

Even before the A.A.A. became law, Wallace wrote to Peek, "there are extraordinary difficulties in building up at once an effective foreign purchasing power for our surplus farm products at a price which is at all satisfactory to our farmers. Also it seems that in case we indulge in a subsidized export trade in farm products, we can very promptly get into inter-

[15] Wallace to Peek, May 12, 1933. Peek Papers.
[16] George N. Peek, *Why Quit Our Own* (New York, 1936), 132.
[17] Edwin G. Nourse, *Marketing Agreements Under the AAA* (Washington, 1935), 206.

national jams of one kind or another."[18] And on May 12, Wallace declared that "we ought to act for the moment as if we were a self-contained agricultural economy." It appeared to many that Wallace was recognizing economic realities. To Peek the Secretary's position represented an admission of defeat and acceptance of the further decline of agriculture.

Peek argued that if the productive facilities of the farm were reduced, industry, not agriculture, would be the greatest beneficiary. His strong feelings on this point were expressed in a radio speech on September 1:

My own view is that we are suffering in this country from an overcapacity of industrial facilities for which both the farmer and the consumer are paying. . . . Agriculture is cutting down its plant but a large part of industry is still trying to maintain boom-time capacity and capital values. This is being done at the expense of farmers and consumers. The public should no longer tolerate it. Industry must reduce its overcapacity. It cannot look for its relief by taking it out of the farmer's hide.

Peek never explained how he thought industrial overcapacity might be reduced, but his statement sounded good to bankrupt farmers.

The conflicts in the department which had been shaping up over policy and personnel reached a near climax in September with the negotiation of a marketing agreement for flue-cured tobacco. Officials of the A.A.A. drew up an agreement and presented it to representatives of the leading tobacco companies on September 15. Company officials objected to it on several counts, but especially criticized the provision which would have limited price increases on manufactured tobacco unless approved by the secretary of agriculture, and that provision which would have given A.A.A. officials limited access to books and records. In offering a counterproposal, the

companies argued that they must be permitted "to manage, conduct and operate their respective businesses with freedom of business policy as heretofore."

Members of the legal department in the A.A.A. who had drawn up the original agreement favored strict control over the tobacco firms. In writing all of the marketing agreements, they took the position that food processors must be strictly regulated. They especially wanted to restrain price increases which might be passed on to consumers and to inspect company books.

There has been a great deal of misunderstanding on this matter of book and record inspection in the marketing agreements. The companies were willing for their books to be opened to the extent necessary to determine that the provisions of the agreement were being honestly carried out. But the legal division and consumer's counsel wanted unlimited right to investigate all of the companies' books and records, including those of affiliated firms in other lines of business not directly concerned with the marketing agreements. The companies did not object to the "standard books and records provision" in the license, just so they were not required to agree to it in the legal contract. They refused to sign away their legal defense against what they considered unwarranted and illegal fishing expeditions. This was considered unjustifiable interference with private enterprise. Peek agreed.

The tobacco buyers took the matter to Peek, and he supported them in objecting to those provisions which seemed like meddling with legitimate business. As finally accepted, the flue-cured-tobacco agreement provided that the companies would buy 250,000,000 pounds of tobacco at the parity price of 17 cents a pound. This was considerably above the current price and the agreement meant some $12,000,000 to this group of tobacco farmers over their 1932 income.

[18] Wallace to Peek, April 28, 1933. Peek Papers.

Chief Counsel Frank and members of his staff strongly opposed the agreement on the basis that it did not extend sufficient control over the tobacco industry. It looked like Secretary Wallace would refuse to approve it, largely upon Frank's recommendation.

Peek was fighting mad. In a memorandum to the President, written October 5, he reviewed the controversy in full. He declared:

The manufacturers feel, because of licensing and other provisions inserted by our group in the first draft of the present agreement and because of charts, specific comments on excessive profits, advertising, and other matters, there is a disposition by some members of our Administration to assume control of the industry as soon as possible. Therefore, they have attempted to determine by definition in the agreement the extent of control intended, because they state the possibility of their undertaking this agreement depends on the extent of the control to be exercised. . . . Some of our representatives have suggested, because of the apparent impasse with respect to these issues, that in lieu of this agreement—

(1) We take direct control of the markets by licensing all buyers at once.

(2) We enter the markets immediately to stabilize prices at or near parity by purchasing flue-cured tobacco.

Arguing that the agreement should be approved as it stood, Peek concluded, "I do not conceive that the Government should take over or control by license or otherwise, any industry which appears to be willing to co-operate with us in attaining these objectives."[19] A few days later he took the question directly to the President, who backed his stand. Wallace then reluctantly signed the agreement.

The fight over the flue-cured-tobacco agreement brought out the long smoldering feud between Peek and part of his legal staff. From the beginning Peek distrusted Jerome Frank, who, incidentally,

had been a member of a law firm active in liquidating the Moline Plow Company. To provide himself with counsel in whom he had confidence, he employed Fred Lee on a personal basis. He gave Lee his full salary as administrator, which meant that Peek was serving without pay. He also hired Glenn McHugh, who had worked on the McNary-Haugen bill in 1925. McHugh did his best to serve as a buffer between Peek and Frank.

Difficulties were sure to arise when Peek tried to work around part of his legal staff. And conditions became worse when Frank brought in a number of young urban lawyers, some of whom were more concerned with social reform than with raising farm prices. Frank told Peek, "What we need are brilliant young men with keen legal minds and imagination." Then he added: "There are a considerable number of brilliant young men who would be willing to join us, partly because of the desire for experience, and partly because of the desire to help us meet the social problems arising from the emergency."[20]

As the A.A.A.'s legal staff was increased to about fifty-five lawyers, Frank employed Alger Hiss, Lee Pressman, Victor Rotnem, Francis J. Shea, and others. That they were bright young men, there is no doubt. And there is equally no question but that some of them held strong collectivist economic ideas. Their real interest was not so much to help raise farm prices as it was to protect consumers and control business.

These super-liberals believed that the capitalistic system was crumbling, that the profit motive was outdated, and that the place of government in the economy must continually increase. For example, Lee Pressman reportedly told some Detroit Milk distributors that the United States government ought to operate the milk business. When he was asked why the government should not also operate

---

[19] Peek, *Why Quit Our Own*, 148–49.

[20] Jerome Frank, memorandum to Mr. Peek, June 16, 1933. Files of the Secretary of Agriculture.

grocery and department stores, he replied, "Why not?"[21]

Disillusioned by the depression and its consequences, these young men had permanent ideas about relieving the nation's social and economic ills. It was later revealed that Pressman and some others in the A.A.A. became members of a Communist group in Washington. They would build a new world. They were not sure just how, but someway they would help usher in the millennium. If a new economic order was desirable, there must be a way. They were idealistic, impractical, and above all inexperienced. They had never plowed corn or met a payroll. Indeed, Jerome Frank's city lawyers had much to learn. One of them, working on a macaroni code, was supposed to have asked: "Just tell me this; is this code fair to the macaroni growers?"[22]

It quickly became clear to Peek that these leftwing urban lawyers were trying to use the A.A.A., particularly its power to license processors, for purposes not originally contemplated. Their talk of limiting profits, regulating business practices, and inspecting books and records all seemed un-American to Peek. And when they tried to incorporate some of these principles in the marketing agreements and codes which were under A.A.A. jurisdiction, Peek balked. The talk and ideas of the young liberals sounded like nonsense to him and he said so. Speaking before the Farm Bureau convention in Chicago on December 12, he strongly upheld the profit system and discounted the

trend of government in business. He said that the "grave concern over the expression of a few ultra-liberals about the government taking over private business . . . is unwarranted." Then he concluded with his familiar statement, "I am in favor of the profit system, but I am in favor of starting with the farmer."[23]

Did Peek really know of Communist influence in the A.A.A.? There is no evidence in the Peek files to indicate that, while he was in office, he knew of any actual card carriers in his agency. Some of Peek's closest friends do not recall ever having heard him make such a charge while he was administrator. Peek had a tendency to group all leftwingers in that category, and "Communist" was a term which he frequently used to stigmatize extreme liberals with whom he disagreed. His belief, however, that there were some potentially dangerous radicals in the New Deal administration was borne out later. Peek was one of the earliest to notice that there were reformers around Washington who would solve the nation's problems in some authoritarian fashion outside of the American tradition. He warned against it, but his warnings went largely unheeded.

Besides the marketing agreements in milk, fruit, tobacco, and other commodities, Peek worked hard to export surpluses abroad. Through the wheat export agreement consummated in October, 1933, he was responsible for sending some 28,-000,000 bushels of wheat grown in the Pacific Northwest to the Far East. A subsidy of around 23 cents a bushel was paid to the export corporation at a cost of over $6,000,000, which came from processing taxes on wheat. China was able to buy American wheat because of a loan of $10,000,000 from the Reconstruction Finance Corporation, 60 per cent

[21] Peek, *Why Quit Our Own*, 150; See also Arthur Krock in the *New York Times*, December 10, 1933, Pt. IV, p. 1.

[22] Lord, *The Wallaces of Iowa*, 358. Actually, this person was probably referring to durum wheat which was used for making macaroni. In speaking of this kind of wheat it was not uncommon to use only the word macaroni instead of macaroni wheat. But it made a good story and was repeated by the anti-Tugwell-Frank faction to show that the young lawyers knew nothing about farming.

[23] G. N. Peek, "Speech before the American Farm Bureau Federation," December 12, 1933. Peek Papers.

of which was designated for wheat purchases.[24]

Along with the tobacco agreement, Peek considered the export of wheat to China one of his most notable successes as administrator. To him it represented the type of government co-operation necessary to dispose of farm products. A regional surplus had been cut down and some $3,000,000 had been added to the pockets of northwestern farmers. Processing taxes, he argued, could better be used to subsidize export in this manner than to pay farmers to reduce production. But despite the apparent success of the agreement, it represented financing our own exports. Without the R.F.C. loan to China the deal could not have been made.

The fact that Wallace, Tugwell, and others in the department were hostile to export dumping did not deter Peek from further activity along this line. In November he authorized the use of $500,000 from processing taxes, in addition to previous sums, to pay losses on butter exports. Secretary Wallace was then at Warm Springs with the President, so Under-Secretary Tugwell was asked to approve the arrangement. He refused. But to make sure that he had the Secretary's support, Tugwell discussed the matter with Wallace by telephone on the evening of November 27. Wallace said that he did not favor subsidizing exports, and would not authorize dumping. This seemed to Peek like another example of interference by the liberals and idealists in the department. He wrote a sharp memorandum to the Secretary, but his arguments were unavailing and the proposal was dropped.[25]

Even a man possessed of much more patience than Peek would have been tried by these difficulties and frustrations. But

[24] Nourse, *Marketing Agreements Under the AAA*, 72–73.
[25] R. M. Littlejohn, memorandum for Mr. Peek, November 28, 1933; G. N. Peek, memorandum for Secretary Wallace, December 1, 1933; and R. G. Tugwell, memorandum for Secretary Wallace, December 2, 1933. Peek Papers.

this was not all. He believed that many policies under the National Recovery Act were militating against agriculture's welfare. Peek favored the general principles of the N.R.A., and he had suggested a voluntary partnership between government and business as early as 1918. However, he believed that industrial prices must be kept in check until farm prices were raised. Otherwise, how could farm parity be achieved? On this question he came into sharp conflict with his old friend and head of the N.R.A., Hugh Johnson.

In July the President announced his Re-employment Agreement to bring employers under a "blanket code." The important provision was for minimum-wage and maximum-hour agreements. Peek saw at once that if the food industries incurred higher costs under this code, they would likely pass them on to the farmer in the form of reduced prices for his products, or higher prices for what he had to buy. That, Peek said, would increase the disparity between farm and industrial prices. He recommended that food industries over which the A.A.A. had code authority should be exempt from the blanket code. His job, he told Johnson, was to raise farm prices, and he could not approve policies which worked against this objective.

The meeting of the Special Industrial Recovery Board on July 19 was hotter than the Washington weather. Johnson, Frances Perkins, Wallace, and Secretary Roper took the position that wages must be raised first. Peek argued that the A.A.A. and N.R.A. must be co-ordinated and wages and farm prices lifted together. The programs should not go in opposite directions, he said. "You mean," Johnson retorted, "you ought to start out and we follow you." "I resent that," Peek heatedly replied, "I resent it for the purpose of the record." On this issue Tugwell fought shoulder to shoulder with Peek, and representatives of the major farm organizations also supported his view. But Johnson's policy of placing labor provisions in the food industry codes prevailed.[26]

By November conditions had become untenable for Peek in the A.A.A. He disagreed with Wallace and Tugwell on so many points that it seemed hopeless to try to continue. The crisis came when Peek attempted to remove Jerome Frank. He wrote to Wallace on November 15, saying that Frank had become "impossible." His complaints centered around Frank's alleged holding up of marketing agreements, and retarding enforcement proceedings under some of the milk licenses. But his real objection was that Frank almost always concurred with Tugwell and Wallace on important issues, and was in a key position to hamper or block Peek's plans.

It was quickly rumored, however, that Wallace would not dismiss Frank. Tugwell, more than anyone else, wanted to get rid of Peek, not Frank, and it was said that he was maneuvering so that Peek would be forced to resign.[27] Wallace had been deeply annoyed by the bickering within the A.A.A. He hated strife and discord. But most of all he was tired of Peek attempting to circumvent him by taking issues directly to the President as he had done in the case of the flue-cured-tobacco agreement.

As early as May 15, the day Peek took office, Wallace had written to Roosevelt, "Mr. Peek's insistence on using you as an umpire between him and myself will involve you unnecessarily in administrative detail." He said that he wanted "a clear and final understanding . . . that I am Mr. Peek's chief."[28] Thus it was not just a matter of firing the Chief Counsel, but a question of Wallace's authority as secretary. Peek always had been restive under

the administrative arrangement. He wanted the A.A.A. established as an independent agency outside the Department of Agriculture and directly responsible to the President. Now he had raised the issue of Wallace's authority and would have to go.

On December 7, Peek had lunch with the President, after which they conferred for two hours. Wallace and Tugwell had been at the White House that morning, and Wallace returned for an hour after Peek departed. As Peek was leaving the President's office, reporters asked him about quitting the A.A.A. Peek replied abruptly: "I am going back to my desk now. I also shall be at my desk tomorrow morning. Beyond that nobody can ever make any plans."[29]

However, Roosevelt had asked him to resign. In fact, Wallace already had conferred with Chester Davis about taking the post. The only remaining question was what to do with Peek. It was a chilling prospect for Wallace and Roosevelt to think of a man of Peek's forcefulness and vocabulary running around outside the administration attacking the farm program. As it was, the A.A.A. had more than its share of troubles at the grass roots. Somehow, he must be kept happy and active within the New Deal framework.

Tugwell suggested sending him as minister to Czechoslovakia! From there he might travel around Europe and find some new markets for American farm products. But this idea was not seriously considered. It was finally decided that, since Peek was so vitally concerned about exporting agricultural commodities, he might be made special adviser to the President on foreign trade. That was it. Such a job would certainly appeal to Peek. It was dignified and sounded important; thus no one would lose face. It was encompassing enough to take all of his tremendous energies.

So on December 15, exactly seven months after he took office, Peek formally

[26] Peek to Johnson, July 13, 17, and 20, 1933; and Proceedings of the Special Industrial Recovery Board, July 18 and 19, 1933. Peek Papers.
[27] See Arthur Krock in the New York Times, December 10, 1933, Pt. IV, p. 1.
[28] Wallace to Roosevelt, May 15, 1933. Roosevelt Papers, Hyde Park.
[29] New York Times, December 8, 1933, p. 1.

tendered his resignation. This was a victory for the "social outlook" group in the A.A.A. Three days later, President Roosevelt wrote, "I want to thank you very warmly for the high character of service you have rendered and to express my genuine appreciation of your willingness to take over the new duties I requested you to assume."[30]

In his last talk with Chester Davis before leaving the A.A.A., Peek said, "Get rid of Jerome Frank and the rest of that

crowd as a condition to your acceptance." Davis, however, believed that he could "handle them." But in January, 1935, Davis called for and shortly got the resignations of Frank and Pressman, in the legal division, and of Fred Howe and Gardner Jackson, top men in the consumer's counsel. Peek's position on the question of personnel had been vindicated.[31]

[30] Roosevelt to Peek, December 18, 1933. Peek Papers.

[31] Peek discusses his problems with this group in his book *Why Quit Our Own*. In 1953 a subcommittee of the Senate Judiciary Committee quoted Peek in its report, *Interlocking Subversion in Government Departments*.

An Agricultural Revolution

■ Higher demand for meat, dairy products, fruits, and vegetables, initiated by World War II and sustained by fuller employment and better living standards thereafter, rapidly translated accumulated knowledge and unused technology into operations on the farm. The result was an increase in agricultural efficiency not equaled in any other twenty-year period of recorded history. On the commercial farms of the nation, in contrast to those that represent merely part-time activities of people with other incomes, the movement toward bigger acreage, less employment, and more product was still going on rapidly in the 1960s. If the graphs in the following selection could be continued to 1965, the results would be even more dramatic. Nowhere else in the world, moreover, were agricultural improvements taking place that were comparable in quality or quantity to those in the United States.

Reuben W. Hecht and Eugene G. McKibben are members of the expert staff of social and physical scientists within the Department of Agriculture.

Reuben W. Hecht and Eugene G. McKibben
Efficiency of Labor*

Today a farmer with mechanical and electrical power, modern machines, im-

* Reprinted from *Power to Produce*, The Yearbook of Agriculture, 1960 (Washington: The United States Government Printing Office, 1961), pp. 317–331.

proved seeds, fertilizers, and pesticides, convenient buildings, and improved breeding stock and feed turns out almost four times as much product each hour of work as a farmer did each hour in the years just before the First World War.

Advances in efficiency of farm labor have resulted directly from fewer hours of farmwork and from greater farm production. Many related and interrelated forces, including engineering and biological developments and economic and social changes, have been behind these basic causes.

During the half century since 1910, farm output per man-hour has risen at an average rate of almost 3 percent a year. This gain has not come about gradually.

For the first decade after 1910, farm output per man-hour rose less than 1 percent a year. The increase was due to the expansion in farm output as the labor used on farms also rose.

The two decades between the First and Second World Wars were characterized by a start of a persistent downward trend in the number of workers on farms. Lack of an effective demand for farm products and other factors held the annual gain in farm output to a modest 1 percent a year, but the gain had a greater influence on raising farm labor efficiency

an average of 1.6 percent a year than the reduction in the amount of labor used on farms had.

The annual increase in farm production and its contribution to the greater labor efficiency that came during the Second World War was without precedent in the history of American agriculture and has not been equaled since. By a fortunate conjuncture of circumstances, farm output rose 3.3 percent annually and was largely responsible for raising production per man-hour to record levels. Efficiency of farm labor rose at the annual rate of 4.8 percent from 1940 to 1945.

The advances in mechanization and the changes that accompanied it have meant an acceleration in the reduction in the man-hours of farmwork since the war. The number of man-hours dropped at an annual rate of 4 percent from 1945 to 1950. Since 1950 the reduction on a percentage basis has been even greater —4.2 percent a year. Expressed in hours of farmwork, the drop in the 5 years following the war amounted to almost

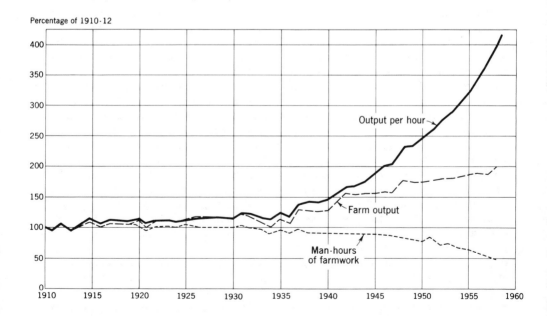

Percentage of 1910-12

Efficiency in Use of Farm Labor, Total Farm Production

750 million man-hours a year. During the next decade the annual reduction was about 500 million hours a year.

The postwar drop in farm labor input is shown also in the number of workers on farms. There were 10 million on farms at the end of the war. Primarily because of the return of workers from war industries and the Armed Forces, farm employment rose for a couple of years, but after 1947 numbers again turned downward.

In the first 5 years after the war, the reduction was only 15 thousand workers a year, compared with an annual drop of about 200 thousand from 1940 to 1945. Farm employment averaged only about 7.4 million workers in 1959: The annual reduction since 1950 has been almost 20 times as fast as during the first 5 postwar years.

On the other side of the labor efficiency ratio—the production side—additions to farm output after the war continued to contribute significantly to the steep upward climb in labor productivity.

Its effect was less than during the wartime period for two basic reasons, one absolute and the other relative: The annual increase in farm production was less than during the war; the accelerated reduction in labor used on farms lowered the relative effect of additions to farm output.

In line with the great strides made in adding tractors and other forms of mechanical power to farms after the war, work animals disappeared rapidly. From 1945 to 1950, the drop in work animals was responsible for additions to cropland for raising products for human use, amounting to 2.6 million acres a year. The horse-and-mule-release of cropland had equaled 2.2 million acres annually during the war and has averaged 1.5 million acres yearly since 1950.

As only about 3 million head of horses and mules were left on farms and ranches at the beginning of 1960, this source of additional output is about exhausted. However, this aspect of farm mechanization was the prime source of greater farm output for the first half decade after the war. Since 1950, greater crop and livestock production resulting from higher yields has been chiefly responsible for additions to farm production.

While greater farm production helped, the reduction in labor used on farms was the chief cause of the steep upward climb in labor efficiency after the war. It rose at the annual rate of 5.2 percent for the first half decade and 6.5 percent a year since 1950.

Many adjustments in organization and management of farms and related industries developed concurrently with the advance in farm technology and labor efficiency. Indeed, they were part of it.

We have said that the farm mechanization phase of the technological progress in farming both lowered the amount of labor used on farms and raised the amount of farm products available for human use. That is true, but it is an oversimplification of the complex and interrelated changes that have been part of the technological revolution in agriculture.

An all-inclusive discussion of labor efficiency in farming would include consideration of most of the forces behind growth in the total economy. The more general of these include human desires; stable government and institutions; public and private research for new and adaptable products and techniques; education, particularly regarding adoption of the innovations; and a favorable economic climate.

Economic forces express themselves through prices and incomes. Many price relationships and changes in the relationships have profoundly affected advances in technology.

An example is the cost of farm labor and the cost of the items that can be substituted for labor. Much of this kind of substitution has taken place, particularly the replacement of work animals by mechanical power.

To simplify the comparison, we assume that wage rates paid to hired workers reflect the cost of operator's time and that of unpaid labor of his family. (This assumption fails to recognize remuneration for management functions performed by farm operators. On the other hand, they and family workers do many jobs that add little to farm income.)

Farm wage rates were more than 200 percent higher in 1958 than in 1925–1929. During those 30 years, the average prices paid for tractors, trucks, and automobiles rose 190 percent; farm machinery, 130 percent; and fuel, tires, and other motor supplies about 30 percent. A comparison with 1935–1939 would show even greater disparity in the rates of increase.

We could cite other illustrations of the relationship of prices that favor the adoption of technology, such as the prices paid for fertilizer and improved seed, whose cost generally has been considerably less than the value of their additions to production.

The increase in size and specialization of farms has been one of the most significant changes in farm structure and organization that have come with the adoption of technology.

About a billion acres have consistently constituted the land base in farming, but the number of farms has dropped from about 6.5 million at the time of the First World War to fewer than 4 million in 1960. Each year the fewer remaining farms, on the average, add land to their operations. More than two-fifths of the transfers of farmland are for the purpose of enlarging farms. They were one-fifth of the purchases in 1950.

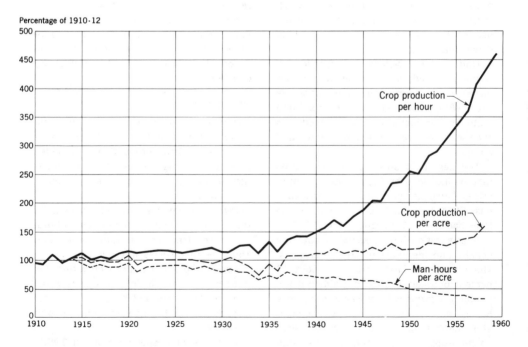

Percentage of 1910-12

Efficiency in Use of Farm Labor, Crops

One might expect that by this time wheat farmers, who were among the first to mechanize, would have pretty well adjusted their operating units to the new machines and methods. A larger proportion of the current transfers of farmland, however, is for farm enlargement in the wheat farming areas than in other parts of the country: Even in the more mechanized areas, innovations are being adopted that save even more labor, and effects of them are being translated into larger farms.

The number of acres is not a reliable measure of size in all farming situations, of course. A poultry farm may have few acres but be a large unit in terms of total investment or in number of birds or eggs produced. Here a major part of the investment is in buildings and equipment that induce large flocks and raise production per hour of labor.

Modern equipment and machines are so expensive in many instances that it is advantageous to the farmer to develop larger farms and enterprises to make full use of the new resources and to hold down unit costs.

Under older systems of farming, a farmer could add acres or animals without increasing proportionally the labor he used. With modern equipment, tools, and methods, the increase in labor needed is even less, relative to the added acres and animals.

The degree of specialization on farms may be indicated by the number of enterprises (such as milk cows or corn) each has. Of 20 major enterprises, the average farm had 5.4 in 1940 and 4.7 in 1954.

Specialization has occurred in both the general and the unusual farm enterprises. The number of farms dropped about 10 percent between 1950 and 1954, but the number of farms with chickens and those having milk cows each fell 19 percent. The number of farmers growing snap beans dropped 35 percent, and the number producing tomatoes, 30 percent. In each instance, the average size of the enterprise was greater in 1954.

Besides raising overall efficiency in farming, specialization has had other effects on farm labor.

One of the disadvantages of specialization is that work may not be provided for all seasons and periods of the year if there are only a few enterprises.

That is particularly significant on farms with a relatively fixed labor force, such as many family farms.

According to the census, workers on farms put in about 5 fewer hours per week in 1959 than they did in 1949. Or on a daily basis—around September 1, 1959—farm operators averaged 9.8 hours of work a day. Hired workers averaged 8.9 hours. Comparable lengths of workdays 10 years earlier were 11.1 and 9.5 hours, respectively.

Specialization, then, has been translated into fewer hours per farmworker as well as into greater production per worker and per hour of work.

We do not mean to stress specialization unduly or to imply the absence of other influences. Many forces have induced changes in input and productivity of labor.

The index of labor efficiency is the ratio of total agricultural output to the input of labor in farm production. The index thus reflects the net effect of all forces that influence either farm production or farm labor.

Myriad influences underlie changes in the two basic indexes of total agricultural output and labor used in farm production. They are themselves interrelated.

For example: Labor used on farms has trended downward for nearly four decades, and the descent would have been greater were it not for the upward trend in farm production.

In terms of a specific crop, in 1950–1954 it took an average of 69 man-hours

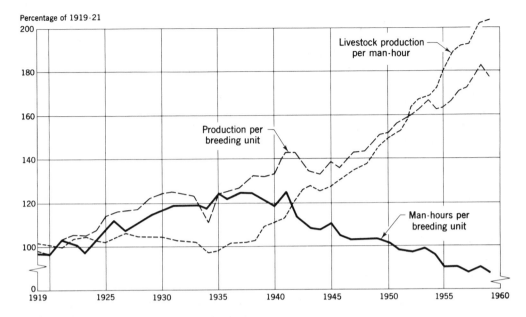

Percentage of 1919-21

Efficiency in Use of Farm Labor, Livestock

to grow and harvest an acre of sugar beets yielding 15.5 tons. The average for the following 4 years was 53 hours per acre, or more than a fifth less, and the drop would have been greater if the yield had not increased. The average yield in 1955–1958 was 17 tons. The combined effect of fewer hours and more tons per acre, including the almost innumerable forces back of these changes, was to raise production of sugar beets per man-hour by more than 40 percent in 5 years.

It is unrealistic in some respects to view farming as a thing apart. When our Nation was young, that could be done because agriculture was largely self-contained. The draft animals, feed, tools, building materials, implements, manure, the family's food and clothing, material for the farmhouse and furniture, and the fuel were all mostly produced on the farm.

Not so today. Now farmers sell most of what they produce and buy what they need on the farm and in the home. There has been a dispersion of jobs or functions from farms to nonfarm business firms.

The modern farmer retains primarily the function of a producer of crops and livestock. This is a different kind of specialization than we discussed previously. The average farmer specializes on fewer enterprises and he also performs fewer functions.

The evolution from self-sufficiency to commercialization of farming may best be portrayed by changes in the distribution of the population and labor force. At the beginning of the 19th century nearly everybody lived in rural areas, and 80 of every 100 persons in the labor force were engaged in farming. Now only 12 percent of the people live on farms, and of each 100 in the total working force, only 9 are farmworkers.

Entirely new industries and service institutions have had their beginning and growth in the increasing tendency of farmers to utilize production supplies originating off the farm.

Complementing this development has been the creation of still another group of business entities with the functions of handling, storing, processing, and distributing food, fiber, and other products from the farm to the consumer. Thus we have three groups of related industries with interrelated functions. Altogether they embrace essentially the functions that the term agriculture denoted 150 years ago.

Their dimensions are large. Consumers in 1954 bought food and fiber worth about 93 billion dollars, or roughly 40 percent of the total consumer expenditures for all products and services.

The total assets of the three segments equaled approximately 220 billion dollars, which was almost three-fifths of the total assets of manufacturing, wholesale, and retail corporations and agriculture.

About 24 million persons, or about two-fifths of the total working force of 64.5 million, engaged in the activities pertaining to agriculture—about 6 million were employed by farm-supplies industries, about 8 million were engaged in farming, and 10 million were in the processing-distribution industries.

The significant point is this: The workers in the farm-supplies industries by taking over functions formerly done by farmworkers have contributed heavily to the advance in farm output per hour of farm labor.

Before going into the extent of this contribution, we should indicate that the processing-distribution workers also do a few functions that were done by farmworkers, but most of their tasks were taken over from housewives.

The processing-distribution workers, that is to say, chiefly perform additional services or processes rather than the functions that farmworkers once did. Processing-distribution workers should be excluded, therefore, in a comparison between farm production or output as it leaves the farmer's gate and the workers who contribute to it.

If we add farm-supplies workers to the farm labor force, however, and compare the sum with farm output, we get a measure of the efficiency of all labor—direct and indirect, farm and nonfarm—that contributes to farm output.

This concept attempts to answer in aggregate a question of which the following illustrates a part of the broader inquiry:

Does using a tractor on a farm still save labor even though we include the miners who dug the iron ore and coal from the earth, the smelter workers who converted these raw materials into steel, the manufacturing workers who fabricated the steel into tractors, and all the other nonfarm workers who assisted in producing and distributing the tractor, the fuel, and the other supplies that it requires?

We cannot give an exact measurement because we lack precise and full data. Some jobs, for example, have been transferred to nonfarm workers and have later been transferred back to farmworkers: Farmworkers once hauled nearly all farm products to a local market. When motortrucks were introduced, many were purchased by commercial truckers, who did a lot of hauling for farmers. When farm trucks became more common, many farmers tended to do their own hauling rather than to hire nonfarm truckers. The exact division of the hauling job between these kinds of workers at a given point in time is unknown.

Estimates by men in the Department of Agriculture indicate that 5 million persons worked in the farm-supplies industries in 1947 and 6 million in 1954. Industrial workers put in about 40 hours a week during this period. Farm-supplies workers therefore spent 10 billion to 11 billion hours in producing goods and services purchased and used by farmers in 1947–1954. At the same time, work on farms took 17 billion to 13 billion hours, or from half to two-thirds of the total.

Farm output per hour of farm labor rose by about 40 percent during the interwar period. When the time of the farm-supplies workers is included, the increase is less—about 30 percent. Since the beginning of the Second World War, the gain in farm labor productivity has been a little more than 150 percent. The inclusion of farm-supplies workers reduces it to about 50 percent.

Thus, when farm supplies are converted to labor and added to the farm labor force, the gain in efficiency is not so great as when only farm labor is considered. The increase is still sizable—more than 80 percent from the end of the First World War to 1958.

The technological revolution has not been limited to agriculture. It has occurred in industrial plants, also; it has meant a gain in productivity of those workers as well as a substantial contribution to the increase in efficiency of workers on farms.

This idea of laborsaving or gain in efficiency of all labor resulting from the adoption of technology is clearer when it is put in terms of a few important farm machines such as cornpickers, cotton-pickers, and milking machines.

First, let us assume that in the late 1950's the average cost of labor going into the production, handling, and delivery of these machines is 2 dollars an hour. Second, let us assume that the total labor represented by one of these machines as received on the job is something less than the delivered cost divided by the average wage. The difference, of course, consists of items—such as natural resources and profit—that do not represent labor.

Two-row mounted cornpickers cost 2,000 to 2,400 dollars delivered to the farm. The farm-supplies labor represented is about 1,100 hours. The use of such a

picker may reduce harvest labor requirements by 5 man-hours per acre and can harvest 80 or more acres in a season. This means a total reduction of more than 400 man-hours annually.

Thus, under usual conditions, only a few years would be required for the reduction in farm labor to equal the nonfarm labor required to produce and deliver the machine. A cornpicker, of course, requires a tractor, fuel, and other supplies produced by nonfarm workers. But here, also, a net saving in labor occurs compared with the farm labor required to raise, feed, and work the animals required under older methods of harvesting corn.

One-row, tractor-mounted cottonpickers cost 4,000 dollars to 8,000 dollars. The off-farm labor used to produce, handle, and deliver such machines may be 2,000 to 4,000 man-hours. Such a picker under normal use will reduce the man-hours needed for cottonpicking from 40 to 50 per acre on 40 to 80 acres. This would be a reduction of farm labor of 1,600 to 4,000 man-hours a year. Again, only a few years would be required to balance reduced man-hours of farm labor against the man-hours of industrial labor required to deliver such a cottonpicker to the user.

A four-unit milking machine costs about 1,000 dollars. The off-farm labor represented must be something less than 500 man-hours. Such a machine will handle 40 or more cows, with an annual reduction of about 30 man-hours per cow compared to hand milking. Thus, the annual reduction of the dairy labor will be 1,200 hours or more. Thus, in many cases, less than a year's use will be sufficient for the reduction in man-hours of dairy labor to balance the man-hours of industrial labor required to make the milking machine available.

These examples constitute further evidence that the increase in time of farm-supplies workers is more than offset by the reduction in time of farmworkers resulting from their use.

Efficiency in farming results from more efficient production of corn, cotton, milk, and other farm products.

How have the different farm enterprises fared in this respect?

How do crops compare with livestock?

If there are differences, what have been the significant causes?

American farmers in 1956–1958 raised more than three times more total crops per hour of labor than they did in 1910–1912. (The 3-year averages are used to add stability.) During the same period, livestock production per hour nearly doubled, and labor efficiency in total farm production rose 2.8 times.

The increase in productivity of the labor spent on crops has been far from uniform among crops and sections and for different parts of the last half century.

There has also been considerable variation during different parts of the period in the relative influence of the two basic factors behind the phenomenal increase in crop production per hour. These causal factors are higher yields per acre, which were largely the result of fertilizer, variety, hybrids, pesticides, weather, and other biological factors, and fewer man-hours per acre, which resulted primarily from mechanization—that is, more effective power sources, machines, and methods.

Man-hours per acre and yield are interrelated. To illustrate: If a greater quantity of fertilizer is applied to a crop and results in a greater yield, additional time is needed to obtain and to apply the fertilizer and harvest and market the higher yield. The relation between yield and time for harvest depends on the extent of mechanization. Additional yield of a highly mechanized crop adds little to the time for harvesting but for crops that are gathered by hand the increase in harvest-time is almost proportional to the added produce.

For the half century beginning in 1910, wide adoption of mechanized and labor-saving methods of producing, harvesting, and marketing crops resulted in a drop in man-hours per acre of crops at the rate of 2.2 percent per year. Mechanization was the prime cause of greater labor efficiency in producing crops. The increase of 0.8 percent per year in yields also contributed, however, and the combination of the two resulted in the substantial rise—3.1 percent annually—of crop labor productivity. Of the gain in crop efficiency, 72 percent resulted from fewer hours per acre. The remaining 28 percent was associated with higher yields.

Between 1910 and 1920, there was a relatively small but still important increase in the labor efficiency of crop production. Crop production per acre dropped slightly. That had a negative effect on labor efficiency. But changes in equipment and methods, the beginning of the trend toward mechanization, was enough to offset the influence of lower yields and to raise the efficiency of crop labor at the rate of 1 percent annually. There was a trend toward the use of larger teams. Tractors were coming into use, particularly in the western wheat areas. The use of the combine was expanding.

During the depression years of the interwar period, the labor efficiency of crop production continued to improve at the slightly greater rate of about 1.5 percent annually. It was partly the result of moderately higher yields per acre, but a developing mechanization was the dominant factor. It was responsible for about two-thirds of the gain during these two decades. The tractor, particularly the general-purpose tractor with pneumatic tires, was widely accepted in these years. The combine harvester-thresher had almost entirely replaced the binder and threshing machine. Extensive use was made of cornpickers. The adoption of field forage harvesters and field pickup hay balers was expanding.

During the war years of 1940–1945,

the increased demand and prices for crop products resulted in an almost explosive combination of biological and engineering developments, which had been incubating during the depression years. The result was an annual increase of crop production per man-hour of nearly 5 percent. Biological developments in crops, soils, and entomology appear to have made contributions about equal to those of mechanization during this period. The use of hybrid seed corn and heavier applications of fertilizer became almost universal. Laborsaving harvesting machines were generally used, except where wartime limitations on steel for their manufacture prevented.

During the period 1945–1950, labor efficiency continued to increase and at the still higher rate of about 5.3 percent per year. Slight increases in yield per acre occurred during this period, but the major contribution to increased production per man-hour resulted from fewer man-hours per acre, which dropped an average of about 5 percent per year. The Korean situation helped maintain farm prices but did not seriously restrict the production of farm machines. Thus, mechanization developed at the highest rate so far attained and accounted for 97 percent of the gain in productivity of crop labor.

Mechanization, as reflected in man-hours per acre, continued at the slightly lower rate of about 4.6 percent per year from 1950 to 1958 and was the most important factor contributing to rapid increase in labor efficiency.

During this period, though, there was also the highest rate of increase of average yield per acre so far attained— nearly 3 percent annually. An important factor was acreage allotments for wheat, cotton, and a few other crops. With the allotments there was strong incentive to use the best agronomic practices on the best acres.

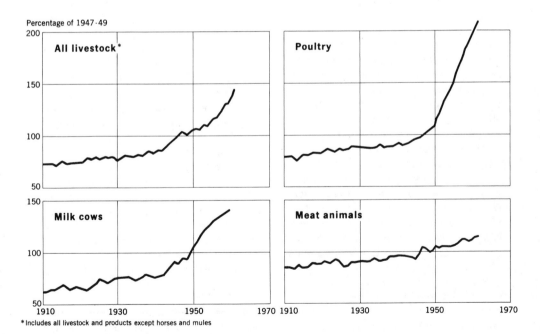

Percentage of 1947-49

All livestock*

Poultry

Milk cows

Meat animals

* Includes all livestock and products except horses and mules

Production per Man-hour, Selected Kinds of Livestock

The combination of this rapidly increasing yield per acre and the reduced labor per acre caused by the continuing rapid development of mechanization resulted in a startling 7.4 percent average annual increase in crop production per man-hour. About two-thirds of this phenomenal gain resulted from advances in mechanization and the other third from greater yields.

The biggest gains in labor efficiency have been for the feed and food grains and oil crops, among them corn, wheat, and soybeans, which are among the most completely and effectively mechanized. Farmers in 1956–1958 produced more than six times as much oil crops, six and two-thirds times as much food grains, and almost six times as much feed grains per man-hour as in 1910–1912.

Even greater gains in efficiency were made in the major producing area of each crop.

For sugar crops, mainly sugar beets, the gain in labor productivity for the past 5 decades has been nearly 300 percent, somewhat less than for crop production as a whole. Production of sugar crops per hour from 1950 to 1957, however, rose more rapidly than for any other group of crops except feed grains. Much progress has been made in mechanizing production of sugar beets, which took about 95 hours per acre during the war but only 53 hours in 1955–1958. Also contributing was a significant increase in yield from 12.7 tons to 17 tons an acre.

For cotton, the gain in labor efficiency also has been just under 300 percent. Picking cotton was about one-third mechanized in 1958. Even less progress has been made in mechanizing chopping and hoeing—the most time-consuming preharvest operation.

Production of hay and forage is well mechanized, but the gain in productivity during 1910–1958 was only about three-fifths that of all crop production. That is because baling, one of the modern methods, does not save a great deal of labor as compared with older methods, most notably in the West, where stacking was formerly the prevalent method. Chopping with a field forage harvester, the most laborsaving modern method, has not increased significantly. In fact, the percentage of the hay crop that was chopped has dropped slightly. Advances in the mechanization of tillage and seeding operations have had less effect on the labor for forage production because many acres of forage crops produce for several years with one seedbed preparation and seeding.

The gain in labor efficiency for vegetable production has also been equally low—170 percent—although for certain vegetables as green peas and spinach for canning and freezing production has been completely mechanized.

The mechanization of fruit and nut production has made still less progress. In many fruit and vegetable crops, particularly those produced for the fresh market, the increase in productivity has been low. That is true also of certain special crops.

Tobacco, for example, is an important commercial crop but still requires nearly two-thirds as many man-hours per unit of production as it did in 1910. Because the manual harvesting of this crop has a high labor requirement, the large increase in yield, more than 60 percent, that has occurred since 1910 has tended to counteract the savings per acre resulting from progress in the mechanization of other operations. In fact, production per man-hour has increased less during this period than the yield per acre, with the result that the man-hours per acre required in 1958 were somewhat higher than in 1910.

What are the possibilities to improve farm labor efficiency further for crop production by mechanization?

The complete or partial mechanization

of harvesting fruit and vegetables is the most challenging. Another important possibility is the completion of the mechanization of the harvesting and handling of difficult crops, such as for cotton and certain fruit and vegetables, where a good start has already been made. Promising starts have been made on the mechanization of the harvesting of such very difficult crops as tobacco, tomatoes, cucumbers, cherries, and blueberries.

Complete mechanization of weed control in all crops offers a good possibility of further improving the work efficiency of crop production. Peak labor demands for manual weed control and harvesting required almost 1.5 million seasonal workers at the peak in 1958.

We can expect that machines will become reliable—that is, less subject to breakdowns and other interruptions. That could improve greatly the work efficiency of crop production.

More effective machines for planting and applying fertilizers and pesticides might increase work efficiency by reducing the labor cost of replanting and by increasing the yield per acre.

The development of more reliable and effective machines and the more extensive adoption of land forming and stone removal will open the way for the use of wider machines at higher operating speeds. That will tend to contribute proportionately to improved work efficiency.

The possibilities of eliminating operations, such as some of the seedbed and cultivating operations in favor of so-called minimum tillage, or combining operations, such as was done with the combine harvester-thresher, are intriguing but quite unpredictable.

For livestock production, farm labor efficiency about doubled from 1910–1912 to 1956–1958. It rose at the rate of 1.5 percent a year. That would appear to be

good progress when considered by itself, but it is only about one-third of the increase for crop production. It seems to have been the result of more effective application of engineering to crop production, because for the four decades following 1920 the gains from animal science, as reflected in production per breeding unit, equaled or surpassed those from plant and soil science.

Production per breeding unit is essentially an average of milk per cow, eggs per hen, and so on. The gain in production per breeding unit was about three-fourths, while the gain in crop production per acre was slightly less than one-half. On the other hand, the reduction in man-hours per breeding unit was less than 10 percent, while the reduction in man-hours per acre of crops was 60 percent.

This gain in production per breeding unit has been continuous throughout the period at a fairly uniform rate. Some acceleration began about 1945, but the gain from 1950 to 1956–1958 was slower. Up to 1937 or so there was little gain in efficiency of labor spent on livestock; the man-hours per breeding unit just about kept pace with the production per breeding unit. The production per man-hour therefore remained virtually unchanged.

Livestock production per man-hour has risen at the rate of 3.7 percent a year since 1950.

The war years were the only period during which the reduction in man-hours per breeding unit was more effective than higher livestock yields in enhancing livestock labor efficiency. Hours per cow, sow, and hen dropped at the rate of 2.4 percent a year and was responsible for more than 90 percent of the gain in labor productivity. There was a great urge to save labor and despite critical shortages of steel and rubber, the number of farms having milking machines more than doubled during 1940–1945. Almost half the farms were receiving central-station electric service in 1945, compared to about a fourth in 1940. Many of the machines and installations that save chore labor depend on electricity.

Declines in man-hours per breeding unit have continued to be a significant factor in greater labor efficiency since the war. They have come through engineering developments, such as more effective buildings and farmstead arrangement; mechanized methods of handling water, feed, bedding and manure; and so on.

Livestock yields also have gone up since the war, however. The average milk cow on farms produced 6,438 pounds of milk in 1959 but only 4,787 pounds in 1945. Rate of lay was in excess of 200 eggs per hen in 1958 and 152 in 1945. Besides, a growing number of the eggs were hatched into broilers; that increases production per hen on farms. These developments were more effective than the reduction in labor in the greater production per man-hour. Since 1950, however, the two basic causes have been about equally responsible for increased livestock labor efficiency.

The dairy and poultry enterprises are the large users of labor in livestock production. The large gains in labor efficiency have been in them.

For meat animals, the gain in labor efficiency was only about a third from 1910 to 1958. This has been a slow but rather constant development throughout the period; it has accelerated somewhat since 1950.

On the other hand, the gain in labor efficiency for dairy production has been over 100 percent. The gain for poultry has been still greater—about 170 percent.

The labor efficiency gains for the egg production phase of poultry are about the same as for dairy, but the production of poultry meat products has been outstanding. Turkeys and broilers have reached commercial status as a farm enterprise since 1940. Turkey production per man-hour has increased nearly 350 percent since 1910, and broiler production per man-hour about 400 percent since 1935.

It is impossible to say exactly what will happen in the way of continued improvement of the labor efficiency of livestock production. It seems certain that for some time the trend will continue to concentrate much of the livestock production in what might be considered livestock factories rather than as secondary or even primary enterprises on general farms. That would mean greater efficiency of the labor spent on livestock.

Chapter Nine

The Status of Labor

■ By the early twentieth century the AFL, which attained two million members in 1904, was by far the biggest American labor organization. Only a few independent unions and the conservative railroad brotherhoods were on the outside. But the whole group of unions had done little to organize large-scale factory industry, unskilled labor, white-collar workers, women, or Negroes. Most unions were socially exclusive and were built around the skilled crafts, such as the building trades or the operation of railroad trains.

Partly because of this limited base, the number of organized workers no more than kept pace with the growing labor force up to World War I. The proportion of organized workers then rose sharply during the war, declined equally sharply in the postwar Depression of 1920 to 1922, and sagged during the prosperous twenties to a lower level than in 1904.

Success in organization was hindered not only by the rigid craft structure of the AFL but also by opposition from employers opposed to strong independent unions. Industrialists organized through associations to prevent the spread of union contracts and the closed shop. Furthermore, the rapidly growing sectors of industry, such as automobiles, communication, and electrical equipment, were those in which unions had never had any strength.

In order to increase consumption by raising wages, the New Deal favored collective bargaining. First the National Industrial Recovery Act of 1933 and then the far stronger National Labor Relations, or Wagner, Act of 1935 gave Federal protection to union organizers and led to new developments in the labor movement. Responding to the government-created opportunity, a group of AFL union presidents led by John L. Lewis of the United Mine Workers formed a Committee for Industrial Organization. They hoped to sponsor the formation of unions embracing all the workers in the industries in which the AFL had organized only a few skilled crafts. After half a dozen years of conflict, sometimes bloody, the committee succeeded in organizing the basic factory industries, but meanwhile the AFL, still dominated by the building trades, had expelled the members of the Lewis group and the unions that supported them. In 1938 these unions, with nearly as many members as the AFL, formed the Congress of Industrial Organizations. In 1939 all union members are estimated to have been equal to 29 per cent of the nonagricultural labor force, compared with 12 per cent in 1930 and an earlier all-time high of 16 per cent at the peak of the postwar boom in 1920.

Unions continued to gain strength during World War II as the War Labor Board enforced collective bargaining. In return for a government pledge to include new workers in war plants in the coverage of existing union contracts, the major labor organizations agreed not to strike the plants. As a result, in spite of a period of general labor peace during the war, both the AFL and the CIO emerged stronger than before.

The kind of labor history briefly sketched here has been written in great detail from the side of both organized labor and the government. But relatively little has been written on the economic history of labor as distinct from the sociologic and political history of unions. There are numerous histories of the sit-down strikes that occurred in the New Deal era and of the rise of the CIO, but there is little beyond conjecture on the effect of organization on labor supply, productivity, and wages. In the absence of any concise and comprehensive analysis of such purely economic factors as they functioned during the exciting days of the New Deal, it would seem more rewarding to concentrate in this chapter on the new and important post-World War II status of labor as seen both from quantitative and qualitative points of view. While neither of the two readings chosen for this purpose directly answers key questions regarding the economic effects of the relatively high level of unionization, both provide facts that the scholar should bear in mind in any economic approach to changing labor inputs and outputs.

Have Unions Passed Their Peak?

■ A number of labor economists argue that present employment trends are distinctly adverse to union growth. Blue-collar factory work, the area that gave organization its big upward push from 1933 to 1953, has been declining in relation to the work of the total labor force. White-collar office work, an area in which unions have been weak, has increased. Furthermore, decentralization of manufacturing means movement of industry into nonunion areas where organizers have had little success, the South, for example.

Irving Bernstein, of the Institute of Industrial Relations of the University of California, Los Angeles, doubts the validity of this argument. According to his figures, and they are as reliable as any others available, the secular trend of labor organization is one of both absolute and real growth. By "real"

Professor Bernstein means union membership in relation to the total labor force. His secular trend does depend, however, on discounting the temporary rise in organization brought about by the Korean War and the stagnation caused by a low rate of economic expansion from 1956 to 1960. Otherwise 1953 would mark the high point, and real percentage would decline from there to 1960.

Irving Bernstein

The Growth of
American Unions, 1945–1960*

During the past decade students of the American labor movement have differed sharply over its rate of growth. There have been two schools of thought. The "saturationist" have stressed structural factors. By the end of World War II, they have argued, unions had penetrated the readily organizable segments of the labor force—male, blue-collar workers employed mainly by large firms in the manufacturing, mining, transportation, and construction industries in the larger urban centers of the North and West. Labor organizations now faced the virtually impenetrable sectors—women, white-collar workers, employees in wholesale and retail trade, the service industries, the professions, government, and in agriculture, little firms, small towns, and the South. Further, the labor movement is disadvantaged by the contemporary labor force shift from blue- to white-collar employment.

The historical school has adopted a broader frame of analysis, emphasizing that many factors in addition to the structural have been at work in determining the rate of union growth.[1] The labor movement is seen as increasing its size in two ways—at a modest pace over

long spans of time and in sharp spurts at infrequent intervals. The forces that have caused secular growth are the expansion of the labor force, the increasing social acceptability of unionism, the growing homogeneity of the working class, and the extension of union security provisions in collective bargaining agreements. In the short run unions have increased their memberships dramatically as a consequence of wars and major depressions, in both of which government tends to intervene to protect the right to organize.

Fifteen years have now elapsed since the end of World War II. It is time to examine the course of union growth during this era in order to determine which of these analyses is correct.

I

This controversy seems preposterous on its face. The answer is a matter of fact: during this period union membership has

* Reprinted by permission from *Labor History*, II (Spring, 1961), pp. 131–157.
[1] Several readers of this paper have observed that this conflict is overdrawn. I have deliberately sharpened the arguments to give discussion of the problem a cutting edge. For expressions of the saturationist viewpoint see Daniel Bell's "The Next American Labor Movement," *Fortune* (April 1953), 204, and his "Discussion," *Proceedings* (1954), Industrial Relations Research Association, 231–36. For the historical analysis see Irving Bernstein, "The Growth of American Unions," *American Economic Review* (June 1954), 301–18. For a somewhat different historical treatment see John T. Dunlop, "The Development of Labor Organization: A Theoretical Framework," in R. A. Lester and Joseph Shister, eds., *Insights into Labor Issues* (New York: Macmillan, 1958).

either increased or it has stagnated. One need only examine the figures to learn what happened. But the rub is in the statistics. There is no internally consistent series for the years 1945–1960.

Ultimately, all measurements of membership depend upon figures submitted by trade unions. The basic difficulty is that unions differ sharply in their definitions of a member. Some count only those who have paid dues; others employ the criterion of "good standing." This affects persons who are unemployed, on strike, in the armed forces, in apprenticeship, and in retirement. The definition significantly influences the count. In 1958, for example, the Bureau of Labor Statistics found that 62 international unions out of a total of 186 had 933,000 "members" who for various reasons did not pay dues. Another difficulty is that some unions do not report accurately. They either inflate the figures to show greater strength than they actually have for institutional reasons, or they inflate or deflate their memberships to avoid payment of per capita taxes to federal bodies or to raise or lower representation at federal conventions. There is, of course, no way of knowing how much of this goes on. In addition, many "international" unions have members outside the continental United States and show them in their statistics. The main concentration is in Canada, while others are located in Puerto Rico, Hawaii, Alaska, and the Canal Zone. In 1958, according to BLS, 1.2 million were in this category, of whom 1.1 million were in Canada. Finally, the agencies that count members nationally rely upon the international unions as sources and do not include the members of organizations confined to one employer or to one locality. BLS estimated that in 1958 over 500,000 persons were members of these smaller organizations. Thus, the reader should bear these qualifications in mind in evaluating the data that follow. That is, they exclude many persons in good standing who do not pay dues, contain some inaccurate reports, include foreign and territorial members, and exclude members of organizations limited to a single locality or employer.[2]

For the purpose of this paper it is necessary to have an annual membership series for 1945–1960 with reasonable internal consistency. Its construction has been an exercise in crazy-quilt making. Leo Wolman of the National Bureau of Economic Research has supplied unpublished statistics for the years 1945–1948. Presumably they are consistent with the earlier data published in his *Ebb and Flow in Trade Unionism* and with the figure for 1953 published by Wolman's student, Leo Troy, in the NBER's *Distribution of Union Membership among the States, 1939 and 1953*. For 1949–1953 I have projected Wolman's series at the rate of growth of the American Federation of Labor, which was the largest labor body in those years. The Bureau of Labor Statistics has published data for the years 1954–1958 in its *Directories of National and International Labor Unions in the United States*, which are the best national figures we have ever had. For 1959–1960 I have projected the BLS series by the rate of growth of union membership in California, whose Division of Labor Statistics and Research supplies the most reliable state figures available.

The resulting series, in addition to its obvious defects, suffers from a significant inconsistency. Wolman's data are markedly lower than those of BLS, and Troy's figure for California in 1953 is substantially below that of the California Division of Labor Statistics for the same year. Since, in my judgment, the BLS and California results are more reliable, it is necessary to adjust the Wolman data and the

[2] For discussions of the complications in measuring union membership, see Bureau of Labor Statistics, Bull. No. 1185, *Directory of National and International Labor Unions in the United States, 1955*, 6–10, and Irving Bernstein, "Measuring with a Broken Yardstick," *Statistics of Labor-Management Relations* (Berkeley: Institute of Industrial Relations, 1956), 15–19.

projection therefrom for the years 1945–1953. Between the last Wolman year, 1953, and the first BLS year, 1954, there is an apparent increase of 4.39 per cent. This, obviously, is unrealistic because the recession of 1954 must have caused a drop in union membership. The California series, in fact, shows a decline of 0.75 per cent. Thus I have taken the spread between these amounts—5.14 per cent—and have added it to the figures for each year between 1945 and 1953.

Table 1 shows the actual membership of American labor unions for the period 1945–1960 as constructed by the above methods. It also reveals what I have elsewhere described as "real" union membership, that is, actual membership expressed as a per cent of the civilian labor force.[3] Since some students of union growth prefer the employment over the labor force series in calculating real membership, Table 1 also gives these data. In my judgment they are not satisfactory because unions have both unemployed and self-employed members as well as farm workers who are not counted in the nonagricultural employment statistics.

For the period as a whole the actual membership of unions rose 5,228,000, or 39.1 per cent. Viewed historically, this is a formidable absolute achievement. The number of members added during these sixteen years exceeded the total size of the labor movement in any year prior to 1937. The percentage of growth is also impressive when one considers the high base. That is, a 1 per cent increase on the 1945 base yielded 133,790 members; for 1930 it was only 29,730, for 1900

[3] My use of the civilian labor force to establish real membership has been criticized on the ground that many persons are counted that unions do not seek to organize. More properly, one should remove them to determine the "union potential" of the labor force. See Benjamin Solomon, "Dimensions of Union Growth, 1900–1950," Industrial and Labor Relations Review (July 1956), 545–46. I concur heartily with this criticism. The trouble for present purposes is that no annual series of the union potential exists. Thus I am forced to employ the labor force series.

but 8,685. Real union membership, however, advanced only modestly, 2.5 per cent between the terminal years of 1946 and 1960. (Here it is advisable to disregard 1945 because the disproportionately large number in the armed forces in that year depressed the size of the civilian labor force.)

There were, of course, significant internal differences within this sixteen-year span of time. Seven phases are notable. The first is the post-World War II boom, which lasted from 1945 to 1949, in which American unions added 1,581,000 members, a gain of 11.8 per cent. During these years real membership was fairly steady at about 24 per cent. This was a time of full employment and of marked increase in consumer prices, both of which contributed to union expansion.

The recession of 1949–1950 formed the second period, which saw a decline in membership of 209,000 in 1950, or 1.4 per cent. Real membership dropped to 23.4 per cent, the lowest point of any year between 1945 and 1960. At this time joblessness was quite severe and consumer prices fell slightly.

The Korean War of 1950–1953 was the third phase and witnessed the most notable advance in union membership—3,133,000, or 21.2 per cent. Here real membership rose to 28 per cent, the peak for the whole period. Conditions were highly favorable for union growth: more than full employment and a sharp rise in the cost of living.

The fourth phase occurred during the succeeding recession of 1953–1955, which saw a decline of 135,000, or 0.8 per cent. Real membership dropped one point to 27 per cent. At this time there was a good deal of joblessness and prices were steady.

During the capital goods boom of 1955–1956, the fifth period, membership rose by 728,000, or 4.1 per cent. In 1956 real membership recovered to 27.4 per cent. At this time there was substantially full employment and a modest rise in prices.

Table 1/ Union Membership, 1945–1960

		"Real" Membership		Alternate "Real" Membership	
Year	Actual Membership[a]	Civilian Labor Force[b]	Union Membership as Per Cent of Civilian Labor Force	Non-agricultural Employment[c]	Union Membership as Per Cent of Non-agricultural Employment
1945	13,379,000	53,860,000	24.8	40,037,000	33.4
1946	13,648,000	57,520,000	23.7	41,287,000	33.1
1947	14,845,000	60,168,000	24.7	43,462,000	34.2
1948	14,916,000	61,442,000	24.3	44,448,000	33.6
1949	14,960,000	62,105,000	24.1	43,315,000	34.5
1950	14,751,000	63,099,000	23.4	44,738,000	33.0
1951	16,211,000	62,884,000	25.8	47,347,000	34.2
1952	16,730,000	62,966,000	26.6	48,303,000	34.6
1953	17,884,000	63,815,000	28.0	49,681,000	36.0
1954	17,757,000	64,468,000	27.5	48,431,000	36.7
1955	17,749,000	65,847,000	27.0	50,056,000	35.5
1956	18,477,000	67,530,000	27.4	51,766,000	35.7
1957	18,430,000	67,946,000	27.1	52,162,000	35.3
1958	18,081,000	68,647,000	26.3	50,543,000	35.8
1959	18,452,000	69,394,000	26.6	51,975,000	35.5
1960	18,607,000	71,056,000	26.2	53,135,000[d]	35.0[d]

a 1945–1948: Leo Wolman, by correspondence.
  1949–1953: Projected from AFL membership.
  1954–1958: Bureau of Labor Statistics.
  1959–1960: Projected from California membership.
b Bureau of the Census.
c Bureau of Labor Statistics.
d Includes Alaska and Hawaii.

The sixth phase took place during the recession of 1957–1958, when membership fell 396,000, or 2.1 per cent. Real membership declined a full point to 26.3 per cent. This downturn saw severe unemployment and, interestingly enough, some increase in prices.

The final period was the recovery of 1959–1960, in which membership rose by 526,000, or 2.9 per cent. Real membership, however, did not recover, remaining at a fraction over 26 per cent. While unemployment diminished, a significant amount of joblessness remained and the size of the civilian labor force leapt upwards in 1960. Further, employment lagged in two sectors in which unions are relatively strong—manufacturing and mining. At the same time prices rose modestly.

II

The discussion thus far has been confined to the American labor movement as a whole. I shall now turn to significant internal differences among industries and among unions.

The distribution of union membership by industry group for the United States is available only for four recent years. NBER supplies data for 1939 and 1953, BLS for 1956 and 1958. Unfortunately, these sources differ in the classification of industries, thereby inhibiting comparisons. Table 2 shows the distribution of union membership for the United States for these years for those industry groups which are comparable.

Table 2 reveals the high concentration of union membership in manufacturing

Table 2/ Distribution of Union Membership in the United States by Industry Group, 1939, 1953, 1956, 1958

Industry Group	1939[a] Number	1939[a] Per Cent	1953[a] Number	1953[a] Per Cent	1956[b] Number	1956[b] Per Cent	1958[b] Number	1958[b] Per Cent
Total	6,517,700	100.0	16,217,300	100.0	18,104,000	100.0	17,968,000	100.0
Manufacturing	2,299,100	35.3	7,312,800	45.1	8,839,000	48.8	8,359,000	46.5
Nonmanufacturing	4,218,600	64.7	8,904,500	54.9	9,265,000	51.2	9,609,000	53.5
Mining and quarrying			c		518,000	2.9	622,000	3.5
Contract construction	889,000	13.6	2,197,800	13.6	2,123,000	11.7	2,324,000	12.9
Transportation			c		2,727,000	15.1	2,712,000	15.1
Telephone and telegraph			c		428,000	2.4	409,000	2.3
Electric and gas utilities			c		323,000	1.8	259,000	1.4
Trade			c		883,000	4.9	852,000	4.7
Finance and insurance			c		51,000	0.3	104,000	0.6
Service industries			c		1,222,000	6.7	1,240,000	6.9
Agriculture and fishing	4,400	d	8,300	d	76,000	0.4	33,000	0.2
Nonmanufacturing (not classifiable)			c		* n.a.		19,000	0.1
Government	418,700	6.4	749,600	4.6	915,000	5.1	1,035,000	5.8

[a] Troy, Distribution of Union Membership.
[b] Bureau of Labor Statistics.
[c] Not comparable.
[d] Less than 1 per cent.

337

industries since World War II. Prior to the war only a little over a third of the labor movement worked in factories. That fraction must have grown markedly during the war and slowly in the postwar period to a peak of just under one half the total in 1956. There was a decline between 1956 and 1958. While membership in manufacturing industries is more sensitive to fluctuations in employment than that in nonmanufacturing, the recession of 1958 probably explains this downturn only in part. There are good reasons for believing that the factory segment of the labor movement is now in a position of secular decline. The leading nonmanufacturing industry groups are transportation, construction, services, government, and trade.

Table 3 expresses these national membership statistics for 1939, 1953, 1956, and 1958 as a per cent of employment, showing the penetration by labor unions of these industrial sectors. For the employed labor force as a whole the proportion of union members rose from 21.5 per cent in 1939 to 35.5 per cent in 1958. The table suggests that the rate of growth slowed down in the latter half of the fifties. Most of this gain was supplied by manufacturing, where membership climbed from 22.8 per cent of employment in 1939 to 54 per cent in 1958. In the same period nonmanufacturing penetration advanced much less—from 20.9 to 27.4 per cent.

By 1958 three industry groups were substantially unionized—transportation, construction, and mining and quarrying. Almost half the persons who worked in manufacturing and in telephone and telegraph remained unorganized. More than half the employees in electric and gas utilities were beyond the union pale. In four industry groups—services, government, trade, finance and insurance—membership was only a minor fraction of the organizable potential.

The California statistics of union membership so far surpass those for the United States in quantity and quality as to justify their examination in detail. That state's Division of Labor Statistics and Research has gathered data from local unions for each year in the period 1945–1960 (for 1945–1950 as of either June 1 or May 1 and for 1951–1960 as of July), which are published annually in *Union Labor in California*. For the years 1945–1949 the Division did not obtain complete coverage; the size of the sample suggests that 90 per cent or more of union membership was included. For 1950–1960 the statistics are complete.

While California's economy differed sharply from that of the United States before World War II, that difference has markedly diminished in the last twenty years. This is evident in the distribution of nonfarm employment in 1958:[4]

	United States	California
Total	100.0%	100.0%
Manufacturing	30.6	26.4
Trade	22.0	22.6
Government	15.6	17.6
Service	12.7	13.5
Transportation, communication, and utilities	7.7	7.8
Finance	4.7	4.7
Construction	5.3	6.6
Mineral extraction	1.4	.8

A somewhat heavier national concentration of employment in manufacturing and mining is compensated for by a moderately higher California percentage of employment in trade, government, service, and construction. Fundamentally, however, the distribution in California is similar to that in the nation.

Further, the widely-held notion that unions are much stronger in California than they are in the United States as

[4] Maurice I. Gershenson, "Shifts in California's Industrial and Employment Composition," *Monthly Labor Review* (May 1959), 516.

Table 3 / Union Membership in the United States as a Per Cent of Nonagricultural Employment by Industry Group

Industry Group	1939			1953			1956			1958		
	Membership[a]	Employment[a]	Per Cent	Membership[a]	Employment[b]	Per Cent	Membership[c]	Employment[b]	Per Cent	Membership[c]	Employment[b]	Per Cent
	(000)	(000)		(000)	(000)		(000)	(000)		(000)	(000)	
Total	6,518	30,311	21.5	16,217	49,681	32.6	18,104	51,766	35.0	17,968	50,543	35.5
Manufacturing	2,299	10,078	22.8	7,313	17,238	42.4	8,839	16,903	52.3	8,359	15,468	54.0
Nonmanufacturing	4,219	20,234	20.9	8,905	32,433	27.5	9,265	34,824	26.6	9,609	35,052	27.4
Mining & quarrying	[d]			[d]	852		518	807	64.2	622	721	86.3
Contract construction	889	1,150	77.3	2,198	2,622	83.8	2,123	2,929	72.5	2,324	2,648	87.8
Transportation	[d]	[d]		[d]	2,899		2,727	2,745	99.3	2,712	2,531	107.2
Telephone & telegraph	[d]	[d]		[d]	746		428	805	53.2	409	771	53.0
Electric & gas utilities	[d]	[d]		[d]	566		323	572	56.5	259	579	44.7
Trade	[d]	[d]		[d]	10,527		883	11,221	7.9	852	11,141	7.6
Finance & insurance	[d]	[d]		[d]	2,038		51	2,308	0.2	104	2,374	4.4
Service industries	[d]	[d]		[d]	5,538		1,222	6,160	19.8	1,240	6,395	19.4
Nonmanufacturing (not classifiable)	[d]	n.a.		[d]	n.a.		n.a.	n.a.		19	n.a.	
Government	419	3,995	10.5	750	6,645	11.3	915	7,277	12.6	1,035	7,893	13.1

[a] Troy, *Distribution of Union Membership.*
[b] Bureau of the Census.
[c] Bureau of Labor Statistics.
[d] Not comparable.

a whole has little merit. In 1953, according to Troy, 35.7 per cent of California's nonfarm employment was organized in comparison with 32.6 for the nation. In fact, California ranked thirteenth among the states, running far behind Washington, Montana, West Virginia, Michigan, Oregon, and Indiana.[5]

Table 4 shows the distribution of union membership in California by industry group (including a breakdown for manufacturing) since World War II. To conserve space, I have chosen key years for the first decade of this period, but have included each year since 1955.

The California labor movement increased in size by approximately 75 per cent between 1945 and 1960, much the greater part of the gain coming from nonmanufacturing industries. Except for 1945, when there was an unusually heavy concentration in aircraft and shipbuilding (i.e., transportation equipment), there has been a remarkably stable relationship between factory and nonfactory union membership, that is, one manufacturing member to two nonmanufacturing members. Similarly, excepting the immediate postwar adjustment, there has been little difference in rate of growth among manufacturing industries. All have increased in union membership and at roughly the same rate. Pretty much the same may be said of nonmanufacturing industries. The expansion of the labor movement in California was accomplished by 1957; since that time it has been unable significantly to add to its size.

Unfortunately, it is not possible to measure union membership as a percentage of employment in California except in a very crude way because the membership figures are compiled by very broad industry groups. In general, California unionism follows the national pattern of penetration. The major deviation is that manufacturing is somewhat less well organized and nonmanufacturing is better organized, especially in construction, trade, and services.[6]

III

There are, of course, marked differences in growth rates among unions. Some conform to the pattern of the labor movement as a whole; others deviate from it. This is evident in the data presented in Table 5.

Production workers in the aircraft-missiles industry are almost completely under collective bargaining agreements, mainly with the Machinists and the UAW, of which the former is larger. Hence the size of the aircraft segment of the IAM is highly sensitive to fluctuations in employment. After the post-World War II shakedown, membership rose slowly until 1950. The expansion that accompanied the Korean War produced a huge increase in membership, which rolled on until 1957. In the late fifties employment of hourly-rated workers declined markedly because of the obsolescence of the piston-engine aircraft, the emergence of the jet, and the shift to guided missiles and electronics. IAM membership reflected this change. The experience of the Machinists, as will be noted shortly, is representative of that of many organizations in heavy manufacturing, mining, and transportation.

Retail trade, by contrast, is only slightly unionized, presenting the Clerks with an enormous organizable potential. While the data are incomplete, they suggest that this union has grown steadily and rapidly since World War II without any special sensitivity to fluctuations in employment.

In Table 6, I have sought to summarize variations in growth rates among sixty-six

[5] Leo Troy, *Distribution of Union Membership among the States, 1939 and 1953* (New York: National Bureau of Economic Research, 1957), 18–19.

[6] Irving Bernstein, "Trade Union Characteristics, Membership, and Influence," *Monthly Labor Review* (May 1959), 531.

Table 4/ Distribution of Union Membership in California by Industry Group, 1945–1960[a]

Industry Group	1945 Number	1945 Per Cent	1949 Number	1949 Per Cent	1953 Number	1953 Per Cent	1956 Number	1956 Per Cent	1957 Number	1957 Per Cent	1958 Number	1958 Per Cent	1959 Number	1959 Per Cent	1960 Number	1960 Per Cent
Total	946,639	100.0	1,200,686	100.0	1,577,900	100.0	1,689,500	100.0	1,736,700	100.0	1,706,200	100.0	1,741,100	100.0	1,755,700	100.0
Manufacturing	435,329	46.0	374,834	31.2	522,000	33.1	549,600	32.5	575,000	33.1	561,100	32.9	574,000	33.0	568,800	32.4
Food and kindred products	98,521	10.4	108,634	9.0	105,000	6.7	108,000	6.4	114,000	6.6	130,600	7.7	132,700	7.6	133,300	7.6
Textiles and apparel	14,669	1.5	26,082	2.2	25,100	1.6	24,500	1.5	22,500	1.3	22,100	1.3	21,400	1.2	21,100	1.2
Lumber and furniture	21,625	2.3	35,964	3.0	43,900	2.8	43,600	2.6	40,800	2.3	39,700	2.3	41,100	2.4	43,200	2.5
Printing, publishing and allied industries	13,553	1.4	20,891	1.7	25,600	1.6	28,800	1.7	29,700	1.7	30,300	1.8	30,600	1.8	31,800	1.8
Petroleum, chemicals, and rubber	23,519	2.5	29,606	2.5	35,800	2.3	35,800	2.1	36,000	2.1	34,200	2.0	34,000	2.0	32,800	1.9
Metals and machinery, except ordnance and transportation equipment	62,054	6.6	71,468	6.0	128,000	8.1	131,100	7.8	141,500	8.1	134,500	7.9	138,800	8.0	136,900	7.8
Transportation equipment	191,752	20.3	59,102	4.9	128,100	8.1	133,000	7.9	144,400	8.3	125,700	7.4	123,400	7.1	115,900	6.6
Paper and allied products	[b]		[b]		[b]		[b]		[b]		15,300	0.9	16,200	0.9	17,000	1.0
Stone, clay, and glass products	[b]		[b]		[b]		[b]		[b]		16,100	0.9	16,400	0.9	16,800	1.0
Other manufacturing	9,636	1.0	23,087	1.9	30,500	1.9	44,800	2.7	46,100	2.7	12,600	0.7	19,400	1.1	20,000	1.1
Nonmanufacturing	511,310	54.0	825,852	68.8	1,055,900	66.7	1,139,900	67.5	1,161,700	66.9	1,145,100	67.1	1,167,100	67.0	1,186,900	67.6
Construction	107,250	11.3	232,557	19.4	285,800	18.1	325,900	19.3	328,800	18.9	326,700	19.1	334,700	19.2	342,600	19.5
Transportation and warehousing	89,848[c]	9.5	151,487	12.6	204,100	12.9	199,200	11.8	201,400	11.6	192,900	11.3	200,800	11.5	192,700	11.0
Public utilities	86,786[d]	9.2	44,689	3.7	60,700	3.8	65,800	3.9	66,200	3.8	70,200	4.1	68,300	3.9	69,700	4.0
Wholesale and retail trade	61,672	6.5	122,385	10.2	185,400	11.7	213,000	12.6	220,300	12.7	202,300	11.9	204,500	11.7	211,300	12.0
Eating and drinking places, hotels and other lodging places	52,257	5.5	80,905	6.7	93,600	5.9	97,700	5.8	100,400	5.8	102,800	6.0	102,900	5.9	106,000	6.0
Motion picture production and distribution, theatres and other entertainment	42,418	4.5	67,016	5.6	76,400	4.8	76,400	4.5	73,900	4.3	77,000	4.5	76,500	4.4	77,000	4.4
Miscellaneous services	43,376	4.6	81,106	6.8	86,400	5.5	97,400	5.8	103,800	6.0	77,600	4.5	79,800	4.6	81,200	4.6
Government	23,135	2.4	38,924	3.2	49,400	3.1	54,200	3.2	57,400	3.3	86,600[f]	5.1	90,000	5.2	96,400	5.5
Agriculture, fishing, and mineral extraction	4,568[e]	0.5	6,423[e]	0.5	14,100	0.9	10,300	0.6	9,500	0.5	9,000	0.5	9,600	0.6	10,000	0.6

[a] California Division of Labor Statistics and Research.
[b] Classified with Other Manufacturing.
[c] Transportation except local service.
[d] Includes local transportation and distribution.
[e] Miscellaneous nonmanufacturing.
[f] Beginning in 1958, locals with majorities employed by government agencies classified in government regardless of type of service performed.

Table 5/ Membership in Machinists Aircraft Lodges and Retail Clerks, 1945–1960

Year	Machinists Aircraft Lodges	Retail Clerks
1945	n.a.	119,000
1946	n.a.	n.a.
1947	62,937	163,000
1948	64,681	n.a.
1949	68,906	n.a.
1950	75,469	n.a.
1951	126,381	170,000
1952	179,827	n.a.
1953	206,004	n.a.
1954	214,854	265,000
1955	203,854	300,000
1956	219,346	300,000
1957	250,499	n.a.
1958	235,049	305,000
1959	216,469	n.a.
1960	n.a.	400,000

International Association of Machinists and Retail Clerks International Association.

Table 6/ Growth of Selected Unions, 1944–1958, 1956–1958[a]

Union	Per Cent Change 1944-1958	Per Cent Change 1956-1958
MANUFACTURING		
Food and kindred products		
Brewery	−27.1	0
Distillery	230.0	32.0
Meat Cutters	193.1	4.9
Packinghouse	66.0	5.1
Average	115.5	10.5
Textiles and apparel		
Clothing	15.7	− 2.3
Garment (ILG)	47.4	− 1.8
Hosiery	−80.4	−41.1
Textile (UTW)	15.0	−54.0
Textile (TWU)	−42.3	− 2.7
Average	− 8.9	−20.4
Lumber		
Woodworkers	33.3	−12.1
Printing and publishing		
Bookbinders	104.2	1.1
Lithographers	156.1	9.6
Newspaper Guild	38.3	4.9
Printing Pressmen	70.0	6.3
Typographical	34.7	11.4
Average	80.7	6.7
Petroleum, chemicals, & rubber		
Chemical	62.3	− 3.7
Oil, Chemical and Atomic	80.2	− 1.5
Rubber	5.7	−10.9
Average	49.4	− 5.4
Metals and machinery		
IUE	n.a.	−30.0
Machinists	49.1	4.5
Steelworkers	20.3	−23.2
Average	23.1	−16.2

[a] Florence Peterson, American Labor Unions (New York: Harper, 1945) and Bureau of Labor Statistics, except SAG and AFTRA from David L. Cole, Is Merger Practicable?

unions, which together hold the great majority of members in the United States. Since no data were available for 1945, I have used those for 1944 published by Florence Peterson in American Labor Unions. The figures for 1956 and 1958 were those reported in the BLS directories. The use of 1956 as a base year suggests the heavy industry watershed noted above. Statistics were not available for a year later than 1958. David L. Cole's study of the possible merger of the Screen Actors Guild and the American Federation of Television and Radio Artists supplied information for those organizations. At the risk of criticism, I have classified unions by industry group. The American labor movement, of course, seldom shows a fine appreciation of jurisdictional lines and many unions have members in more than one industry. For the present purpose, however, I think this categorization is helpful.

The percentage changes from 1944 to 1958 reveal the great growth of the labor

Table 6/ Growth of Selected Unions, 1944–1958, 1956–1958[a]—*Continued*

Union	Per Cent Change 1944-1958	Per Cent Change 1956-1958	Union	Per Cent Change 1944-1958	Per Cent Change 1956-1958
Transportation equipment			Railway & Steamship Clerks	26.2	3.1
Auto	− 2.4	−22.2	Street, Electric Railway	− 0.3	−13.3
Boilermakers	−66.9	−12.2	Teamsters	125.5	3.7
Marine and Shipbuilding	−80.0	25.0	Transport	42.1	3.8
Average	−49.8	− 3.1	Average	36.0	−3.8
Paper			**Public utilities**		
Paper Makers	115.3	3.8	Communications	93.5	− 1.4
Pulp, Sulphite	120.0	0			
Average	117.7	1.9			
			Trade		
			Retail Clerks	205.0	1.7
Stone, clay, and glass			Retail, Wholesale	146.2[b]	36.0
Glass, Ceramic	38.2	− 0.4	Average	175.6	18.9
Glass Bottle Blowers	122.9	3.6			
Potters	4.9	−13.3			
Average	55.3	− 3.4	**Eating places and hotels**		
			Hotel and Restaurant	63.4	− 1.1
NONMANUFACTURING					
Construction			**Entertainment**		
Bricklayers	144.8	3.6	Musicians	162.9	2.3
Bridge, Structural Iron	31.4	3.7	Screen Actors	82.7[c]	19.9[d]
Carpenters	39.2	− 1.8	Stage Employees	29.2	29.0
Electrical (IBEW)	139.6	11.1	Television and Radio Artists	61.6[c]	11.4[d]
Hod Carriers	19.1	2.3	Average	84.1	15.7
Operating Engineers	180.0	40.0			
Painters	31.8	−15.0			
Plumbers	96.8	4.9	**Miscellaneous services**		
Average	85.3	6.1	Building Service	271.4	13.0
Transportation and warehousing			**Government**		
			Federal (NFFE)	20.0	− 8.2
			Government (AFGE)	122.2	− 6.2
Air Line Pilots	314.1	23.6	Letter Carriers	83.3	1.9
Locomotive Engineers	−34.0	− 5.3	Post Office Clerks	150.0	3.0
Locomotive Firemen	−34.8	−19.2	State, County, and Municipal	300.0	33.3
Longshoremen (ILWU)	12.0	−20.0	Average	135.1	4.8
Maintenance of Way	44.1	−18.7			
Maritime (NMU)	−55.6	0	**Mining**		
Railroad Trainmen	2.1	− 8.0	Mine (UMW)	0	n.a.
Railway Carmen	63.7	20.9	Mine, Mill	0	0
Railway Conductors	−36.8	−19.8	Average	0	0

[a] Florence Peterson, *American Labor Unions* (New York: Harper, 1945) and Bureau of Labor Statistics, except SAG and AFTRA from David L. Cole, *Is Merger Practicable?*
[b] 1950–1958.
[c] 1950–1959.
[d] 1957–1959.
[e] 1953–1959.

movement between these years. Only eleven of the sixty-six unions suffered a decline in membership. The Brewery Workers lost out largely because of raids by the Teamsters; the Hosiery and Textile Workers saw a shift from the union to the nonunion sectors of their industries; the Boilermakers and the Shipbuilding Workers were caught in the postwar collapse of the shipyards; the UAW suffered from employment attrition in the auto, farm implement, and aircraft industries; and the railway operating crafts, the Maritime Union, and the Street Railway Employees found themselves in declining industries. These organizations, however, were exceptional, as most unions expanded. Among industry groups, notable gains in rank order were made in air transportation, building service, trade, government, truck transportation, paper, food, public utilities, construction, entertainment, printing and publishing, eating places and hotels, stone, clay, and glass, and petroleum, chemicals, and rubber. It is worth observing that these are mainly nonmanufacturing classes and that the unions in heavy manufacturing, mining, and rail and ship transportation are conspicuously absent.

The percentage changes between 1956 and 1958 reveal a quite different picture. Here the number of shrinking unions rose to twenty-eight, of which fifteen were in manufacturing and thirteen in nonmanufacturing. Notable losses were suffered in textiles and apparel, lumber, petroleum, chemicals, and rubber, metals and machinery, transportation equipment, and rail transportation. There is the probability that the same was true in mining if one considers only employed members. Even two construction unions—the Carpenters and the Painters—declined at this time although the former may have suffered its losses in its lumber locals. The main areas of growth between 1956 and 1958 were in food, printing and publishing, paper, construction, air and truck transportation, trade, entertainment, building service, and government. These results reflect in part the 1958 recession.

Historically union membership in the United States has concentrated in a few large organizations which have tended to set the tone for the labor movement. Thus it is interesting to see how these internal shifts have affected large unions. In Table 7, I have ranked the fifteen biggest organizations for 1944 and 1958.

The changes are significant. Most dramatic is the rise of the Teamsters Union, which ranked fourth in 1944 and first in 1958 by virtue of more than doubling its membership. The building trades made notable gains: the Carpenters moved from sixth to fifth, the Hod Carriers from ninth to eighth, the IBEW from twelfth to sixth, and the Operating Engineers entered the top group in 1958. The Teamsters, it should be noted, have a stake in the construction industry. Several other nonmanufacturing organizations advanced: the Hotel and Restaurant Employees moved from fifteenth to tenth, the Railway & Steamship Clerks from fourteenth to twelfth, and the Retail Clerks entered the big fifteen. The Meat Cutters, which has a large nonmanufacturing membership, made thirteenth. The principal losers were the large industrial unions that were the mainstay of the old CIO—the UAW, the Steelworkers, the UMW, the UE, and the Textile Workers. The only organization to hold its own in this group was the Clothing Workers. The manufacturing unions affiliated with the old AFL did better: the IAM made third in each year and the ILG moved from thirteenth to ninth.

IV

I shall now turn to an intensive examination of the "saturationist" analysis. Before doing so, however, I must stress the importance of the fact that we know little in a systematic way of how unions organize. The only method that is charted is the election procedure of the National Labor Relations Act. It is hazardous to draw general conclusions from this information. Unions in many industries lack legal recourse to the NLRB; other organizations which are eligible to use the Board prefer other methods; the United Mine Workers during much of the period under examination refused to qualify itself under the Taft-Hartley Act. For these and perhaps other reasons only a limited number of labor organizations normally seek to organize through the election procedure of the NLRB and they are heavily concentrated in manufacturing industries. From 1946 to 1959 the factory segment of NLRB collective bargaining elections fluctuated between 64.1 and 78.4 per cent of all such elections.[7]

There are many other methods by which unions organize, some acting through the employees, others through an employer, and still others through another labor organization. The union may conduct an organizational drive, sign up enough members to demand a contract, and persuade the employer either voluntarily or after a strike to begin collective bargaining. In an expanding bargaining unit covered by a union or closed shop new employees automatically become members. In the case of a corporation already under agreement which opens a branch plant the union may extend the existing contract to the new unit, often with the consent or even active support of the employer. Similarly, a master agreement in a multi-employer unit may be extended to a new or hitherto unorganized firm. Or the union may disregard the employees and organize the employer under a union security provision which automatically makes his people members. Finally, unions may add to their ranks from the membership of other

[7] National Labor Relations Board, *Annual Reports*, 1946–1959.

Table 7/ Ranking of Fifteen Largest Unions, 1944 and 1958

Rank	Union	1944 Members
1	Auto Workers	1,052,000
2	Steelworkers	798,000
3	Machinists	665,900
4	Teamsters	629,200
5	Mine Workers	600,000
6	Carpenters	600,000
7	Electrical Workers (UE)	430,000
8	Boilermakers	400,000
9	Hod Carriers	400,000
10	Textile Workers (TWU)	342,000
11	Clothing Workers	325,000
12	Electrical Workers (IBEW)	313,000
13	Garment Workers (ILG)	300,500
14	Railway & Steamship Clerks	286,000
15	Hotel and Restaurant	267,000

Rank	Union	1958 Members
1	Teamsters	1,418,246
2	Auto Workers	1,027,000
3	Machinists	992,689
4	Steelworkers	960,000
5	Carpenters	835,000
6	Electrical Workers (IBEW)	750,000
7	Mine Workers	600,000
8	Hod Carriers	476,598
9	Garment Workers (ILG)	442,901
10	Hotel and Restaurant	436,315
11	Clothing Workers	376,000
12	Railway & Steamship Clerks	360,899
13	Meat Cutters	325,304
14	Retail Clerks	305,000
15	Operating Engineers	280,000

Florence Peterson, *American Labor Unions*, and Bureau of Labor Statistics.

unions by raiding or by merger; or a powerful organization, frequently the Teamsters, may compel an employer to deal with a weak union. There is little firm knowledge on the incidence of these techniques or their distribution among industries and unions.

With this qualification, I shall now turn to an assessment of the roadblocks to union growth stressed by the saturationists. They point out, first, that women are less well organized than men and that the prospect is for a larger female proportion of the labor force. Both points are valid. In the mid-fifties, according to BLS, only about 16 per cent of the females in the labor force were union members in contrast with 31 per cent of the males. Further, the proportion of women has been rising secularly—17.7 per cent of the labor force in 1900, 21.9 in 1930, 25.3 in 1940, 30.3 in 1955. Ewan Clague, the Commissioner of Labor Statistics, anticipates a figure of 33.4 per cent by 1965.[8]

In fact, we know nothing about the comparative propensity of men and women to join unions. In the abstract there is no reason to anticipate a difference, because the economic and social forces that shape the decision work on both sexes. Women, that is, tend to be as indifferent or as militant as men. The difference in the membership rate, rather, is to be explained largely by the fact that women work primarily in industries and occupations into which unions have not made a deep penetration, primarily office, sales, and services. In those areas both sexes are relatively unorganized.

The California data suggest that there is a modest secular rise in the rate of female union membership. In 1941 only 11 per cent of the state's members were women. The proportion increased to 22 per cent in 1945 because of the withdrawal of men from the civilian labor force during the war. It declined to 15 per cent in 1948 and then rose to 19 per cent in 1950. Between 1950 and 1959 the female proportion stabilized at about 19 per cent of California's union membership. That is, female membership grew at the same rate as male during this decade when the state's labor movement added 387,000 workers to its rolls.[9] This analysis suggests that sex by itself is probably not a significant impediment to union organization.

The second saturationist argument is that unions, which have in the main organized large corporations, now face the tougher small firms. Here there is no certainty as to fact in general, although it is the case in manufacturing. A big anti-union employer, obviously, has greater resources than a little one; the UAW had more trouble organizing General Motors than the typical parts supplier. The great majority of NLRB elections that unions have won have been in units with fewer than 100 employees—83.8 per cent of the total in 1959. Union representatives in both manufacturing and services have informed me that their organizations could unionize many more small units if they wished. The question is only in part whether the job can be done; more often it is whether it is worth the expenditure in time and money in view of the potential return. In recent years the labor movement seems normally to have answered this question in the negative. Many unions, as well as the AFL-CIO, have been operating under restricted budgets.

The saturationists, third, make the same contention about small towns. Again, it is not an assured (though a probable) fact that big cities are better organized than little ones. Exceptions come readily to mind. In California, for example, Fresno and Bakersfield are more highly unionized than Los Angeles. In that state between 1954 and 1957 the three leading areas in rate of union growth—the Southeast, Santa Barbara-Ventura, and the Sacramento Valley—had no great cities. In California, and I suspect elsewhere, the industrial spillover from cities to satellite communities in

---

[8] Bureau of the Census, *Historical Statistics of the United States*, 64; Ewan Clague, "The Shifting Industrial and Occupational Composition of the Work Force During the Next Ten Years," *The Changing Character of American Industry* (Washington: AFL-CIO, 1958), 4.

[9] California Division of Labor Statistics and Research, *Union Labor in California, 1941–1959*.

expanding metropolitan areas has brought unionism to small towns.[10]

On the other hand, the atmosphere of a community can influence the propensity to unionize. Historically, for example, this factor made the difference between "closed-shop" San Francisco and "open-shop" Los Angeles. For all practical purposes, there are no longer large cities in which anti-union sentiment predominates. Some small cities of this sort remain, largely in the South and in the Plains states. However, this does not in itself prove that small towns are harder to organize.

The fourth roadblock to union growth, the saturationists argue, is agriculture. It is, of course, a fact that virtually no farm workers belong to labor organizations and that they are denied the benefits of the National Labor Relations Act. The obstacles to unionization are formidable. Even here, however, there are long-term forces at work—mechanization, a rising skill level, and a rapidly shrinking labor force —that suggest that some day organization may come. It is not without significance that, as this paper is written, the most serious campaign in a generation to unionize California's farms is underway.

The fifth saturationist contention is that government employees are hard to unionize. It is true that public workers are not as highly organized as those in manufacturing, mining, and construction. Yet, as Tables 2, 3, 4, and 6 demonstrate, both actual and real union membership among government employees have been rising in the United States and in California. There are many reasons for this development: the narrowing of historic fringe benefit differentials between private industry and government, the growing variety in public employment, the increased willingness of government instrumentalities to experiment with collective

bargaining systems, and the shift of some properties, especially in local transit, from private to public ownership. In fact, the State, County, and Municipal Employees, the largest government union, grew at a faster rate between 1956 and 1958 than any of the sixty-six organizations listed in Table 6 except the Operating Engineers.[11]

Sixth, the saturationists argue that the South is a formidable regional bar to unionization. Here analysis is hobbled by the virtual absence of membership statistics. The latest estimate is Troy's, which showed that the South Atlantic, East South Central, and West South Central areas lagged far behind the rest of the nation in 1953. A study by H. M. Douty of manufacturing workers covered by collective bargaining agreements in 1958 suggests that the gap may have narrowed in recent years. He found that 46.1 per cent of southern factories had bargaining agreements covering a majority of their workers in contrast with 67.9 in the Northeast, 72.6 in the West, and 76.5 per cent in the North Central. Douty also concluded for the nation as a whole that the number of workers covered by agreements was the same as the number of union members. Frederic Meyers has found significant unionization in Texas not only in manufacturing but also in nonmanufacturing industries: virtually 100 per cent in telephone and telegraph and on the railroads, 80 per cent in transit and interstate trucking, 50 per cent in construction, and 25 per cent in electric utilities.

It is popular to conceive of the South as a monolith; in fact, there are significant internal differences. Douty discovered for manufacturing a high degree of unionization in primary metals, petroleum and coal products, transportation equipment, paper, tobacco, stone, clay and glass, machinery,

[10] Bernstein, "Trade Union Characteristics," 532–33.

[11] Paul A. Brinker, "Recent Trends of Labor Unions in Government," Labor Law Journal (January 1961), 13–22.

chemicals, and printing and publishing. The low incidence industries were textiles, lumber, furniture, and apparel. In general, both Meyers and Ray Marshall have emphasized that unions have been most successful in organizing newer and larger units (notably branch plants of nation-wide corporations) and have found the going tougher in the older and smaller establishments (especially in textiles). As the South has industrialized, the propor-tion of the former has risen and unions have thereby gained.[12]

In the light of these findings, fragmen-tary though they are, it would be incorrect to regard the South as the Sahara of the labor movement. Unionism, though still markedly behind in that region, has made notable gains. This is confirmed by the regional distribution of NLRB collective bargaining elections: prior to the Korean War the South accounted for less than 20 per cent; in the late fifties its share rose to about 25 per cent of these elections. Certain unions, especially the Teamsters and District 50 of the United Mine Workers, have invested in vigorous organizing campaigns in the South with not insignificant success. As the region industrializes, one might reasonably an-ticipate the further growth of union membership.

This is not to say that the saturationist hypothesis is wholly invalid. It seems to explain those industries into which unions have failed to penetrate deeply—textiles, hosiery, lumber, and furniture. In all probability it also explains the weakness of unionism in some southern com-munities.

[12] Troy, *Distribution of Union Membership*, 22; H. M. Douty, "Collective Bargaining Coverage in Factory Employment, 1958," *Monthly Labor Re-view* (April 1960), 345–49; Frederic Meyers, "The Growth of Collective Bargaining in Texas—A Newly Industrialized Area," *Proceedings* (1954), Industrial Relations Research Association, 286–97; Ray Marshall, "Some Factors Influencing the Growth of Unions in the South," paper presented to Industrial Relations Research Association, De-cember 1960.

Finally, and with great emphasis, the saturationists stress the white-collar bar to unionization. The American labor move-ment in membership, leadership, and tradition is predominantly blue-collar. In 1958, according to BLS, only 2.2 million trade unionists, just 12 per cent of the total, were in nonmanual occupations. Of the twenty-nine members of the Exec-utive Council of AFL-CIO at that time only two—the presidents of the Railway Clerks and the Retail Clerks—were from white-collar organizations. In addition, the labor force is undergoing a secular shift away from manual to nonmanual employ-ment. In 1910 professional and technical workers, managers, officials and proprie-tors, clerical and sales workers accounted for 22 per cent of the labor force; by 1956 this share had risen to almost 40 per cent and for the first time exceeded the number of manual workers. "The most important occupational development that we foresee," Ewan Clague has written, "is a more rapid increase in employment among white-collar workers than among the blue-collar workers."

There is a tendency to lump all white-collar workers together. In fact, they have significant differences. A professional engi-neer, a motion picture star, a railway clerk, a telephone operator, a postal clerk, a checker in a food market, a secretary in the central office of a large corpora-tion, and a secretary in a lawyer's office have as little in common with each other as they have with manual workers. They are divided by differences in education, income, employment regularity, status, and relationship to the employer, all of which shape their propensity to unionize. Further, the shift to white-collar employ-ment has been uneven. Within the manu-facturing group, for example, the per-centage of manual workers declined sharply between 1944 and 1959 in air-craft, petroleum, and chemicals; fell moderately in machinery, steel, paper, stone, clay, and glass; and dropped only slightly in rubber, shipbuilding, and textiles. Thus, it is hazardous, if not impossible, to generalize about the organization of white-collar workers as a whole.

This conclusion is reinforced by an examination of the distribution of union membership within nonmanual occupations. They are strongly organized on the railroads and in telecommunications. In public agencies extensive unionization exists in the postal service, with much less in other federal agencies and in state, county, and municipal employment. There is uneven organization of the clerical staffs of manufacturing firms. Virtually no unionism exists in banking, finance, and real estate, although there is some in insurance. In retailing, unions have made significant penetrations into department stores, into food, drug, and variety chain stores, and into mail-order houses, but into little else. Professional people in the entertainment field are almost completely organized, as are the air line pilots. A substantial number of newspaper reporters and editors are union members. Only a slight percentage of school teachers, nurses, engineers, scientists, architects, draftsmen, and technicians are in labor organizations.

It is precisely in the white-collar area that union growth has made impressive strides in recent years. The expanding organizations, as Table 6 demonstrates, have been the Air Line Pilots, the Railway Clerks, the Teamsters (with a substantial membership in retail and wholesale trade as well as in clerical occupations), the Retail Clerks, the Retail, Wholesale, and Department Store Union, the Musicians, the Screen Actors, AFTRA, the postal organizations, and the State, County, and Municipal Employees. Few serious students of the labor movement regard the present low level of organization among white-collar people as permanent. Jack Barbash has recently written, "When the white-collar person becomes a baby sitter for an automated machine, pride of work

gets drained out of his job, and he is going to try to join with his fellows. . . . Once the white-collar worker gets over the initial trauma of being in a union, he behaves like a bricklayer."[13]

This is not to say that the organization of nonmanual workers on a massive scale is likely to come about either quickly or dramatically. In all probability the growth will occur differentially by continuation of those expansionist tendencies already evident and by the gradual emergence of new ones. Certain areas, for example, banking, finance, real estate, and office employees in very small units, will be organized in the distant future, if at all. In order to achieve the unionization of white-collar people it will be necessary for the labor movement to adapt itself in structure and in outlook and for Congress to amend the National Labor Relations Act, which presently denies certain nonmanual workers the benefits of the statute. The organization of these workers is presently and prospectively the Number 1 challenge to the American labor movement. There is no reason to regard it as insurmountable.

V

Daniel Bell wrote in 1953: "In 1946 U.S. unions had organized about 15 million workers—48 per cent of the 31 million potential members. . . . Since 1946 the working population has expanded but union membership has remained stationary."[14] As Table 1 demonstrates, his

[13] Clague, "The Shifting . . . Composition of the Work Force," 16–21; Everett M. Kassalow, "Occupational Frontiers of Trade Unionism in the United States," paper presented to Industrial Relations Research Association, December 1960; Industrial Union Department, AFL-CIO, "Summary Report of Staff Seminar, White-Collar Workers in Industry," New York, December 1–3, 1960; Solomon, "Dimensions of Union Growth," 549–59; Barbash is quoted in Daily Labor Report, December 27, 1960, A-3.
[14] Bell, "The Next American Labor Movement," 204.

figure for 1946 was more than 1 million too high and his estimate for 1953 was almost 3 million too low. In fact, between 1946 and 1953 American unions added 4.2 million actual members and their proportion of the labor force advanced 4.3 per cent. In the entire period between the close of World War II and 1960 the American labor movement grew in size by more than 5 million and real membership rose 2.5 per cent. As the discussion in the preceding section indicates, I do not believe that the saturationist arguments taken together have general validity. Only a handful deserve any weight and that in relatively narrow sectors: small towns in the South and the Plains states; the textile, hosiery, furniture, and lumber industries in the South; some white-collar areas—banking, finance, real estate, and office employees in small units.

Thus, I think the saturationist analysis must be dismissed as a general proposition. There is no difficulty in fitting the period 1945–1960 into the historical theory. It was an era dominated by the slow, secular rise of union membership, actual and real. There was a secondary war which stimulated the growth rate, and no major depression occurred. In these features this period paralleled the years 1897–1914. In that earlier era union membership, actual and real, grew gradually except for the acceleration given the rate by the Spanish-American War, and there was no deep economic downturn.

In one respect the years since 1945 constitute an aberration: in no prior period in the history of the American labor movement has so large a proportion of its constituency worked in manufacturing industries. This has made membership more sensitive to fluctuations in employment than at any other time, at least during the twentieth century. This is because employment in manufacturing is more sensitive to the cycle than is employment in nonmanufacturing. The decline in the manufacturing share of total

union membership, which became evident in the late fifties, constitutes, I suspect, a permanent resumption of the pre-World War II pattern. If this proves to be the case, union membership in the future should be less sensitive to employment fluctuations than it was in the recent past.

This shift from manufacturing to non-manufacturing unionism suggests several probable aspects of union growth in the future. First, it is likely to come quietly, in a fashion unlike the great manu-facturing breakthrough of the thirties. The pattern has already been laid down by such organizations as the Retail Clerks and the State, County, and Municipal Employees, which grew rapidly in the fifties without major strikes and with little public attention. Second, there are likely to be significant changes in the centers of power within the labor move-ment. The relative gains of the Teamsters, the building trades, the Hotel and Restau-rant Employees, the Railway Clerks, the Meat Cutters, and the Retail Clerks at the expense of the industrial unions in manu-facturing and mining have been noted. This trend should continue to the ad-vantage of most of these nonmanufactur-ing organizations. They may well be joined in size by such presently modest unions as the Building Service and the State, County, and Municipal Employees. Third, we may expect the leadership of the labor movement increasingly to reflect its grow-ing white-collar base. In some nations in which nonmanual organization is highly developed, notably the Netherlands and Germany, the white-collar group supplies a disproportionately large share of labor leadership.

Finally, it is necessary to note and explain the fact that between 1956 and 1960 actual union membership did not grow and real membership fell. As already indicated, I do not think the saturationist hypothesis offers a useful explanation. This was the time when the revelations of the McClellan Committee blackened the public's "image" of the labor movement. While this factor, undoubtedly, explains the stagnation in part, I think it is only in small part. The Teamsters, who suffered most from the exposures, actually expanded during these years. Far more fundamental, in my judgment, was the failure of the American economy to grow.

Output did not advance significantly and there was a persistent and large lump of unemployment. The growth of the labor movement is inextricably linked to the growth of the economy. If union membership expands in the future, it will do so only as part of an expanding economic system.

The Power of Unions

■ The executives of companies that were forced by labor militancy and its support by government to enter into contracts with unions necessarily developed a new interest in labor relations. Also, the stake of the modern professional manager in the welfare of his company as an organization of fellow employees probably made him less resistant to worker demands than owner-managers had been. But for whatever reasons, unions were able after World War II to negotiate contracts not only increasing real wages but providing numerous fringe benefits, such as pensions, sick leave, and vacations with pay.

In the following selection, an article for business executives, J. B. S. Hardman, editor and writer on labor matters, discusses organized labor as a social force in mid-century America. In doing so, he illustrates the inevitable interweaving of such economic factors as wage rates, the power structure of unions, and the social ideas of both labor and management in the advanced industrial state.

J. B. S. Hardman
Labor in Midpassage*

Organized labor is a great and ever-expanding social force in the American community. Rich in resources, in numbers, and in influence, labor is spurred on by a significant objective and a vital idea inherent in the simple logic of the union's day-to-day performance.

This is not meant to suggest that the

members and the leaders of unions are all or even predominantly committed to a centrally recognized social philosophy, or driven by a myth of "manifest destiny," except for those few who are dedicated to an ideological creed. Just the same, it is not reasonable to "sell labor intellectually short" or to assume that it is devoid of a theoretic content merely because theorists are classed by most labor leaders (and also by most business-

* Reprinted by permission from *Harvard Business Review*, XXI (January-February, 1953), pp. 39–48.

men) as "long-hairs" and therefore not worthy of serious attention. What has labor, a practical, workaday proposition, they ask, got to do with theory, an intellectual pursuit? But the labor movement makes sense—the kind of sense in which it is possible to trace a central pattern of labor union behavior, not a model or a preconceived concept but one that represents a generalization based upon and evolved from analyzed experience and observation.

Big Labor in a Big Nation

The increasingly wide realization of the mounting significance of labor in American life is interestingly, if not altogether convincingly, expressed in Professor Sumner H. Slichter's characterization of our national community as a *laboristic society,* "a society in which employees are the most influential group in the community and in which laws, policies and institutions largely reflect the interests of employees."[1] However, the wide recognition of labor's increasing stature in the nation is not accompanied often enough by a sufficient understanding of the nature of organized labor's enhanced power and therefore of its specific social significance in our "system of countervailing powers" (to use Professor Galbraith's definition of a society which, while in effect a widely multifarious, contradictory organism, strives for adjustment within reason and under law[2]).

We have lately grown accustomed to speaking of Big Government, Big Business, Big Labor, Big Everything. But bigness is not an objective yardstick; bigness in this instance is not so much an *absolute* measure of what *is* as a *relative* measure of what *was.* Our world has not really increased in size; if anything, it has grown

smaller. The point is that at the same time it has achieved immense gains in knowledge, in working capacity and resources, in mastery of its natural setting, in the courage and originality of its thought. And, needless to say, our virtues are not the only things which have expanded.

Bigness is to be recognized as a fact of mid-twentieth century American life; and if there is something wrong with the mammoths of industry, labor, administration, and so on, fault if any is to be found not with the size of the particular units which are erring but with their respective failure to equate their performance with the progressive, socially positive needs of society. Indeed, such fault really lies in democracy's failure to coordinate adequately the functioning of such units. We must have Big Democracy to match the other "Bigs."

Contest of Social Powers/ Labor, as a big part of a big nation, can help make or break that kind of democracy. In labor's cooperation with other forces lies the key. And, obviously, cooperation cannot operate single-handedly. Yet the concept of organized labor as *the enemy* is still all too prevalent in management circles today. "We spend too much time wrangling with organized labor as though organized labor was our preordained enemy . . . ," wrote the chairman of a national industrial enterprise in a letter to the editor of the *New York Times,* June 10, 1952. The same enemy-orientation exists on the other side of the line, also calling forth reaction in kind. There are exceptions of course—lots of them, and on both sides— but even a little of what is no good can be very bad. The intricate, interdependent, extremely sensitive American industrial society of today rests upon contests over stakes in social power, but is allergic to brawls and dogfights.

The important thing to remember is that labor is an aspect of social history, as are

---

[1] *What's Ahead for American Business* (Boston, Little, Brown and Company, 1951), p. 126.
[2] *American Capitalism* (Boston, Houghton Mifflin Company, 1952).

both management and democracy itself, and no constructive resolution of today's contest between social powers is possible if this fact is ignored.

A review of "the labor situation" in this period of heightened national and international tensions is generally expected to be, and rarely turns out not to be, either a defense of or an attack upon one side or the other of the basic factions in the labor-management feud. Neutrality fares none too well where basic social interests are contested. Nevertheless, it is possible to be both objective without being neutral and critical without being antagonistic. The intellectual basis for such a frame of mind may perhaps be gained from Mr. Frank W. Abrams' admonishment to management—advice which could be heeded by labor as well—to "recognize true long-term interests, as distinguished from interests that may seem real because they are more immediate."[3]

Motives and Aims

Can labor be said to function and act in a group manner? Or is it only a loose conglomeration of many unions, each pursuing its own ends, often working at cross purposes? The jurisdictional feuds, internecine fights of special interests, and bitter orientational disputes that labor is often subject to, all lead many people to think the latter. Yet there is evidence that the labor movement possesses a sense of direction and social value judgments, and hence is in effect unified in broad objectives although not in any formal way.

Spokesmen for organized labor have ever so often claimed that labor is not motivated by any long-range aims or central ideology. "We have no ultimate aims. . . . We are all practical men. . . .

[3] "Management's Responsibilities in a Complex World," *Harvard Business Review*, May 1951, p. 30.

We are going on from day to day." Thus spoke Adolph Strasser, leader of a cigarmakers' union, in 1885. His statement has been quoted time and time again to emphasize labor's divorcement from roadmaps, end-aims, and isms. So has Samuel Gompers' statement in 1913, before the United States Commission on Industrial Relations, that "the intelligent common-sense workmen prefer to deal with the problems of today, the problems with which they are bound to contend if they want to advance, rather than to deal with a picture and a dream which have never had, and I am sure will never have, any reality in the actual affairs of humanity. . . ."

These men were not the "kidding" kind. Were they expressing a deep-rooted conviction; or were these statements only eyewash, intended as protective coloration in a setting of antagonism toward unions, of distinctly unfriendly laws and courts, and of government administrations "neutral" only to management and actively hostile to labor? The latter conclusion may well be the correct one; "Aesopian" language was known long before witnesses for the prosecution in trials of Lenin-Stalinite operatives of the American Communist cadres reported discovery of its use.

But what urges labor on, in our present circumstances, with most of the old evils eliminated or mitigated? Some time ago, a prominent publisher-editor said at a dinner conference of business leaders, labor officials, and intellectuals:

We have been holding numerous informal gatherings, with or without dinner, with competent, representative men discussing management-labor relations and the over-all labor problems in our democratic country. Discussion has always been carried on at a high objective level, aboveboard, pointed, and at all times candid. Yet somehow we seem to have been skirting the core of the matter that puzzles us most, and never really getting to it at all—namely, just what, clinically speaking, is the labor movement or, for that matter, who is it and what makes it tick? We haven't gotten the right answers. Yet we need to know them.

The need is indeed a real one. Why are the answers so difficult to find? Conceivably dinner conferences and round-table discussions in which "representatives of all sides and shades of opinion" take part do not provide quite the right means for getting at the facts. Not all those who know will tell freely what they think at such politically interdenominational get-togethers, hesitating to speak with complete frankness in such rapid-fire exchanges of bits of thought for fear that what they would say, unless fully documented and spelled out, might injure their side's public relations.

Certainly, the more than two-dimensional "something" that makes unions tick cannot be understood from statements of membership numbers, of collective bargaining coverage, of wage and hour progress, or of other purely factual data, however accurate and authentic they may be.

Our search here is for deeper motivations and aims such as will account (1) for the amazing regenerative capacity of unions, their ability to arise Phoenix-like to renewed life and vigor from the flames of defeat and even destruction, and (2) for the expanding effect which unions appear to have on the pattern of development of our democratic system. These two facets of American unionism are in reality but a single social phenomenon— the continuous and never-ceasing (even though receding at times) urge of the people in a free nation to widen and to intensify their scope of competent intervention in the national life. This has always been true of Americans, so why are so many people overwhelmed by the fact that men who wear overalls part of the day are influenced by the same motivations and desires on the whole as those who wear business suits?

Political Citizenship/ The traditional consideration of the working man as a plant personnel G.I. and of the labor union as strictly a "bread 'n' butter" enterprise has a record of long acceptance. It dies hard. That the worker in industry is also a member of the national community, a political citizen, is considered somehow irrelevant. It is admitted that as a worker he might be concerned with the passage or the defeat of a special legislative item, but such political or rather legislative interest on his part is looked upon as incidental to his eight-hours-a-day shop life and not likely to set in motion a chain of reactions linking his proletarian essence with his civic entity. This "piecemeal" view of labor people as part-worker and part-citizen, each leading his respective part-time life independent of the other, simply will not hold water, certainly not red American blood. A man is not a worker eight hours a day, a citizen four hours a day, a family man twelve hours a day. He is all things all the time, though he is more of one thing at one time and more of another thing at another.

Workers are people—a non-dramatic but true fact; and as a rule they are in the habit of viewing their lives as a whole, of integrating and interrelating their interests and outlook. The socio-political and psychological fragmentation of the human being as a worker, whatever it may accomplish for specific ends, is of no help in the effort to achieve a realistic view of labor unionism as a whole. Labor does "make sense" when looked upon as an organic part of the American people, its history, its political and cultural milieu, its psychological attunement and élan.

Unions are *economic* organizations only in the purely technical sense that they are dealing with such matters as wages, hours, and living costs and that these involve economic data. There is where their narrow "economism" ends. Beyond that they are associations of people in the same social categories, working for hire, and preoccupied with improving or reforming human relations in the process of work, and this is essentially a *political* objective.

According to most of our books, American unionism as a body has been no part or affiliate of any political party. But labor unions have never, at least for any significant length of time, been apolitical. In fact active participation of labor in politics marks union history all the way back to the first quarter of the nineteenth century. And recent years, following the national economic breakdown in the late 1920's and the early 1930's, have seen heightened and highly activized union participation in politics.

Of great pertinence to the widening area of union activity is the fact that the operational basis and scope of collective bargaining are no longer what they used to be. The process has expanded so that those who used to sit around the old bargaining table would be hard put to recognize it. The outside has intruded, and it is no longer sensible or feasible to suggest that true and free collective bargaining can only be achieved by inviting government and public boards to keep out of the picture. Government's "meddling" in business is more than a passing phenomenon; it is here to stay—and the recent election is most unlikely to change matters.

Sense of Participation/ This intensive politicalization of the union process, indeed of the whole industrial process, has in recent years affected large numbers of union members, extending far beyond the coterie of union officers and staffs and even the relatively small-numbered "bargaining committees." Although only a few will actually stand up and speak up in the bargaining room or before Congressional committees and administrative setups, multitudes are involved—indirectly, it is true—in the immediate, intermediate, and follow-up stages of the bargaining relation

ship which has developed into virtually continuous action on one level or another.

There is no minimizing the sense of participation and achievement experienced by thousands of second-rank and third-rank union activists—to cite but a few instances: 10,000 shop stewards in the UAW-CIO, 12,000 in the Railway Clerks-AFL, 25,000 in the IBEW-AFL, 73,600 in the Steelworkers-CIO, 10,000 in the CIO textile union, and 10,000 in the ILGWU-AFL. As they report to shop and plant meetings, to local union membership meetings, these men are given the feeling that they are in the mainstream of important events and have their hands on the pulse of vital happenings. Union life acquires something of the quality and drama of a presidential election, except that it is continuous, intimate, and bears closely on the daily existence of its members. This is not true, of course, of all industries, but is typical enough to make labor men feel that they "make the news."

This sense of participation that unions engender in their members and the consequent feeling of power explain in no small measure the phenomenon of the particularly pronounced present-day union "ticking." Its momentum makes the difference between organization and movement, between the static and the dynamic in organized labor.

The present complexity of union behavior is quantitatively different from union behavior of old, but not qualitatively. The old battles were against poverty; now the goal has shifted, the sights have been raised. It is status that the unions are fighting for today. The latest objectives are human dignity and security. Participation in government is simply one of the instruments by which unions hope to gain their ends.

Has labor gained any victories in this fight? Well, to take one small but perhaps significant measurement, it was not very long ago that all pullman porters, for instance, were called George or John; and as for elevator operators, they were just nameless. Now, at company expense, notices in pullman car vestibules and store elevators advise us that this sleeping or parlor car is served by Matthew A. Johnson, Jr., and that this elevator is operated by Michael Stevenson. The privilege of being identified was previously limited to bank presidents, vice presidents, and cashiers. Now it has come down the ladder of social gradations.

Accumulation of Power

American unions play a vital role in the material welfare of about two-fifths of the nation's wage-earning labor force. Although there is a question whether or not they can substantially affect their members' actual voting or cause important shifts in political party loyalties (witness the overwhelming Taft victory in Ohio in 1950 despite united union opposition), they do shape the political consciousness of many millions. That is why it makes such a great difference to the fortunes of the democratic process in American life whether unions are merely a series of self-centered and possibly self-sufficient enterprises or whether they are integrated in their own communities (formally or otherwise) and thus constitute together a definite part of the nation's social structure.

At least, practical trade unionists do not doubt that theirs is a coherent "movement." Most of them, however, do not realize the implications that ideologists or theorists read into the term. When pressed, the unionists would probably be hard put to define what they mean by it except to say, "Why, that is what we all are . . . all of us together . . . raising hell if need be or giving one another a helping hand in an emergency." They sense the power that derives from working together, and that is basic; they see the meaning of the movement in the fact of their unity and in what they seek to achieve by joint effort.

Rallying behind Issues / There have been instances over the years when almost the entire union movement has rallied behind certain issues. First of all, there have been several situations where the destiny of the whole labor movement appeared to be at stake; the defense of Haywood, Moyer, and Pettibone in the first decade of the century and of Tom Mooney in the second decade are notable examples.

Then there was the 1919 drive to organize steel labor; although centrifugal tendencies soon put in an appearance, the attempt was initially made under what was an unprecedented degree of labor unity. Again, in the 1930's and through the years of the New Deal, cohesion more often than not outdistanced parochialism. Even the sharp and often violent schism expressed by the formation of the CIO, first as the Committee for Industrial Organization within the AFL and then as the Congress of Industrial Organizations completely apart from the parent union, was in one sense a display of labor unity which simply happened to operate in separate organizations, along two parallel lines, toward essentially identical aims.

In the absence of an extraordinary urge or virtual danger, however, most of the national unions, even those of an alert and sociopolitically sensitive disposition, prefer to go it alone. This tendency was well illustrated in the case of the United Labor Policy Committee of 1951.

That committee, it will be recalled, was formed following labor's walkout from the National Wage Stabilization Board in 1951. The setting up of the committee—as an organized, cooperative, coordinating agent for the continuing purpose of the several national labor federations and the significant nonaffiliated independents, the International Association of Machinists (then outside the AFL) and the Railroad Brotherhoods—was viewed by participants and by competent, detached outsiders as of far-reaching importance. The issue involved was the ability of the several union groupings to work together. Also at stake was the answer to the vital question whether labor is fit to participate in government. The *New York Times* of March 22, 1951, reported:

At the first joint meeting of its kind since the split fifteen years ago between the American Federation of Labor and what became the Congress of Industrial Organizations, top leaders predicted the welding of the two main wings of labor into a powerful united movement as a result of the conference. . . .

The action of the top labor leaders who walked out of all defense organizations where labor was represented is being ratified daily by the rank and file. The four groups represented by the United Labor Policy Committee are being bombarded with messages indicating the desire of unionists in the lower echelons to force recognition of labor's demand for "status" in the defense production program.

Apparently the strongly worded protests of the labor spokesmen have caught fire among their local members. Telegrams, letters, telephone calls have swamped the offices of the American Federation of Labor, the Congress of Industrial Organizations, the International Association of Machinists, and the Railway Labor Executives' Association.

But some eight or nine months later, the ULPC was dissolved. The AFL, breaking up the "accouplement" (to borrow one of John L. Lewis' pithier terms), said in effect that the un-"welding of wings" was done in the name of even greater organic unity—which would all come later on, of course.

Cohesive capacity obviously had proved to be weaker than had been supposed. It is unwise, however, to conclude from this that labor is not a movement, after all, but merely an amorphous mass of unions. In the rather trying months since the dissolution of the ULPC, union organization has grown neither stronger nor weaker; so the tentative experiment in coordination has merely lent support to the idea that the incidence of formal unity of central bodies, or an approximation of such unity, need not necessarily make or

break labor's powers of resistance, its primary striking force being paramount in the national unions. The final determinant is the power that is possessed by the unions "on the ground floor." At the same time, it is possible that had the over-all economic and political situation seemed to be less secure for organized labor, the need for central unity would have been pressing enough to create a more lasting alliance.

A Social Movement/ Labor is a movement, not primarily because its affiliated parts "hold hands," so to speak, but because its activity falls within the interplay of social forces in a democratic nation. The degree of its over-all unity is neither the proof absolute nor the refutation of labor's validity as a social movement. It is the reality of its functioning as a social force rather than the details of organization or the specifics of the unity concept that qualifies it as a factor in national life.

The abiding motivation or driving force behind the labor movement in America throughout its history has stemmed from more than one solitary urge or one realized need, and that explains the variety of interpretations. Its motivations are complex; their content and emphasis vary. But a social movement is never irrevocably committed to consistency or obliged to proceed on an even keel. It cannot be forced into a strictly one-track way. Union action is pragmatic and experimental. The following generalities, however, *can* be made:

1 Labor unions are simultaneously defense and offense organizations. In the classic words of the Webbs, they are "continuous associations of wage earners for the purpose of maintaining or improving the conditions of their working lives." To validate this double task they endeavor to *create and to accumulate power by organization;* and this is the inherent aim of unionism.

2 Unions seek to use that organized

power to achieve job control, job security, and other shop rights, along with the establishment and development of collective bargaining, which of course is a vital form of the utilization of union power.

3 Parallel with the operation of the collective bargaining institution, however, and with a view to placing it upon a solid foundation, unions engage their power of organization to wrest recognition from the extant social order. They expect to be treated as fullfledged, participating equals in the democratic processes of decision-making which sustain the American nation as a going concern.

4 The power which unions create by way of mass organization, and which they utilize to affect a rearrangement of prevailing social, economic, and political relations, is *social power*. Though directed by a single segment of society, it is, because of its mass origin and uses, a contributory force in the social fabric of American life. It is not a force against society but a constituent element in the functioning of the whole of society.

5 Social power, built and put to use by executives and leaders, and used to affect human relations, is a human affair. In consequence, the operation of the union movement as generator of social power calls forth and emphasizes a kind of labor leadership able and prepared to cope with the complex tasks of community living which tend to diversify and to enrich social progress. It is true, of course, that hold-overs and surviving yes-days are as much a fact of labor life as of any other section of life. Enough change has occurred, however, whether by turnover or overturn, to bring into play in the labor hierarchy types of leaders and modes of leading that are consonant with the changing times and scenes.

6 The rise of the newer labor leadership, no matter how spotty and slow, has reflected and in turn influenced the activistic, socially minded mood of the rank and file of the unions. It has proved to be of constructive significance in the social revival that animated "the generation which had a rendezvous with destiny" and which grew up in the years of hardship and strife, from the recovery in the 1930's to the war and the troubled peace of the 1940's and on to the present unsettled start of the 1950's. Thus the accelerated organization and broad social awareness of labor have gone hand in hand with the course of the nation as a whole.

Such an interpretation of the power motivation of the American labor movement does not fit in with Professor Charles E. Lindblom's dire prognosis that the growing power of unionism will eventually destroy the private enterprise system.[4] Nor, obviously, does it jibe with the traditional Socialist or Communist class-struggle concept of unionism. The power motivation of American unionism is rooted in the historic dynamism of the American people, and it lacks the "we versus they" bias of the European labor movement. Perhaps because it does not suffer from an inferiority complex, it is immune to any Messianic obsession.

Power accumulation is what most active unionists would submit as the *raison d'être* of their organizations (whether or not it is seen as such by those whose professional business or intellectual hobby it is to analyze and theorize about labor). Unionists might not all phrase their views in that manner, but movements live not by words but by what the words stand for.

The Use of Power

Up to this point the argument has been that labor unionism is power-motivated, i.e., that its central drive is to achieve power through organization; and obviously labor now possesses considerable power. The question then logically arises: What does labor do with this power?

[4] *Unions and Capitalism* (New Haven, Yale University Press, 1949).

Active Membership/ The reported total of dues-paying members in the AFL, CIO, UMW, the Railroad Brotherhoods, and lesser nonaffiliated unions is about 16 million. These 16 million comprise about 200 international unions, operating through some 70,000 local unions and well over 1,000 state and city or regional delegated bodies. In addition there are countless organizations of members or of delegated representatives set up to perform various temporary or continuing functions and assignments. This multiplicity of the union setup is not in itself necessarily proof of great strength (it might even be construed to indicate weakness), but it is indicative of widespread concern with the business of the unions.

About 3 million union members are actively involved in the work of these organizations, performing minor executive tasks, participating in decision-making on the various levels of union activity, taking part in or acting upon officers' proposals in matters of pay and other work terms. Of these 3 million, about one in every five or six serves on a committee or holds an elective or appointive office—and usually without remuneration except for being compensated for expenses incurred in connection with his duties, such as loss of regular work time. (Under many of the 50,000 collective bargaining contracts in force, the employers pay for such loss of time involved in the discharge of duties included in the contract.)

About 15,000 or 20,000 elected or appointed union officers service the national unions, and probably an equal number are employed full time by local unions or local central bodies to direct, administer, and supervise activity or to organize those not yet unionized. Organization is from 80% to almost 100% in a majority of the nation's vital and economically strategic industries.

In contrast to today's figures there were at best 2 million actual dues-paying members in the union movement in 1932.

Unionism "turned the corner" in the mid-1930's. By the war's end in 1945, the organized union movement was stronger and more effective than ever in terms not only of organization but also of bold economic and political assertiveness. But no unions were forgetting that only ten years earlier union security was the exception rather than the rule. That psychological fact is of great importance to an adequate appreciation of present labor-industry and labor-government interrelations.

Public Strength/ Even more important than its quantitative or membership aspect is the mobile strength of unionism, its command of a following, its resources, its public influence. There was in 1945 no general acceptance by the public of the fact that the new strength of labor was a lasting phenomenon. Many remembered the dissipation in the 1920's of the considerable strength which labor had acquired in World War I and immediately after. It was generally expected that the same thing would occur after World War II. Accordingly, labor's ability to hold its own was gingerly challenged in several politically and economically important areas.

The results were mixed. The various bitter strikes of 1945–1946, the bargaining bickerings in the steel, automotive, transportation, and electrical equipment industries, and the accompanying political tensions—not yet forgotten by labor—indicated neither victory nor surrender for either side. Another contest of strength came in 1947 with the passing of the Taft-Hartley Labor-Management Relations Act over labor's mobilized opposition. And just last year we had the protracted dispute over wage rates and union shop in the steel industry.

On the other side of the picture, attesting to the internal strength of unions, is the virtual disappearance in recent years of the phenomenon of strike breaking in major industries. Management has given up trying to bribe workers with good pay and a bonus to turn "scab" in strike-bound or strike-threatened industries.

Equally significant has been the testing of the popularity of the union shop. The Taft-Hartley Act made the granting of the union shop by an employer to employees contingent upon NLRB-supervised secret balloting and upon a majority vote of all workers eligible to vote in the respective bargaining units. The logic behind this provision was that, given the chance to express themselves with impunity, beyond the alleged terrorizing reach of a union, the workers would vote against the union shop. Results proved to the contrary. In 44,587 shop and plant elections held since the enactment of the law to determine the issue, all but 3% of the units voted for the union shop. Of the total individual votes cast, more than 91% were *for*, less than 9% *against*.

This was conclusive enough to prompt Senators Taft and Humphrey in 1951 to move for and secure a favorable vote on an amendment to the act permitting collective bargaining negotiations for a union shop without recourse to preliminary balloting by the workers involved. And earlier in that same year the Railway Labor Act was amended to legalize contract negotiations for the union shop, formerly banned by it.

In the light of developments during and since 1946, then, it is reasonable to conclude, on the one hand, that although by no means able to dictate their own terms completely, unions *are* sufficiently entrenched so as not to fear dislocations in their organizational setups; and, on the other hand, although strong enough to bear the difficulties imposed on them by the Taft-Hartley Act, the unions have proved politically powerless to prevent the passage of unfriendly legislation.

The Logic of Power

The power that comes into being with the growth of unionism is aroused to action by the environment in which labor lives as well as by the logic of its own business at hand. Labor brings about a continuous shift of power at the expense of the environing social groups or classes. Thus unionism proceeds from the attainment of its immediate objectives to positions from which it can be said to challenge the balance of social power in the present political and economic social order. Would labor go so far as actually to attack this foundation? Any answer must be speculative and tentative at best.

Labor leaders do not sit up nights plotting what to do with their power. They know pretty well in broad daylight what they want power for—what they have always wanted it for: to strengthen organization, to make easier and less costly the task of maintaining and improving the conditions of the working lives of the members. The only difference is that maintenance and improvement in 1952 represent a much more difficult and complex 'task, involve additional and varied means, and reach out into areas of which the men of, say, 1902 did not even know.

So labor men do not think about "taking over things." But neither are they satisfied that "what was good enough for my old man is good enough for me"; in this their feeling is as American as corn on the cob or apple pie, and it is one that certainly is not limited to the laboring classes. "We'll cross that bridge when we come to it" is their usual answer to questions of how they will use their accumulated power in the future.

Co-determination/ The issue of what labor is actually out to get in the long run was brought out in a concrete case in the labor section of the magazine *Business Week*, December 1 and 8, 1951, commenting on a resolution, passed unanimously by the 1951 convention of the CIO. This resolution, which expressed sympathetic receptiveness to the idea of "co-determination" (i.e., the plan legislated in the German Ruhr heavy industry under which labor representatives sit on the industries' governing boards with power equal to that of management), read in part:

> Industrial policies which should be brought under democratic [co-determinative] direction . . . include among others . . . stable price ceilings to protect purchasing power and guard against inflation, and decisions on production levels, on the rate and nature of capital investment, on the rate and nature of technological change, on the size and location of industrial plants, and on the development and conservation of natural resources.

The late CIO President Philip Murray was quoted as having said in urging the resolution:

> I would liken this plan to the plan that was promulgated in Germany. . . . [It] does not propose socialization of American industry. . . . I believe the time has come when there ought to be a reorientation of our thinking within the CIO, that we ought to be thinking in terms of tomorrow.

And *Business Week*'s editorial comment was:

> That is not, of course, socialism; it does not contemplate the expropriation of capital and the nationalization of business. But it certainly isn't capitalism, the essence of which is that the owner runs the enterprise. It is, if label is required, a latter-day form of syndicalism.

To bolster his criticism of the Murray statement of attitude, the *Business Week* writer submitted two points. One was that the idea endorsed by Mr. Murray was "a mishmash of Marx, Sorel, Papal Encyclicals, IWW slogans, Mussolini labor syndicates, and Weimar Republic politics. How such a cross-pollinated seed will grow in the American climate remains to be seen." The other was that "the leaders of labor, to stay leaders, must never let too great a gap develop between their thinking and the thinking of their followers."

But if Mr. Murray's thinking was wrong, it surely is only because *he* was wrong,

not because the ideas are similar to those nurtured in other lands. We all live by ideas from everywhere. Only in Stalinia is all wisdom native, all things invented and all discoveries made on native soil.

As for not allowing "too great a gap" between the thinking of the leaders and the followers, it depends upon what is considered too great and what is considered to be the task of leadership. The poet Carl Sandburg suggested: "The drum major who turned a corner when the band didn't became a has-been leader." But, tragic as it may be to the leader to lose his following, it is an even greater tragedy for the followers if their leaders are only drum majors.

Mr. Philip Murray's statement was neither a mishmash nor a potpourri but a proposal altogether within the concept of a free society with a modicum of traffic regulation. Perhaps if what he was referring to should actually come to pass— i.e., American labor representatives sitting on management boards, having equal rights with representatives of stock owners, under an umpire—capitalism would not be the same as we have been accustomed to know it. But is today's capitalism what it was in the days of our fathers? And what living human arrangement continues for long unchanged? In this generation at least we seem to be making remarkably quick adjustment to changes in material actualities and in the human relations which are affected by such actualities.

Readers will recall without undue strain of memory the bloody battles of about a decade ago around the Ford plants at Dearborn, Michigan, and elsewhere, with union organizers (Walter Reuther leading them and being atrociously beaten up) and the armed forces of the company in virtual deadly combat. And then, as reported in the newspapers, the following exchanges took place:

> In Washington to address the U.S. Chamber of Commerce convention, genial Henry Ford II decided to drop in on CIO President Phil Murray.

Appearing unannounced in the CIO offices, young Ford introduced himself to Molly Lynch, Murray's secretary, and asked to see her boss. "I don't have an appointment," Ford explained, "so if he's busy, please don't bother him."

Somewhat aghast, Miss Lynch said she would call Murray from a meeting immediately.

"That's very kind, but I'll wait until he's through."

So the ruler of the mighty Ford empire patiently waited for the head of the CIO to finish his meeting. It was not a long wait. When Murray came out, the two men greeted each other warmly and went into Murray's office for a chat.

No sociological conclusions are invited—except perhaps that "of such is life."

I am not trying to make a case for co-determination or, as far as that is concerned, for any particular development; certainly co-determination is not desirable if it cannot be made to work in America—whatever the theoretical arguments on either side are. Rather, I am simply asking for understanding of labor and what makes labor tick, confident that society will resolve whatever issues are involved if such understanding exists in adequate measure.

The basic point of this discussion has been that labor builds social power. But all power is expansive and can be explosive. Hence it seems only common sense for intelligent society to give due sway to what is *reasonable* in power and thus to minimize the likelihood of breakup. The potential dynamism of labor, it should always be remembered, is altogether "in the father's image"; it is fully in character with the broad, ever-growing expanse of our American society. If we do not want to change the dynamic quality of the American people, then we do not want a tame, visionless labor movement, led by drum majors fearful of being a step ahead.

Conclusion

The political functioning of our industrial society is very different from what it was a generation ago, and far more different from what it was a half-century back. The form of our government outwardly remains, as designed by the founding fathers and their sons, majority government, the party system, the three coordinate branches of legislative authority, administration, and judicial interpretation and adjustment. The content of our political system has, however, greatly changed and continues to change. Indeed, to all practical intents and purposes, the American people have been for quite some time now a constitutional convention in continuous session, sitting as a committee of the whole, and devising political adaptation to industrial, economic, and cultural changes.

The changes were necessitated by the fact that we have become a nation of substantial groups of the citizenry, each identified and practically unified by "clear and present" special interests and desirous of having those interests realized. The general welfare as we now see it is the sum total of all special interests, properly coordinated, and mutually interrelated by due process—or even logrolling. Each interest represents a socially significant function and power bloc, actual or potential, and the nation is really becoming ever more a confederation of power blocs, contending, coalescing, cooperating, making war or peace with one another as the case may be.

Of course, congressional government continues as the supreme legislative power of the American democracy, and the decisions of the individual voters are the source of that power. But congressional enactments tend to become mostly enabling laws, and they increasingly delegate quasi-legislative authority to a growing and already vast network of executive agencies, commissions, and administrators. When the Federal Trade Commission was set up, and later on the Interstate Commerce Commission and the Federal Reserve Board, the beginning was made of a process of divesting the congressional government of the kind of authority with which the framers of the Constitution had endowed it.

Thus there came about what publicists like to refer to as the revolution of our time. And revolution it is, except that it has taken place by legislative process, not by smashing windows. This is the democratic way our people have chosen—or wandered into—or both—to resolve conflicts between what is and what is getting to be. We can do better than cry about what is happening. We could hardly do worse than ignore the facts as we see them.

The maintenance of healthy, progressive equilibrium among groups, blocs, and powers is the essential problem of this period in our history if we propose to preserve the "ramparts of freedom" without obstructing the compulsive forces of our dynamic growth. If the evidence of experience is to be the basis of judgment, the growing labor community in this nation is actively sympathetic with this reading of our future in the making.

Chapter Ten

America in World Economic Development

■ In the first half of the twentieth century the United States went through radical changes in its economic relations with the rest of the world, chiefly as a result of war. Before 1914 the United States was paying out more in interest and dividends to foreigners for the large investments they had made in America during the nineteenth century than the nation was receiving in new foreign investment plus returns on the growing United States holdings in other countries. Barring important balancing items such as ocean freights, tourist expenditures, and transfers of specie, a nation in this situation should have an excess of merchandise exports over imports, and in the early twentieth century this was the case. Imports of goods had not exceeded exports since 1893 and had not exceeded them one year after another since the late 1880s. Thus American businessmen became used to a favorable merchandise trade balance. But Americans were investing more and more abroad and seemed bound to reach a condition where interest and dividend payments coming into the country would exceed those going out, so that, given the usual nature of international trade, there would be a tendency toward an unfavorable merchandise trade balance.

World War I abruptly brought the reversal in money obligations that had been approaching. European holdings in the United States were liquidated, and private and public loans totaling many billions of dollars were made to friendly foreign governments. But as the financial outflow went in the form of goods, an unfavorable trade balance did not develop. The value of the excess of American exports above imports from 1915 to 1921 came to about $20 billion.

If world, particularly European, economic stability was to be restored after 1918, the United States faced this choice: to try actively to collect the interest and principal of the debts through accepting a large annual surplus of imports over exports, or to keep imports down through high tariff duties and preserve the favorable merchandise trade balance by shoring up European purchasing power through continued loans and investments in amounts larger than the sum of return payments. Congress in 1922 and again in 1929 decided, without much reference to balance-of-payments problems, to keep duties high. Since in the long run international payments have to be made in specie, goods, or services, the government's policy led to an essentially unstable situation. As long as Americans were willing to continue lending and investing abroad at a high rate, foreign markets for American goods would hold up, but since every new loan or investment involved the expectation by Americans of return payments, the process had a tendency ultimately to be self-defeating.

Another sudden break came, however, with the panic of 1929. American investment abroad dried up, and payments on existing foreign obligations in the form of goods were either kept out by the tariff or else found no market in the Depression. As a result the entire system of international payments ceased to function. The merchandise trade that remained was often negotiated on a barter basis that involved no balance of payments.

World War II accentuated the creditor position of the United States, but some lessons had been learned. In this war aid to the Allies in goods was chiefly under the lend-lease plan, which involved little or no expectation of repayment. At the end of the war a mixture of realistic assessment of possibilities and the fear of the spread of communism produced a new attitude of responsibility toward friendly debtors. Instead of trying to collect wartime advances, the United States gave these nations additional funds to aid their recovery. Such foreign aid and external investment preserved highly favorable merchandise trade balances in spite of the fact that from 1934 on, the average of American tariff duties had been greatly reduced by reciprocal trade pacts, giving foreign nations easier access to the American market.

In the late 1950s new problems arose. The United States was spending billions of dollars on military forces all over the world, and tourist expenditures, nonmilitary foreign aid not supplied in the form of American goods, and sharp annual increases in the foreign investment of American business combined to produce additional drains of dollars. As a result, in spite of a very high surplus of merchandise exports above imports, the overall payments balance was unfavorable to our country. Because of this and the speculative buying of dollars and foreign depositing in American banks, Europeans, in particular, came to hold enough dollars in cash to menace the United States gold supply if all this "hot" money should be presented for redemption in specie.

Thus this volume ends in the twentieth century on the note on which the preceding volume began in the seventeenth—the unsolved problems of international payments.

Some Mechanics of International Trade

■ The effects of the efforts of European citizens and their governments to turn American holdings into cash at the beginning of World War I illustrate strikingly the thinness and imperfection of stock exchanges as markets and the problems involved in large international transfers of currency. The actual sums withdrawn before the gold current was reversed in direction in 1915 were small by international standards, yet they produced panic and the closing of the New York Stock Exchange for two months.

Cleona Lewis, who was a member of the staff of the Brookings Institution, devoted a lifetime of research to international finance. Her account of the European selling also provides a general picture of the types of foreign holdings in the United States that had accumulated over the many decades during which the United States looked to Europe for capital.

Cleona Lewis
War-time Liquidation*

During the four and a half years of the World War, the creditor countries of Europe disposed of a large part of the American investments they had accumulated during the preceding century. In this way the principal belligerents were able to supply part of their war-time needs for American wheat, cotton, oil, munitions, and other commodities. All classes of European investments in the United States were thus scaled down considerably: security holdings, foreign control of enterprises established in the United States, and short-term credits extended to Americans by foreign commer-

cial, industrial, and banking concerns. Some offsetting investments were made during the period, particularly by non-Europeans. On balance, however, the aggregate investment of foreigners was reduced from about 7.2 billion dollars in the summer of 1914, to about 4 billions at the close of 1919.

Liquidation Began Early

During the month that intervened between the assassination of Archduke Francis Ferdinand and the outbreak of war in Europe there was active and persistent foreign selling of American securities, particularly rails. Early in July financial writers noted that German holders were beginning to sell their American securities, Dutch capitalists were showing an "indisposition" to add to their holdings, and the French press was criticizing American securities in general. They attributed the movement to the recent failure of a New

* Reprinted by permission of the publishers from America's Stake in Foreign Investments (Washington: The Brookings Institution, 1938), pp. 114–130.
Note: The aggregate estimates given in this chapter include all classes of foreign investments, while many estimates currently quoted omit the direct and short-term items and also, in 1919, the properties held for foreign account by the Alien Property Custodian.

York wholesale dry-goods firm having a large indebtedness to certain German and French banks, and to the difficulties some of the railroads were experiencing. In particular they mentioned the Interstate Commerce Commission case against the New York, New Haven and Hartford, in which the misdeeds of the road were recited at length, to the distress of bourse officials in Paris and Berlin who had recently listed some of the road's securities. Also unsettling was the formation of a bondholders' committee for the Missouri Pacific and uncertainty regarding the probable effects of the Cincinnati, Hamilton and Dayton receivership on Baltimore and Ohio securities—companies in which there was large foreign ownership.[1]

As the month wore on this selling movement gained momentum, representing in the main the sale of actual securities in comparatively small lots, on direct orders from abroad.[2] Finally, with Austria's declaration of war on Serbia, followed shortly by Germany's entry into the war, the torrent of foreign-owned American securities pressing into the New York market became tremendous, bringing back all grades of American stocks and bonds. There were clear indications that the liquidation was not essentially speculative in its origin, but represented the outpouring of securities that had been locked up as permanent investments.[3]

On Monday, July 27, began the "temporary" suspension of trading on some of the principal stock exchanges of Europe, which rapidly spread to other financial centers. The London Stock Exchange remained open officially until Friday, but earlier in the week its members had stopped doing business and jobbers had stopped quoting either buying or selling prices. Finally, on Friday morning with a deluge of selling orders brought in by the overnight cables, and with Thursday's stock prices at new lows throughout the list and bonds beginning to show substantial losses, the Board of Governors decided that the New York Stock Exchange must close. Meanwhile, the foreign exchange market had been completely demoralized by the inordinate demand for remittances. Sterling demand bills at Thursday's close were quoted at $5.50, and cable transfers at $6.35. Gold exports to Europe, unusually large early in July, continued in increasing amounts.

Under authorization by a committee of the Stock Exchange, members of the Exchange resumed trading in an unofficial way shortly after the formal closing of the institution. No quotations were officially given out, and little other information was made available, except that these transactions were limited by two important conditions imposed by the Stock Exchange Committee. No sales were permitted at prices below those last recorded at the Exchange, and all transactions were required to be reported to the stock exchange clearing house.

To avoid these restrictions, a center of trading developed in New Street. When the New Street price for a given security had advanced above the lower limit set by the Committee's rules, further trading was usually transferred to the "clearing house" market. By the third week of August, a number of securities were selling well above the clearing house minimum. On November 28, the Exchange was reopened for restricted trading in bonds; on December 12 restricted trading in stocks was permitted; and finally, on December 15, 1914, unrestricted trading was restored.

The return of securities from Europe continued. But as the warring nations bought more and more goods in America, the fall in the exchange value of the dollar was stopped and the climb back

[1] Commercial and Financial Chronicle, 1914: July 4, p. 7; July 11, pp. 81–83; July 25, pp. 224, 228.
[2] The same, July 25, 1914, p. 230.
[3] The same, Aug. 1, 1914, p. 297.

to par begun. When par had been passed —before the end of 1914—and the dollar still continued its upward trend well into 1915, the belligerent governments became increasingly aware of the importance of the claims held by their people against various American debtors. Shortly thereafter Great Britain began mobilization of the American securities held by her nationals.

Britain's Mobilization of American Securities

At the outbreak of the War, British investors, like those of other countries, began selling a portion of their American securities, and in this way helped provide the funds needed for Britain's increased import requirements. The flow of dollars from these sales—far from sufficient for war needs—was supplemented at an early date by American commercial and bank loans, and later by loans sold to the American public. In some of these transactions collateral was required, part of it in the form of American securities. The British government, therefore, found it necessary to mobilize the foreign securities held in the country, to furnish a basis for further borrowing in the United States and in general to give support to the pound sterling.

The first step was taken in July 1915 when the treasury instructed the Bank of England to buy American securities in London for sale in New York. Six months later insurance and trust companies were asked to submit lists of the issues they were willing to sell or loan to the government. At the end of the year a special committee known as the American Dollar Securities Committee was appointed to take charge of these transactions, and shortly afterward published a list of 54 dollar securities wanted by the treasury. Soon the list had grown to 909 issues that the treasury wanted to borrow or buy for use as collateral with American banks or for sale in New York.

The plan became more and more comprehensive as time passed. From a position of one among many bidders in the market in the middle of July, the British government in February 1917 became the sole purchaser to whom holders of foreign securities were permitted to sell. The entry of the United States into the War in April 1917 eased the strain on the British treasury, but until the control was removed and the Dollar Committee dissolved at the end of March 1919, American securities occupied an important place in Britain's war-time financing and in the plan by which for almost four years the pound was maintained at a practically uniform rate of $4.76.

The government's pressure for dollar exchange caused British corporations to curtail their mortgages on American real estate, to the distress of some of the borrowers. In September 1917, when southern financiers were conferring with their congressmen regarding the difficulties raised by the withdrawal of this capital, British loans on cotton and other farm lands of the South aggregated about 110 million dollars. The following month it was arranged by the British and American treasuries that British companies need not further reduce their investments in American mortgages, though they were required to remit their income to Great Britain as they collected it.[4]

At the beginning of the War, British investors held about 3.7 billion dollars (par value) of American shares and bonds, or about five-eighths of the foreign-owned total.[5] By the close of 1919 they had sold about 70 per cent of their holdings, or about 2.6 billion dollars, and still retained

---

[4] The Chronicle, Sept. 15, 1917, p. 1046; the Statist, Nov. 22, 1919, p. 1123.
[5] With common shares included at market values, instead of par, the British total is 3.4 billion dollars. This adjustment makes the estimate for Great Britain fully comparable with that given on p. 366 above for all classes of foreign investments in the United States.

about 1.1 billions. The greatest liquidation was in railway securities, of which some 2 billions were sold and about 800 millions retained. Of other American securities a little more than a half billion were sold and about 325 millions still remained in British hands.

British-controlled enterprises in the United States amounted to perhaps 600 million dollars in July 1914, or as much as all other foreign-controlled enterprises in the country combined. By the end of 1919 some few of the companies had been sold, but control of most of them was still with the British.

With the dissolution of the Dollar Securities Committee at the end of March 1919, the British government vacated its monopoly position in the market for foreign securities. However, the British treasury continued to accept certain issues on loan, and made some additional purchases, until the plan was brought to an end in March 1922.

French Investments Greatly Reduced

In the decade preceding the War the French had floated a number of large loans for certain railways and for the municipality of New York. This flow of funds was reversed during the weeks between the Sarajevo assassination and the declaration of war, and the return of American securities from France was under way. On May 8, 1915 the Minister of Finance, M. Ribot, stated that the French had resold to America more than 41 million dollars of their American bonds and shares.

During the months that followed, large blocks of securities were bought up by the French government and by private interests for forwarding to New York, where they were sold or used as collateral for loans. For the first loans made to France no collateral was required. As that country's indebtedness accumulated, however, American bankers making new advances

of funds usually requested the deposit of American and other securities as a safeguard against loss.

During the four and a half war years, more than 35 million dollars of the Chicago, Milwaukee and St. Paul loan issued in Paris in 1910, and almost 38 million dollars of the Pennsylvania Company loan taken in Paris in 1906, were sold by the French—the greater part of these having been acquired by the French government before the end of 1915. In September 1915 French bankers sold 1 million dollars, par value (or about 6.6 million dollars market value) of Utah Copper Company stock. In December, Kuhn, Loeb and Company made arrangements for the purchase of a Central Pacific loan issued in Paris in 1911, and eventually bought up almost 25 million dollars of the original 48.2 millions issued. By the close of 1915 French holdings of United States Steel common and preferred were 2 million dollars less than at the end of March 1914, and an additional 3 millions were sold before the end of 1919.

In the spring of 1916 the French treasury's requirements for foreign exchange, particularly for dollars, resulted in a mobilization plan somewhat similar to that already in effect in Great Britain. The Minister of Finance inserted a notice in the *Official Journal*[6] for May 5 listing securities that the government wished to acquire by purchase or loan, and the terms offered. The plan did not prove a complete success, French capitalists in many cases finding it more profitable to sell their securities direct to foreign buyers than to dispose of them to the French government.[7] But whether through the government or through private sales,

[6] *Journal officiel de la république française*, May 5, 1916, p. 3909 and May 24, 1916, p. 4627.
[7] Harold G. Moulton and Cleona Lewis, *The French Debt Problem* (1925), p. 350; André Théry, *Les grands établissements de crédit français* (1921), pp. 218–20; Jules Décamps, *Les changes étrangers*, 2d ed., pp. 304–05.

the French liquidated about 70 per cent of their portfolio of American securities, the greater part of their sales being accomplished before America joined forces with the allies. In dollar terms, however, French sales were of minor importance, representing an aggregate par value of perhaps 250 to 275 million dollars—or about one-tenth of the amount sold by the British.

After the War, many securities that had been used as collateral for American loans were returned to France. For example, on February 26, 1919, the Bankers Trust Company shipped twenty cases of French-owned securities to the Minister of Finance in Paris, the loans that they secured having matured and been paid off. This was part of a 100 to 125 million dollar lot of stocks and bonds that had been in the Bank's vaults for two years. Another 100 million dollar lot was released April 1, with the payment of the 100 million dollar government loan falling due on that date.[8] These return shipments were made up largely of French and foreign securities, since the bankers accepted as collateral the bonds of many countries, but they included some American issues.

For one reason or another the greater part of the direct investments of the French were also thrown on the market during the War. Southern Aluminum Company, representing an investment of 5.5 million dollars, was sold out early in 1915. A large French interest in the Midwest Refining Company was sold to Standard Oil of Indiana sometime between 1917 and 1920. Their other large investment in American oil, the 8 million dollar Union des Petroles d'Oklahoma, was bought up by the Pure Oil Company in 1918 and 1922. In all, little remained here except the properties needed for facilitating French trade with the United States.

[8] The Chronicle, Mar. 1, 1919, p. 822.

German Liquidations

War-time pressure for foreign currencies was fully as great in Germany as in the allied countries. In August 1916, the German government took a foreign security census, preliminary to the complete control established the following March. This showed that about 4,060 million dollars of foreign securities, including those of all foreign countries, remained in German hands and that not less than 500 millions had already been exported.[9] The figures currently accepted were somewhat higher, since it seemed likely that there was some evasion in answering an inquiry whose purpose was known to be the detection and later acquisition by the government of foreign currency assets of all sorts.

Germany's transactions with other countries were always under the close surveillance of the allies. Securities shipped to the United States—whether American securities returning here or German bonds bought by American bankers—were likely to be intercepted. American bankers and brokers known to have had dealings with Germany were put on the British black list. In March 1916 about 10 million dollars in securities, mailed from Holland and thought to be of German ownership, were seized by British authorities and turned over to the Prize Court.[10] In December, a small block of mark bonds bought by the State Commercial and Savings Bank of Chicago and mailed to the United States were also seized by the British on the Danish steamer *Frederick VIII* and turned over to the Prize Court.[11] Thus, there was little if any opportunity for Germany to use her foreign portfolio as a basis for Ameri-

[9] *Wirtschaft und Statistik*, No. 2, 1923, p. 64; Harold G. Moulton and Constantine E. McGuire, *Germany's Capacity to Pay* (1923), pp. 279, 288.
[10] The *Chronicle*, 1916: Mar. 18, p. 1009; Apr. 15, p. 1407.
[11] The same, Dec. 30, 1916, p. 2399.

can loans. To acquire dollar exchange she had to sell her holdings outright, largely through the agency of the neutral nations. It is believed that before April 1917, when the United States came into the War, she had disposed of the greater part of the pick of her American securities. Estimates of such liquidations have ranged upward from a minimum of 300 million dollars.[12] It is, of course, possible that some sales were made through neutral markets even later than April, until such activities were curtailed by the Alien Property Custodian.

The Office of the Alien Property Custodian was created by an act of Congress approved October 6, 1917, and was filled by a presidential appointment sixteen days later. Its function was to take over and liquidate all classes of enemy-owned property, including both the physical properties of foreign-controlled enterprises in the United States and the enemy-owned securities of American enterprises. In fact, a move looking toward the sequestration of securities had begun early in April when the New York Stock Exchange issued a call for information regarding alien enemy accounts, including both securities and money.[13]

The remnant of Germany's holdings of American bonds and shares thus taken over was disposed of for some 275 million dollars. Other properties handled by the Custodian, when sold under the hammer, brought about 275 millions additional, though the value on a going-concern basis would probably have been larger.[14] By amendments to the Trading with the Enemy Act, July 11, 1919 and June 5,

1920,[15] by the Winslow bill of March 4, 1923,[16] and by the "Settlement of War Claims Act of 1928,"[17] the proceeds of these sales, with interest, were returned to the dispossessed German owners.

When the Office of the Alien Property Custodian was closed at the end of June 1934, the trust property still on hand had a book value of 65.8 million dollars, and payments already made to enemy aliens, including Austrians and Bulgarians, had amounted to about 596 million dollars.[18] As indicated above, Germany's portion of the total probably was some 550 million dollars more or less. Thus, about 550 millions remained at the close of 1919 (out of about 950 million dollars invested in the United States before the War), this amount representing the claims of German nationals against an American government official acting as trustee for their confiscated properties.

Other Creditors

Aside from the sales of the principal belligerents, liquidation was under way by other creditors of the American economy. At this same time, however, some foreigners were acquiring new investments in the United States. Among the latter were the Canadian railway companies, particularly the Grand Trunk, that were buying additional rail securities for the purpose of extending their control over certain American roads near the northern border. Between 1914 and the close of 1919 such purchases amounted to almost 17 million dollars, a small figure in comparison with the sales by other creditors.

The Netherlands sold many classes of American securities, reducing the total holdings of that country considerably, but at the same time acquired new oil prop-

[12] This minimum is from John Maynard Keynes, *The Economic Consequences of the Peace* (1920), p. 177; a much higher figure is indicated by the Royal Institute of International Affairs, *The Problem of International Investment* (1937), p. 131.
[13] The *Chronicle*, Apr. 14, 1917, p. 1445.
[14] This is exclusive of German ships confiscated in American ports at the outbreak of the War, which were valued at 34.2 million dollars.

[15] 41 Stat. L. 35–68, 977–80.
[16] 42 Stat. L. 1511–16.
[17] Passed Mar. 10, 1928. 45 Stat. L. 254–79.
[18] *Report of the Alien Property Custodian*, 1932, p. 3; 1933, p. 2; 1934, pp. 6–7.

erties. The Royal Dutch-Shell group, in which the Dutch held control, increased their investment in California oil from about 17.7 million dollars in 1914 to 38.5 millions at the end of 1919. Switzerland, with her franc at a premium in terms of the dollar, increased her investments in American securities after the United States entered the War. In 1917 and 1918 blocks of American Liberty Loan bonds and treasury certificates were reported to have been sold in Central and South America, in the Philippines, and in Scandinavian countries.[19]

Further indications of the mixed trends in the transactions of this group of countries are furnished by United States Steel Corporation data showing holdings of its stock, common and preferred, on March 31, 1914 and December 31, 1919. Par value figures for all countries except the United Kingdom, France, and Germany are given below, in millions of dollars.

Country	March 31, 1914	December 31, 1919	Change
Holland	38.6	14.8	−23.8
Switzerland	0.4	0.5	+ 0.1
Canada	7.8	7.2	− 0.6
All others	1.4	2.1	+ 0.7

On balance this group probably reduced its holdings of rails by as much as 50 per cent, with a small reduction in their holdings of other securities.

Short-term Credits

During the War, shifts in America's foreign trade brought some shifts in the country's short-term indebtedness. Available data show that after 1914 short-term debts to Europe were increased by

deposits made for war purposes, but that these were drawn down to approximately the pre-war level within a year after hostilities had ended. Meantime, an increased volume of short-term commercial debts had been incurred in other parts of the world. The net result was that the aggregate amount of this class of indebtedness was increased from roughly 450 million dollars at the beginning of the War to approximately 800 millions at the close of 1919.

The bulk of our war-time exports went to Europe, while imports from the Orient and from South America were taken in increasing amounts. With the growth of imports from Japan, and with payment by means of gold shipments prohibited, Japanese credits accumulated in New York banks. A relatively small portion of such funds was invested in the security markets. The greater part was put at the disposal of Great Britain, or bought up by the Japanese government. By the end of January 1918 not less than 100 million dollars had thus been loaned to the British treasury and used for the purchase of American goods. During the succeeding nine months, additional accumulations of about 200 million dollars had been bought up by the Japanese government and left to their credit in the United States. Such balances reached their peak at the end of 1919, and were reduced thereafter as world trade began readjusting to post-war conditions.[20]

In a similar way claims against the United States accumulated to the credit of the Argentine government. American business men made payment for their Argentine imports by deposits to the credit of the Argentine government's account with the Federal Reserve Bank of New York. After reaching a total of about

---

[19] The Chronicle, Aug. 11, 1917, p. 549; Oct. 12, 1918, pp. 1432–33.

[20] Harold G. Moulton, Japan (1931), pp. 286–91, 539; the Chronicle, Aug. 11, 1917, p. 549; and 1918: Jan. 26, p. 337; Aug. 24, p. 743; Oct. 12, p. 1423.

97 million dollars late in 1918, the account was scaled down by about 20 million dollars in 1919 and fully repaid the following year.[21] By the same mechanism a 20 million dollar commercial credit was extended to the United States by the Uruguayan government and a 4.5 million dollar credit by Bolivia in 1918. Both loans were repaid the following year.[22]

So long as gold shipments were permitted, Spain received payment in gold for a large part of the important war materials she furnished the United States, but after the embargo was imposed, war purchases in Spain also necessitated American borrowing. During the latter part of 1918 bank credits amounting to 250 million pesetas, or about 50 million dollars, were made available to the American government—on the deposit of American treasury bonds and the guarantee of the American bankers arranging the transaction. This short-term debt was repaid the latter part of 1919 and the spring of 1920.[23] The purchase of the Virgin Islands from Denmark early in 1917 put funds at that country's disposal.[24] And in 1919 the proceeds of a 10 million dollar loan to the Philippine Islands were left in this country to the credit of the Insular Treasurer.[25]

Throughout the War the allied governments deposited with American banks the unexpended balances of the loans advanced to them by the United States

treasury. Standing to the account of the French government were also the dollars made available by the United States government in return for French francs used in paying the expenses of the American Army abroad. Various neutral nations of Europe also accumulated funds here, representing payments received for shipping and other services and goods they had furnished the United States. The proceeds of some Canadian loans were deposited with banks in the United States in anticipation of payments to be made for American exports. Mexican deposits were also of sizable proportions, and smaller amounts were held for the account of many countries throughout the world.

Figures compiled by the Federal Reserve Board show that on June 25, 1919 short-term indebtedness to foreigners amounted to 1,049 million dollars, of which 644 millions were payable to Europeans and 405 millions to all other creditors.[26] During the latter part of the year and the early part of 1920, these were drawn down by foreigners who were paying off some of their war-time indebtedness. An unofficial investigation—in which the principal banks of New York and Boston, and members of the American Manufacturers Export Association, and of the Exporters and Importers Association cooperated—showed that on July 1, 1920 the total of this short-term indebtedness to foreigners had been reduced to 500 million dollars: 238 millions payable in Europe, and 262 millions in countries elsewhere.[27] Similar data have not been published for the close of 1919, but judging

[21] The Chronicle, 1918: Jan. 12, p. 129, Jan. 26, p. 339, May 11, p. 1952, June 15, p. 2495; and 1920: June 5, p. 2340, June 12, p. 2437; Annual Report of the Federal Reserve Board, 1919, p. 324, and 1920, p. 391.
[22] The Chronicle, July 6, 1918, p. 17; Aug. 13, 1921, pp. xxv, 680.
[23] The same, Aug. 11, 1917, p. 549; 1918: Oct. 26, p. 1612, Nov. 16, p. 1872; The Fitch Record of Government Finances, 1918, p. 359; Annual Report of the Federal Reserve Board, 1919, p. 323, and 1920, p. 391. Only 155 million pesetas were actually used. Federal Reserve Bulletin, December 1921, p. 1409.
[24] The Chronicle, Aug. 11, 1917, p. 549.
[25] The same, May 10, 1919, p. 1874.

[26] Federal Reserve Bulletin, December 1921, p. 1410. The Bulletin states that these figures cover practically all transactions and bank balances except the peseta debt to Spain and some other comparatively insignificant holdings and remittances which were not reported. The same, pp. 1262, 1401, 1409.
[27] From an article by John H. Williams, published in the Journal of the American Bankers Association, August 1922, and reprinted in the Chronicle, Aug. 19, 1922, p. 839.

from the trends indicated in paragraphs above and from Federal Reserve Board figures showing the reduction in these balances during the first half of 1919,[28] the total outstanding at the end of December 1919 probably amounted to 800 million dollars, of which the European portion approximated 425 million dollars, and the non-European about 375 millions.

For all countries combined, foreign holdings of the various securities issued by American corporations were reduced from a total of roughly 5.4 billion dollars in

[28] On Dec. 31, 1918 the figures were as follows: total outstanding, 1,214 million dollars; payable in Europe, 831 millions; payable elsewhere, 383 millions. *Federal Reserve Bulletin,* December 1921, p. 1409.

the summer of 1914 to about 1.6 billions in 1919. Direct investments were reduced from approximately 1.3 billions to 900 millions. Short-term credits payable to foreigners increased from 450 millions in 1914 to about 800 millions in 1919. Sequestrated property in the United States, held by the Alien Property Custodian for the account of foreigners (a new category of foreign claims that came into existence during the War), amounted to approximately 662 million dollars at the close of 1919.

In short, during the course of four and a half War years, America's foreign creditors had "collected" some 3 billion dollars of their former claims, reducing them from a total of 7.2 billion dollars in the summer of 1914 to approximately 4 billions, all classes of indebtedness included, at the close of 1919.

The Problem of an Underdeveloped World

■ After World War II Americans quickly learned that either economic depression, with consequent unemployment, or lack of sufficient industrial development to produce a substantial middle class opened the door to communism. Accordingly, the 1948 Marshall Plan for financial aid was designed to put Western Europe on its feet economically so that middle-class parties could control politics, and the 1949 Point Four program for technical assistance was geared to speed the movement of less developed areas to higher levels of income and productivity. The first aim was achieved with surprising ease; within a decade Western Europe was enjoying unprecedented prosperity, and generally conservative governments were in control. But how to aid effectively the underdeveloped nations was still an unsolved problem. Jacob Viner, one of the foremost economists of the world on matters of international economic relations, assesses the relationship between the United States and the underdeveloped nations as seen in the early 1950s. Viner was then at Princeton University.

Jacob Viner
America's Aims and the Progress of Underdeveloped Countries*

It is my assignment to speak of American interests in the question of the economic development of so-called underdeveloped countries. The first interest with which I will deal, and the one, I believe, which is going to be given major weight as long as the present international tension continues, will be the security interests of the United States.

We are seeking willing and strong allies. We are seeking the maintenance and the development of overseas sources of strategically important raw materials. We probably also are seeking to strengthen our own internal morale by offering evidence of a willingness to deal generously out of our riches with less-well-endowed peoples.

The second set of interests which underlie our national policy are economic in nature. It is the belief of our government, in its Executive Branch at least, and the belief of many Americans, that other countries which play a role in the international economic network of which we are a part contribute positively by their prosperity to our own prosperity. They give us growing and profitable markets for our exports. They give us good sources of supply for the goods which we desire to import. They feed us with ideas, designs, and technical innovations, as we feed them in turn. While prosperity is not, perhaps, as some enthusiasts have held, indivisible, it tends at least to be contagious, and we are more likely to prosper if the outside world is also prospering than if it is declining or remaining stagnant. Even under the freest of trade conditions there is economic rivalry as well as eco-

* Reprinted from Bert Hoselitz (editor), *The Progress of Underdeveloped Areas*, by permission of University of Chicago Press. Copyright © 1952, pp. 175–202.

nomic co-operation between nations; but it is a fundamental assumption of our current economic policy that, in general, our mutuality of economic interests with the outside world far surpasses our conflict of interest therewith.

There is also, I am convinced, a genuine humanitarian interest on the part of the American people in the welfare of the masses of people elsewhere who are living in a state which seems to us, and increasingly to them, one of distressful misery. The floor of Congress is not ordinarily the platform from which the more generous impulses of the American nation receive their most outspoken and vigorous expression. The Administration, which lives closer to Congress and has to respond to its views more fully than do those whose operations are confined to the academic lecture hall or the pulpit, has to be guarded in revealing any feelings of generosity to other peoples, lest Congress charge it with giving away the substance of the American people to gratify a soft-minded humanitarianism. It is not easy, therefore, to prove to foreign skeptics that a genuine sympathy on the part of large sections of the American people for the economic plight of low-income peoples is influencing American policy. I believe it nevertheless to be a fact—one which a properly concluded public opinion poll would verify and which we could verify for ourselves if we were to examine our own motives.

We have, I insist, interests in the welfare of foreign peoples going beyond our own national security and commercial prosperity. We want them also to have some participation in the good material things of this life which we enjoy and perhaps in some cases overvalue and are overboastful about. We want the common man and his wife and his children to have not only Coca-Cola and chewing gum and ice cream, not only modern plumbing, automobiles, refrigerators, and electric lighting, but also good health and good diet, good education and good prospects of betterment in life. We would like others also to enjoy the benefits and the virtues, as we see them, of political democracy, of social security, and of freedom from degradation of human dignity and from overarduous, overlong, or servile toil. These, and other things, we want other people to enjoy in fuller measure than they do now and in fuller measure even than some of our own underprivileged do as yet.

American philanthropy abroad is not a seedling of recent planting. It is an unexpected tribute to our national modesty that there seems to be no American history of our record in this connection and that the only account I have found reference to was published in Hitler Germany. Americans in times of calamity abroad have generally given aid on a commendable scale, individually and through private or official agencies. Much more important has been the systematic contribution of American religious organizations and of American missionaries to poor relief, to education, and to health in underdeveloped countries. I should also mention as an item in our record the contributions of our charitable foundations, and especially the Rockefeller Foundation, in pioneering the way for aid in public health work such as, in connection with Point IV, our government is now engaged in learning how to do on an official basis.

Humanitarian activities on a large scale and directed toward foreign countries grew to significant proportions only as the Western world accumulated economic surplus and only as it became psychologically possible to extend aid to the foreign needy without its being too obvious that there was unmet need at home. Charity has always begun at home, and it was late in modern history before it ceased to end there also. International philanthropy was a by-product of modern capitalism, of its development of a prosperous middle class with religious and moral awareness of obligations extending beyond national boundaries. Its early American manifestations were an offshoot largely of those of Europe. It has grown since World War I to new dimensions; it is now largely conducted under governmental auspices and from governmental financial resources; and the American share therein has become by far the largest. Peoples in need are now more vocal about their needs than they used to be, and we are now better informed about conditions elsewhere than formerly. The growth of relevant statistical information has made the disparity between our levels of living and those of other peoples more conspicuous than hitherto, and it is probably also greater in fact. Two world wars and widespread strife have spread ruin and hunger over wide stretches of the earth. Our participation in the two wars was shorter than that of our enemies, or our allies, and the actual fighting did not touch our home territory. For all these reasons, and, no doubt, others as well, our contributions in recent years to relief of need abroad have been on a much larger scale, have been directed toward a much greater area, and have been much more systematic in plan and execution than there is parallel for in our own past history or in the past or present experience of other countries.

While I would insist that our foreign-aid activities have been in some degree of a genuinely humanitarian character, it is, of course, undeniable that the American interest in the needs of other peoples has been stimulated, and the scale of American response to such needs has been permitted to grow to its recent dimensions, largely from considerations which, while thoroughly respectable, were not primarily philanthropic in character. It is with these considerations that I now propose to deal.

First, there have been economic considerations, some of which have been clearly rational and others, I think, misguided. It was genuinely enlightened self-interest on our part, for instance, to aid in the recovery of the economic health, which war had undermined, of those countries which had been in the past and could again be profitable economic partners for us. Not so easy to defend has been the argument repeatedly invoked by the government and in Congress that foreign aid was needed to maintain our current or future exports, even if this meant that directly or indirectly the exports would in effect be given away. In the first place, during most of the postwar period our exports have been embarrassingly large instead of distressfully small, as far as the availability of domestic markets for them and their impact on inflation and employment at home were concerned. In the second place, the predictions at the end of the war of the imminence of mass unemployment which only extraordinary measures, like foreign aid, involving huge federal budgetary deficits, could avert were an inexcusable aberration of my profession, or of a part of it, for which due penance is still to be exacted. Third, a reasonably well-managed economy should never get into such a state that government spending unjustified by its immediate object becomes an acceptable means, as compared to other available alternatives, of restoring or maintaining balance in a national economy. Finally, there was in some of the advocacy of foreign aid at least a hint that the mercantilist delusion that exports, aside from benevolent sentiments toward their recipients or interest in the imports by which at once or later they would be repaid, were a national good in themselves. In any case, economic considerations, wise and foolish, were important supports for our program of foreign aid.

Undoubtedly of most importance, however, in the Administration, in public opinion, and above all in Congress, in obtaining support for a series of large-scale programs of foreign aid, was the strategic consideration, the consideration of national security. Throughout most of our history our people has not felt that its national security faced any formidable external threat. We have therefore been too much disposed to regard with disdain and to apply disparaging terms to the foreign policies of other countries which did not consider themselves to be so fortunately situated. Even Woodrow Wilson and Franklin D. Roosevelt, each for a time, refused to distinguish between policies designed to carry out wilful aggression and policies designed for defense against aggression and applied to both aggressive policies and defense policies, with undiscriminating opprobrium, the label of "power politics." Today, we are ourselves deeply enmeshed, if not in "power politics," then in "security politics," and it is now the role of other countries to irritate us by refusing to make fine distinctions between plans of aggression and plans of defense.

In any case, hostilities were barely over before we became convinced—somewhat belatedly, I can say, without undue benefit of hindsight—that our national security faced a major external menace from expansionist communism. Given this menace, we came to believe that aid to needy potential allies and to needy countries in general which were not yet caught in the Soviet net could make a valuable and even vital contribution to our national security, now and hereafter.

When Congress approved the Anglo-American loan, someone commented that Molotov was Britain's most successful foreign minister. Let us recall the circumstances at the time. The loan was large; the terms of repayment and of interest were, on past standards, very generous; then, as always, there was considerable anti-English feeling in this country; taxes were high; and neither Congress nor the public had received clear warning in advance that aid to England was contemplated after Lend-Lease had terminated. Nevertheless, Congress approved the loan. Russian diplomacy, in its timing, if not in its general direction, seems to be beyond the understanding of non-Communists. In any case, Soviet Russia had chosen just this critical moment to deal with us and to speak of us unkindly, and the *Congressional Record* is there as demonstration that Molotov speeded the loan through Congress and as evidence at least that without his aid it would have failed of passage. The hostility and the apparent menace to us of Russia are continuing to operate to make us more responsive to programs of foreign aid than we otherwise would be, which is another supporting instance for the maxim that it is an ill wind that blows no one any good.

It seems that we no longer have a monopoly of the atom bomb. We do, however, have a monopoly of the resources available for economic aid on a large scale to other countries. Russia is fully aware of this and apparently attaches considerable weight to it, for she is engaging in counterpropaganda which asserts, not only that recipient countries will have to pay dearly, in sacrifice of their independence, for such aid, but also that aid received from abroad yields no lasting benefit and that the only economic progress which is genuine and durable is that which is accomplished by one's own effort and resources. I can conceive this sour-grapes propaganda as being successful with their own people, but it should find hard going in countries to which American aid has actually been extended.

Using calendar-year 1950 data, the United States government gave in outright grants to Europe and its colonial dependencies, to the Far East, to Latin America, to the Near East, to United Nations activities, and in contributions to international philanthropic agencies, about 4.5 billion dollars, of which about 80 per cent went to Europe. Private charitable remittances abroad amounted to about 500 million dollars. Government external loans, net, were only about 150 million dollars, and private investments abroad were around 1 billion dollars. This makes a grand total of about 6 billion dollars, net, of grants and loans, public and private, of which about five-sixths were grants and about three-fourths were public.

These are substantial figures. But this new term "foreign aid" includes ambiguously loans on a nearly commercial basis, loans on special terms, and grants. If all of it is to be regarded as philanthropy, then we should remember, as we can be sure that the recipients do, that a minor but significant fraction of it is philanthropy at 3 per cent or more per annum. Also, if loans and grants are treated alike, and private investment is included, the scale on which foreign aid is being extended is not out of line with past experience. Before World War I, England, which was then the leading international lender, was investing abroad at an annual net rate of about 8 per cent of its national income and about 50 per cent of its annual savings. If we were to match such rates today, our foreign aid in the form of private and public loans and of grants would have to exceed their actual current rates several fold.

There are important differences in character, of course, between American foreign aid today and the British export of capital before World War I. We are in the main making outright grants. Our governmental loans are at low interest rates, with the interest subject in some cases to cancellation, and the terms of repayment are flexible and otherwise moderate. Except for the American private investment, moreover, none of the American loans is being made on a strictly commercial basis in the expectation of remunerative interest or dividend returns. The British export of capital before World War I, on the other hand, was all strictly private and was all governed exclusively by the expectation of greater profit to the investors than would be derivable from investment at home.

There are still other differences. The British lending was at high contractual rates of interest. While the actual yields on the earlier lending, after defaults and conversions, were not very different from the rates on loans we now are charging, the lenders then were unconcerned as to the productivity of the investments for the borrowing countries except as this might affect the prospects of repayment, and they accepted high contractual rates of interest as adequate compensation for poor prospects of productive investment and mediocre prospects of repayment according to schedule. The American government, on the contrary, is very much concerned with the productive use of the grants and loans it makes and is probably only mildly concerned with the interest yield or even with ultimate repayment of principal.

Before 1914 a large part of international investment consisted of direct investment in private enterprises and in loans to private firms. Later on, the doctrine evolved that these loans had been the means of economic exploitation of, and imperialistic domination over, the debtor countries. There was some basis for this interpretation. The record is clear, however, that the great bulk of the capital which went to underdeveloped countries carried with it no real threat to the independence of the debtor countries and that, when there was wasteful or exploitative investment, the shortcomings of local governments were at least as much responsible as the malice or cupidity or indifference to local interests of the foreign investors. Today, in any case, the governments of debtor countries are more alert to such dangers and perhaps also better qualified to cope with them, and the danger in particular of creditor-country designs against

their territorial sovereignty, to whose realization their state of indebtedness may contribute, can be taken as nil.

Americans in particular must not be too disdainful of the benefits which flowed to debtor countries from foreign investment before World War I. European capital investment greatly speeded up the rate of economic development of this country and made it a much less painful process as far as pressure on the current standard of living was concerned. American debtors, moreover, like other debtors, did not always pay their debts.

Economists in the underdeveloped countries have additional criticisms to make of the past record of international investments. They assert that these investments, insofar as they were not loans to wasteful and corrupt governments, went largely to the development of sources of supply of foodstuffs and raw materials for the investing countries and thus helped to fasten on the undeveloped countries an agricultural and raw-material pattern of production, labeled by them a "colonial" pattern, which added to instead of removing the obstacles to the industrialization which they now generally regard as essential to true economic progress. They claim also that the European capital went largely to the countries least in need of it, to countries which already had relatively high per capita incomes and capital resources. They cite the United States, Canada, Australia, and New Zealand as illustrations of this. They point out that even capital-exporting countries which had large colonial empires, England and France, did not make large investments in their own low-income colonies but permitted their surplus capital to flow in the main to less needy areas.

This is a fairly accurate transcript of the record. International investment in the past was largely unplanned and was conducted by private interests in pursuit of their own advantage. Neither benefit to the countries to which the capital went nor benefit to the countries from which it came was of direct concern to the investors. Such benefit did result, but it came as an incidental by-product, not as a major objective, of the investment.

One exception, however, needs to be pointed out, namely, the instances where governments, mainly French and German, steered foreign investment in certain directions for reasons of national political and strategic interest. The most notable case was the great flow of French capital to Russia from the early 1890's to 1914, mostly in the form of loans to the Russian government. These loans were an important factor in the formation and maintenance of the Franco-Russian alliance, and French private investors were induced to place their savings in them by the combined efforts of the French government, of the large French banks, and of the French press in promoting their sale, and by the exclusion from the Paris money market, through government regulation and informal pressure, of competing foreign investment outlets for French savings. Russia borrowed largely for railroad construction purposes. While these railroads made a contribution to Russian economic development, they were largely designed and located with strategic considerations in the foreground. The French loans to Russia thus bore a close resemblance to the program of military aid to western Europe which we are now embarking on. One important difference, however, is that our present program takes the form exclusively of intergovernmental grants and loans, whereas the French aid to Russia involved the necessity of persuading individual French investors that Russian government bonds were good investments.

It is more generally an important difference between the international finance of pre-World War I and of the interwar period, on the one hand, and of the present time, on the other, that the relative importance of private investment has greatly shrunk.

Heavy taxation and wartime impairment of capital have greatly reduced the amounts of private capital available for foreign investment. Capital export controls in the lending countries and new hazards to the investor in the capital-poor countries in the form of, among other things, political unrest, fear of confiscation and expropriation, discriminatory taxation and regulation, and a widespread hostility to the foreign capitalist are operating as formidable obstacles to international private investment. The United States is now the only important net exporter of capital. American private investment abroad is of small dimensions. What there is, is largely concentrated in mining investments, notably in the petroleum field, where extraordinarily high short-run profit prospects offset the also extraordinarily high appraisals of the political and other risks. If there are excluded a few favored spots, such as Canada and some of the Caribbean countries, it is probably substantially true that in the absence of very special circumstances no American private capital will now venture abroad unless the prospects are good that, aside from political risks, the returns will amortize the investments within five years or so.

Great as is the contribution to economic development which international investment has made in the past and can make in the future, there is sometimes a tendency to exaggerate its importance as compared to other types of international economic co-operation. Much of the contribution of international investment itself has been indirect, through acting as carrier for the transmission of technology and of administrative capacity and through the migration to sparsely settled areas which it has facilitated. But the most important form of international economic co-operation has been and will continue to be ordinary and routine foreign trade. England in the nineteenth century and the United States at its recent peak of foreign financial aid made a much greater contribution to the economic growth and prosperity of other countries by their ordinary trade with them than by foreign investment or foreign grants. We should not move into the establishment of foreign aid as a permanent institution which merely provides other countries on a loan or grant basis with dollars which, were it not for our trade barriers, they could earn by export to us. We should not use foreign aid as conscience-money payments for our tariff.

I turn now to the question of the nature and functions of economic development itself. What manner or kind of economic development are the underdeveloped countries seeking? And what kind have we good reason, whether in terms of our national economic interest or on humanitarian grounds, to wish to promote? Even we are not so rich that we could respond to all the requests for aid which would come from other countries if they were free to choose whatever form of economic development seemed most attractive to them and to call upon us to meet by unconditional loans or grants any consequent deficits in their international balances of payments. But I will leave aside the economic limitations which exist on our capacity to render foreign aid.

In the literature on economic development, both the immensity of which in the last decade and the scarcity of which earlier are almost beyond belief, the term is used with great ambiguity of meaning. Often it is used so as not necessarily to mean more than growth in national indexes of aggregate production or income. Such growth could come solely or mainly as a result of mere growth of population, with no improvement and even with impairment of average income or average output. For countries other than the one directly in question, the nature of the economic growth may not be, from the strictly economic point of view, a matter of much concern. It is even conceivable that, for some other countries for which it is an important export market or source of

supply of essential foodstuffs or raw materials, the economic growth of a particular country which is mainly the consequence of growth in its population and involves no major change in its standards of living or in its allocation of productive resources may be the most beneficial type of growth. But why should any country want growth of this kind for itself, especially where it means chiefly that more persons are there to endure a substandard level of existence?

One might just as well ask why Chicago wants to be a still bigger city than it is already or why an overgrown university wants still further growth. Welfare rests on prestige, and prestige goes with size for many minds. To the native of India, it is likely to seem a self-evidently good thing that there should be as many Indians as possible, even if they be wretchedly poor and sick and illiterate. Earthly misery may be regarded as an unimportant prelude to eternal paradise in a later life. Numbers are widely supposed to bring military strength of themselves, and military arithmetic, rightly or wrongly, in comparing the power of different countries, turns first to a merely quantitative comparison of their populations.

Economic growth which is merely the result of growth of a population which was and remains miserably poor, ill fed, ill housed, ill governed, unwashed, untutored, and unhealthy seems to me a menace to be avoided rather than an objective ardently to be pursued. That many do not share this view, however, is only too apparent. Take a look at even the sophisticated literature on economic development, as issued by the United Nations, by governments (including our own), and by learned men from the universities, and see how much of it neither presents nor seeks statistical evidence or criteria of desirable economic development which could not be fully met by a country swarming with ever more crowded and ever more miserable population, provided only its national indexes of total production or aggregate income, or total exports, continued to rise. There have been important state papers in which mere growth in this sense, without explicit qualification or reservation, has been treated as a matter for congratulation if it has occurred and as a goal to be striven for in the future.

A second kind of growth, a more attractive one, would be growth in per capita output and per capita income, whether or not accompanied by growth in population or in aggregate production or income. But even such growth, if associated with an increasing inequality in the distribution of income, is consistent with an increase both in the absolute numbers and in the percentage of the total population which is living in squalid and diseased poverty. If associated with mass immigration, this kind of growth is even consistent with no one being better off than his parents were at the same age.

It would be a superior kind of growth, to my taste at least, if it involved, in addition to an increase in the average income, an improvement in the standard of living of the majority of the people. It would be better still if there was not associated with it the impairment in the standard of living of any class, and especially of any low-income class, of the population. Economic growth which met even these tests, however, would be consistent, if population were simultaneously growing, with a growth in the absolute number of those living in a state of economic misery.

I would suggest, therefore, that we accept no program of economic development as a fully satisfactory one, entitled to our support and aid, unless it is designed to promote, among other improvements, an absolute decrease in the numbers of those living at less than some minimum level of income.

It may be objected that this would mean setting a utopian standard, which perhaps not even the United States has met. I am, indeed, not at all sure that the number of persons in the United States now living in a state of crushing and degrading poverty is not greater than the number so living in, say, 1900. If so, then in this important respect at least ours is also an "underdeveloped" country. In any case, it is healthy for us to realize that many of the evils of "underdevelopment" which appeal to our consciences when we see them in less-privileged countries are present also, though in less degree, in our own country, and that those who suffer from them here have even more obvious claims on us to promote their removal.

There are differences, of course, in the causes and the appropriate remedies for extreme poverty as between a rich country and a country in which poverty is general. I do not pretend to be well informed in this field, but I would suppose that the major factors responsible for the persistence of large clusters of extreme poverty in this country are race discrimination, the incomplete assimilation of our immigrant population, and the impoverishment and social deterioration which have occurred or persisted in "distressed areas" which have not enjoyed the full impact of American economic progress in general. In some cases, perhaps, these areas should be given back to the Indians or to the wilderness, and their present inhabitants should be attracted to locations where an acceptable standard of living is attainable. If our foreign-aid program is to have any of the characteristics of a global attack on poverty, it will be rational, and it will make the program more acceptable at home, if as part of it or parallel with it we systematically attack our domestic manifestations of "underdevelopment."

Corresponding somewhat to these different concepts of economic development are two radically different approaches to the planning of economic development. The distinction between the two approaches is rarely clearly perceived, and I have never encountered a systematic discussion of it. It lies only half-concealed, however, in much of the literature, and it is implicit in much of governmental planning. I label the two approaches as, first, the "humanitarian," or, perhaps, the "sentimental," and, second, the "aristocratic." These, I concede, are not altogether satisfactory labels, and I adopt them only for lack of better ones.

The humanitarian approach calls for investing directly in the amelioration of the poverty of the lowest-income groups of a country a large fraction of the surplus resources above meager subsistence available from domestic resources or obtainable by loan or otherwise from abroad. This means applying available capital resources to improvement of the health and diet of the poorest classes, to extension of the facilities available for their general and technical education, and, where they are self-employed, to financing their acquisition of more and better tools and more and improved land.

To this approach, three kinds of objections are raised in the underdeveloped countries themselves or are implicit in the character of the development programs which they actually adopt.

First is the argument that in most underdeveloped countries the available capital resources are such that, if they were applied to the direct amelioration of the living and working conditions of the masses of the poor, they would have to be spread so thinly that they would be absorbed in a negligible improvement of their current standard of living, or in costs of administration, without any permanent betterment resulting.

Second, it is argued that a modest addition to the income of the poor would have as its chief short-run result a reduction in mortality rates and/or an increase in marriage and birth rates, with the only lasting result an increase absolutely and relatively in the numbers of miserably poor.

Finally, it is argued that such procedure would weaken the forces leading to the domestic capital formation on which long-run improvement must largely depend on transferring ownership and command of income from those who would apply it to building up the material productive capital of the country to those who would use it up in current consumption without productive aftermath.

These arguments perhaps suffice to indicate the nature of what I have called the "aristocratic approach." Stated positively, it runs along the following lines:

Available resources that can be wrested from current unproductive consumption should be invested in large part not only in the most productive forms of physical capital equipment but in those capital facilities whose returns will go where they will be used for further investment, so as to contribute indefinitely to the process of capital formation. Insofar as there results currently any increase in current income available for current consumption, it should as far as practicable be directed toward those sections of the population, whether class, racial, religious, or regional groups, which can be most relied upon to use the increased income not in relief of current misery or in the support of larger families but in strengthening their long-run productive capacity by better education, by increased savings, and by providing themselves with more abundant or more efficient productive equipment. Exponents of this approach would deny lack of any sympathy with the economic distress of the miserably poor, but they would insist that, given the shortage of resources, the only way lastingly to ameliorate their position is first to help those who will thereby add to the economic strength and the capacity for progress of the country as a whole, and only when large enclaves of economic health and strength have thus been built up to invest resources in the gradual extension of their prosperity to the masses below.

The aristocratic approach could have been termed a "Malthusian" approach, because it rests on a belief in the existence of a Malthusian tendency for populations with low standards of living to absorb any increments of income in mere increase of numbers instead of improvement of living standards and because the remedy it proposes is one of the two remedies which Malthus proposed, although not the one which he most emphasized and which is most associated with his name.

Whether or not the issue is ever seen as sharply as it has here been presented, or faced as frankly, everywhere in poor countries choices are being made, more or less knowingly, as between these two approaches. Let me give you some concrete illustrations which could be extended almost indefinitely.

Shall a poor country put any additional resources available for expansion of its educational facilities into extending and raising the quality of its secondary education and its colleges or into a campaign against the illiteracy of the masses?

Shall a poor country distribute its tax burden so as to hit lightly margins of income which if left untaxed would be likely to be saved, or shall it tax them relatively heavily because they represent superior "ability" to bear taxes?

Shall national policy in general favor the relatively more prosperous small landlords, small-scale manufacturers, and the professional classes or low-income farm and urban labor?

Shall urban populations be favored over rural, even if the former have higher real incomes on the average, because urban dwellers are likely to have smaller families, and in greater degree to use increased income to accumulate capital and to raise their standard of living, than are rural families?

There is here a basic problem, calling for difficult decisions, which poor countries must either deliberately face or deal with by indirection, compromise, or blundering improvisation. It is a problem which our country must also face if it is to proceed with large-scale promotion of economic development abroad and if its programs are to have clear-cut and well-considered objectives. It will be difficult, here and abroad, perhaps as much here as abroad, to face the issue frankly and to indicate frankly the choices that are being made, for, whatever the choice, it will have unpleasant associations. There will be a tendency—there is a tendency—here and abroad, to flinch from the issue or to fudge it.

The aristocratic approach clashes with our humanitarian impulses. In many countries it may no longer be politically practicable. It presents a vulnerable point of attack for Communist propaganda. It makes the paper solutions of communism seem more attractive to many. Communism promises aid to the depressed classes while denying that under communism the problem of excess population can arise and insisting that only under communism can disposable income be effectively mobilized, by forced saving, for long-run economic development. The humanitarian approach, on the other hand, in the absence of Communist ruthlessness and discipline, may lead to a race between technological progress and population growth, which is liable to be won by the latter and to culminate in universal misery, the recurrent threat of famine, and cultural and moral stagnation or even deterioration.

I yield to others, for the time being at least, the answer to this question. I venture only to insist that it is a most serious question and that there probably is no easy answer to it; but ignoring it, or refusing to acknowledge its existence and to examine its significance, is liable to result in its being answered by the course of history in a manner which no one would welcome in advance.

I turn now to another question which

is a matter of lively concern, and of some debate, in a number of underdeveloped countries. Shall they, in programming and planning their economic development, make their primary objective industrialization and urbanization, or shall they concentrate their investment in agricultural improvement and development? This is not by any means an issue wholly independent of the one which I have just been discussing, but I must leave their interrelations for you to explore on your own.

In many quarters it is claimed, often on the basis of reasoning and evidence of incredibly low quality, that industrialization automatically and necessarily leads to improvement in average income. Sometimes argument, good or bad, is dispensed with, and industrialization is tacitly, or by arbitrary definition, taken as synonymous with improvement in per capita income. Let me give you an illustration from an American economist who, I am sure, knows better: "Industrialization, as defined in this paper, comprehends the sum total of the factors that have made and will continue to make for increase in net output per worker and/or per capita."

Many complex and troublesome questions could be neatly and decisively settled if this mode of defining terms were to be generally followed. For instance: "Industrialization can be defined as the growth in urban manufacturing which results when taxes are laid on agriculture, or on rural industries in general, to provide the subsidies to keep non-self-supporting urban industry going, with all-round lowering of per capita real income as a consequence."

Underdeveloped countries do want industrialization. They frequently also want that industrialization to be largely in heavy industry and in large-scale units. It is now a stereotype that industrialization means urbanization, that cities are synonymous with progress, and that urban populations everywhere are more prosperous than the surrounding rural ones. To what extent urban per capita *real* incomes are genuinely higher than agricultural ones and, to the extent to which they are higher, whether the industrialization and urbanization are the cause or the effect of higher national per capita incomes are questions which have rarely if ever been competently and objectively examined.

The actual facts are, I am convinced, much less simple and one-directional than are the current dogmas. It is conspicuously apparent that in some underdeveloped countries the scanty capital resources have by subsidization or direct government action been directed into premature or misdirected industrialization projects and that much of the urban industry which is allegedly high-income-yielding in such countries is really a parasitic growth supported by direct and indirect levies on rural industry which, while it may be returning only low incomes to those engaged in it, at least is earning those incomes.

On the ancient debate as to the relative virtues of urban and rural life, I will make only three comments. First, it is apparently a universal phenomenon that predominantly agricultural countries take a romantic view of cities and that industrialized countries look at the countryside through rose-colored glasses. Second, there is a general tendency to exaggerate the extent to which industrialization necessarily involves urbanization. In many countries, I am sure, the economically most promising opportunities for industrialization, at least in its earlier stages, lie outside the large cities and even in the open countryside—such activities, for example, as cotton gins, seed-crushing plants, sawmills, tile and brick kilns, hydroelectric plants, fruit-sorting and fruit-packing plants, fertilizer plants, cement mills, mining, and light cottage industry in general. Third, granted that cities are needed as civilizing and educative centers, they rise in adequate degree for these purposes in even predominantly agricultural countries, as governmental, educational, professional service, and marketing and transportation centers, provided the rural population is prosperous enough to need and want urban services in substantial proportions.

The one wrong way to attack the problem of urban industrialization versus development of primary industries is to adopt a dogma that one is inherently superior to the other and then to promote the expansion of the favored one by subsidizing it as the cost of the one which is out of favor. The one correct general principle, or so at least it seems to me, is to make decisions in terms of projects or related groups of projects rather than of wholesale categories and to base these decisions on careful estimating of prospective long-run returns to what is to be invested, always with reference to what types of resources, material and human, are needed for different types of development and what types of resources are relatively abundant in the country in question. In some underdeveloped countries such investigation would no doubt lead correctly to programs of industrialization, including heavy-industry, large-scale plants and rapid urbanization. In many of them, however, probably in most of them, it is highly likely that it would lead, at least for decades or even generations to come, to the concentration of the available resources for development on primary industry, on agriculture, on village industries, on transportation and power facilities, and on improvement of education and health.

Land reform is often one of the most urgent needs. What constitutes land reform, however, is often not a simple matter. It always is used to mean a system of land tenure different from the one which prevails, but sometimes it means larger units, or collectivization, as in the Communist countries; and sometimes it means the breaking-up of large estates into small holdings. That the substitution of peasant-proprietorship for large holdings can sometimes constitute a great reform from the points of view both of productivity and of social peace and progress, Ireland offers a conspicuous example. I suspect, however, that we take too readily for granted, even with respect to American conditions, that small-scale owner operation is necessarily superior economically to tenancy. Whether it is or is not, I would suppose, depends on many circumstances: the quality and efficiency of the landlord class, the ability of small proprietors to finance the equipment of their farms with adequate productive facilities, their ability to apply without supervision advanced methods of cultivation and soil conservation and to assemble farms of adequate size to permit efficient operation. Here, again, sound policy must operate on the basis of careful examination of the local circumstances, cultural and political, as well as economic, rather than on maxims and arbitrary dogmas.

I can say only a few words on a matter which is of great importance in the realm of economic development but which in the present-day uncritical enthusiasm is often given little consideration until it forces itself directly upon the attention by quickly reducing to obvious failure overambitious or overimpatient or otherwise ill-designed or ill-managed programs—that is, the host of obstacles to economic development in the form of poor natural and human resources, of cultural patterns resistant to change, of deficient government, and of scarcity of capital. Rapid economic progress has come only to few countries and usually only for limited periods of time. Except for temperate-climate countries richly endowed by nature and originally empty of population or nearly so, it has never come to regions with high birth rates. We have presumably learned from past experience how to avoid earlier mistakes, and the great accumulation of technological knowledge gives modern peoples a much greater degree of power of control over their physical environment; but we still do not know how to work miracles. What may be the equivalent of a miracle, however, is the present possibility that countries which have gained an advanced stage of economic prosperity and accumulated great capital resources, and especially the United States, will make available on generous terms their knowledge, their personnel, and their capital to aid the less-advanced countries in the difficult process of escaping from mass poverty.

I will turn now, as my last topic, to a consideration of what we can reasonably be expected to do for underdeveloped countries, as well as what they must be left to do for themselves.

We can, of course, make free grants to them, and we can lend them capital on moderate terms of interest and repayment, working out with them ways by which this can be done on an adequate scale on fair and safe conditions for both creditors and debtors. I do not believe that, where the winning of allies in a tense situation of great-power conflict is not an important and durable factor, outright grants will or should play an important role. International sharing is even a less practicable procedure politically than voluntary domestic sharing and is less likely to work smoothly and without breeding tensions and animosities than programs which frankly demand mutuality of interest and benefit for both those who give and those who receive the aid. There is no historical experience which supports the view that national benevolence on a global scale, without expectation or prospect of a counterflow of readily visible and material benefit, is a sturdy plant which can thrive for a protracted period of time.

We can give valuable assistance to underdeveloped countries by making capital available to them on generous terms and also by sharing with them our store of technical knowledge and lending them our skilled personnel, which, incidentally, when done under government auspices, is apparently an extremely expensive operation per expert capita. I believe, however, that the most important single means available to us of rendering mutually beneficial aid consists in proceeding further in the reform of our commercial policy which began in 1934. A reduction of our trade barriers, which after fifteen years of being whittled away still remain formidable, can be of greater benefit to other countries than all the much-advertised grants, loans, and technical aid. It is probably true, however, that it is even more difficult to get really significant cuts in the American tariff through Congress than to persuade it to give money away.

Given the level of our trade barriers, we buy much more from other countries, and pay better prices for our imports, when we are prosperous than when we are having one of our periodic, though not inevitable, depressions. Other countries have been insisting, unilaterally and through the United Nations, that we owe it to the rest of the world, as well as to ourselves, to stabilize our economy. Our boom-and-bust record is one of the most effective elements in the psychological warfare which Soviet Russia is conducting against us.

The great depression of the 1930's, in its intensity and duration, was a phenomenon without excuse and unlikely to be repeated. We have ample knowledge of ways in which, without weakening and even with strengthening of the free-enterprise foundations of our national way of life, we can prevent depression from being severe or protracted. If we should fail to act accordingly should the occasion arise, it will be because of a cultural lag comparable to but less excusable on our part than the stubborn resistance to change of the Hopi Indians and of other primitive peoples which, in our more private conferences, the anthropologists have been emphasizing, if I understood them—which is not to be taken for granted—as invulnerable barriers to the acceptance of even the most urgent and the most rewarding economic reforms.

Sophisticated public opinion in other non-Communist countries shares—and indeed surpasses—my confidence that we do not have to submit to the recurrence of major depressions. Much of it, however, would not agree with me that we can escape the cycle without largely abandoning our free-enterprise system and is, in any case, without confidence that we will, in fact, conquer our instability. Many foreign observers, especially if they are socialists, regard us as in this respect a backward people, clinging stubbornly to the obsolete social patterns of behavior which, they believe, darken our economic prospects and threaten ruin to themselves if they should become too closely involved with us. This does not make them reluctant to accept outright grants from us if there are no unpalatable conditions attached to them, but it does lessen their eagerness to borrow from us even on what on past experience would appear to be very generous terms. It also contributes to their unwillingness to plan for their future development along lines which involve a large measure of dependence on exports, and especially on exports to us, and leads them to press us for guaranties, of a kin which it seems unlikely that we will ever be willing to concede, that we will not permit our annual supply of dollars to the outside world to fall below stated minimums.

This lack of confidence in us as an economic partner may wear off in time, as year after year depression fails to make its much-heralded appearance. Let us suppose, however, that we will no longer have major depressions; that we will continue to lower our trade barriers; that we will give and lend abroad, both publicly and privately, on a large scale and on generous terms; and that international tension will subside so that our aid will go to genuine economic development rather than to rearmament. Even then,

what we can contribute to the economic progress of underdeveloped countries will be of minor importance as compared to what they must do for themselves.

Countries do not achieve economic progress by default. If they attain it at all, they do so by fashioning their government policies and their social patterns so as to foster economic development rather than to hinder it. They must steer their educational programs so as to provide the needed skills and attitudes. As incomes rise, they must divert increased proportions of them from current consumption to capital formation. They must develop reasonably efficient government and good credit facilities and must provide for their middle class incentives to enterprise and for their working classes incentives to productive effort. They must succeed in providing the masses of their peoples at least the minimum standards of health, of education, and of social security that are essential prerequisites of genuine economic progress and in arousing in their upper classes the public spirit and the leadership without which domestic effort and foreign aid will come to naught.

What this amounts to, if we consider the advantages enjoyed by us and the handicaps which they must carry, is that, to make real progress, perhaps even to hold their own, the underdeveloped countries must marshal greater effort, must husband their resources more carefully, and must practice greater social discipline than, aside from strategic considerations, we will be urgently called upon to do. Most of these countries are living in a vicious circle of low productivity, poor health, inadequate education, and meager equipment with capital. In the worst cases the circle may not be breakable without both heroic effort and discipline and substantial external aid.

In addition to all this, if there is to be real hope of genuine betterment of economic conditions in those underdeveloped countries which already have a high ratio of population to natural resources, they must find some solution of the population problem which will prevent all the product of more abundant capital equipment and of improved methods of production from being sunk in the support of increased numbers on a bare subsistence level.

It seems certain that most of the underdeveloped countries will rely heavily on government planning and government initiative to achieve the economic progress they aspire to, and I feel fairly certain that most of them will go further in this direction than will be to their long-run advantage. But what the proper division is between government initiative and private enterprise must depend largely on the extent to which the general public is able and disposed to exercise the needed initiative, enterprise, and skill. In some countries the masses of the people are probably too poor, too ignorant, and too bound by old patterns of behavior to do much for themselves; and, if there is to be progress, it must be initiated and, for a time at least, largely conducted from above. In some cases, government itself will not be able to recruit sufficient talent for these purposes from domestic sources, and there will be need for importation of skilled personnel from abroad.

There will be cases where governments will waste scarce resources on grandiose projects; there will be corruption and graft; many projects will be failures; some projects will fail despite the most honest and intelligent planning. There are few of the underdeveloped countries whose prospects of rapid economic development, if objectively appraised on the basis of present circumstances, warrant a high degree of optimism, whatever degree of help, within the limits of reasonable expectations, they may get from outside sources. Most countries, if their peoples are to be satisfied with their rate of progress, will have to move forward at a much more rapid rate than did in the past century those countries which are now the most advanced;

and many of these countries have disadvantages of poor natural resources, unfavorable climates, and populations already dense, which neither western Europe, the British Dominions, nor the United States, had to face. At best, the attainment by the now underdeveloped countries of satisfactory standards of living for the bulk at least of their peoples will be a slow, painful climb up a very arduous path. Foreign aid cannot reasonably be expected to do much more than to make the climb somewhat less arduous.

We should be sympathetic, therefore, if their first efforts do not immediately yield spectacular results. We should make our advice and counsel readily available, but we should not press it upon them. We should not, in complacent satisfaction with our own prosperity, take for granted that we will always be able to give them better solutions for their problems than those they would find for themselves. We should especially beware of assuming that what has worked well with us, whether it be forms of government, tax systems, factory design, or agricultural technique, is necessarily suitable for them.

There will inevitably be a strong temptation on our part to make acceptance of our advice and supervision a condition of our extension of aid. We must exercise great self-restraint in this connection. We cannot, of course, be unconcerned if our aid is patently misapplied or misappropriated. We must, however, avoid patterns of aid which involve us in detailed interference with the internal affairs of other peoples. In that direction lies only frustration, friction, and failure. Once we have approved of a claimant as deserving of aid and as having an acceptable plan for its use, we must then, as a general rule, leave it to its own devices, hope for the best, and not expect too much. That, after all, is very much how our people deal with our own governments, federal and local, how our federal government deals with Congress, and how the federal government and Congress deal with us. We must leave it to other peoples to initiate their own social revolutions, to do their own purging of the inefficiency, extravagance, and corruption of their governments, and to find their own ways of adapting ancient cultural patterns to the requirements of modern economic progress. They may make a mess of it, but that is a risk they must be permitted to take. It is a lesser risk, in any case, probably for them, and certainly for us, than would be involved if we undertook to manage their affairs for them, a role in which we have had no experience and in which no country has had highly successful experience.

There is one more issue on which something should be said, although to attempt an adequate consideration of it would unduly protract this paper, and this is the question as to the extent to which we should administer our foreign aid ourselves or intrust it to United Nations organizations. We are now doing both, but the bulk of our aid is granted by us directly to the recipient countries. There is no doubt that most countries would strongly prefer receiving aid via the United Nations. It must not be taken for granted, however, that the United Nations would attach less stringent conditions or administer grants more laxly and more generously than we do. We are very sensitive to the charge of "imperialism," to which the United Nations, as a multinational institution, is scarcely susceptible. The United Nations might in many cases be more disposed to encroach on national autonomy, and its encroachments might more readily be tolerated, than would be the case if it were a single great power which was interfering. There is not much actual evidence as yet to aid judgment, but it is possible that recipient countries might take contractual obligations to a multi-

national agency more seriously, and treat them as less susceptible to unilateral deviation, than obligations to a single government which might have political and other reasons for refraining from pressing vigorously for adherence to pledges. It is probably an open question as to whether we, or the United Nations, would be a more efficient or more economical administrator of foreign aid, although it is already evident, if we may judge by prevailing salary scales and scales of staffing, that both will be expensive on the domestic standards either of this country or of the recipient countries.

There are at least two important reasons, however, why we must, for the time being at least, reserve to ourselves the control over the allocation and the use of the bulk of our foreign aid. As long as we are the donors of an overwhelming proportion of the foreign aid being granted, the United Nations will in the main reflect the views and attitudes of claimant countries rather than of donor countries. As long as strategic and military considerations continue to be important, we cannot surrender to the United Nations, which includes the Iron Curtain countries, "neutralist" countries, and border-line countries, in which regional and other species of log-rolling have already attained a high level of efficiency, and in which Soviet Russia has veto power, the decision as to how and for what purposes our aid is to be allotted.

Should, however, the international tension subside, and should a return to world prosperity make less unbalanced the ratio of donor to recipient countries, it would become desirable on many counts, some of which I have here suggested, that international aid should be made, exclusively or predominantly, a function of multinational agencies.

Chapter One
Political and Social Factors
in Industrial Development

Economic and business thought in this period is covered in Sidney Fine, *Laissez-faire and the General Welfare State: A Study of Conflict in American Thought, 1865–1901* (1956); Joseph Dorfman, *The Economic Mind in American Civilization, 1865–1918* (1949); Richard Hofstader, *Social Darwinism in American Thought, 1860–1915* (1944); Edward Kirkland, *Business in the Gilded Age: The Conservative's Balance Sheet* (1952); and Thomas C. Cochran, *Railroad Leaders 1845–1890: The Business Mind in Action* (1953).

The political side of industrialization may be found in Ida Tarbell, *The Nationalizing of Business, 1878–1898* (1936); Matthew Josephson, *The Robber Barons: The Great American Capitalists, 1861–1901* (1934) and *The Politicos, 1865–1896* (1938); Thomas C. Cochran and William Miller, *The Age of Enterprise: A Social History of Industrial America* (1961); and Chester M. Destler, *American Radicalism, 1865–1901* (1946). For the Progressive period, consult Harold V. Faulkner, *The Decline of Laissez Faire, 1897–1917* (1951); Gabriel Kolko, *The Triumph of Conservatism: A Reinterpretation of American History, 1900–1916* (1964); and Robert Wiebe, *Businessmen*

391

and Reform: A Study of the Progressive Movement (1962).

Many excellent studies have been written recently on the regulation of business. See especially Gabriel Kolko, Railroads and Regulation, 1877–1916 (1965); William Letwin, Law and Economic Policy in America: The Evolution of the Sherman Anti-trust Act (1965); Hans Thorelli, The Federal Antitrust Policy: Origination of an American Tradition (1955); Lee Benson, Merchants, Farmers and Railroads; Railroad Regulation and New York Politics, 1850–1887 (1955); and James W. Hurst, Law and Economic Growth (1964).

Blake McKelvey studies The Urbanization of America, 1860–1915 (1963). Samuel P. Hays, The Response to Industrialization, 1885–1914 (1957) presents new interpretations. See also Lewis Atherton, Main Street on the Middle Border (1954); A. M. Schlesinger, The Rise of the City, 1878–1898 (1933); and Constance M. Green, American Cities in the Growth of the Nation (1957).

Chapter Two
Railroads and
Economic Growth

A survey of the expansion of nineteenth-century railroads is George R. Taylor and Irene Neu, The American Railroad Network, 1861–1890 (1956). On a regional basis, see Robert E. Riegel, The Story of Western Railroads (1926); Oscar A. Winther, The Transportation Frontier, Trans-Mississippi West, 1865–1890 (1964); John F. Stover, The Railroads of the South, 1865–1900: A Study in Finance and Control (1955); and Richard C. Overton, Burlington Route (1965).

For special topics one of the best is Paul W. Gates, The Illinois Central and Its Colonization Work (1934). See also Richard C. Overton, Burlington West: A Colonization History of the Burlington Railroad (1934), as well as his Burlington Route.

See Julius Grodinsky's works, The Iowa Pool: A Study in Railroad Competition, 1870–84 (1950); Transcontinental Railroad Strategy, 1869–1893: A Study of Businessmen (1962); and Jay Gould: His Business Career (1957). For quantitative information, consult Harold Barger, The Transportation Industries, 1889–1948: A Study of Output, Employment, and Productivity (1951) and Melville J. Ulmer, Capital in Transportation, Communications, and Public Utilities: Its Formation and Financing (1960).

Chapter Three
The Business Structure
of Industrialism

The list of books on individual businessmen and companies continues to grow. For an analysis, see Thomas B. Brewer, "Approaches to Business History: A Bibliographical Study," The Southwestern Social Science Quarterly, vol. 42 (June, 1962). Some of the standard works are Burton J. Hendrick, The Life of Andrew Carnegie (2 vols., 1932); Allan Nevins, A Study in Power: John D. Rockefeller, Industrialist and Philanthropist (2 vols., 1953); William T. Hutchinson, Cyrus Hall McCormick (2 vols., 1930 and 1935); and Joseph H. Appel, The Business Biography of John Wanamaker (1930). Company histories include Boris Emmet and J. E. Jeuck, Catalogues and Counters: A History of Sears Roebuck and Company (1950); Ralph and Muriel Hidy, Pioneering in Big Business, 1882–1911 (1955); Allan Nevins, Ford: The Times, The Man, The Company (2 vols., 1954); and Marquis James, The Metropolitan Life: A Study in Business Growth (1947).

The organization of business is presented in several older books such as H. R. Seager and Charles A. Gulick, Jr., Trust and Corporation Problems (1929), and John Moody, The Truth about the Trusts (1904). For more recent work in this area, see Walter Adams, The Structure of

American Industry (1954); Alfred D. Chandler, Jr., The Railroads, the Nation's First Big Business (1965); and works cited under Chapter 1 above pertaining to the antitrust movement.

The development of investment banking may be seen in Henrietta Larson, Jay Cooke, Private Banker (1936); Frederick L. Allen, The Great Pierpont Morgan (1949); and Lewis Corey, The House of Morgan (1930). The growth of one type of financial intermediary is covered in Morton Keller, The Life Insurance Enterprise, 1885–1910: A Study in the Limits of Corporate Power (1963). Closely connected with capital problems are the money difficulties of the period. Milton Friedman and Anna Jacobson Swartz give an interpretation in A Monetary History of the United States, 1867–1960 (1963); there is a more politically conscious book by Irwin Unger, The Greenback Era (1964). For the Federal Reserve System consult J. Lawrence Laughlin, The Federal Reserve Act: Its Origin and Problems (1933). Business-cycle theory is developed by Rendigs Fels in American Business Cycles, 1865–1897 (1959); there are three articles by Samuel Rezneck on the depressions in the 1870s, 1880s, and 1890s, respectively, in The Journal of Political Economy, vol. 58 (December, 1950); American Historical Review, vol. 61 (October, 1955); and The Journal of Political Economy, vol. 61 (August, 1953). See also Wesley C. Mitchell, What Happens during Business Cycles: A Progress Report (1951).

Quantitative studies for this period often overlap earlier and later years. See Harold Barger, Distribution's Place in the American Economy since 1869 (1955) and the articles in National Bureau of Economic Research, Trends in the American Economy in the Nineteenth Century (1960). Other quantitative studies include Daniel Creamer et al., Capital in Manufacturing and Mining: Its Formation and Financing (1960); John Kendrick, Productivity Trends in the United States (1961); two works by Simon Kuznets, National Product since 1869 (1946) and Capital in the American Economy: Its Formation and Financing (1961); Simon Kuznets and Dorothy S. Thomas (eds.), Population Redistribution and Economic Growth in the United States, 1870–1950 (3 vols., 1957–1964); William H. Shaw, Value of Commodity Output since 1869 (1947); and Raymond Goldsmith, A Study of Saving (2 vols., 1955).

Chapter Four
Agriculture and Labor
in an Expanding Economy

The indispensable book on agriculture for this period is Fred A. Shannon, The Farmer's Last Frontier, 1860–1897 (1945). For special topics, see Mary Wilma M. Hargreaves, Dry Farming in the Northern Great Plains, 1900–1925 (1956); works on the range cattle industry by E. E. Dale, Ernest O. Osgood, and Louis Pelzer; Alvin S. Tostlebe, Capital in Agriculture: Its Formation and Financing since 1870 (1957); Allen G. Boque, Money at Interest: The Farm Mortgage on the Middle Border (1955); and Paul Gates, Fifty Million Acres: Conflicts over Kansas Land Policy, 1854–1890 (1954).

The general works cited for labor in the bibliography at the end of the preceding volume (under Chapter 4) are useful for this period. More specific studies include Lloyd Ulman, Rise of the National Trade Union (1955); Norman J. Ware, The Labor Movement in the United States, 1860–1895 (1929); Lewis L. Lorwin, The American Federation of Labor (1933); and Philip Taft, The A. F. of L. in the Time of Gompers (1957).

Quantitative studies on labor include Clarence D. Long, Wages and Earnings in the United States, 1860–1890 (1960) and Paul Douglas, Wages in the United States, 1890–1926 (1930).

Chapter Five
Changing Foreign
Economic Relations

Important books and interpretations have appeared in a field receiving new attention. See Walter LaFeber, *The New Empire: An Interpretation of American Expansion, 1860–1898* (1964); L. H. Battistini, *The Rise of American Influence in Asia and the Pacific* (1960); Ernest R. May, *Imperial Democracy: The Emergence of America as a Great Power* (1961); Charles Vevier, *The United States and China, 1906–1913* (1955); D. M. Fletcher, *Rails, Mining and Progress: Seven American Promoters in Mexico, 1867–1911* (1958); Foster R. Dulles, *The Imperial Years* (1956); and William Appleman Williams, *The Tragedy of American Diplomacy* (1959).

These should be supplemented with older standard works such as B. H. Williams, *Economic Foreign Policy of the United States* (1929); J. F. Rippy, *The United States and Mexico* (1926); Leland H. Jenks, *Our Cuban Colony* (1928); Charles F. Remer, *Foreign Investments in China* (1933); Julius W. Pratt, *America's Colonial Experiment* (1928); and Scott Nearing and Joseph Freeman, *Dollar Diplomacy* (1925). Capital imports are considered in L. H. Jenks, *Migration of British Capital to 1875* (1927); Herbert Feis, *Europe, the World's Banker, 1870–1914* (1930); and Clark C. Spence, *British Investments and the American Mining Frontier, 1860–1901* (1958).

Chapter Six
Government and the Economy

The best starting points for a study of the 1920s and the 1930s are George Soule, *Prosperity Decade: From War to Depression, 1917–1929* (1947), and Broadus Mitchell, *Depression Decade: From New Era through New Deal, 1929–1941* (1947). Besides the Hoover Memoirs (3 vols., 1952), see Harris G. Warner,

Herbert Hoover and the Great Depression (1959). Many volumes have been done on Franklin D. Roosevelt, and all contain material on the relationship between government and business. Consult especially those by Arthur Schlesinger, Jr., Frank Freidel, and William E. Leuchtenburg. Of special interest is Daniel R. Fusfeld, *The Economic Thought of Franklin D. Roosevelt and the Origins of the New Deal* (1956). No work exists on the NRA except contemporary volumes by Leverett S. Lyon, Hugh S. Johnson, and Charles R. Roos. To this point no scholar has attempted to synthesize economic growth during World War II, with the exception of the brief volume by Eliot Janeway, *The Struggle for Survival: A Chronicle of Economic Mobilization in World War II* (1951). The acceptance of government responsibility for the economy is described by Stephen K. Bailey, *Congress Makes a Law: The Story behind the Employment Act of 1946* (1950).

A great deal has been written on antitrust activity. Recent studies include W. L. Baldwin, *Antitrust and the Changing Corporation* (1951); V. A. Mudd, *Government and Business* (1950); S. N. Whitney, *Antitrust Policy: American Experience in Twenty Industries* (2 vols., 1955); George W. Stocking and Myron W. Watkins, *Monopoly and Free Enterprise* (1951); and George W. Stocking, *Workable Competition and Antitrust Policy* (1961). Government aid to business since 1920 has been given scant attention, but a few general works exist, such as E. Davenport and S. R. Cooke, *The Oil Trusts and Anglo-American Relations* (1923); Walter Adams and H. M. Gray, *Monopoly in America: The Government as a Promoter* (1955); and M. A. Copeland, *Trends in Government Finance* (1961).

Chapter Seven
A New Type of Capitalism?

For the growth of the automobile industry, the best survey is John B. Rae, *American*

Automobile Manufacturers (1959). See also Ralph C. Epstein, The Automobile Industry: Its Economic and Commercial Development (1928); and vols. 2 and 3 of the Ford study by Allan Nevins. A survey of air transport is Henry L. Smith's Airways: The History of Commercial Aviation in the United States (1942). For other new industries, consult G. L. Archer, History of the Radio to 1926 (1938); J. G. Glover and W. B. Cornell, The Development of American Industries: Their Economic Significance (3d ed., 1951); Williams Haynes, The American Chemical Industry (6 vols., 1945–1954); and Forrest McDonald, Insull (1962).

The changing structure of the corporation may be studied in Walter Adams and H. M. Gray, Monopoly in America (1955); A. A. Berle, Jr., and G. C. Means, The Modern Corporation and Private Property (1932); A. D. H. Kaplan, Big Enterprise in a Competitive System (1954); Thomas C. Cochran, The American Business System, 1900–1955 (1957); G. C. Means, The Corporate Revolution in America (1962); R. L. Nelson, Merger Movements in American Industry, 1895–1956 (1959); and G. W. Nutter, The Extent of Enterprise Monopoly in the United States, 1899–1939 (1951).

On management, see Hugh G. J. Aitken, Taylorism at Watertown Arsenal: Scientific Management in Action (1960); Peter Drucker, The Practice of Management (1954); R. A. Gordon, Business Leadership in the Large Corporation (1945); and F. X. Sutton et al., The American Business Creed (1956).

The emphasis on research is covered in C. F. Carter and B. R. Williams, Science in Industry (1959); the work by the Editors of Fortune called U.S.A.: The Permanent Revolution (1951); and Leonard S. Silk, The Research Revolution (1960). Changes in technology are discussed in Robert A. Brady, Organization, Automation, and Society: The Scientific Revolution in Industry (1961).

Interest has been focusing in recent years on the relationship between business, wealth, and society. Some studies have been quantitative, such as Simon Kuznets, Share of Upper Income Groups in Income and Savings (1953); Robert J. Lampman, The Share of Top Wealth-holders in National Wealth, 1922–1956 (1962); and Gabriel Kolko, Wealth and Power (1965). Most have been oriented toward the social influence of business. See Kenneth E. Boulding, The Organizational Revolution: A Study in Ethics of Economic Organizations (1953); Marquis Childs and Douglass Cater, Ethics in a Business Society (1954); and Arthur H. Cole, Business Enterprise in Its Social Setting (1960).

Chapter Eight
The Big Change in Agriculture

Agriculture in the 1920s and 1930s has been the subject of several studies. See John D. Black, Agricultural Reform in the United States (1929); James H. Ahiedeler, Farm Crisis, 1919–1923 (1957); John Hicks and Theodore Saloutos, Agricultural Discontent in the Middle West (1951); Russell Lord, The Wallaces of Iowa (1947); Orville H. Kile, The Farm Bureau through Three Decades (1948); and John L. Fulmer, Agricultural Progress in the Cotton Belt since 1920 (1950). Almost all studies of New Deal agricultural policy were contemporary, but a recent study dealing partly with the period is Gladys L. Baker and Wayne D. Rasmussen et al., Century of Service: The First Hundred Years of the United States Department of Agriculture (1963). For the post-World War II years consult Murray Benedict, Can We Solve the Farm Problem? (1955); Murray Benedict and Oscar C. Stine, The Agricultural Commodity Programs (1956); and Edward Higbee, Farms and Farmers in an Urban Age (1963). Statistical material is found in Harold Barger, American Agriculture, 1899–1939 (1942); and the Department of Agriculture yearbooks.

Chapter Nine
The Status of Labor

The best account of labor in the 1920s is Irving Bernstein, *The Lean Years: A History of the American Worker, 1920–1933* (1960). See also Selig Perlman and Philip Taft, *History of Labour in the United States, 1896–1932* (1935); a quantitative study by John D. Durand, *The Labor Force in the United States, 1890–1940* (1948); and M. J. Nadworny, *Scientific Management and the Unions, 1900–1932* (1955). Irving Bernstein, *The New Deal Collective Bargaining Policy* (1950) is an important work on the 1930s. In addition, use Clyde E. Dankert, *Contemporary Unionism in the United States* (1948); Milton Derber and Edwin Young eds.), *Labor and the New Deal* (1947); Walter Galenson, *The CIO Challenge to the AFL* (1960); and Eveline M. Burns, *The American Social Security System* (1949). Labor is covered in chapters in general books on the postwar period, such as Ralph E. Freeman (ed.), *Postwar Economic Trends in the United States* (1960); and Harold Vatter, *The U.S. Economy in the 1950's* (1963). See also Arthur J. Goldberg, *AFL-CIO: Labor United* (1956); Richard A. Lester, *As Unions Mature* (1958); Sidney Lens, *The Crisis of American Labor* (1961); and William H. Miernyk, *Trade Unions in the Age of Affluence* (1962).

Chapter Ten
America in World
Economic Development

One of the best general books dealing with trade is Wendell C. Gordon, *International Trade: Goods, People, and Ideas* (1958). For the 1920s, see Muriel F. Jolliffe, *The United States as a Financial Centre, 1919–1933* (1935); Ilse Mintz, *Deterioration of the Quality of Foreign Bonds in the United States, 1920–1930* (1951); and J. Brandes, *Herbert Hoover and Economic Diplomacy* (1962). New Deal policy is covered in James C. Pearson, *The Reciprocal Trade Agreements Program: The Policy of the United States and Its Effectiveness* (1942), and H. B. Hinton, *Cordell Hull* (1942). Many volumes already cited for the 1920s and 1930s contain chapters dealing with the international position of the United States. The post-World War II era has not yet received much attention from economic historians, but consult Seymour E. Harris, *The European Recovery Program* (1948); Seymour E. Harris (ed.), *Foreign Economic Policy of the United States* (1948); Howard S. Piquet, *Aid, Trade, and the Tariff* (1953); William A. Brown, *The United States and the Restoration of World Trade* (1950); and Don D. Humphrey, *American Imports* (1955).